GRAPHIC ARTISTS GUILD HANDBOOK

Pricing & Ethical Guidelines

THIRTEENTH EDITION

Dedication

To the hundreds of volunteers from all aspects of the graphic arts industry who, over the past 37 years, have given their time and freely shared their insights, expertise, and business practices to make this handbook an essential resource for graphic artists and their clients. If there were a Lifetime Achievement Award for volunteers, it would undoubtedly go to illustrator Simms Taback. He was part of that visionary group that gave birth to the first edition, and his perseverance, hard work, and direction helped the book grow from a 20-page booklet to the over 350-page volume it is today. Without the collective contributions and continued support of Simms and all the other volunteers, a project of this magnitude would not be possible. Their efforts make the handbook the standard industry reference it is today.

HANDBOOK

GRAPHIC ARTISTS GUILD

Pricing &

EDITION 13

Ethical
Guidelines

LAURA SMITH ART COM

Published in the United States of America by the Graphic Artists Guild, Inc.
32 Broadway, Suite 1114
New York, New York 10004 USA
Telephone: 212.791.3400
Fax: 212.791.0333
www.graphicartistsguild.org

Executive director
Patricia McKiernan

President
Haydn S. Adams

Project consultant/Handbook Subcommittee Chair
Sara Love

Project consultant
Simms Taback

Executive editor
Patricia McKiernan

Project manager/editor
Deborah Kantor

Art direction
Sara Love
saralove.com

Cover design & illustration
Laura Smith
laurasmithart.com

Book interior design & prepress production
Jon Sholly and James Sholly
commercialartisan.com

Indexer
Wendy Catalano
lastlookeditorial.com

Proofreader
Karen Kingsley
kingsleyink.com

Cover printing
Lehigh Phoenix

Interior printing & binding
Maple Vail Book
Manufacturing Group

Distributors to the trade in the U.S.
HOW Design Books
(A Division of F+W Media Inc.)
800.283.0963

Direct-mail distribution
Graphic Artists Guild
212.791.3400
www.graphicartistsguild.org

ISBN-13: 978-0-932102-15-7
ISBN-10: 0-932102-15-8
2 3 4 5 6 7 8 9

Contents

APPENDIX

CONTRACTS & FORMS

Foreword

I started my art/photo rep business in 1980 and never dreamed of the education path I would eventually follow. Growing up I was fairly certain of my future as a nurse or maybe a librarian—not an art rep and a teacher. So it is my honor and privilege to be asked to write this Foreword for the *Graphic Artists Guild Handbook: Pricing & Ethical Guidelines.*

First published in 1973, the *Handbook* was one of the very few books dealing with educating artists in business practices. It gave me information resources and credibility when I first became involved with education as a faculty advisor at Orange Coast College in 1988. Due to the *Handbook's* influence, the college's art department became one of the first to devote a full semester to a business class. I went on to teach the class at several colleges. My first publisher found me through the teaching of that class, and my career in education really got rolling. The journey continues today with the publication of the 13th edition of the *Handbook.*

The journey is of education: educating ourselves, each other, and our clients. Education is the process by which society deliberately transmits its accumulated knowledge, skills, and values from one generation to another. Every time I pick up this book, I am truly amazed at the scope and the volume of information it presents.

Throughout my own career journey, the *Handbook* has been by my side. I have used it in teaching my college courses and referenced it in my workshops. As an educational tool, the *Handbook* is as important now as it was back in 1973. I can turn to any page and find credible, reliable information and learn from the experiences of others. Whether we are dealing with peers or clients, one of our biggest fears is always lack of confidence. The *Handbook* delivers that confidence and credential because it presents industry standard business practices. It is not just YOU talking; you have an entire industry to support your point of view.

I'm always asked when I speak at conferences, "Do these business practices work?" My answer is always the same, "*They* work when *you* do." The key to good business practices is to incorporate what you read in this 13th edition into your day-to-day business and career life.

Read the *Handbook* "again for the first time." Use highlighters and sticky notes for your favorite parts. Keep a copy on your desk and give copies to your clients. Come to this edition with an open mind and heart. You will be enriched and rewarded in doing so.

Maria Piscopo
Art Rep/Author/Creative Services Consultant

Foreword dedicated to Jill Youmans (1949-2003)

President's Prologue

Designers, illustrators, and artists of all ages, it gives me great pleasure to write the introduction to the *Graphic Artists Guild Handbook: Pricing & Ethical Guidelines, 13th Edition.*

Much like a trapeze artist who relies on solidly built equipment to fly through the air, I have had this book to help me soar through the graphic arts business. I never took a business course, and yet I was determined to run my own business right out of college. The thrill of flying through the air looks like a lot of fun—from the ground. However, once perched atop a two-square-foot pedestal looking at the ground 40 feet below, with a net somewhere in between and a flying bar coming at me, the job looks completely different.

It's in those times when the *Handbook* is there for you. The Graphic Artists Guild's mission is to protect the economic interests of graphic artists; so from adequate pricing structures to solid contracts, this book will help you make it safely to the next pedestal.

The Graphic Artists Guild, early in its inception, saw a need to write down the standards and practices of the graphic arts profession, not as law, but as a way for creators and buyers of graphic art to communicate clearly. After all, trapeze artists are only as successful as the partners with whom they work. The *Handbook* serves as a guide to this language and cultural understanding.

Copyright protection is at the heart of our sustenance as graphic artists. Keeping current and informed on copyright issues enables artists to sell, and clients to purchase, only the rights necessary for their specific needs. Copyright knowledge makes for better contracts, fewer misunderstandings, and better business experiences for all.

It truly is a circus out there—especially lately. In the past few years, it might have seemed that you were a trapeze artist standing on the pedestal, trying to figure out how to swing across to the other side (often, without a net). The *Graphic Artists Guild Handbook: Pricing & Ethical Guidelines, 13th edition* will help you get there—all you have to do is reach out and take the first step. After all, the show must go on.

Haydn S. Adams
President, Graphic Artists Guild

How to Use this Book

The 13th edition of the *Graphic Artists Guild Handbook: Pricing & Ethical Guidelines* continues to be a work in progress, evolving to meet the changing needs of graphic artists and their clients. It seeks to be as neutral and objective as possible and aims to promote the understanding that fees and terms are always negotiable between buyer and seller.

To some, the prices shown in the book will be too low; for others, too high. Still others may complain that prices don't reflect the current economy. The Guild recognizes that the level of expertise, years of experience, and reputation of the graphic artist will affect what is charged, as will the cost of living and size of the market where an artist works. This book covers many different specialties within the graphic arts; some have been hit much harder by the recessionary economy than others, due to its impact on the clients and media they serve. In general, graphic artists are reporting that their smaller clients have been affected the most by the sluggish economy, a trend reflected in lower pricing at the low end of the pricing ranges.

It is intended that the *Handbook* be what it says it is—*guidelines,* and only guidelines, for the seller and buyer to use to arrive at fair and equitable pricing for the work under consideration. The pricing charts, based on the latest feedback and reviewed by outstanding practitioners for each discipline, are not meant to be specific set prices. It is up to the individual graphic artist to determine how to price work—after taking into account all the factors related to the work.

So much information is packed into the *Handbook* that readers may miss valuable wisdom in their effort to quickly find a suitable contract or price. We suggest reading the book cover to cover and becoming familiar with issues that affect all disciplines. At the very least, read the chapter introductions; they will give you an overview and help direct you to specific information.

- The first six chapters examine the complex legal, technological, and financial considerations that influence how graphic artists conduct business, including copyright issues and equitable contracts.

- Following a chapter on salaries and trade customs within the industry, six chapters cover, in depth, the many trade practices unique to the specific disciplines, enabling both art buyers and graphic artists to understand and appreciate the demands on time and talent reflected in the ranges of fees being paid.

- The book concludes with sample forms and contracts and a glossary of terms used in their development; every artist should make the effort to become familiar with these terms.

Acknowledgments

Judith Stagnitto Abbate
Haydn S. Adams
Daren Bader
Scott Bakal
Lauri Baram
Urshula Barbour
Pamela Barcita
Diane Barton
Robert Becker
Deborah Benson
Annie Bissett
Marty Blake
Rebecca Blake
Theresa Bower
Brian Lee Boyce
David Cain
Adrianne Caporusso
Meredith Carle
Paul Carlos
Frederick H. Carlson
Laurie Ann Carlson
Jean Cassels
Ophelia M. Chambliss
Stephanie Chaparian
Alicia Cheng
George Chiang
Marcos Chin
Robert W. Clarida, Esq.
Cory Clarke
Matthew Cohen, CPA
Susan Conway
Carol Coogan
Cheryl A. Cook
Tad Crawford, Esq.
Gene Czebiniack
Traci Daberko
Mike Dammer
Beau and Alan Daniels
Libby Davidson
Roy Delgado
Rebecca Dolan
Debbie Donarummo
Bil Donovan
Colleen Doran
Marion Dorfer
Laurie Douglas
Ali Douglass
Terre Dunivant
Becky Eason
Pamela Esposito
Joanne Fink
Carla Francheschi-Green
Mark Frankmann
Jim Frazier
Dale Gladstone
Susi Goldberg
Rick Grafe
Anita Grien
Sam Gross
Holly Hagen
Samantha Hahn
Leslie Ellen Harris, Esq.

Staciellen Heasley, Esq.
Anne Keenan Higgins
Gareth Hinds
Tara Hogan
Sarah Holden
Dianna Jacobsen
Sue Jenkins
Iskra Johnson
Diana Kappa
Linda Joy Kattwinkel, Esq.
Cecile Kaufman
Larissa Kisielewska
Gary Koeppel
David Koeth
Jim Kopp
Josh Korwin
Charles Kreloff
Susan McGee Krukonis
Adam Larson
Richard Laurent
Matthew LeBaron
Cheryl Leisenring
Jonathan Lemon
William Levin
Pam Levy
Jennifer Lilya
Sara Love
Suzanne Lucas
John MacDonald
Jim Mahfood
Jen Manion
Wendy Lyon Martin
Angela Martini
Jacqueline McCarthy
Evelyn McCauley
Claudia McCue
Matthew McElligott
Tara McPherson
George Middleton
James Montalbano
Patricia Morley
Julie Metz
Clara Applewhaite Mitchell
Raymond Mongroo
Jody Nebesnick
Scott Neely
Betsy Nelson
Eileen O'Connell
Rachel O'Donnell
Regina Ortenzi
Ken Orvidas
Richard Osaka
Megan Patrick
Daniel Pelavin
Cheryl Phelps
Diane Piemonte
Maria Piscopo
Diana Ponce
Catherine Post
Allison Puff
Adam Questell
Chris Reed

David H. Reuss
Kathleen Rietz
Robin Riggs
Francine Rosenfeld
Marc Rosenthal
Nancy C. Sampson
Douglas Schneider
Tobias Schwarz
Kirsti Scott
Andrea Selby
Lisa Shaftel
Ed Shems
Yuko Shimizu
Suzanne Silk
Elizabeth Silver
Lauren Simeone
Julie Sims
Mark Simon
Mark Simonson
Laura Smith
Phyllis Stevens
Louisa St. Pierre
Marc V. Stress
Gordon Studer
Susan Swan
Kristina Swarner
Simms Taback
Billy Tan
Pepper Tharp
Melissa Turk
Robert Uncapher
Courtney Vagliardo
Renita Van Dusen
Gregory T. Victoroff, Esq.
Ilene Weingard
Brian T. Whitehill
Renee Winfield
Mary Jo York
Christian Zagarskas
Judy Francis Zankel
Mary Jo Zazueta

American Institute of Graphic Arts
Animation Guild, Local 839, IATSE
Aquent
Bernhardt Fudyma Design Group
The Creative Group
D*MNGOOD®
F+W Publications
Game Developer magazine
Gerald & Cullen Rapp
HOW magazine
The July Group
The Licensing Letter
Mendola Artists
Readex Research
Ross Culbert & Lavery, Inc.
Society for Environmental
  Graphic Design
U.S. Copyright Office

Many thanks to the hundreds of graphic arts professionals—both Guild members and nonmembers—who have contributed their expertise over the years to this cooperative effort, including those who completed the pricing questionnaires that are the basis for the most current pricing data.

PROFESSIONAL RELATIONSHIPS

This chapter provides an overview of how illustrators and graphic designers conduct business, and it examines many professional relationships they may encounter during their careers. Ethical standards for doing business with graphic artists are stressed.

VIRTUALLY all areas of commerce and communications use graphic arts. Graphic artists often specialize, focusing their talents to serve particular markets within the communications industry, such as magazine or book publishing, or they work for corporations, manufacturers, retailers, advertising agencies, broadcasting companies, or for-profit and nonprofit institutions. Clients may be individuals, small companies, or conglomerates. Some clients purchase art and design on a regular basis, while many are first-time, one-time, or infrequent buyers. No matter how clients work, the graphic artist has to present a professional face to all buyers.

Today, the role of the visual communicator is both simpler and more complicated. Much of the new media blurs the distinctions between disciplines; and visual artists, increasingly, must be adept at multiple disciplines. In general, illustrators and graphic designers differ in that illustrators create commercial artwork that conveys an idea pictorially for a specific purpose, while designers are professional visual problem solvers who work with the elements of typography, color, illustration, and photography to create all types of commercial visual communication tools. Illustrators and graphic designers may work in both print and digital media.

Because these lines have gotten fuzzy, employers may be uncertain about who, exactly, they need, and/or they try to get two for the price of one. Artists need to be clear on the various components of a project and why they're being hired. Artists also must ensure that clients are clear about what's required and who's the appropriate artist for the work.

For clients, it is important to understand what illustrators and graphic designers do—and how they differ—in order to understand how to initiate and sustain professional relationships with them. Establishing and maintaining good working relationships between graphic artists and clients are vital to the health and prosperity of the profession.

Illustrator Professional Relationships

A client may commission artwork from an illustrator directly or indirectly, through an artist's representative or other agent. Clients occasionally contract with an art director, design firm or studio, advertising agency, or packager to hire illustrators for a particular project. The Guild recommends that both parties sign a written agreement prior to starting work. For more information about contracts, refer to Chapter 5, Essential Business Practices and Chapter 6, Standard Contracts & Business Tools.

Client

As experts in their fields, clients communicate their needs and objectives to graphic artists regarding the product and the market. Using their particular style and expertise, illustrators offer solutions to the client for the visual communications problems posed. Ethical professional practices, as well as the ability to describe problems effectively and envision winning solutions, form the practical basis of a successful partnership between client and illustrator.

During initial meetings, the illustrator and client discuss the problem in terms of the client's objectives and possible solutions, fees, usage, and contract terms. These discussions should create an agreement that addresses the concerns of both parties.

Regular art buyers usually have staff specifically responsible for all purchasing; these are art directors or other employees with expertise in commissioning art assignments. In a large corporation, for example, the art director, art buyer, or stylist probably has some experience in professional practices and pricing.

Art director

In many organizations, art directors manage a number of projects or accounts simultaneously. They are responsible for finding the illustrators, negotiating the terms of the jobs, and supervising assignments to ensure their proper execution within prescribed budgeting and time constraints. Art directors base their choices of talent on their knowledge of the client's concerns and on the diverse styles of the artists available. To find illustrators, an art director consults talent sourcebooks, advertising directories, and major trade publications. In addition, an art director may call in artists to present their portfolios or review artists' web sites, place ads in publications or with professional organizations (such as the Graphic Artists Guild's *JOBline News,* described later in this chapter under Sources of Illustration & Design Talent), or contact employment services.

When speaking with illustrators, art directors need to be familiar with the project's schedule, the budget, how the artwork will be used, and a variety of other factors. Illustrators then negotiate appropriate rights, terms, and fees with the art director. The art director may then send the artist a confirming purchase order, or the artist may send the art director a proposal or contract and later, when turning in the artwork, an invoice and delivery memo. The factors used to determine the terms of agreement are thoroughly described throughout this book.

LIMITED RIGHTS

Following are categories for the purchase of limited rights, which may range from one-time to extensive use. All rights granted should be clearly detailed in the purchase order, including a specific market, medium, time period, and geographic region: for example, national (region), consumer magazine (medium), advertising (market), rights for a period of one year (time). Exclusivity within the markets purchased is usually guaranteed. Non-competing rights may be sold elsewhere, unless the purchase order stipulates otherwise. Sale of the original artwork or sale of the copyright (which is sometimes erroneously called a buyout) is a separate transaction.

In-house presentation & research: Usage is generally purchased at the lowest rates in the advertising market, since the material will be used only in-house for presentation or in front of small groups. Agreements permitting more extensive uses generally require that additional fees must be paid.

Test market: Artwork is historically purchased at low rates for use in a limited number of markets, and an artist's agreement should stipulate additional fees if use is expanded.

Displays, trade shows, public relations.

Electronic: This use is growing in frequency as Internet communications continue to expand. Electronic rights may be purchased in addition to other rights and should include additional charges (for instance, a percentage of the publication fee).

Point-of-purchase: Usage includes all point-of-sale materials, such as signs, leaflets, shopping cart posters, catalogs, brochures, counter displays, and so on.

Outdoor: All posters that are not point-of-sale, including those used for billboards, painted bulletins, transit, and bus shelters, are in this category.

Publication: Usage includes newspapers, magazines, Sunday supplements, in-house publications, and any material included as part of a publication, such as freestanding inserts or advertorials.

TV use: Only television rights.

Design firm or studio

Design firm and *design studio* are often used interchangeably depending on the image the business wants to project. Therefore, the distinction between the two is blurred. However, a design firm is often thought of as a larger organization with more employees on staff, offering a full range of graphic art services, while a studio may be a sole proprietorship consisting of only the designer/owner or a small organization of two to three partners. However, this does not mean that a studio cannot be a full-service business. Established studios often have arrangements with other independent contractors, such as illustrators, Web designers, photographers, editors, etc., who they can call on to provide specialty or complementary services when the need arises. A larger design firm might have one or more illustrators on staff, or it may also subcontract illustrators when needed.

Studio can also refer to the workplace of a self-employed illustrator or fine artist. In this situation, the client would hire and work directly with the illustrator.

Advertising agency

Artwork for advertising agencies is usually purchased by an art director and an art buyer, who work together to select the illustrator to be used on a job. An art buyer is responsible for calling in a selection of artists' portfolios for review by the creative group, who choose an illustrator based on the style of art needed and the portfolio submitted. After an illustrator is selected, the art buyer and the illustrator are mutually responsible for negotiating the purchase of usage rights from the illustrator as well as the budget, schedule, trafficking, and invoicing of each assignment.

At the time of assignment, most agencies provide illustrators with a purchase order that details the rights purchased, ownership of the art, delivery dates for sketches and finished art, prices for the completed assignment, the cancellation fee at sketch and finish stages, and any additional expenses that will be covered, such as delivery charges or shipping. All terms in a purchase order or contract are open to negotiation until both parties reach agreement.

An understanding or contract has been reached when both parties sign the purchase order. As independent contractors, illustrators are responsible for sending a contract that describes the terms of the understanding. A letter of agreement does this nicely; for a sample form, see the Appendix. Rights purchased may be in any or all of a number of categories, which should be spelled out in the purchase order. (See sidebars: Limited Rights and Multiple Rights.) Each illustrator decides independently how to price each use of his or her work.

Packager

Packagers, who work predominantly in book publishing, coordinate all the components of a project and either present the finished concept to publishers for execution or manufacture the books themselves and deliver bound volumes to the publisher. Like publishers, packagers contract with illustrators, designers, and writers, and all negotiations are handled as if the packager were the publisher. Because of the relatively small size and weak financial strength of packagers compared with publishers, the importance of a written agreement cannot be overemphasized.

Artist's representative/broker

Illustrators, textile designers, and other artists need to connect effectively with their markets. Some artists are as adept at solving visual problems as soliciting business, researching new markets, coordinating directory ads, designing and following up on promotions, and negotiating contracts and rights. But others are more skilled at solving visual problems than at marketing or promoting their own talent.

In an ideal world, artists would concentrate solely on creating their art. In order for this to happen, the best solution is to have a representative or agent who spends time, energy, and resources seeking work for artists. Professional representatives, skilled at representing artists' interests, are often more adept at negotiations than the artists themselves, resulting in better terms and higher fees than artists could secure on their own. For artists who are comfortable delegating business tasks, a professional agent can contribute thousands of dollars in additional revenue and hours of additional creative time. This arrangement is very cost-effective for the artist because representatives are compensated only when they find work for their clients; it is therefore in their interest to find the best outlets for their artists. Although the agent works for the artist, the best artist-agent relationships are mutually beneficial partnerships.

But not every situation is ideal. If an artist feels that he or she is just another portfolio, or if a representative continually fails to secure work for an artist while insisting on receiving commissions for work secured by the artist, such relationships should be critically evaluated. Some agents will offer lower fees to ensure a good personal relationship with a buyer, at the expense of the artist whose interests they have pledged to protect. Obviously, relationships with representatives who engage in questionable practices should be avoided. In these cases, having any agent may be worse than having no agent.

FINDING A SUITABLE REPRESENTATIVE

Representatives who handle a number of artists often concentrate on a particular style or market. For example, one rep may represent artists with highly realistic, painterly styles, while another may concentrate on humorous work. Some representatives have cultivated strong contacts in advertising, while others have extensive networks in the editorial or children's book market. Illustrators need to research which representatives are best able to serve their needs.

Research A good place to research the talent and clients handled by particular representatives is in the major sourcebooks and talent directories (for further information, see the Sources of Illustration & Design Talent section later in this chapter). *American Showcase, The Black Book, the Directory of Illustration, Workbook,* and others display many pages of advertising that are placed, in whole or in part, by artist's representatives. Interested illustrators can easily determine which representative is the best fit. Similarly, agents seeking additional talent often use these books to locate suitable unrepresented artists.

Contact The illustrator should contact likely representatives to see if they are interested in seeing samples of his or her work. When sending samples, it is important to note that published work is not necessarily as important as imaginative work.

Artists should always trust their own first impressions of a representative; as the rep impresses the artist, so he or she will impress prospective clients. If an artist feels compatible with a representative and the rep is interested in setting up a partnership, references should be checked. The best place to start is by talking with artists currently working with the rep, as well as with those formerly repre-

CONSIDERATIONS WHEN HIRING AN ARTIST'S REP

When an artist thinks his or her career has reached the point where it would benefit from professional representation, the following should be considered:

Be objective about your talent & stature. A reputable agent is interested in representing highly marketable talent—successful artists who no longer have time to cold-call new clients or follow up with existing clients. Although an entry-level artist could benefit from the services of a representative, most agents do not take on someone who is untried and unknown. There are exceptions if the artist has a style that will sell.

Identify & target your market. A frank appraisal of one's work and target market is necessary to make the best match with a rep. An artist with a sketchy, humorous style would not be suitable for an agent who represents predominantly painterly styles. Similarly, if one's work is best suited for the editorial or book cover market, pursuing a representative with a strong agency clientele would not be very productive; though reps will, on occasion, seek out artists with strong potential to cross over into other markets. In other cases, a rep with only one fashion illustrator will push for that artist, should opportunities arise, but the fashion illustrator needs to make sure the rep has contacts in the fashion market. Opportunities will rarely come up for a fashion illustrator among children's book artists. Having a clear vision of your work and the direction in which you want to go is essential. You need a rep who shares that vision and wants to pursue that direction.

Seek aesthetic compatibility. An artist needs to know that his or her work fits well with the work of other artists represented. Even if an artist might seem to compete with other artists in a group, a good rep will not form a relationship with an artist unless sufficient opportunities are available. Or an artist may deliberately select a rep who does not represent other artists with competing styles.

sented. Talking to other artists is the best way to separate good from mediocre or incompetent agents among the large number of representatives working in the industry.

Among the questions to ask are: How much work did the representative generate over the year? Does the agent promote artists individually or as a group? Was the relationship productive for both parties? Were payments received promptly? Did the representative share in advertising and promotional expenses? What financial responsibility for yearly promotional costs did the artist carry? How were disputes, if any, resolved? If the relationship was terminated, why was it, and on what terms?

Talking with clients who have worked with the rep is another approach. It is reasonable to ask a prospective rep for clients' phone numbers; how the rep responds will provide clues about his or her business ethics. Another helpful practice is visiting the agent's office to see the physical layout, how portfolios and artists' samples are handled, and what business procedures are used.

REACHING AN AGREEMENT

Artists' representatives have the authority to act on behalf of the artists they represent. They can commit the artist legally, but only in matters agreed upon in the artist-representative contract. Therefore, all terms and conditions of artist-representative arrangements should be discussed in detail, negotiated as needed, and confirmed in writing. Artists should have a lawyer read any contract and make certain the terms are clearly understood before signing. The Guild's Artist-Agent Agreement and Surface/Textile Designer-Agent Agreement can be found in the Appendix. If a more casual relationship is preferred, the Guild recommends that both parties, at the least, sign a memo that describes each person's responsibilities.

The most important issues to be considered when negotiating an artist-agent agreement are:

Commissions & fees Traditionally, artists pay reps a commission of 25 to 35 percent for all jobs executed, excluding expenses. Most U.S. artists pay 25 percent; artists outside the United States pay the higher rate. Textile design commissions have historically ranged from 25 to 50 percent of the fees paid, excluding expenses. Expenses not billable to the client are generally subtracted from a flat fee before the commission is computed. Expenses billed to the client as line items on an invoice are normally reimbursed to the person who incurred the expenses and are paid separately from any commission. Policies concerning stock and reuse sales should be discussed and negotiated in detail.

House accounts Clients that the artist contacted and developed before signing with a rep are called "house accounts." Most artists do not pay commissions on house accounts that they service themselves, and they generally pay a lower commission on house accounts that the rep services. A problem may occur when the artist initiates contact with a client, but no jobs begin until after a rep agreement is signed. Artists may become dissatisfied with a rep if they have to pay commissions on accounts they feel they cultivated. To avoid this problem, the artist and the rep should negotiate prior to signing an agreement how work that materializes from such clients will be handled.

Exclusivity or nonexclusivity Reps usually expect an exclusive arrangement with an artist for at least North American markets, but they often agree that the artist may continue to work directly with any previously established house accounts.

In one kind of nonexclusive relationship, artists are free to promote their work in all markets, even those handled by the representative. In another nonexclusive arrangement, representatives handle only certain markets, such as advertising or publishing, or certain geographic areas, and artists retain the right to promote their work in other areas. In considering this type of agreement, artists should take into account the situation that occurs when an art director who changes jobs has a personal relationship with one rep and does not want to call another one.

Exclusivity or nonexclusivity is a crucial issue in any contract, since artists should feel that all their work will be marketed in the best possible manner. Representatives who ask for exclusive contracts should be willing to identify the other artists they represent, so artists can ascertain that they will not be competing against other artists in the group or lose jobs that might otherwise go to them. Artists who accept a rep's demand for exclusivity may wish to consider negotiating exclusivity for their particular style or genre within a group. Any artist-rep arrangement can be negotiated if it offers the potential for mutual benefit for both parties.

Expenses While all expenses are negotiable, artists are generally responsible for expenses related to their art, including the duplication of chromes and other display material. The rep provides the portfolio, but the artist retains ownership of the material in it. Any agreement should state that these pieces remain the property of the artist and that they will be returned to the artist upon termination of the relationship.

Reps are generally responsible for their selling expenses, such as phone calls, overnight deliveries, messengers, insurance, and entertaining clients. Directory advertising and direct-mail promotion expenses are generally split in the same ratio as commissions, with the rep paying 25 to 35 percent and artists paying only their share of the actual costs, not published rates. Artists should expect that any savings from discounted page rates, printing, or other expenses will be credited to them.

Reps should get the artist's authorization ahead of time for any expenses the artist is obligated to pay, such as costs for directories, web sites, and promotional mailings. These expenses should be itemized and are deducted from the artist's fees.

Billing procedures In most cases, the agent handles billing, but this depends on the negotiated agreement. The party responsible for billing is obligated to send the other party copies of all purchase orders and invoices. If there is no purchase order, a copy of the canceled check should be supplied. The invoice should reflect exact terms. One practical benefit of this procedure is that if the person handling the billing dies, declares bankruptcy, or reorganizes, the other party has proof of what is owed.

If the rep handles billing, it is his or her job to maintain an up-to-date record-keeping and reporting system to inform artists about their finances. If a rep fails to keep an artist regularly informed about all billing and payment transactions, there is a problem, and the artist should move quickly to terminate the relationship.

It should be noted that accurate record keeping is not just the rep's responsibility. The Guild recommends that artists maintain complete records of all paperwork and log any oral agreements. Monitoring finances and making sure payments are timely will benefit the artist's business.

Timely payment If artists believe that payments take longer than they should, they may request that the rep copy all incoming checks so they may see the dates when they were mailed. If the rep refuses, artists may request that all payments go directly to them.

Finder's fee Occasionally, a special opportunity is presented to an artist by an agent or broker, even though a formal relationship does not exist between them. Traditionally, in such special circumstances, the agent receives a finder's fee of 10 percent of the negotiated fee or advance. Because no formal relationship exists, this is usually a one-time fee, and if that client assigns more work, no additional commissions would be due. Occasionally, an artist will ask a rep to negotiate a difficult deal that the artist has secured, paying 10 percent or more, on a one-time basis.

Differences Even in the best relationships, differences may arise between artists and reps. Reps may become dissatisfied with artists who refuse what seem to be good jobs. Artists may become dissatisfied or discontented paying commissions to reps who they feel are not doing enough to generate more work. The rep and the artist must clearly express their concerns and explore why new work is not coming in. Perhaps the rep needs to try a new marketing approach, or the artist needs to develop a new style. If the relationship cannot be improved, the artist may need a different rep. In that case, they need to terminate their agreement amicably.

Termination This is a sensitive area for both artist and agent. Each party should be allowed to terminate with 30 days' written notice. After termination of services, an agent may continue to receive commissions for an agreed-upon period of time—usually three months after the termination date—on work that was generated from accounts developed by the agent. If an agent has represented an artist for more than six months, the right to receive commissions after termination is often increased by one month for each additional six months of representation. For example, after two years of representation, the agent would receive commissions for six months after termination. Royalty compensation on assignments contracted during the association continues until the client ceases payment on those projects.

Although circumstances can vary, artists rarely agree to give agents commissions on assignments obtained more than six months after the effective termination date. Of course, if an agent is entitled to receive a commission on an assignment obtained within the agreed-upon time, even if it started after the end of the termination period, it is due if the client's payment arrives after that time. This right, however, should not apply to house accounts. If an artist does not want to continue to pay commissions to a former rep, a lump sum settlement may be preferable and may be negotiated based on the previous year's earnings.

All termination terms should be negotiated at the beginning of a relationship. Most agents do not show artists' work during termination periods unless an artist specifically requests it, and agents should forward all inquiries about the artist to the artist. Agents should return to the artist all artwork, portfolios, tear sheets, promotions, and any other images created solely by the artist at the end of the 30-day termination period, if not sooner.

Bankruptcy Very rarely, a rep has been known to declare bankruptcy and fail to pay the artist's fees. The best way for artists to prevent that is to be sure the artist-agent contract contains a clause that prohibits the agent from commingling the artist's fees with the agent's income and expenses.

Legally, the rep works for the artist and is obligated to protect and promote the artist's interests. Yet, legalities aside, the most practical, win-win model is that the artist and the rep are two independent businesses working together to improve both businesses. The best relationship is a rep and an artist who work symbiotically so that both businesses grow. It is in the rep's best interests to see an artist succeed. It is in the artist's interests to help establish his or her rep's reputation in the field.

WHAT TO DO & NOT DO
IF YOUR AGENT DECLARES BANKRUPTCY

- An artist may file a proof of claim with the court. This form is usually attached to the notice of the bankruptcy case mailed to creditors (or it can be obtained from a bankruptcy lawyer). This places the debtor on formal notice of the amount claimed to be owed, and it will give the artist a share of whatever payments are made to creditors.

- Depending on the amount of money at stake, an artist may, singly or with a group of similarly affected artists, consult a bankruptcy lawyer, who can evaluate the contractual provisions of the artist-agent agreement. This will determine if the artist has any rights to payments, any possible lien rights, or any possibility of personally suing the agent outside of the bankruptcy case (to do this, one has to get the permission of the bankruptcy court in what is referred to as "dischargeability litigation"). The artist may even be able to make a claim against the bank.

- An artist should not try to collect his or her fee directly from a client. Once bankruptcy has been declared, an estate is created that includes all the property in which the agent has an interest. Therefore, a bankruptcy petition operates as an automatic stay, which legally bars the artist from trying to collect a debt from the bankrupt agent, and may even bar the artist from trying to collect from the client. It is the bankruptcy court's responsibility to decide whose money is whose.

  In Chapter VII bankruptcy cases, a bankruptcy trustee is appointed to reduce the estate to cash and make distributions. If the artist goes to a client and asks for his or her portion of the fee, the bankruptcy trustee can go to the court and argue that the artist has violated the automatic stay by collecting money owed to the bankruptcy estate. If the court rules in the artist's favor, he gets to keep the money and the trustee loses. If the court rules in the trustee's favor, the artist has to refund the money and may be liable for a significant additional sum for the knowing violation of the automatic stay. The trustee may not contest the matter, but that may not be a risk the artist wants to take.

- An artist should not file a claim in small-claims court because that also violates the automatic stay. (Any action in violation of the automatic stay is legally considered a nullity, whether the person knows about the bankruptcy or not.) A knowing violation of a stay could be considered contempt of court and subject the violator to legal sanctions, which could damage the artist's case.

- In a Chapter VII bankruptcy case, the contract between the artist and agent is automatically terminated when the agent files for bankruptcy. A letter from the artist informing clients of the severed relationship would be appropriate (though it will not resolve the collection issues discussed above). In a Chapter XI bankruptcy case, the artist may not be able to terminate the contract (for reasons that are too complex to discuss here), in which case a letter to clients would not be a good idea.

Graphic Designer Professional Relationships

Graphic designers are hired to communicate ideas. Whether they design books or billboards, movie posters or television graphics, corporate identity programs or web sites, designers take the client's message and, by selecting a combination of type, color, imagery, and texture (which is often accomplished by printing techniques), transform the content into an informative, persuasive piece of visual communication.

To be effective, graphic designers need to combine aesthetic and strategic judgment with project management skills to create effective, timely marketing strategies for their clients. Designers usually execute projects at the client's request, taking the client's need, and formulating an effective selling tool, product, promotion piece, or strategy to meet a specific objective. Sometimes, they collaborate with market researchers and public relations specialists to help formulate design concepts. Often, they are called upon to advise clients on what they should be doing, diverting them from a comfortable approach to a more daring one.

Graphic designers play a multitude of roles when working with clients, including acting as consultants, teachers, and even shepherds. Often clients' questions provide opportunities for designers to help the clients understand how best to present and promote themselves, which is the purpose of a consistent, imaginative corporate identity program, for example.

Although one tends to think of graphic design in terms of print media, today's designers often need to anticipate future needs and consider how their design solutions will work on the Internet or in three dimensions as well as in print. Such re-purposing of design is essential today when multiple applications are in demand. (For further discussion of designing for electronic media, see Chapter 9, Web Design & Other Digital Graphic Arts.)

Client relationships

Because graphic design exerts such a tremendous influence on a company's image, service, or product, most businesses consider it a necessary component of their overall business strategy. Clients hire graphic designers to develop and provide a marketing approach and a creative direction for their visual communication needs and then to coordinate all production details through final delivery. In providing this service, designers often coordinate their art direction and design services with copywriters, illustrators, photographers, and printers and bill the client for the entire package. As professional consultants, they assess the feasibility of a project based on their experience, knowledge of the market, and available resources. There are many advantages and disadvantages to this all-inclusive practice, and designers may choose instead to have all vendors bill the client directly.

Sometimes, though, clients choose to develop a project and then bring in a designer. This is usually inefficient. Many decisions will already have been made about matters requiring a designer's input, which may lead to unnecessary delays, additional costs, and inadequate solutions. The earlier a designer is called in to consult on a project, the more efficient it is for them to help develop the most effective solution for a design objective. The designer can contribute a fresh perspective, strategy, and aesthetic viewpoint that influence the project's impact, cost-effectiveness, and success.

A client may seek a long-term relationship with a graphic designer or design firm, particularly when planning a series of projects that need design continuity. When such a relationship is envisioned, a designer may be retained as a consultant during the early stages of a project to help strategize, plan, schedule, and budget.

FACTORS FOR CLIENTS TO CONSIDER WHEN HIRING A DESIGNER

Many design clients do not work with designers regularly and are, therefore, unaware of the trade customs and procedures that designers follow. To find a designer, a prospective client should ask friends, business colleagues, and graphics industry professionals (such as illustrators, photographers, or printers) to recommend design firms and then study examples of their work. When a client sees pieces s/he admires, the client should find out who designed them and investigate the designer's professional background. The client also should be sure to inquire about the designer's specialties, reputation, dependability, and working relationships. Then the client can invite the designer to present a range of work in a variety of budget categories to provide an overview of the designer's capabilities, as well as anything else that may be relevant to the anticipated project.

A number of variables contribute to a successful relationship with a designer.

Talent/Expertise Talent may be difficult to define, especially for corporate clients who like to rely on measurable standards when conducting business. Clients must often judge design talent based on such intangibles as perceptions of the designer's presentation and the designer's ability to effectively communicate an understanding of the client's needs and objectives. Standard measurements of talent/expertise are based on evaluation of the firm's portfolio, references, and design proposal (described later in this chapter). The client needs to assess if the designer developed an idea or concept successfully as well as if s/he used type, color, paper, ink, and imagery effectively for the message and the intended audience. Does the work command attention and have impact? Does it fulfill its function and purpose? Did the designer find innovative ways to solve unique problems?

Chemistry In any creative process, personalities count, and being able to communicate easily is essential. Clients need to establish a comfortable working rapport with designers.

Reputation It may be prudent for a prospective client to interview other clients or vendors with whom a designer has worked and ask if the designer behaved like a team player, delivered on time, stuck to the budget, and paid bills in full. If necessary, a credit check should be run.

Capacity The scope and scale of the client's project and/or the design firm's capability to accommodate a client's special needs often dictate the choice of the design firm.

Location While today's electronic technology makes physical proximity to the client less and less important, geographic closeness may facilitate better communication. A face-to-face relationship may create a stronger bond and feeling of involvement than a telephone or e-mail relationship. But this is not true in all cases, and conducting business at a distance is becoming more frequent, especially if the designer's particular location is advantageous to the client.

Subcontractor relationships

Design firms, art directors, or other art buyers who assume creative control of a project for a client often subcontract with independent contractors for work or services they cannot provide themselves, such as illustration, photography, web design, copy editing, and proofreading. Payment is due to these contractors in a timely manner, no matter when designers receive payment from the client. The designer and the independent contractor should sign separate subcontractor agreements.

Bidding on a project

Designers are chosen to work on projects in two ways. They either respond to a Request for Proposal (RFP) or, most often, prepare their own proposal in competition with other design firms.

RESPONDING TO AN RFP OR DESIGN BRIEF

Often when a client needs a designer for a major project, the client prepares a Request for Proposal or a design brief that contains all the background information, objectives, and specifications for the project that a design firm needs in order to create and submit a proposal. The RFP is a great tool for client and designer alike because it focuses on all aspects of a future project. It helps the client get bids that are based on the same specifications, so the client is able to compare "apples to apples." And it gives the designer all the information needed to formulate an accurate proposal without endlessly questioning a prospective client.

There are drawbacks to responding to an RFP. One is that designers generally do not know who they are competing against. Did the potential client send the RFP to 50 firms, or did the client do some research and offer the RFP to a pre-selected group of three firms? (This can easily be resolved by asking the client who received RFPs.) Another drawback is that sometimes a highly developed RFP leaves the designer out of the critical phase of advising and helping to plan the client's marketing strategy. On the other hand, receiving a well-developed RFP is usually a positive indication of an organized client and is a time-saver for the designer.

Writing proposals is a very time-consuming process, and it is often difficult to assess the prospective client. Designers need to determine, using whatever criteria they find appropriate, whether or not the project is interesting or lucrative enough to spend hours preparing a proposal. A typical RFP or design brief includes:

Background Information about the company or organization, including its size and primary services or products.

Audience General information about the target audience. This helps convey the general scope of the project.

Objectives Objectives can be as broad and general as "keeping the audience informed about our company," or they can be as specific as "get registered users of our product to order the upgrade."

Vehicle What is the piece to be created? A brochure, newsletter, web site, identity program, packaging, or other item?

Look & feel General direction about company positioning and its target market: for example, "a cutting-edge design that appeals to tech-savvy Gen-X readers who surf the Internet daily" or "a down-to-earth style that appeals to college-educated women over 50."

Specifications Rights needed. Print: finished size, folds, colors, paper weight, etc. Digital: file format, resolution, etc. Quantity. Packaging, mailing/shipping requirements, etc.

Time frame Goal date for final deliverable. Is a specific event or mailing distribution date being targeted?

Preliminary schedule Date when client-provided materials are due to designer. Dates for initial concepts, revisions, final art.

Other questions Will the designer handle printing? Are there other services that the designer must provide, such as finding writers, photographers, and illustrators? What is the final deliverable—disk, film, or printed piece?

Proposal review criteria How will the client choose the designer? Will there be an interview? Should the designer include work samples or a portfolio with the proposal?

DEVELOPING A DESIGN PROPOSAL

Often when bidding on a project, graphic designers develop their own proposals. They use initial meetings and research to understand the client's objectives and conceptualize possible directions. They also determine the target audience, desired response, and the overall effect to be achieved. Responsible clients communicate limitations clearly at the beginning of a project, such as budget and deadlines and all the elements they will provide, such as text, photographs, artwork, or charts.

It is important for both client and designer to discuss specific directions about what is being bid upon. Being specific ensures that both parties will be able to avoid surprises in the scope and estimates of the project once the proposal is accepted.

Based on these initial discussions, designers establish their fees, often taking a combination of factors into consideration, including scope of services (what they will provide), project value, usage, market conditions, schedule, client budget (what can be accomplished for the money allotted to the project), hours expended, and gut instinct. The value the client expects to derive from the work is an increasingly important factor. For example, a company desiring top talent to develop a new identity program may be willing to pay a substantially higher fee than one calculated solely on expended time. Conversely, a designer may create a company greeting card for a long-term client as a client accommodation for substantially less than the market rates. While it may help a designer to walk through a project step-by-step, calculating the time needed for every activity and multiplying that time by the appropriate rate(s),

Parts of a Design Proposal

PART 1: DESIGN & PRODUCTION PROCESS

Design and production can be divided into three phases. Some designers prefer to divide their process into five phases: orientation; design development; design execution; prepress/production; and on press. Feel free to devise a system that is easiest and most workable for you.

Phase 1: Describes the design phase of the project, including what form the design presentation will take, how many versions will be presented, the client approval process, and the time frame.

Phase 2: Explains the production process, which occurs after client approval of the design phase. Includes assigning illustration and/or photography, copywriting, typesetting, proofreading, supervision of those components, print/production time estimates, and client approval schedules.

Phase 3: Final production: After client approval of the previous phases, final production begins. Depending on the end product(s) a design firm has been commissioned to produce, this phase may be a matter of going on press and/or supervising the fabrication or manufacturing of products within a prescribed schedule. If designers are involved with developing PowerPoint presentations, web sites, and multimedia presentations, programming them is part of this phase.

PART 2: FEES

Fees and expenses may be handled in a number of ways. During the first phase, the design office may arrange to bill on a project basis. If clients prefer to be billed on a project basis, they usually establish an acceptable cap on the total amount billed. The project is outlined in briefer form than for Part 1, including the fees required for design, copywriting, photography, illustration, and so on.

It is important to explain what these fees include (design, layout, type specification, preliminary proofreading, production, and so on) and, more importantly, what they do not include (out-of-pocket expenses, author's alterations, overtime charges, photographic art direction, long-distance travel, etc.). The latter expenses, including markups for account handling and supervision (typically 15 to 25 percent), should be stated and estimates of charges should be included if possible.

When supplying production prices for printing, be sure to state that these estimates are based on rough specifications and are budget estimates only. More exact quotations can be furnished at the time the final design mechanicals or comprehensives are reviewed by the printer.

PART 3: PAYMENT SCHEDULE

Many design projects are quoted and billed by phase, with an initial fee representing 30 percent of the total estimated fee and reimbursable expenses. An outline of the payment schedule should be provided.

Another method of payment is a monthly breakdown of the fee in equal increments (often called a retainer). This method allows the designer to predict income over a long project and discourages the client from attaching a value to each phase that may be misleading, since few projects follow the phase development in a strictly sequential way.

PART 4: RIGHTS, USAGE & CREDIT

Discuss usage, ownership of rights and artwork, credit lines, approvals, interest charged for late payments, and any other terms (such as sales tax, confidentiality, or termination) deemed necessary. For clarification of these items, see the standard contracts in Chapter 6, Standard Contracts & Business Tools.

Signature lines for both client and designer and the date that the agreement is signed should follow. Both parties should retain a signed original and a copy.

PART 5: COLLATERAL MATERIAL

Include material that will help sell your abilities to the client. These may include background material or biographies, awards, and a list of other clients and examples of work completed for them.

FIGURE 1—1

the designer should view that information as a material guideline and not discuss projected hours with the client. As a rule, a designer's work should be judged for its value, as are the services of an experienced consultant or advisor, rather than by the time expended, as is the work of a vendor.

Once designers assess all these variables, they write a design proposal that spells out the scope of services, the client's responsibilities, and the estimated fees, expenses, and schedules.

What to include The proposal includes many of the following factors: an overview of the client's market; objectives and requirements of the project; research, art, and other components that will be developed or commissioned by the designer; typography, programming and other production services; printing requirements; intended use of the printed piece; and a schedule. In addition, designers frequently prepare documents explaining relationships with subcontractors (illustrators or photographers), billing procedures, and contract terms.

A proposal begins with an overview—a clear, concise description of the project. It includes a disclaimer that says that any prices and fees quoted are based on rough specifications of the items listed; if the items change, fees will change accordingly.

Proposals, like the projects they reflect, are divided into parts. These include a description of design and production; a description of fees; a payment schedule for the phases of work involved; rights, usage terms, and conditions; and collateral material to help sell the designer's abilities to the client.

Defining and describing the project phases helps facilitate the billing process and ensure the work will not proceed to the next phase until payment is received according to the agreed-upon schedule. These checkpoints also give clients clear, tangible input at appropriate times as the project develops. (See Figure 1-1 for parts and phases.)

Targeting the proposal The information supplied in the proposal is only for the design direction already discussed, specified, and agreed upon by the client and designer at their initial meetings. Since clients often compare a number of proposals before choosing a designer for the job, a proposal needs to be clear and thorough enough to be reviewed without the designer present.

The organization and appearance of a design proposal can be crucial in winning a job, especially when a design firm is competing against others. A proposal's appearance reflects a designer's ability and expertise as much as the information contained within it. Consequently, proposals should be organized logically, well written, well designed, and professionally presented.

When preparing a proposal for a new client, it helps to include collateral material, such as promotion pieces, reprints of published work, examples of similar projects produced by the designer, biographies of the designer and subcontractors involved in the project, and so on.

It is customary for project descriptions and cost proposals to be submitted to clients as a complimentary service. If a creative proposal—one that entails solutions to a client's objective—is submitted, any fees and expenses incurred on a client's behalf and with the client's consent are billable.

If the client accepts the proposal, the terms and conditions are expressed in writing and are signed by authorized representatives of both the client and the designer or design firm. Always make at least two copies of the proposal for both client and designer to retain as original signed copies if the commission is accepted. When signed by both client and designer, a proposal is legally binding as a contract.

It is important to note that any changes requested by the client beyond the scope outlined in the design proposal are considered "author's alterations" (AAs) and are billable. Additional services may include changes in the extent of the work, in the scheduling, and in the complexity of elements, and/or changes after client approval has been given for a specific stage, including concept, design, composition, and file production. AAs can become expensive to the client because changes are usually billed at an hourly rate. They may also increase the difficulty of completing the project within the time scheduled, causing overtime charges. It is the designer's responsibility to keep the client informed of any additional services that may be required by issuing timely change orders outlining the changes and to obtain the client's approval, also in writing, of related additional costs before any changes are implemented and additional fees incurred.

Standard contracts, like those in the Appendix, do not provide the detailed explanatory material required in proposals for complex, multiphase projects. Those proposals are much more comprehensive than the contracts provided in this book. However, these contracts can be used as outlines or models.

Getting started

Once the agreement is signed, the designer begins researching the project in greater depth. Before exploring any design directions, the designer reviews his or her findings with the client to make sure they agree. Then, with various design concepts in mind, the designer prepares a presentation showing general directions and formats for the project. Depending on the client's needs and the understanding between the client and the designer, the presentation may be "tight" or "loose." Preliminary renderings, or "comps" (an abbreviation for "comprehensives"), show the layout of the piece and are presented to the client for approval. Once approved, or revised and approved, the designer begins assembling the elements and services necessary to carry out the project within the client's agreed-on budget and time frame.

With the client's approval and/or involvement, the designer makes key decisions on the specific look of the work, including the use of illustration or photography. Since few clients buy art on a regular basis, the designer negotiates with individual artists on the client's behalf and within the scope of the client's approved art budget. In this regard, designers often assume the responsibility for educating the client on the intent, content, and ethics of trade customs and copyright law.

Designers must also remember their own responsibility to the artists whose work they are considering. The increased practice of using images from artists' portfolios and talent sourcebooks at the presentation or comp stage—without permission—prompted the Graphic Artists Guild to initiate the "Ask First" campaign to educate designers, art directors, and other art buyers to respect private intellectual property and the copyright laws that govern it. Art or photography should not be copied or borrowed for any use, including client presentations or comping, without the creator's permission. In addition, portfolios must be returned intact and in good condition (an unfortunate side effect of misusing sample work without permission has been damaged artwork and portfolios).

Sources of Illustration & Design Talent

Several resources are available to clients and graphic artists to find and/or promote talent.

Employment & recruitment agencies

Employment agencies in various cities around the country refer graphic designers to clients for a fee. They operate in the same way that most employment agencies do, but specialize in visual communications markets. Often these agencies are listed in trade magazines and telephone books.

Recruitment and search agencies (often referred to as headhunters) are a unique talent resource for a firm in need of specialized employees. To the person seeking a position, they represent an employment resource that might not be readily available through other channels. These agencies are actually variations on employment agencies. Recruitment agencies receive the job description from the client, and their task is to find the proper person. Client relationships are confidential, and job descriptions need not be made public. They are, nonetheless, subject to equal opportunity employment laws.

Recruiters often place ads in local newspapers to advertise positions. Because the recruiting agency's fees are paid by the client seeking an artist and not by the artist who is placed in the position, the term "fee paid" in the advertisement indicates that the job candidate has no financial obligation to the agency. (For more about employment, see the Employment Issues section in Chapter 3, Professional Issues, and the Labor Market section in Chapter 4, Technology Issues.)

Advertising directories & magazine annuals

Advertising directories are widely known and used sources of talent. These directories generally showcase a specific type of work, such as illustration or graphic design. Artists purchase space in a directory where they display representative work and list a contact address for either the artist or the artist's representative. Several of these directories have online versions. Other annual publications are compilations of juried shows. Directories and annuals also provide references for the types and styles of work being done in the field.

Among the best-known national directories for illustration are *The Alternative Pick* (Altpick.com), *American Showcase* (http://web.showcase.com/products.asp), *The Black Book, Chicago Talent,* the *Directory of Illustration* (http://directoryofillustration.com/), and *Workbook.* Directories of juried shows for illustration include *American Illustration, Art Directors Annual,* and the *Society of Illustrators Annual.* Those for design include the *AIGA Annual* (www.aigadesignjobs.org/public/default.asp), *The Alternative Pick* (Altpick.com), *Art Directors Annual, The Black Book* (www.blackbook.com/index.php), *Communication Arts Design Annual* (www.commarts.com/), *Graphis* (www.graphis.com/), *Print Regional Annual,* and *Workbook* (www.workbook.com/). Many publications sponsor juried shows in areas of special interest, such as dimensional illustration, humorous illustration, and international design and illustration.

All of the graphic design magazines hold yearly competitions and feature the winners in special annual issues. Directories and magazine annuals can be purchased directly from the publishers or at most art supply stores and well-stocked bookstores.

The Internet

The Internet is a valuable resource for artists and clients alike. Illustrators and graphic designers can showcase and market their work on their own web sites or on portfolio sites devoted to the work of many artists. As mentioned above, many of the print directories and annuals have online counterparts. For example, animation, design, illustration, photography, type, and web design talent can be found at Altpick.com http://altpick.com/, the online version of *The Alternative Pick.* Clients can search for talent by name or artistic specialty.

Guild resources

The Portfolio section of the Guild's web site enables prospective clients to search online for artists by specialty and artistic style and to preview their work before making contact www.graphicartists-guild.org/theguild/member-portfolios/.

JOBline News is a national employment resource published weekly as an e-newsletter by the Guild's New York Chapter. It lists job opportunities in all areas of the graphic arts, ranging from independent contractors to part-time, long-term, and full-time staff positions. *JOBline News* is a free benefit for Guild members. Employers can post their job openings at affordable rates (for details, e-mail jobline@gag.org).

Some Guild chapters also collect information on employment possibilities available in their geographic areas. Others offer a number of different forms of referral services.

Ethical Standards

The Graphic Artists Guild, established by graphic artists, is mandated by its constitution to monitor, support, and foster ethical standards in all dealings between graphic artists and art buyers. This is accomplished through Guild programs for members, through cooperation with related organizations, and through legislative activity on local, state, and federal levels.

The Graphic Artists Guild's Grievance Committee

As part of this responsibility, the Guild has a grievance committee that addresses issues of professional relationships to help members resolve disputes with clients over violations of agreements and commonly accepted trade standards. Misunderstandings and disputes in the graphic communications industries are inevitable due to the nature of business interactions. The Guild believes that many disputes result from a lack of awareness, or disregard, of common standards of professional practices. Such problems can be reduced, and mutually beneficial and productive business practices can be advanced through discussion and negotiation. The Grievance Committee seeks to improve professional relations between artists and buyers by fostering an ongoing dialogue with all involved parties.

As with all other Guild programs, this committee draws from members' experiences in the field, tracks industry standards, and publicizes any changes in the field that affect contracts and trade practices.

The Code of Fair Practice for the graphic communications industry

The Joint Ethics Committee was established in 1945 and financed by three leading New York City art organizations to address concerns of artists and art directors working in the graphic communications field regarding growing abuses and misunderstandings and an increasing disregard of uniform standards of conduct. In 1948, the Committee wrote and published a Code of Fair Practice for the industry.

The intention of the Joint Ethics Committee's Code of Fair Practice, which was revised in 1989, was to uphold existing laws and traditions and to help define an ethical standard for business practices and professional conduct in the graphic communications industry. Designed to promote equity for those engaged in creating, selling, buying, and using graphics, the Code has been used successfully since its formulation by thousands of industry professionals to create equitable business relationships. It has also been used to educate those entering the profession about accepted codes of behavior. See Figure 1-2 for the full text of the Code of Fair Practice.

The ramifications of a professional's behavior (both positive and negative) must be carefully considered. Although the Code provides guidelines for the voluntary conduct of people in the industry, which may be modified by written agreement between the parties, each artist should individually decide, for instance, whether to enter art contests or design competitions, provide free services, work on speculation, or work on a contingent basis. Each artist should independently decide how to price work.

As used in this text, the word artist should be understood to include creative people and their representatives in such fields of visual communications as illustration, graphic design, photography, film, and television.

(For more information about the Guild's history of promoting ethical standards, see Chapter 14, The Graphic Artists Guild.)

★　　　★　　　★

The Code of Fair Practice

ARTICLE 1 Negotiations between an artist or the artist's representative and a client shall be conducted only through an authorized buyer.

ARTICLE 2 Orders or agreements between an artist or artist's representative and buyer should be in writing and shall include the specific rights which are being transferred, the specific fee arrangement agreed to by the parties, delivery date, and a summarized description of the work.

ARTICLE 3 All changes or additions not due to the fault of the artist or artist's representative should be billed to the buyer as an additional and separate charge.

ARTICLE 4 There should be no charges to the buyer for revisions or retakes made necessary by errors on the part of the artist or the artist's representative.

ARTICLE 5 If work commissioned by a buyer is postponed or canceled, a "kill fee" should be negotiated based on time allotted, effort expended, and expenses incurred. In addition, other lost work shall be considered.

ARTICLE 6 Completed work shall be promptly paid for in full and the artwork shall be returned promptly to the artist. Payment due the artist shall not be contingent upon third-party approval or payment.

ARTICLE 7 Alterations shall not be made without consulting the artist. Where alterations or retakes are necessary, the artist shall be given the opportunity of making such changes.

ARTICLE 8 The artist shall notify the buyer of any anticipated delay in delivery. Should the artist fail to keep the contract through unreasonable delay or nonconformance with agreed specifications, it will be considered a breach of contract by the artist. Should the agreed timetable be delayed due to the buyer's failure, the artist should endeavor to adhere as closely as possible to the original schedule as other commitments permit.

ARTICLE 9 Whenever practical, the buyer of artwork shall provide the artist with samples of the reproduced artwork for self-promotion purposes.

ARTICLE 10 There shall be no undisclosed rebates, discounts, gifts, or bonuses requested by or given to buyers by the artist or representative.

ARTICLE 11 Artwork and copyright ownership are vested in the hands of the artist unless agreed to in writing. No works shall be duplicated, archived, or scanned without the artist's prior authorization.

ARTICLE 12 Original artwork, and any material object used to store a computer file containing original artwork, remains the property of the artist unless it is specifically purchased. It is distinct from the purchase of any reproduction rights. All transactions shall be in writing.*

ARTICLE 13 In case of copyright transfers, only specified rights are transferred. All unspecified rights remain vested with the artist. All transactions shall be in writing.

ARTICLE 14 Commissioned artwork is not to be considered as "work for hire" unless agreed to in writing before work begins.

ARTICLE 15 When the price of work is based on limited use and later such work is used more extensively, the artist shall receive additional payment.

ARTICLE 16 Art or photography should not be copied for any use, including client presentation or "comping," without the artist's prior authorization. If exploratory work, comprehensives, or preliminary photographs from an assignment are subsequently chosen for reproduction, the artist's permission shall be secured and the artist shall receive fair additional payment.

ARTICLE 17 If exploratory work, comprehensives, or photographs are bought from an artist with the intention or possibility that another artist will be assigned to do the finished work, this shall be in writing at the time of placing the order.

(Continues on next page)

---

* Artwork ownership, copyright ownership, and ownership and rights transferred after January 1, 1978, are to be in compliance with the Federal Copyright Revision Act of 1976.

FIGURE 1—2

The Code of Fair Practice (Continued)

ARTICLE 18 Electronic rights are separate from traditional media, and shall be separately negotiated. In the absence of a total copyright transfer or a work-for-hire agreement, the right to reproduce artwork in media not yet discovered is subject to negotiation.

ARTICLE 19 All published illustrations and photographs should be accompanied by a line crediting the artist by name, unless otherwise agreed to in writing.

ARTICLE 20 The right of an illustrator to sign work and to have the signature appear in all reproductions should remain intact.

ARTICLE 21 There shall be no plagiarism of any artwork.

ARTICLE 22 If an artist is specifically requested to produce any artwork during unreasonable working hours, fair additional remuneration shall be paid.

ARTICLE 23 All artwork or photography submitted as samples to a buyer should bear the name of the artist or artists responsible for the work. An artist shall not claim authorship of another's work.

ARTICLE 24 All companies that receive artist portfolios, samples, etc., shall be responsible for the return of the portfolio to the artist in the same condition as received.

ARTICLE 25 An artist entering into an agreement with a representative for exclusive representation shall not accept an order from nor permit work to be shown by any other representative. Any agreement that is not intended to be exclusive should set forth the exact restrictions agreed upon between the parties.

ARTICLE 26 Severance of an association between an artist and a representative should be agreed to in writing. The agreement should take into consideration the length of time the parties have worked together as well as the representative's financial contribution to any ongoing advertising or promotion. No representative should continue to show an artist's samples after the termination of an association.

ARTICLE 27 Examples of an artist's work furnished to a representative or submitted to a prospective buyer shall remain the property of the artist, should not be duplicated without the artist's authorization, and shall be returned promptly to the artist in good condition.

ARTICLE 28 Interpretation of the Code for the purposes of arbitration shall be in the hands of a body designated to resolve the dispute, and is subject to changes and additions at the discretion of the parent organizations through their appointed representatives on the Committee. Arbitration by a designated body shall be binding among the parties, and decisions may be entered for judgment and execution.

ARTICLE 29 Work on speculation/contests: Artists and designers who accept speculative assignments (whether directly from a client or by entering a contest or competition) risk losing anticipated fees, expenses, and the potential opportunity to pursue other, rewarding assignments. Each artist shall decide individually whether to enter art contests or design competitions, provide free services, work on speculation, or work on a contingency basis.

FIGURE 1—2

LEGAL RIGHTS & ISSUES

This chapter discusses the many legal aspects involved in doing business as a graphic artist. Of paramount concern are understanding and protecting copyright, both in the United States and internationally. Other issues, such as work-for-hire and fair practices, are also included.

NOTE: The information contained in this chapter does not constitute legal advice; proper advice from a legal professional should be sought where necessary.

RECOGNIZING

the need to stimulate the spread of learning and the dissemination of ideas, our nation's founders provided protection for creators of intellectual property when they wrote the U.S. Constitution. Article I, Section 8 empowers Congress to "promote the progress of science and useful arts by securing for limited times to authors and inventors the exclusive right to their respective writings and discoveries." This established the foundation for our copyright laws, which acknowledge artwork as intellectual property that is traded in the marketplace as a valuable economic resource.

In today's visual world, the works created by graphic artists are among the most powerful vehicles for communicating ideas in our society. A successful illustration can sell a product. A successful logo can evoke a company's goodwill in the public mind. A successful poster can move an entire population to action.

Like other creative professionals—actors, musicians, dancers, writers, photographers—graphic artists occupy a special place in our society and economy. Their unique vision, skill, and style enable them to attract clients, sell their work, and earn their livelihood. Like other professionals, graphic artists provide their highly skilled services and creative input within a framework of professional standards and ethics. But the work of graphic artists is vulnerable and requires the maximum protection of our laws, not only to prevent unauthorized exploitation but also to ensure that artists can continue to work without economic or competitive disadvantages.

The Graphic Artists Guild

The Graphic Artists Guild's constitution and membership mandate is to "promote and maintain high professional standards of ethics and practice, and to secure the conformance of all buyers, users, sellers, and employers to established standards." Further, the Guild seeks to "establish, implement, and enforce laws and policies…designed to accomplish these ends." The organization's legislative agenda, therefore, is based on the needs and desires expressed by its members and its constitutionally mandated goals.

One of the primary goals of the Graphic Artists Guild is to help buyers recognize the value of graphic art to their businesses and the importance of fair and ethical relationships with graphic artists. The Guild upholds the standard of a value-for-value exchange, recognizing that both client and artist contribute to a successful working relationship.

The Guild monitors and influences public policy developments, including legislative initiatives at the local, state, and federal levels, and regulatory actions by a range of agencies. Additionally, the Guild has advocated for state laws to encourage fair practices and protect artists' authorship rights; federal legislation closing the work-for-hire loophole of the U.S. Copyright Act, strengthening protections against infringement, and creating tax equity for artists; developing a national standard for artists' authorship rights (known as "moral rights," discussed below); and extending the copyright term to conform to the European standard, which is life plus 70 years. The Guild drafted model legislation and lobbied locally and nationally on these issues. Its early successes in California, Massachusetts, New York, and Oregon created a wave of interest in artists' rights legislation. The Guild's former Atlanta Chapter helped win protection for artists in Georgia by requiring printers to obtain written authorization of copyright clearance for all print orders over $1,000. The Guild spearheaded the "Ask First" initiative, organizing a coalition of creators and publishers' organizations to advance a copyright awareness campaign designed to educate users of images about appropriate and ethical practices. The Guild also reached out to gallery artists in the fine arts communities by co-founding Artists for Tax Equity (AFTE), a coalition representing nearly one million creators that successfully lobbied Congress for exemption from an onerous tax provision.

Copyright

Graphic artists' livelihoods depend on their ability to claim authorship of the pieces they produce. They build their reputations—and thus their ability to attract clients and build a career—on the basis of past performance. Indeed, artists' careers succeed or fail because of their skill and style in communicating the ideas and messages society needs to disseminate. Artists' rights to control the use of their original creative art are defined primarily by copyright law, which also provides the basis for pricing and fair trade practices.

Copyright law was created to extend limited monopolies that provided economic rewards and protections to artists and other creators. This encourages the dissemination of creative works, thereby serving the public interest. The current copyright law (Copyright Act of 1976) became effective January 1, 1978.

In 1998, the Digital Millennium Copyright Act (DMCA) was enacted; it implemented two 1996 World Intellectual Property Organization copyright treaties. The bill's most significant feature is that it affirms that copyright applies in digital network environments as well as in print, film, and recording media. The bill makes it a violation of U.S. law to circumvent any copyright protection mechanism in the digital environment and to remove any copyright management information that owners of intellectual properties attach to a digital document, such as the title and other information identifying the work and the names of, and other identifying information about the author and the copyright owner of the work, including the information set forth in a notice of copyright.

The law also limits infringement liability for online service providers who unwittingly transmit material that infringes on a copyright. Finally, it clarifies and strengthens the continuing policy role of the Copyright Office. (For a more complete discussion of the DMCA, see the Digital Millennium Copyright Act section later in this chapter.)

A bundle of rights

An artist's copyright is actually a bundle of individual rights. These broadly include the rights to copy (commonly known as the "right of reproduction"); to publicly display, distribute, and perform; or to create a derivative work from an existing work. Each specific use can be transferred outright or licensed separately for a specific length of time. Fees are determined primarily by the value agreed upon for the specific rights. Any rights not transferred explicitly in writing remain the property of the creator.

The ability to sell or license limited usage, or limited rights, to a work of art for a fee is an issue of basic fairness. The true value of a work, however, is difficult to determine (particularly before the work has been executed), considering that the potential economic life of the work is the length of time granted by copyright law, which is currently the author's life plus seventy years. Therefore, negotiations over the price of a commissioned work are normally based on the initial rights the client wishes to purchase.

Transferring rights

An agreement to transfer any exclusive (but not nonexclusive) rights, or to transfer all rights (which are by their nature exclusive), must be in writing and signed by the artist or the artist's agent. Those rights not specifically transferred in writing are retained by the artist. Nonexclusive rights, which can be transferred to more than one client at a time, may be transferred orally.

For contributions to collective works, such as magazines, anthologies, and encyclopedias, where there is no signed agreement, the law presumes the transfer of only nonexclusive rights for use in that particular collective work. All other rights remain vested with the artist. Exclusive or all-rights transfers must be in writing to be valid.

Copyright is separate from the physical art and is sold separately. State laws in New York and California require the transfer of the original, physical art to be in writing. These laws were passed after successful lobbying by artists to stop clients from insisting that transactions transferring reproduction rights only also included the sale of the original.

Termination of rights transfers

Transfers of copyright made by the artist after 1977 may be terminated by the artist or his or her heirs during a five-year period beginning 35 years after execution of the transfer. This "right of termination or reversion" feature of the 1976 Copyright Law, Section 203, is particularly important when transfers or licenses are for exceptionally long periods of time and when artists who have since become successful wish to regain rights to their early work.

Artists or their heirs whose grants of rights are approaching 35 years should contact the Copyright Office for forms and procedures. The formalities of termination are detailed; the exact form of notice is specified by, and must be filed with, the Copyright Office. (U.S. Copyright Office, 101 Independence Avenue SE, Washington, DC 20559-6000, (202) 707-3000.) Artists will lose the opportunity to reclaim rights to their creations, unless the grants otherwise terminate, if they fail to comply with the proper procedures.

The right of termination does not apply to works that have been created as work-for-hire (the artist is not considered the "author" in such circumstances), nor does it apply to transfers of copyright interests made through a will. Notwithstanding termination, the transferee may continue to exploit any derivative works created prior to termination.

Transfers made prior to January, 1, 1978, may also be subject to termination after fifty-six or seventy-five years, under Section 304 of the Copyright Act. The mechanics and timing of such terminations are spelled out in the statute. In addition, the Supreme Court has held that an author's pre-1978 grant of renewal-term rights terminates automatically if the author does not survive into the start of the renewal term.

Licensing rights

Licensing copyright rights to a client to use a work for a particular purpose for a particular length of time or in a particular geographic area means the artist is still the owner of the copyright for any uses not licensed and wholly after the term of the license has expired. For instance, an artist can license the right to make copies of a work, display it, and make derivative works from it. Each of these licenses has a value that may be much higher than the value of selling the work outright and transferring all rights to the buyer. The market will determine those values; what has no particular value today may have great value tomorrow. If artists license rather than transfer rights, they will be able to take advantage of any value the work may have in the future or any uses that were not thought of when it was created.

For example, an artist creates an illustration for a magazine cover, but then the magazine wants to use it for a promotional poster. The magazine has to go back to the artist for another license to use it on the poster and pay the artist an additional fee for that use. If a graphic designer is hired to create a logo for a company that wants widespread use of the logo on all its products and merchandise, the designer must be paid accordingly for transferring all the rights to the company so it can use the design in any way it wants. (The designer may want to stipulate in the agreement that he or she may use the logo for promotional purposes.) If a designer is only paid to create a company logo for stationery and business cards, then it should be spelled out in writing that the company cannot use the logo for other uses, such as on uniforms and for a twenty-foot sculpture on the company campus. Although the artist should in theory retain all rights not expressly granted, the best approach is to state explicitly what each party may or may not do with the work. A "silent" agreement invites misunderstandings.

Licensing is a business decision. Only the individual can decide what terms or length of time best suit the client and the situation. When in doubt, it is always good business to keep, control, and defend copyright rights. A discussion of short- and long-term licensing agreements are provided in Chapter 6, Standard Contracts and Business Tools, and examples are provided in the Appendix: Contracts & Forms.

Transfer of electronic rights

A landmark legal ruling in 2001 addressed the issue of electronic licensing as applied to freelance authors. Its influence is potentially much broader and could affect the terms for electronic licensing of work by all independent creators. (See also the Legal and Ethical Issues section in Chapter 4, Technology Issues.)

The U.S. Supreme Court affirmed a reversal of a 1997 district court opinion in *Tasini, et al v. The New York Times,* which had ruled in favor of a number of publishers (including *Newsday*, a subsidiary of Times-Mirror; Time Inc., a subsidiary of Time Warner; Mead Data Central Inc., former owner of Lexis-Nexis, a subsidiary of Mead Corporation.; the Atlantic Media Company; and University Microfilms International) and against a number of authors who owned copyrights to individual articles previously published in periodicals. The authors claimed infringement by the publishers and owners of electronic databases that made the articles available on electronic databases without the authors' permission or additional compensation. The district court originally held that the publishers were protected by the privilege of "collective works" under Section 201(c) of the Copyright Act. The Court of Appeals for the Second Circuit reversed that ruling. The publishers then appealed that reversal to the Supreme Court, which affirmed the Second Circuit in the summer of 2001.

The authors based their copyright claim on the fact that they each owned the copyright to their individual articles and these copyrights were infringed when the publishers, after printing the articles, provided them to electronic databases without the authors' consent or additional payment. The publishers did not dispute that the authors owned the copyright to their individual works. Rather, the publishers asserted that they each owned the copyright in the "collective works" that they produced and were afforded the privilege, under Section 201(c), of "reproducing and distributing" the individual works in "any revision of that collective work." The issue was this: whether one or more of the electronic databases could be considered a "revision" of the individual periodicals from which the articles were taken, as the district court originally held.

Section 201 provides that as to "contributions to collective works (such as an article, illustration, or a photograph), the copyright in each separate contribution is distinct from the copyright in the collective work as a whole (such as a magazine or newspaper) and is vested initially in the author of the contribution (the writer/photographer/ illustrator)." A collective work is defined as a "work, such as a periodical issue, anthology, or encyclopedia, in which a number of contributions, consisting of separate and independent works in themselves, are assembled into a collective whole." In other words, there are two distinct copyrights: the individual copyright of the contributors and the copyright to the collective work of the publisher, which covers the selection and arrangement of the articles and contents, but not the contents itself.

The language the courts were asked to explain is found in Section 201(c), which affords a privilege to authors of collective works: "In the absence of an express transfer of the copyright or of any rights under it, the owner of copyright in the collective work is presumed to have acquired only the privilege of reproducing and distributing the contribution as part of that particular collective work, any revision of that collective work, and any later collective work in the same series."

The Supreme Court, like the Court of Appeals, found that the most natural reading of the "revision" of "that collective work" clause is that the Section 201(c) privilege protects only later editions of a particular issue of a periodical, such as the final edition of a newspaper. The court found that this interpretation protects the use of an individual contribution in a collective work that is somewhat altered from the original in which the copyrighted article was first published, but that is not in any ordinary sense a "later" work in the "same series."

Relying on the statutory definition of a "collective work" (which lists as examples "a periodical issue, anthology, or encyclopedia"), the court found support for its reading of the revision clause. While issues of periodicals are often updated by revised editions, anthologies and encyclopedias are altered through the release of a new version, which would be a "later collective work in the same series." Therefore, the court rejected the publishers' contention that electronic databases are revised, digital copies of collective works and found that it could not be squared with basic canons of statutory construction, or with the way the databases are actually used by their subscribers.

Therefore, both the use of print-only articles on databases such as Lexis and the "image-based" representation of complete pages included in CD-ROM compilations are not protected by the publishers' Section 201(c) privilege. To hold otherwise, the court concluded, would create a right in a collective work that would cause the exception to swallow the rule, giving publishers rights in a collective work that would in effect subsume the exclusive rights reserved to the individual contributors.

Only one author in the Tasini case had a written contract with his publisher that required payment for additional uses of the article. The Court of Appeals had rejected the lower court's ruling that the authors were not due additional compensation, but the Supreme Court remanded the case to the district court for determination of a proper remedy.

Copyright notice

Since 1989, U.S. copyright law automatically protects original artwork from the moment of its creation even without inscribing a copyright notice. It is best, however, for artists to have their copyright notice appear with their work whenever it is published, placed on public display, or distributed; this helps avoid certain risks of infringement. The copyright notice can be placed on the back of an artwork or, when it is published, adjacent to the artwork. Other reasonable placements of the copyright notice for published works are specified in Copyright Office regulations, available at www.copyright.gov/. Pieces in an artist's portfolio should have copyright notices on them, including published pieces when the artist retains the copyright.

The elements that make up a copyright notice are Copyright or ©; the year of first publication; and the name of the corporation or the artist's name, an abbreviation of the name, or an alternate designation by which the artist is known: © 2001 Jane Artist, for example. The form and placement of the notice should be understood by artist and client and should be reflected in a written agreement. When use of the art has been temporarily granted to a client, the notice should be in the artist's name; however, it may be placed in the client's name for the duration of the use, if the client holds an exclusive license. The clients' other alternative would be to obtain a copyright for the collective work in which the licensed work is contained.

Copyright registration

Because current copyright law automatically "protects" original artwork from the moment it is created, even without a copyright notice, an artist always has the right to assert a claim for copyright infringement even if he or she has not previously registered the work in question. This is an improvement over previous law, when copyrights could be lost permanently if a work was published without registration or with incorrect notice. Artworks are protected, whether or not they are published or registered. However, the bulk of the benefits that the copyright law offers to artists are available only through formally registering the art with the U.S. Copyright Office of the Library of Congress.

BENEFITS OF REGISTRATION
Registration establishes a public record of the artist's claim to authorship and is a necessary prerequisite to asserting any copyright claim in court. As long as a work is registered any time from its creation to five years after first publication (known as "timely registration"), then the court will consider this timely registration to be prima facie evidence of copyright ownership. Prima facie evidence means that the burden is on the infringer to disprove the copyright's validity, rather than on the artist to prove that the copyright is valid.

The benefits of registration increase if a work is registered within three months of publication or prior to a particular infringement: the artist is entitled to recover statutory damages for infringement. Additionally, such registration allows the prevailing party to recoup attorney's fees at the judge's discretion. This is useful when evaluating whether an infringement is worth pursuing.

Damages are considered by a court only after infringement has been proven. If a work has been registered in a timely fashion and before an infringement has occurred, the court determines recovery by multiplying the number of works infringed times an amount specified by the copyright statute: a sum between $750 and $30,000 that the court considers just. Because this range is determined by the statute, these are called "statutory damages." If the copyright owner can prove to the court that the infringement was willful and not inadvertent, the statutory damages may be increased to $150,000 per work infringed. Because damages are based on the number of works infringed, not on the number of infringements of a single work, in some situations it would be more advantageous to go for actual damages; for example, if a defendant copied one of your designs onto greeting cards, then put it on coffee mugs, then on t-shirts, and sold millions of each, the defendant is still only liable for one award of statutory damages. Obviously, in that situation you would go for actual damages instead, which would be higher.

Thus, there are many incentives, both positive and negative, for following the procedures and ensuring timely registration. If a work is not registered within five years of publication, registration will not be considered prima facie evidence by the court. Additionally, if an infringement occurs before registration, the right to attorney's fees and statutory damages is lost. Recovery will be limited to the amount of actual damages that can be proven: essentially, whatever profits may be attributed to the infringement. That puts a major burden on the artist pursuing an infringement claim because he or she will have to prove the infringer's gross profits. After that, the infringer must prove what portion of the profits are not attributable to the copyrighted work. Since an artist never knows when an infringement may occur, it is prudent to register early. Not only are statutory damages easier to obtain than actual damages, they can run much higher.

REGISTRATION METHODS, FORMS, & FEES
Fortunately, registration is relatively easy. Three options for registering are now available: two types of paper registrations (using traditional paper forms or the new CO fill-in form) and online registration, which was launched July 1, 2008.

Paper registrations The types of works that can be registered as basic claims are visual arts works, as well as literary works, performing arts works, sound recordings, motion pictures, and single serial issues. Form VA (visual arts) and the easier Short Form VA are used to register pictorial, graphic, or sculptural works, including works originally created by computer and multimedia. Other registration forms may be needed at certain times by graphic artists. If audiovisual work is created, including motion pictures and animations, then Form PA is appropriate. When an artist creates both art and text in a work, and the text predominates, Form TX should be used and the description should indicate "text with accompanying art." Generally, Form TX is also used to register computer software, including any graphics that are part of screen displays generated by the software. All forms come with line-by-line instructions.

Traditional Paper Forms. The fee for registration by paper of a basic claim in an original work of authorship is $65. The Copyright Office supplies, upon request, free registration forms with instructions as well as informational circulars (The Office is eventually phasing out traditional paper forms, so they are no longer available for download from the web site). However, informational Copyright Office circulars are still available online in PDF format. Specific circulars numbered 40, 40a, 41, and 44 are especially helpful for registering visual arts.

Circulars may be accessed online at www.copyright.gov/. Circulars, as well as forms, also may be obtained by writing to Information Section LM-401, Copyright Office, Library of Congress, 101 Independence Ave., SE, Washington, DC 20559-6000, or they can be requested from the Forms Hotline at 202-707-9100. Allow two to three weeks for delivery. Once received, the forms should be reserved as masters and photocopies used for future registrations. Although the Copyright Office will accept photocopied applications, they must be clear, legible, and on a good grade of 8 1/2 x 11-inch white paper, suitable for automatic feeding through a photocopier. The forms should be completed in black ink and photocopied double-sided (not on two separate sheets) and head to head (so when the sheet is turned over, the top of page 2 is directly behind the top of page 1). Short Form VA, however, is only one-sided.

Fill-In Form CO. For $50, paper registration of basic claims can also be accomplished with the new fill-in Form CO, which can be used for categories of works usually registered on Forms VA, TX, PA, SR, and SE. The advantages of using Form CO are it's less expensive and the Office can process it much faster and more efficiently, due to 2-D barcode scanning technology, than it can a paper form completed manually. Form CO, which can be downloaded as a PDF from the Copyright Office web site (http://www.copyright.gov/forms/), allows you to insert the text into the form on your computer and then print out the completed form.

Online registration In an effort to serve the public more efficiently and effectively, the Copyright Office established its Electronic Copyright Office (eCO) in 2008, which offers online copyright registration of the basic claims listed in the paper registration section above. For filing basic claims, this is the Office's preferred method of registration. (For a list of types of registrations that are not available online, go to the eCO web site (http://www.copyright.gov/eco/index.html).

The advantages of online registration over paper registration include:
- A lower filing fee ($35) for a basic claim
- Faster processing time
- Online status tracking
- Secure payment by credit or debit card, electronic check, or Copyright Office deposit account
- Ability to upload certain categories of deposits (copies of artwork) into eCO as electronic files.

Before using the online service, it is recommended that you review the eCO Tips and eCO FAQs sections for important details and guidelines about the process. An online eCO Tutorial is also available, which walks you through the process step-by-step.

SUBMITTING APPLICATIONS

Paper The following are needed to submit a paper application for basic registration:

- The registration form, completed manually or by using fill-in Form CO.
- (1) copy of an unpublished work; (2) copies of a published work.
- A check or money order for the required registration fee.

Tearsheets are acceptable as copies of published work. Transparencies, photographs, photocopies, and CD-ROMs are acceptable for both published and unpublished work, as long as all the copyrightable content of the artwork is shown. Originals should never be sent to the Copyright Office for registration purposes. The artist should keep photocopies of all work submitted with each registration form for easy reference.

Completed forms, artwork documentation, and the fee should be mailed to Register of Copyrights, Copyright Office, Library of Congress, 101 Independence Ave., SE, Washington, DC 20559-6000. To expedite the processing of your claim, use the appropriate four-digit zip code extension (-6211 for visual arts work and -6238 for motion picture or other audiovisual work). Be sure to include your zip code in your return address and a daytime telephone number where you can be reached. (For an example of a VA form, see the Appendix: Contracts & Forms.)

Applications should be sent by an express mail service rather than by regular mail. Courier services offer a more accurate record of delivery than the U.S. Postal Service (unless a package is registered, sent by certified mail, or a return receipt is requested) and less likelihood of damage or loss in transit. It is essential to have an accurate record of the delivery date and proof of delivery, in the event that it is necessary to expedite a registration in progress for the purpose of filing a lawsuit or to trace an application in the rare instance that it is lost during processing.

Online Submitting an online application involves three simple steps, done in the following order.

1. Complete the application.
2. Pay the associated fee
3. Submit your work

Payment options include paying with a credit/ debit card or ACH transfer via Pay.gov or through a Copyright Office deposit account. Pay.gov is a secure, web-based application operated by the U.S. Treasury Department that allows users to make online payments to government agencies. The Office also maintains a system of deposit accounts for those who frequently use its services. An individual or a firm may establish a deposit account, make advance deposits into their account, and charge copyright fees against their balance via eCO.

If the artwork being registered meets the requirements for depositing with electronic files, then the entire application can be submitted online, or the registrant has the option of completing the forms and paying online but depositing artwork as hard copies sent by mail/courier. If the artwork does not qualify for electronic depositing, then the latter method must be used. Both unpublished works and works published only electronically can be deposited electronically. The eCO web site provides a complete list of the classes of work that can be deposited electronically, as well as acceptable file formats and other specifications for electronic deposits.

Payment is required before the system will prompt you to upload copies of your work as an electronic file or print out a shipping slip if you intend to submit hard copies of your work. The shipping slip must accompany your hard copy deposit when it is shipped.

REGISTRATION OF COLLECTIONS

Artists can save money on both paper and online registration fees by registering a number of works on one application for a single fee as a "collection." No additional forms are required for registration of collections.

The criteria for registering work as a collection is determined by whether a work is considered published or unpublished. "Unpublished work" includes any work that has not been published at the time it is sent to the Copyright Office. Even if an artist knows that the work will be published the next week, if it is unpublished at the time a completed application is sent to the Copyright Office, it may be registered with other works as unpublished work. "Published" means that copies of the work have been made available to the public by sale or other transfer of ownership, or by rental, lease, or lending. The offering to distribute copies to a group of persons for the purposes of further distribution, public performance, or public display also constitutes publication. A public performance or display of a work does not in itself constitute publication.

The definition of "publication" in U.S. copyright law does not specifically address online transmissions. The Copyright Office asks the applicant, who knows the facts surrounding the distribution of a work, to decide whether posting work online makes it "published" or "unpublished" for purposes of registration. Thus, you can choose how you want to register such works. To learn the specifics about registering online work, refer to *Circular 66: Copyright Registration for Online Works,* available as a downloadable PDF on the Office's web site.

Unpublished works Any number of related unpublished artworks may be grouped under a single title and registered together for a single fee ($65 for Form VA; $50 for Form CO; $35 online), if the collection is by the same author and owned by the same claimant. It is not necessary to list the individual titles of the works, but they should be given a collection title, in a way that makes it possible to identify them later in the event that copyright registration becomes an issue. For example, a series of drawings may be given a name or date and the individual drawings numbered in the following manner: "Spring Still Life Series, 2010, drawings 1–15" or "Drawings by Artist, Series 1, 2010." If works are individually titled, Form CON must be used to list the individual works by number and title. If the deposit is submitted in the form of a digital file, the file name of each image must also be included. The art does not have to be registered again when published.

It is more economical for an artist to register all images for a job, including rough sketches, as an unpublished collection for one fee as soon as finals are submitted to the client. Otherwise, once the final artwork is published, it has to be registered separately from the unpublished images that were created for the same job. To make sure that copyright registration occurs—and happens in a timely manner—it should be a routine function scheduled in the artist's workflow for a project or assignment. Although registration fees should not be charged to the client as line items, they should be figured into the artist's cost of doing business when calculating rates.

Published works The only published works that may be registered as a collection on a single form for a single fee are multiple works owned by the same claimant that were actually first published as a collection in a single unit of publication, such as all of the illustrations for one book, one magazine article, or one corporate report. Another example of a published work that meets the criteria of a collection for a single registration is a game consisting of game board, playing pieces, and game instructions.

GROUP REGISTRATION

Published artworks, which were created for periodicals (including newspapers) within the same 12-month period and which included the individual artist's copyright notice, may be submitted for registration (by paper only) as a "Group" at the same cost as a single registration. To qualify for group registration, the works must be editorial illustrations (not advertising images) by the same individual author (not an employer or other person for whom the work was made for hire), and must all have the same copyright claimant. Examples of visual artwork eligible for group registration include cartoon strips, drawings, and illustrations. Group registration for illustrations in periodicals requires that Form GR/CP be completed in addition to the appropriate VA or Short VA form. As many GR/CP forms as needed should be used to list the titles of all the images.

Groups of images that are created for other media (such as catalogs or brochures) or that are not used for editorial purposes (displays, storyboards, advertising, etc.) must be registered as a Collection (see above).

The accompanying artwork (or deposit) for works published in periodicals is one copy of the entire newspaper section or periodical in which each contribution was first published.

Older works that haven't been registered yet may also be registered as a Group by year for one fee/one registration. In effect, only one fee is being paid for an entire year of work.

Group registration (by paper only) is also available for published photographs, using additional Form GR/PPh/CON. However, some of the qualifying criteria for registering photographs as a group differ from those for artwork: all the photographs must be by the same photographer, regardless of whether the author is an individual or an employer for hire; be published in the same calendar year; and have the same copyright claimant(s). One copy of each photograph must be included with the forms.

Note that while these forms allow group registration of work covering an entire year, the post-publication grace period for the strongest copyright protection is only three months. It would be wise for an artist who works for a great many periodicals and newspapers to submit group registration forms four times a year to ensure the strongest copyright protection.

PROOF OF REGISTRATION
The Copyright Office receives more than 600,000 registrations annually, so an immediate acknowledgment or receipt of a paper application will not be sent. However, the status of online applications can be tracked online. The registration process for paper registrations can take up to 18 months. If there is any difficulty or question about the registration, the Copyright Office will contact the registrant during that interval. There is also a "Special Handling" procedure that can result in a registration in ten to fifteen business days, but this is much more expensive ($685 vs. $35–$65), and it can only be used in certain circumstances, such as when a lawsuit or business transaction requires immediate registration. If the application cannot be accepted, a letter will be sent explaining why it was rejected.

After registration is granted, the registrant will receive a certificate from the Copyright Office that takes effect from the date the application (complete with fee and deposit) was received in acceptable form. An artist does not have to receive the certificate before publishing, copying, or displaying a registered work, nor does the artist need permission from the Copyright Office to place a notice of copyright on any work, whether registered or not.

Automatic copyright renewal

The Copyright Act of 1909 required that copyrights expiring after the initial 28-year term had to be renewed by submission of a specific renewal form to extend protections for another 28 years (the renewal registration fee is $75). Because of this onerous provision, many valuable works, such as the famous Frank Capra movie *It's a Wonderful Life* fell into the public domain, to the detriment of their creators or the creators' heirs. In 1992, the Automatic Renewal Act was passed to protect the "widows and orphans" of authors who did not, or could not, register the copyright's renewal. The law provides that copyrights secured prior to 1978 live out their 28-year first term and, if renewed, an additional 67-year second term. Although this renewal term is automatically provided for works first published or registered in 1964 or later, the Copyright Office does not issue a renewal certificate for these works unless a renewal application and fee are received and registered in the Copyright Office. Works initially created after 1978 are automatically protected for the lifetime of the author plus 70 years, without need for renewal, but with no renewal available thereafter. As with pre-1978 copyrights, the Act provides for termination of long-term grants of rights.

Fair use

Copyright owners have the exclusive right to reproduce or sell their work, prepare derivative works (such as a poster copied from a painting), and publicly perform or display their work. Anyone who violates these rights is infringing on the copyright and can be penalized and prevented from continuing the infringement.

There are, however, some limitations on artists' exclusive control of their work. One such limitation allows for so-called "fair use" of a copyrighted work, including use for such purposes as news reporting, teaching, scholarship, or research. The law does not specifically define fair use, but courts will resolve the question of whether a particular use was fair by examining, for instance, the purpose and character of the use; the nature of the copyrighted work; the amount and substantiality of the portion used in relation to the copyrighted work as a whole; and the effect of the use on the potential market for, or value of, the copyrighted work. For example, under certain circumstances, a magazine may use an artist's work to accompany or illustrate an article about the artist's life. Fair use also permits artists to display a work executed for a client on a work-for-hire basis in their portfolio.

Fair use is a possible defense against an accusation of infringement that may be used both by the artist incorporating someone else's copyrighted work into his or her own work and by someone using the artist's work without permission. Because the boundaries of fair use are vague, it is a defense that can be easily abused. Fair use protects the use of quotations in commentaries and reviews and, by extension, protects parody, satire, and caricature. Because of this "free speech" aspect, fair use is often put forth as a justification for freely using copyrighted works in situations where use should clearly be compensated. One example is in academic settings, where works may be copied and distributed to a class rather than purchased, sometimes to the detriment of the market for the author's work. The free speech aspect of fair use is also cited by ideologues opposed to the concept of copyright protection, who wish to enjoy the benefit of others' creativity without being burdened by the necessity of paying for what they use. These "information-wants-to-be-free" advocates forget that all creative work comes at a price. Creators deserve to be compensated for their work; when their compensation is safeguarded, the public benefits, for the promise of compensation creates an atmosphere where creativity flourishes.

A few artists and designers who expect the copyright laws to protect their work sometimes abuse the rights of other artists and designers. For example, creators of collage often cite "fair use" as a defense for appropriating pieces of someone else's work. Collage is a gray area. Even if only a small portion of the work is used, that alone may not be sufficient to mitigate the infringement. It will depend upon whether the court thinks the collage is sufficiently "transformative," that is whether the underlying work is being used for a purpose fundamentally different than the purpose of the original use. Collage artists are safer relying on public domain sources, creating their own materials, or obtaining permission.

Similarly, some agencies and design firms routinely use published and unpublished images without permission to develop comps for client presentations and other such uses. If the four "fair use" factors were applied to these circumstances, the defense against infringement would likely fail. (In 1996, the Guild organized 16 industry organizations behind the "Ask First" campaign, which is a copyright awareness program intended to end unauthorized use of images in client presentations.)

In 1993, a Working Group on Intellectual Property Rights was formed as part of the Clinton administration's Information Infrastructure Taskforce. The Working Group decided to convene a Conference on Fair Use (CONFU) to bring together copyright owner and user interests to discuss fair use issues and, if appropriate and feasible, to develop guidelines for fair use of copyrighted works by librarians and educators. Meeting regularly in public session, CONFU grew from the 40 groups invited to participate in the first meeting in September 1994 to the approximately 100 organizations that finally participated in the process.

In December 1996, the Working Group issued an interim report that included three sets of proposed guidelines dealing with digital images, distance learning, and educational multimedia, but they were unable to come to a consensus on those guidelines after two years of meetings and negotiations among the participants. As a result, some groups have accepted the proposed guidelines and others have not. The final Report on the Conference on Fair Use is available on the U.S. Patent and Trademark Office web site (www.uspto.gov).

Artists' liability: privacy & likeness issues, copyright infringement

All illustration or design has the potential for invasion of privacy issues. For example, the advertising or trade use of a living (and in many states, even a deceased) person's name or likeness without permission is an invasion of privacy, and claims may be in the hundreds of thousands of dollars for an infringement. "Advertising or trade" means virtually all uses other than factual editorial content of magazines, newspapers, books, and television programs; it includes print and TV ads, company brochures, packaging, and other commercial uses. Public and private figures are protected equally. (See Rights of Celebrity Privacy, later in this chapter.)

The test of "likeness" is whether an ordinary person would recognize the complainant as the person in the illustration. It need not be a perfect likeness. The best protection in these cases is a signed release from the person whose likeness is used (for a model release form, see the Appendix: Contracts & Forms), and any contract should provide for this if a problem is likely to arise.

If an artist copies another work—a photograph, for example—in making an illustration, the photographer or copyright holder might sue for copyright infringement. The test of an infringement is whether an ordinary person would say that one work is copied from the other; the copying need not be exact.

Given the substantial amount of photography used as reference for illustration, as well as the frequent incorporation of photographs into designs, everyone, particularly freelance artists, should exercise extreme caution in this area. Of course, common themes and images, such as squares or triangles, are in the public domain and may be used freely. Infringement requires copying substantial protectable portions of a work, so a mere similarity in style or concept will not constitute an infringement.

Because of privacy and infringement risks, many advertisers and publishers carry special liability insurance to cover these types of claims. That, however, may not provide complete protection, particularly for the freelance artist, who may be sued along with the client. Sometimes clients insist that artists incorporate images that might infringe on someone's right of privacy or copyright. Artists need to incorporate an indemnification clause in their agreements that hold the artist harmless in this situation. A sample indemnification clause reads as follows:

You [client] agree to indemnify and hold [artist] harmless against all claims, including but not limited to claims of copyright or trademark infringement, violations of the rights of privacy or publicity or defamation, arising out of use of [the work].

Many contracts today require an artist to warrant that the work does not infringe on any other work, and they demand that the artist hold the company harmless for any action arising from breach of this warranty. It is possible to rewrite and limit these clauses to minimize the artist's liability. For example, artists can rewrite the warranty clause so that they are not responsible for infringements arising from any reference or textual material provided by the client. Artists can also limit the warranty so that it does not infringe "to the best of the artist's knowledge and belief." And they can limit liability to court judgments arising from an actual breach of warranty, rather than any action taken against the company.

Compulsory licensing

A provision of copyright law dealing with compulsory licensing permits a noncommercial, educational broadcasting station to use certain published work without the artist's consent so long as the station pays the government-set royalty rate. (Some published works, such as dramatic ones, are not covered by this license.) If the broadcaster does not pay the license fee, or underpays it, the use will be considered an infringement.

Programs produced independently for airing on public stations are eligible for compulsory licenses, but the license does not extend to secondary (after broadcast) markets such as merchandising, toys, books, or videocassette sales.

Copyright extension

As a participating member in the Coalition of Creators and Copyright Owners, the Graphic Artists Guild long advocated extending the term of United States copyright law from life-plus-50 years to life-plus-70 years, which would bring it into harmony with most other Berne Convention signatories. The Copyright Term Extension Act, passed by the 105th Congress and signed into law by President Clinton in 1998, did just that. Approximately 20 organizations in the coalition supported extending the term of copyright for the following reasons, among others:

- Artists and other authors now live longer, and the term of copyright needs to reflect that. Further, currently created works now have greater value for longer periods of time.
- A longer term of copyright is good for American business. In 2007 United States copyright and related industries accounted for over 11 percent of the gross domestic product ($1.52 trillion) and exported goods and services totaling more than $126 billion per year. More than 11.7 million Americans worked in copyright industries, and they accounted for over 8.5 percent of the nation's employment.

- Term extension allows the United States to continue to be a leader in international copyright. Intellectual property generally, and copyright in particular, are among the brightest spots in our balance of trade. Copyrighted works the world wants are overwhelmingly those created in the United States.
- The primary reason for passage of this law was to bring U.S. copyright terms into harmony with other Berne Convention signatories so that European copyright owners would not have an unfair advantage over U.S. rights holders.
- Term extension discourages retaliatory legislation and trade policies by other countries. The European community extends protection to foreign copyrights under the "rule of the shorter term," which limits protection in the European community to the length of the term in the home country. Failure to extend the United States term would protect United States copyrights for the shorter term of life-plus-50 only, while protecting European copyrights for the longer term. This would have placed United States copyright holders at a tremendous disadvantage in the global marketplace.
- Worldwide harmonization facilitates international trade and a greater exchange of copyrighted property between countries.

For reasons of simplification, the 20-year term extension was applied across the board to all copyrights, including works-for-hire, which have been extended from 75 to 95 years. This is a major drawback for artists seeking to reclaim their copyright. The Graphic Artists Guild strenuously opposed lengthening the copyright term of works-for-hire, as it might provide an incentive for more work-for-hire agreements. More importantly, since work-for-hire agreements do not exist in most other countries that signed the Berne Convention, this extension creates disharmony with practices in other countries. The constitutionality of the term extension was challenged in the U.S. Supreme Court. The challenge was defeated when the court upheld the Copyright Term Extension Act in January 2003.

Digital Millennium Copyright Act

The Digital Millennium Copyright Act (DMCA) of 1998 added several new sections to copyright law, including one of particular concern to graphic artists. Section 512 limits online service provider liability by preventing a service provider from incurring monetary liability for copyright infringements carried by its service in relation to the following four areas: transitory communications (e-mail), system caching, storage of information on systems or networks at the direction of users (web sites), and information location tools (browsers).

While this may not seem relevant to graphic artists, it does have important ramifications in two areas: the removal or blocking of infringing material and the terms of service imposed by online service providers. The first area is of particular concern because of the *Kelly v. Arriba Soft Corporation* case. Photographer Les Kelly sued Arriba Soft for vacuuming his images off the World Wide Web and displaying them on its commercial search engine without his knowledge or permission. In November 1999, a U.S. district court in California ruled that the search engine's unauthorized copying and display of Kelly's copyrighted images falls under "fair use" and that the DMCA had not been violated as Kelly had charged. Because of the huge impact this decision can have on the DMCA and on intellectual property rights on the Web, Kelly appealed. On appeal (July 2003), the Ninth Circuit Court partly affirmed and partly reversed the decision. The court held only that Arriba Soft's creation and display of low-resolution thumbnail images was fair use. While there was no final ruling on the full-size high-resolution images, this case is widely interpreted as indicating that such full-size copies constitute infringement. After failure to reach a settlement, a default judgment in Kelly's favor was obtained on the remaining issues on March 18, 2004.

The Arriba Soft site (ditto.com) and browser are "information locators" within the meaning of Section 512. To avoid liability, such a provider must not know that the material on its site is an infringement. If it has the right and ability to control the infringing activity, the provider must not receive a financial benefit directly attributable to the activity. Upon receiving notice of infringement, the provider must expeditiously remove or block access to the material. In the case of ditto.com, the site will remove material upon receiving objections.

If an entity qualifies as a service provider (for criteria, see the Copyright Office web site, www.copyright.gov), complies with the statute, and (1) adopts and reasonably implements a policy of terminating, in appropriate circumstances, the accounts of subscribers who are repeat infringers, and (2) accommodates and does not interfere with "standard technical measures," it will not be liable for the infringements of subscribers. This means that the service provider cannot interfere with a copyright owner's watermarking or other protective measures.

To avail themselves of the protections offered in Section 512, service providers must file the name of a designated agent with the Copyright Office to receive notification of claimed infringements. The service provider is eligible for limitation from liability only if it does not have actual knowledge of the infringement. Section 512 (c)(3) provides for a notice and takedown procedure, under which a copyright holder submits a notification to the provider's designated agent. The notification, made under penalty of perjury, must describe the elements of the infringement. To retain its exemption from liability, the service provider must promptly remove or block access to the material identified in the notification.

The service provider is protected against claims from the allegedly infringing subscriber by taking down the material, but it must promptly notify the subscriber that it has done so. The subscriber may serve a counter notification, under penalty of perjury, that the material was wrongly removed. Unless the copyright holder files an action against the subscriber, the service provider must put the material back up within 10 to 14 business days after receiving the counter notification.

This procedure offers graphic artists and other copyright holders rapid relief from online infringements pending resolution of a copyright dispute, rather than requiring a matter to be first adjudicated through the court system. Note, however, that to preserve blocking or disabling, the claimant must file a court action in a very short period of time. A completed copyright registration is necessary to embark on any court action. Given the long lead-time that registration requires or the alternative, the high cost of a "Special Handling" registration, it is clearly unwise to leave work unregistered and particularly unwise to post any unregistered work online.

The requirements of Section 512 generally specify that the service provider must not modify transmitted material, must not have knowledge that the material is infringing, and must not receive any financial benefit directly attributable to the infringing activity. This raises interesting issues regarding provider terms of service. Many service providers claim for themselves a nonexclusive copyright interest in their subscribers' material as part of their terms of service. These have included claims of the right to alter the work, prepare derivative works, and make use of the works in various ways that potentially offer financial benefit. The requirements of Section 512 call the legality and enforceability of these terms of service claims into question.

The obvious conclusion is that all creators should register their work and familiarize themselves with the provisions of Section 512 so that they may be prepared to make use of the protections it offers. To learn more about Section 512 and other aspects of the DMCA, visit the Copyright Office web site (www.copyright.gov).

States' liability for copyright infringement

The U.S. Copyright Act, in establishing sanctions (monetary damages, fines, injunctions) against infringement, intended these sanctions to apply to "anyone who violates any of the exclusive rights of the copyright owner." According to the Copyright Office, "anyone" was meant to include states, state institutions, and state employees. But in 1985, the Supreme Court ruled in a five-to-four decision that the Eleventh Amendment to the Constitution, which generally grants states immunity from lawsuits and monetary judgments in federal courts, could not be negated by Congress except by explicit and unequivocal language. Subsequent courts decided that under this test, the Copyright Act's language was not specific enough and so opened the door for many state-funded institutions to use copyrighted materials without permission, without paying or giving credit, and without fear of reprisal from the copyright owner.

In 1990, Congress attempted to correct this inequity by passing the Copyright Remedy Clarification Act, so that states and their agents would once again be subject to all penalties and sanctions for copyright infringement. Grassroots lobbying by the Guild and its members helped obtain passage of this new law. Unfortunately, the Supreme Court has held that the 1990 legislation exceeded Congress' power to alter Eleventh Amendment immunity, so the states are once again free to infringe copyrights without legal penalty. In 2006, a lawsuit filed against San Diego State University seems to strike down a key piece of this legislation, stating that: "Any State, any instrumentality of a State, and any officer or employee of a State or instrumentality of a State ... shall not be immune, under the Eleventh Amendment ... from suit in Federal Court ... for a violation of any of the exclusive rights of a copyright owner..." Theoretically, this means that states are subject to copyright infringement suits; however, it leaves open the possibility that a state could argue that the person committing the infringement did so as a private citizen, not in his or her formal capacity, which would remove liability from the institution.

Orphan works

In January 2005, the Senate Judiciary Committee and the House Judiciary Committee's Subcommittee on Courts, the Internet, and Intellectual Property asked the Register of Copyrights to study the issue of "orphaned" copyright works and to report back to the Senate Judiciary Committee.

The U.S. Copyright Office defines "orphan works" as "copyrighted works whose owners are difficult or even impossible to locate." These works are problematic because they are still protected within their terms of copyright, but their copyright owners cannot be contacted, for a variety of reasons, by potential users who seek permission to use the works.

The issue was brought to Congress's attention in 2004 as part of an unsuccessful lawsuit against the Federal Government (*Kahle v. Ashcroft*) regarding the length of the term of copyright. The purpose of the lawsuit was to repeal updates in U.S. copyright law from 1976 to the present that redefined copyright ownership, extended the length of copyright protection, brought U.S. copyright law into compliance with the Berne Convention, and criminalized Internet piracy as copyright infringement. The plaintiffs in the case argued that current copyright laws effectively protect all works and for too long, delaying too many works from becoming public domain and creating a larger class of orphan works. This delay, they argued, impedes the progress of science because it

restricts the use of many works that would never have been registered in the first place or would not have been renewed after the death of their author.

Normally, the Graphic Artists Guild's position on the issue of usage is that as creators of original work, graphic artists who own the copyrights to their images are entitled to full protection of copyright under U.S. copyright law for themselves and their heirs. If a potential user is unable to contact the copyright owner to get permission to use an image, then the user does not have permission—period.

However, the issue of use of orphan works is not as simplistic as it appears at first glance. It is made complex by the existence under U.S. copyright law of two distinct classes of copyright owners, which has created two categories of orphan works:

- Works created by individual living authors who still own their copyright or deceased authors whose copyright has passed to their heirs, and who are not able to be located either because they have not kept their contact information current with the U.S. Copyright Office, their names are not on their work, or they never registered their work at all.
- Works created under a work-for-hire agreement (or works in which the author's rights were bought out in full), where a business or corporation owned the copyright, and that business or corporation is defunct and its assets—including intellectual property rights—were not sold or assigned to anyone else. In these circumstances, the works are truly orphaned because although no one owns the copyright, the term of copyright has not expired, and therefore, the work does not qualify for public domain status.

Closer examination reveals numerous unique situations that merit individual consideration for very compelling reasons, especially within the second category of works. An especially compelling argument for releasing the copyright on orphaned works and allowing them into the public domain pertains to preserving artistic works in danger of being lost forever, such as the need to restore decomposing silent films made in the 1920s by Hollywood studios long defunct. A parallel situation exists for old books that are out of print.

The Guild's position on the orphan works issue is that it is too complicated to be resolved with an all-or-nothing ruling. Instead, usage requests for orphaned works should be handled on a case-by-case basis by the U.S. Copyright Office, not by repealing U.S. copyright law and violating the Berne Convention.

Pressure from non-profit users, such as universities, libraries, archives, and museums, led to the request by Congress that the U.S. Copyright Office propose a solution to the problem at the beginning of 2006. The Copyright Office's proposed amendment to U.S. copyright law regarding "orphan works" was discussed by the appropriate Congressional subcommittees, and those committees held hearings that included "interested parties." Those interested parties included the Coalition on Orphan Works, comprised of numerous groups of creative professionals from the United States, Canada, and Europe, including the Graphic Artists Guild.

In April of 2008, the House and Senate both introduced similar bills, S. 2913 and H.R. 5889. The Guild continued to urge inclusion of Useful Articles and Notice of Use clauses while reinforcing the inadequacy of current database technology to protect artist rights.

The Guild Board of Directors voted unanimously to oppose the Senate bill, calling S. 2913 incomplete, insufficient and indifferent. The Senate passed S. 2913—The Shawn Bentley Orphan Works Act of 2008—by "hotline" on September 26, 2008. The House version of the bill was never passed.

The Guild argues there is no current way to identify copyright owners of visual art regardless of what active steps the owner may take to protect his or her legitimate ownership rights. Until an image-searchable, comprehensively populated, database technology is available that doesn't impose undue burden on artists, the Guild focused its lobbying efforts on two bill provisions to provide a reasonable means of copyright protection:

- Excluding useful articles from being subject to the legislation, because the art on these items are the most vulnerable to infringement. This clause limits commercial use but not to the extent the Guild originally sought. This exclusion was in both versions of the 2008 bills.
- Including a Notice of Use clause requiring users to file a copy of the allegedly orphaned artwork in a publicly accessible database within the Copyright Office. This would make it possible for artists to proactively determine if their work has mistakenly been identified as being orphaned. This clause was in the 2008 House version.

The Guild acknowledges these compromises are not preferred ideals but decided to support the House version of the bill because it included a Notice of Use clause. That support was instrumental in ensuring that the Senate version of the bill did not get passed into law. It remains to be seen what Congress will do about Orphan Works in 2010 and whether the 2008 bills will survive.

Additional information on copyright

For further information on copyright, artists can send for a free copy of the Copyright Information Kit from the Copyright Office, Information and Publications Section, Library of Congress, 101 Independence Ave., SE, Washington, DC 20559-6000; consult the Copyright Office web site at www.copyright.gov; or call the Public Information Office at 202-707-3000 for recorded information available 24 hours a day, seven days a week.

Information specialists are on duty from 8:30 A.M. to 5:00 P.M. (EST) Monday through Friday except holidays. The TTY number is 202-707-6737.

Work-for-Hire

"Work-for-hire" is a provision of the U.S. Copyright Act intended as a narrow exception to the general rule that the artist or author who actually creates the work owns the copyright to it. The provision confers initial authorship and ownership to the employer or other hiring party who commissions the work, leaving the artist with no rights whatsoever. While such a result may be justifiable in a traditional employment setting, the freelance artist, considered to be an independent contractor for all purposes except copyright, has no access to the usual employee benefits that may compensate for the loss of that copyright and the future earnings it may represent.

Under the law, a work made for hire can come into existence in two ways: an employee creating a copyrightable work within the scope of employment; or an independent contractor creating a specially ordered or commissioned work in one of several categories, verified by a written contract signed by both parties and expressly stating that it is a work-for-hire.

An employed artist is usually defined as one who works at the employer's office during regular business hours on a scheduled basis, is directed by the employer, and works with tools supplied by the employer. More importantly, an artist is considered an employee if he or she is entitled to employment benefits and has taxes withheld from his or her paycheck. (For further details, see the CCNV v. Reid section later in this chapter, and the Employment Issues section of Chapter 3, Professional Issues.)

Even as an employee, an artist may negotiate a separate written contract with the employer, apart from the employment agreement, that transfers copyright ownership to the artist in some or all of the work created in the regular course of employment. And it is also possible, though highly unusual, for an artist working under a work-for-hire agreement to receive royalties according to a written contract.

Work-for-hire criteria

Work created by a freelance artist, by contrast, can be work-for-hire only if the following two conditions are met: the artist and the client sign an agreement stating that the work is for hire, and it falls under one of the following nine categories as enumerated in the law:

1. A contribution to a collective work (such as a magazine, newspaper, encyclopedia, or anthology).
2. A contribution used as part of a motion picture or other audiovisual work.
3. A supplementary work, which includes pictorial

illustrations, maps, and charts, done to supplement a work by another author.
4. A compilation (new arrangement of preexisting works or data).
5. A translation.
6. An atlas.
7. A test.
8. Answer material for a test.
9. An instructional text (defined as a literary, pictorial, or graphic work prepared for publication and with the purpose of use in systematic instructional activities).

Works that fall outside these categories are clearly ineligible to be work-for-hire, even with a signed contract. Not so clear are works like comic books, print advertising, or web sites. Some clients may add fallback language in a work-for-hire contract that provides for all-rights transfers if a work is deemed not for hire. Creators should resist signing such contracts and should challenge them if a commissioned work does not fall within the specified categories. Ultimately, the courts may have to determine a particular work's eligibility.

These criteria apply only to work done on special order or commission by an independent contractor. If there is no written agreement, if the agreement does not specifically state that the work is made for hire, if such an agreement is not signed, or if the work does not fall into one of the above categories, then there is no work-for-hire, and the artist automatically retains authorship and copyright ownership.

By signing a work-for-hire contract, a freelance artist becomes an employee only for the purposes of copyright law and for no other purpose. In addition to losing authorship status, the freelance artist receives no salary, unemployment, workers compensation, or disability insurance benefits; nor does he or she receive health insurance, sick pay, vacation, pension, or profit-sharing opportunities that a company may provide to formal, salaried employees. When a freelance artist signs a work-for-hire contract, the artist has no further relationship with the work and cannot display, copy, or use it for other purposes such as in the artist's portfolio except by relying on a claim of fair use. The client, now considered the legal author, may change the art and use it again without limitation.

Some clients still attempt to gain windfall benefits from work-for-hire where there was no signed agreement by claiming that extensive supervision, control, and direction made the artist an employee, and therefore the work was for hire. The Supreme Court resolved the issue in *CCNV v. Reid,* affirming that, in virtually all cases, commissioned works executed by independent contractors cannot be works-for-hire unless the work falls into one of the nine specified categories listed above and a written agreement stating the work is for hire has been signed by both parties.

The Graphic Artists Guild is emphatically opposed to the use of work-for-hire contracts. Work-for-hire is an unfair practice that strips the artist of the moral right of paternity—the right to be recognized as a work's author (see section on Moral Rights later in this chapter). It gives art buyers economic benefits and recognition that belong to the creative artist. Such contracts devalue the integrity of artists and their work by empowering buyers to alter the work without consulting the artist and by preventing artists from obtaining any payment for the future use of their work.

Work-for-hire abuses

Clients who insist on a work-for-hire arrangement may resort to other means that, while unethical, are not prohibited under current copyright law. Some businesses coerce freelancers by denying assignments to artists who do not accept work-for-hire. Some clients attempt to designate a work as for hire after the fact by requiring that the artist endorse a payment check or sign a purchase order on which work-for-hire terms appear (usually in fine print). Unless this confirms a previous oral agreement, artists who encounter this should request a new payment check (see *Playboy Enterprises, Inc. v. Dumas*) or cross out the incorrect work-for-hire statement.

Some work-for-hire contracts understood by the artist to be for a single project may actually have work-for-hire language that covers all future work. Artists entering the industry are especially vulnerable to such blanket work-for-hire agreements; unfortunately, by the time they have the reputation to resist work-for-hire, clients already have the artist's agreement on file.

With the growth of technology, and as-yet-unimagined vistas opening in digital media, many clients have begun adding increasingly broad rights ownership language to contracts. Artists should be alert to any clauses buying "all electronic rights" or "all rights in all media now in existence or invented in the future in perpetuity throughout the universe." These overly broad grants of rights effectively give the purchaser indefinite and unspecified use of a creator's work without additional compensation or input into uses. Such clauses can be as damaging to artists as traditional work-for-hire arrangements; artists lose valuable sources of future income and control over their images and reputations. Historically, artists and other creators have been able to withstand such onslaughts by negotiating strenuously, both individually and collectively. (For more information on artists' negotiating options, see Chapter 5, Essential Business Practices.)

LEGAL CLARIFICATION
The following two court cases illustrate ways in which clients have forced work-for-hire arrangements on artists in order to circumvent copyright law, resulting in artists losing control of their images. Although the final rulings in both cases favored the artists and severely limited the potential for work-for-hire abuses, the language of the decisions was not strong enough to eliminate abuses entirely.

CCNV v. Reid In 1989, the Supreme Court ruled unanimously that the employee clause in the Copyright Act could not be applied to independent contractors. If the relationship between the artist and the hiring party was determined to be one of conventional employment based on the application of a rigorous test of 13 factors (based on English common law), then the created work would be considered made for hire.

This landmark case involved freelance sculptor James Earl Reid versus homeless advocate Mitch Snyder and the Community for Creative NonViolence (CCNV) over a commissioned sculpture created by Reid, but conceived and partly directed by Snyder. Even though there was no written contract between the parties, and even though sculpture does not fall into any of the nine categories of specially ordered works, the district court found Reid to be an employee because he was under Snyder's "supervision and control" and awarded the copyright to CCNV. The Supreme Court reversed this ruling.

The factors the Supreme Court relied upon in deciding James Reid's employment status were:

- The hiring party's right to control the manner and means by which the product was accomplished.
- The skill required.
- The source of the "instrumentalities" and tools.
- The location of the work.
- The duration of the relationship between the parties.
- Whether the hiring party had the right to assign additional projects to the hired party.
- The hired party's discretion over when and how long to work.
- The method of payment.
- The hired party's role in hiring and paying assistants.
- Whether the work was part of the regular business of the hiring party.
- Whether the hiring party was in business.
- The provision of employee benefits.
- The tax treatment of the hired party.

The Court made it clear that no one of these factors is determinative, but that all factors must be examined. In applying them to the Reid case, the Court found Reid clearly to be an independent contractor, not an employee.

The practical consequences of this landmark decision are that some clients have reexamined their policies of insisting on work-for-hire from freelancers, determining that it is more desirable and economical to purchase only the specific rights needed. Those clients who insist on work-for-hire must comply strictly with the requirement for written agreements that state expressly that a work is for hire and the work must also fall within the nine statutory categories.

Although the Supreme Court decision narrowed one loophole, others remain. Under the "joint authorship" provision of the Copyright Act, a work may be presumed to be a collaborative effort between the artist and the client, granting each party the right to exploit the work independently of the other without regard to the importance of their respective contributions—if each party's contribution is copyrightable—so long as profits are accounted for and divided equally. This can only result, however, if both parties intend the work to be jointly owned, a condition that is difficult to meet when credit and creative control are given to the artist.

Playboy Enterprises, Inc. v. Dumas The practice of introducing back-of-check contract terms, used by some clients to force a work-for-hire arrangement, was severely limited by a 1995 federal court decision in the case of *Playboy Enterprises, Inc. v. Dumas.* Let stand by the U.S. Supreme Court, the Second Circuit Court of Appeals unequivocally rejected declarations of a work-for-hire agreement after the contract was fulfilled. The Appeals Court did not agree, however, as the Graphic Artists Guild argued in its amicus curiae brief, that work-for-hire agreements must be established in writing before work begins.

The case of *Playboy Enterprises v. Dumas* resulted from an attempt by the widow of artist Patrick Nagle, Jennifer Dumas, to stop Playboy from selling new editions of her late husband's work that had been commissioned by Playboy. He had endorsed checks with work-for-hire language on the back; therefore, claimed Playboy, the company was the legal author of the work and sued the widow for copyright infringement.

The Court decided "that the written requirement can be met by a writing executed after the work is created, if the writing confirms a prior agreement, either explicit or implicit, made before the creation of the work." The language of the decision may unfortunately open the door to a flood of court actions if unscrupulous clients claim there was an "implicit" work-for-hire agreement, prior to creation, when in fact none existed.

The Graphic Artists Guild strongly recommends that artists and clients confirm all assignments in writing before work begins, detailing the terms of the agreement and the specific rights licensed. This professional practice avoids any confusion, misunderstanding, or legal action concerning the rights sold.

Artists confronted with incorrect work-for-hire language on the back of checks may consider crossing it out and writing "deposited without conditions" to mitigate the attempted rights grab.

Rights of Celebrity & Privacy

Artists are occasionally asked by clients to reproduce or imitate images of recognizable individuals. The potential for right of publicity infringement in such cases is serious and underscores the need for including indemnification clauses protecting artists in all contracts.

The right of publicity

Unlike copyrights and trademarks, the right of publicity is not created by federal law but by the laws of each individual state. These laws vary greatly in their details, but most states recognize a general right for a person to control the commercial use of his or her name, likeness, and other aspects of "personal identity." In an obvious example, every state in the union would prohibit The Gap from selling T-shirts bearing the likeness of Monica Lewinsky without her permission. Some states have enacted statutes to govern these rights, some rely on "common law" principles developed by the courts, and some, like California, recognize both.

Not surprisingly, these state laws are extremely inconsistent. In New York, the right of publicity is written into the state civil rights statute, which provides that "any person whose name, portrait, picture, or voice is used within this state for advertising purposes or purposes of trade without the written consent" of the subject may be sued for injunctive and monetary relief. Significantly, this right extends to "any person" in New York, not merely to celebrities or people in the public eye. So in New York, at least, it is illegal to market a sketch of the corner grocer as a poster for Boar's Head cold cuts, no matter how unknown he may be.

In California, the statute covers largely the same conduct as the New York law, but it can also protect the rights of the deceased, both famous and obscure. Under New York law, once a person is dead they have no more right of publicity: witness throngs of vendors selling unauthorized John Lennon merchandise outside the Dakota apartment building where Lennon used to live. As long as those vendors sell their wares only in New York and do not otherwise violate the trademark laws (merchandise that suggests a false endorsement by the singer might be actionable under the federal Lanham Act, for example, even if it did not violate state law), they are doing nothing wrong because under New York law, Lennon's right of publicity died with him. Wisconsin law also limits coverage to living people.

Those same vendors could not operate legally in California. The California statute allows the heirs or survivors of a deceased "personality" to continue to control that person's right of publicity for 50 years after death, provided they register with the Secretary of State and pay a small fee. Indeed, even without filing the necessary paperwork, the heirs of a deceased person can enjoin unauthorized uses in California; but they cannot recover monetary damages until they have complied with the statutory formalities.

Other states go even further in granting post-mortem rights of publicity, with Indiana and Oklahoma protecting the right for 100 years after death and Tennessee, home of the late Elvis Presley, recognizing it in perpetuity, so long as it continues to be used for commercial purposes. Other states, such as Washington, provide for a 10-year post-mortem right for ordinary people but offer 75 years of protection for those whose images have "commercial value." Accordingly, it seems safe to assume that even the long-deceased may have enforceable rights of publicity somewhere.

Exceptions

There are several limitations and exceptions to the right of publicity, most importantly those involving First Amendment protection for "newsworthy" images. The same likeness of Monica Lewinsky that would be prohibited on a T-shirt may be permissible as an illustration for an article in a commercial publication if two conditions are met. First, the image must bear some reasonable relation to the content of the article. Second, the article must concern a matter of legitimate "public interest," a broad concept that encompasses everything from hard news to celebrity gossip. As the courts have defined it, virtually any story or article will qualify as a matter of public interest, so long as it is not merely an advertisement in disguise. Moreover, if the story itself is legitimate and the image is reasonably related to it, the likeness can also be used on posters and billboards advertising the publication, on the theory that the protected nature of the initial use extends to advertisements for the protected speech.

In addition, both California and New York recognize a "fine art" exception, also rooted in the First Amendment. The California statute exempts "single and original works of fine art," which would appear to be limited to unique works, not including mass-produced reproductions. It is unclear whether the term fine art in this section is intended to apply only to works of "recognized quality," as determined by expert opinion, or to any original work in a graphic or sculptural medium. It is also unclear whether "works prepared under contract for commercial use" could qualify for the exemption. The California Art Preservation Act defines fine art as only works "of recognized quality," but not including works made under contract for commercial use, while the California Resale Royalties Act applies to "an original painting, sculpture, or drawing, or an original work of art in glass." The Right of Publicity statute does not include any definition of the term fine art. The statute clearly provides, however, that, as with newsworthy publications, advertisements for legitimate works of fine art, such as gallery posters, do not violate the statute.

In New York, there is no direct statutory language regarding fine art, but the courts have recently interpreted the statute to exempt two- and three-dimensional works of art from the law. In Simeonov v. Tiegs, the Civil Court held that an artist who created a plaster casting of model Cheryl Tiegs could "sell at least a limited number of copies" of the work without violating Tiegs's right of publicity because such activities did not amount to a use of her likeness "for purposes of trade." In this case, the New York statute was read to permit the sale of reproductions, at least in small numbers, to avoid creating a possible conflict between the state statute and the First Amendment. A recent case involving artist Barbara Kruger went further, finding no "purpose of trade" with respect to T-shirts, refrigerator magnets, and other items sold in the gift shop of the Whitney Museum. The ruling stated that those items were merely reproductions of a Kruger work being shown at the Whitney, and the Kruger work was itself clearly protected under the First Amendment. In California, however, the standard is more subjective. Rather than focusing on whether there is a "purpose of trade," California courts look at whether the artwork on the item is "transformative." Artwork is transformative if it is perceived as "primarily the artist's own expression rather than the subject's likeness." Under that standard, the courts have held that a realistic portrait of the Three Stooges, when reproduced on fine arts prints as well as T-shirts, was a commercial use in violation of the Stooges' rights of publicity. On the other hand, caricatures of Johnny and Edgar Winter in a comic book were held sufficiently transformative not to infringe the Winters' publicity rights.

Obtaining permission: when and from whom?

If none of the exceptions apply to a particular project, and the subject has not been deceased for at least 100 years, a graphic artist may decide that permission is required. If possible, think about this issue sooner rather than later. Under both the New York and California statutes, the subject's written consent must be obtained before the use occurs. Also, it is necessary to obtain permission from all the proper parties. In a recent case, *Wendt v. Host International, Inc.*, a corporation licensed the rights to make life-size robotic replicas of the characters "Norm" and "Cliff" from the TV series Cheers. Even though the copyright owner of the show granted permission, George Wendt and John Ratzenberger, the actors who portrayed the characters, brought a successful action for violation of their rights of publicity under California law.

There has been some discussion in recent years about creating a single federal right of publicity statute that would eliminate the confusing inconsistencies in the various state laws, but no such change in the law is expected any time soon. Until it happens, the prudent graphic artist has only two choices: master the byzantine laws of all 50 states or get those model releases.

Moral Rights

Moral rights are derived from the French doctrine of *droit moral,* which recognizes certain inherent personal rights of creators in their works, even after the works have been sold or the copyright transferred. These rights stand above and distinct from copyright. The doctrine traditionally grants artists and writers four specific rights:

1. The right to protect the integrity of their work to prevent any modification, distortion, or mutilation that would be prejudicial to their honor or reputation.
2. The right of attribution (or paternity) to insist that their authorship be acknowledged properly and to prevent use of their names on works they did not create.
3. The right of disclosure to decide if, when, and how a work is presented to the public.
4. The right of recall to withdraw, destroy, or disavow a work if it is changed or no longer represents their views.

The Berne Convention

Moral rights have long been an integral part of copyright protection laws in most European nations, but were largely rejected and ignored in the United States. In 1886, the United States refused to join the Berne Convention, a worldwide multinational treaty for the protection of literary and artistic works that accepted moral rights as a matter of course. Member nations participating in Berne are required to frame their copyright laws according to certain minimum standards and to guarantee reciprocity to citizens of any other member.

After 100 years, economic realities and skyrocketing foreign piracy forced the United States to seek entry into the Berne union. By that time, the 1976 Copyright Act had brought the United States closer to other Berne standards. For example, duration of copyright was extended from a term of 28 years, renewable only once, to the life of the creator plus 50 years. Regulations eliminating the necessity of placing a notice on a work as a requirement for bringing a lawsuit were also implemented.

Several states have enacted various forms of moral rights statutes, due in great part to the Guild's involvement. Certain moral rights elements have also been protected in state and federal courts, which saw them as questions of unfair competition, privacy, or defamation. The totality of the American legal system, therefore, persuaded Berne administrators that the United States qualified for membership.

In 1988, the United States became the eightieth country to sign the Berne Convention, thereby extending protection to American works in 24 nations with which the United States had no separate copyright agreements. This also succeeded in stemming the loss of billions of dollars in royalties to copyright owners. Although works are now protected the moment they are created, and the Berne Convention does not require copyright notice, it is still advisable to affix a copyright notice (© 2010 Jane Artist or Copyright 2010 Jane Artist) because it bars the defense of innocent infringement in court and also because it affords international copyright protection in those countries that are members of the Universal Copyright Convention (UCC), which still requires a copyright notice on a work. Although foreign works are currently exempt from the American registration requirements as a precondition for filing a lawsuit, American works still have to be registered with the U.S. Copyright Office before their creators can sue for infringement. Both foreign and U.S. authors must register in order to be eligible for statutory damages and attorney's fees.

The Visual Artists Rights Act

Most of the cases that have brought moral rights problems to the public's attention revolve around mutilation of works of fine art. Some memorable cases include Pablo Picasso's *Trois Femmes,* which was cut into one-inch squares and sold as original Picassos by two entrepreneurs in 1986; the destruction and removal of an Isamu Noguchi sculpture from a New York office lobby; and the alteration by the Marriott Corporation of a historic William Smith mural in a landmark Maryland building.

A case widely publicized in the graphic arts arena involved Alberto Vargas's series *The Vargas Girls,* which ran in Esquire magazine. After Vargas's contract with Esquire expired, the magazine continued to run the series under the name *The Esquire Girls* without giving Vargas credit. Vargas brought Esquire to court, but lost the case. The court found that he had no rights left under the contract, including the right to his own name.

Moral rights legislation at both the state and federal levels has been proposed and supported vigorously by the Graphic Artists Guild since the late 1970s. Successes in California (1979), New York (1983), Maine and Massachusetts (1985), and other states, established the momentum to advance a federal version.

By presenting testimony about the problems that illustrators and designers face, the Graphic Artists Guild has been able to broaden state legislation. For instance, members of the Graphic Artists Guild have strongly argued that the appearance of their artwork with unauthorized alterations or defacement can damage an otherwise vital career. The state bills that the Guild helped to pass recognize artists' ongoing relationships with the work they create.

The Visual Artists Rights Act (VARA), Section 106A of the Copyright Act, was finally enacted by Congress in 1990. Although the act is a positive first step toward comprehensive moral rights legislation, unfortunately, it has limited application and, ironically, may invalidate, through federal preemption (discussed below), many state statutes that may be far more protective.

The law covers only visual arts and only one-of-a-kind works that are defined as paintings, drawings, prints, photographs made solely for exhibition, and sculptures, existing in a single copy or in a limited edition of 200 or fewer copies, signed and numbered consecutively by the artist. Specifically excluded are any kind of commercial or applied arts (advertising, promotion, packaging); posters, maps, charts, and technical drawings; motion pictures and other audiovisual works; books,

magazines, newspapers, and periodicals; electronically produced work; any work-for-hire; and any noncopyrightable work.

The moral rights protected are limited to those of attribution and integrity. To be actionable, a distortion, mutilation, or other modification of a work must be intentional. Mere natural deterioration is not actionable unless caused by gross negligence. In addition, the act places two burdens on the artist: to prove that a threatened action would be "prejudicial to his or her honor or reputation" and, if the goal is to prevent destruction of a work, to prove that it is "of recognized stature." Since no guidelines are provided for either standard, their meaning will have to be determined in the courts on a case-by-case basis.

The law stipulates that these rights exist exclusively with the artist during his or her lifetime and may not be transferred. They may be waived, but only by an expressly written and signed agreement. In the case of a joint work, each contributing artist may claim or waive the rights for all the others. The act also contains special provisions for removal of works that are parts of buildings (murals or bas reliefs), including a procedure to register such works.

A potential problem of the law is that it arguably invokes the doctrine of federal preemption and can be read to supersede any existing state laws that protect equivalent rights against mutilation and defacement. Among the questions that will probably have to be answered in the courts are whether the state statutes, many of which apply to other visual works or extend greater protections, are completely preempted or only partially so, and whether they may be invoked after the death of the artist. So far, a lower court in New York has held that VARA does preempt state law regarding attribution rights.

Resale Royalties

Another time-honored French doctrine, like moral rights, that transcends rights of copyright and ownership of the original work in most Berne signatory countries is known as *droit de suite.* It grants to creators a share in the value of their works by guaranteeing a certain percentage of the sale price every time a work is resold.

In the United States such rights, known as resale royalties, exist only in California. A provision for resale royalties had been part of the original draft of the Visual Artists Rights Act, but it was later dropped because of strong opposition from art dealers, auction houses, and museums. Under the Act's authority, the Copyright Office conducted a study of adoption of resale royalty legislation and recommended against it, concluding that anticipation of potential royalties does not provide proper incentive for artists to be creative. Incredibly, the study suggested that resale royalties might actually have an adverse economic impact on artists, because buyers, anticipating having to pay a future royalty, might lower the amount they were willing to pay. The Copyright Office did suggest, however, that the issue be reexamined if the European Community (EC) decided to harmonize existing *droit de suite* laws to extend resale royalty to all member states, which the EC did in July, 2001.

Practices Governing Original Art

Well-known illustrators can command high prices for the sale of original art. Many graphic artists also sell their work through galleries, to collectors, and to corporations. Original art may be exhibited, used as portfolio pieces, given as gifts, or bequeathed as part of an estate. Concern for protecting ownership of an original work stems not only from artists' interests in obtaining additional income from the sale of the original, but also from their interest in protecting their reputations and careers.

Ownership of the physical art, while separate from ownership of copyright, is similarly vested with the artist from the moment it is created. Selling the artwork does not transfer any rights of copyright to the buyer, just as selling the right of reproduction does not give a client any claim to the physical artwork.

The work may be given to the client temporarily so reproductions can be made, but the client must take reasonable care of it and return it undamaged to the artist. Of course, separate fees can be negotiated with a client or any other party who wishes to buy the physical artwork. The artist who wishes to sell original art should stipulate on the invoice or bill of sale the extent of any copyright interest that is also being sold with the original. To be able to license any copyright interest he or she has decided to keep, the artist should also keep a reproduction-quality transparency on file.

Laws Defining Fair Practices

The Fair Practices Act, signed into law in Oregon (Sections 359.350 to 359.365 of Rev. Stat., 1981), California (Section 988 of Civil Code,1982), and New York State (Sections 1401 & 1403 of Arts & Cultural Affairs Law and Artists' Authorship Rights Law, Article 12-J of General Business Law, 1983), clarifies who owns the original work of art when reproduction rights are sold. This legislation was drafted by the Guild's attorneys based on concerns raised by Guild members.

The Act provides that an original work of art can become the property of a client only if the sale is in writing. The passage of this act reinforces one of the premises of the copyright law: works of art have value beyond their reproduction for a specific purpose, and this value rightly belongs to the

artist who created them. The Fair Practices Act prevents clients from holding on to originals unless they have written sales agreements with the creator. In those states where it applies, this act solves problems that can arise when clients believe they have obtained ownership of the original art when in fact they have only purchased rights of reproduction, or when they believe they have obtained an original through an ambiguous oral agreement.

In Oregon and California, the law also provides that any ambiguity about the ownership of reproduction rights shall be resolved in favor of the artist. For artists whose livelihoods depend on resale of reproduction rights and on sales of original works, the law is critical.

Another important piece of legislation that prevents unauthorized reproduction of artwork was enacted by a Georgia statute in 1990. The Protection of Artists Act requires commercial printers to obtain written affidavits from their clients attesting that the artist has authorized the reproduction of the work when the printing of the art (painting, drawing, photograph, or work of graphic art) costs $1,000 or more. Echoing federal copyright law, the Georgia law separates the ownership of artwork from the right to reproduce it and puts clients on notice that bills of sale or purchase orders must state explicitly the extent of the rights purchased. Any client or printer who uses or reuses artwork without the written permission of the artist is subject to misdemeanor penalties. The Atlanta Chapter of the Guild was instrumental in getting the law passed.

Trademarks

A trademark may be a word, symbol, design, or slogan, or a combination of words and designs, that identifies and distinguishes the goods or services of one party from those of another. Trademarks identify the source of the goods or services. Marks that identify the source of services rather than goods are typically referred to as service marks. Normally, a trademark for goods appears on the product or its packaging, while a service mark is usually used to identify the owner's services in advertising. The protection given to trademarks and service marks is identical, and the terms are sometimes used interchangeably.

While a copyright protects an artistic or literary work and a patent protects an invention, a trademark protects a name or identity. For example, Adobe is used as the trademark for certain software products, Mickey Mouse is a trademarked character for Disney, and Amtrak is a service mark for railroad service. Product names and logos are the most traditional forms of trademarks. Sounds, such as jingles, can also be used as trademarks, as can product shapes or configurations such as Coca Cola's distinctive bottle shape.

Trademark protections can last indefinitely if the mark continues to be used for source identification.

A valid trademark gives the owner the right to prevent others from using a mark that might be confusingly similar to the owner's mark. If anyone else uses the mark for similar goods or services, and it is similar in sound, connotation, or appearance, then the first user can prevent the latecomer from using the mark. The test for infringement is whether there would be a likelihood of confusion as to the source of the goods and services.

For maximum trademark protection, a party using a trademark in interstate commerce should register it for $375 (paper filing) or $325 (electronic filing) with the U.S. Patent and Trademark Office (PTO) (mailing address: Commissioner of Trademarks, P.O. Box 1451, Alexandria, VA 22313-1451). You can access forms through the Trademark Electronic Application System (TEAS), at http://www.uspto.gov/teas/index.html. For information about applying for a trademark, click Basic Facts about Trademarks. If you need answers to specific trademark questions, please contact the Trademark Assistance Center at 1-800-786-9199 (or 571-272-9250) or consult the PTO web site at www.uspto.gov. It is recommended that a search be conducted to determine whether the trademark is already in use by another party, since the application fee will not be refunded if the application is rejected. Trademark searches, preparation, and application filing for trademark registration can be done online.

The owner of a federal trademark registration may give notice of registration by using the ® symbol, which can only be used after the mark is registered (the Graphic Artists Guild logo, the Guild's service mark, appears in print with an ®). Trademark owners who do not have federal registration may only use the symbol TM for trademarks. The symbol SM is used for service marks.

While not mandatory, federal registration protects the trademark throughout the United States, even in geographical areas in which the trademark is not used. Federal registration is legal evidence of trademark ownership and the exclusive right to use it in interstate commerce. As in copyright, someone with a federal registration can be eligible for special remedies, including attorneys' fees and enhanced damages, when willful infringement is proved. Unlike copyright, however, there is no requirement to register a trademark before suing for infringement. Also unlike copyright, trademark registration only applies to a particular product or service, not to the entire universe of possible uses. Thus, different parties may each have valid registrations for the same or similar trademarks, such as "Cadillac" for automobiles and cat food, provided there areas of business are sufficiently unrelated that consumers would not be confused by the similarity.

Legal cases involving artists

In the past two decades, there have been several legal cases involving the work of artists and photographers that have raised concerns for graphic artists and their clients about potential trademark Infringement liability.

LANDMARK BUILDINGS
A relatively new application of trademark law has been attempted by the owners of landmark buildings, such as the Chrysler Building, Rockefeller Center, or the Flatiron Building in New York City, who are trying to prevent use of illustrations or photographs of their buildings on everything from advertising to note cards and textbooks. The problem is now affecting illustrators and graphic artists who work either on assignment for a client or are selling stock. Clients are increasingly reluctant to use these images in the face of demand letters by large corporate building owners requiring that creators of images supply property releases or clear the usage rights. In many cases this simply results in another work being chosen for the job. No one wants to risk legal action or having to pull an advertisement after it has been created. Few creators can afford to be caught in a lawsuit over usage rights.

For instance, the New York Stock Exchange, alleging trademark violation, sued a casino in Las Vegas for building a model of its facade on their gambling floor. The Stock Exchange ultimately lost the suit.

It is important to note that a 1999 ruling by the Federal District Court for the Northern District of Ohio held in favor of photographer Chuck Gentile against the Rock & Roll Hall of Fame. It denied the museum's request to stop the sale of a poster with a night photograph taken by Gentile of the Rock & Roll Hall of Fame. The ruling stated that (1) the Rock & Roll Hall of Fame's building design was not used as a trademark, so the poster could not infringe trademark rights; (2) Gentile did not use the poster as a trademark, so he was not infringing any alleged trademark rights; and (3) the use of the identifying phrase "Rock & Roll Hall of Fame" under the photograph was fair use and did not infringe any trademark rights. This ruling was affirmed by the Sixth Circuit Court of Appeals.

While this decision cannot be construed to mean that no photograph or illustration of a building could ever violate a trademark, it seems very difficult after this decision for the owner of a building to convince a court that an image of a building infringed any trademark rights. This decision supports the position that, in most situations, a photograph or illustration of a building does not violate the building owner's trademark and additional permission is not required by law. Since trademark infringement turns on issues of confusion as to the origin of goods and services, it is still advisable to analyze each use on a case-by-case basis.

TRADEMARKS IN PAINTINGS
One 1995 case that threatened the artist's right to reproduce a trademark in a painting involved the use of celebrity animals and images associated with professional sports. Visual artist Jenness Cortez

was sued by the New York Racing Association (NYRA) in July, 1995 for her use of the Saratoga Race Track, including the use of the word "Saratoga," in her original paintings, etchings, and lithographs. NYRA claimed the right to a portion of the income derived from the sale of her work. In August 1996, a U.S. district court dismissed the case, saying Cortez's work was covered by the First Amendment. In a strongly worded decision affirming that artists can include trademarked images or symbols in their paintings, the judge noted, however, that the artist does not have the right to gratuitously include trademarks that are not already part of a particular scene. Although Cortez was subsequently sued by the owner and agents of the horse Cigar for trademark infringement and unauthorized use of the horse's image, that case was also settled in Cortez's favor in 1997.

Trade Dress

Graphic artists need a way to protect against copycats who capitalize on successful projects by passing off work that is stylistically similar at a lower fee. Although an artist's style cannot be copyrighted, the relatively new concept of "trade dress"—that part of trademark law that protects an established look—can be used by artists to support their claims of imitation.

It is important for artists to understand the difference between what is protected under copyright law and what is protected under trademark law. Copyright protects the tangible expression of an idea fixed in some tangible, reproducible format (written word, music, or image). By contrast, according to J. Thomas McCarthy, a pre-eminent expert on intellectual property law and the author of McCarthy on Trademarks and Unfair Competition, the purpose of a trademark, service mark, or trade dress is to identify one seller's goods and distinguish them from goods sold by others. A trademark or service mark is a specific word, symbol, design, slogan, or combination of words and designs that identifies and distinguishes a product or service. Trade dress, on the other hand, protects a product's total image and overall appearance. Trade dress is defined by a work's overall composition and design, including size, shape, color, texture, and graphics. Therefore, trade dress also includes a product's packaging and labeling. Generally, the law governing trade dress (a 1988 amendment to Section 43(a) of the Lanham Act) permits civil actions against any person whose trade dress is likely to cause confusion "as to the origin, sponsorship, or approval of his or her goods, services, or commercial activities by another person."

Legal cases supporting trade dress

The Lanham Act was amended in 1988 to make the act consistent with decisions that had been made by the courts in trade dress cases. One that is of particular interest to designers is the 1986 Missouri case, Hartford House, Ltd. v. Hallmark Cards, Inc. Hartford House, Ltd., one of the manufacturers of Blue Mountain Cards, claimed that Hallmark Cards' Personal Touch product line was confusingly similar to Blue Mountain's Airebrush Feelings and Water-Color Feelings lines of greeting cards. The district court determined that the trade dress—overall appearance or arrangement of features—of the two Blue Mountain lines of cards had acquired a "secondary meaning" and that there was a likelihood of confusion among card purchasers as to the source of the cards. "Secondary meaning" refers to the public's perception of the cards' appearance as a Blue Mountain brand, not just an aesthetically pleasing design. The district court granted a preliminary injunction against Hallmark.

Hallmark appealed, but the U.S. Court of Appeals for the Tenth Circuit affirmed the lower court's decision that certain greeting cards in the Blue Mountain lines were protected under trade dress since they contained inherently distinctive and uniform features that combined in an overall look that consumers could recognize and attribute to Blue Mountain. Some of these distinguishing features included:

1. A two-fold card containing poetry on the first page and the third page.
2. A deckle edge on the right side of the first page.
3. A high quality, uncoated and textured art paper for the cards.
4. Lengthy poetry, written in free verse, typically with a personal message.
5. Appearance of hand-lettered calligraphy on the first and third page with the first letter of the words often enlarged.
6. The look of the cards primarily characterized by backgrounds of soft colors done with air brush blends or light watercolor strokes, usually depicting simple contrasting foreground scenes superimposed in the background.

Since Hallmark could have used other designs that were not so similar to Blue Mountain's as to make them virtually indistinguishable, Hallmark was prohibited from marketing or advertising certain cards in its Personal Touch line that were found to cause consumer confusion.

It is important to note that the ruling in the Blue Mountain case does not mean that artistic style on its own can be protected under trademark law. The court specified: "Blue Mountain has not been granted exclusive rights in an artistic style or in some concept, idea, or theme of expression. Rather, it is Blue Mountain's specific artistic expression, in combination with other features to produce an overall Blue Mountain look, that is being protected. This protection does not extend the protection available under trademark law and does not conflict with the policy of copyright law."

Given that unfair competition by imitators is one of the critical issues affecting the graphic arts industry today, it is vital for artists to understand trade dress law so that they can include it in their arsenal. Since trade dress includes the design and appearance of a product as well as that of its container and all elements making up the total visual image by which the product is presented to consumers, in order to claim trademark or trade dress rights, an artist must prove that the look of a product performs the job of identification, in the way that the Blue Mountain cards were found to have done. If it does not do this, then it is not protectable as a trademark, service mark, trade dress, or any other exclusive right.

The challenge for graphic artists is to prove that their services are eligible for "branding," as in any other business that provides services or manufactures products, and to convince the courts that these "services" are distinctive and protectable as trade dress. The most encouraging development in this area is a 1992 New York decision, *Romm Art Creations v. Sincha International,* which found that an artist's style was "inherently distinctive" and thus protectable against "slavish imitations" by a competitor. The decision has been criticized, however, and artists continue to face judicial skepticism when asserting trade dress rights in style per se.

One of the next arenas for trade dress legislation is Internet design. Although specific guidelines have not yet been legislated, cases regarding trade dress protection have cropped up concerning the overriding appearance of a web site. In 2007, in *Blue Nile, Inc. v. Ice.com, Inc.,* the plaintiff sued the defendant for copying the overall "look and feel" of the plaintiff's retail jewelry web sites, including the design of the plaintiff's search pages. Although the court requested more information before it could rule definitively, the court held that it was possible for the web site's look and feel to merit trade dress protection if the plaintiff's copyright did not already cover the issue. This case addressed two important questions:

1. Whether "look and feel" infringements of a web site qualify as trade dress infringements, and
2. Whether these infringements are preempted by existing copyright law. This particular case was settled, but the issues are likely to arise again.

International & Canadian Copyright

Any discussion of this subject begins with the proviso that there is no such thing as international copyright law. Each country has its own copyright laws. Artists are protected under each country's laws through the copyright relations their home country shares with other countries.

In practical terms, this means that a U.S. artist is protected by copyright in most other countries, although that protection may be to a different degree than in the United States. For example, moral rights, discussed earlier in this chapter, are protected differently, depending on the country. In some countries, such as France, there is much greater moral rights protection for all creators of copyrighted works than in many other countries. In still other countries, such as Canada, moral rights protection for visual and fine artists does not extend as far as it does in France, but the protection extends to all creators of copyright materials, unlike the situation in the United States.

Copyright laws around the world protect artists and provide them with negotiating power. All copyright laws are based on the same principles. The copyright laws provide a certain copyright culture within a country and help set industry standards in contractual relationships. For instance, because of the work-for-hire provision in the U.S. Copyright Act, it is common practice in certain industries, such as the film industry, to require writers and other creators to assign all their rights. In Canada, where there is no work-for-hire provision, screenwriters retain the copyright to their scripts and license the rights to a licensee/producer to make a film out of it.

As the graphic communication industries adapt to the global economy, graphic artists can easily reside in one country while serving clients in another. Political boundaries no longer limit business relationships between artists and buyers, though U.S. immigration laws do set quotas that limit the number of professionals who live and work in the United States. (Highly qualified professionals can be awarded special visas if a union such as the Guild finds they have exceptional credentials.) Canadian and European artists often serve U.S. clients, and vice versa. Given the phenomenal expansion of the global economy, which can only continue to grow, it is in the Guild's interests to improve standards for all graphic artists around the world. Establishing contact and signing agreements with graphic arts unions, or organizations in other countries, will help ensure that all artists compete on talent and portfolio, not on price.

Canadian/United States rights

The following section highlights and contrasts the important features of Canadian copyright law as it applies to the visual communications industries.

REGISTERING COPYRIGHT
Copyright is automatic in Canada and always has been. There is a voluntary registration system but, unlike in the United States, no deposit system where artists send in a copy of their works. Canadian registration of copyright and licenses relating to works have much less stringent provisions than in the United States. Canadians will find much more space in U.S. contracts devoted to copyright registration and documentation issues (often standard clauses). There are no copyright notice provisions under Canadian copyright law, although Canadian creators generally include a copyright notice to remind the public that copyright does exist in their works.
DURATION OF COPYRIGHT

There is no renewal of copyright in Canada, nor are there any works that fall into the public domain and that then may once again be protected by copyright. With only two exceptions, a literary or artistic work in Canada is protected for 50 years after the death of the author. One of the exceptions involves engravings, which are defined in the law as "etchings, lithographs, woodcuts, prints, and other similar works, not being photographs." Engravings published at the time of an author's death are subject to the life-plus-50 rule. However, engravings unpublished at the time of an author's death are protected until publication and for 50 years thereafter. The other exception involves photographs made on or after January 1, 1944: they are protected for 50 years from the end of the calendar year when the initial negative or other plate was made from which the photograph was directly or indirectly derived. If no negative or other plate was made, then they are protected for 50 years from the end of the calendar year in which the initial photograph was made. A work that is being exploited in both Canada and the United States may be licensed for a part of the duration of copyright or for its full term.

REVERSIONARY INTEREST PROVISO

In Canada, where the author of a work is the first owner of the copyright (it is not a product of employment, a government work, or a commissioned engraving, photograph, or portrait), any copyright acquired by contract becomes void 25 years after the author's death. This does not mean that the term of copyright is affected. It means that, if specific conditions apply, any subsequent owner of copyright will lose his or her rights 25 years after the author's death. At this time, the copyright becomes part of the author's estate, and only the estate has the right to deal with the copyright. Conditions affecting this reversion include when the author disposes of the copyright by will for the period following the 25-year limit. Thus, the reversion may be avoided by the author bequeathing copyright for the period between 25 and 50 years after his or her death.

It also does not apply when a work is part of a collective work or when a work or part thereof has been licensed to be published in a collective work such as a magazine or an encyclopedia.

COMMISSIONED WORKS

Under Canadian law, a special rule applies only to commissioned engravings, photographs, or portraits. For these works, the person ordering the work is deemed to be the first owner of the copyright if the following conditions are met:

- The person ordering the work has offered valuable consideration, such as money or services.
- The work was created because of the order and was not created prior to the order being made.

This holds true provided there is no agreement between the commissioner and the creator stating that copyright subsists with the creator of the work.

While at first glance this appears to be more limited than U.S. work-for-hire, it is in fact more broad. Unlike in the United States, where it must be agreed in writing that a work is for hire, it is assumed in Canada that the commissioning party owns the rights unless a written agreement exists to the contrary. That's why U.S. artists who assume they retain their rights under a Canadian contract that contains no mention of ownership of copyright may be in for a nasty shock. When the art purchaser is based in Canada, it is highly likely that the contract will be based on Canadian law.

Canadian law is limited to three very specific types of works, but insofar as published illustrations are regarded as "commissioned engravings," the provision applies to all commissioned illustrations, and not merely those in the nine categories delineated under U.S. law. Thus, a U.S. artist dealing with a Canadian company should make sure that the disposition of rights is clearly spelled out and that he or she fully understands any unfamiliar terminology.

EMPLOYMENT WORK

In Canada, three criteria must be met in order for works made during employment to belong initially to the employer:

- The employee must be employed under a "contract of service."
- The work must be created in the course of performing the contract.
- There must not be any provision in a contract that states that the employee owns the copyright (such a contract need not be in writing).

One important distinction between the U.S. work-for-hire and the Canadian employment works provision is that in Canada, notwithstanding that the employee does not own the copyright, the employee continues to retain the moral rights. An employee can never license these moral rights, though he or she can waive them.

DIGITAL RIGHTS

Although an agreement may govern only one jurisdiction, say, North America, certain rights, such as those for the Internet or World Wide Web, are not necessarily subject to geographical division. This means that by virtue of licensing Internet rights, artists are granting a de facto worldwide license.

MORAL RIGHTS

Under Canadian law, there are three types of moral rights:

- The right of paternity.
- The right of integrity.
- The right of association or disclosure.
  These rights are discussed at length previously

in this chapter in the section on Moral Rights (especially The Berne Convention).

Even when an artist transfers copyright and even when the work is owned by an employer, the artist has moral rights unless they are waived. Moral rights in Canada last for fifty years from the date of a creator's death (at the end of that calendar year). Upon death, they can be passed to an artist's heirs, but not otherwise transferred. Artists can agree not to exercise one or more of their moral rights, and this is something artists working with a Canadian company should be aware of.

The United States has moral rights protections for limited works of visual art under the Visual Artists Rights Act (see section earlier in this chapter). The duration depends on when the work was created and/or transferred. If the work was created after June 1, 1991, the rights endure for the life of the artist. If the work was created prior to June 1, 1991, and the title has not been transferred to another party, the rights have the same term as ordinary Section 106 rights, as determined by Sections 302–304 of the Copyright Act. If the artist transferred the work prior to June 1, 1991, he or she has no moral rights to the work.

FAIR USE/DEALING AND EXCEPTIONS

Canada does not have a fair use provision but has a similar, though much narrower, provision known as the "fair dealing provision." Generally, it is used only for quotations from a book or article and does not apply beyond that, except, for example, in cases of multiple copying for classroom use as in the United States.

In addition, Canada has fewer exceptions that allow free uses of copyrighted materials. With the passage of a 1999 copyright revision bill, there are many more exceptions than in the past, primarily for schools, libraries, archives, and museums. Even with the changes, in certain circumstances a U.S. artist may find that certain free uses of work in the United States may be uses for which permission must be requested and paid for in Canada. The converse is also true. Canadian artists may find that there may be free uses of their work in the United States for which they would be paid in Canada. Generally, such provisions cannot be reversed by contract but are subject to the copyright statutes in the respective countries.

GOVERNMENT WORKS

In the U.S., there is no copyright protection for government-created works. However, the government can own copyright in works created for it by independent contractors (as opposed to government employees), e.g., stamp artwork. In Canada, the government owns the copyright to works produced by its employees, and sometimes by independent contractors/consultants, and any use of government works requires permission from the government. Thus, a Canadian artist whose work incorporates some government works will probably have cleared copyright to that

work before including it in his or her work. A U.S. artist on the other hand, may not have cleared copyright to a U.S. government work incorporated in his work. In this situation, although permission may not be required from the U.S. government for use of the work in the United States, permission will be required when the same work is used in Canada. Therefore, an American artist should be careful in making any warranties and representations regarding copyright clearance of works incorporating any government materials when those works are used in Canada.

GOVERNING LAW

Parties to an agreement are generally free to choose the state/province whose law will govern the agreement. That is usually settled by negotiation. The contract should state under which jurisdiction the contract is to be interpreted, especially when work is to be created, performed, or delivered in more than one jurisdiction. It is usually in the artist's best interests to have his/her own state/province's law govern the contract for ease of access to a lawyer in that jurisdiction as well as for convenience (especially when considering costs), should court action be necessary.

Remember that an agreement on governing law does not in itself determine the jurisdiction where a suit may be filed, only the law under which that suit will be decided. It is possible to agree that a contract will be judged by U.S. law but adjudicated in Canada, or vice versa. It is also possible, and sometimes more desirable, to agree upon the governing law without specifying a jurisdiction for adjudication, which leaves the aggrieved party with the freedom to file suit in the most convenient location.

More and more agreements are now subject to mediation and binding arbitration in a place halfway between the cities of the contracting parties. This can at least limit costs and travel time. A lawyer should be able to ensure that the laws of another jurisdiction are compatible with any contractual relationship.

PROFESSIONAL ISSUES

This chapter provides a summary of important business issues, including taxation, employment status, cancellation and rejection fees, working on speculation, and entering contests and competitions, and is designed to aid both buyers and sellers of graphic art.

PROFESSIONAL

issues involve a variety of factors affecting the way artists and designers work. Changes in business practices, taxation, copyright, or other laws can dramatically impact a creator's business, so can emerging trends or practices that vary from accepted customs. Artists, designers, and their clients need to be aware of the following major factors when working on visual communications projects.

Sales Tax

States have widely different policies regarding sales tax. In those that have one, the rate usually ranges from 3 to 9 percent, and it is levied on the sale or use of physical property within the state. A number of exemptions exist, including special rules for the sale of reproduction rights.

Generally, sales tax is applicable for end sales or retail costs only, not for intermediate subcontracting. An artist may have to file forms showing that materials were intermediate and thus not taxable. Services, including the services of transferring reproduction rights, are not subject to sales tax. Transfers of physical property to a client (original art or designer's mechanicals) are generally not subject to sales tax if they are part of a project that will later be billed to a client by a design firm or other agent.

Variations by state

Many tax laws are unclear in relation to the graphic communications industry, though efforts have been made to clarify them (see the New York State section later in this chapter). If artists are doubtful about whether to collect sales tax, it is safest, of course, to collect and remit it to the state sales tax bureau. Note, however, that one accountant advised that if you do charge sales tax, and it is found during an audit that you should not have, you are liable to repay that amount to the client. If artists are required to collect the tax but do not, they, as well as their clients, remain liable, and it may be difficult to try to collect the tax from clients on assignments that were performed in the past if an audit or another review determines that sales tax is owed.

Consulting an experienced accountant to determine your specific responsibilities for your state is the best course of action. If you are required to collect sales tax, most states require you to register as a vendor and as a collector of taxes on the state's behalf. You will be issued what is known as a resale number enabling you to purchase certain materials, free of tax, for the creation of products to be resold to your clients.

The following examples of California, Minnesota, New York, and Wisconsin illustrate the great variation in state sales tax regulations.

CALIFORNIA

Following a random audit in 1993, the Board of Equalization (BOE), one of California's taxing agencies, ruled that children's book and stamp illustrator Heather Preston was required to pay sales taxes on four years' worth of royalties for book and rubber stamp illustrations. But she found peculiar catches. The authors of the books Preston illustrated, who turned in hard-copy manuscripts, owed no sales tax on their royalties. And had Preston sent the work electronically, rather than in hard copy, she would likely not have owed sales tax. On June 21, 1996, following an unsuccessful appeal to the BOE, Preston filed a lawsuit to recover sales taxes and interest on the ground that the BOE had improperly attempted to treat the grant of use rights as a "transfer of tangible property."

The BOE considers even a temporary transfer of hard-copy artwork or the transfer of digital artwork on a storage disk to be a transfer of "tangible personal property" (a physical product rather than a service or intellectual property such as reproduction rights) and therefore subject to sales tax. Written work is recognized as "authorship," which renders the transfer of tangible elements, such as a physical manuscript, "incidental to the true object" of the sale and, therefore, excluded from tax. Transfers of tangible personal property are considered taxable unless specifically exempted by the state legislature.

Preston lost her case at trial, and the California Court of Appeals rejected her appeal on procedural grounds. In the spring of 2000, the California Supreme Court agreed to hear Preston's case. The Graphic Artists Guild wrote the Supreme Court in support of Preston's appeal and filed an *amicus curiae* (friend of the court) brief. On April 2, 2001, the seven justices of the California Supreme Court ruled in favor of Preston, unanimously agreeing with her position that the copyright licenses had been wrongly taxed under California law; however, the majority concluded that the transactions constitute "technology transfer agreements." The decision means that a fair rental value for the artwork or computer disks transferred for the purpose of accessing the copyright interest is subject to tax. The Court remanded the matter of determining the value of the "rental" portion of Preston's transactions to the lower court.

The Guild has uploaded several useful PDF files on the Northern California Chapter's web site to assist California artists and designers seeking sales tax relief from that state's Board of Equalization in light of the historic *Preston v. State Board of Equalization* victory. The files can be found at http://norcal.gag.org/salestax/index.html.

Shortly before Preston filed her original suit, cartoonist Paul Mavrides won an appeal of his back taxes assessment. Mavrides's case, which was supported by the American Civil Liberties Union, the California Newspaper Publishers Association, the Cartoonists Legal Defense Fund, and more than 30 other organizations, differed in significant respects from Preston's. In Mavrides's case, the BOE attempted to collect sales tax from cartoonists for the first time following the 1991 repeal of the newspapers' exemption from the sales tax. The ruling in his successful appeal was made narrowly, exempting the work of cartoonists who both draw the pictures and write accompanying script as authors when their work is published in books, magazines, or newspapers but not when in greeting cards, posters, or displays.

In 1996, the Northern California Chapter of the Graphic Artists Guild determined that a surprisingly high percentage of its members—estimated as high as 20 percent—had been subject to sales tax audits. Members reported widespread inconsistency, errors, and overzealous enforcement by auditors. In concert with the Guild's National Advocacy Committee, the Chapter began working to change California's tax law so that illustrators, graphic designers, and photographers would have the same exclusion from sales tax that authors of written manuscripts enjoy, based on equal treatment under federal copyright law and California civil code. Subsequently, the Guild was the lead sponsor of two bills in the California Legislature, both of which initially failed to pass in a form adequate to provide the necessary relief.

Finally, on February 7, 2002, in a long-awaited victory for the California arts community, the California Board of Equalization voted to clarify the sales tax regulations affecting illustrators, photographers, cartoonists, and designers. The change benefits graphic artists in four ways:

- It virtually exempts sales tax on all reproduction rights (including royalties) on the artwork of graphic artists.
- It exempts sales tax on artwork delivered on computer disk if returned on disk.
- It exempts sales tax on print design when the designer buys printing.
- It clearly specifies that commercial photographers working in the advertising and publishing fields are considered graphic artists.

In 1999, the Guild represented California's graphic arts industry as an interested party when the Business Tax Division of the BOE began a major revision of the 1974 regulation affecting the advertising industry. The Guild was successful at having provisions inserted in the new regulations that set uniform conditions where none previously existed, greatly cut the tax burden on graphic artists, and reduced their exposure to audits. The following provisions were approved by the BOE and went into effect on January 5, 2000:

- Reduced the taxable portion of graphic design and illustration jobs based on the fact that part of the fees paid are for "conceptual services" rendered. The regulation presumes that 75 percent represents a reasonable allocation for these nontaxable services.
- Excluded web site design and hosting from taxation, as well as transfers of artwork by remote communications (modem).
- Limited taxability of reuse and royalties to one year from the time of contract.
- Excluded the design of environmental signage from taxation.
- Applied changes to the advertising regulation uniformly to other industries where artists and designers are affected.

It is important to note that artists who take advantage of any of these exemptions must be sure to separate taxable and nontaxable charges on all invoices and carefully document the exemptions.

All artists and designers engaged in business in California are required to obtain a California seller's permit and to comply with applicable sales and use tax regulations. Businesses that do not have these permits are exposed to more extensive audits and face additional penalties than those that comply.

While it is not required, the Graphic Artists Guild strongly recommends that artists working in California take advantage of a provision in the California Taxpayers Bill of Rights and obtain binding information by filing a document called a "Section 6596 Query." This is a personal letter from you to the BOE requesting information on how sales tax regulations specifically apply to your individual business. Answers given over the telephone are nonbinding and frequently inaccurate, but a written response from the BOE provides protection from contrary interpretations by an auditor during an audit.

To learn more about the Northern California Guild Chapter and its tax campaign, go to http://norcal.gag.org/salestax/index.html.

MINNESOTA

In 1993, Minnesota passed a rule that the sale of an advertising brochure is no longer considered the sale of "tangible personal property" (a physical product rather than a service or intellectual property such as reproduction rights); it is now considered part of the sale of a "nontaxable advertising service." Since an ad agency sells a nontaxable service, it must pay tax on all taxable "inputs" (all the components of an advertising product provided by outside vendors such as illustration, photography, or copywriting) used to create the brochure, including commissioned artwork. In most cases, inputs can no longer be purchased tax free, so illustrators may have to collect sales tax when selling work used in advertising brochures.

NEW YORK STATE

For years, many practitioners in New York State were told different things by different people, including accountants and other professionals, and consequently were subjected to substantial sales tax assessments if audited. In 1990, a coalition of the American Institute of Graphic Artists (AIGA), the Graphic Artists Guild, and the Society for Environmental Graphic Design (SEGD) met with representatives of the New York State Sales Tax Authority to establish guidelines for how graphic designers and illustrators should charge sales tax for their services. The guidelines, which were reviewed and approved by the New York State Tax Department in 1992, answer the two most frequently asked questions about sales tax:

- When are graphic designers and illustrators expected to charge sales tax on their services, and when are their sales exempt from tax?

- When are graphic designers and illustrators expected to pay sales tax on the materials, equipment, and services they buy, and when are those purchases exempt from tax?

Charging sales tax New York State sales tax law imposes a tax on the sale of tangible personal property. Many local authorities add their own sales tax to that imposed by the state. The resulting sales tax must be charged in addition to other charges, stated as a separate item on any invoice, and paid by the purchaser. Payment of sales tax by the seller (in this case the graphic designer or illustrator) or failure to itemize it on an invoice is prohibited. Mixing taxable with nontaxable items on an invoice makes the entire invoice subject to sales tax.

Exemptions from charging sales tax Six areas of exemption are relevant to graphic designers and illustrators working in New York State:

1. **Terms for resale:** When tangible personal property passes through intermediate owners, taxes are deferred until it reaches the final purchaser. An example is any item purchased in a store. Sales tax is paid by the end customer at the over-the-counter sale; the retailer does not pay tax when purchasing from the wholesaler; the wholesaler does not pay it when purchasing from the manufacturer. Consequently, any item purchased for resale may be purchased tax-exempt if the purchaser has a properly completed resale certificate. The responsibility for collecting the tax then falls on the seller when the item is sold to the final purchaser.
2. **Exempt use:** If the final sale is for an exempt use—for instance, promotional materials delivered to a client in New York that will be distributed out of New York State—the vendor must verify the tax-exempt status by obtaining an exempt use certificate from the purchaser.
3. **Sales to exempt organizations:** Nonprofit and educational institutions and most federal and New York State governmental agencies have tax-exempt status. In this instance, the vendor must verify the tax-exempt status by obtaining an exempt organization certificate or government purchase order from the purchaser.
4. **Grants of reproduction rights:** At the end of a creative process, if only specified restricted rights are transferred, but there is no transfer of ownership of tangible personal property (for example, the original, physical artwork or 50,000 brochures), the transaction is not taxable. Grants of rights are not subject to sales tax.
5. **Tax-exempt services:** Purchases of certain services that do not result in the transfer of tangible personal property are, by their nature, not taxable. Likewise, services provided by writers, copyeditors, and proofreaders are also exempt if there is no transfer of tangible personal property. However, if a writer writes an article and then sells it to a magazine, that transaction is taxable.
6. **Out-of-New York State sales:** The sale of work to out-of-state clients, delivered out-of-state, is not subject to sales tax, but there must be evidence of out-of-state delivery.

Payment & collection of sales tax Whether a graphic designer's or illustrator's services are taxable in New York State depends upon whether there is a final transfer of tangible personal property. If there is, the entire contract is taxable, including all consultations, designs, preparation of artwork, and so on. If the graphic designer or illustrator sells the rights to comps, mechanicals, computer data, printed materials, or fabricated materials such as exhibits or signs to the client, the graphic artist's services are considered to be transferable personal property.

The results of graphic designers' or illustrators' services are not considered transferable personal property if the artists do not provide printing or fabrication services, if they grant reproduction rights only, or if they retain ownership of all the designs, comps, mechanicals, or computer data and transfer them only temporarily for reproduction, to be returned—unretouched, unaltered, and undisplayed.

In most cases, graphic designers and illustrators may discover that some of their projects are taxable and some are not. The importance of setting up taxable and nontaxable work in separate contracts cannot be stressed enough. Graphic designers and illustrators must remember that the onus is always on them to prove that a project is nontaxable. Therefore, all agreements, invoices, and digital layouts or illustrations should have very clear language stating that ownership remains with the graphic artist, that only rights for reproduction are being granted, and that any graphic representations or artwork are being transferred temporarily solely for the purpose of reproduction, after which they are to be returned—unretouched, unaltered, and undisplayed—to the graphic designer or illustrator.

Corporate identity and logo programs are a special case. Conceivably, one could state in a contract that only specific, limited reproduction rights are being granted. In practice, however, the prospect of a client not having complete rights to their own logo or corporate identity system is not credible. Therefore, such a project is considered a taxable sale.

If a graphic artist or illustrator is required to charge sales tax, he or she should consult an experienced accountant to determine specific responsibilities. The artist will have to register as a vendor and, as a collector of taxes on the state's behalf, will be issued a resale number that will enable the artist to purchase certain materials, free of tax, for the creation of products to be resold to clients.

Exemption documents needed Graphic designers and illustrators in New York State need two exemption documents when making tax-exempt purchases: the resale certificate and the exempt use certificate. The resale certificate is only for items or services that are part of the item being sold—for example, the illustration board used to make a mechanical. The exempt use certificate is for items used in the production of the final product that do not become an actual part of it—for example, watercolors used to create an illustration that will be scanned into a computer and sent to the client electronically. Resale certificates cannot be used to purchase anything that does not substantially result in the tangible property being created.

Graphic artists are required to keep accurate records of (1) all items so purchased and (2) projects for which they were used. They are also required to retain the subsequent invoice that indicates that sales tax has been charged on that item directly or on the item into which it has been incorporated. It is essential that graphic designers and illustrators keep clear, thorough records of all projects, including all purchases for each project, so that in the event of an audit they can accurately show that they paid sales tax on purchases that required sales tax to be paid.

A graphic designer or illustrator is entitled to purchase services or materials for resale or production without paying tax, even if sale of the final product will be exempt from tax—for example, to an exempt client or if the final product will be shipped out of New York State.

The resale certificate may not be used if the services do not result in a sale, such as when unrestricted reproduction rights are granted or if the contract is for consultation alone, with no tangible end result. On such projects, the designer must pay tax on all equipment, supplies, and services used.

Equipment, such as computers and laser printers, that is used predominantly for the production of work for sale (more than 50% of the time) may also be purchased exempt from sales tax by submitting an exempt use certificate to the vendor. This means that if only half the artist's work results in taxable sales and this equipment is used only half the time on design work, then the equipment is actually being used only 25% of the time to produce work for sale. It is therefore subject to full tax when purchased.

Special considerations in New York City On certain purchases, only New York City sales tax is payable; New York State sales tax is not. Artists working in New York City should check with their accountants for current tax rates. These purchases are:

- Consumable materials used to produce work for sale that are not to be passed along to the client as part of the final product, including knife blades, masking tape, tracing paper, sketch paper, and markers.
- Maintenance and repair services for equipment used predominantly to produce work for sale, such as a computer, laser printer, fax machine, or copier.

- Freelance services used during the production of work for sale, including those employed to work on presentation materials or digital layouts that are part of a contract on which sales tax will be charged.

When any of the above items or services is purchased, the graphic designer or illustrator must use a valid resale or exempt use certificate to be exempt from the state sales tax, even though the local city tax is being paid.

From a practical standpoint, it is easy to ascertain whether the services of independent contractors are subject to the New York City tax because they work on specific projects. With consumable materials and maintenance and repair, it is not always as clear. It may be simpler to pay the full New York City sales tax rather than guess which projects they may be used on.

Graphic artists working in New York City also need to be aware of other special considerations concerning their purchases:

- If most projects are not taxable, it may be simpler to pay tax on all the equipment, supplies, and services you purchase, just to be safe and to simplify matters in the event of an audit.
- Where projects may result in a taxable sale, it is permissible to divide the project into two entirely separate contracts, one that is taxable and one that is not. For example, if a client wishes the designer or illustrator to provide printing and fabrication services, one contract can be set up for design and production of the artwork and an entirely separate contract for printing and fabrication. The design and production contract must specify the transfer of limited reproduction rights only, and the client must be able to terminate the relationship and go elsewhere for printing or fabrication services. A separate contract providing printing services is taxable (subject to the other relevant exemptions described above, such as exempt purchaser or out-of-state delivery). It is essential to keep the two contracts entirely separate: separate proposals, separate agreements, and separate invoices. If any part of a contract is taxable, the entire project is taxable. A contract cannot include some items that are taxable and some that are not.

The Graphic Artists Guild strongly recommends that graphic artists consult experienced accountants or tax lawyers to determine tax liabilities under these guidelines. Because of their familiarity with an artist's business, these professionals are best suited to answer questions. An alternative is to contact the New York State Department of Taxation and Finance, http://www.tax.state.ny.us/nyshome/how_to_reach.htm. This web site offers contact info, either by mail, phone or e-mail depending on your specific need. If a graphic artist finds that any ruling is contrary to these guidelines, notify the Graphic Artists Guild immediately.

WISCONSIN

Effective October 1, 2009, Wisconsin imposed state and county sales taxes on "the sale, lease, license, or rental of specified digital goods and additional digital goods at retail for the right to use the specified digital goods or additional digital goods on a permanent or less than permanent basis and regardless of whether the purchaser is required to make continued payment for such rights." The law defines "additional digital goods" as the following, if they are transferred electronically: 1) greeting cards; 2) finished artwork; 3) periodicals; and 4) video or electronic games.

"Finished artwork" means the final art used for actual reproduction by photomechanical or other processes or for display purposes. It also includes drawings, paintings, designs, photographs, lettering, paste-ups, mechanicals, assemblies, charts, graphs, and illustrative material, regardless of whether such items are reproduced.

Consequently, graphic artists in Wisconsin must charge sales tax on final projects delivered via e-mail and the Internet or on CD and DVD. The tax should be applied to only the final purchased product, not on communications, sketches, or proofs delivered electronically.

Taxable freelance services

It is important for freelance graphic designers and illustrators to understand that services they use, such as those of freelance layout artists, may be taxable. Each state makes its own laws in order to stimulate a certain type of business or service. Artists should contact an accountant in the state or locality in which their business is located or per-formed to find out exactly what services are taxable.

In New York State, freelancers must charge sales tax on their services to the graphic designer or illustrator, unless the exemptions outlined previously apply. When the graphic designer or illustrator's services result in a taxable sale, he or she may issue a resale certificate to the freelancer for the work.

In certain circumstances, artists who use free-lance services should, for their own protection, pay any tax due directly to the state—for example, if the freelancer is a student and not registered as a vendor or if the freelance supplier does not bill and collect the tax. A specific fill-in section on the sales tax reporting form, entitled "Purchases Subject to Use Tax," is provided for this purpose.

When a freelancer works on a project that does not result in a taxable sale for the artist—where reproduction rights only are being granted to the client—then the artist must pay full tax on the freelancer's fee.

As part of routine record keeping, graphic designers and illustrators should keep carefully receipted invoices from freelancers showing that, where appropriate, sales tax has been charged and paid. If the evidence is not clear-cut, sales tax authorities will expect the artist to pay the taxes.

Deductibility of Artwork

There is a popular misconception that artists donating their art to a charitable organization may deduct the "fair market value" of the work. Current law, in fact, distinguishes between "personal property" and "inventory." While anyone may donate personal goods to any charity and deduct the fair market value, businesses may deduct only the actual cost of producing the item. Artists, therefore, may deduct only the cost of producing the work: the price of the canvas, paint, and other materials. If an artist sells an original work, the buyer of that work may donate the piece as personal property and be eligible for the tax deduction of the amount paid for it. As a result, historically, artists have either withheld their valuable originals or sold them to private collectors.

In February 2003, a new bill to amend the Internal Revenue Code of 1986, S.287, was introduced into the Senate by Sen. Patrick J. Leahy of Vermont. The bill seeks to change artwork deductibility allowances by providing a deduction equal to fair market value for charitable contributions of literary, musical, artistic, or scholarly compositions created by the donor. If the bill (which was referred to the Committee on Finance in January, 2009) passes, artists will be eligible for the tax deduction currently enjoyed by the art buyer. This bill is in the first step in the legislative process. Introduced bills and resolu-tions first go to committees that deliberate, investigate, and revise them before they go to general debate. The majority of bills and resolutions never make it out of committee.

Although it does not affect artists and their artwork directly, legislation signed into law by President Clinton on August 10, 1993, contained a number of significant provisions affecting tax-exempt charitable organizations described in section 501(c)(3) of the Internal Revenue Code (IRC). Since January 1, 1994, deductions have not been allowed under section 170 of the IRC for any charitable contribution of $250 or more unless the donor has a receipt from the charity written at the time of the donation. The respon-sibility for obtaining the receipt lies with the donor, who must request it from the charity. The charity is not required to record or report this information to the Internal Revenue Service (IRS) on behalf of donors. Generally, if the value of an item (or group of like items) exceeds $5,000, the donor must obtain a qualified appraisal and submit an appraisal summary with the return to claim the deduction.

Employment Issues

Clients should be aware that the Internal Revenue Service takes a dim view of independent contractor relationships. From the government's perspective, employers use so-called independent contractors to evade employment taxes. If independent contractors are hired, the employer should be able to justify this designation in the event of an audit. If the IRS successfully reclassifies independent contractors, the very existence of a firm can be threatened. (For a complete discussion of work-for-hire, consult the Work-for-Hire section in Chapter 2, Legal Rights & Issues.)

In recent years the Internal Revenue Service has cracked down on advertising agencies, design firms, publishers, and others by examining whether artists providing graphic design, illustration, or production services are actually freelancers or employees. In audit after audit, the IRS has determined that so-called freelancers are, in fact, employees based upon their analysis of the actual working relationship between the client and the graphic artist. Especially vulnerable to IRS scrutiny, and a significant risk to the hiring party, are artists who work as full-time freelancers. One West Coast comic book publisher, for example, went out of business after six-figure penalties were imposed by the IRS for misclassifying its employees as independent contractors.

There are advantages and disadvantages of each classification for both the artist and the hiring party. Independent contractors are paid a flat fee, simplifying the employer's bookkeeping; and depending on the freelancer's fee structure, the art buyer may realize significant savings on taxes, insurance, and other fringe benefits. Independents retain some control over their copyrights, time, and business tax deductions for materials, overhead on private workspace, and so on. But independents always risk loss of payment when work is rejected or canceled or when they work on speculation, while employees are guaranteed at least the legal minimum wage.

NOTE: Portions of the above section were reprinted from *Communication Arts* with permission of Tad Crawford. ©Tad Crawford, 1993.

Social Security tax (FICA)

When classified as an employee, 6.2 percent of a graphic artist's gross income up to $106,800 is paid by the employer for Social Security tax; the remaining 6.2 percent of income for the total Social Security tax payment is withheld from the artist's paycheck. Independent contractors must pay the full 12.4 percent FICA tax on their adjusted gross income.

The Social Security tax rate for 2009 is 15.3 percent (the same as 2008) on self-employment income up to $106,800 (it was $102,000 in 2008). If your net earnings exceed $106,800, you continue to pay only the Medicare portion of the Social Security tax, which is 2.9 percent, on the rest of your earnings. There are two income tax deductions that reduce your tax liability. The deductions are intended to make sure self-employed people are treated in much the same way as employers and employees for Social Security and income tax purposes.

First, your net earnings from self-employment are reduced by an amount equal to half of your total Social Security tax. This is similar to the way employees are treated under the tax laws in that the employer's share of the Social Security tax is not considered income to the employee.

Second, you can deduct half of your Social Security tax on the IRS Form 1040 (line 29). This means the deduction is taken from your gross income in determining adjusted gross income. It cannot be an itemized deduction and must not be listed on your Schedule C.

Benefits & insurance

All employees are entitled to receive unemployment, disability, and workers' compensation insurance coverage. Depending upon specific company policy, employers may also be obligated to provide optional fringe benefits such as paid vacations, comprehensive medical and hospitalization insurance, employer-funded pension plans, or profit sharing to every employee. Independent contractors must purchase their own disability coverage and have no access to unemployment insurance or workers' compensation. Furthermore, independent contractors must provide their own vacations, medical coverage, and retirement plans.

Tax deductions

Independent contractors can reduce their taxable income significantly by deducting legitimate business expenses. Employees may also deduct expenses, but only for the amount exceeding 2 percent of their adjusted gross income.

Job security

Employees do not enjoy the freedom of working for whomever they want, as independent contractors do, but they do enjoy the security of a regular paycheck. One advantage employees have is the legal right to organize for the purposes of collective bargaining, a right denied to most independent contractors. Since November 1993, the Graphic Artists Guild has represented one group of employees in a collective bargaining agreement with its employer, Channel Thirteen/WNET Educational Broadcasting Corporation in New York City. As a result, the Guild has been instrumental in broadening the definition of graphic artists eligible for union representation and benefits and improved attributions and program credits.

Work-for-hire

All work created by employees, unless otherwise negotiated, is done as work-for-hire, which gives authorship and all attendant rights to the employer. Negotiating those rights back, while possible, is not easy. In contrast, independent contractors are recognized as the authors of their work and control the copyright unless they sign a contract that specifically states the work is a "work-for-hire."

Determining employee status

The IRS has a 20-factor control test (Revenue Ruling 87-41, 1897-1CB296) that it uses to clarify the distinction between employees and independent contractors. The control test is easy. Is the person subject to the control of or by the firm?

The guidelines, however, are too general to resolve every situation. Often some factors suggest employee status, while others suggest independent contractor status. Key factors that the IRS looks at include:

Instructions: Is the worker required to obey the firm's instructions about when, where, and how work is to be performed? If the firm has the right to require compliance with such instructions, the worker is likely to be an employee.

Training: Training a worker suggests that the worker is an employee. Training may consist only of having a more experienced employee fill in the newcomer on office procedures, or he or she might be required to attend meetings or read files and/or correspondence.

Integration: If a worker's services are part of a firm's operations, this suggests that the worker is subject to the firm's control. This is especially true if the success or continuation of the firm's business depends in a significant way upon those services.

Personal services: If the firm requires that the services be performed in person, this suggests control over an employee.

Use of assistants: If the firm hires, directs, and pays for the worker's assistants, this indicates employee status. On the other hand, if the worker hires, directs, and pays for his or her assistants; supplies materials; and works under a contract providing that he or she is responsible only to achieve certain results, that is consistent with independent contractor status.

Ongoing relationship: If the relationship is ongoing, even if frequent work is done on irregular cycles, the worker is likely to be an employee.

Fixed hours of work: That suggests the worker is an employee controlled by the firm.

Full-time work: If the worker is with the firm full time, that suggests the firm controls the time of work and restricts the worker from taking other jobs. That shows employee status.

Work location: If the firm requires that the worker be located on the firm's premises, that suggests employment. That the worker performs the services off-premises implies being an independent contractor, especially if an employee normally has to perform similar services at an employer's premises.

Workflow: A worker required to conform to the routines, schedules, and patterns established by the firm is consistent with being an employee.

Reports: A requirement that reports be submitted, whether oral or written, suggests employee status.

Manner of payment: Payment by the hour, week, or month suggests an employee, while payment of an agreed-upon lump sum for a job suggests an independent contractor.

Expenses: Payment of expenses by the firm implies the right to control company expenses, and thus suggests employment status.

Tools and equipment: If the firm provides tools and equipment, it suggests the worker is an employee.

Investment: A significant investment by a worker in his or her own equipment implies being an independent contractor.

Profit or loss: Showing a profit or loss (due to overhead, project costs, and investment in equipment) is consistent with being an independent contractor.

Multiple clients: Working for many clients suggests independent contractor status. However, the worker could be an employee of each of the businesses, if there is one service arrangement for all clients.

Marketing: The marketing of services by a worker to the public on a regular basis indicates independent contractor status.

Right to discharge: If the firm can discharge the worker at any time, this suggests employment. An independent contractor cannot be dismissed without legal liability unless contract specifications are not met.

Right to quit: An employee may quit at any time without liability, but an independent contractor may be liable for failure to perform, depending on the contractual terms.

A MATTER OF INTENTION

The IRS may argue that workers with a very peripheral connection to the firm—for example, mechanical artists or illustrators—are employees. The penalties for unintentional misclassification of an employee are serious, but not nearly as serious as the penalties for intentional misclassification. If the misclassification is unintentional, the employer's liability for income taxes is limited to 1.5 percent of the employee's wages. The employer's liability for FICA taxes that should have been paid by the employee is limited to 20 percent of that amount. The employer has no right to recover from the employee any amounts determined to be due to the IRS. Also, the employer is still liable for its own share of FICA or unemployment taxes. Interest and penalties may be assessed by the IRS, but only on the amount of the employer's liability.

On the other hand, if the misclassification is intentional, the employer may be liable for the full amount of income tax that should have been withheld (with an adjustment if the employee has paid, or does pay, part of the tax) and for the full amount of both the employer and employee shares of FICA (though some of it may be offset by employee payments of FICA self-employment taxes). In addition, the employer is liable for interest and penalties computed on far larger amounts than when the misclassification is unintentional.

PRECAUTIONS & SAFEGUARDS

After conducting a careful review of how their workers should be classified under the IRS's 20-factor control test, a client or firm may remain uncertain of what is correct. A wise approach is to err on the side of caution and, when in doubt, classify workers as employees.

If the firm believes a worker is an independent contractor, the two parties should negotiate a carefully worded contract that accurately sets forth the parties' agreement and is legally binding. To be most effective, in the event of an IRS challenge, the contract should state that the worker is an independent contractor according to the 20-factor test. The parties must then adhere to the contract. If a firm already has such a contract in place, it should be reviewed with the IRS test in mind and to confirm whether the parties are in fact following its terms.

To protect themselves from an IRS audit and any potential penalties, many clients treat every artist as an employee, even those who are clearly independent. In such cases, clients withhold appropriate taxes from creative fees and issue end-of-year W-2 forms rather than a Form 1099. To counter the potential loss of copyright (since works created by employees are considered works-for-hire unless otherwise negotiated), artists should clearly establish themselves as independent contractors, preserving authorship and copyrights and attempt to reclaim the rights to their works from the hiring party through negotiation.

Cancellation & Rejection Fees ("Kill Fees")

Historically, cancellation and rejection fees have been widely accepted by clients and artists alike, even when contracts are verbal or no cancellation or rejection provision is included in a written document. Whether they are paid, and where on the spectrum a particular cancellation or rejection fee is set, depends upon the specific circumstances of each case and upon the artist's determination to require such fees to be paid in an amount commensurate with the effort invested. For example, if preliminary work is unusually complex or the assignment requires completion on a very short deadline, artists may demand higher cancellation or rejection fees.

Another consideration often taken into account is whether the graphic artist declined rewarding assignments from other clients in order to complete the canceled assignment in a timely manner.

Traditionally, freelance graphic artists are entitled to remuneration if a job is canceled or rejected, according to the following conditions.

Cancellation provision

Clients usually pay the artist a cancellation fee if the assignment is canceled for reasons beyond the artist's control.

- If cancellation occurred prior to the completion of the concept or sketch phase, current data indicates the average cancellation fee is approximately 25 percent of the original fee for illustrators and approximately 40 percent for graphic designers.
- If cancellation occurred after the completion of preliminary work and prior to the completion of finished work, current data indicates the cancellation fee is between 30 and 65 percent (with an average of approximately 50 percent) for illustrators and between 45 and 100 percent (with an average of nearly 80 percent) for graphic designers.
- If cancellation occurred after the completion of finished work, the average cancellation fees currently range between 65 and 100 percent of the original fee.
- Previous data indicates that all necessary and related expenses (such as model fees, materials, or overnight shipping fees) are paid in full.
- In the event of cancellation, the client obtains all the originally agreed-upon rights to the use of the completed work upon payment of the cancellation fee (except in royalty arrangements; for more information on that, see Chapter 5, Essential Business Practices). Even though the client chooses not to exercise a particular reproduction right at this time, that right is transferred to the client when the purchase is completed with payment. Depending upon the understanding between the parties, the specified right may revert back to the artist if not exercised within a specific period of time.
- If preliminary or incomplete work is canceled and later used as finished art, the client usually is contractually obligated to pay the unpaid balance of the original usage fee.
- Graphic artists and clients may agree to submit any dispute regarding cancellation fees to mediation or binding arbitration.

Rejection provision

According to current and historical data, clients may agree to pay the artist a rejection fee if the preliminary or finished artwork is found not to be reasonably satisfactory and the assignment is terminated.

- If rejection occurred prior to the completion of the concept or sketch phase, current data indicates the average rejection fee to be approximately 21 percent of the original fee.
- If rejection occurred after the completion of preliminary work and prior to the completion of finished art, current data indicates the rejection fee to be between 27 and 58 percent.
- If rejection occurred after the completion of finished art, the average rejection fees currently range between 53 and 100 percent of the original fee.
- All necessary and related expenses are customarily paid in full.
- In the event of rejection, the client has chosen not to obtain any rights to the use of the artwork. Therefore, many artists refuse to permit rejected work to be used for reproduction by the client without a separate fee.
- Artists and clients may agree to submit any dispute regarding rejection fees for mediation or binding arbitration.

Speculation

Speculative ventures, whether in financial markets or visual communications industries, are fraught with risk. Individuals who choose this course risk loss of capital and incur expenses. Artists and designers who accept speculative assignments, whether directly from a client or by entering a contest or competition, risk not being paid for the work, take valuable time from pursuing other paying assignments, and may incur expenses out of pocket. In some circumstances, all the risks are placed on the artist, with the client or contest-holder assuming none—for example, buyers who decide only upon completion of finished art whether or not to compensate the artist. This situation occurs in agreements where payment depends on "buyer's satisfaction" or "on publication." Typically, when a prospective client requests that work be created on speculation, there is too little information available to the artist to create a truly successful work because a true partnership has not been created due to the tentative nature of the speculative project.

Creating your own products

Many individual artists and designers, acting as entrepreneurs, create their own work and use those works in a variety of ways, including consumer-oriented products, such as a book showcasing their work, limited edition prints, calendars, computer mouse pads, and T-shirts, to name a few. This work can be sold directly to the consumer through various channels, including craft shows and web sites. This is also one way truly innovative work is produced. In a more speculative arrangement, an artist may choose to put together a book of his or her work and submit the book to a publisher who agrees to pay an advance against a royalty on sales. The artist and the publisher share the risks on

their mutual investment, and the compensation to both parties is speculative, meaning both depend on the market response to the product.

Contests & Competitions

In 1980, the Graphic Artists Guild, together with Designers Saturday (DS), a furniture manufacturers association, developed a competition to meet two goals: to produce high-quality art for the DS annual show and to provide a competition that is ethical and appropriate for professional artists. Around the same time, the Guild had received complaints from artists around the country concerning the unethical nature of most contests they were asked to enter. The results of the experiment with DS were so successful that the Guild decided to see if other competitions and contests could be structured to accomplish the goals met by the DS model.

Survey

In an effort to gain a clearer picture of the competition scene across the country, the Graphic Artists Guild Foundation, with a supporting grant from the National Endowment for the Arts, conducted a nationwide survey of art and design competition holders, as well as an informal poll of jurors and competition entrants.

- By far, the largest and most expensive competitions are those operated by associations ancillary to the advertising industry, such as art directors' clubs and graphic design industry trade magazines. The purpose of these competitions is to honor excellence within their own communities. While these competitions do not require that original art or graphic design be submitted, the sponsoring organizations often charge high entry fees for members and nonmembers alike. These competitions generally attract the highest volume of entrants.
- Contests requiring submission of new, original artwork have attracted the fewest number of entries from professional artists. Most professional artists reported that they did not want or could not afford to take time from income-producing projects to create original work for a contest on a speculative basis. The most popular type of competition for this group is based on work already produced or published.
- In most cases, the process for selecting a jury for competitions appears to be quite good. Jurors, on the other hand, noted that the criteria or process for judging the work is often vague or poorly articulated.
- All-rights transfers by all entrants to the contest holder is an inappropriate requirement.

The 1980 study resulted in the establishment of a list of guidelines for fair competition for three types of art contests or competitions: competitions held by art-related organizations or associations to award excellence in the field, contests where all entries are created specifically for the contest and where the winning entries are used for commercial purposes, and contests held by nonprofit organizations or where the winning entries are used for nonprofit purposes. The principal purpose of the guidelines is to enable competition or contest holders and entrants to make their own independent judgments concerning the way fair contests and competitions should be run and whether and on what terms to participate in them. Thanks to these guidelines, many unethical and problematic practices relating to contests and competitions no longer exist.

Awards for excellence in the field

1. The call for entry shall clearly define all rules governing competition entries, specifications for work entered, any and all fees for entry, and any and all rights to be transferred by any entrants to the competition holder.
2. Jurors for the competition and their affiliations shall be listed on the call for entry. No juror or employee of the organization holding the competition shall be eligible to enter the competition.
3. Criteria for judging the entries and specifications for the artwork to be submitted in all rounds shall be defined clearly in the call for entry as a guide to both entrants and jurors.
4. Deadlines and process for notification of acceptance or rejection of all entries shall be listed in the call for entry.
5. Any and all uses for any and all entries shall be listed clearly in the call for entries, with terms for any rights to be transferred.
6. For the first round, tear sheets, slides, photographs, or other reproductions of existing work shall be requested in order to judge the appropriateness of style, technique, and proficiency of the entrants. This round shall result in the choice of finalists. If samples from this round will not be returned to the entrants, that fact shall be clearly listed in the call for entries.
7. If the competition ends in an exhibition, hanging or exhibition fees paid for by the entrants shall be listed in the call for entries.
8. After the first round, the jury may request original art for review. The competition holder shall insure all works against damage or loss until the work is returned to the artist. All original artwork shall be returned to the artist. Any fees charged to the artists for the return of artwork shall be clearly listed in the call for entry.
9. Artwork shall not be altered in any way without the express permission of the artist.
10. All entries and rights to the artwork remain the property of the artist unless a separate written transfer and payment for the original have been negotiated.

11. If work exhibited by the competition is for sale, any commission taken by the competition holder shall be listed in the call for entries.

Contests for commercial purposes

1. The call for entry shall clearly define all rules governing contest entries, specifications for work entered, any and all fees for entry, and any and all rights to be transferred by any entrants to the contest holder.
2. Jurors for the contest and their affiliations shall be listed on the call for entry. No juror or employee of the organization holding the contest shall be eligible to enter the contest.
3. Criteria for judging the entries and specifications for the artwork to be submitted in all rounds shall be clearly defined in the call for entry as a guide to both entrants and jurors.
4. Deadlines and process for notification of acceptance or rejection of all entries shall be listed in the call for entry.
5. Any and all uses for any and all entries shall be clearly listed in the call for entries, with terms for any rights to be transferred.
6. For the first round, tear sheets, slides, photographs, or other reproductions of existing work shall be requested in order to judge the appropriateness of style, technique, and proficiency of the entrants. This round shall result in the choice of finalists. If samples from this round will not be returned to the entrants, that fact shall be clearly listed in the call for entries.
7. The number of finalists chosen after the first round should be small. The finalists shall then be required to submit sketches or comprehensive drawings for final judging.
8. Agreements shall be made with each finalist prior to the beginning of the final stage of the work (Graphic Artists Guild contracts or the equivalent can be used). The agreements shall include the nature of the artwork required, deadlines, credit line and copyright ownership for the artist, and the amount of the award.
9. Any work of finalists not received by the required deadline or not in the form required and agreed upon shall be disqualified. All rights to the artwork that has been disqualified shall remain with the artist.
10. The winners shall produce camera-ready or finished art according to the specifications listed in the call for entry. Artwork submitted shall not be altered in any way without the express permission of the artist.
11. The value of any award to the winners shall be at least commensurate with fair market value of the rights transferred. The first-place winner shall receive an award that is significantly greater than that of other winners.
12. The contest holder shall insure original artwork in its possession against loss or damage until it is returned to the artist.

Contests for nonprofit purposes

1. The call for entry shall clearly define all rules governing contest entries, specifications for work entered, any and all fees for entry, and any and all rights to be transferred by any entrants to the contest holder.
2. Jurors for the contest and their affiliations shall be listed on the call for entry. No juror or employee of the organization holding the contest shall be eligible to enter the contest.
3. Criteria for judging the entries and specifications for the artwork to be submitted in all rounds shall be clearly defined in the call as a guide to both entrants and jurors.
4. Deadlines and process for notification of acceptance or rejection of all entries shall be listed in the call for entry.
5. Any and all uses for any and all entries shall be clearly listed in the call for entries, with terms for any rights to be transferred.
6. For the first round, tear sheets, slides, photographs, or other reproductions of existing work shall be requested in order to judge the appropriateness of style, technique, and proficiency of the entrants. This round shall result in the choice of finalists. If samples from this round will not be returned to the entrants, that fact shall be clearly listed in the call for entries.
7. The number of finalists chosen after the first round should be small. The finalists shall then be required to submit sketches or comprehensive drawings for final judging.
8. Agreements shall be made with each finalist prior to the beginning of the final stage of the work (Graphic Artists Guild contracts or the equivalent can be used). The agreements shall include the nature of the artwork required, deadlines, credit line and copyright ownership for the artist, and the amount of the award.
9. Any work of finalists not received by the required deadline or not in the form required and agreed upon shall be disqualified. All rights to the artwork that has been disqualified shall remain with the artist.
10. The winners shall produce camera-ready or finished art according to the specifications listed in the call for entry. Artwork submitted shall not be altered in any way without the express permission of the artist.
11. The value of the award should, if possible, be commensurate with the fair market price for the job, though exceptions may be made depending on the budget and use of the artwork for the contest.
12. The contest holder shall insure original artwork in its possession against loss or damage until it is returned to the artist.

Some problems persist

Over the intervening years since the above guidelines were developed, graphic artists have raised other concerns: Who is judging the work? Is the work or the artist being judged? Are competitors who are unknown and unconnected treated as fairly as those whose work is familiar to judges? In 1998, in an effort to keep informed about the latest practices, the Guild sent surveys to 40 associations, publications, sourcebooks, and paper companies that sponsor competitions and contests. The survey asked a number of questions, including: Are entrance fees reasonable? Is speculative work required? What rights are entrants asked to give up? How are submissions handled and returned? What are the odds of winning? Twenty-one competition holders responded.

The results of the survey were both reassuring and troubling. On the one hand, the study indicated that most sponsors of annual competitions are reputable organizations making good faith efforts to design fair and ethical contests and competitions. They are not guilty of the kinds of questionable practices engaged in by one-shot contest holders, such as the manufacturer who requests original artwork created on speculation to which the artist must sign over all rights. On the other hand, the study revealed that some contests are still conducted in ways that are ethically ambiguous.

The most troubling area involves judging. When entries are identified by artist, the likelihood increases that judges will vote for friends and colleagues or for names they recognize. Of course there is no way to prevent judges from recognizing an entrant's work, even without an attached name. And in certain cases, such as book competitions, it is impossible to remove the name of the illustrator. But more could be done to create a firewall between judges and judged. A numerical coding system would ensure both anonymity and proper identification of entries. Entrants could be asked to mask their signatures and credit lines from flat art and disks.

Being a competition judge can add a prestigious feather to an artist's or designer's cap, but it also seems to improve the chances of winning. Temptations are inevitable when judges are permitted to enter their own work, no matter what safeguards exist. Though the competition holders surveyed insisted that their rules prevent bias and promote impartiality, the Guild's analysis of the judging raised some questions about the appearance of bias.

Some artists refuse to enter certain competitions because they believe the judges will not choose their work. Though that may seem unlikely to some, it is not if competition and contest holders draw continually from the same pool of judges. Competition and contest holders could eliminate bias and promote impartiality by both excluding judges from entering competitions and looking for ways to expand the pool of judges so competitions and contests do not appear to be closed enterprises.

These measures would open up the process and create conditions that would allow new, unfamiliar talent to emerge.

What is the real value of contests and competitions to the award winners, and how does that compare with the value derived by the sponsors? It is difficult to measure the benefits to winners because they involve intangibles such as exposure and prestige. But trade publications, for example, have much to gain. Not only are competitions and contests a source of considerable revenue from entrance fees ($35 and higher per image), magazines fill their award issues with work they do not have to commission. A search of art contests and competitions for all types of visual media found entry fees as high as $200 per work. Competitions involving digital media and media with motion tend to have much higher entry fees than those for print media. Nor should the artist assume that contests with no entry fees are in their best interest. The sponsors of these contests are often looking for art, designs, illustrations, logos, etc. that they can use on their products or marketing materials—in other words, free art and design services.

Contests and competitions may be part of every graphic artist's marketing plan, but entering them requires time, energy, thought, and money. Artists and designers need to analyze competitions and contests with care, weigh the value of the awards offered, estimate the chances of winning, and evaluate whether safeguards create an open, even-handed contest or competition.

Final Note

Each artist should decide individually whether to enter art contests or design competitions, provide free services, work on speculation, or work on a contingent basis and what to charge for his or her work. The purpose of this book is to inform the artist fully so that he or she can make educated decisions about pricing work and negotiating fair agreements.

★   ★   ★

TECHNOLOGY ISSUES

This chapter discusses the ongoing effect technology has on all aspects of the visual communications industry—from the way graphic artists create their work to how it is reproduced. Also covered are related legal, ethical, health, and employment issues.

TECHNOLOGICAL

advances that brought about the change from traditional to digital publishing, image making, and image processing transformed the tools, the terms, and the jobs that were familiar to clients and graphic artists since the advent of offset printing in the Middle Ages. The scope of this change was as revolutionary as the introduction of the Gutenberg movable-type printing press was in its day.

Today, commissioned design and illustration are primarily created using the computer to produce a digital file or final form. Technology raises a number of concerns about the cost of doing business. Some of these concerns include the high costs of purchasing, maintaining, and upgrading hardware and software as well as the time and effort required to learn a particular program and keep abreast of the latest applications. Legal and ethical issues include the ease of copying and altering computer-generated art or reflective artwork scanned into a computer, which places new or extended uses of copyrighted material in jeopardy.

Workplace Changes

Workplace changes involving job responsibilities, functions, health concerns, and compensation levels were also affected by the changes in technology. In some fields, respect for graphic artists' skills and their mastery of technology are reflected in the compensation they receive. At the same time, many employers attempt to redefine office staff who are trained in the rudiments of desktop publishing as graphic artists or, likewise, to use skilled graphic artists as temporary secretarial help. And some graphic art service buyers continue to abuse markets with attempts to obtain extended rights or work-for-hire authorship transfers from artists at less-than-market rates, creating a windfall of media-ready assets for the buyer.

Technology's Negative Impact on the Profession

The same advances in technology that have created labor-saving devices and instant global communication have also spawned a proliferation of electronic and online businesses that threaten the graphic arts profession.

Digital art

Some entrepreneurs have set themselves up in the business of supplying ready-made electronic art. They hire illustrators to create clip art for rights-free CDs that provide some up-front income, minimal royalties, and wide exposure of an artist's work. Buyers of the CDs are then free to copy or alter the art without further compensation to the illustrator. (See the Royalty-Free Distribution sidebar later in this chapter and the Maximizing Income section in Chapter 5, Essential Business Practices.) Stock house sales of specific rights to an artist's work provide some additional income from existing work without loss of rights and give some measure of protection, though they generally yield lower fees. Many veteran artists believe that these efforts are driving creators out of the illustration business as salaries and/or prices fall, inexpensive art proliferates, and sources of future income are diminished.

Logo mills

Graphic designers are facing similar assaults on their profession by companies that devalue professional design services by competing unfairly on price with shoddy design, sub-standard services, unfair labor practices, and with no regard to copyright. So-called "logo mills" are online operations that hire "designers" at ridiculously low rates to pump out off-the-shelf logos that are marketed to consumers at cut-rate prices. Most of these pre-made logos are simply pieced together clip art with mundane type treatment. The same logos are sold over and over again. Buyers can pay higher prices to get a "unique" logo, which means the company promises not to resell the design and the buyer simply owns the copyright as part of the package. "Customization" may consist of little more than providing the same logo in a different color scheme or with adjustments to the font.

A second type of logo mill offers "original" logos. The price of their services is based on the number of concepts, rounds of revisions, and designers working on the project (the greater the number, the higher the price), yet their prices are still below the prevailing market rates for professional design services. Their success, despite such low prices, is due to their abusive labor practices, which treat designers as just another expendable commodity instead of highly-trained professionals. Logo mills are the digital sweatshops of the design world. In one such company, designers work on a per project basis (earning $25–$40 per project) in extremely competitive conditions with no assurance of continued work and no copyright fees. Designers sign up for a project on a first-come, first-served basis. Since multiple designers work on a project, they "compete" to have their design accepted by the client. Successful designers are awarded points as well as a monetary bonus. Designers are required to critique each other's work with points being deducted from those whose work is panned. A loss of points means that the designer's fee will be lowered on future projects.

Logo mills have an insidious impact on the perception among business owners regarding copyrights. By simply ignoring the existence of copyrights in their pricing structure, logo mills are completely devaluing copyrights. The result is a business community that increasingly is unaware of the existence or value of copyright and unwilling to pay what to them seems to be an unfair or unnecessary fee tacked on to a job. It will be up to designers to confront this perception and educate clients.

Online freelancing

Another type of business proliferating in cyberspace is online freelancing, which preys on graphic artists eager to find work. These companies seldom allow artists to retain the rights to their work. They also denigrate the graphic arts profession by marketing themselves to potential clients as full-service creative businesses offering services at a fraction of the cost of a traditional ad agency or design firm and having a community of thousands of graphic artists at their disposal; however, in reality, the thousands of artists are actually freelancers who "bid" on posted jobs. In one worst-case scenario, artists are lured into working for free under the guise of a contest; they must do all of the work upfront at their own expense to be considered as a contestant. The online business negotiates the "award," keeping a percentage for itself, as well as all work submitted (even from those who lose the contest), and the "winners" and "losers" alike have no rights to the work they created. Technology will continue to exert a powerful influence on the graphic arts industry. The best way graphic artists can protect themselves from technology's often overwhelming effects is by staying informed about such issues as professional practices, pricing considerations, ethical and legal concerns (especially copyright), health issues, and the labor market.

Professional Practices Influenced by Technology

In response to the technological revolution, graphic designers and illustrators changed how they do business.

Considerations for graphic designers

Today's designer consults with the client, creates a concept and a layout, and specifies type for the client's copy in a page layout program. The designer researches or assigns photography or illustration; scales and crops the visual images; oversees the creation of color separations; prepares the final digital file for the printer; obtains client approvals; and buys and oversees paper stock, printing, die cuts, cutting, binding, and shipping.

Photographs and illustrations are scanned, first in low resolution for scaling, cropping, and positioning in the digital page layout. Other illustrations and charts may be created in various programs, stored in any of a number of file formats, and imported into the layout. Then the artwork is scanned in a high-resolution form and may be retouched digitally to correct for scanning defects or damaged originals. Any alterations or other manipulation should be done either by the original artist or with permission. Finally, the high-resolution images are positioned in the electronic page layout.

Translating color from a light-based RGB monitor to an ink-based CMYK printing press can never be perfect. For that reason, numerical breakdowns of colors are used both on the computer and on the press so that the printed colors will appear as the designer intended. Responsibility for color correction and trapping is among the more important areas of client/artist/vendor communication for graphic designers and illustrators. Graphic designers should consult with the printer who's producing the final communication piece for instructions on setting up final files. Today, most printing plates are made directly from computer files, eliminating the film separation process. Preparing digital files for accurate translation to an image setter is called "electronic production," "preparation for prepress," or "preflighting." It is most often shortened to

"prepress," although prepress is, more accurately, the actual production of the output materials on machines.

Designers and printers now have overlapping, and often varying, in-house capabilities. Designers must be familiar with the abilities and quality levels of their suppliers. Which imaging center or printer scans the best high-resolution image? What kind of proofs should the client see and at what stages?

PRECAUTIONARY STEPS
General guidelines to improve prepress preparation of electronic files are available from Specifications Web Offset Publications, www.swop.org. Following the computer-ready electronic files (CREF) guidelines, however, is not enough to ensure that a particular job will achieve the desired end result. No guidelines can be fully comprehensive for this continually changing industry, nor can they reflect the requirements of all imaging centers. Also, no legal defense absolves a graphic artist of financial responsibility if electronic files are not printed or reproduced correctly.

Graphic artists should obtain specific guidelines from the intended imaging center and the printer, in writing if possible, at the beginning of each project, as it is often difficult to determine who is to blame and who must absorb the cost of corrections when things go wrong. Each job is different, but the graphic artist should be sure to provide the correct scan resolution when preparing all electronic files for prepress and thoroughly discuss desired line screens. A comprehensive proofing schedule for each project should also be arranged among client, designer, imaging center, and printer.

If the graphic artist has prepared digital files correctly, following the imaging center's guidelines, the artist is not likely to be financially responsible for imaging errors although software/hardware incompatibilities between artist and an imaging center are common and can be difficult to trace. Problems in fonts, software, or hardware owned by the imaging center and certain industry-wide problems may not be the fault of any party; solving them is considered part of the imaging center's overhead. Although, including desired fonts, for example, in the digital file diminishes problems. Errors resulting from poor communication, misunderstanding, or faulty equipment are corrected by the responsible party. For this reason, all instructions should be written and confirmed, and proofing schedules adhered to.

AREAS OF POSSIBLE PROBLEMS BETWEEN DESIGNERS AND CLIENTS
The client may be tempted to micromanage a work in progress, requesting many changes and alternatives or making many unnecessary changes. It is more efficient if the client reserves comments and changes until the designer presents the work at appropriate stages of the project.

Clients sometimes assume that digitally produced comps are finished art or that such work can be revised quickly and without cost. They may not understand that even seemingly simple changes, for example, in the size of a logo, require fine-tuning (at an additional cost) if quality is to be retained. Designers must continually educate clients about software and hardware limitations and clearly explain the parameters of work included in each job estimate. It's also important for graphic artists to include a fee, specified upfront, for author's alterations (AAs), which are changes made by the client after content has already been approved.

It benefits the designer to discuss all intended uses before a job begins so that he or she can present an appropriate estimate that reflects all rights being bought and any physical property—disks or files—being transferred. Care must be taken to specify the limits of the rights being transferred for fonts, commissioned art, style sheets, and other copyrighted data that a client wishes to purchase. A client may wait until a job is nearly finished to request ownership of a digital file or design template, so it is best if these rights are negotiated before an invoice for the complete job is submitted.

Ownership of electronic files Major areas of misunderstanding between clients and designers involve electronic file ownership, especially with the increasing use of PDF files (see below) and all related monetary transactions. Some clients routinely expect that electronic files will be turned over to them without cost. Industry standards separate the sale of original work from the sale of usage rights. Ownership of the electronic file is a sale of extended usage rights to a design, which is priced differently than limited, or one-time, use. Similarly, creating a template for ongoing use by a client should also be handled separately. Unless terms are clearly defined, sticky situations may occur when clients are sent PDF files or when designers are sent another designer's electronic files for a job.

Unlike illustration, graphic design work is not specifically protected by copyright, so designers should use specific, well-written contracts that can give them the same protections as copyright. Designers need to define and protect usage rights in all contracts with clients (for example, see the Graphic Designer's Estimate and Confirmation Form and the Graphic Designer's Invoice in the Appendix: Contracts & Forms). Designers also need to spell out usage rights on all disks, CDs, and any documentary material accompanying the product, as well as PDF files and web sites.

For example, the following statement should be put on a label on a disk or CD that is sent to a client: "This disk/CD and all information contained herein is the property of Designer. This disk may not be copied or otherwise transferred and must be returned to Designer within thirty (30) days of use, unless otherwise provided for by contract."

The following statement should appear at the beginning of a PDF file or on a web site: "The Designer retains ownership of all original artwork, design elements, and other graphic information contained herein. The Designer herein retains all rights except for those explicitly transferred. Such artwork, design elements, and other graphic information may not be copied or otherwise transferred, and must be returned to Designer within thirty (30) days of use, unless otherwise provided in the Designer/Client Agreement."

Adobe Acrobat PDF Using Adobe Acrobat PDF (Portable Document Format) files means designers can instantly send designs generated on both Macs and PCs anywhere in the world to be viewed on Adobe Reader, which is available free to clients. Adobe's PDF technology brought about revolutionary changes in how designers present designs to, and acquire approvals from, clients, and how they distribute final art to publishers or printers.

This comping, soft-proofing, file preparation, and transfer method, using Adobe Acrobat Distiller, allows designers to convert layouts into relatively small files that can be viewed and printed with accurate fonts, colors, and print-quality-resolution photographs. Or the same files can be e-mailed to separate marketing, account, and corporate contacts involved with a particular project, whether they are in a cyber cafe in Amsterdam, a corporate office in Tokyo, or a home office in Cleveland. The files can then be e-mailed back with comments and approvals.

Time and expenses spent printing, packing, and shipping are drastically reduced, as are approval time frames and time-to-market schedules. A value-added aspect to the process is that if the client has a color printer, as many corporate clients do, they can generate full-color prints of designs and use them for review and approval.

Another growing use of PDF is to send final advertising art to newspapers and magazines for printing. The process of preparing files is different for each publisher. The publisher's production department will have an instructional sheet or web page explaining the entire process to its specifications.

Once prepared, the PDF is either e-mailed or placed on an area of a Web server through a file transfer protocol (FTP). The method is similar to moving a file from one computer folder to another, except that it takes place over the Internet.

There are drawbacks to using PDF technology. Designers must include the production time needed to create PDF files and prepare e-mail correspondence. That generally takes less time than traditional output methods, but the client is not going to see any real savings at this phase, though the designer may see a slight increase in productivity.

As noted earlier in the chapter, color calibration on individual monitors varies dramatically. Over time, even the same printer may show color differently. A client may have an older, darker monitor that does not show accurate color, resulting, for example, in a medium purple appearing black. In that case, the client can check the designs for type, content, and composition but not color. Or the designer may need to send the client Pantone chips, a final laser print, or a matchprint proof produced by traditional means.

Keep in mind that PDF technology also raises critical issues about retaining control of one's work, which can lead to copyright and usage rights problems. Because all the fonts and art are generally embedded in the file, perfect copies can be distributed internally or on the Internet with no way for the designer to track usage.

Considerations for illustrators

The artistic approaches to electronic illustration are as varied as they are in traditional media, although the methods of conceptualizing and researching an illustration remain much the same. Access to one's own previously created art, stock photography, copyright-free art, or other reference material may speed up a particular job or mean that some research is done on-screen or online.

Many illustrators first do a rough of their drawings on paper and fax the sketch they select to the client for approval. Or they scan the selected sketch into the computer, import it into a software program, and submit it to the client by e-mail. Some illustrators use the sketch as a rough template for the finished illustration. Other illustrators draw and revise their illustration directly on the computer. Still others take a collage-like approach, scanning their own photographs, drawings, or other reference material into the computer to use as elements in the finished piece. (Care must be taken that such material is in the public domain or that permission is obtained from the copyright owner. For more information, see the Legal and Ethical Issues section later in this chapter.) Yet other illustrators use the computer only at the very end of the creative process to add type or tweak color. Of course, drawing, typography, and color are all only as flexible and variable as the artist's software program allows.

Once the illustration is completed as an electronic file, the illustrator must now prepare the work for the client's designated output. If it is to go directly to print or color separations from a digital state, the artist may deliver the illustration electronically by modem or by a portable storage medium such as a disk. Clients and illustrators also use File Transfer Protocol (FTP) to exchange information and images. When working with clients who have FTP capability, you can log onto their drive space securely and upload or download directly to them so that they immediately receive the illustrations. Since electronic illustrations tend to require huge amounts of storage, large storage media may be required, such as internal or external hard drives, flash drives, CDs, or DVDs. Another approach is to post art to a secure web site and provide password-protected access to a client for viewing and approval. To protect their copyright and work inventory, artists should keep a backup copy of the finished art.

While it is unlikely the client will request a transparency or other non-digital form of art, the output cost is billed to the client and ownership of the tangible copy remains with the artist. If film output is requested, the client is billed for the film. (It is important to note that the client's receipt of film does not automatically confer reproduction rights other than those agreed upon. Multiple or long-term usage must be specifically negotiated.) Prior to printing, the art director may order color proofs or a small JPEG file via e-mail for client approval and so that the artist or designer may make any final adjustments. (California artists should note that the form of delivery has an impact on whether or not they owe sales tax, also known as a use tax. See the Sales Tax section in Chapter 3, Professional Issues.)

AREAS OF POSSIBLE PROBLEMS BETWEEN ILLUSTRATORS & CLIENTS

Problems can develop between illustrators and their clients, which often can be attributed to misunderstandings and miscommunication.

Sketches At the sketch stage, clients may mistakenly assume that multiple concepts, color treatments, or sketches for an assortment of proposed page layouts are easy, quick, and cost-free. Good communication between a client and an illustrator about artistic requirements and what the illustrator usually supplies may help avoid this kind of potential conflict.

In current trade practice, the number or scope of sketches that the illustrator presents before an additional fee is negotiated is generally discussed and included in the letter of agreement between artist and client. The average number is usually three sketches. A change in the shape of an illustration, unless occurring quite early in the sketch stage, is considered a revision and is usually billed.

File maintenance In current practice, clients are responsible for maintaining an illustration in good condition after its delivery to ensure successful printing and safe return. Electronic files require special care in this regard, as many storage media are vulnerable to loss or damage.

A client holding a backup of electronic art for use in the near future should, with the artist's permission, make additional backups with a note that this does not grant any additional rights of reproduction. Clients who delay printing or who have purchased long-term rights to a work should make transparencies or any necessary archival backups. Illustrators are responsible for having their own backup copies for tracking work inventory and copyright protection.

Output methods

Work produced digitally can be output in many ways—from low to very-high-resolution print or photographic methods. Resolution, when referring to printed results made from electronic data, means the number of dots per inch (dpi) used to render the electronic information on the output—the more dots per inch, the higher the quality of the image.

Resolution in printing is measured on a continuum of quality—from 72 dpi of a coarse, low-resolution printer through 3,600 dpi of high-resolution image setters. Higher-resolution output methods are sometimes called image setting; in general, they provide resolution at or above 900 dpi. Resolution of 72 dpi is normally used for web sites and low-resolution versions of work to show the client before the full version is sent. The industry norm requires an EPS TIF image in the range of 200-400 dpi to be sent for print, but this may differ by client or by media.

DIGITAL COLOR OUTPUT

There are many different brands of color printers, ranging in capability from low to high resolution. Graphic artists must become familiar with them and choose the right one to fit the desired mix of quality and cost for each project. Thermal wax (thermal transfer), ink jet, color laser copier, and dye sublimation are four common printer types, and each manufacturer and model varies in capability.

Raster image processors (RIPs) are hardware devices or software that interpret digital information sent to the printer or image setter. They are used for digital proofs as well as digital color output.

DIGITAL PROOFS

Digital high-end proofs for checking color can be made from electronic files. Although the quality available from digital color printers is constantly being improved, many graphic artists continue to rely on traditional matchprints and bluelines for final client approval before printing. They enable the graphic artist to check for color accuracy and spot errors, such as areas mistakenly specified as overprints, which will not show up on an Iris print. Virtual Proofing Systems are also becoming more commonplace. They demand SWOP protocols.

TRADITIONAL MEDIA OUTPUT

Traditional media output such as photographic transparencies can be output from files via a number of software programs. Digital cameras now record images that can be imported into imaging software.

Transparencies can be made in various sizes and resolutions from electronic files by an output device called a film recorder. CDs, DVDs, and flash drives are also used to store photographic output, notably the work of web or multimedia designers. While you still may find places that can create slides and transparencies from digital files, the need for these services has quickly declined and/or has completely disappeared. Today, most illustrations are handled digitally, and the need to supply film is non-existent.

DIRECT DIGITAL OUTPUT

Computer-generated art may go to production for direct-to-plate printing without ever being seen on a reflective surface. The original screen image is faithfully reproduced, with resolution based on the file's specifications.

Many presentations are made directly from a computer monitor or, after being output from the computer on different media, are used in slides, overheads, or videos. In-house or external communications may take place directly by modem or networks between computers, or artwork may be stored on a CD, DVD, or flash drive.

Pricing Considerations

Computer use has compressed job skills in many fields, making it a challenge to define and break down the billable services involved in a project, although both designers and illustrators surveyed consider the computer a major factor in the general pricing structure. Other major factors that determine pricing include the scale and scope of the project, the intended use and the market, the turnaround time and deadline, the rights of reproduction being purchased, and all the other factors that affect the cost of doing business. Graphic artists also frequently incorporate into their estimates overhead costs, such as invested capital, training, and necessary downtime for troubleshooting problems that are inherent to using hardware and software.

Pricing computer-generated art & design

Graphic artists and clients have found that pricing computer-generated art and design requires good artist-client communication, production management skills, and a careful periodic review of costs and time use. Specific factors to be considered include the following:

OVERHEAD

Studio overhead costs will be incurred for hardware and software purchases and for maintenance, upgrades, and business growth. Formal training costs must be included as overhead, along with a budget for continuing professional education.

Graphic artists working on desktop computers may initially invest $10,000 or more in hardware and software to meet their clients' needs effectively. This does not include training time, upgrade requirements, and time lost due to hardware and software problems.

TIME

A graphic artist may find it more efficient to work on a computer, or some projects may take longer than work produced with traditional media. Yet having all the project data in a digital file can save time when moving from comps to finishes, making alterations, or creating multiple applications from one overall concept. Graphic artists can create their own image and layout libraries to save time as opportunities arise. Since it may take a long time to learn to use many software programs and since hardware has speed limits, time should be scheduled for work in traditional media as well as for necessary approval time.

CREATIVE FEE VS PRODUCTION COSTS BREAKDOWN

Most graphic artists using computers reported in a recent survey that they structure their pricing by separating their creative fees from their expenses (including any work done outside the studio). Like any business, the artist simply bills for each service provided and adds customary markups when appropriate.

At first it may seem difficult to separate the many components of an electronic publishing project. Scanning, image manipulation, page composition, prepress, and color separation preparation (if necessary) all seem to merge when producing a job. The graphic artist may feel there is no clear point at which creation is complete and production begins. And refinements such as scaling, moving, and kerning seem to continue throughout the electronic production process.

Once identified, the time, overhead, or skill required for each stage of production may not correspond to the figures both artists and clients have been accustomed to. Artists have found that billing accurately, by using either an hourly rate or a fee for services, may prove that some stages cost more than when using traditional methods, while other production stages may be simpler, faster, and less expensive.

Graphic artists report that forcing electronic production into traditional pricing structures does not work. New price breakdown categories such as scanning, image manipulation, page composition, color separation creation, and trapping more accurately reflect services performed using the most recent creative and production methods. In the long run, introducing current production steps into the billing process will improve artist-client understanding and help minimize arguments over revisions or errors.

Postproduction costs for imaging center output (such as video, transparencies/slides, film), use of removable media, delivery services (including messenger services and overnight couriers), peripheral equipment rental, and purchase of specific software to meet a job requirement are typical expenses that are billed separately to the client. Other expenses to be reimbursed may include subcontractors' fees, supplies, travel, and long-distance phone calls. Consultations and client meetings may sometimes be billed separately.

A 15 to 20 percent markup is common in most fields, however, be prepared to submit actual receipts. Expenses should be approved by the client in the original estimate and should be billed at 10 to 20 percent over cost without client approval (unless job specifications change, which should be confirmed in writing). It's also wise to set a price over which the designer needs to receive separate, specific approval from the client for expenses that arise once the project is underway. For more information, refer to Chapter 6, Standard Contracts and Business Tools.

Revisions are probably the single largest factor affecting the final charge. Ongoing communication keeps the client informed about revisions that must be billed. This can sometimes mean several adjustments to the original cost estimate. Taking care of that while the job is underway avoids an unpleasant incident when the client receives the final bill. It also allows the client to limit or stop revisions before budget allocations or deadlines run out. Immediately submitting an overage bill for unexpected changes or revisions, and getting it signed before performing the work, is a good way to manage these costs and avoid unpleasantness once the job is complete and memories are dim.

Design projects are especially vulnerable to soaring revision costs when clients believe that changes are easy to make and when it is not clearly spelled out when, how often, and in what form clients may approve work in progress. As deadlines approach, approval time may be compressed or skipped—a shortsighted tactic that may result in high correction costs. Client awareness and clear communication about when revisions become chargeable is necessary.

Another area prone to revision charges is prepress costs where a page composition or imaging center error or software bugs can cause problems as a job goes to output or to press. Careful communication with the imaging center about specifications required to make the graphic artist's electronic files compatible and usable by image setters and printers is necessary. The creation of accurate color separations is a particularly fine operation and must be carefully monitored by the graphic artist.

Legal & Ethical Issues

Copyright laws apply to electronically created art and design, as they do to any visual or audiovisual work. Copyright protection occurs at the time the work is created and put in tangible form and is vested in the creator except in the case of a traditional, salaried employee, where copyright is held by the employer unless otherwise negotiated. Certain nonexclusive rights may be transferred verbally, but transfer of exclusive rights or of the copyright itself must be done in writing. It is also possible to copyright computer source codes as text, protecting the work as it is expressed in fundamental computer language. (For general information about copyright, see the Copyright section in Chapter 2, Legal Rights & Issues.)

Applying copyright to digital art

The following copyright ownership provisions generally affect electronic artwork and design: control of reproduction rights, creation of derivative works, distribution, performance, and joint works. The easiest way to avoid copyright infringement is to confirm that permission has been obtained in advance, in writing, and for any intended use of copyrighted art, such as making a composite.

RIGHTS OF REPRODUCTION

Reproduction rights give the copyright owner the exclusive right to reproduce or make copies of the image. Grants of reproduction rights may be limited in the number of copies, length of time, geographic area, exclusivity, market, edition, and so on, as agreed by the rights purchaser and the copyright owner. (For a discussion of the 1999 *Tasini v. The New York Times* case that defines rights of reproduction in electronic media, see the Transfer of Electronic Rights section in Chapter 2, Legal Rights & Issues.)

Retrieving a copy of art in digital form on a screen is probably exempt from infringement under a copyright exception for loading programs. Be aware that scanning a work into a computer, for example, does constitute making a reproduction. Court cases have held that substantive editing of movies for television constitutes infringement.

One lawsuit that involved failure to pay for second-use rights may also help define what constitutes a derivative work (see below). Eighteen plaintiffs in *Teri J. McDermott, CMI, et al. v. Advanstar Communications, Inc.* sued the largest U.S. publisher of medical and trade magazines for allowing their illustrations, for which they only granted first North American print rights, to be reprinted in at least 27 countries over a period of more than 20 years. The artists also were able to document instances of cropped signatures, intentionally dropped attributions, and cases where the images were intentionally changed, cropped, flopped, and recolored.

DERIVATIVE WORKS

A derivative work is one that is based on one or more preexisting works. It may be termed a modification, adaptation, or translation, and applies to a work that, according to copyright law, is "recast, transformed or adapted." Most substantial alterations, including editorial revisions, of an image probably constitute creation of a derivative work. A derivative work created with the permission of the original copyright holder is itself copyrightable. Created without permission, it can be considered infringement.

The creator of the derivative work has rights to contributions that may be considered original and copyrightable from their additional creative input but has no rights to the underlying work (whether it was copyrighted or copyright free). The degree of originality is weighed by courts in deciding whether a derivative work is itself copyrightable. In most cases, combining images in an electronic composite constitutes the creation of a derivative work of each of the contributing images. A derivative work in which both the original and the second artist have equal, tangible creative input can be a joint work, with copyright held by both parties, if such agreement is made at the time of the work's creation (see the Joint Works section later in this chapter).

The dividing line between an unauthorized derivative work that infringes on another copyright owner's rights and a new original work that may make reference to an existing image is still blurred. Some court cases have established several important criteria to help determine whether a work is derivative:

Substance (importance of the borrowed content's quality) How much of the meaningful content of a work has been reproduced? This may be a very small portion of a work in terms of size, but the crucial nugget that delivers the main idea. Another measure of substantial content is whether the element taken is unique, recognizable, or identifiable.

Extent of work copied (sheer volume) How much, literally, of a work has been reproduced? The specific quantity of permissible copying can only be determined in court, and that is a situation generally to be avoided.

Access Did the second artist have access to the original work? If so, a court or jury may infer that a work was copied intentionally. Most copyright infringement cases depend on a "person-in-the-street" test. If the lay observer, seeing the original art and the altered or copied work side-by-side, says that copying took place, infringement exists. Juries are required to search for similarities, not differences, in arriving at a decision.

A retouched photograph, for example, where the final image is not substantially different from the original, would probably not be considered a derivative work. Courts have found such changes to be primarily mechanical and thus not original. But the courts may view changes resulting from digital image manipulation as artistic, rather than mechanical, thereby creating substantial originality.

A pre-existing work of art or design used as a base from which a substantially different final work is developed will not likely be held to be a derivative work. This makes it all the more compelling for graphic artists to specify grants of rights with regard to image manipulation up-front and in writing.

DISTRIBUTION RIGHTS

The right to control distribution of a work remains the copyright holder's unless it is sold. Once sold, that particular item may be resold, passed on, rented, and so on, though it may not be copied or used for derivative works.

It is assumed that electronic distribution is considered the same as distributing a printed version of a work. Purchase of electronic rights is negotiated separately. Technology can now be used to imbed in any type of work—text, image, or computer source code—electronic copyright management information that identifies rights holders, permitted uses, exclusions, and appropriate fees for a particular use. Electronic delivery systems permit potential users to choose a work, indicate intended uses, and pay appropriate usage fees with the click of a mouse.

PERFORMANCE RIGHTS

Works that are part of certain multimedia, such as video broadcasts or Power Point presentations, also involve performance rights, which may require explicit licensing. A court held in one case that a video game was "performed" (played) without authorization by the end-user in a public arcade.

JOINT WORKS

If two or more artists create a work with the intention that their contributions be merged into inseparable or interdependent parts of a unitary whole, the result is a joint work according to copyright law. Joint authorship must be intended at the time the work is created and implies co-creation of the piece from conception to fulfillment. Modification by a second artist of a piece by a first artist does not constitute joint authorship, but it is a derivative work (see previous section on Derivative Works).

Joint authors hold copyright as "tenants in common." Either creator can license any rights to the work, providing that the proceeds are shared equally.

Protecting copyright

Protection of creative work under copyright law is still enforced most efficiently by the contracts under which work is commissioned or licensed. Contracts should be clear about rights granted, usage, and duration of time for which a license is granted. Grants of rights licensing work for any use should specify what is granted and how it will be used; all other rights should be reserved to the artist or copyright holder. (For information about contracts, see Chapter 6, Standard Contracts & Business Tools.)

The importance of spelling out the usage rights the client is purchasing in the graphic artist's estimate and in the letter of confirmation cannot be overemphasized. Most legal problems between artist and client arise because the original terms and any later changes were not expressed clearly in writing. The invoice should not be the first time a client sees or hears of copyright. Clients must be equally careful to assess their usage needs in relation to their budget at the start of a project, as historically, most artists adjust their fees according to the rights purchased.

ROYALTY-FREE DISTRIBUTION

Some entrepreneurs have been selling an artist's entire inventory, royalty free, on CD disks. Others are commissioning artists to supply a large number of pieces of art on a particular theme or in a certain style for sale on CDs. They offer artists royalties on sales of the physical CD, but the artist is not paid royalties for any additional uses, and the rights are sold outright. Purchasers of the resulting royalty-free art have access to hundreds of images they may use in any way, such as altering, manipulating, combining, or otherwise changing, for placement on products, in ads, or as characters in feature films.

Many artists are concerned about the impact royalty-free art is having on the industry. While participating artists may generate significant money up-front, many artists feel that flooding the market with low-cost images is lowering the value of images overall. Clients, they believe, are reluctant to commission original works when low-cost images are readily available. This is particularly worrisome when an art director or designer can take copyright-free works and manipulate or combine them to create new artwork. Some graphic artists who do this are going so far as to copyright the new artwork under their own name, as well as split copyright ownership with stock agencies through which their work is distributed.

Others, however, believe that such practices broaden the recognition of an artist's work, and clients will still be interested in new and original material. Royalty-free art also makes available, say proponents, otherwise costly work to clients who ordinarily could not afford first-time-rights fees.

Both proponents and opponents of these practices agree that such availability is likely to reduce the amount of newly commissioned art and may reduce some fees. A long-term alternative scenario is the institution of a mechanism for monitoring rights purchases similar to those in the music and theater industries.

In specifying rights of reproduction for digital art and design, graphic artists should specify the number of copies permitted, the form in which they will be made, the degree of resolution, limitations on scaling up or down, and so forth. Quality control is a legitimate negotiating point that affects the artist's reputation and income. Other specified limitations usually include the number of appearances or length of time the rights are being licensed for, the market, the media, the geographic area, and the degree of exclusivity. Recent surveys show that payment may be by flat fee or by royalty on either a straight percentage basis or a sliding scale. Royalties may differ for uses of the same piece in different markets.

Assigning the entire copyright, all rights, or granting complete reproduction and derivative-work rights entitles the receiving party to manipulate the art or design at will. Some artists and designers are interested in granting broad rights licenses. Many artists and designers prefer to control their work tightly and restrict image manipulation subject to their approval. Each artist or designer determines what constitutes appropriate compensation for the scope of the licensing rights granted.

Written agreements should be used to grant the right to create a derivative work from an existing image. By granting a general right to prepare a derivative work, an artist permits the client to do anything to the artwork to create something new. Therefore, specifying the resulting intended image may better protect one's rights. As with the license of any copyrighted image, intended markets, rights of reproduction, and so on, granted to any derivative work should be clearly specified.

As digital markets proliferate, publishers have new types of projects in which to use art. Many of these will be derivative works, compiling text, image, and sound. An appropriate license should be negotiated that briefly describes the product and specifies that the client is licensing the right to use the art in the product described. A storyboard, outline, or comp may be attached to help explain the project.

Contracts should specify whether alteration or modification will take place, whether derivative works will be created, or, if the art does not yet exist, whether the creators will collaborate equally to devise a new, original joint work with a shared copyright. Advance discussion of these issues can help avoid awkward and unpleasant situations.

A contract may specifically prohibit manipulation. One such limiting phrase is "This work may not be digitally manipulated, altered, or scanned without specific written permission from the artist." An alternative is "This license does not give [Buyer] the right to produce any derivative works and [Buyer] agrees not to manipulate the image except as we have agreed in writing, even if such manipulation would not constitute a derivative work."

Without a contractual restriction, the art could be altered to the point where it no longer resembles the original piece enough to be judged a derivative work and thus would not constitute an infringement. Including a limiting phrase gives the artist the ability to prevent unauthorized manipulation, copyright infringement, or a breach of contract.

, While typefaces are not copyrightable, the software that produces them is. Owning such software usually implies a license for personal use; it cannot be lent or copied.

ELECTRONIC DEFENSE

Be aware that unauthorized use of electronic media may be particularly difficult to monitor. While contracts are the clearest overall legal copyright protection, a preemptive line of defense may be taken electronically. For example, artwork intended for presentation but not for reproduction can be provided in a low-resolution form that is unsuitable for further use.

Technological approaches are developed continually to ensure protection and to monitor the appearance or alteration of a work. Encryption, or programming an invisible protective code into the body of a work, may be useful, though determined hackers can break most codes. Experts have also discussed imbedding a self-destructing key in an electronic image so that after a certain number of uses it can no longer be accessed. Digital pictures can also be labeled visibly so that notice of ownership and the terms of any license always accompany the image. Other types of "watermarking" can be as simple as imbedding a copyright notice, ©, in an image that will be visible if reproduced.

As always, creating a paper trail and keeping good records can help prove infringement. For example, it is good business practice to keep copies of all written agreements and records of telephone conversations in which changes were discussed. Saving copies of work in stages may also help prove that an infringement has been made. And saving reference images with a record of their sources and rights agreements can protect against infringement claims by others.

DEFENSE ON THE INTERNET

Web sites, businesses, and service providers are proliferating at a truly astounding rate on the Internet, but except for some restrictions on the transmission of adult-oriented material, the only federal regulation on these electronic arenas is the Digital Millennium Copyright Act (DMCA) of 1998, which added several new sections to the copyright law. One of these, Section 512, prevents a service provider from being sued for copyright infringement carried by its service and covers four areas: e-mail communications, system caching, information storage on systems or networks on web sites, and browsers. Requirements imposed on service providers have important ramifications for creators in two areas: the removal or blocking of infringing material and the terms of service imposed by online providers. (For a thorough discussion of the DMCA, see the copyright section in Chapter 2, Legal Rights & Issues.) While there are no specific new developments in this legislation, ten years after its enactment, there is considerable conversation about its efficacy and limitations. The Graphic Artists Guild anticipates that additional legislation will crop up in this area in the future.

One area of particular interest to graphic artists was argued in the *Kelly v. Arriba Soft* case. The U.S. District Court ruled in November, 1999 that photographer Les Kelly's copyright was not infringed when Arriba Soft (now ditto.com) downloaded his images from the Internet and displayed them on its commercial search engine without his knowledge or permission; the court found that the unauthorized copying and display was "fair use." Because of the huge impact this decision would have on the DMCA and on intellectual property rights on the Web, Kelly appealed. On appeal (February 2002), the Ninth Circuit Court partly affirmed and partly reversed the decision and requested additional briefing as to whether the use of Kelly's images was a "display" under the Copyright Act. For a more detailed and updated explanation of this case, see Chapter 2, Legal Rights & Issues.

Discussion of intellectual property law with regard to the Internet is ongoing, but currently consists of more questions than answers. What goes online and how it is used mix the copyright, commercial, and contractual interests of many parties. Online vendors, for example, may be more interested in getting out a lot of information to attract customers and be less motivated to monitor what happens afterwards. A publisher or original creator, though, wants to maintain control.

Legislation is currently under consideration to address many of these issues. A few of these bills follow. The PIRATE Act (Protecting Intellectual Rights Against Theft and Expropriation Act of 2004) would let federal prosecutors file civil lawsuits against suspected copyright infringers. The bill was introduced in the United States Senate as S. 2237 by Orrin Hatch (R-UT) and Patrick Leahy (D-VT) on March 25, 2004. It passed the Senate by a unanimous vote on June 25, 2004, and was referred to the U.S. House Committee on the Judiciary on August 4, 2004.

The Inducing Infringement of Copyrights Act (INDUCE Act), is a bill introduced in the United States Senate which targets "whoever intentionally induces any violation" of copyright. The name came from an earlier version named the "Inducement Devolves into Unlawful Child Exploitation Act." The proposed legislation was introduced as S. 2560 by Senator Orrin Hatch on June 22, 2004, and was then referred to the U.S. Senate Committee on the Judiciary. As of printing, this bill appears to be dead.

The Digital Transition Content Security Act (DTCSA, H.R. 4569) is a bill introduced by House Judiciary Committee Chairman James Sensenbrenner Jr., a Wisconsin Republican, on December 16, 2005. The bill was backed by Democratic Rep. John Conyers. Its goal is "To require certain analog conversion devices to preserve digital content security measures," i.e., plugging the analog hole. The bill effectively proposes mandating use of the Veil Rights Assertion Mark technology into new video-handling consumer devices.

Creators and publishers may sometimes be at odds. For example, freelance writers who are members of, and others who are supported by, the National Writers Union brought the *Tasini v. The New York Times* lawsuit in late 1993 against one database operator and five large media companies, alleging infringement of their copyrights through unauthorized reproduction of their articles on electronic databases and CDs with no additional compensation. (For an update on this case, see the Transfer of Electronic Rights section in Chapter 2, Legal Rights & Issues.)

Graphic artists have been asked to sign broad contracts agreeing that their work may appear on unlimited electronic media or in future technologies—as yet undiscovered and unnamed—as a condition of licensing a supposedly one-time right and for no additional payment. Others have received checks in payment for work performed under traditional one-time rights contracts that attempt to grant the client additional rights not discussed and/or unremunerated by way of new terms stamped on the back of the check. (See the *Playboy Enterprises Inc. v. Dumas* section in Chapter 2, Legal Rights & Issues.) As the law is currently written (though yet untested), termination rights permit a graphic artist to void even a global all-rights agreement as long as the artist retains authorship by not signing a work-for-hire agreement and if the work is registered in a timely manner (thereby providing evidence for a claim).

Strengthening copyright protections

Stock agencies can play a role in preventing and monitoring unauthorized use of art by using contracts stating that the image may not be manipulated without the artist's permission and that the artist must be given the first opportunity to make any desired changes. Requesting printed samples of all stock work also helps the artist monitor the image's appearance. Agencies can protect their own and their artists' interests by conducting random checks of the media to spot unauthorized uses. (See the Stock Houses section of Chapter 5, Essential Business Practices.)

Illustrators who do not work with stock agencies need to maintain control over their intellectual property and to take advantage of secondary markets for their work. The American Society of Media Photographers established a copyright licensing cooperative for photographers and illustrators, called Creative Eye, in 2002. Its objective is to provide a means for photographers and illustrators to address such concerns as market standards, licensing methods, rights protection, and licensing fees for the reuse of their images

(More information about Creative Eye may be found under Some Useful Web Sites in Chapter 15, Resources & References.)

Some observers foresee the establishment of more copyright licensing and monitoring organizations similar to ASCAP and BMI, which oversee the use of songs and music and collect and distribute compulsory licensing fees (royalties) to their members. In 2008, the Copyright Clearance Center (CCC), a not-for-profit company founded in 1978 and dedicated to making it easy to use and share published content, launched the Ozmo beta site (www.ozmo.com). Ozmo is a web-based service for licensing independent, or user-generated, content for commercial use. Ozmo makes it easy for photographers, artists, bloggers, researchers and others to license their work to content buyers such as marketing firms and advertising agencies, who are increasingly incorporating user-generated content into their work.

Ethical practices

Copyrighted electronic images require the same respect as any other copyrighted images—permission for use—under federal copyright law. No one, for example, should make unauthorized or pirated copies of application software. Model releases should be obtained from any recognizable people.

Editors and other artwork buyers may want to crop or otherwise manipulate an image, and digital retouching makes that incredibly easy. Clear contractual terms spelling out the artist's rights and a good relationship with an editor or art director ensure that the artist will be involved throughout the editorial process so the best aesthetic results can be obtained. All changes should be discussed with the artist, and the artist should be given the first opportunity to make them or to approve changes that the art director or client would like to make. No image manipulation should take place without the artist's knowledge and permission, and any changes should be made on a duplicate copy of the art. Artists who know how to make changes electronically and who are willing to do so will have more control over their final art.

A traditional exception is for low-resolution images provided by sources such as stock houses. Many of these are used in presentations, with the expectation that rights to the image will be purchased if the concept is approved. In 1996, the Graphic Artists Guild spearheaded the "Ask First" campaign in response to the increased use of sample or portfolio images in presentations without the artists' permission.

Health Issues

There is a high risk of becoming seriously injured from working on computers for extended periods of time. Repetitive motion disorders, an umbrella term describing a large number of repetitive strain injuries that include the musculoskeletal disorder, carpal tunnel syndrome, are not specific to computer users, but are frequently suffered by them. The most recent major study on musculoskeletal disorders (MSD) in the workplace was conducted by the National Academy of Sciences (NAS) and the Institute of Medicine in 2001. It concluded that there is strong scientific evidence, supporting the findings of earlier studies done in 1997 by OSHA and in 1998 by NAS, that exposure to ergonomic hazards in the workplace causes musculoskeletal disorders. The study calls MSD a national problem, estimating that 1 million people lose time from work each year due to these disabling injuries and that ergonomic problems cost the economy about $50 billion annually in compensation costs, lost wages, and lost productivity. The report warned that MSD-related problems are expected to increase in the future due to the changing nature of work, the aging of the workforce, and the rising number of women entering material handling and computer jobs. For graphic artists, injuries can occur to the hands, arms, wrists, shoulders, back, and eyes. Headaches and chronic fatigue are also reported. A physician or clinic specializing in occupational health may be able to provide proper diagnosis and correct treatment.

While employers are responsible for creating a safe work environment, independent creators should make a safe setup a priority to avoid future disability. A number of preventive measures can reduce the risk of injury. The design of a workstation, including desk height, chair posture, and placement of keyboard, copy stand, and monitor, are important. Overhead lighting should be indirect and glare-reduced. Correct posture at the computer and taking frequent breaks are good ways to reduce stress and hand, wrist, arm, back, shoulder, and eye strain. A 15-minute break for each two hours of work is recommended by the Communications Workers of America; hourly breaks are ideal. Allowing the eyes to focus farther away than the screen distance, such as out a window, is recommended during a break, as is doing simple hand stretches.

The ergonomic quality of some hardware and furniture must be improved. For example, one stylus widely used in broadcast design is too thin for some hands to hold comfortably. Wrapping it with masking tape or foam from a hair curler has been found to help prevent RSI. Similarly, broadcast designers may use a foot pedal to minimize the injurious effect of constantly calling up a menu with a hand tool.

For a list of organizations that provide publications and information on artists' health issues, see Chapter 15, Resources & References.

The Labor Market

The employment situation is changing rapidly. When computer use became widespread a few decades ago, many companies attempted to exploit the illusory ease of working with them and refused to pay competitive fees. Now many agencies and companies are hiring staff, and web design is providing a huge area of work for graphic artists. In the process, traditional distinctions between job categories are blurring. For instance, web programmers are becoming designers, and designers are becoming web programmers.

Unfortunately, many things about the job market have not changed. Job titles and responsibilities are still poorly defined. Classified advertisements frequently describe entry-level jobs as requiring "knowledge of Quark, InDesign, Photoshop, and Illustrator" but offer low starting salaries that fail to acknowledge the extensive education and ongoing training needed to acquire and maintain those skills. One classified ad in *The New York Times* advertised for a "Receptionist/Graphic Designer," certainly a *prima facie* case for the need for certification in the industry.

Though many employers have begun to acknowledge the high level of expertise that graphic techniques require, increased employer education is needed. A standard hierarchy of jobs recognizing required skill levels would be a beginning, although that may be difficult given the rapidly changing technology. This state of flux challenges the interpretive skills of every job seeker: Do employers want someone to answer phones who also can lay out a form, or do they want someone who can program design elements into a web site? Since the actual job descriptions are murky, the help wanted ads describing them are also. It's a time-consuming challenge to find work and to define job responsibilities once hired.

Temporary employment agencies

Temporary agencies, while providing work for many graphic artists in advertising agencies and large design studios, do not aid in the recognition of, and compensation for, computer artists' skills. Temporary agencies advertise that they can supply artists who have mastered a wide array of software applications and are familiar with many hardware systems but then only pay artists rates comparable to what secretaries earn, while charging the client two to three times that rate. On the other hand, most of the major agencies in the graphics arts sector—Aquent, The Creative Group, and Paladin—offer benefits (health insurance and 401K plans after a qualifying period) and more favorable rates and handle taxes as well.

For a variety of reasons, some skilled graphic artists opt to be temporary workers, hired for the duration of a specific project. These artists are often required to sign blanket contracts that ask them to release more rights of privacy and personal financial information than is relevant to the scope of their job. Some of these contracts would be considered extreme even by regular employees, who generally enjoy better compensation and benefits. This practice may have originated because companies request extremely protective contracts from other temporary workers, such as software developers, systems analysts, and computer consultants who have access to important corporate information and financial data. Such conditions rarely apply to a temporary graphic artist, and the same contracts should not be used.

Other employment issues

Closely following salary in importance are issues of workplace stress, including long hours of work, unrealistic deadlines, and repeated changes to projects in progress. A 14-hour workday is all too common among graphic artists in staff positions. These conditions lead to high levels of burnout and injury. One graphic artist was hospitalized for stress after working 41 hours in three days.

The continuous learning curve required of graphic artists working with computers is another stress. Keeping up with new software programs or the latest versions may necessitate expensive training programs, and upgrading hardware can be very expensive. One benefit of an in-house job is that many employers provide on-the-job training, especially if an assignment requires special competence.

Some employers still retain the mistaken impression that working at computers takes no time, and they fail to build proofreading and correction time into production schedules. In addition, an increasing number of business people without production experience work as creative managers. Too often companies, misunderstanding the technical expertise required for computer-generated work, believe that designers can be easily replaced. When they are faced with expensive errors and poor quality, however, many begin to view these jobs with greater understanding and appreciation.

Signs indicate that respect for well-trained professionals is growing, as is greater understanding that the quality of a job often depends on the expertise of the designer, rather than the equipment used for the job. Even though similar equipment is available elsewhere, the best designer does the best work. Although corporations do not yet universally understand the many valuable skills graphic artists bring to a job, skilled graphic artists may eventually be recognized with better pay, when and if they demand it.

Organized labor in the United States would like to see American industry follow the lead of Western European countries—emphasize high-level skills and reward them with high wages that make them competitive in the new technological era. This view stresses building a workforce with unique, high-level, well-paid skills, rather than settling for reducing the U.S. worker's standard of living.

Communication companies of the future

Alliances of artists who contribute varied creative, technological, and technical skills that provide clients with the widest possible range of services at the best possible price are being formed. A group of specialists may form a company for the sole purpose of bidding on a single project, then disband it when the job is completed and form a new "skills cluster" for the next project. Or, a professional group may be assembled by the client to fulfill a project. Whether called strategic alliances, teams, skills clusters, joint ventures, or the "virtual corporation," such groupings often include designers; animation, broadcast, and multimedia specialists; page composers; and prepress and print specialists.

Strategic alliances are cost-efficient and quality-oriented. Ideally, they attract work that is closely tailored to each artist's skills and preferences and that encourages maximum creativity, flexibility, and job variety. A disadvantage is that alliances may mean less regular employment and more reliance on per-project work. Graphic artists may be pressured to hop from alliance to alliance, and indeed may prefer doing that.

Freelance jobs and hiring may expand, to help companies maximize their use of expensive equipment purchased under the misperception that a computer can create by itself. New jobs evolve continuously, and the traditional divisions between the design and illustration disciplines are becoming increasingly blurred. Some segments of the industry may incorporate graphic skills into earlier editorial stages as the creative process becomes more multimedia and team-oriented and as creation and production continue to merge. Graphic artists and production personnel may be called upon to play a larger consulting role to educate clients about new skills that are integral to the electronic age.

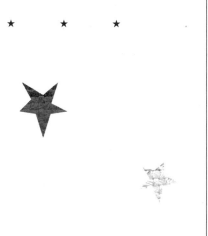

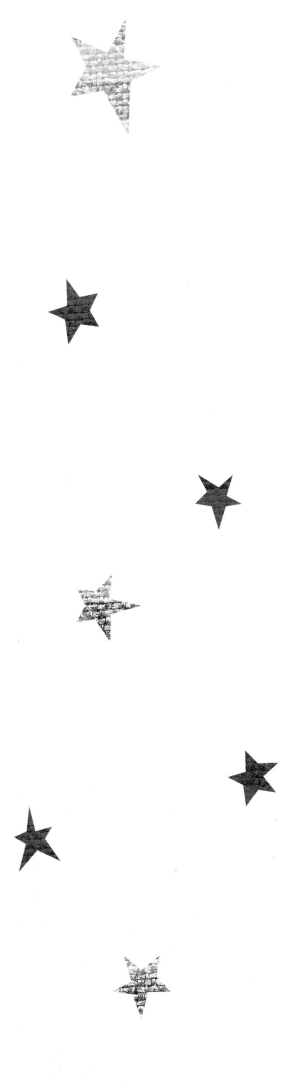

ESSENTIAL BUSINESS PRACTICES

This chapter discusses the fundamental business management issues common to all professionals in the graphic arts—from preparing for the negotiation, to the negotiation process itself, to keeping track of payment schedules, to collection options when deadlines are not met. It also includes marketing and self-promotion strategies that self-employed artists must practice on an on-going basis to attract prospective clients and to ensure that their business is growing, with new jobs continuously coming in. It concludes with finding financially rewarding ways to resell work.

SUCCESSFUL

graphic artists develop the business skills necessary to market and maintain their careers. This knowledge allows them to negotiate with clients to reach agreements that are mutually beneficial, as well as to manage the record keeping necessary to assure prompt and accurate payment for their work. As business people, graphic artists need to understand contract terms, copyright basics, and customary business practices. As creators, graphic artists have the right to share in the economic benefits generated by their creative product and, where possible, to seek out and generate additional opportunities. Securing these economic interests and rights is a graphic artist's responsibility.

The project cycle is a process that graphic artists will experience hundreds of times in their careers. It starts with negotiating the terms for a new project with a potential client. The artist then decides how to price the work based on the parameters determined in the initial negotiation with the buyer. Usually, there are additional discussions about the terms of the project, which might include such parameters as schedule, credits, and usage. The terms are determined prior to signing an agreement and beginning the work. Throughout the project, certain bookkeeping and tracking functions must be performed in order to be assured of compensation, or to have recourse for other collection options in the end.

Successfully repeating this process over and over not only builds client loyalty and trust, it fosters financial well-being throughout a career. Graphic artists have little professional purpose without a buyer or user of their services. The client-artist relationship is one of the most important professional relationships a graphic artist can have. Fair, honest, and straightforward business practices on both sides cultivate rewarding and lasting relationships—the key to success. For background on current copyright law, see Chapter: 2, Legal Rights & Issues.

Negotiating & Evaluating the Terms of an Offer

Graphic artists must be able to analyze and evaluate the terms of an offer when potential clients want to purchase their talents. Understanding the scope of work and the terms of a contractual agreement is crucial. Only then can one skillfully negotiate mutually beneficial terms to reach financial and personal goals.

Negotiation can be learned and mastered. In negotiations, each party seeks to accommodate its own needs as well as those of the other party. An atmosphere of mutual trust and collaboration should be established so that both sides can create a "win-win" agreement. Approaching negotiation with a "winner-take-all" attitude can do more harm than good, undermining the mutual professional respect necessary for long-standing relationships and repeat business.

Throughout the negotiation process, finding compromises that are necessary to reach a workable agreement can be taxing for both parties. Compromise is attained more readily if the two parties approach negotiations with a professional attitude and manner that sincerely wants to develop solutions that meet their respective needs.

The Guild has found that a common source of complaints is the failure by both sides to communicate effectively before work is started. Both graphic artists and clients must know and articulate their needs to each other in a straight-forward, clear manner. Such frankness will reduce the chances of a misunderstanding or conflict, as will putting the agreement into writing.

Both graphic artists and clients have goals when entering negotiations. Most clients need to stay within an established budget for obtaining appropriate artwork or graphic design while a graphic artist needs to find work that will earn enough to cover overhead expenses and make a reasonable profit. The graphic artist must determine if the client's budget is sufficient for the requested work. Remembering that value is not measured solely in dollars, graphic artists need to carefully consider all the benefits of a job, not just the fee. Sometimes exposure on a high-profile project, good portfolio samples, or flexibility on deadlines can make up for lower fees. Sometimes taking a job may help you to establish a relationship with a new client. The more information each party has about the other, the more effective the negotiation.

Graphic artists need to know the budget and many other factors to accurately price a given job. They also need to have a good sense of current market forces, which is one of many reasons why this book was developed. Similarly, clients who use this book to keep abreast of current standards and contract terms are better equipped to establish more accurate budgets and to determine what rights to buy. The Guild encourages graphic artists and clients to adhere in all negotiations to the standards of the Joint Ethics Committee's Code of Fair Practice (see Chapter 1, Professional Relationships). Of course, in the end, if either graphic artists or clients find that the other party prevents them from achieving their essential goals, then the negotiation breaks down and the parties seek to fulfill their needs elsewhere.

Some graphic artists may be reluctant to ask questions or raise objections to a client's demands, for fear of appearing to be difficult or argumentative. Guild members report, however, that as long as discussions are carried out in an appropriately professional manner, clients appreciate graphic artists who articulate their needs, since it prevents future misunderstandings. Above all, graphic artists need to remember that a client is not "the enemy" and that client relationships need to be cultivated.

Preparing to negotiate

Since negotiation can be stressful, preparation is very important. Knowing you have the right information, as well as knowing the parameters of what to ask for or relinquish, will give you the confidence needed to be successful. Being objective helps you respond with agility so that the opportunity to negotiate the right job at the right price will not slip away. Though the deal at hand may seem crucial for success, it is usually not the case. Most graphic art careers are built upon hundreds of projects, not one.

ASK THE RIGHT QUESTIONS
Be prepared at the beginning of every negotiation to get the information necessary to evaluate the project. In order to do this, draw up a standard agenda or checklist that outlines the topics to be covered, and fill it out while having preliminary discussions (sometimes by telephone) with the potential client. Include a job description, due dates, fees, expenses, and other pertinent notes. Writing down such information as a standard business practice will reduce stress and will positively affect what you agree to in negotiations.

DETERMINE YOUR REQUIREMENTS
Graphic artists need to know what their highest expectations are for a project as well as a list of minimum requirements, such as a "no-lower" fee, no work-for-hire, and a reasonable deadline. Creating this list sets the parameters for negotiation and prepares you to walk away from a job if the client cannot meet your minimum requirements.

DETERMINE THE CLIENT'S NEEDS
Both sides begin a negotiation by stating a set of demands based on their needs. These demands should not be confused with underlying needs, which a skilled negotiator strives to discern. For example, when the problem stated is, "My company is looking for a first-class brochure that we can produce for under $10,000," several underlying needs are not being directly articulated. The client may

actually be saying, "I want top-quality work at an economical price. Can you accommodate me and make me look good, or do I have to worry that what you do may not please my boss?" Knowledgeable and skillful questioning helps determine not only what kind of brochure is required to effectively meet the client's needs, but also whether some other solution might better solve the client's problem within the established parameters.

The answer to a stated problem is not always obvious. That's why it is critical to try to discern the other person's true needs and expectations. In responding to the client, a skilled negotiator responds positively to the underlying meaning of what is being said and shows a personal interest and regard for solving problems. It is important to remember that most clients' needs extend well beyond the purely visual solution. Sometimes their own success rides on the success of a project.

RESEARCH THE CLIENT

Learning as much as you can about a potential client makes negotiating easier. It helps to have a general understanding of the client's market and typical media for which that market buys art. See Figure 5-1 for examples of market categories and media. You can often find very specific information about a client, such as its products, services, key personnel, philosophy, and business culture, by doing an Internet search, which should include visiting the client's web site. In addition to the wealth of information available on the Web, business libraries contain valuable information about the marketplace. Directories for corporations and advertising agencies, such as those published by Standard Rate & Data Service, Inc., show revenue, circulation, media buys, officers, and so on. Publication directories list information about magazines: circulation, advertising rates, key staff, and other important data. Subscribing to major trade magazines may also be helpful. Consulting with other professionals who have worked for a client may also provide valuable background information.

Dealing with common tactics

Tactics are used during every negotiation, and it is important to understand them and not take them personally. Separating emotional responses from calm, detached observations of an opposing party's tactics can help defuse their effectiveness. Consider the following examples:

LIMITED AUTHORITY

A client's negotiator claims to lack the authority to make decisions. That enables the client to make rigid demands, forcing the graphic artist to offer concessions in the interests of moving forward. One possible solution is to treat the project under discussion as a joint venture and recruit the other person as a "partner." By emphasizing terms that create a partnership, and sharing a stake in decisions, the client's negotiator is encouraged to represent the graphic artist's needs and goals.

PHONY LEGITIMACY

The negotiator states that the offer is a "standard contract" and cannot be changed. In such cases it helps to remember that contracts are working documents designed to protect both parties in an agreement. The graphic artist should not feel pressured to sign standardized contracts if the terms are not correct. Unfavorable sections or terms can be struck out. If necessary, the graphic artist can make alterations using the explanation that "my attorney has instructed me not to sign contracts with these conditions" (see Chapter 6, Standard Contracts & Business Tools).

EMOTIONS

Anger, threats, derisive laughter, tears, or insults may seem convincing and may, in fact, be genuine, but they are also tactical maneuvers. Listen carefully to the point of the message and separate it from the style of delivery. Never escalate an emotional situation.

Special issues with phone calls & meetings

It is important to master the special skills needed to negotiate both on the phone and in face-to-face meetings. Each type of negotiation has advantages and disadvantages. Phone meetings enable participants to refer to written materials for support, and being in one's own environment may bolster confidence. It is always easier to refuse someone over the phone.

Negotiating by phone also has disadvantages. If a difficult demand has to be made, it may be easier to do it in person. It is difficult to judge the reaction to what is being said without seeing the other person's face. And it can be hard for both parties to maintain focus on what is being said, making it more difficult to establish the rapport and partnership so important to any successful negotiation.

PHONE CALLS

As recommended above, a simple agenda or checklist should be used, outlining all the points to be covered. This helps keep the conversation centered on the important matters at hand and prevents the problem of omitting important details. Some individuals go as far as to prepare scripts for particularly difficult situations where performing under pressure may cause confusion.

Taking notes during phone conversations is recommended. Graphic artists must simultaneously understand the aesthetic requirements of a project, agree on the business arrangements, and establish rapport with the client. Written notes of the project details provide valuable reference points and alleviate misunderstandings during the project.

If a discussion becomes difficult or gets bogged down, the graphic artist should end the call and plan another call for after he or she has had a chance to consider the project. This gives the artist additional time in which to make a decision. In fact, many graphic artists make a practice of not accepting a job during an initial call. They take time to thoroughly evaluate all terms before accepting the work.

MEETINGS

Create environments for meetings that are comfortable and relaxed, whether in one party's office or in a neutral space. Always arrive on time, well rested and prepared to make a thoughtful presentation. Planning goes a long way, and an unusual, thoughtful, and creative presentation establishes the graphic artist's expertise—and makes a sale.

Examples of Market Categories & Media

The following are examples of market categories and typical media for which each market buys art. Within each category, there may be more media than space allows to be listed here.

ADVERTISING
Animation
Client presentation
    -Preproduction, comps
Collateral & direct mail
    Brochures, direct mailers,
    flyers, handouts, catalogs
Display & exhibit
Magazines/magazine supplements
Newspapers/newspaper
    supplements/advertorials
Online
    Web sites;
    electronic publications/periodicals
Outdoor
Packaging
    Products, CDs, DVDs, videos,
    software, food
Point of sale
    Counter cards, shelf signs, posters
Poster
    Film, theater. concert, event
Presentation
Television/cable TV
Other

EDITORIAL
Educational
Audiovisual
Encyclopedia
Magazine
Multimedia
Newspaper
Online/database
Television/cable TV
Other

INSTITUTIONAL
Annual report
Audiovisual (video, PowerPoint, etc.)
Brochure
Corporate/employee publication
Presentation
Other

MANUFACTURING
Apparel
Domestics
Electronics
Food & beverage
Footwear
Home furnishing
Jewelry
Novelty & retail goods
    Paper products, greeting cards, mugs,
    posters, calendars, giftware, other
Toys & games

PROMOTION
Booklet
Brochure
Calendar
Card
Direct mail
E-newsletter
Poster
Press kit
Sales literature
Other

BOOK PUBLISHING
Anthology
CDs/Online
Educational text
Mass market
Trade
Electronic books
Other
    Hardcover or soft-cover editions, covers,
    jackets or interiors, etc.

FIGURE 5—1

- **Refrain from small talk** unless the content relates to the business at hand. A well-placed word here and there helps establish credibility, but chatter can be perceived as a lack of respect for the client's time.
- **Observe.** A lot about the client's personality can be learned from physical clues such as the office environment (wallpaper, furniture, desktops, artwork, and photographs). Body language also provides information about the client. Notice whether a seat is offered and whether the client consults a watch constantly and is not focused on the discussion. Understanding behavioral clues may give the graphic artist information that is advantageous for negotiating.
- **Listen.** People appreciate someone who is alert, attentive, and understands what is being said. It may be useful to use active listening techniques, such as, "Let me see if I understand correctly: You are saying that...." Listening effectively helps determine and address the other party's needs and expectations. Listening actively, with nods of agreement, encourages the other party to communicate.

Discuss money last

Money should be the last item on the agenda in a negotiation, for several reasons. It is the area where most disagreements occur. In the early stages of a negotiation, it is important to focus on areas in which it is easiest to reach agreement, such as the job description, difficulty of execution, usage and reproduction rights, deadlines, and expenses. These factors all define the value a job holds for the client. Delaying a discussion of money until later in the negotiation process also provides more time for an understanding, or even a feeling of partnership, to develop between the two parties. Negotiating about money before reaching agreement on other terms of the project is premature and could prove to be costly.

Sometimes parties set an arbitrary limit from which they say they will not deviate, such as "I will not pay more than $25,000," or "I will not accept less than $3,000." These figures or conditions are often set arbitrarily. Do not allow the price quotation to become a focal point that inhibits negotiating terms that are agreeable and beneficial to both parties.

Also, do not feel obligated to respond right away if someone starts a negotiation with the statement, "I only have $500, but I think you'd be great for the job." One can acknowledge the statement and still discuss the fee later when there is more of a foundation for a working relationship and more facts on which to base requests for more money.

When the discussion appropriately turns to money, it is advisable to first outline or summarize all the variables that will go into the project; then try to get the client to make the first offer. It is advantageous to get the client to make the first offer, or better, to tell you the budget. Depending on how it is presented, a first offer is rarely a final offer and should be looked at realistically in terms of what the client expects in terms of services, deliverables, and usage. You are negotiating at this point and should already know what your "bottom line" is. It is appropriate to ask for higher compensation if the offer is too low, but you should weigh the risk of losing the job by refusing to negotiate price. Sometimes, if the client refuses to meet your minimum requirements, you can negotiate an accommodation such as reducing a license from three to two years, requesting 500 samples to mail out as your next promotion, or bartering for in-kind services such as computer equipment or ad space.

ESTIMATES

At any time during negotiations, a potential client might ask the graphic artist for an estimate—even before all the details of the project have been discussed. When asked for an estimate, the artist should not feel pressured to give a figure immediately. The wiser tactic is to say, "I'll call you later with a quote." This will give you time to weigh your needs against the terms and scope of the project. It is good business for both parties if you estimate costs accurately, but also make sure that you will be adequately compensated if unforeseen circumstances arise. Artists should be aware that when offering an estimate made up of a range of figures that brackets the desired price in the middle, many clients will hear only the lower figure.

BIDS

Graphic artists are asked sometimes to bid on jobs. It is important to clarify the nature of the bid and to find out with whom you will be competing. Ask who the other bidders are to determine if they are of comparable talent. If the client refuses to disclose the name of the competition, at least explain why it is to the client's advantage to choose you despite your price. Awarding work based on price rarely results in the best quality.

A client sometimes requests a bid in order to establish a budget and should say so when making the request. This gives you an opportunity to build a relationship with the client for future work. It should be understood that the information is for budget purposes only and that the terms and pricing for the project will be negotiated when the project actually happens. Often the parameters and the scope of work change significantly from the time a project was conceived to when it becomes a reality.

KNOWING WHEN TO STOP

An essential element in every successful negotiation is knowing when to stop. Getting greedy when things start to go well or pushing for unreasonable concessions could lead the other party to abandon the process. Fair and equitable negotiating will help you win repeat business and reap the monetary rewards you seek.

When negotiation fails

Negotiation cannot guarantee favorable terms. Sometimes one party must either yield to unfavorable conditions or give up the opportunity. After you have evaluated the situation objectively, you may decide to protect yourself from an agreement that may be detrimental by walking away from it. Sometimes, no matter how hard you try, you just cannot make it work. It is an ill-founded notion to assume that a deal must be made at any cost.

Both parties should determine what their courses of action will be if the negotiation ends without agreement. Each party should make a realistic assessment of how much leverage they have in negotiation. Assessing the alternatives always clarifies a negotiating position.

Remember that not every negotiation will end in a deal. Two parties can "agree to disagree" amicably and part ways, with the hope of trying to negotiate again at a later date. Power is also knowing when to say "no."

Deciding on the Price

Graphic art is commissioned in highly competitive and specialized markets. Prices are negotiated between the buyer and the seller, and each graphic artist sets his or her own prices. These prices usually depend upon many factors, including how the buyer intends to make use of the art, the size and prominence of the client, the client's budget, the urgency of the deadline, the complexity of the art, and the graphic artist's reputation. Both historical and current practices reveal that the factors often considered in pricing decisions vary from discipline to discipline; the information in this chapter should be supplemented by reading corresponding sections within each discipline.

Usage factors

Setting prices for art involves usage, which depends on how, where, and for how long the art will be used (or reused).

USAGE RIGHTS

To encourage the free flow of ideas, copyright law vests the creator of every artistic or literary work with a bundle of rights that can be divided and sold in any number of ways (for more detailed descriptions of these rights, see Chapter 2, Legal Rights & Issues). The price of graphic art is primarily determined by the extent and value of its use, or "usage." Graphic artists, such as photographers, writers, and other creators, customarily sell only specific rights to their creative work. The graphic artist specifies which rights of reproduction are being granted for the intended use, so learning how to define usage of work is critical for both illustrators and graphic designers.

Some inexperienced clients assume they are buying a product for a flat fee, with the right to reuse or manipulate the art or design without the permission of the graphic artist. Some purchase agreements are more like licensing agreements in that only the exclusive or nonexclusive right to use the work in a specific medium (such as magazine cover, point-of-purchase display, or billboard), for a limited time period, over a specific geographic area, is sold, or "granted."

The basic standard of sale for a commissioned work of art is "first reproduction rights" or "one-time reproduction rights." Graphic artists should consider the value of the full potential of their work when estimating the value of "exclusive," "unlimited," or "all-rights" agreements. Current data indicate that reuse, more extensive use, use in additional markets, or international use receives additional compensation. Under copyright law, the sale of the original physical art or design (including digital media) is not included in the sale of reproduction rights and is more often a separate transaction.

In some cases (corporate logos, advertising, product identity), the buyer may prefer to acquire most or all rights for extended periods of time. Surveys report that buyers and sellers both consider additional fees for such extensive grants of rights to be usual and customary. In other cases, the buyer has no need for extensive rights. When negotiating transfers of rights, it is the graphic artist's responsibility to identify the buyer's needs and negotiate the appropriate usage.

Selling extensive or all rights, at prices usually paid for limited rights, is like giving the buyer unpaid inventory of stock art, thereby depriving the artist, and other artists, of income from additional uses and future assignments. Purchasing more rights than are needed deprives the public of access to the work and is expensive and unnecessary. If buyers ask for an all-rights or work-for-hire agreement to protect themselves from competitive or embarrassing uses of the work, a limited-rights contract with exclusivity provisions can be easily drafted by the graphic artist, which will more appropriately meet the buyer's needs and more adequately remunerate the artist.

Grants of all rights should specify the category, the medium of intended use, and the title of the publication or product. Grants of rights may also specify, where appropriate, edition, number of appearances, and geographic or time limitations, for example, advertising (market category) rights in a national (region) general-interest consumer magazine (medium) for a period of one year (time). A common formula for editorial assignments is one-time North American magazine or newspaper rights. Designers may choose to limit how their work will be used—for instance, in a particular brochure and not as the basis for the client's annual report.

INTERNATIONAL USES

Determining the value of work to be used outside the United States follows the same general guidelines as for other uses. In addition to the length of time, how and where the material will be used are important variables to consider. For example, selling rights to a French-language European edition of a consumer magazine includes distribution in France, Belgium, and Switzerland. A country's economic condition also plays a role. A license for distribution in Japan might be considered more valuable than one for China because a higher percentage of the population would be reached.

ROYALTIES

Both graphic artists and clients have found that a royalty arrangement is a good way to compensate the value an artist contributes to a project; this is the accepted method of payment in book publishing and all types of licensing. A royalty is the percentage of either the list (retail) or the wholesale price of the product that is paid to the graphic artist based on the product's sales. Royalty arrangements often include a nonrefundable advance payment to the artist in anticipation of royalties, which is paid before the product is produced and sold. Royalties are not appropriate in cases where the use of the art does not involve direct sales or where a direct sale is difficult to monitor (see Maximizing Income later in this chapter).

REUSE

In most cases, illustration is commissioned for specific use. Rights that were not transferred to the client and were reserved by the artist can be sold. Also, rights completed under a specified grant of rights or rights not exercised within a specified period of time return to the artist and may be sold again. Subsequent uses of commissioned art, some of which are called "reuse," "licensing," and "merchandising," have grown dramatically in recent years, creating additional sources of income for artists. While many artists are concerned about the resulting drop in new commissions, a significant number of artists have taken advantage of these new markets to enhance their income. The Maximizing Income section in this chapter describes these opportunities.

Working arrangements

The particular working arrangement is another factor that is considered when determining the price of a job.

PER DIEM RATE

Sometimes graphic artists are hired on a per diem, or day rate, basis. Surveys of graphic artists and clients have found this to be a perfectly acceptable work arrangement and method of compensation, provided that it accurately reflects the work required and is agreed to in advance by both graphic artist and buyer.

Per Diem Rate Formula

Annual rent, utilities, insurance, employees' salaries and benefits, advertising and promotion, outside professional services, equipment, transportation, office and art supplies, business taxes, entertainment, and other expenses: _____

Add a reasonable salary: _____

Total: _____

Divide by 230 working days per year: _____

Add 10%-15% profit margin: _____

Per Diem Rate: $ _____

FIGURE 5—2

A day rate, coupled with an estimate of the number of days needed to complete the work, art direction, consultation, and/or travel, gives both parties a starting point from which to calculate a rough estimate. A word of caution: some jobs look deceptively simple, and even the most experienced graphic artists and clients sometimes find that greater expenditures of time are needed than were anticipated. When negotiating an estimate, both parties often address questions concerning complexity, degree of finish, delivery time, expenses, and general responsibilities, and they agree that an estimate is just that and is not assumed to be precise.

Guild members have found that one method of estimating an appropriate per-diem rate is to first total all direct and indirect business costs, adding in a reasonable salary. Divide this total by 230 annual business days (52 weeks minus six weeks' vacation, holiday, and sick time). Then add to this figure a reasonable profit margin, which usually ranges from 10 to 15 percent. See Figure 5-2 for a per-diem formula.

HOURLY RATE

Whether pricing on a fee-for-use basis or per diem, graphic artists must know what it costs them to conduct business so they know whether the fee received for a particular project amounts to profit, breaking even, or loss. Calculating the individual cost per hour of doing business enables graphic artists to evaluate their financial progress.

Industry professionals use the following method to establish an hourly rate: First, total all direct and indirect business expenses for a year, including rent, utilities, insurance, employees' salaries and benefits, advertising and promotion, outside professional services, equipment, transportation, office and art supplies, business taxes, and entertainment. Using the actual figures in your Schedule C for IRS Form 1040 makes this easy. Include a reasonable salary that reflects current market conditions (see Chapter 7, Salaries & Trade Customs). Divide the total by 1,610, which is the number of hours worked in an average year (52 weeks minus 6 weeks' vacation, holiday, and sick time). Add to this figure a reasonable profit margin, which usually ranges from 10 to 15 percent. The resulting hourly rate, based on a 35-hour workweek, covers all costs of doing business, including the graphic artist's own salary. Most self-employed graphic artists indicate that they divide the annual overhead figure by a much smaller number of working hours to allow for time spent on such non-billable work as writing proposals, billing, and self-promotion. A figure from 20 to 45 percent less, or roughly 900 to 1,300 hours, has been found to be more accurate and practical. See Figure 5-3 for an hourly rate formula.

When considering a project, it is important to accurately estimate the number of work hours. Many graphic artists say that multiplying this estimate by the hourly rate demonstrates whether the client's fee for the project will at least cover costs. If it will not, negotiating with the client for more money, proposing a solution that will take less time, or searching with the client for another mutually agreeable alternative is recommended. Many large jobs, such as corporate design projects, require that the hours involved be used as a gauge to measure if the project is on budget.

Recent surveys indicate that design firms usually have at least two hourly rates: one for principals and one for employees. The difference is related to salary level. For example, in the graphic design field, hourly rates for a principal range from $150 to $350, and for studio staff, $65 to $120.

Advertising factors

Some illustrators and designers working in advertising and editorial print media markets check advertising page rates as another factor in gauging fees.

Advertising page rates vary according to the type and circulation of a magazine and therefore provide a standard for measuring the extent of usage and serve as a good barometer of a magazine's resources. For example, *Women's Health* (ranked 2nd on the Advertising Age "A list of magazines") has a circulation of 1.35 million copies. It receives $138,075 for each full-page, four-color ad sold. Obviously, *Women's Health* delivers a potential market to its advertisers that makes this cost worthwhile. *Fast Company* (ranked 6th), with a 2009 North American circulation base of 725,000, receives $76,980 for each full-page, four-color advertisement. The same four-color ad in *Popular Mechanics* (circulation 1.2 million copies) costs $125,770. The regional consumer magazine *New York* (circulation 425,000) charges $67,700 for each full page four-color ad sold, while the specialty consumer magazine *Scientific American,* worldwide edition (circulation 665,000) charges $76,100.

Magazine advertising page rates and circulation information can be found in the September issues of trade journals such as *Folio, Advertising Age,* and *Adweek*, and in publications issued by Standard Rate & Data Service, Inc., which are available in most business libraries. Most magazines also post their media kits online. The media kit details circulation, specifies ad sizes and deadlines, and posts rates for the various types and styles of advertisements accepted.

Other pricing factors

INFLATION
During periods of inflation, the change in the government's Consumer Price Index (CPI), which measures cost-of-living fluctuations, is another variable to be considered when calculating an appropriate fee. As the costs of printing, paper, distribution, advertising page and TV rates, and other items in the communications industry rise as time passes, so should prices paid for commissioned art. Such costs are generally reviewed annually, and any increases in the inflation rate are taken into consideration, say industry professionals. The CPI may also decrease, as we saw in 2008, which usually accounts for stagnant or declining fees.

CONSULTATION
If a job requires extensive consultation, recent surveys indicate that graphic artists frequently estimate the number of hours or days required, multiply them by their individual rate, and add a consultation fee to the basic project fee. It is not uncommon, especially for a brief consultation to solve a particular problem, for the consultation fee to be substantially higher than the normal hourly

---

Hourly Rate Formula*

Annual rent, utilities, insurance, employees' salaries and benefits, advertising and promotion, outside professional services, equipment, transportation, office and art supplies, business taxes, entertainment, and other expenses: _____

Add a reasonable salary: _____

Total: _____

Divide by 1,610** hours worked per year: _____

Add 10%-15% profit margin: _____

Hourly Rate: $ _____

* Based on direct/indirect business costs

** Divide by 900 to 1350 hours if graphic artist is self-employed, to allow for time spent on non-billable work such as writing proposals, billing, and self promotion.

FIGURE 5—3

rate. The nature of the project, proposed usage, unusual time demands, and travel requirements are factors to consider when estimating a consultation fee.

Billable expenses

The cost of supplies and services that an artist needs to purchase or rent in order to complete a job needs to be budgeted for when determining the price of a job. These expenses vary by industry and by project

FOR GRAPHIC DESIGN

Graphic designers traditionally bill clients for all expenses involved in executing an assignment, while textile designers and illustrators often absorb expenses for such things as art supplies because those costs tend to be modest. Necessary costs related to producing a job, such as model fees, prop rental, research time, production or printing, shipping, and travel expenses, are usually billed to the client separately. These expenses, even as estimates, are generally agreed upon and set down in the original written agreement. Often a maximum amount is itemized beyond which a designer may not incur costs without the client's authorization.

When graphic artists are required to advance sums on behalf of their clients, surveys show that it is customary to charge a markup as a percentage of the expense to cover overhead and provide adequate cash flow. Dimensional illustration, for example, often requires substantial outlays for rental or purchase of materials and photography needed for a reproducible final. Current data indicate that markups are in the range of 15 to 25 percent, with most charging 20 percent.

FOR COMPUTER GRAPHICS & ILLUSTRATION

Graphic artists need to consider their capital investment in computers and software in their fees. Those who rent or lease equipment or use out-of-house service bureaus must maintain strict records of all expenses in order to bill the client. Billable expenses usually include rental or leasing fees, transportation to and from the equipment, and any costs incurred in recording work as hard copy or on film or videotape. Fees paid for technical assistants and the cost of research, reference, and preparing raw art (from photos or line art) for digitizing camera input are also billed as expenses. Expenses, such as purchases of equipment or technology to meet specific demands of the job or the purchase of a new font, are usually considered assets rather than expenses billable to a client.

Graphic artists also usually follow the markup conventions outlined above for equipment rental, particularly when they have spent time negotiating for rental time or purchasing supplies and services. Recent data show that billable rates for renting hardware for video animation and special effects systems, for example, run around $150 per day, with software costing from $150 to thousands depending

on its sophistication. Any graphic artist working with video animation systems should consider the revision cycles for technology and software updates as part of a regular review of expenses and charges.

Other contractual considerations

Graphic artists should consider a variety of other items, including cancellation and rejection fees, credit lines, samples, and liability for portfolios and artwork, when preparing to negotiate a contract.

CANCELLATION FEES

In the past, such a fee has sometimes been referred to as a "kill fee," but this term has become outmoded and may be misunderstood by clients. According to current and historical data, clients usually pay a graphic artist a cancellation fee if an assignment is canceled for reasons beyond the artist's control. The amount of the fee can range from 30 to 100 percent, with 50 percent being fairly usual. (For a more detailed discussion of such fees, see Chapter 3, Professional Issues.)

Upon cancellation, all rights to the artwork, as well as possession of the original art, generally revert to the artist. Under a royalty arrangement, however, the client may demand all the originally agreed-upon rights to use the artwork upon payment of the cancellation fee.

When determining an appropriate cancellation fee, many artists take into account a project's advance and any anticipated royalties. For example, suppose an illustrator completes the work for a 32-page children's picture book for which the artist received a $5,000 advance against a 5 percent royalty, and then the job is killed. If the initial print run were to have been 10,000 copies, with each book listing at $12.95, then the anticipated royalty would have been $6,475 (10,000 x $12.95 x 5%). After the $5,000 advance is subtracted, the anticipated royalty would have been $1,475. That would be the appropriate cancellation fee.

When flat-fee projects are canceled, data indicate that all necessary and related expenses (such as model fees, materials, or overnight shipping fees) are paid in full.

Cancellation terms should be stipulated in writing, in contracts, and on confirmation forms and purchase orders. Otherwise, artists report, negotiating these fees at the time cancellation occurs makes it more difficult to protect their investment of time and resources. Artists also have found that contract language that makes payment of fees contingent upon the buyer's receipt of the artwork, not upon publication, anticipates the possibility of cancellation after acceptance and has helped ensure timely payment.

REJECTION FEES

Clients may agree to pay the graphic artist a rejection fee if the preliminary or finished artwork is not found to be reasonably satisfactory and the assignment is terminated. The amount of the fee varies widely, usually from 20 to 100 percent, depending upon the degree of the work's completion. (For a more detailed discussion of rejection fees, see Chapter 3, Professional Issues.)

By rejecting the artwork, the client has chosen to forfeit any rights to its use. Therefore, many artists refuse to permit the client to use rejected work for reproduction without a separate fee.

CREDIT LINES

Illustrators usually incorporate their signatures into their artwork, and they are typically reproduced as part of the piece. For important pieces, especially when a letter of agreement spells out the terms of usage and payment, artists may request specific credit lines as part of the agreement. For some, this may mean a printed credit line with copyright notice; for others, merely the reproduction of the signature in the artwork. In some cases, as is traditional in magazines, both forms of credit may be agreed upon.

A copyright notice can be added to the credit line simply by adding © and the year of publication before the artist's name—for example, © 2010 Jane Artist. Such a copyright notice benefits the artist without harming the client.

Surveys show that some magazine photographers' contracts require that their fees be doubled if an adjacent credit line is omitted. Given the modest rates for editorial work, it is not surprising that the value of the credit line is as important as the fee. This does not yet constitute a trade practice, but it is becoming more common and has also been adopted by some designers and illustrators.

SAMPLES OF WORK

It is a courtesy for clients to provide artists with samples of a finished piece as it was reproduced. This piece, often called a "tear sheet," shows the project in its completed form and can be displayed in an artist's portfolio. Even if clients purchase the copyright to artwork, artists' use of their original art in their portfolios is permissible as fair use (and is not competitive with the copyright owner's uses), except in cases of work-for-hire, when the client's permission must be obtained.

LIABILITY FOR PORTFOLIOS & ORIGINAL ART

If an artist's portfolio is lost by an art buyer, the law of "bailments" (the holding of another's property) makes the buyer liable for the "reasonable value" of that portfolio, if the loss arose from the buyer's carelessness. If the portfolio contained original art such as drawings, paintings, or original transparencies, the amount in question could be substantial. The same potential liability exists with commissioned artwork that a client has agreed to return to the artist. A model Holding Form for use by surface and textile designers, which can be modified for use by other disciplines, is provided in the Appendix: Contracts & Forms.

The value or appraisal of originals, transparencies, and other lost items can be verified by obtaining simple written assessments from a number of the artist's clients, art directors, or vendors and then by presenting the figures to the party who lost the work or to a court. An independent appraisal by a professional appraiser is also credible. The full value of the work may be nearly impossible to calculate, since no one can be certain what the work will be worth over the life of the copyright, which is currently the artist's lifetime plus 70 years (see the Copyright Extension section in Chapter 2, Legal Rights & Issues). One factor that can affect a work's value is whether it is generic or specific. Generic works (a bald eagle soaring in flight) may have more potential for economic exploitation than specific works (a brand of laundry detergent). Artists may also need to prove that their work has generated additional income through transfers of rights.

The risk of losing original work can be minimized. First, whenever possible, artists should avoid letting original art out of their possession. Instead of submitting portfolios of finished work, it is preferable to provide transparencies, color copies, or digital files. Second, the artist should have "valuable paper" insurance that protects against the loss or damage of valuable artwork in the artist's studio, in transit, or while in the client's possession. That, however, is still not enough protection, since, as with any insurance, deductibles must be met, and claims may lead to prohibitive premiums or a complete loss of coverage.

Buyers need effective systems for tracking and storing original art in their offices. They should provide a record of receipt of every portfolio and maintain a tracking system within the organization. There should also be a system in place that logs original art when it comes into the studio and when it is sent to a supplier such as a printer or a color separator. The risk of damage or loss to original art or portfolios is minimized if buyers avoid keeping portfolios overnight and on weekends. Finally, suppliers and vendors should understand that they might be held liable for any losses they cause as a result of damage to, or disappearance of, any original art.

In addition to record-keeping and tracking systems, buyers should minimize their legal risks by purchasing suitable insurance since absolute guarantees of protection of original art are impossible.

Keeping Track

Maintaining a system for documenting each project from start to finish will benefit the artist in a number of ways.

Written agreements

A letter of agreement or a contract should be kept on file for each work assignment. Graphic artists assume certain risks if they start to work on an assignment prior to having a signed, written agreement. While an oral agreement may be enforceable, a written agreement protects both the client and the graphic artist by confirming the terms before memory fades or a misunderstanding arises.

A written agreement also demonstrates that both parties are professionals who treat their resources with care. When used properly, it can be a valuable tool that helps both parties clarify their needs and reflect their concerns, and can specifically address any issues raised in negotiations. Should a client refuse to pay, a written agreement protects the graphic artist's rights and offers various types of recourse, including negotiation, collection services, arbitration, and, as a last resort, a lawsuit.

The document can be as simple or as complicated as the situation requires—from an informal letter of agreement, purchase order, or invoice to a comprehensive contract requiring the signatures of all parties. It should describe the project, name specific rights that are being transferred, describe the disposition of the original art or design, define cancellation fees, and spell out other terms, such as expenses.

Formulating letters and contracts, or analyzing contracts offered by clients, requires a thorough working knowledge of copyright, business law, and related terminology. Graphic artists can become familiar with these areas by carefully studying Chapter 2, Legal Rights & Issues, for copyright information; Chapter 6, Standard Contracts & Business Tools, for all types of standard contracts; and Chapter 15, Resources & References, for additional resources.

When a client uses a work-for-hire clause in a design contract or demands all rights to artwork, every effort should be made to determine the client's real needs. Often such terms have been added to the contract by a lawyer trying to anticipate every possible contingency, but such terms are usually excessive and, if priced accordingly by the graphic artist, make the work too expensive for the client. Through study and practice, graphic artists can learn how to rephrase contractual terms to meet their requirements and negotiate to win the client's agreement. Knowing how to do that is a valuable asset for every graphic artist.

OTHER INCLUSIONS IN AN AGREEMENT

Letters of agreement, contracts, and purchase orders should contain the following:

- Names of the graphic artist and client, including the name of the client's authorized buyer or commissioning party.
- A complete description of the assignment or the project.
- The fee arrangement, including fees for usage, consultations, alterations, travel time, cancellation, and reimbursement for billable expenses.
- Payment terms, including a schedule for advances, monthly service charges for late payment, expense estimates and/or maximums, and royalty percentages and terms, where applicable.
- Specifications regarding when and how the original work will be returned.
- Any agreement regarding copyright notice requirements and placement of the credit line.
- Assignment of rights described in specific terms, normally naming a specific market category, medium, time period, and geographic region (see Chapter 2, Legal Rights & Issues, as well as Chapters 8, 9, 10, 11, 12, and 13, which cover specific disciplines).
- Assignment of responsibility for obtaining releases for the use of people's names and/or images for advertising or trade purposes.

Record keeping

A standard record-keeping system helps facilitate accurate billing, bill tracking, fee collection, and tax liabilities. Being able to track invoices allows the graphic artist to remind buyers of outstanding obligations and to take whatever follow-up steps are necessary to obtain payment. It also provides a paper trail in the event that a disagreement or misunderstanding interferes with completing a project or receiving payment.

Graphic artists may find it helpful to set up a job file for keeping track of individual assignments and a job ledger for tracking all assignments within given time frames.

JOB FILE

A common method of record keeping is to set up a folder or labeled envelope for each assignment. All information pertaining to the job is kept in this file. This includes such things as written agreements, business letters, invoices, memos, sketches, layouts, notes about phone calls or meetings, messenger and expense receipts, e-mail messages, itemized hours spent on the job, etc. This information will prove very helpful as reminders or clarification to you or your client about the facts if there are misunderstandings or disagreements at any point in the project. Other information that should be stored in this file is copies of outside vendor invoices. It is very important that information is filed in a timely way to maintain accuracy. The file then provides a single, complete record of the entire project.

Identifying information is usually recorded on the folder cover. This may include the job number, the title of the project, the buyer's name, and the delivery date. If the job is complex, the job file should be subdivided into sections to permit easy access to information. All sketches and drawings should be retained at least until after payment is received.

JOB LEDGER

A job ledger contains standard columns for information such as the job description (job number, client, description of artwork, delivery date), rights granted (usage, status of original artwork), fees and expenses (advance or payment schedule, reimbursable expenses, sales tax, and so on), and billing information (invoice amount and date, payment due date, amount and date received, late penalties, balance due, artwork returned date). Using a job ledger, an artist can determine at a glance the status of each aspect of a job. The ledger's format can vary from a printed journal sold in stationery stores to a form specifically created by the artist, sometimes by customizing off-the-shelf software.

CHANGES TO THE ORIGINAL AGREEMENT

Getting paid on time and in full is the entitlement of any businessperson, and having a signed, written agreement; a complete understanding of the negotiated terms of that agreement; and accurate records help ensure timely and proper payment of fees. It is particularly important to confirm in writing any changes that alter the original agreement and to record additional fees resulting from them. The Guild's model business forms incorporate a number of these measures and can aid graphic artists in securing their rights.

Billing procedures

When signing a contractual arrangement, the buyer promises to make a specific payment in return for the graphic artist's grant of usage rights or sale of work. The graphic artist's invoices serve as formal notice to the buyer that payment is due; in many businesses an invoice is mandatory for the buyer to authorize a check and see that it is issued. Whenever possible, an invoice should accompany delivery of the finished art or design. A copy of the invoice may also be sent to the accounting department, if the business is large enough to have one, to facilitate prompt processing.

To encourage timely payment, graphic artists often incorporate payment terms into their billing process. One common procedure is to charge penalties for accounts that are past due as a percentage of the total, as allowed by law. Another procedure is to withhold rights of usage until full payment is received (see the section on Extension of Payment Time under Collecting later in this chapter).

If the parties have not specified a payment due date, the generally accepted practice is payment within 30 days of delivery of the art or design. When a partial payment is due, or costs are to be billed during the job, the invoice or statement should be delivered as needed. Oral requests for payment do not substitute for invoices, but serve as reminders in the collection process. If cancellation or rejection of the job occurs, the buyer should be billed immediately, according to the agreement, or if such a provision is absent, according to the standards discussed in Chapter 3, Professional Issues.

Wording of invoices should be accurate and complete to avoid payment delays. Billing may be expedited by including such instructions as "Make check payable to Jan Artist or J. Artist Associates."

Sales & use taxes

States have varying policies regarding sales and use taxes (for detailed information on sales taxes, especially in California and New York, see Chapter 3, Professional Issues, or the web site: http://www.tax sites.com). In states that have sales taxes, the rate usually ranges from 3 to 9 percent, and it is levied on the sale or use of physical property within the state. A number of exemptions exist, including special rules for the sale of reproduction rights.

Generally, services, including the service of transferring reproduction rights, are not subject to sales tax. Transfers of physical property to a client (original art or mechanicals) should not be taxed if they are part of a project that will later be billed to a client by an illustrator or design firm. Sales tax is usually applicable for end sales or retail costs only, not for intermediate subcontracting, so an artist may have to retain forms showing that materials were intermediate and thus not taxable.

Many tax laws are unclear in relation to the graphic communications industry. In any case, where graphic artists are unsure whether to collect tax, it is safest to collect and remit it to the state sales tax bureau. Graphic artists as well as their clients are liable for uncollected sales tax, and it may be difficult, if not impossible, to collect such taxes from clients whose final bills have been invoiced without including sales tax.

Checks with conditions

Some clients attempt to add terms to the contract or to change terms after the work is completed by listing conditions on the check, for example, claiming that endorsement transfers all reproduction rights and/or ownership of the original art to the payer. A 1995 U.S. Supreme Court decision (*Playboy Enterprises, Inc. v. Dumas*) let stand a lower court decision giving creators mixed rights when faced with additional contract terms after the work is completed (see discussion in Chapter 2, Legal Rights & Issues, and Chapter 3, Professional Issues). It has always been the Guild's opinion that endorsement of such a check does not constitute a legal contract, especially if it conflicts with the previous contract.

When confronted with checks with conditions, an artist has at least three options:

1. Simply return the check and request that a new check be issued without conditions. If the conditions on the check violate a prior contract, refusal to issue a check without conditions will be a breach of contract.
2. If an artist has signed a contract or sent an invoice that restricts the client's rights of use and if the artwork has been used already, the artist should strike out the conditions on the check and deposit it. In this case the artist should probably not sign the back of the check, but instead use a bank endorsement stamp, which eliminates the need for a signature.

    If the artwork has not yet been used, the artist should notify the client in writing that he or she is striking out the conditions on the check. If the client does not respond within two weeks, the check can be safely deposited.
3. If the artist has neither signed a contract with the client nor sent an invoice restricting use, the check should be returned in order to protect all rights. Along with the check, the artist should include an appropriate invoice restricting usage. Of course, this can be avoided by specifying in writing which rights will be transferred before beginning the assignment.

Tracking invoices

Once an invoice has been sent to the client, the graphic artist should track the outstanding invoice through the record-keeping system until it is paid. Keeping a folder marked "accounts receivable" is the simplest way to organize these records. Copies of all invoices sent to clients, which should include the graphic artist's job number and the billing date, should be kept in this folder in order of payment due date. This folder should be reviewed at least once a month. When payment is received, the invoice should be moved to the job file.

Graphic artists who use a paper job ledger or accounting software can determine at a glance which payments remain outstanding by referring to the "payment due date" column. When payment is received, the date is entered under "payment received date."

Accurate, timely information on cash flow should trigger follow-up steps to collect past-due fees or other outstanding obligations.

Collecting

Once a project that meets the client's specifications has been completed and delivered, it is natural to expect that payment will be made as agreed to in the contract. Taking routine precautions in advance, such as clearly detailing payment and related terms in the written agreement, is the artist's best insurance against payment problems.

However, graphic artists who do not receive timely payment will want to implement appropriate and efficient collection strategies if they are to avoid loss of income and time. Invoices become more difficult to collect as they get older, so prompt action is important. Figure 5-4, Step-by-Step Collection Strategy, details the actions graphic artists can take to collect outstanding fees. Note that this strategy does not represent legal advice; actions with legal ramifications should not be undertaken without consulting a qualified attorney (a list of Volunteer Lawyers for the Arts groups, by location, is provided in Chapter 15, Resources & References).

Prevention

The first step in any collection strategy is prevention. When dealing with a new client, be sure to ask for and check credit references. Then call the Better Business Bureau and credit-reporting agencies such as Dun & Bradstreet to verify the firm's worthiness.

The next logical step is direct communication with the client to determine why payment has not been made. Subsequent steps depend on the client's response and the nature of the problem. In most cases, the client will explain that the reason is a cash-flow problem. In other cases, the client may dispute whether monies are owed or how much. A direct discussion may clarify the problem and lead to a solution. If one discussion is not sufficient to resolve a delay, misunderstanding, or dispute, graphic artists can take advantage of the support services of the Graphic Artists Guild's Grievance Committee (for members only), or clients may be willing to try mediation or arbitration.

If the graphic artist encounters an unreasonable or evasive client, however, more forceful measures may be required, such as engaging a collection agency, suing in small-claims court, or initiating a legal suit.

Common causes of nonpayment

Graphic artists usually learn why the payment has not been made during the first contact with the client. Following are some of the more common causes and basic strategies for responding to them. A more detailed explanation of strategies for dealing with nonpayment is covered in the next section.

GRAPHIC ARTIST'S ERROR
Perhaps an invoice was not provided, was sent to the attention of the wrong person, was incomplete or illegible, or did not document reimbursable expenses. The artist must correct the error to expedite the payment process.

BUYER'S ERROR
Once a project is delivered, the client may be involved in the next project and forget to process the check. One purpose of an invoice is to serve as

a physical reminder; the client should not be expected to send the check automatically, without an invoice, and oral requests for payment are not sufficient.

If the cause of nonpayment is oversight, a new due date should be established and the client requested to follow up personally. The graphic artist should send a letter or e-mail confirming when payment will be made.

DISPUTES AND MISUNDERSTANDINGS

Some disputes are caused by unintentional actions or ignorance about professional standards and practices. For example, a client may make an incorrect assumption (such as assuming it is fine to delay payment when experiencing cash-flow problems) or may be unaware of appropriate professional conduct in a particular situation. The graphic artist should instruct the client in the proper procedure, agree on a new payment date, and write a letter or e-mail confirming the new schedule.

BANKRUPTCY

If a client files for bankruptcy, there may be little a graphic artist can do except join the list of unsecured creditors. If the client is forced to liquidate assets to pay creditors, a percentage of the fee may ultimately be paid to the graphic artist.

Another problem in a bankruptcy may be getting original artwork or design returned, especially if the trustee or court assumes that everything in the client's possession is an asset. Graphic artists must state that the work belongs to them and cannot, therefore, be considered an asset of the bankrupt party. While New York State has passed legislation that protects the work of gallery artists if a gallery files for bankruptcy, those protections are not extended to graphic artists unless their work is similarly on exhibit.

Strategies for dealing with nonpayment

The following represent a progression of strategies to use in cases of nonpayment, from simple remedies for client oversight to more drastic measures when a client refuses to pay.

DIRECT NEGOTIATION

Unless complex legal matters or large amounts of money are at issue, direct negotiation is usually the most appropriate approach. A phone call or a personal visit may be the most effective way to resolve a payment problem. It is important in this kind of negotiation to remain objective and realistic at all times. It is in the graphic artist's best interest to behave professionally when dealing with the client or anyone in the client's firm.

Always refer to the written agreement when contacting the client. Well-negotiated agreements usually foresee possible areas of dispute and specify the client's obligations and the graphic

artist's rights. If necessary, remind the client of provisions in the agreement providing alternatives or penalties; they are there to provide negotiating leverage. If the reason for the payment failure violates the agreement or professional standards, the graphic artist should inform the client of the correct procedure. If necessary, cite the appropriate professional standards in the industry's Code of Fair Practice (see Chapter 1, Professional Relationships).

Alternatively, the artist might send a brief, businesslike letter with a copy of the original invoice attached and marked "Second Notice." Remind the client of the overdue payment and request that he or she handle it immediately. All correspondence (letters and invoices) should be sent by certified mail, return receipt requested. Copies of all correspondence and memos of discussions between the parties should be kept in the job file. Establishing a paper trail with the proper documentation may be crucial later.

At this stage, the graphic artist can assume that human error, or red tape, was involved and that the call or letter will clear things up. These reminders often prove sufficient and forestall the need for stronger measures—until it becomes clear that nonpayment is deliberate.

EXTENSION OF PAYMENT TIME

Clients may claim a cash-flow problem (not having sufficient funds on hand to pay). It may be difficult to verify whether this is legitimate or an evasive maneuver. It is not unusual for the client to blame a late payment on the company's computer; however, long intervals between programmed payments are unlikely. Exceptions to automatic payments are made all the time. In this case, insist that a handwritten check be authorized immediately and paid within a week.

If the cause of the delay appears to be legitimate and future payment will clearly be made, the graphic artist may wish to accommodate the client and grant a reasonable extension, with the new payment deadline confirmed in writing. Granting extensions should be viewed as the discretion of the graphic artist, not the client's right. Some graphic artists may demand a service fee, often a percentage of the outstanding balance, as compensation for the delayed payment. Graphic artists who employ this practice should make sure to stipulate it in the written agreement. This practice should be used particularly when longer extensions are granted.

FINAL NOTICE LETTER

After direct negotiation has been attempted, a client may still refuse to make payment. The client may fail to respond to the graphic artist's letters and calls, give unreasonable explanations, not address the issue at hand, or not make payment according to the newly negotiated terms.

As a last effort before turning to stronger alternatives, the graphic artist should send a final notice letter (Figure 5-5). The basis of the graphic

Step-By-Step Collection Strategy

Caution and restraint should be exercised in all communications with clients so that there is no question of harassment, which is a violation of the federal Fair Debt Collection Practices Law.

STEP 1. At the completion of the project, the artist should send an invoice to the client clearly stating the amount owed by the agreed-upon due date. If appropriate, the artist can include a notation that a late payment penalty fee will be applied to all overdue balances. (Many businesses assess a late fee of 1.5 to 2 percent of outstanding balances due.)

STEP 2. If the client does not make timely payment, the artist should send a follow-up invoice. A handwritten or stamped message to the effect of "Have you forgotten to send your payment?" or "Payment overdue—Please remit promptly" may help speed payment. If appropriate, the artist should include on the follow-up invoice any applicable late payment penalty fee incurred to date as part of the balance due. To help expedite payment, the artist may include a self-addressed stamped envelope or his or her express mail account number for the client to use in mailing back the payment.

STEP 3. If the client does not make payment within 10 days of the follow-up invoice, the artist should call the client as a reminder that payment is due.

Sample "Phone Script"

"Hello, Mr. Client.
This is Joe Talent at Ads & Such, and I'm calling to remind you that payment for the [name of project] that was delivered to you on [date] is now over [X] days past due. When can I expect to have payment in my hands?"

At this point the client will probably give the artist a reason for the delay, which should be listened to patiently. It could have been simply an oversight, and the client will agree to send payment immediately.

STEP 4. If payment is not received within 10 days of the phone call, the artist should send a "Second Notice" that payment is overdue and expected within 10 days of this notice. The Second Notice allows for possible human error or "red tape" that may have caused the delay and presents the client with another copy of the overdue invoice and a self-addressed envelope to simplify and speed payment.

Sample "Second Notice" Letter

Dear Mr. Client:

Ten days ago I spoke with you about the outstanding balance of $[amount] owed for the [project] Ads & Such delivered to you on [date]. You agreed to make payment within 30 days of acceptance, and now, [X] days later, you have still not settled your account.

This may be merely an oversight, or your payment has crossed this letter in the mail. If there are other reasons payment has not arrived that I should be aware of, I hope you will call me immediately.

Please do not jeopardize your credit record by failing to respond to this request. If payment has been sent, accept my thanks. If not, please send a check or money order for $[amount] in the enclosed return envelope no later than [date—usually 10 days from the receipt of the letter].
Sincerely yours,
Joe Talent
President, Ads & Such
Enc: copy of original invoice [marked "Second Notice"], *return envelope for payment*

STEP 5. If the client does not make payment within 10 days of the Second Notice, the artist can send the client a "Final Notice" letter. It should state that if payment is not made within three days, the debt will be turned over to either a collection agency, the Graphic Artists Guild's Grievance Committee, or an attorney (see sections later in this chapter for more information on these options). See Figure 5–5 for sample wording for a Final Notice Letter.

Up to this point, a number of reasonable efforts have been made and sufficient time has elapsed to allow the buyer to respond or pay the debt. The artist has established a "paper trail" of documentation verifying the continued indebtedness and the artist's attempts to collect. If the buyer still fails to respond or pay, or acts evasively, the artist may reasonably assume that the buyer is avoiding payment intentionally. More severe courses of action are discussed in the Strategies for Dealing with Nonpayment.

FIGURE 5—4

artist's claim should be stated briefly, with a demand for immediate payment of any outstanding balance. The final notice letter should apprise the client that the graphic artist is determined to pursue his or her legal rights and further legal action will be taken unless payment is received.

THE GRAPHIC ARTISTS GUILD GRIEVANCE COMMITTEE

The Graphic Artists Guild Grievance Committee provides guidance and assistance to members in good standing who need to resolve differences with clients. Guild members in need of this service should contact the National Office.

Members may not claim the support of the Grievance Committee until the committee has reviewed the case and notified the member that the case has been accepted. The Grievance Committee may refuse a case if the member has begun formal litigation.

The committee reviews grievances at its earliest opportunity. If it determines that the grievance is justified, the committee contacts the member. A plan of action is recommended and appropriate support provided, ranging from direct communication with the client to testimony in court supporting the member in any follow-up litigation. It is crucial that the member participate fully and keep the committee advised of subsequent developments.

The Grievance Committee will not offer assistance in a dispute involving questionable professional conduct on a member's part, such as misrepresentation of talent, plagiarism, or any violation of the Joint Ethics Committee's Code of Fair Practice (see Chapter 1, Professional Relationships).

The following information is required when submitting a grievance (a standard grievance form is available upon request):

Contact information: the member's personal and business names, addresses, phone and fax numbers, and e-mail address.

Client information: the name of the client, the name and title of the appropriate party, and the relevant addresses and phone and fax numbers.

The exact job description.

Statement of grievance: the nature of the grievance, including a chronological narration of facts and the respective positions of the parties.

Resolution attempts: the names of any agencies and persons (collection agencies or lawyers) contacted regarding the grievance and the result of such contacts.

Copies, not originals, of relevant documents substantiating the grievance: purchase order, written agreement, invoice, correspondence, receipts, and so on.

Desired remedy: a statement of what the member would consider an appropriate solution of the grievance.

Sample Final Notice Letter

Dear Mr. Client:

Your account is now [X] months overdue. Unless your check or money order in the amount of $[amount] is received within [usually three days] from receipt of this letter, I will be forced to pursue other methods of collection.

You can preserve your credit rating by calling me today to discuss payment of this invoice.

If I do not hear from you within [three days], I will be forced to turn your account over to a collection agency [or attorney or the Graphic Artists Guild Grievance Committee].*

Very truly yours,
Joe Talent
President, Ads & Such
Enc: copy of Invoice [marked "Final Notice"], return envelope for payment

* The Guild's Grievance Committee handles disputes for members only. Guild members should call the National Office for information.

FIGURE 5—5

MEDIATION & ARBITRATION

Mediation and arbitration, based on the services of an impartial outside party, are long-established processes for settling disputes privately and expeditiously. A mediator, acting as an umpire, does everything possible to bring the parties to agreement, but he or she cannot impose a decision upon them. If the parties cannot reach an agreement, they must proceed either to arbitration or to court to resolve the dispute. An arbitrator acts as a judge, reviewing the evidence presented by both sides and then making a legally binding decision.

Submitting to mediation or arbitration is voluntary, although signing a contract with such provisions establishes the client's consent to those procedures. Should a party in the dispute not appear for arbitration, a binding decision may be reached in that party's absence.

Mediation and arbitration are speedier and far less expensive than suing in court. The conciliatory and private atmosphere may be more appropriate for parties who have had, or would like to have, a long business relationship. These services may also be relevant if the graphic artist's monetary claim exceeds the monetary limit of small-claims court. Arbitrators' fees, which are usually split between the parties, are relatively moderate and normally consist of a flat fee plus expenses. Either party may choose to use an attorney in arbitration proceedings, but it is not required, and such costs are borne by that party.

The American Arbitration Association is available in many cities around the country, and its services may be requested in other localities. Mediation and arbitration may also be sponsored by some volunteer arts-related lawyer groups, including Volunteer Lawyers for the Arts in New York City and California Lawyers for the Arts in San Francisco (see a complete list in Chapter 15, Resources & References).

COLLECTION SERVICES

If voluntary dispute resolution such as mediation or arbitration is not available or has not produced the outstanding check, commercial collection agencies will seek payment on the graphic artist's behalf. Collection agencies make escalated demands on the client through letters, phone calls, visits, and/or legal services.

Collection agency fees, in addition to routine expenses, generally range from 10 to 50 percent of the monies actually recovered, depending on the amount of money involved and how much time has lapsed since the work was first invoiced (older invoices are more difficult to collect). If the agency engages a lawyer, his or her fee is included.

Before signing an agreement with a collection agency, the graphic artist should review it carefully to determine the actions the agency will take and what it will charge. Of particular concern is dealing with an agency that may use practices that could be deemed unprofessional, since they may reflect unfavorably on the graphic artist.

SMALL-CLAIMS COURT

When all else fails, the legal system may offer a way to remedy the problem. Small-claims courts give a grievant access to the legal system while avoiding the usual encumbrances, costs, and length of a formal court proceeding; in contrast, the small-claims procedure is streamlined, speedy, and available for a nominal fee. Many small-claims court cases are heard by arbitrators rather than judges. This does not prejudice one's case and may even expedite a decision.

Graphic artists may bring claims seeking a monetary judgment to small-claims court. Besides nonpayment for a completed assignment or project, other claims may include nonpayment for canceled artwork, for purchase of original art, for unauthorized reuses, or for unreturned or damaged art.

Graphic artists can handle their own cases in small-claims court with a little preparation. Information is readily available from flyers prepared by the court, how-to publications, and, perhaps best: local rules books. The court clerk, or in some localities a legal advisor, is often available to help with preparation. Small-claims forms are also known as "trespass and assumpsit" claims forms.

Each state's small-claims court has a dollar limit for what it considers a small claim. Amounts in excess of the limit require litigation in civil court. Considering the high cost of pursuing a claim through civil court, the graphic artist may decide it is more economical in the long run to reduce the claim to an amount that qualifies as a "small claim," especially if the amount in dispute is only slightly higher than the court's limit. The claim, however, must be made with the understanding that the balance above the court's limit is forfeited permanently. One possible way to avoid this is to split a larger amount into several small claims to be pursued individually—for example, if a client owes a large sum made up of payments due from several assignments.

COLLECTING AFTER A JUDGMENT

Should a client fail to pay after the court has rendered its decision or affirmed an arbitration award, the law authorizes a number of collection remedies. The graphic artist gains the right, within limitations, to place a lien on the client's funds and assets. Available funds, such as bank accounts or a portion of an individual's salary, may be seized by a sheriff or marshal and turned over to the graphic artist. Similarly, the proceeds of property, such as a car sold at public auction, may be used to settle the debt.

CONSULTING OR HIRING A LAWYER

A lawyer can assist in a number of ways and at different stages in the collection process. A lawyer may initially be able to provide enough information and advice so the graphic artist can pursue his or her own collection efforts. An initial consultation, whether in person or by phone, can confirm what the relevant law is and whether the graphic artist's position is supportable under the law. The lawyer may be able to advise about available resources, chances for successful resolution, and other legal matters.

For simple payment-due problems, a general practitioner or a collection lawyer may be hired to perform services similar to that of a collection agency. The psychological effect of receiving a lawyer's letter or call often produces a quick resolution to a dispute.

When a dispute must be cleared up before payment can be made, engaging a lawyer to negotiate with the client might be helpful. The lawyer may be able to take a more forceful role on the graphic artist's behalf and may bring about a fairer and quicker settlement. A lawyer's presence and negotiation skills may also avoid a lawsuit. When the problem is resolved, and if it proves advisable, a lawyer can provide a written agreement to bring complex issues to a final and binding close.

If the dispute involves the graphic artist's legal rights in, and economic control over, artwork, a lawyer specializing in art-related law should be selected. It is important that the lawyer is familiar with applicable copyright laws and trade practices, as well as the business aspects of the artist's profession. In addition, an attorney's expertise in a specific area should be verified through direct questioning and by checking references. If you think your case might actually go to trial, do not hire an attorney who has no litigation experience, no matter how great he or she may be at negotiating contracts.

The Graphic Artists Guild offers its members access to its Legal Referral Service by contacting the Guild's National Office. Fees and expenses should be negotiated directly between the member and the attorney and are the sole responsibility of the member.

Lawyers' fees and structures vary. Some charge a flat fee; others charge a percentage of the monies recovered. Initial one-time consultation fees may be low. Graphic artists should discuss fees with the attorney before requesting and/or accepting advice or assistance. Graphic artists with limited income may want to take advantage of volunteer arts-related lawyer groups. Most Volunteer Lawyers for the Arts organizations place limitations on income for assistance eligibility (see Chapter 15 for a list of organizations).

SUING IN CIVIL COURT

Suing in civil court, or federal district court, is not usually necessary to resolve a payment or other dispute. Court should be considered a last resort, to be used only if all other options for resolving the problem have been exhausted. If big guns are brought out in a lawsuit early in a dispute, there's nothing to fall back on, but if other options have been exhausted, the only remaining choice is a court case, with an attorney's help.

Other cases that must be brought to civil court include monetary claims that exceed the small-claims court limit. Violation of copyright laws can be resolved only in federal court; current law requires that a work's copyright is registered with the U.S. Copyright Office before a federal case for copyright infringement can be initiated. Other nonmonetary issues, such as suing for the return of original artwork or other contractual breaches, must also be taken to civil court.

The graphic artist does not necessarily have to hire a lawyer in order to sue. The law allows a person to appear as his or her own lawyer; in disputes where the issue is clear, graphic artists will usually not be at a disadvantage if they represent themselves. For disputes that do not involve large sums of money, a lawyer may be hired to advise the graphic artist on how to prepare the case, rather than for formal representation, which will help keep legal costs down.

When a lot of money or complex legal issues are involved, it is prudent to hire a lawyer. In such cases, the fee structure and expenses should be discussed with the lawyer at the outset. An attorney usually will bill time either by the hour or work for a contingency fee. Attorneys who accept a contingency (generally, $1/_3$ of an award or judgment, plus expenses) feel confident that they have a good chance of winning and are willing to risk their time to pursue it. If an attorney will accept a case only by billing time, it may be a signal for the graphic artist to re-evaluate the chances of winning the case or to review the amount that can realistically be recovered.

Marketing & Self Promotion

One of the most vital, but frequently neglected, aspects of being a graphic artist—which applies to all artists in all disciplines who function as independent contractors—is marketing and self promotion. Every graphic artist should see promotion as a top priority in maintaining a consistent, steady flow of work. It is best to avoid the obvious dilemma: when it is busy, there's no time for it; when it is not, it is too late.

Graphic artists need to show potential clients their work and position themselves advantageously to develop ongoing client relationships or to get more work or a better type of work. Promotion also enhances the studio's image or identity. It shows a creator's thinking: his or her ability to innovate, attract attention, and articulate a unique style or approach.

Keys to successful marketing include establishing a clear identity for a studio or firm, targeting desirable clients, and routinely reminding prospective clients of available services through ongoing promotion.

Establishing an identity

Pinpointing the kind of work you want to do, what interests you most, and what you do best helps define a clear identity for your studio or firm. If you have trouble doing that, it may be useful to hire a management consultant to help you devise a marketing plan.

Targeting clientele

Defining the ideal clients and then creating a market strategy to target those potential clients is critical. If you want to develop new business in a particular area, such as banking or health care, research into departments in those organizations that use graphic art services, followed by direct mailings, is crucial.

Maintaining a contact list

An essential aspect of good marketing is compiling and maintaining a list of contacts and updating it at least once a year to keep it fresh and relevant. Lists targeted to particular industries can be purchased, or the artist can ask for referrals from current clients, business acquaintances, suppliers, or generous colleagues. Also available are marketing consultants who can help graphic artists develop lists and devise mailings based on what has worked for other clients in the past.

Scheduling promotions

To be effective, graphic artists need to schedule promotions at key intervals throughout the year. An example might be a series of postcards with a common theme but with changing copy sent out periodically (monthly, bi-monthly, etc.) or postcards with a seasonal theme or message sent out four times a year. Sending out an attractive and creative periodic marketing piece that also contains useful information will be appreciated by the client. The information might be something that is helpful to the artist-client relationship of the targeted clientele, or it might be tips on a more general subject that most people would find interesting or useful.

At the very least, try to make a memorable statement at least once a year. Sending out a tear sheet with a recent illustration or a press release about the latest award in a trade magazine annual acts as a timely reminder; including an enticing reference to a web site makes the piece doubly effective. Some graphic artists send out a self-designed or self-illustrated holiday card to clients and colleagues. A holiday card accomplishes both social and business purposes: it lets clients know they are thought of and appreciated; it keeps the artist in the clients' minds; and it showcases the artist's creativity (especially talents that the client might not normally see). Clients are known to keep memorable holiday cards on display in their offices. To stand out from the crowd, artists might send out a unique greeting for a holiday other than the December holidays or for a holiday that ties in with the image that they want to project (e.g., a design firm that wants to promote green design might send out a card on Earth Day).

For major and repeat clients, some artists expand the holiday card concept to a gift that showcases their talent. The most common are useful items that keep the artist in the client's mind all year, such as a calendar. Other artists hold annual events to thank clients and supporters, such as a studio open house with artwork offered at discounted prices.

Ongoing promotion

Staying on the radar screen of existing and prospective clients is vital. Though most people do not like sending out cold mailings or making cold calls, they are among the many traditional ways of attracting new business. The artist should do them only if he or she enjoys doing them; otherwise, they may be a waste of time. The best marketing plans integrate a combination of strategies that utilize print, electronic media, and face-to-face communication and that cross-promote among the three. For example, the artist's web site, an e-letter, or a postcard can be used to announce his/her upcoming exhibit. Likewise, the exhibit not only showcases the artist's creativity but also provides opportunity for the artist to meet and engage with prospective clients, discuss business services, and have business cards and brochures on hand for attendees to take with them. Marketing plans should be continually adjusted by artists, based on what strategies prove to be the most and least successful for their particular situation. Colleagues, vendors, and friends should also be targeted in promotional efforts because they can be a source of referral to new clients or they might become future clients themselves.

Increasingly, artists are finding the Internet to be a source of many alternative ways to attract new clients and to keep existing clients interested in them. Some of the online tools graphic artists are using for marketing and promotion are:

- **Personal Web Sites**
  For visual creators, a personal web site is becoming more and more of a necessity for creating a business identity, describing and promoting services, and displaying examples of work. Keep it fresh by updating info and changing images frequently. Don't forget to promote the web site by including the URL in any print materials you send out or by including live links to it in e-mail and other electronic media.

- **Links to Personal Web Sites**
  To drive business to your site, include a live link to your site from wherever you can. Make sure you are linking from sites with which you want to be associated. Many professional organizations offer their members a link from their web site to those of their members. An example is the Member Portfolios section of the Graphic Artists Guild web site (www.graphicartistsguild.org). Potential clients and art buyers can search the portfolio section by artistic discipline. Full Members can choose up to three disciplines under which to be listed.

- **Portfolio Web Sites & Pages**
  Portfolio web sites are sites specifically designed for creative professionals to display their work—for a monthly or annual fee. Some allow you to sell your work from the site. The amount of text allowed varies but usually includes at least the artist's contact information and an artist's statement. These sites often provide layout and design options for displaying your work. They can be a relatively inexpensive alternative for artists who don't have their own web site. However, before posting your work on one of these sites, read its terms and conditions section to make sure you are not relinquishing any copyrights by posting your work.

  Some professional organization web sites offer its members a portfolio "page" to display work. The cost of displaying work is either nominal or offered free as a benefit of membership.

- **Online Directories**
  These are online versions of established advertising directories (see the Sources of Illustration and Design Talent section in Chapter1). For an annual fee, artists can display their work, list their disciplines and artistic styles, and provide their contact information. Many include a live link to the artist's personal web site.

- **Social Networking Sites**
  Social networking sites are the electronic equivalent of the business networking event. Artists are increasingly using these sites for

visibility and to connect with professionals working in the same or related fields. The best sites are those that are more business-oriented and which offer opportunities to be recommended by others and to post availability for work. Personal and professional information can be changed or updated at any time. Being listed on a social networking site also increases your visibility in search engines on the Internet.

- **E-letters**

E-letters are informative e-mails sent periodically (monthly, bi-monthly, etc.) to keep graphic artists in the minds of existing and prospective clients. To stand out from normal e-mail communication, e-letters should contain a certain amount of formatting and styling, especially color, and include a business logo and images where appropriate. The most attractive ones look more like print pieces than e-mail, but they have all the advantages of electronic media (low cost, immediacy, ease of editing and tailoring to targeted specific audiences, and reaching large numbers of people). The information included in an e-letter can range from the purely business (new services offered, recent jobs, change in contact info, etc.) to a mix of business and general interest information. They can also be targeted to specific clients or businesses. However, regardless of the kind of information included, e-letters should provide something that the recipient will find useful, interesting, or entertaining, either in the text and images or through live links to other useful resources. Remember, the purpose is for you to stand out in the receiver's mind.

- **Blogs**

The best feature of blogs is their interactive capability, which enables bloggers to share information and solutions to problems with other people in their field as well as with prospective clients. Artists can create their own blog on or linked to their web site, or they can increase their visibility by contributing to other professionals' art, business, communication, or technology-related blogs on a regular basis. Many professional organizations have blogs on their web sites where members can share information with each other. Blogs are an excellent way to demonstrate your expertise on a particular subject that ties in with the services you provide, without doing a hard sell. They also reveal something about your personality in a way that traditional self-promotion does not. Blogging also has the added benefit of increasing your ranking on search engines. However, if you decide to create your own blog, be aware of the time it takes to post messages frequently in order to keep it fresh and make it a resource that people will want to keep coming back to.

It may help to think of your career as a long-term promotion or identity campaign. It is actually a building process. It lets clients know you have longevity and staying power. If you persist, promotion should pay off, but you have to be willing to invest both time and money to make it work. Whatever you do, make sure you get noticed. The first rule of promotion is to get the client's attention.

There are numerous resources available for the graphic artist to learn more about marketing and self-promotion: books, magazines, web sites, local Chambers of Commerce, courses, workshops, and presentations at conferences and trade shows. For a list of books about marketing and self promotion, see Chapter 15, Resources & References.

Maximizing Income

Maximizing the income potential of artwork both enables artists to sustain and improve their business and provides art buyers with options for solving their needs. While reuse—the sale of additional rights to existing artwork—has long been standard practice, this market has exploded in recent years, while licensing and merchandising markets for new artwork have also grown. Stock illustration—existing artwork whose rights are sold for other uses—is a highly controversial issue within the visual communications industry. Artists are generally wary of stock agencies that dominate the resale market and tend to undercut prices for illustration, preferring to control stock sales themselves, while graphic designers appreciate the easy access to affordable artwork that stock provides. In the best of all worlds, commissioned illustration and stock sales should be complementary rather than competing markets.

Reuse

Reuse is an opportunity for all artists and an important area of income for many. The artist, authorized agent, or copyright holder sells the right to reproduce artwork originally commissioned for one specified use for new or additional uses. By trade custom, the term "stock art" in general illustration markets means copyrighted artwork for which the user negotiates a pay-per-use license or use fee. It also includes typographic alphabets (usually prepared in digital form and licensed to buyers by type houses) and typographic dingbats, usually sold as clip art.

Reuse may also be called "second rights" (though it may actually be the third, fourth, or fifteenth time the rights have been sold). In publishing they are called "subsidiary rights" and are grants of usage in addition to what the project was originally commissioned for, such as when a chapter from a book is sold to a magazine before the book is published. In merchandising, where existing art may sell for many different uses to many different clients, grants of usage rights are called "licensing."

Selling reuse rights represents a logical step in extending the value of artwork through the length of the copyright. Over the artist's lifetime plus 70 years, judicious control of a work's copyright and uses can generate a lot more income for an illustrator than the original rights grant. One source calculated that advertising and corporate sales of mostly photo stock accounted for 65 percent of the total use of stock art; textbook, trade, and educational publishing accounted for 15 percent, with magazines and newspapers taking another 15 percent.

The growing market for reuse fuels the debate about whether stock illustration sales reduce new commissions or harm artists by overexposing or undercontrolling the appearance of an illustration. The continuous improvements and growth in technology heighten the debate. Methods of cataloging and presenting stock art have improved dramatically, thanks to advances in computers, CDs, and the Internet. Digital technology has increased compact storage, as well as enabled quicker searches, retrievals, and presentations; reduced the risk of artwork being swiped or copied; and accelerated transmission and digital delivery to platemaking or electronic end products. And technology also enables graphic artists to customize existing images to meet the needs of a new client and charge fees that reflect the customized image.

Reuse may be sought by the original client, who wishes to expand the original project or use it in a new campaign. Or a prospective buyer may want to use art seen in a directory, stock catalog, or other promotional material. Some buyers may even plan a proposed project around a particular image; if the desired image is not available, they will have to be flexible about using other work that is available or commission original work. Sometimes artists envision and market a reuse; for example, an artist may propose using an existing image for a greeting card, calendar, or editorial insert.

The aesthetic is different when using existing artwork rather than commissioned illustration; the art buyer knows exactly what he or she is getting. The client's risk of being unfavorably surprised is avoided. On the other hand, an element of creativity is eliminated, as is the traditional excitement of collaboration between art director and illustrator and the thrill of creating/receiving a superlative new illustration.

The economic climate and the growth in uses of stock illustration are creating new niches for existing artwork. It is up to each artist to seek them out in order to better fulfill the artwork's potential value. Artists interested in reselling rights must make individual marketing decisions about the best avenues for reuse sales for their inventory of images.

Any discussion of reuse is predicated on an artist's control and ownership of rights. Artists who relinquish control by accepting work-for-hire and all-rights conditions are forever locked out of reuse markets and other sources of potential income.

WHO SHOULD HANDLE REUSE SALES?

Artists, stock agencies, and artists' representatives may each claim they know the stock market best and can negotiate the most appropriate reuse fees.

Artists Many artists like to handle their own reuse sales, but there are advantages and disadvantages to that arrangement. On the one hand, artists have to handle all the usual record keeping connected with an illustration assignment without the excitement of creating a new image. On the other hand, a little paperwork can produce welcome additional income from an inventory of existing images.

Handling reuse sales themselves allows artists to determine the client's needs firsthand and to custom-tailor the agreement, fee, and quality of the artwork's reproduction. Knowing their own body of work, artists may come up with more options or an image better suited to the client's needs, while at the same time establishing a relationship that might result in future assignments. If a potential client contacts an artist with a possible commission but an insufficient budget, the artist can suggest reusing an existing image that conveys a similar message. Artists may feel they are best qualified to set reuse fees because of their knowledge of their own work relative to the field, their reputation, and their comfort with negotiating.

To handle sales of reuse rights, artists must be willing to maintain accurate records of usage rights agreements for all illustrations (see the section on Keeping Track, earlier in this chapter); monitor sales to prevent conflicts and unauthorized usage; handle contracts, invoices, and shipping; and manage all the other usual overhead tasks of the illustration business. (Artists may also need to warehouse slides or transparencies of any artwork they do not store electronically.) Artists who maintain careful records can sell reuse rights to images that could not be handled through a stock agency (agencies often require images with completely or widely available rights). If necessary, artists may be able to negotiate the reversion of desired reuse rights from a client.

Reuse pricing is as complex as pricing for original commissioned art, and no percentage of an original commissioned fee has been set that is common to all markets. The primary criterion for setting pricing should be how the client chooses to use the work. If the client derives great value from its reuse of the work, then the artist should feel free to set a fee, commensurate with the new use, that is higher than that for the original use. Artists should also take the usual factors—size, geographic region, exclusivity of market, time frame, and media—into consideration when setting reuse prices.

Some markets, such as greeting cards, corporate advertising, and textbooks, are known to pay 50 to 100 percent of an original commissioned rate for reuse. Others, such as editorial, usually pay a percentage of the commissioned rate. Resale rights are usually sold at less than the rate of commissioned work, though not if the artist controls the sale and determines that the new use warrants a higher rate. Fees vary wildly on reuse and resale, depending on the use, the medium, and the exposure of the original artwork. Generally speaking, it is wise not to commit to a reuse/resale fee in your original contract. Just stipulate that there will be a reuse/resale fee to be negotiated later. When the request is made, base the fee on the factors outlined above.

To maximize stock illustration sales, some artists feature images available for resale in targeted promotions or on their web sites. If art is featured on a web site, it needs to be displayed in a format that is protected against unauthorized use.

Artists' representatives Artists' representatives may sell reuse rights on behalf of artists as part of the normal artist-agent agreement. Reps are in a good position to negotiate reuse fees, custom-tailor reuse agreements to the clients' needs, and monitor compliance with purchase agreements. Often these agreements are handled just like newly commissioned work: the artist usually receives 75 percent of the fee, with 25 percent going to the rep. Artists usually retain the right to refuse a sale; they also receive tear sheets of the final printed piece.

Though this type of contract has been standard for commissioned artwork, reps may choose to handle reuse differently than commissioned art. For example, while the usual artist-agent split of 75-25 percent is a clear advantage to the artist over the 50-50 percent split of usual stock agency agreements (see below), reps may change the percentage split to match those in stock agreements if they want their businesses to more closely resemble stock agency marketing. Artists are always free to negotiate more favorable terms.

Many reps prefer to handle reuse sales of images originally commissioned through their efforts, or appearing on promotional materials carrying their name, rather than have the artist or a stock house manage them. Having negotiated one-time or limited rights in the initial agreement, reps often feel they deserve the opportunity to market the rights that were reserved to the artist through their efforts. Artist-agent contracts should specify whether the rep will handle such sales and, if so, whether that is an exclusive arrangement. Artists and reps whose relationships predate the rise of the reuse market can attach a letter of agreement to their contract, detailing the new arrangements.

Artists' reps who have long-standing relationships with their artists and handled the initial agreement with the client are well positioned to market reuses that both protect the artist's reputation and avoid stepping on the original client's toes. Some reps also handle reuses of images that did not originate with them. Among the marketing techniques employed by some reps are establishing a special stock division on terms similar to those at stock agencies and developing special promotions of images judged to be particularly marketable. It may take a different kind of marketing to achieve successful, sustained reuse sales; the clients are not necessarily the same as those for commissioned work. Only the particular artists' rep can decide whether it is in his or her interest and ability to pursue stock illustration sales.

Stock agencies Stock illustration was introduced by stock agencies or houses that were already established as sources of stock photography; several illustration-only agencies, including international ones, have since been founded to handle stock art. The gross worldwide revenue for the stock art market, both photography and illustration, was estimated to be $1.8 billion in 2007—a huge leap from $200 million in the mid-1990s. Of primary concern to illustrators is that stock illustration sales may, as with stock photography, reduce the demand for originally commissioned work.

Though stock illustration evolved from stock photography, the significant differences in how artwork and photography are created affect each genre's opportunities in the stock market. Photographers create many images in the course of doing business; illustrators create fewer images over their lifetime. This means that illustrators have fewer potentially income-producing copyrights. But the growth of the stock illustration business argues that a market exists. As demand grows, illustrators hope the market will provide them with additional, and more lucrative, sources of income.

Stock agencies market images to prospective buyers through catalogs, directories, direct mail, CDs, the Internet, and other promotions. The artist grants the agency the right, usually exclusive (though in some cases this is negotiable), to resell selected images from the artist's existing work to specified markets for a certain length of time (usually up to five years or for the shelf life of the promotional vehicle in which the work appears), for a fee set by the agency.

A rollover clause used to be common in agency contracts, whereby artists must notify the agency within 30 days of the five-year completion to end the agreement. If such notification is not received, the contract is automatically renewed for another five years. In actual cases, stock agencies stated that they would not hold artists to this stringent requirement; nonetheless, rollover contracts put the burden on the artist and make renegotiation

---

SOME CONSIDERATIONS ON CHOOSING A STOCK HOUSE

Artists may want to ask the following questions of a stock house when considering a relationship:

• What markets is the house strongest in?

• What portion of its sales is below the set minimum fee level?

• How many artists is the house working with?

• What are the names of artists it represents who would be willing to provide references?

more difficult. These days computer tracking makes it easy for agencies to notify artists of contract terminations, and some prominent agencies have taken rollover clauses out of their contracts.

The stock agency and the illustrator usually split the proceeds of whatever rights the agency sells. Interviews with major illustration stock houses indicate that the usual agency-artist splits can range from an 80/20 split (depending on the agency, you may get the 80 percent or you may get the 20 percent) to 50/50. Many of the newer royalty-free stock houses give artists a flat fee for each use, which is the least profitable option. Increasingly, there is no difference between domestic and foreign rights, although, if another agency is involved, you may earn 40-30-30 for foreign sales, with 40 percent withheld by the foreign agency. The royalty-free agencies are changing the face of stock photography and illustration, making them increasingly competitive and less profitable. Stock agencies usually quote reuse prices, though still negotiable, by referring to in-house charts that rely upon such factors as market, reproduction size, print run, and number of photos to be used as benchmarks. For instance, a large sale of many images may result in a low price per image, with the profit to the agency derived from search fees charged to the client for each hour the agency's staff searches their libraries.

Artists may find that fees negotiated by stock agencies are significantly lower than they would negotiate for themselves. Agencies send out periodic checks with sales reports, usually quarterly or monthly, that list the sale, the client's name, and sometimes the media in which it appeared, but not the terms of the reuse. Many artists feel the last information is vital in order to accurately calculate the income generated from each reuse. Although some agencies request tear sheets, they do not guarantee that they will send samples to the artists.

Artists under contract to a stock agency do not have the right to refuse a sale, except by indicating in the contract any off-limit markets such as pornography or cigarette and liquor advertising. Some agencies do contact artists at their discretion to discuss a proposed sale.

Some stock agencies grant clients the right to alter, tint, crop, or otherwise manipulate images; others do not. This right is usually listed in the agency's delivery memo, which states standard terms governing the client's purchase of rights, but it is usually not addressed in the artist-agency contract. Very few agencies discuss intended alterations with the artist or arrange to have the client contact the artist to discuss changes.

When a client commissions new work from an artist through a stock agency and the agency acts as agent and negotiates the fee with the client, the agency usually takes a 25 to 30 percent commission—depending on the stock house—and in this economic climate, fees are up for grabs. Increasingly, anything goes. When new work is commissioned through a stock agency for an illustrator who has a representative, the agency allows the rep to negotiate the price and takes a smaller finder's fee (usually 10 percent) or has the buyer contact the rep directly.

Some unrepresented illustrators do not wish to have a stock agency represent them for commissioned work. Illustrators have negotiated artist-agency contracts in which the artist handles the fee and contract negotiations directly with the client and pays the agency a 10 percent finder's fee for attracting new work rather than a full rep's commission. Some agencies do not request a finder's fee for commission referrals. However, beware of the terms of the contract—most demand payment for the life of your work with the client. And many will charge fees well in excess of the 10% suggested here unless you negotiate otherwise.

Occasional errors or abuses have occurred with agencies reporting fees received. These would be minimized if artists received a copy of the agency-client delivery memo or invoice with regularly reported sales and income, allowing them to verify prices and terms of sales. Ensuring that artists see the terms of sale and a sample of the published result would also aid in monitoring the client's compliance with the delivery memo. Some artist-agency agreements include the right to audit the agency's books by a certified public accountant.

ADVANTAGES AND DISADVANTAGES OF WORKING WITH STOCK AGENCIES

There is no question that artists want to maximize the income potential from a lifetime of work, leaving all such revenues to their heirs. There is, however, considerable controversy in the industry about how best to do that.

Arguments in favor of artists marketing artwork through a stock agency

- Agencies offer the artist the chance of generating high-volume reuse sales for little additional work on the artist's part.
- Artists have more time to create while the agency does the selling.
- Artists can pick particular images to be licensed to an agency while retaining others to market personally.
- Stock agency sales may help introduce an artist's work to new clients or new markets.
- The burden of keeping up with new technology and markets is left to the agency.
- Some agencies are expert at getting their images before buyers.

In short, the stock agency offers artists the possibility of additional sales for less work on their part.

Arguments against artists selling reuses through stock agencies

- The artist does not determine or negotiate the fee for a sale.
- The artist pays a high commission (50 percent or more) for each sale.

- The artist yields control over the integrity of the art or where it appears.
- Many stock houses are now large, impersonal corporations that seek control and rights to art that may not be in the artist's best interests.
- Increased use of stock may negatively affect the market for originally commissioned works.

Advantages for clients to use stock agencies

- Agencies provide complete, available images that can be delivered immediately with ensured results.
- An art director saves time negotiating directly with the agency, rather than with the artist, client, and/or the designer.
- Digital catalogs offer the art director a large number of images without liability for loss of original artwork.
- Stock may serve as an introduction to an artist's work that leads to commissioned assignments for future needs.

Disadvantages for clients to use stock agencies

- Clients miss the chance to discover the artist's skills as a problem-solver and creative collaborator.
- Searching through large numbers of files is time-consuming, and the cost of the designer's time plus the use fee may exceed the price of custom art.

TRADE PRACTICES & CONTRACTS FOR REUSE SALES

The artist, agent, or stock agency must be clear about which reproduction rights were transferred to the previous buyer and which the artist retained. It is, of course, illegal to sell a usage that breaches an existing contract on exclusivity of market, time frame, geographic region, and so on. It is accepted practice that an artist or agent will not sell a use that competes with another use, though the definition of competing uses may be hard to articulate. In general, a reuse should not be in the same market and time frame or for a competing client or product.

Paperwork relating to the sale of an image should always be reviewed carefully if there is any doubt about rights previously sold. Contracts for reuse rights, whether drawn up by artists, their reps, or stock agencies, should state clearly what usage is being granted and the intended market, the size of the reproduction, the print run, the length of the agreement, and so on. Other negotiating points might include reasonable payment schedules, alteration policies, access to accounting records, receipt of copies of delivery memos, and tear sheets. (For more information on artist-agent agreements, see Chapter 1, Professional Relationships.)

Artists who wish to have their stock illustration sales conducted by artists' representatives or agencies should discuss all reuse agreements and contracts carefully so all terms are fully understood and agreed upon by both parties. Artists considering prewritten contracts should remember that many points are negotiable; they may wish to consult a lawyer and/or other artists before signing a contract.

Artists considering signing with a stock illustration agency or artists' rep may also want to review a copy of the firm's standard delivery memo or invoice, which states the standard terms by which a client buys rights. Information such as whether tear sheets will be provided or alterations permitted is usually located in this agreement rather than in the contract the artist signs.

CLIP ART & RIGHTS-FREE ART

Grants of reuse rights for art sold as stock are not the same as clip art. Clip art consists of images that, once acquired, come with a grant of license for any use (though specific terms depend on the license agreement). Clip art can be any artwork that is in the public domain or camera- or computer-ready art to which all rights have been sold by the artist, with the understanding that such art may be altered, cropped, retouched, and used as often as desired. Clip art is available to the public in books and on CD. Some clip art distributors pay the collection artist a royalty on sales and give them name credit.

Clip art competes with both commissioned art and stock illustration. With increased digital imaging capability, designers can create new artwork solely by combining and altering clip art, although that may not be cost-effective when one considers the designer's investment of time and effort against the cost of a commissioned illustration.

One controversial way to market an artist's entire inventory as clip art is on rights-free CDs. Companies usually offer artists royalties on sales of the original disks but not on any additional uses, since all rights are sold outright. The purchasers may then use the work in any way they choose, including manipulating, combining, or otherwise changing the original for placement on products, in ads, or as characters in feature films.

Selling artwork on rights-free CDs gives the artist the opportunity to sell a large number of images at one time for an up-front fee and to receive royalties on sales of the CDs. Some illustrators fear that the release of many rights-free images at low fees will flood the market with low-priced images, discouraging art buyers from purchasing original work at more desirable rates.

The availability of rights-free art on CDs has also created new options for graphic designers, who have increased technological means of manipulating them. On the other hand, designers lose the experience of working with a knowledgeable and creative illustrator to generate new and exciting artwork made for their specific needs.

In the mid-1990s, well-known illustrator Seymour Chwast released a sizable inventory of his work on a CD, with some restrictions for high-revenue use. He reports that its release has not limited the amount of new work he has been offered. Each disk carries a label telling the user that rights to corporate or brand identities, logos, trademarks, symbols, or other images must be negotiated separately for use on merchandise to be sold, such as greeting cards or clothing. He did not establish a system to monitor all uses, both legal and illegal, of his work.

ONLINE SALES

Reuse sales (as well as general illustration sales) on the Internet are evolving rapidly and are often the preferred method of purchasing stock since it allows buyers to research numerous images themselves. Whereas only a handful of agencies sold illustrations online in 1997, today the marketplace is flooded with them. Some online services are set up to enable the buyer to locate an image by describing it in simple language or in keywords. This service is usually free until an image is chosen, but online registration is often required prior to being permitted to search the images.

UNAUTHORIZED REUSE

Reproduction of an image without the artist's or copyright holder's permission constitutes unauthorized reuse. It involves copyright infringement, and the infringer may be liable for attorney's fees and statutory damages if pursued in court. The same may be true of unauthorized alteration of an artist's image (for more information, see Chapter 2, Legal Rights & Issues, and Chapter 4, Technology Issues).

An art user who wishes to "pick up" an image from an already published source should first contact the artist to arrange for permission and payment of an appropriate usage fee. Failure to reach the artist is not sufficient excuse for unauthorized use of an image; legal due diligence (an earnest, concerted effort to obtain the necessary information) must be demonstrated.

Stories abound of artists' portfolio work being used without permission for client presentations. Digital images have made it even easier for those who engage in questionable business practices to produce "ripamatics" and include them in presentations—and artists are rarely, if ever, consulted, much less compensated. For instance, in 1995 one photographer's representative received a five-figure settlement from a major advertising agency when the photographer's portfolio was returned with the transparencies torn from the expensive matting. The agency had had the images duplicated, even though the rep had denied permission to do so. The issue surfaced again when *Direct* magazine reported that an artist sued after an agency allegedly had an illustration recreated by another illustrator with only slight changes for a large, direct-mail campaign for a major client—with no payment to the original artist. The case stirred debate among artists' groups, agents, reps, and directory publishers about how to stem this abuse.

In addition to the obvious issue of infringement, illegal comping directly affects the work of pre-production artists, whose livelihoods depend upon assignments to create comps, storyboards, and animatics. As the practice of illegal comping persists, these artists are finding it harder to secure work. In 1996, the Graphic Artists Guild brought together more than a dozen professional organizations in the "Ask First" educational campaign to inform the industry about the harmful aspects of these practices.

Artists who display their work via digital catalogs can use electronic watermarks, digital time stamping, and registries to protect their copyrights. Such methods clearly indicate ownership for protected art, as opposed to rights-free clip art, and are available as software. All such efforts have some merit, but the only sure way to protect one's electronic property is by registering the work with the Copyright Office (see the Copyright section of Chapter 2, Legal Rights & Issues). However, some stock photo houses permit limited comping use of their images, so it's important to check this when reviewing their client agreement.

An artist, artists' rep, or stock agent who notices an unauthorized reuse will usually contact the infringer and request an appropriate fee. Other remedies include legal action, which may involve receiving damages and court fees from the user. For instance, in late 2000, celebrity photographer Michael Grecco added Corbis to the $8.7 million suit he had brought against the Sygma agency in 1998, after discovering several new unlicensed uses of his work.

Both artists and buyers should clearly specify in writing the particular rights bought or sold, including whether the client has permission to scan or alter the art electronically. While vigilance and follow-through are important, a well-written agreement is currently the best overall protection for all parties' rights.

Licensing & merchandising

Licensing is big business, presenting tremendous opportunities for graphic artists of all disciplines to generate revenue in new markets. In 2008, retail sales of licensed products in the United States and Canada totaled $59.1 billion. According to the Licensing Industry Merchandisers Association (LIMA), manufacturers paid $5.7 billion in licensing royalties in the United States in 2008.

TOP SIX LICENSING ROYALTY REVENUE CATEGORIES

The estimated 2008 licensing royalty revenues for the top six categories are listed below in millions of dollars:

Entertainment	$ 2605
Trademarks/Brands	$ 975
Fashion	$ 775
Sports (leagues, individuals)	$ 740
Collegiate	$ 208
Art	$ 154

Source: International Licensing Industry Merchandisers' Association (LIMA). Annual Licensing Industry Survey, June 2, 2009.

LICENSING CATEGORIES

LIMA tracks licensing categories. In 2008, the top six categories in royalty revenue were entertainment, trademarks/brands, fashion, sports, collegiate, and art.

Entertainment, with 2008 royalty revenue of $2.6 billion, is the largest category in the licensing world. It includes movie properties such as *Shrek*, television properties such as *Sponge Bob*, and entertainment/personality properties such as Marilyn Monroe or George Clooney. The corporate brands category, with 2008 royalty revenue of $975 million, encompasses everything from Kellogg's to GE to Harley Davidson. Fashion licensing, with 2008 royalty revenue of $775 million, features names such as Tommy Hilfiger and Ralph Lauren. Sports licensing ($740 million in 2008) includes individual teams, the NFL, NASCAR, etc., and collegiate licensing ($208 million) involves both the name of a university, as well as its sports teams.

ART LICENSING

Like all other categories of licensing (except collegiate), art licensing was affected negatively by the consumer spending slump of 2008, with royalty revenue of $154 million (down from $175 million in 2007). Nevertheless, art licensing has been one of the top six in royalty revenues out of nine licensing categories for the past several years. In 2008, the $5.15 billion in retail sales of art-licensed products (up $2.9 billion since 2005) came from the following product categories (percentages show a category's share of the total sales, rounded to the nearest percent):

7 %	gifts and novelties
3 %	home décor
4 %	housewares
5 %	paper products
10 %	accessories
12 %	apparel
7 %	publishing
12 %	food and beverage
7 %	health and beauty
5 %	infant products
8 %	toys and games

Art licensing basics Two terms are of particular importance in licensing: licensor and licensee. The artist or owner/creator of the design or property is called the licensor. The entity that acquires the rights to use the design or property is referred to as the licensee. In art licensing, artists license the right to reproduce their work on a specific product (e.g., a photo album), in a certain territory (e.g., North America, Australia, worldwide, etc.), for a specified period of time (which is usually two to three years), and sometimes for a particular distribution channel (e.g., mass market, specialty, home shopping, etc.). The artist/licensor maintains the right to license the same design in North America for a different product—perhaps a magnet or a mug—or to license the rights for the same product to a manufacturer who will only sell the product in

LICENSING CATEGORIES

Some of the many categories in which artists can license their designs include

Accessories (jewelry, buttons, headbands, etc.)
Apparel (T-shirts, hats, other clothing items)
Crafts (stickers, scrapbooking items, rubber stamps, craft kits, etc.)
Domestics (bedding, rugs, and throws)
Electronics (cell phones, screen savers, electronic games)
Games/toys (everything from puzzles to plush)
Garden (flags, banners, birdhouses, gardening products)
Gift and collectibles (candles, picture frames, boxes, figurines)
Gift Packaging (gift wrap, tissue, bags, cards)
Home décor (wall paper, wall décor, etc.)
Home Furnishings (lamps, tables, chairs, etc.)
Housewares (tabletop, kitchen, etc.)
Infant products (bibs, baby bedding, baby clothing, diapers)
Kitchenware (cutting boards, coasters, towels, trivets, etc.)
Novelty (magnets, key chains, pencil toppers, etc.)
Party (paper goods, balloons, decorations)
Personal care (soap, fragrances, etc.)
Pet products (food bowls, treats, clothes, etc.)
Publishing (books, calendars, bank checks)
Stationery & paper goods (greeting cards, stationery, notepads, etc.)
Tabletop (melamine, ceramic, china, glassware)

Asia, South America, or somewhere else in the world not specified in the first licensing agreement.

The artist should avoid entering "all rights" licensing agreements because a single licensee does not produce product in every category. The ability to license the same design in different product categories and territories allows artists to maximize the earning potential of a particular image. It is extremely important to keep a "rights database," to track which rights have been licensed for each design.

Payment methods: flat fee vs. royalty Unlike other categories of licensing, art licensing does not necessarily involve royalties. Artists can license their work based on either a flat fee payment or on a royalty basis.

The advantage to a flat fee license is that the artist receives money up front, and therefore will not be dependent on the design selling successfully to get further income from it. Also, manufacturers tend to pay a higher flat fee than an advance against royalties. For example, a flat fee for a greeting card design generally ranges between $275 and $500, while an advance—if one is offered—against the average 5-percent royalty tends be between $100 and $250. Because the gift and stationery industries are facing economic challenges, many manufacturers have stopped offering advances. They feel that they are spending tens of thousands of dollars to bring a product to market and that the artists should share in the risk.

Royalty rates vary depending on the industry: the print industry, for example, pays a 10 percent royalty, while the gift industry pays royalties between 5 and 8 percent. Rates also vary by distribution channel. For example, if a product is sold in the mass market (i.e., a major retailer, such as Wal-Mart or Target), the artist may only get a 2- or 3-percent royalty while the same product could receive an 8-percent royalty if sold in the specialty market (retail gift stores). However, the higher royalty may not generate the largest income. Artists must also take into consideration the potential volume of sales. Artists who have a product at Wal-Mart will invariably make more money, even at a 3-percent royalty rate, than they would if the product were sold in a gift store at an 8-percent royalty.

Royalty rates are also negotiable. If no advance is offered, an artist may ask for a higher royalty.

When working on a royalty basis, there is a difference between licensing an existing illustration and asking an artist to spend time creating something new. If a company commissions a design on a royalty basis, it is appropriate for it to pay the artist an advance in order to cover the time the artist must spend creating the artwork. If the company just wants to license an artist's existing work, an advance is not as critical, as the artist has not had to spend additional time and will start receiving royalty income sooner than if an advance has to be paid off. In other words, no advance means that the artist receives the royalty income sooner.

Some companies, especially start-up concerns, may not have an effective distribution system in place, and if they can't get the product into stores, there will be no sales, so they won't be paying any royalties on it. Artists are advised not to work on a royalty arrangement with start-up companies.

To determine if a royalty arrangement is appropriate, an artist should first ask how many pieces the client plans to produce for its initial and subsequent manufacturing runs. Then the artist can evaluate the options and strike the best deal.

Creating licensable artwork It is important for an artist who is thinking of entering the licensing market to understand why companies manufacture product and what types of designs they are looking for before creating designs specifically for licensing. Many of the companies that license art manufacture gift items. Art appropriate for Christmas and other seasonal needs, as well as life events (birth, birthday, wedding, etc.) is always sought by licensees.

In the competitive licensing world, it is advisable for artists to provide their artwork in a format that is easy for their licensees to apply to product templates. The best way to do that is to create a "themed collection"—a group of coordinated images that an art director can mix and match to create a saleable product line. This includes a central illustration (or a pair of illustrations) with coordinating frames, borders, background patterns, and icons. It is important to provide these digitally, in layered PhotoShop files.

Developing a marketing plan One step in developing a marketing plan is to become familiar with the different categories in which artists can license their designs. See the sidebar for a sample of licensing categories.

Artists should select and prioritize the categories in which they wish to find a licensee, and then research each one to identify those licensees that have a good reputation. Resources and methods for researching categories include:

Trade shows
Magazines
Web sites
Books
Licensing consultants
Networking

There are trade shows geared to each of the categories above. Attending them can help artists identify companies they would like to approach. If attending a trade show isn't feasible, it is possible to gain a lot of information about a company by surfing the Internet and reading trade magazines and books on art licensing. *Art Licensing 101* by Michael Woodward is very informative. A licensing consultant can also help artists identify companies to approach, and networking with other artists who are licensing their work already is an effective way to get information about which manufacturers are easy and desirable to work with. There is an e-mail licensing group on Yahoo, which many designers find helpful (http://groups.yahoo.com/group/TheArtofLicensing/).

Licensing agents The advantage of working with a licensing agent is that agents have contacts with creative directors at a number of companies and can get their client's work seen by the right people. Agents usually handle all the marketing, contract negotiation, billing, and paperwork, so artists are able to concentrate what they do best—create art. Often agents also provide valuable advice on trends, colors, and themes. The main disadvantage of working with agents is that they generally take a 40- to 50-percent commission and sometimes require a monthly retainer until a licensee is secured. Another disadvantage of agents is that because they represent more than one artist, they cannot focus exclusively on the needs of an individual artist. (For more about working with agents, see Chapter 1, Professional Relationships.)

An artist-agent relationship is similar to a marriage—a good one takes work. Licensing agents often specialize in specific product categories or property types, so it makes sense for graphic artists to contact agents in their specialty. Once such an agent is found, the Graphic Artists Guild recommends interviewing the artists the agent already represents to get an idea of what can be expected from the relationship. Some artists hire a licensing consultant (who charges hourly for advice) to help determine if having an agent is in their best interest. Before signing with an agent, artists are advised to be sure they are comfortable with the agent's contract, especially the termination clause.

Protecting ideas Whether dealing with potential licensees or with a licensing agent, graphic artists should be careful to protect their ideas by copyrighting their work and by using a nondisclosure agreement, which protects ideas that are not yet fixed in a tangible, copyrightable form. A model nondisclosure agreement is found in the Appendix.

Licensing resources Three good sources for licensors, licensees, and licensing agents are the *North American Licensing Industry Buyers Guide, The Licensing Letter,* and the International Licensing Industry Merchandiser's Association (LIMA). Another excellent book on licensing is *Licensing Art & Design* by Caryn Leland. Model licensing agreements, reprinted with permission from the book, appear in the Appendix: Contracts & Forms. (For contact information and additional resources, see Chapter 15, Resources & References.)

Limited-edition prints

While original artwork may sell for thousands of dollars, lithography and serigraphy have made the collection of limited-edition prints, numbered and signed by the graphic artist, within reach of the average collector. Art for limited-edition prints may be created independently by graphic artists or under contract with a gallery or publisher. Recent survey data show that payment is made on a commission or royalty basis, and an advance is usually included. Both the advance and the payment to the artist vary, depending on, among other factors, the size of the print run, the number of colors printed, and the selling price. A typical financial arrangement for limited-edition prints is for the graphic artist to receive an advance against 50 to 67 percent of gross sales revenues, with the gallery receiving a commission of 25 to 50 percent. In many cases, the prints are submitted to a gallery on spec. The gallery receives a similar commission, although it is more likely to be on the lower end if it's placed on spec. If the gallery or publisher is responsible for all production costs, advertising, and promotion, graphic artists traditionally receive less.

A typical edition ranges from 100 to 250 prints. Each print is usually numbered and signed by the graphic artist. The agreement usually guarantees the artist a certain number of proofs to use in any way he or she wishes. Artists should be aware that limited editions numbering 200 or fewer are granted special moral rights protections under the Visual Artists Rights Act (see Chapter 2, Legal Rights & Issues).

Marketing can make or break a limited-edition venture. Market research should be conducted prior to entering into a binding agreement, making significant outlays of money, or investing time in creating the art. The market for limited-edition prints is regulated by law in a number of states, including California, Georgia, Hawaii, Illinois, Maryland, Michigan, Minnesota, New York, North Carolina, Oregon, and South Carolina. Extensive disclosures or disclaimers may have to accompany limited-edition prints sold in these states.

Trade practices for graphic artists creating limited-edition prints are the same as those for greeting card, novelty, and retail goods illustration (see Chapter 10, Illustration Prices & Trade Customs).

Standard Contracts & Business Tools

This chapter describes why contracts are needed to define and protect business relationships. Seven different types of contracts are explained; contract terms are defined in the Glossary at the back of the book. This chapter also includes advice on what to do when things go wrong. Sample contracts for various graphic art assignments can be found in the Appendix: Contracts & Forms.

CONTRACTS

increasingly define the business side of graphic arts as the professional landscape of the graphic artist has changed dramatically over the last 15 years. Digital media, new technology, growing competition in the workplace, and the consolidation of publishing venues have all placed new demands on artists and on the companies who hire them. While clients routinely ask for more considerations, often without additional compensation, artists struggle to retain control and to bolster the value of their work.

At first glance, contracts may inspire dread, but they can make doing business much easier. When the basic concepts are understood, contracts can protect both the artist and the client. And contracts can provide a common working language by which each job can proceed. With a little time and patience, graphic artists can learn not only how to read their clients' contracts but also how to structure agreements that best represent their own interests.

The Importance of Contracts

There are always two perspectives on an assignment. Clients may assume they own more rights than the artist's fee dictates or that a kill fee represents 25 percent of the agreed-upon price. The graphic artist may expect to be paid immediately upon delivery, while the client routinely pays 30 days or more after publication. To avoid confusion and misunderstanding, a well-written contract defines the working relationship of the client and the artist, the use of the finished work, and how changes in the scope of the project are to be handled.

Most contracts provide:

- A definition of the project or assignment.
- Limitations on the use of the work.
- Terms for such professional issues as payment and artist's credit.
- Protection in the event of a dispute.

The most important fact to remember when reading a contract is that the person or business who drafts the contract is concerned with rights and controls that are advantageous to them. Their objective is to get the other party to agree to the protections laid out in the document. As independent contractors, artists should make every effort to present their own contracts. This may not always be possible, so having a clear understanding of contract language is important.

Graphic artists have the same advantages as clients when they read contracts. Although the legal language may seem daunting at first, every clause contains basic principles and concerns regarding the specific assignment and affecting general studio policy. With a little common sense and a glossary (see the Glossary for definitions of terms introduced in this chapter), artists can learn to understand and negotiate many legal documents.

How contracts protect

A contract is an agreement, whether oral or written, that defines the obligations and responsibilities of each party. One party makes an offer, usually containing terms that benefit that party. The second party considers the offer and negotiates terms to reflect their needs. Ideally, each party should benefit equally from the contract. Once both parties agree to the terms of the contract and sign it, the agreement is legally binding.

In written contracts, obligations are defined in paragraphs (clauses), and all terms within a contract are potentially subject to negotiation before the agreement is finalized. Clauses in graphic art contracts typically set business standards for payment and kill fees, the number of roughs or comps, alterations, licensing and copyright transfers, and dispute resolution.

Contract clauses also provide limitations on unauthorized uses of the finished work. Each party is notified that certain behavior is expected and that a breach of that behavior can result in legal proceedings. At times contract language may seem harsh, but the intent is to protect the signers from potential misunderstandings as the job proceeds.

It is important to understand and agree to terms before starting a job. Should an artist start a job after seeing a client's contract but without signing it, it could be argued that the artist has accepted the terms and that the contract is binding. By making sure all terms are agreed upon before starting, the graphic artist enjoys the protections of a binding contract.

Agreements that are straightforward, clearly written, and customized to the project and its use provide a positive work environment for both client and artist. The content should reflect the best interests of all parties, or at least an agreeable compromise. One-sided documents that require a signature without possibility of negotiation are not advantageous to either party.

Seven Basic Types of Contracts

Contracts can be as simple as an oral agreement or as complex as a multi-page document. Regardless of the scope of the project, a written contract is always advisable. Seldom will one standard contract be appropriate for every job, so flexibility and customization are key to drawing up contracts. Here are some of the more common types of contracts, ranging from the most simple to the more complex.

1. Oral agreement

While written agreements are always preferred, circumstances do not always allow for them. Thus, many jobs are assigned over the phone, where usually just the bare essentials are discussed: the work needed, the timeline for the work, where the work will be used, how it will be reproduced, and the compensation. The graphic artist orally accepts the client's terms over the phone or in person with a simple handshake. This type of agreement is legally binding. If a dispute arises over the terms of the agreement, however, proving what was actually intended can be difficult. Often one party's memory contradicts another's, and there is no set rule to determine what evidence will be allowed for review by the courts. If there are no witnesses or documents to prove the specific terms of the agreement, either side could prevail.

If a graphic artist has built a long-standing relationship with a client, an oral agreement may be adequate. Before accepting an oral agreement, certain things should be considered: Are you dealing with the owner of the business or a representative of the owner? Who will be accountable if there is a dispute in the agreement? Are you willing to take a risk with this person?

2. Letter of agreement or engagement

If an assignment is initiated by an oral agreement as described above, the artist will have more legal protection if he or she finalizes the deal with a one-page document defining the project. Called a "letter of agreement," this document can be very simple and should include a project description, what is due, when it is due, usage and ownership rights, kill fees, and so on. It is advisable to have a standard letter of agreement on file in your computer, which you can tailor to the project and fax to the client if time is limited.

3. Purchase order

Historically, companies have used purchase orders (POs) to assign work to contributors or to track jobs from assignment to payment. POs often resemble invoice forms, with a tracking number and a statement of the assignment and terms, which often appears in small print on the back or the bottom of the order. Many POs now function as contracts, including assignment of rights and more general terms, and require the graphic artist's signature before the job starts or before the artist's invoice can be processed for payment.

Purchase orders, however, can present a problem for the graphic artist. Because they are often general boilerplate documents, automatically sent out by buyers with each assignment, they do not clearly state the expectations and obligations of both parties for a specific assignment. Should a dispute about terms arise, graphic artists run the risk of not being as well protected as they would be with a custom contract. If there are unacceptable terms on a PO, the artist should cross them out using the addendum procedure outlined later in this chapter under "Working with client's contracts."

4. Working contract

This document is what everyone recognizes as a contract, complete with legal language and clauses. Regardless of its length, a working contract can be written in clear, concise language or convoluted, confusing terminology. Either way, artists are often intimidated by the appearance of a contract and for this reason do not properly review it before signing. It cannot be stressed enough how important it is to understand the meaning of each clause in a contract before signing it. If read with patience, even the most confusing contract can be understood.

Traditionally, detailed working contracts are usually used for more complex jobs that require periodic payments or royalties, such as books or other major commissions. As the electronic marketplace grows and the nature of corporate business changes, graphic artists must expect to deal with clients' growing demands for greater rights and control over projects. Increasingly, longer, more complicated contracts are used for such seemingly simple jobs as editorial assignments that in the past were covered by simple letters of agreement.

One strategy for coping with such client demands is for graphic artists to create their own working contracts that reflect their studio policies and basic business standards. The standard contract can then be customized to suit particular projects. Artists need to be prepared to deal with client contracts—always considering a contract a first offer to be negotiated. A client's contract, when properly negotiated, protects both parties equally.

5. Post-project "contracts"

Terms in small type at the bottom or on the back of a graphic artist's invoice, on the back of a client's check, or even on a purchase order sent from the client after receiving the artist's invoice are all examples of post-project contracts. The legality of such after-the-fact documents is questionable and subject to varying interpretation in the courts. Usually they do not require two signatures, which erodes their authority as agreements between two parties.

Using post-project contracts is not a smart business strategy for either artist or client. It is always best to promote open communication by using standard contracts and letters of agreement that can be easily customized, offered for discussion, and signed before the job begins. That way the job proceeds with all terms and expectations understood and agreed to by both parties. The time and expense invested in preparing them is minimal compared with the legal costs that may result if a dispute arises.

INVOICES

Invoice contracts are sometimes used by graphic artists and artists' representatives who do not want to alarm or intimidate clients with lengthy contracts. As with POs, the terms are usually preprinted and are not specific to the assignment at hand. It is important to point out that invoice contracts provide little legal protection, since no signatures are involved. To be legally binding, such forms must conform to an oral or written agreement made before the work was started.

CHECKS

Check contracts are the trickiest. Sometimes an artist receives a check for services rendered, but the amount represents less than the full, agreed-upon fee. Endorsing and cashing a check that states "payment in full" could possibly be considered acceptance by the artist of the lower payment for all the services rendered. In the 1995 federal case of *Playboy Enterprises, Inc. v. Dumas,* the court decided that payment in this form is not legal unless the check restates a "prior agreement, either explicit or implied, made before the creation of the work." (For a more detailed discussion of this case, see Chapter 2, Legal Rights & Issues.)

It is very important to note that in New York State this type of activity is legal and is considered payment in full. This could possibly hurt the artist. Before cashing any check that represents less than the agreed-upon amount, it is always advisable for the artist to verify that the check was not sent in lieu of full payment.

For a discussion of other problems associated with terms added to a client's check, see the Checks with Conditions section in Chapter 5, Essential Business Practices.

6. Boilerplate contract

A boilerplate contract contains generic or formulaic language (standard terminology). There are two definitions of a boilerplate contract. One is a document used as a general template for a wide range of projects, with clauses and elements that are altered to fit a particular project before the contract is offered. As a matter of studio policy, graphic artists should design their own boilerplate letters of agreement and working contracts for ongoing use. Then the graphic artist has a basic contract that can be customized as needed for each assignment.

Although never clearly labeled as such, a boilerplate contract can also be used as a multiple-use contract, designed to cover a wide variety of projects with no customization. Multiple-use contracts, provided by both large and small companies, can be recognized by their obvious general clauses, especially in the assignment of rights and licensing. They must be carefully reviewed and negotiated because they typically request many more concessions than are realistic for the project at hand.

To deal effectively with non-customized boilerplates, graphic artists need to establish their own studio policy (see the Using Contracts section later in this chapter) that defines general terms and expectations for various assignments. This sets a business standard that the graphic artist can work from when negotiating all contracts, but especially standard contracts with general clauses.

7. Retainer agreement

Although retainer agreements are most often used by attorneys and accountants, they are also used with increasing frequency by graphic designers and sometimes by illustrators.

When signing a retainer agreement, the graphic artist agrees to work for the client for a specific amount of time over a given period or on a particular project for a fee paid according to an agreed-upon schedule. Often the schedule includes an initial payment, which reduces the graphic artist's risk; otherwise the designer is virtually extending credit to a possibly unknown client. The payment also guarantees the designer's availability for the duration of the project.

Retainers may take several forms:

1. **Annual retainer:** Payment schedules vary, but the client usually agrees to pay a substantial fee upon signing—30 percent is recommended—and the graphic artist guarantees to be available to work for the client as needed. The agreement may include a specific number of hours or days devoted to the client's needs, with additional time billed as used. Payment for time not used is forfeited, or can be accumulated throughout the year as credit.
2. **Project-based retainer:** This type also involves a substantial fee upon signing—30 percent is recommended—to retain the graphic artist's services as a one-time deposit against future billings. Hourly rates are set, and the client is kept informed of the hours billed against the retainer. After the retainer hours are used, regular hourly billing continues. If the fee is not completely used, the remaining amount may or may not be refundable.
3. **Service retainer:** This agreement covers longer-term commitments of six months to a year, with payments made in monthly installments. Design services are billed against this retainer, which is very similar to a level billing program where annual project fees are set with a client, who pays the fees in equal installments.

The service retainer is different from the more traditional annual retainer, which is usually based on hourly billing. The problem with hourly billing is that the client may lose control over costs—especially if the clock keeps ticking. In a project-based agreement, both sides know exactly what fees will change hands.

The advantages to the graphic artist of working on retainer are guarantees of long-term designer/client relationships, multiple projects, and a steady cash flow. Among the disadvantages are clients calling too often about minor issues and expecting priority over non-retainer clients. Clients may also question whether they are getting all the services they are paying for. A retainer relationship may sometimes limit the graphic artist's ability to compete for other assignments.

Among the advantages of retainers to the client are cost savings, since retainer work is usually done at a 10 to 15 percent discount. (Additional billable hours may or may not be discounted.) A graphic artist who is on retainer is fully aware of the company's needs and products and gives preferential treatment to the company—two benefits that are increasingly valued in this age of tight deadlines.

What a Contract Should Include

Contracts in the visual communications industries usually cover four issues: copyright use, payment, legal, and working relationship.

Copyright use issues

In the graphic arts, the value of a particular work of art or design depends on its use. An illustration used for a small local magazine has one value; the same illustration used in a worldwide advertising campaign is worth far more. A logo designed for a local mom-and-pop store has much less value than a logo used by a global corporation. Use determines price. (For more on use and value, see the Copyright section in Chapter 2, Legal Rights & Issues.)

Under copyright law, the exclusive use of a design or artwork licensed by a client must be transferred in writing. To avoid any future dispute between client and artist, it is always best to clearly specify which uses are agreed upon in a written contract. As important as it is to specify where and how a work is going to be used, it is equally important to stipulate where it cannot be used. A contract should describe in detail exactly where, how, and how long a work can be used, including the following issues:

Type of medium/product: Where will the finished work appear: in a magazine, in a newspaper ad, on a web site, on a CD cover, or on a billboard? Or in multiple media? In the age of multimedia it is extremely important to be specific about each medium where the work will be used, since each use helps define the final value of the work.

Category of use: What is the intent of the use: advertising, editorial, corporate, institutional, book? To understand the difference in value between a single magazine page and a multi-market campaign, it may help to study the many charts detailing survey results that appear in preceding chapters of this book.

Geographic area of use: How widely will the work be used: North America, Europe, all over the world, on planets yet to be discovered? As the span of the marketplace increases, so does the work's exposure, which can increase its present and future value.

Duration of use: How long will the work be used: for one time, for one year, for two editions? Limitations on duration of use allow graphic artists to control the exposure of their work and to receive fair market value in each venue where their work appears.

All-rights terms: Such clauses allow clients unlimited use of a work, including in multiple markets and in any way the client may see fit. An all-rights clause (also called a "buyout," which is a misleading term and one to be avoided) is often used for logos, in advertising, or in other areas where a design appears so frequently that keeping track of usage is impossible. An artist who agrees to all-rights terms should always consider appropriate compensation.

Ownership of original art: Who retains the original? Giving a client the right to artwork or to a design for a specified use or a particular period of time is different from selling the client the physical artwork or sending the client an electronic file. The sale of original art is often a secondary market for graphic artists and is, by law, a transaction separate from the transfer or sale of reproduction rights.

Licensing third parties: Many clients specify the right to resell or transfer their agreed-upon rights to others. This can be for resale purposes or to allow the work to flow through normal channels of manufacture and distribution. Keep in mind that transferring the right to license to a client may effectively remove the artist's control over the work and divert any potential resale revenue from the artist.

Exclusivity: Who has the right to license, use, or resell the artwork? "Exclusivity" means that only the client can use the art for the agreed-upon purposes for the time specified and that the artist or designer cannot resell the art to, or adapt it for, any other person or concern within the same medium, category of use, or type of product for the time period stipulated in the contract. "Nonexclusive rights" means that while the client can use the art for the agreed purposes, the artist can also resell the work to other clients.

Many contracts, especially editorial ones, may combine exclusive and nonexclusive terms. For example, a magazine may ask for exclusive terms for 60 days from the date of publication. After 60 days, the contract stipulates nonexclusive terms, allowing the magazine to continue to use the image while the artist is free to resell the work to other clients. Nonexclusive rights can extend the use and value of artwork to clients; the artist should consider this added value when determining the price of the work.

Work-for-hire: A work-for-hire clause vests authorship of art or design in the client. The graphic artist hands over all rights to the client, including copyright, all preliminary concepts, and even the original. By signing a work-for-hire contract an artist becomes, in effect, an employee of the client for copyright purposes only, but with none of the benefits or compensation usually associated with employment. Note that the contract need not specifically include the words "work-for-hire" or "work made for hire" to qualify as such. (For a thorough discussion of work-for-hire, see Chapter 2, Legal Rights & Issues.)

Payment issues

How much will be paid for a particular use or design? When is payment due? Are there penalties if it is not paid on time? All these issues fall under this category.

Fee/estimate: What is the monetary value of the final work? A variety of factors are used to estimate and set fees: media and geographic areas in which the work will appear, frequency of use, and allocation of a variety of rights.

Additional expenses: If the contract is part of an estimate, how much is estimated for expenses? If outside vendors are used, who will pay their costs and when? Are delivery fees and supplies, such as blank CDs, paid for by the client or the graphic artist? Will the client be notified if expenses exceed the original estimate by a certain percentage? When is payment for the expenses carried by the graphic artist due from the client? Will those expenses be marked up?

Kill/cancellation fees: If a project is canceled for reasons beyond the control of the graphic artist, the project is considered "killed." Typical charges for services rendered can be 25 to 50 percent if the work is killed during the initial sketch stage, 50 percent if killed after completion of the sketch stage, and 100 percent if killed after the final design is completed.

"Rejection" is used when an assignment is canceled due to client dissatisfaction. Perhaps the final art deviates from the agreed-upon sketch or the style is different from the artist's portfolio or samples shown to obtain the job. Common cancellation fees are one-third of the total fee if canceled before completion of final art, and 50 to 100 percent after the final artwork is completed.

Determining whether a job is killed or rejected may become a matter of common sense and negotiation. Both the graphic artist and the client need to realistically evaluate the causes for terminating the project and negotiate payment accordingly. Contracts should provide a clear directive that the client, in killing or canceling the project, gives up any agreed-upon copyright transfer or license. Any future use is subject to renegotiation.

Payment schedule: When are payments due? For large projects, payment is often divided into scheduled segments, called "progress payments." An example is a percentage upon signing, a percentage due after approval of the initial designs, and the remainder, plus expenses, upon delivery of the final work. Smaller jobs may simply require payment at delivery or net 30 days after delivery of the artwork.

As with any schedule, specific deadlines can be crucial, and the graphic artist should consider whether the final payment plan is realistic. There is a big difference between 30 days after receipt of the invoice and 30 days after first use, which may be delayed for many reasons beyond the artist's control.

Late-payment fees: When is a payment late and subject to penalties? After 30 days? Some artists charge a penalty fee (such as 1 1/2 percent of the total), due every month that the balance remains unpaid. As an incentive for timely payment, some artists offer clients a small discount (such as 2 percent) if payment is received within a short period of time after the invoice date (for example, 15 days).

Client alterations: Any changes requested by the client that are integral to the original assignment are usually considered part of the process and not client (or author's) alterations. When changes go beyond the original, agreed-upon scope of a project, they are billable beyond the agreed-upon price. These changes can be billed by the hour (the artist's hourly rate is often stipulated in the contract) or by an additional fee agreed upon at the time of the change.

If the nature of the assignment changes in the middle of the project, the graphic artist may assume that the client is liable for an additional fee and increased expenses. It is important to specify such expectations in the initial contract. It is also important to discuss the change in the original assignment with the client so there is no misunderstanding at the time of completion and billing.

Taxes: What taxes are due, and who pays them? Some taxes to consider are state sales tax and transfer taxes. (See the Sales Tax section in Chapter 3, Professional Issues.)

Default/legal fees: How will the matter be settled should the client fail to pay the bill? If there is a dispute regarding rights or use, who will cover the expenses incurred in the resolution of the dispute? (See the Remedies section under Legal Issues, below.)

Legal issues

Clauses in this category define responsibilities over such legal issues as questions of ownership, libel, and recourse in disputes.

WARRANTY

A warranty is an assurance by the creator that the work is original and unique, created solely by the artist or designer for the buyer. It protects the buyer from legal action based on the art or design supplied to them by the graphic artist.

A warranty may also guarantee that the graphic artist holds the exclusive rights to the artwork or design, has the authority to sell the agreed-upon rights, and that no one else may claim these rights. Typical warranties of this type may state that "to the best of the artist's knowledge," the artist has not infringed on any person's copyright in creating the artwork.

Some buyers want to be assured that nothing in a work is considered "obscene" or "indecent." This may be a matter of personal taste that is beyond the artist's control. If a client is adamant about certain issues, this language ("no explicit sexual references") should be clearly stated in the wording of the contract.

INDEMNITY

Indemnity is a common clause in contracts that seek to exempt or protect the client and/or the graphic artist from damages or liability in actions brought by third parties. Should someone other than the client or graphic artist sue one of the parties, this clause protects the other from also being brought into the lawsuit. Similarly, graphic artists should insert wording into any contract that will protect them if a client causes the work to be subject to any litigation.

An indemnity clause should be negotiated based on the scale and scope of the work. A typical indemnification clause reads: "Artist holds client harmless from and against any and all judgments and related costs and expenses arising out of, or concerning artist's rights in, the material provided."

REMEDIES

Remedy clauses map out agreed-upon courses of action by which a disagreement or breach of contract can be resolved. Solutions in remedy clauses include negotiation, mediation, arbitration, and court action. Several points should be considered:

Types of remedies Will the claim be taken to an arbitrator or mediator agreed upon by both parties or appointed by only one party, or will the dispute be settled in court? It is important to note the difference between arbitration and mediation. Arbitration by a neutral party results in a binding decision, enforced by a court. In mediation, an impartial mediator seeks to facilitate an agreement between the two parties. A mediator can be appointed by a judge or another third party, such as an arts mediation service, but the resolution is binding upon the parties only if the parties agree to it in writing. Does agreement to use arbitration or mediation waive all rights to otherwise pursue additional settlement in court? (It may or may not; see the When Things Go Wrong section later in this chapter.)

Geographic area Where will resolution of the dispute be pursued? Individual cities, counties, and states all have different laws and codes that govern and affect a final ruling in a dispute. If the client and the graphic artist do business in different locales, a remedy clause should specify where arbitration or court action will take place.

Legal expenses Who will pay legal costs, such as lawyers and research, should a dispute arise? Clients often try to establish that the graphic artist bears full financial responsibility regarding expenses incurred in the settlement of a dispute. This responsibility often extends beyond the client/graphic artist relationship to actions by third parties who feel the work has somehow infringed on their rights.

Cure provision A cure provision is a clause in the contract that gives an infringing party a certain amount of time to "fix" a mistake before any legal action is taken. Such a provision is necessary for both parties because often circumstances beyond anyone's control create situations adverse to the agreement; for example, late delivery of supplies by a third party could cause the graphic artist to miss a deadline. The typical cure provision gives a party approximately 30 days to cure the breach.

Working relationship issues

This category describes areas in a contract that define the basic working elements of a project: the function and facets of the job, what is expected and when, who approves the work, and so on. The following is a standard list for any assignment:

Project description: The project description is one of the main considerations in setting compensation for the work. Be sure to include the project name, a thorough description of the project, uses, and copyright transfers. Both parties benefit when the scope of the project is described in as much detail as possible.

Work stages and scheduling: What is expected at the various stages and when: pencil roughs, color comps, camera-ready mechanicals? What is the responsibility of each party at each stage? How many ideas will be presented in the initial stages, and how many revisions are reasonable under the stated fee schedule? Is there a penalty for missed deadlines? Number of revisions, scheduled sign-offs, and time allowed for turn-around are important considerations governing the work. Both graphic artist and client should strive to set realistic expectations for each stage.

Approval process: Who accepts and approves the work, and when? How long does the client have to review and sign off on concepts, comps, or final art without upsetting the final delivery date? The contract may include language that specifies a monetary penalty for missed deadlines, especially at the final deliverable stage.

Final artwork and return of originals: What form should the final deliverable work take: reflective art, transparency, electronic transmission? Is final art to be hand-delivered, mailed, express-mailed, or e-mailed? When should the artist expect the original artwork to be returned? What would be appropriate compensation in the event of damage or loss of the original? Does the artist receive tear sheets or finished samples? Delivery and care of the artwork as well as samples of the printed work are all concerns that should be governed by the contract.

Using Contracts

The more proactive artists are in managing their businesses, the less intimidated they are by unreasonable situations. By its nature, all creative work, which straddles the line between the personal and the practical, is not the average business transaction. The following three suggestions enable a graphic artist to adopt a proactive stance.

Create a boilerplate contract

Start by drafting a basic studio contract based on the ones in this book. Study contracts sent by clients and incorporate appropriate clauses into a boilerplate contract. Also compare notes with other professionals in the field about what clauses should be included.

Save the boilerplate contract as a template in your computer. Then customize the contract by changing, adding, or removing clauses to suit a particular job and print it out on studio letterhead. By designing your contract to look as professional as possible, you project businesslike authority, and your contract will be taken more seriously.

Follow the same procedure to draft your own letter of agreement for less complicated jobs and store it for future use.

Establish a studio policy

Being proactive means anticipating the needs of your business as well as your clients before assignments come in. Setting a studio policy eliminates possible problems and conflicts before they arise.

Using an established policy depersonalizes the process of negotiation. Policies can be quoted whenever something unpleasant arises, such as: "Our policy is no returns without receipt." So the artist is not saying "no;" the studio is saying "no." In reality, the artist and the studio are one and the same, but clients are less likely to question a business policy than to badger an individual.

As a businessperson, it is easy to establish a list of policies that support your work. Prepare a written statement, and then practice stating the studio policy aloud. Try saying: "I'm sorry, but we have a studio policy of not signing work-for-hire contracts." With practice, the phrase will sound natural and convincing.

In addition to establishing priorities, studio policies help pinpoint difficult or problem clients. Should a job sound confusing or the client undependable, the artist can simply say, "This job sounds terrific. Let me send you our standard letter of agreement so that you are aware of our studio policy. When you are ready, just sign and return the letter, and I'll get started on the work." The letter communicates to the client the terms under which you will and will not consider a job.

Here are some recommended studio policies:

- Do not ever work on projects without a signed agreement.
- Do not accept work-for-hire terms.
- Do not accept all-rights terms (or buyouts).
- Do not do work on speculation.
- Refuse contracts that deny the artist the opportunity to negotiate terms.
- Establish a studio minimum for work.
- Do not quote estimates on the spot; allow time for reflection.

Here's another policy to consider:

- Establish a policy of delaying before signing a contract. No matter how exciting the prospect of the job, set aside an hour to read over the contract, remembering that any agreement must benefit both parties, not just one.

Working with clients' contracts

When a client says, "I have a contract to fax you," do not automatically assume it is unfavorable to you. But also do not assume it incorporates your best interests. Every contract offers an opportunity to work out an agreement. Tell the client you are looking forward to seeing the contract. Then follow these steps:

Get acquainted: Make a copy of the contract. Then read through it carefully without interruption, using a pen to make notes and a highlighter to mark problem areas.

Isolate problem areas: After the first read-through, pause and read it again, noting any areas you do not understand and repetitive clauses. Occasionally a client's legal department may try to establish a right in several clauses spread throughout a document or insert a clause under an inappropriate heading. Write additional notes in the margin.

Compare notes: Does the contract reflect what the client said when assigning the job? Is the client saying one thing and the contract another? Does the contract ask for more rights or terms than initially discussed? Does the stated fee support what the contract requests? If not, make notes about the items that are beyond the scope of the assignment and estimate what is needed to cover the additional work.

Start the rewrite process: Methodically cross out sentences and rewrite passages that are unreasonable. (Remember, negotiation takes place between two parties.) Be aware of the client's concerns, as well as your own. Although the client may have submitted a one-sided contract, it is important to alter the contract so it reflects a reasonable agreement. An invaluable skill in client negotiations is understanding both sides of the transaction and working in good faith toward a common understanding. The goal is for both parties to sign an agreement that supports an ongoing working relationship. Keep that in mind during the rewrite.

Alter the original: Now copy your changes neatly onto the original contract, using a ruler and a thin black pen (do not obliterate the original). Put your initials in the margin next to each change. Should changes to a clause be so extensive that an addendum is required, cross out the entire clause and write "See addendum" next to the section. Compile all the addenda on separate sheets; title each one with the clause number, the name of the clause, and the title "Addendum" so the client can easily locate the original clause in the contract. For instance: "Section 4. Grant of License Addendum," followed by the rewritten clause. Then attach the addenda to the contract.

Send it to the client: Fax or mail the altered contract with a cover letter thanking the client for sending it. Be sure to alert the client to any alterations by stating something like: "Please note that I have made substantial changes in the contract sent. The changes occur in Sections 3, 5, and 8. Please feel free to contact me should you have any questions regarding these changes." Then conclude with a positive statement and a polite request: "I am looking forward to starting the project as soon as I receive the signed contract."

Prepare for a reaction: Arriving at an appropriate contract often involves a series of back-and-forth compromises. Expect questions about the reasons behind the revisions and deletions. Be prepared to explain why alterations were made. If the client insists on reinserting a deleted clause, try to negotiate additional compensation for it. As in all business transactions, but especially phone conversations, remain calm, businesslike, and personally removed from the issues.

Determine, in advance, your minimum requirements: Be prepared to turn down the job if they are not met. Remember that not all negotiations result in projects.

Negotiation

Negotiation is discussed in depth in Chapter 5, Essential Business Practices. Some of the more important points are summarized below.

When negotiating a contract, act as professional as possible and strive for a win-win solution. Create a document that lists standard points you want to cover or an agenda that outlines topics to be covered, and refer to the document whenever negotiating, particularly over the phone. Whether a project is interesting purely for the money, because it is a valuable showcase, or because it will help establish a working relationship with a new client, using a standard agenda may influence what you agree to during negotiations.

In addition, you may want to develop a "position paper" with several questions that will help evaluate any negotiation: (1) What value—monetary or otherwise—will I derive from this job? (2) Is the compensation sufficient to cover my time and expenses? (3) What payment would I like for the job? (4) What payment am I willing to accept? (5) What is the lowest acceptable price? (6) Can I afford not to do the job? (7) What will I do with the time if I turn it down?

Determine the client's real goals

When clients try to insert work-for-hire clauses in contracts or demand all rights to artwork, an effort should be made to determine the client's real goals.

Such terms may have been put in a contract by a zealous lawyer trying to anticipate every possible contingency. But such terms usually are excessive and, if priced accordingly, make the work too expensive.

Most art directors and creative service personnel who commission art and design have little or no understanding of contract and copyright issues. They are too busy managing a number of creative projects in unusually hectic, high-pressure surroundings, and, like artists, most of them would prefer to spend their time in creative pursuits rather than administering legal details. So if the artist has a clear understanding of what contract amendments should be added and how to word them, some problems will be avoided.

Keep written records

Keep thorough written records of every negotiation, including the initial checklist that should include a job description, due dates, fees, and expenses, notes on the person representing the client, records of follow-up meetings and phone calls, hours on the job, sketches or layouts, contracts, invoices, all e-mail correspondence, memos, and business letters. This is the "job packet" that provides a paper trail in the event that a disagreement or misunderstanding interferes with completing the project and receiving payment.

Discuss money last

- Discussion of money is where most disagreements occur; focus first on areas where agreement can be reached.
- The price of a project cannot be determined until all the factors that define the project are thoroughly discussed and agreed upon by both parties.
- Deferring discussion of money gives time for both parties to develop a relationship based on working toward a common goal.
- Negotiating on price before reaching agreement on services, deliverables, and usage is premature and can prove to be costly.

Stay calm and professional

Tactical problems may occur, especially if emotions become involved, so try to stay calm, cool, and collected at all times, even if the client does not. If the person you are negotiating with claims to lack decision-making authority on terms, talk about the project as a joint venture and solicit the person as your newfound "partner." That may inspire the person to negotiate with his or her boss to defend your needs. If a contract states that it is a "standard contract" and cannot be changed, remember that contracts are working documents that should protect both parties. Do not agree to sign a standard contract if it does not protect you. Do not be afraid to strike out unfavorable sections or terms. If necessary, the defense "My attorney has instructed me not to sign contracts with these conditions," may be used to suggest alterations.

Think it over

Do not ever feel obligated to respond immediately, especially if a client starts a negotiation with "I only have $500, but I think you'd be great for the job." The artist can acknowledge the figure and still find creative ways to ask for more money. For instance, try selling the client usage of an existing piece of art (stock). (See the Maximizing Income section in Chapter 5, Essential Business Practices.)

It is always best to tell the client you will call back after you've had a chance to think about the project. Then take time to review the terms and note any points you want to change. If a project has many variables, you might consider discussing it with an associate or consulting the Guild's Legal Referral Network (see the Member Benefits & Services section in Chapter 14, The Graphic Artists Guild).

It is important to note that negotiation will not lead to a good contract in every situation. In some relationships the balance of power is so skewed that one party must either yield to unfavorable conditions or give up the opportunity, but it is possible to maximize assets and protect yourself from an agreement that may be detrimental to you.

Remember that not every negotiation is destined to end in an agreement. Two parties can "agree to disagree" amicably and part ways, possibly trying again at a later date. The ability to approach negotiation with levelheaded objectivity, keeping it in perspective, gives a skilled negotiator the attitude necessary to obtain the most favorable agreement.

Before Calling a Lawyer

Though some contracts may appear incomprehensible at first glance, the more contracts you read, the more you will understand. In most circumstances, consulting with a lawyer is not necessary. For smaller projects the cost of a lawyer could easily be more than the assignment fee! Sometimes, especially in the beginning, you just need help with a particular clause. Here are some less expensive ways to come to terms with contracts:

Network: Call fellow graphic artists, talk openly about contracts, and ask their opinions. Establish a network or support group with other artists in your field to share information about contracts and companies. Join graphic artist chat boards on the Internet. Two excellent examples are the ispot (www.theispot.com) and the Community Forums on the Graphic Artists Guild web site (www.graphicartistsguild.org), available only to Guild members, which include a forum devoted to advocacy issues and forums for various specific artistic disciplines.

Find a coach: Seek experienced graphic artists as business mentors. A free lunch in exchange for advice can help avoid future business headaches. If you are a Guild member, call your chapter's contract point person. Although they are not lawyers, point people can often answer simple questions, provide coaching through a difficult negotiation, or suggest other resources.

Read and grow wiser: In addition to this book, many books educate artists about contracts and business matters (see those listed in Chapter 15, Resources & References). The Internet has many sites that provide business support to graphic artists; a number of them are hosted by artists. For more help with contracts, check out the Contract Monitor section of the Guild site (www.graphicartistsguild.org).

When to Call a Lawyer

When writing or negotiating a contract, there are situations when you should consult a lawyer:

- For large and/or complicated projects involving complex royalty or licensing issues.
- For projects requiring lengthy schedules and/or penalties.
- For licensing work in multinational markets.

When Things Go Wrong

At the other end of a legal negotiation is the question of what to do when things go wrong after a contract has been signed. The fact that the contract exists at all is usually a deterrent to a violation of terms, but when an agreed-upon clause is violated, it becomes a breach of contract.

There are many ways to address a contract breach, most of them without incurring great expense. No matter what method you use, once you know things are going wrong, it is essential to maintain a thorough paper trail to document your side of the case.

Establish a paper trail

- Keep copies of all letters sent to the client.
- Reflect on your memory of key conversations and oral agreements before, during, and after the job was completed. Write notes for future reference.
- Record all telephone calls made regarding the dispute, including the date and year of the call. Take notes about the content of each call, the people involved in the conversation, and what was agreed/not agreed to. If necessary, follow up each conversation with a brief letter recording your understanding of the conversation. That allows clients to respond if they feel the facts are inaccurate. Keep the

telephone log as a separate file, and do not write on the contract.

- Set up specific dates when you expect an agreed-upon action to be taken. Send all correspondence by certified mail, return receipt requested, and file the receipt with a copy of the letter for future reference.
- Keep a folder with all receipts, notes, and papers regarding the problem.

A word on etiquette: As in negotiating, strive to keep all correspondence and discussions calm, businesslike, and neutral. Shouting or threatening only limits communication, hardens positions, and prolongs the negotiation process. Showing clients that you are serious and methodical can be much more effective than acting in a way that will alienate them. Help the client solve the problem by offering reasonable solutions. Your goal is to encourage the client to work with you to find a solution.

Take action to resolve the problem

There will be times when the client has no intention of solving the problem. Like any other businessperson, the graphic artist has a wide range of available options, depending on the scope and severity of the problem. The following list of actions is scaled from minor to major breaches of a contract (Refer back to the Collecting section of Chapter 5, Essential Business Practices for a more in-depth explanation of these actions.):

Write to the offending client, asking for a remedy to the problem. Mention that you plan to use the contract to prove your point, if needed, in court. Spell out specifics. This is your first brick when laying a foundation for action if going to court.

Negotiate one-on-one: Try to avoid potentially expensive arbitration or legal fees by offering to sit down and negotiate a resolution. Even in extreme circumstances, it is always better to attempt to negotiate before entering the legal system. (Review the Negotiation section in Chapter 5, Essential Business Practices.)

Mediate: Mediation is an informally structured but more aggressive style of negotiation in which an impartial third party is brought in to facilitate the discussion between disputing parties. If the parties are able to resolve their differences with the mediator's assistance, the resolution is written up as a Memorandum of Agreement, which is then signed by both parties and the mediator. Such a memorandum constitutes an enforceable contract between the parties. The Volunteer Lawyers for the Arts organization provides low-cost or free mediation services for artists, with fees based on a sliding scale. (For a list, see Chapter 15, References & Resources.)

Arbitrate: Arbitration is similar to mediation except that the proceedings are more formal and the resolution is handed down to the parties by the arbitrator, rather than arrived at by the parties themselves. The arbitrator's rulings are legally binding upon both parties, and arbitration rulings usually cannot be appealed.

Many associations offer arbitration, including:

- The American Arbitration Association, 800-778-7879
- The American Bar Association Dispute Resolution Program, 202-662-1680
- Judicate West California, 800-488-8805

Consider small-claims court: If the breach is payment-related and the fee is within the allowable range, small-claims court is often an inexpensive way to recover damages. States vary as to maximum amounts allowed in small-claims cases. Many books exist to help you navigate through small-claims court.

Call arts organizations for referrals: Check with local arts organizations for legal groups that specialize in the arts, such as Volunteer Lawyers for the Arts and other nonprofit organizations. Often these organizations can also refer you to local mediators and arbitrators.

Join a professional organization: If you are a member of the Graphic Artists Guild, for instance, you can contact your chapter's contract point person. That volunteer has a wealth of local references, such as Guild-sanctioned lawyers, and can suggest useful negotiating tactics.

Just the Beginning

Although this chapter won't prepare you for a legal career, you should now feel more confident in reading, negotiating, and even drafting simple contracts for your business. By making these business practices an integral part of your studio policy, you will protect your business and minimize disputes. And you will project a professionalism that clients appreciate.

See the Glossary for definitions of important legal terms. Samples of a variety of contracts and business forms are found in the Appendix: Contracts & Forms.

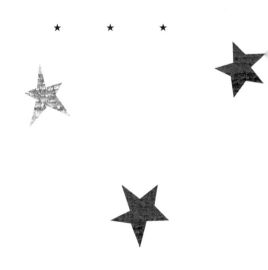

SALARIES & TRADE CUSTOMS

This chapter summarizes employment conditions and salaries for graphic artists—usually graphic designers—who work on staff. Trade practices and employment conditions vary widely, depending on the field. That's why it is important to consider employment conditions in addition to salary when applying for a salaried position.

SALARIED

graphic artists are usually employed solely by one company. Unless the artist or designer can negotiate a written agreement that states otherwise, all art created on company time is considered work-for-hire (for more information on work-for-hire, see Chapter 2, Legal Rights & Issues). Depending upon the responsibilities of the graphic artist and the employer, moonlighting for a competitor may be contractually or ethically prohibited; some employers may require employees to sign non-compete contracts and/or confidentiality forms. A salaried graphic artist's income is frequently limited to what the artist receives from the employer. Freelancing on the side, however, while not encouraged, may be an important source of additional revenue.

Many disciplines overlap in salaried jobs. For instance, an art director may also produce illustrations, designs, or lettering. In fact, few salaried graphic artists specialize so rigidly that they work only in one area; the special responsibilities of a particular position dictate which talents are required.

Employment Outlook

In a belt-tightening economy, there is an increased emphasis on cost-effectiveness. The Creative Group, a national specialized staffing firm, reports in its *2009 Salary Survey* that many hiring managers are becoming much more selective about the marketing programs and personnel in which they invest. To keep labor costs down, many are using freelancers on a more frequent basis and hiring full-time professionals only when there is an ongoing need. However, companies are under pressure to reach increasingly segmented audiences that expect information and entertainment to be personalized and delivered on demand. To remain competitive in this environment, businesses are increasingly turning to digital media for the flexibility it offers. Their challenge is finding professionals who are able to manage projects across a variety of platforms, ranging from print advertising to social and mobile media.

What does this mean for the graphic artist who is looking for employment or trying to avoid being a casualty of downsizing? According to The Creative Group, in today's economy, the most highly prized creative professionals are those who possess diverse skill sets. For example, those who can design for print and also are proficient in Flash, Cascading Style Sheets (CSS), and HTML are highly sought. Project managers who can oversee both traditional and interactive marketing projects are also in high demand.

As more and more companies focus on building dynamic web sites to serve as effective sales tools, professionals who can help them attract customers by developing eye-catching digital design and functionality are especially valued. E-learning has also become a high growth area as more universities and businesses offer online courses, training, and staff development. Graphic arts specialties in strong demand in the e-learning field are 3-D animators and modelers (salaries for these positions are covered in Chapter 12, Animation Prices & Trade Customs).

The American Institute of Graphic Arts (AIGA) also publishes an annual salary survey. In the *AIGA/Aquent Survey of Design Salaries 2009,* AIGA Executive Director Richard Grefé predicts that the demand for design services will increase rapidly once the economy recovers: "Design is essential to success in all sectors—in business and government, health and education—as the U.S. economy shifts toward a knowledge-based economy, where information design and communication design create substantial value." While waiting for this recovery, it is recommended that graphic artists take advantage of the slow economy by using downtime to increase and develop their array of skills—especially digital skills, their proficiency with software, and their understanding of non-print media and platforms.

Salary Ranges

The salary ranges listed in this chapter reflect the current market for professional graphic artists holding staff positions. The salaries are based on a traditional 35-hour workweek with a benefits package that includes vacation, holiday, and sick pay. For health insurance, employees are frequently required to contribute part of their premiums and to use health maintenance organizations (HMOs). Bonuses, stock options, and retirement plans are available, but these benefits usually depend upon company policy regarding salaried personnel and are often reserved for those in creative, supervisory, or executive functions.

Hiring Practices

Generally, larger companies, particularly those that produce a significant amount of in-house graphic art for advertising, catalogs, corporate graphics, newsletters, and packaging, hire a full-time art staff and use freelance talent to supplement it. When there is no in-house staff or when the company chooses to subcontract a specific project or an area of a large project, such as a special advertising campaign, corporate identity program, or annual and quarterly reports, then independent agencies or design firms may be hired to work on retainer.

Agencies and corporations have downsized their art departments since the early 1990s, a trend that seems to favor freelancers over staff. These companies sometimes hire back the same individuals to work as full-time freelancers on the same projects but at a lower rate and without benefits. Even if the flat fee paid is greater than the salary previously earned, the loss of benefits—and the cost of replacing them—is significant, frequently resulting in a lower total income. This cost-cutting business practice has serious tax implications for both the employer and the graphic artist. For further discussion, refer to the Employment Issues section of Chapter 3, Professional Issues.

Graphic artists who work as full-time freelancers should be aware that the law guarantees time-and-a-half salary for work in excess of 40 hours per week. And if artists provide 1,000 hours of service, they are entitled to receive all the benefits regular employees enjoy.

Employment Conditions

Graphic artists should consider conditions of employment as well as salary when applying for a salaried position. Some of the conditions for full-time workers to consider include policies, benefits, job description, and the performance review process.

Policies

Many employers have written staff policies outlining how a company relates to its employees. New York State companies, for example, are required by law to notify employees "in writing or by publicly posting" about their policies on sick leave, vacations, personal leave, holidays, and hours. Other items that may be included are employee grievance procedures, causes for discipline (up to and including discharge), criteria for salary increases and promotions, and parental leave. A written staff policy reveals much about the working environment and the potential employer's attitude toward the staff.

Benefits

All companies are required to offer such basic benefits as minimum wage, unemployment insurance, workers compensation, and short-term disability insurance. Most companies also offer a benefit package to their employees that may include health, long-term disability, and/or life or dental insurance plans. Such benefits are at the discretion of the employer and are not currently required by law. Benefits are often related to company size, with smaller companies offering fewer benefits. Larger companies and corporations often offer pension, profit-sharing, and stock option plans, and sometimes daycare facilities or childcare subsidies. An employee may qualify for a company pension depending on the plan specifications and the number of hours he or she works. Staff artists should check with their employer for details.

Job description

Just as a contract between a client and a freelance artist reflects their understanding of their relationship, a written job description can define what is expected of artists during the term of their employment. The Graphic Artists Guild strongly recommends that all artists taking a salaried position request a written job description, since it will help both employer and employee avoid assumptions and expectations not shared by the other party. A written description is also useful in the event a job changes significantly during the term of employment. Such changes may reflect greater responsibilities or functions, justifying a new title or greater compensation. If such changes are made, the job description should be rewritten to reflect the new title, duties, salary, benefits, and start date. It is also useful for the artist to obtain an official "offer letter" on company letterhead, stating the salary, title, start date, and benefits and signed by the hiring authority.

Performance review

A periodic (semiannual or annual) evaluation of job performance is helpful to both employer and employee. A formal review gives the employer the opportunity to discuss job performance and changes in job description and allows employees to gauge their performance and raise questions about their job expectations. Performance reviews also allow employer and employee to suggest ways to improve the "product" or the employee's function. When handled well, job performance reviews can pinpoint potential problems and help maintain good and productive relationships between employer and employee. The results of the job performance review should be kept on file, and employees should be allowed access to their file.

While many of the above conditions of employment are not mandatory, they help both employer and employee develop and maintain good relationships during the term of employment.

Salary Overview

Keep in mind that in most corporate settings each job title has a salary range, and new employees are often hired at the low end of the range to provide room for future raises. According to the *AIGA/Aquent Survey of Design Salaries 2009,* in the graphic design industry, the median salary for an entry-level designer in 2008 was $35,000, compared with $60,000 for a senior designer, $70,000 for an art director, $90,000 for a creative director, and $90,000 for a partner/principal/owner. Many design firms that took part in the survey reported that their businesses were relatively solid, although the economy had already slipped into a recession. Compared to the previous year, the core design positions—senior designer, designer, entry-level designer—held constant in compensation. All other positions saw declines in median salaries except for web designers and developers, who saw modest increases. Although those results may seem disheartening at first glance, they are not as dire as one might have predicted, considering the dramatic downturn that the global economy experienced since the third quarter of 2008.

Regional differences in pay scales still exist, but they vary by the type of job. The 2009 AIGA/Aquent survey showed that designers and entry-level designers in the Pacific region reported the highest median yearly wages of $50.000 and $40,000 respectively. However, for the higher-level titles, the Middle Atlantic states paid the highest median salaries: owner/principal ($120,000), creative director ($115,000), art director ($80,000), and senior designer ($69,000). New England, which was the highest paying region in 2006, was the second or third best paying region in four job titles. AIGA/Aquent's 2009 survey also revealed that median pay rates between in-house corporate and design-firm/studio designers were the same ($45,000); however, the lower and higher ends of the salary ranges were greater for designers working in design firms ($40,000–$55,000) compared to corporate in-house designers ($37,000–$52,000). It should be noted, however, that freelance designers were included in the design-firm group. For senior designers, the median salary was higher for those working in design firms ($62,000) compared to those working in corporate departments ($60,000), and the salary range was also higher for studio designers ($52,000–$75,000) compared to corporate designers ($50,000–$70,000). For entry-level designers, there were no differences in median salaries or salary ranges between the two types of employers.

Design Salaries

Entry-level designer. An entry-level designer is one to two years out of school and requires mentoring in all aspects of design conception and implementation. $30,000 to $40,000.

Designer. A designer is responsible for the conceptualization and design of graphic applications such as collateral material, environmental graphics, books and magazines, corporate identity, film titling, and multimedia interfaces, to completion. $38,000 to $53,000.

Senior designer. A senior designer is responsible for conceptualization and design of solutions to completion. In some firms, a senior designer directs the work of one or more junior designers, who generate comps and create layouts and final art. In some cases, senior designers do not manage staff but are designated "senior" because of their authority in design decision-making. $50,000 to $72,000.

Art director. The art director establishes the conceptual and stylistic direction for design staff and orchestrates their work, as well as the work of production artists, photographers, illustrators, prepress technicians, printers, and anyone else who is involved in the development of a project. The art director generally selects vendors and, if there is not a creative director on staff, has final creative authority. $54,500 to $81,000.

Creative/design director. A creative director or design director is the creative head of a design firm, advertising agency, or an in-house corporate design department. In all of these positions, key responsibilities can include the development of graphic design, advertising, communications, and industrial design publications. $70,000 to $120,000.

Owner, partner, principal. An owner, partner, or principal holds an equity position and has major business responsibility for a firm with employees. $60,000 to $128,000.

NOTE: The salary figures and job descriptions in the above two sections are reprinted with permission from the American Institute of Graphic Arts (AIGA) and excerpted from the *2009 AIGA/Aquent Survey of Design Salaries.* Please note that the salaries/wages listed above are national median annual salaries and do not include additional compensation such as benefits, bonuses, etc. For regional differences and total compensation levels, contact the AIGA for information on how to receive a copy of the full survey.

Production Salaries

Production artist. Assists design teams in graphic production of collateral, packaging, display, and advertising projects. Typical duties include pre-flight formatting, in addition to collecting, processing, checking, and uploading files. Should be adept in using software applications such as InDesign, Illustrator, Photoshop, ImageReady, QuarkXPress, and FlightCheck. Must have solid knowledge of printing processes, keen attention to detail, and troubleshooting skills. $35,250 to $46,000 with one-to-three years' experience; $44,500 to $50,000 for three or more years' experience.

Production coordinator. Provides logistical support to the creative or production department. Duties may include tracking and scheduling projects, filing summary reports, pre-flight formatting of collateral, archiving, communicating with vendors, and managing invoices. Requires strong organizational skills and the ability to manage multiple assignments at once. Must understand database and project-management software and be familiar with design programs. $36,750 to $47,750.

Digital artist. Creates and modifies images for print and/or the Web, including photographs and illustrations, using software tools. May have basic drawing skills combined with knowledge of design programs such as Illustrator, Photoshop, FreeHand and Dreamweaver. Requires strong technical skills, and artistic and conceptual-thinking abilities. $37,750 to $48,500 for one-to-three years' experience; $47,750 to $62,000 for three or more years' experience.

Production manager. Oversees production of a wide variety of projects. Duties include project planning, workflow management, vendor negotiations, print buying, cost control, quality control, logistical coordination, and press checks. Often supervises traffic coordinators and print buyers; may manage small design studio. Requires strong project-management skills and knowledge of design software applications. $53,000 to $70,750.

Studio manager. Responsible for the general management of a design studio. Duties include establishing internal project goals, reviewing employee schedules, assigning projects, managing resources, writing and distributing detailed project schedules, overseeing quality control, ensuring deadlines are met, and coordinating release of projects as necessary. Requires excellent communication and organizational skills, and an eye for detail. $53,500 to $72,250.

Motion graphics specialist. Creates animated and video artwork for a variety of mediums, such as the Web, television, and movies. Projects may include commercials, movie clips, stand-alone presentations, trailers, title sequences, and post-production work. Should be proficient in Flash, After Effects, Premier, Final Cut Pro, and Photoshop. Requires design ability and willingness to embrace new design, video, and audio technologies. $56,000 to $87,500.

Production director. Directs general production operations. Duties include those listed for production manager but with stronger work experience within each function. Manages staff and systems of production departments; oversees information and cost management; and develops, maintains, and enables standards policies consistent with company interests. Requires advanced, broad-scope technical and industry knowledge, 10 or more years of production management experience, and exceptional communication and managerial skills. $72,000 to $92,250.

NOTE: The above section is reprinted with permission from *The Creative Group 2009 Salary Survey,* ©2008 Robert Half International. Ranges are for average starting salaries and represent national averages. Please note that ranges are for wages/salaries only and do not include additional compensation such as benefits, bonuses, etc.

Salaries for Internet & Digital Media Services

Web production artist. Prepares art for online production. Enters content into web sites, including graphics, video, text, and related links. Manages graphics and production requests, and maintains web production schedules. Must be proficient in web programs and design software, and be familiar with file formats and optimizing graphics for the Web. Knowledge of content management systems and digital-video encoding is a plus. $42,500 to $59,000.

Web content writer. Writes clear and compelling website content, including articles, product descriptions, online advertisements, promotional copy, e-newsletters, blogs, and podcast scripts. Edits and repurposes existing print copy for the Web and plans and crafts e-mail marketing campaigns. Requires strong writing and editing skills. HTML and search engine optimization skills are a plus. $42,750 to $61,000 for one-to-five years' experience; $59.500 to $82,500 for five or more years' experience.

Web animator. Creates and designs animated images and motion graphics for web sites, video games, CD-ROMs and DVDs. Requires an art or design background, and knowledge of software such as Flash, Director, Photoshop, Illustrator, and ImageReady. Knowledge of Maya, After Effects, Final Cut Pro and 3D Studio Max is helpful. $46,000 to $66,000 for one-to-five years' experience; $62,750 to $88,750 for five or more years' experience.

Web site designer. Designs Internet and intranet sites that accurately reflect an organization's goals, objectives, and identity. Creates the concepts, artwork, and layout for sites and other online projects based on creative briefs and client meetings. Uses web-page and design software such as Dreamweaver, Flash, Photoshop, Illustrator, InDesign, ImageReady, Fireworks, and WYSIWYG editors. Should be familiar with web protocols such as HTML, CSS, XML and JSP. Understanding of web design issues, including browser usability and cross-platform compatibility is necessary.

Requires design and troubleshooting skills, as well as an eye for detail. $46,750 to $71,500 for one-to-five years' experience; $67,500 to $97,750 for five or more years' experience (Senior website designer).

Multimedia designer. Creates and executes creative concepts for interactive media, including web sites, presentations, online games and videos, kiosks, CD-ROMs, and DVDs. Knowledge of web architecture, web design, multimedia communications, and interface design is required, as is proficiency in software programs such as Flash, Final Cut Pro, After Effects, Dreamweaver, and PowerPoint. Working knowledge of print design software is helpful. Strong visual style, willingness to embrace new technologies, and thorough understanding of how typography, layout, color, images, and interactivity impact user experience also are necessary. $48,750 to $70,250 for one-to-five years' experience; $70,750 to $102,500 for five or more years' experience (Senior Multimedia Designer).

Interactive project manager. Plans, organizes, and executes multimedia projects. Meets with clients to understand needs, determine specifications, and coordinate planning. Strong interpersonal skills and an eye for detail are essential, as is the ability to communicate effectively with both technical and creative teams. This position also may be known as "project leader" or "media consultant." $61,250 to $88,250.

NOTE: The above section is reprinted with permission from *The Creative Group 2009 Salary Guide,* ©2008 Robert Half International. Ranges are for average starting salaries and represent national averages. Please note that ranges are for wages/salaries only and do not include additional compensation such as benefits, bonuses, etc.

Illustration Salaries

Illustrator. Conceptualizes, paints, and draws images used in a variety of materials and publications. Must be able to convert complex and abstract ideas into compelling visuals. Specialized illustrators may possess expertise in areas such as technical, medical, architectural, scientific and cartoon illustrations. In addition to artistic talent, may require knowledge of design programs such as Illustrator, Photoshop, Painter and Flash. $37,500 to $49,750 for one-to-three years' experience; $48,750 to $69,250 for three or more years' experience.

Specialized illustrator. Conceptualizes and creates illustrations for technical manuals, brochures, catalogs, presentations, animated productions, television commercials, movies, computer games, or set and exhibit designs. Must have knowledge of Photoshop, Illustrator or similar design software. Requires strong artistic, organizational, and research skills. $60,000 to $84,250, requiring five or more years' experience.

NOTE: The above section is reprinted with permission from *The Creative Group 2009 Salary Guide,* ©2008 Robert Half International. Ranges are for average starting salaries and represent national averages. Please note that ranges are for wages/salaries only and do not include additional compensation such as benefits, bonuses, etc.

Graphic Design Prices & Trade Customs

This chapter describes many different business environments in which graphic designers apply their talent and skill. Their clients include corporations, small businesses, manufacturers, non-profit organizations, advertising agencies, publishers, retailers, entrepreneurs, and educational institutions, encompassing all facets of commercial, social, and cultural life.

GRAPHIC

designers use design elements—color, typography, illustration, photography, animation, and printing or programming techniques—to organize ideas visually in order to convey a desired impact and message. In addition to exercising aesthetic judgment and project management skills, the professional graphic designer draws on experience in evaluating and developing effective communication concepts and strategies that enhance a client's image, service, or product. For a general discussion of the scope of what designers do and how they get work, review the Graphic Designer Professional Relationships section in Chapter 1.

Graphic design is applied in a wide variety of visual communications, including, but not limited to, outdoor advertising and printed materials such as magazines and books, packaging and products, and identity systems and promotional campaigns for business and industry through logos and collateral promotion, including annual reports, catalogs, brochures, press kits, and direct mail packages. Graphic design talent is also crucial to electronic communications and advertising on the Internet and other digital platforms and to the broadcasting and film industries. (For more information on electronic communications, see Chapter 9, Web Design & Other Digital Graphic Arts.)

Graphic designers work either as freelancers or as salaried employees at a design firm or other entity, where they may be principals or staff designers. Graphic designers generally work with or hire other graphic designers, illustrators, production artists, and photographers. Almost all graphic designers buy and sell art.

Traditionally, a small design firm has one to nine employees; a medium-sized firm has ten to 49 employees; and a large design firm has 50 or more employees. The vast majority of design firms in the United States are small or medium-sized and are run by graphic designers who are the principals or partners of the firm. Because the level of experience of a design practice, the scope of project services provided, and the overhead expenses may vary considerably, graphic design is one of the most difficult areas for which to identify pricing practices. Most design firms negotiate a project fee, while a freelancer's base fee is often billed at an hourly rate. Regardless of whether or not a freelancer starts with a base hourly rate for time, each project is unique and needs to be priced according to the variables and components of the project as well as the end usage. See Figure 8-1 for Median Hourly Freelance Rates.

A Note about Pricing in the Current Economy

Many graphic designers have reported stagnant or even declining fees since the last edition of this book was published. Factors negatively affecting pricing include the recessionary economy which has impacted most areas of design since late 2008. Other factors, such as the increasing transition from print- to electronic-based media and outsourcing work overseas, have slowly eroded specific industries, such as publishing, for several years now. Print designers working in these fields are not only being asked by their clients to do the same work for less payment, but they are seeing less and less work coming their way. While designers may feel pressured to lower fees to keep work coming in, it is not recommended, especially for established clients. Once fees are reduced, it is very difficult to raise them again. Plus, designers who do this are leaving the impression in the client's mind that they were being charged higher than necessary to begin with. Some designers are reporting being asked to do work at fees that make it impossible to make a living. When the cost of living is steadily climbing, it is financial suicide to start charging less for services.

Designers who feel they cannot compete in today's economy without lowering their fees need to negotiate more favorable terms, such as a higher royalty rate, increased usage fees, more visible credit, promotional opportunities, etc., to help offset the lower fees. Educating clients and savvy negotiating are more crucial than ever in the present economic climate. It is inevitable that electronic media will continue to make inroads into print media. Opportunities for design work are already shifting from print to digital formats. It is recommended that print designers take advantage of the current slowdown in work to increase and hone their digital skills so that they are more marketable in areas where there are growth and opportunity.

The Written Agreement

Since designers work with a variety of graphic resources, it is important that all conditions and expectations are spelled out in writing in a contract, letter of agreement, or purchase order before the work begins. (See Chapter 6, Standard Contracts & Business Tools, for more detailed information about these documents, and the Appendix: Contracts & Forms for samples of each type.) The following points should be considered:

Payment: For larger projects, it is customary for a third of the payment to be made upon signing the agreement, a third upon approval of design comps, and the final third within 30 days of delivery of digital files for production.

Rights: Most contracts include a section specifying how, when, where, and the duration for which the design will be used. The extent of use determines which copyrights the client needs and may be a factor in establishing appropriate fees. Graphic designers are often entitled to credit and copyright, unless another arrangement is negotiated.

Subcontractors: Designers often contract with freelance illustrators, designers, and photographers for work on a limited-use basis for specific projects. Unless specified otherwise in writing, it is assumed that the creator owns the copyrights to the work, not the client or the designer. It is fairly common, therefore, for copyrights to be held by several different contributors to a project, who may all deserve the same acknowledgment and rights on the piece or group of pieces. (For a more in-depth discussion of these and related issues, see Chapter 2, Legal Rights & Issues.)

In addition to copyright concerns, all terms and conditions of working with independent artists should be clearly outlined in writing and reviewed prior to the commission. These standard customs are detailed in a contract, letter of agreement, or estimate and confirmation form. (See Chapter 6, Standard Contracts & Business Tools.)

Reimbursable Expenses: In addition to the designer's fee, expenses reimbursed by the client typically include subcontractors' fees, digital output and file storage, supplies, travel, overnight couriers, and messenger services. Data indicate that the markup for these services usually ranges from 15 to 25 percent. The markup reimburses the designer for supervisory and handling time and helps ensure that all work is done to the designer's specifications and standards of quality. Reimbursable expenses can be billed monthly, upon completion of project phases, or upon completion of the project.

Responsibilities of the client: The client is usually responsible for copywriting, providing copy in an electronic form, proofreading, and sometimes press approval.

Consultation fees: When a graphic designer is called in by a client to advise on a project or design decision, consultation fees are often based on an hourly rate. Consultation fees usually range from $75 to $250 per hour.

Median Hourly Freelance Rates Graphic Design

DESIGNER	$65
SENIOR DESIGNER	$80
CREATIVE DIRECTOR	$100
ART DIRECTOR	$100
PRINT PRODUCTION ARTIST	$50
PRINT PRODUCTION MANAGER	$65

FIGURE 8—1

General Trade Practices

The following trade practices have been used historically for graphic design and thus are accepted as standard.

1. The intended use of the design, the price, and the terms of sale must be stated clearly in the contract, letter of agreement, or purchase order.
2. The use of a design influences the price. If the design will be featured over an extensive geographical area or is an all-rights sale, fees are significantly higher than when used locally, within a selected area, or for limited usage.
3. Designers charge higher fees for rush work, often adding 50 to 100 percent. A job may be considered a rush if the designer is requested to do the work on a greatly abbreviated schedule.
4. If a design will be used for something other than its original purpose, such as for an electronic database or on a web site, the designer should negotiate reuse arrangements with the original commissioning party with speed, efficiency, and respect for the client's needs. Note that the secondary use of a design may be of greater value than the primary use. Although there is no set formula for reuse fees, surveys indicate that designers add a reuse fee ranging from 50 to 125 percent of the fee that would have been charged had the work been originally commissioned for the anticipated use.
5. Return of original artwork, computer disks, or digital files to the designer should be automatic and should be done in a timely manner, unless otherwise negotiated. Note: This may affect sales tax requirements.
6. If a job is canceled through the fault of someone other than the designer, a cancellation fee is charged. Depending upon the stage at which the job is terminated, the fee paid should reflect all work completed or hours spent and any out-of-pocket expenses. (See the Cancellation and Rejection Fees section in Chapter 3, Professional Issues.)
7. A rejection fee is usually agreed upon if the assignment is terminated because the client finds the preliminary or finished work to be less than satisfactory. Depending on the reason for the rejection, the rejection fee for finished work is often equivalent to the charge for the number of hours spent on the job.
8. Designers considering working on speculation assume all risks and should take them into consideration when offered such arrangements. (See the Speculation section in Chapter 3, Professional Issues.)
9. The Graphic Artists Guild is unalterably opposed to the use of work-for-hire contracts, in which authorship and all rights that go with it are transferred to the commissioning party, and the independent designer is treated as an employee for copyright purposes only. Under a work-for-hire arrangement, the independent designer receives no employee benefits and loses the right to claim authorship or to profit from future use of the work forever. Note: Corporate logo designs are ineligible to be done under work-for-hire contracts because they do not fit its legal definition, but all-rights transfers of such work to clients are common. (Additional information on work-for-hire contracts can be found in Chapter 2, Legal Rights & Issues.)
10. No new or additional designer or firm should be hired to work on a project after a commission begins without the original designer's knowledge and consent. The original designer may then choose, without prejudice or loss of fees owed for work completed, to resign from the account or to agree to collaborate with the new design firm.
11. Major revisions or alterations initiated by the client (author alterations, or AAs) are usually billed at the designer's hourly rate. In such cases, the designer will apprise the client of anticipated billing and obtain authorization prior to executing the additional work.
12. Designers are entitled to a minimum of five samples of the final piece.

NOTE: All prices for design in this book are based on independent surveys of the United States and Canada that were reviewed by experienced professionals in the various disciplines in which they work. These figures, reflecting the responses of established professionals, are meant as a point of reference only, and do not necessarily reflect such important factors as geographical differences in cost of living; deadlines; job complexity; reputation and experience of a particular designer; research; technique or unique quality of expression; and extraordinary or extensive use of the finished design. (See related material in other sections of this book, especially in Chapter 5, Essential Business Practices, and Chapter 6, Standard Contracts & Business Tools.)

Corporate Graphic Design

Corporate graphic designers specialize in business communications, identity programs, brand standards, signage, internal and promotional publications, and annual reports for companies and institutions such as hospitals, universities, and museums. A team specializing in this area of design may include a principal of the firm, an art director, designer(s), production manager, copywriter, and project manager. Or a graphic design department can consist of one person, who handles multiple functions.

Since graphic design projects often involve long-term strategic research and development, corporate designers are frequently brought in at the earliest planning stages. Many corporate design offices work on retainer and also act as design consultants in peripheral areas in addition to their main projects. They may be involved in the creation of brand standards or a brand's graphic standards.

It should be noted that quality print versions of annual reports, a mainstay of corporate graphic design, are becoming rare. Companies are increasingly replacing printed reports with online versions, which are better. It is projected that larger firms will rely more and more on their online versions, designing and producing them in-house, with the work being done by their website designer. Mid-size companies will put their annual reports online, too, for economic reasons, but as 8.5″ x 11″ PDFs. Not-for-profits will continue publishing printed annual reports because they use them for thanking donors and for fundraising.

Phases of a project

A corporate design project begins once a client accepts the design proposal outlining the scope of the project, its budget, schedule, and the terms under which it will be executed. Design projects are often quoted and billed by phase, with an initial fee representing 10 to 33 percent of total estimated fees and reimbursable expenses. With new clients, web site projects, and very costly projects, some designers request as much as a 50 percent initial fee to ensure that they will be paid if the project is canceled in mid-schedule. See Figure 8-2 for Corporate Graphic Design fees.

A project might be broken down into three or five phases, depending on the amount and complexity of the work being done or on how much detail the client wants to see. Below is an expanded five-phase project. Often, in a three-phase project, Phases 2 and 3 (Concept Development and Design Refinement) are combined as are Phases 4 and 5 (Design Implementation and Production). An example of a three-phase project is given under the Corporate Identity section.

Phase 1. **Planning:** This phase is concerned with gathering information and establishing design criteria. It often requires spending a great deal of time with the client to define the needs, objectives, and problems to be solved.

Phase 2. **Concept development:** After the designer and client have reached an agreement concerning the basic project, visual solutions are pursued that meet the stated objectives. This phase results in a presentation showing only the ideas that the design team feels are viable, appropriate, and meet the prescribed criteria.

Phase 3. **Design refinement:** At this stage, the design team refines the accepted design, which may include general format, typography, color, other elements, and the assignment of illustration and/or photography. A final presentation may be made to the client explaining the refined applications. Any changes in budget and/or schedule are agreed upon at this point.

Phase 4. **Design implementation:** Decisions on all related art direction, including commissioned illustrations and photography, typography, copywriting, layouts or digital files, and all other elements, are final at this point. Designer errors or printer errors (PEs) are not billable after this point, but all AAs are. The client may make changes in files or on press only through the designer. Conversely, the designer may execute design alterations, either in files or on press, only with the client's final approval.

Phase 5. **Production:** This phase only applies to design projects that have specific deliverables. It may be a matter of going on press, supervising the fabrication or manufacturing of products, or launching a web site. Supervision is the key to this phase, since achieving the designer's vision depends on the precision and quality attained in this final step. After the end product is approved, the project is considered billable.

Corporate identity

The objective of a properly executed corporate identity program is the accurate visual presentation of an organization's unique personality. The client's initial focus may be on the development of a new "mark" or logo, but a complex procedure involving several phases and a wide range of expertise is required to furnish a full-fledged, professionally executed corporate identity program.

A typical three-phase corporate identity program includes the following:

Phase 1. **Planning:** This phase of the program focuses on gathering information and establishing design image criteria. A creative brief is developed by the designer after interviewing the client. A significant sampling of visual materials is collected and evaluated, and interviews are conducted with various relevant audiences. Communication objectives, a plan of action, and a nomenclature (hierarchy and system of language to be used within the identity system) are established.

Phase 2. **Design development:** In this creative phase, design ideas for the mark, logo, or other primary identification device are developed. Applications to stationery and signage must also be presented to demonstrate the versatility of each design. Recommendations are also made regarding color schemes and secondary typography. The design selection process should be made according to the approved image criteria, not based on individual taste or subjective preference.

Phase 3. **Implementation:** This phase of the program is where the brand is expanded beyond the logo concept. Sufficient application formats must be developed to visually demonstrate the nature of the corporate identification system. Guidelines (usually in the form of a brand standards manual or a brand's graphics standards manual) establish the management-endorsed design policy and implementation procedures. Rules governing proper usage of the program's design elements, formats, templates, and nomenclature are presented, including reproduction materials for graphics and color guidelines.

Finally, organizations that want to make the most effective use of a visual corporate identity program either contract for a long-term consulting agreement with the design firm or establish a properly administered in-house communications department. A third option is to utilize a combination of both.

Branding design

In our increasingly consumer-driven society, designers are asked to create distinctive visual images or campaigns to identify a particular brand or commodity. Often, a sense of differentiation or exoticism is evoked by a brand campaign to captivate the consumer.

Thanks to rapidly changing communication technologies, branding is also a response to the proliferation of information anywhere, any time, in any form. A unique and identifiable look associated with a certain product makes its design—including advertising, packaging, and direct mail promotion—more important than ever.

Designers use the usual tools of form, color, texture, graphics, typestyle, and other imagery to evoke emotions connecting a consumer to a brand so the consumer will continue to buy it. Designers who specialize as brand identity consultants need to have a special understanding of the universal emotional, psychological, and visceral meanings of color, shape, and form. They usually also take into account the brand essence,

---

Comparative Fees for Corporate Graphic Design

ORGANIZATIONAL IDENTITY DESIGN	LARGE CLIENT	MEDIUM CLIENT	SMALL CLIENT
Comprehensive branding/ID[1]	$35,000–175,000	$15,000–100,000	$5,000–50,000
Comprehensive Internet web site[2]	$20,000–50,000	$10,000–40,000	$3,500–30,000
Logo design project[3]	$20,000–50,000	$6,000–25,000	$2,000–10,000
Stationery system[4]	$4,000–15,000	$2,500–7,500	$1,000–5,000

[1] Usual and customary fees for comprehensive research, consultation, and design audit; design of an integrated identity system including links to divisions and affiliates; presentation of 3 to 6 schematics; final applications to business papers and other corporate formats; and implementation guidelines.

[2] Usual and customary fees for research and design of all visual aspects and elements of web site look and feel; organization and architecture of corporate web site, including site map and informational hierarchy and relationships; supervision of illustration, photography, and animation; coordination with programmers and information architects.

[3] Usual and customary fees for research and application of primary logo identity to all corporate materials including advertising, business papers, signage, and in-house publications; presentation of 3 to 6 schematics; final applications to stationery; implementation guidelines.

[4] Usual and customary fees for research and design of letterhead, envelope, mailing label, and business card only; presentation of up to 3 comprehensive layouts showing format.

LIMITED CORPORATE PROJECTS	LARGE CLIENT	MEDIUM CLIENT	SMALL CLIENT
Annual report[5]	$25,000–150,000	$10,000–30,000	$5,000–25,000
Newsletter[6]	$7,000–25,000	$3,500–15,000	$2,000–10,000

[5] Research and design. Number of pages (as well as text versus financials) varies greatly, especially for large clients. Presentation of up to 3 comprehensive layouts showing format; supervision of illustration and photography.

[6] Research and design of 12-page, 2-color newsletter, presentation of up to 3 comprehensive layouts showing format; supervision of illustration and photography.

OTHER IDENTITY CAMPAIGNS	POLITICAL[7]	RECORDING ARTIST[8]
World tour	–	$18,000–75,000
National campaign or tour	$25,000–250,000	$7,500–20,000
Statewide campaign	$15,000–50,000	–
Local campaign or engagement	$2,500–25,000	$2,500–10,000

[7] Design of a complete marketing program to apply concept and logo to posters, bumper stickers, buttons, direct mail, outdoor advertising, banners, podium placards, and other collateral.

[8] Design of a consistent visual identity to include recording cover(s), print and newspaper advertising, security badges, crew ID cards, point of sale displays, merchandising material (team jackets, T-shirts, souvenir books, and posters).

The pricing ranges in the chart do not constitute specific prices for particular jobs. The buyer and seller are free to negotiate, with each designer independently deciding how to price the work, after taking all factors into account.

FIGURE 8—2

brand loyalty, marketing considerations (such as demographics and psychographics), and other factors when working on a branding design. Armed with that knowledge, brand designers show that well-defined, well-designed brand imagery can produce big dividends for many commodities.

Billing

Billing is handled in a number of ways. During the first phase, the designer will arrange to bill on either an hourly or project basis. If clients prefer to be billed on a project basis, they usually establish an acceptable limit ("cap") on the total amount, but the designer needs to clearly spell out at the onset of a project that the client cannot request unlimited revisions without additional compensation.

Bills for expenses usually include a markup (except for costs incurred for client-approved travel). Sales tax is rarely included in expense estimates and is usually billed periodically or at the end of the project along with AAs, which are billed at a predetermined hourly rate. Some vendors (such as printers) in some states may require proof of resale (such as a resale permit issued by the county or state) prior to billing; otherwise, sales tax may be added to the invoice.

Costs related to production or printing are the responsibility of the client and may be billed by the studio or directly to the client, depending on the particular designer's practice. The printer and all other professionals working with the designer are accountable to the designer and are ethically bound to follow the designer's directions while working on the project, regardless of who pays the printer. This becomes a matter of practicality as well, since the designer orchestrates many elements and must control them to ensure consistency.

Advertising & Promotion Design

Advertising designers must have a sophisticated knowledge of marketing, sales, and advertising print production in addition to design skills. Because they are experts in a variety of disciplines, they can successfully coordinate a company's visual identity with its marketing. Consequently, more and more of these designers are being asked by clients to replace advertising agencies. In these cases, designers often apply for agency status to be eligible for the "agency discount" when placing advertising with magazines and newspapers.

Advertising agency fees are usually tied to the total advertising budget, usually a 15 to 20 percent commission for creative work and media placement. In today's competitive marketplace, many clients negotiate to lower this fee if their advertising budgets are large enough to be leverage for more favorable terms, or they negotiate for a monthly retainer fee.

Specific trade customs

It is common practice for several agencies to pitch the client (known as the "account") on speculation, presenting ideas for upcoming advertising campaigns. The investment and risks involved are usually accepted by advertising agencies because of the tremendous ongoing rewards that may be gained from media placement, should the agency win the account. Graphic designers, who do not enjoy the media placement commissions, must assess these speculative risks much more critically. Since ideas are a designer's stock in trade, it is the industry's standard not to do work on speculation.

The designer's role is to work as part of a creative team comprised of a copywriter, an account executive, and/or a public relations professional. When the designer works as part of a team, the proposal presented to the client usually includes a strategy as well as a design solution.

Since the Internet is becoming an increasing presence and revenue source (for survival and profit) for most newspapers and magazines, designers have to be able to create artwork for both. It is best to ask ahead of time if both Web and print media will be used because each requires a different preparation of artwork. When designing for dual formats, the artwork needs to be created first in RGB at a high resolution (at least 300 ppi) and then optimized to 72 dpi for the Web. Then the RGB artwork is converted to CMYK with the resolution of 300 ppi maintained as a minimum for print production. When images are converted from RGB to CMYK, they can suffer a loss in quality, since RGB has a larger color spectrum than CMYK has. This loss is especially apparent when converting graphics that include vivid color images (such as bright flowers) or photos with fluorescent colors (e.g., safety equipment); this drastic "dulling" effect needs to be compensated by adjusting hue and saturation. To be on the safe side, many designers will design to accommodate possible additional future use. For example, if they only create for the Web or some other digital platform, and the artwork is 72 dpi, which is "low resolution," it cannot be used for print, which is 300 ppi and considered "high resolution." A designer can always "res-down" artwork from 300 to 72 dpi but cannot "res-up" from 72 to 300.

Pricing

The designer agrees to work with an advertising agency for at least the length of the entire advertising campaign, a long-term rather than project-based relationship. Traditionally, most graphic design firm fees have been based on hourly or per-project estimates, and designers have not enjoyed a percentage of the ongoing revenue generated from a successful campaign, although many alternative arrangements are possible. For example, the designer may handle only the creative work and not the placement. Traditionally, in this case, some designers have charged 10 percent of

Comparative Fees for Advertising & Promotion

Usual and customary fees based on concept and design of:

1. Campaign using 3 to 5 different sizes and shapes employing the elements of photography or illustration, headline, subhead, body copy and company logo or sign off.

2. Presentation of 3 to 5 layouts, 2 revisions, and a final comprehensive for each component indicated and supervision of art and photography.

3. Unlimited use within the specified media for 1 year from date of first placement.

Consumer Magazine

	COVER	SPREAD	FULL PAGE	HALF PAGE	QUARTER PAGE
GENERAL INTEREST *(Reader's Digest, People Weekly)*					
	$7,000–12,000	$10,000–20,000	$5,000–10,000	$3,000–7,500	$2,000–5,000
SPECIAL INTEREST *(The New Yorker, Atlantic Monthly)*					
	$5,000–10,000	$5,000–10,000	$3,000–7,000	$2,500–6,000	$1,500–3,000
SINGLE INTEREST *(Golf Digest, Scientific American)*					
	$6,500–14,000	$5,500–10,000	$5,000–9,000	$3,000–6,500	$2,000–4,000

Business Magazine

	COVER	SPREAD	FULL PAGE	HALF PAGE	QUARTER PAGE
GENERAL *(Fortune, Business Week, Forbes)*					
	$5,000–8,500	$7,500–15,000	$5,000–10,000	$3,500–7,500	$2,500–5,000
PROFESSIONAL *(Architectural Record)*					
	$5,000–8,000	$6,000–11,000	$5,000–10,000	$2,500–5,000	$1,750–4,000
TRADE & INSTITUTIONAL *(Convene, Hospitals)*					
	$5,000–7,500	$6,000–10,000	$5,000–9,000	$2,500–5,000	$1,750–3,500

Newspaper

	FULL PAGE	HALF PAGE OR SMALLER
NATIONAL, MAJOR METRO, OR CIRCULATION OVER 250,000	$5,000–12,000	$1,500–8,000
MIDSIZE METRO, OR CIRCULATION 100,000–250,000	$5,000–10,000	$2,500–7,500
SMALL METRO, OR CIRCULATION UNDER 100,000	$2,500–8,000	$1,500–5,000
WEEKLY NEWSPAPER	$2,500–7,000	$1,500–4,000

Outdoor

	NATIONAL	REGIONAL	LOCAL
Billboard	$5,000–15,000	$2,500–10,000	$2,500–7,000
Bus & Transit	$5,000–40,000	$2,000–25,000	$1,500–15,000
Station Posters	–	$5,000–15,000	$1,500–10,000

The pricing ranges above do not constitute specific prices for particular jobs. The buyer and seller are free to negotiate, with each designer independently deciding how to price the work, after taking all factors into account, including both print and online channels.

FIGURE 8—3

the total advertising budget for the duration of the campaign. The designer may also negotiate a retainer, or an hourly rate based upon a total estimated number of hours. Or the designer may be hired to create a single ad and, in that case, negotiates a price based on the type of placement. For instance, a full-color, full-page advertisement in Rolling Stone magazine usually commands a higher fee than a small black-and-white ad in a limited-run trade publication. (For more information, see Chapter 5, Essential Business Practices.)

Graphic designers who specialize in advertising and promotion design often handle posters and press kits, in addition to the design and placement of magazine and newspaper advertising. They may also handle outdoor advertising and promotion, as well as online graphics for web and e-mail promotions, so consistent application of graphic design is essential across all channels of advertising. Since designers working in this field hire other graphic

Comparative Fees for
Collateral Design

Usual and customary creative fees for concept and design of up to 3 layouts, 2 revisions, and final comprehensive for each component, photo research for stock images, and supervision of art or photography. Does not reflect reimbursable expenses billed separately.

Direct Mail Package[1]

CLIENT SIZE	SIMPLE	COMPLEX
SMALL	$2,500–7,500	$3,500–10,000
MEDIUM	$2,500–10,000	$5,000–20,000
LARGE	$3,000–15,000	$7,500–25,000

Press or Media Kit[2]

	SIMPLE	COMPLEX
SMALL	$1,500–5,000	$2,500–6,000
MEDIUM	$2,500–6,000	$4,000–15,000
LARGE	$3,000–8,000	$5,000–25,000

Product & Service Catalog

	SIMPLE	COMPLEX
SMALL	$1,500–5,000	$3,000–15,000
MEDIUM	$2,000–6,000	$4,000–20,000
LARGE	$3,000–15,000	$5,000–50,000

Brochure Design

CLIENT SIZE	6 PANELS, 4 X 9"	8 PAGES, SELF COVER, 8.5 X 11"	16 PAGES, SELF COVER, 8.5 X 11"
SIMPLE			
SMALL	$1,000–3,000	$1,500–5,000	$3,000–7,500
MEDIUM	$2,000–5,000	$2,500–8,000	$4,000–10,000
LARGE	$2,500–7,500	$3,500–12,000	$5,000–15,000
COMPLEX			
SMALL	$1,500–7,500	$2,500–9,500	$5,000–15,000
MEDIUM	$2,000–10,000	$3,500–15,000	$6,000–25,000
LARGE	$3,000–15,000	$4,500–25,000	$7,000–50,000

[1] Design of a basic package including outer envelope, personalized letter, brochure, reply card, and return envelope.

[2] Design of basic kit including cover or folder, letterhead for text, and formatting for other insert material.

The price ranges above do not constitute specific prices for particular jobs. The buyer and seller are free to negotiate, with each designer independently deciding how to price the work, after taking all factors into account.

FIGURE 8—4

artists on a freelance basis and purchase art and photography on behalf of their clients, they must have a good working knowledge of advertising illustration and photography, including trade customs that govern both fields.

The price ranges in Figure 8-3 assume limited use of advertising design with up to five insertions within a specified media for one year. Surveys indicate that unlimited usage within the same media generally increases fees by 150 to 200 percent; unlimited use in any media increases fees by 75 to 200 percent; and a complete transfer of copyrights increases fees by up to 100 to 200 percent. All reimbursable out-of-pocket expenses incurred, including digital file preparation, are billed separately.

Collateral Design

Graphic designers who specialize in collateral material create brochures, catalogs, press kits, and direct mail packages. While clients generally retain advertising agencies to handle major campaigns for products and/or services, they often commission or retain a design firm to furnish these pieces.

Like advertising designers whose work is intended to elicit a specific response, collateral designers must have a sophisticated awareness of advertising, marketing, and sales. They often receive art and photography from the client or need to research stock images, so it is important to know how the rights to those visuals are transferred. If additional rights are needed, their transfer should be negotiated before the design or production stages. Graphic designers traditionally sell specific uses to the client—for example, first-time print runs. See Figure 8-4 for Collateral Design fees.

Package Design

Artists who design packaging understand the relationship of design objectives to technological and marketing requirements, materials and their limitations, government regulations affecting the package, and printing and reproduction processes. Many branding and graphic design firms create packaging as part of a client's total project. There are also some design firms that specialize only in packaging design. Package design is a demanding discipline, combining advertising, form, function, and style—and can involve months of market research, development, and test marketing.

The scope of a package design project can range from a single component, such as a simple hang tag or a label, to numerous components, including shipping containers. Not only does the number of components affect pricing, but so do the size of the business, the scale of the distribution range of the product (international, national, regional), and usage rights. The ranges of fees for package design, shown in Figure 8-5, reflect these factors.

Entertainment packaging

Entertainment Packaging is a separate entity unto itself. Unlike package design for products, it is package design for the artist/musician or a film/filmmaker. Both are very different art forms with different approaches.

MUSIC

Music packaging is about showing visual concepts of the music on the album. An "album," whether on CD or vinyl, is a collection of songs. In creating the booklet, the art director and designer try to create a visual experience for the band's audience to coincide with the music. The main purpose of the booklet's interior is to deliver liner notes, a more in-depth glimpse of the band, their philosophy, and their music at this moment in time. Each album concept changes with the latest music. Some artists require lyrics in all of their booklets; some are more interested in the photographs, the production credits, and the visuals that move their message. Most Pop artists prefer photography on the covers of their albums, while Jazz, New Age, Rock, or Alternative music may prefer an illustration, paintings, or a conceptual photograph on their covers, with the band or artist's image on the back cover. It is the responsibility of the project's art director to fit the right photography or illustration and design with the music. While photography is the mainstay of most music projects, having a good retouch artist on hand is an essential part of creating the finished booklet.

The components of music packaging include a CD booklet, tray card, and a CD label. The CD also may have stickers. The newest component that package designers are responsible for is a Digital PDF booklet for online downloads, which may contain lyrics or production notes and photos of the artist or band.

FILM

Today, all film packaging is DVD/Blu-ray Discs, soon to be replaced by the digital downloads of films over the internet.

DVD/Blu-ray packaging is driven by the movie studio's marketing machine and must convey a two-hour film with a powerful image and some great marketing copy. All the art created for films is called *key art*. Whether the designer is creating the original one-sheet movie art or the DVD package, both are referred to as key art. Key art involves creating a logo/title treatment and a really powerful image to capture the main theme of the film.

Movie key art is designed to be seen on a large one-sheet poster at the movie theaters, while DVDs are designed to pop out at a much smaller size from video store shelves that display multiple titles. Rarely is the key art from the movie one-sheet used for the DVD packaging. The logos and the images are usually changed to reflect the smaller size and the newest marketing tactics, such as "Academy Award Winner," etc. The new key art is created from scratch, including the film's title treatment. In this process, several key art

Comparative Fees for
Package Design

Based on concept and design, presentation of 3 to 5 layouts, finished comp, supervision of illustration or photography, and final art. Does not include any reimbursable or out-of-pocket expenses such as service bureau output or production expenses that may be billed separately.

CATEGORY	GENERAL	SPECIALIZED CONSUMER	CONSUMER TEST RUN
RETAIL PRODUCTS			
APPAREL	$10,000-30,000	$15,000-35,000	$6,000-8,000
DOMESTICS	$10,000-25,000	$15,000-30,000	$4,000-7,000
ELECTRONICS	$10,000-20,000	$10,000-20,000	$6,000-10,000
FOOD/BEVERAGE	$10,000-50,000	$8,000-30,000	$5,000-15,000
FOOTWEAR	$10,000-25,000	$10,000-25,000	$2,000-6,000
GIFTS/NOVELTIES	$8,000-20,000	$8,000-30,000	$5,000-20,000
HOME FURNISHINGS	$12,000-25,000	$12,000-25,000	$5,000-10,000
HOUSEWARES	$6,000-15,000	$10,000-20,000	$3,000-8,000
TOYS/GAMES	$12,000-40,000	$15,000-30,000	$5,000-15,000

CATEGORY	MAJOR DISTRIBUTION	LIMITED DISTRIBUTION	RE-RELEASED PROPERTY
FILM (DVD/BLU-RAY)[1]			
MAJOR STUDIO RELEASE	$6,000-10,000	$2,500-8,000	$2,500-5,000
INDEPENDENT RELEASE	$3,000-5,500	$1,250-3,750	$850-3,000
DOCUMENTARY/FOREIGN	$4,500-8,500	$2,500-3,500	$750-1,000
TV/CABLE PRODUCTION	$3,500-10,000	$1,250-5,000	$1,500-4,000
MUSIC ALBUM[2]			
POP/ROCK	$5,500-10,000	$2,500-5,000	$2,500-3,000
CLASSICAL/JAZZ	$4,500-8,000	$1,000-4,000	$1,500-3,000

	PDF (DOWNLOAD ONLY)	CONVERSION FROM PRINT-DESIGNED CD TO PDF	
DIGITAL BOOKLETS	$500-3,000[3]	$500	

CATEGORY	GENERAL	SPECIALIZED CONSUMER	CONSUMER TEST RUN
SOFTWARE/DIGITAL GAMES[4]			
BUSINESS SOFTWARE	$20,000-50,000	$5,000-15,000	$7,000-10,000
EDUCATIONAL SOFTWARE	$15,000-40,000	$5,000-15,000	$5,000-12,000
COMPUTER/VIDEO GAMES	$15,000-40,000	$6,000-15,000	$7,000-15,000

[1] DVD packaging is mostly a wrapper format that slides in a plastic case or a cardboard Digipak®. It includes key art, title treatment, billing block, and DVD label art. It is very common to design the DVD package plus the Blu-ray packaging and disc labels, a screener package for the retail buyer ("not for sale"), a trade ad, sell sheet, etc. Sample pricing for total DVD/Blu-ray package: $10,000 (Independent Release); $20,000 (Major Studio Release); $30,000+ (blockbuster film, such as *Avatar*).

[2] Albums are mostly CD packaging; a few are covers for vinyl.

[3] Price depends on size of booklet and distribution of artist.

[4] Based on concept and design of box enclosure, media label, and PDF for online manual.

The price ranges above do not constitute specific prices for particular jobs. The buyer and seller are free to negotiate, with each designer independently deciding how to price the work, after taking all factors into account.

FIGURE 8—5

comps are created. Most studios require more than 2-3. Depending on the size of the budget, up to 10 comps are required.

The design of the DVD package includes a disc label and a wrapper that slides into a plastic case. A secondary package uses a Digi-Pak format, where the key art is printed on cardboard boxes. The wrapper includes a front cover, spine, back cover with scenes from the movie, a synopsis, a specific billing block for the credits in the movie, and a barcode. It is customary for one design studio to work on all the assets for the film. It is very common to do the DVD plus the Blu-ray packaging and disc labels, as well as a screener package for the retail buyer ("not for sale"), a place card for rentals, a trade ad, a sell sheet, etc. Budgets can range from $10,000 a campaign at an independent studio to $20,000–$30,000 for a mid-size campaign at a larger movie studio.

Most movie studios create the design budget for each campaign, however designers should make sure to keep track of the revision hours and whether the work has veered off the initial scope of the project. It is helpful to remind clients when they stray out of their own budget in time and scope due to excessive revisions.

While key art for films involves photography, the end product is more like photo illustration. Art directors rarely have the luxury to reshoot the actors in a studio setting, due to the fact they are off on other movies. The original costumes and hair styles are long gone by the time the DVD/Blu-ray art is being created. Unlike other kinds of packaging design, having a great photo imaging person/illustration artist/Photoshop artist in the design studio is essential to working on key art packaging.

PRICING

The pricing of music packaging is affected by how big the recording artist's name is in music sales. Film packaging is similarly affected: the bigger the actors and the greater the film's success at the box office, the larger the marketing budget for the film's release at the DVD level. Since less prominent or newer artists and smaller films have fewer sales, their budgets are smaller. To work within budget without sacrificing fees, designers need to downscale the project. For example, photo shoots might be reduced from one day to a half day and shot in a studio rather than on location. The booklet size might be reduced to 6 pages, compared to a 16-page booklet for a premium act.

Hollywood takes all rights to package design so designers must be compensated well for design work because there will be no further compensation. Usage rights for U.S. distribution are built into a designer's fees. However, usage rights for merchandising (i.e., putting the package design on a T-shirt or a poster) can, and should, be negotiated separately. The factors affecting entertainment package design are reflected in the ranges of fees listed in Figure 8-5.

Publication Design

Publication designers create the format and look of printed magazines, tabloids, and newspapers, or online e-zines and white papers (usually PDFs). These have an editorial point of view and often contain advertising.

Specific trade customs

Today, approximately 60% of publication design is executed by designers on the publisher's staff and 40% is done by freelance or independent designers. Non-staff designers may be hired to design the format for a new magazine or tabloid; redesign an existing magazine or a special issue, section, or feature within a magazine; or develop a magazine prototype used by an editorial team to pitch a new magazine, either in-house or to a publishing company. Frequently, freelance or independent designers continue on after a job is finished as consultants for periodic oversight, either on retainer or for a fee based on an estimated number of hours per issue. The freelancer may work with one or more staff associate art directors, assistant art directors, and/or designers and production artists. This is common in large publishing companies that have numerous publications (such as trade/technical journals or how-to magazines).

At the planning stage for each issue of the publication, the key editorial staff (most often the editor-in-chief, section editors, and key writers for the issue) meet with the art director and appropriate staff to hold a story and cover conference. During this session, the strategy for several issues is mapped out, with a major focus on the current issue. A direction is established, and concepts may be determined at this time. Then the art director commissions art for the issue within yearly budget constraints. That may involve locating new creative talent (illustrators and photographers) whose styles are appropriate for the new design. Since editors assume authority for the publication, they have approval over dummies and storyboards. The publisher most often has final approval over the entire package, and revisions are frequently required.

Freelance designers who are commissioned to work on publications are often expected to sign all-rights or work-for-hire contracts. Designers may choose to weigh all their options before accepting assignments under these conditions. (For more information, see the Work-for-Hire section in Chapter 2, Legal Rights & Issues.)

Pricing

Because name plates (logos) are the anchors of most magazines, they are the anchors of most magazine design work. Consequently, fees for magazine design are front-loaded toward logo design since its development takes place at

Comparative Fees for
Publication Design

Creative design fees are largely dependent on the complexity of the assignment, the number of pages, circulation, production needs and schedules, the client's budget, the design team, deadines, and printing schedules. Experienced designers work collaboratively with editors/publishers in establishing creative and workable design solutions for a publication. The following data are based on normal conditions and do not reflect any reimbursable or out-of-pocket expenses.

Consumer Magazine

	CIRCULATION*	GENERAL INTEREST*	SPECIAL INTEREST*
STARTUP	Over 1 million	$50,000-100,000	$30,000-70,000
	500,000 to 1 million	$50,000-100,000	$20,000-60,000
	100,000 to 500,000	$30,000-90,000	$15,000-50,000
	50,000 to 100,000	$20,000-50,000	$10,000-25,000
	Under 50,000	$20,000-50,000	$10,000-25,000
REDESIGN OF EXISTING FORMAT	Over 1 million	$40,000-80,000	$25,000-50,000
	500,000 to 1 million	$40,000-80,000	$25,000-50,000
	100,000 to 500,000	$30,000-70,000	$15,000-45,000
	50,000 to 100,000	$20,000-45,000	$12,000-25,000
	Under 50,000	$15,000-25,000	$10,000-20,000
LAYOUT AND EXECUTION OF EXISTING DESIGN	Over 1 million	$20,000-35,000	$20,000-30,000
	500,000 to 1 million	$20,000-35,000	$15,000-25,000
	100,000 to 500,000	$15,000-30,000	$10,000-20,000
	50,000 to 100,000	$15,000-30,000	$10,000-20,000
	Under 50,000	$5,000-15,000	$5,000-10,000

Trade Magazine

	CIRCULATION*	GENERAL INTEREST*	SPECIAL INTEREST*
STARTUP	Over 1 million	$20,000-75,000	$20,000-60,000
	500,000 to 1 million	$15,000-75,000	$15,000-50,000
	100,000 to 500,000	$10,000-60,000	$10,000-35,000
	50,000 to 100,000	$10,000-50,000	$7,500-25,000
	Under 50,000	$10,000-30,000	$7,500-20,000
REDESIGN OF EXISTING FORMAT	Over 1 million	$25,000-70,000	$20,000-50,000
	500,000 to 1 million	$25,000-70,000	$20,000-50,000
	100,000 to 500,000	$20,000-60,000	$10,000-30,000
	50,000 to 100,000	$15,000-50,000	$7,500-20,000
	Under 50,000	$6,000-25,000	$3,500-15,000
LAYOUT AND EXECUTION OF EXISTING DESIGN	Over 1 million	$20,000-40,000	$15,000-30,000
	500,000 to 1 million	$20,000-40,000	$15,000-30,000
	100,000 to 500,000	$15,000-30,000	$10,000-20,000
	50,000 to 100,000	$15,000-30,000	$7,500-15,000
	Under 50,000	$10,000-20,000	$6,000-15,000

*Note: Some designers do not differentiate pricing by circulation figures or type of magazine. Primary factors that may affect pricing are creative ideation, scope of work per issue, and number of pages. Others offer clients a per-page rate if number of pages fluctuates.

(Continues on next page)

FIGURE 8—6

Comparative Fees for
Publication Design (Continued)

Corporate/in-house

	CIRCULATION	64-PAGE SELF-COVER MAGAZINE	12-PAGE SELF-COVER TABLOID/MAGAZINE
STARTUP	Over 100,000	$20,000-60,000	$5,000-20,000
	50,000 to 100,000	$20,000-60,000	$5,000-15,000
	25,000 to 50,000	$15,000-40,000	$3,000-10,000
	Under 25,000	$9,000-30,000	$3,000-10,000
REDESIGN OF EXISTING FORMAT	Over 100,000	$20,000-30,000	$5,000-15,000
	50,000 to 100,000	$20,000-30,000	$5,000-12,000
	25,000 to 50,000	$12,000-25,000	$4,000-10,000
	Under 25,000	$12,000-22,000	$3,000-8,000
LAYOUT AND EXECUTION OF EXISTING DESIGN	Over 100,000	$20,000-25,000	$7,500-15,000
	50,000 to 100,000	$20,000-25,000	$4,000-12,000
	25,000 to 50,000	$15,000-20,000	$3,000-10,000
	Under 25,000	$6,000-20,000	$3,000-8,000

The price ranges in the chart do not constitute specific prices for particular jobs. The buyer and seller are free to negotiate, with each designer independently deciding how to price the work, after taking all factors into account.

FIGURE 8—6

the beginning of the project. If logo design is not required (an existing magazine wishes a new design without changing its name plate), the design fee will be weighted more toward cover design.

Standard procedure is to bill the design and development fee in segments, no matter what the size or cost of the job. For larger projects, a third of the payment is usually made upon signing the agreement, a third upon approval of design comprehensives, and the final third within 30 days of delivery of electronic files or printed pieces. For smaller projects, half is customary at the outset, with the balance due upon submission of final layouts. Billable expenses and production charges are invoiced regularly (usually monthly) to help the designer manage out-of-pocket expenses.

Fees for publication design vary as widely as the magazines themselves. The complexity of the work involved is always an element. Some other factors affecting price are the magazine's audience (consumer, trade, or corporate/in-house), size (number of pages), numerical and geographical circulation, production, whether the publisher is an individual or small or large corporation, the size and stature of the designer or design firm, and the urgency of the schedule. The lower end of the fee range is appropriate for a redesign that only requires the designer to create one or two cover designs and a few inside spreads. If the client requires a full-blown dummy issue to demonstrate every possible variation that might occur in the magazine, a proportionately higher fee is customarily charged. Another factor that affects fees is whether the freelance design team has to provide written guidelines and electronic templates for the in-house art department to use. See Figure 8-6 for Publication Design fees.

Book Jacket or Cover Design

Book jacket designers create the look of the jacket or cover of a book, or of a series of books, using the graphic elements of typography, illustration, photography, and/or specially designed letterforms.

The publishing industry has two major categories: Trade, and Education. What defines the titles within those categories is how much money the book can potentially make in the marketplace, and how much of a budget is assigned to the title. For trade books, the categories of *mass, major, minor* and *young adult* determine how much money will be spent on a particular title. Within the publishing organization, a book may be identified as an A-, B-, or C-level book, based on market research and potential sales. Once a trade book reaches the store shelf, publishers often depend on the consumer "judging the book by its cover" as a way of guiding their purchasing behavior.

For textbooks, the categories are *college,* and *el-hi (elementary/high school).* Unlike the purchasing scenario of a trade book, where people are generally purchasing the book for themselves, in the education market, someone other than the end user is making the purchasing decision. Therefore, the cover image and overall design is meant to appeal to the purchaser, rather than the end user.

The relationships between cover design & book categories

MASS MARKET

Mass-market books are designed to appeal to a broader market and are sold predominantly through mass channels that extend beyond traditional trade outlets. Mass-market sources may include newsstands, drug stores, chain and department stores, in addition to bookstores and libraries. For the client, a mass-market book is often produced in a standard size and format and has lower production costs. The cover design of a mass-market title is critical to its sales.

MAJOR TRADE

Trade books are designed for a specific target audience in either specialized or general consumer markets and are sold primarily through bookstores. Trade books are traditionally hardcover, but soft cover editions often follow the first printing. For most major trade books, the cover image is a key factor in driving the sales of the book.

MINOR TRADE

The cover design for a minor trade book might be a soft cover edition of an existing hardcover title, with a new design that is targeted to be repurposed into a market segment, or designed to fit a specific genre or category.

TEXTBOOK

Textbooks are designed for classroom use rather than general consumption. There are several ancillary components to textbook design. The cover is designed to appeal to specific grades, subject matters, and sometimes, specific geographic locations.

Specific trade customs

After accepting the job, the designer is given a brief synopsis of the book and a marketing and

---

Comparative Fees for Book Jacket or Cover Design

A usual and customary fee for a typical cover design project includes the presentation of (3) comprehensive design concepts, which show both the front cover and spine treatment. The fee may also include supervision of illustration and/or photography as it applies. In many cases, designers are required to also perform the production task of providing the client with a digital file, following the clients template and measurements. The fee does not include billable expenses. The client is purchasing rights to only one of the submitted comps and usage rights for only the first edition.

Hardcover

	ONE CONCEPT	ADDITIONAL CONCEPTS (PER SKETCH)	VOLUNTARY TERMINATION (% OF FEE)
MASS MARKET*	$1,000–2,500	$300–750	50%
MAJOR TRADE*	$1,000–2,500	$750–1,000	50%
MINOR TRADE	$1,000–2,500	$225–500	50%
TEXTBOOK	$1,000–2,500	$150–500	50%
YOUNG ADULT	$1,000–2,500	–	50%

* Sometimes pricing is broken down into $500 for a range of concepts and $500-1,000 for the final selection.

Paperback

	ONE CONCEPT	ADDITIONAL CONCEPTS (PER SKETCH)	VOLUNTARY TERMINATION (% OF FEE)
MASS MARKET	$1,000–2,800	$250–750	50%
MAJOR TRADE	$1,200–2,500	$300–750	50%
MINOR TRADE	$950–2,500	$200–750	50%
TEXTBOOK	$725–2,500	$225–500	50%
YOUNG ADULT	$800–1,200	–	50%

The price ranges in the chart do not constitute specific prices for particular jobs. The buyer and seller are free to negotiate, with each designer independently deciding how to price the work, after taking all factors into account, including any online editions, such as e-books or downloadable electronic formats.

FIGURE 8—7

sales strategy. The purchase order (PO) or contract usually reflects terms (deadlines and credit) and fees that are agreed upon in writing by the publisher's art director and the designer.

Copyright and credit for the designer should be agreed upon before work begins. When credit is given, it usually appears on the back flap or on the back of the cover, though it occasionally appears on the copyright page. If other commissioned elements such as illustration, calligraphy, or custom fonts appear on the cover, they should be credited as well. Book jacket designers should specify on the invoice that the artwork is prepared only for the named edition and title and the ISBN number specified (if available).

Pricing

Many designers usually sell one-time reproduction rights; however, current practice varies. With some unethical publishers, artists may find their work appearing on the paperback edition or in electronic form as an e-book, years after a hardcover jacket was issued, without additional payment; reputable publishers pay for additional paperback and electronic rights. Designers should clarify this provision in a written agreement with the publisher, as well as any additional payments for use of the art by another domestic publisher, by book clubs or foreign publishers, or by film, television, or other media.

The client's right to make additional use of the finished art is usually limited to advertising and promoting the original edition for which the contract was signed. If other rights are negotiated, a statement of those rights should appear on the designer's bill if they are not reflected in writing at the time they are negotiated. The bill should also state that all other rights are reserved by the designer and that original art should be returned to the designer (if it is not a digital file).

The designer may prepare from two to four sketches or comps for presentation, which are supplied to the client most commonly in digital form (as PDFs or JPEGS) or alternatively as color prints if the client prefers. Another one or two variations may be requested. If more than three comps are required, industry sources indicate that it is customary for an additional fee to be paid.

Generally, the comp should be as close as possible in appearance to the finished piece. Such tight comps can entail expenses, and traditionally all out-of-pocket expenses in the sketch stage are billable to the client. For instance, high-quality color prints that may be used in comps are billable directly to the client. However, many clients approve JPEG or PDF proofs on screen, and there is no printed comp.

The nature of publishing leads to a high rate of rejection of comp presentations. Current industry practices indicate that this risk is accepted by designers and publishers, who agree to a rejection fee, reflecting the amount of work completed at the time of the project's termination. Recent data indicate that the usual rejection fee is half the agreed-upon design fee for an accepted job. Any incurred expenses also are paid.

Once the comp is approved, the designer purchases the high resolution stock art or executes or commissions the illustration, lettering, or other graphic elements used in the finished art. Production costs for necessities such as, but not necessarily limited to, photographic processing, type, and digital output are generally billed by the designer in addition to the design fee. Such costs are directly assumed by the client. Current data indicate that markups and handling fees for outside services are in the range of 15 to 25 percent. These are applied to cover expenses incurred (for type or hard-copy output) when the publisher does not pick them up directly. See Figure 8-7 for book jacket design fees.

Interior Book Design

Book designers develop the style and visual flow of a book's interior by combining the graphic elements of typography, illustration, and photography. The job description for book designers ranges from highly creative to somewhat mechanical.

Book design categories

There are four basic book design categories: mass market, trade, college textbook, and elementary through high school-level textbook (el-hi). Some unusual projects or books for small presses may not fit into those categories. In such cases, designers traditionally use their hourly rates as the basis for a fee. If the design is to be used for a series of books, a reuse fee should be negotiated.

MASS MARKET

Mass market book interior designs, when called for, are usually simple and low-budget. These books can be a page-per-page reduction of the trade version or printed on low-quality paper with a type of press that cannot reproduce fine detail.

TRADE

The complexity of design for trade books is determined by the genre and specific format of the book:

Simple: A straightforward book such as a novel or short book of poetry. Design includes a layout showing a title page, a chapter opening, a text spread, and front matter spreads. Simple books are generally done in-house but may be given to a freelance designer if the publisher is small and does not have an in-house design department.
Average: General nonfiction, poetry, anthologies, or illustrated books designed on a grid system. Design may include front matter (half title, title, copyright, dedication, acknowledgments, preface, contents, list of illustrations, introduction, ad card), part opening, chapter opening, text with three to six levels of heads, tabular matter, illustrations and/or photographs, extracts, footnotes, and simple

Comparative Fees for Interior Book Design

Trade

	SIMPLE[1]	AVERAGE[2]	COMPLEX[3]
ADULT	$800–1,000	$1,200–1,500	$2,000–5,000

College Textbook

	SIMPLE[1]	AVERAGE[2]	COMPLEX[3]
Four-color	$1,500–2,500	$3,000–5,000	$6,000–10,000
Two-color	$1,200	-	-

El-hi Textbook

	CONCEPT SKETCHES	DESIGN PROTOTYPE
BASAL	$50–60 Per page	$750–1,200 Per page

[1] Simple includes novels and nonfiction, with two to four elements, chapter numbers, text, extract.

[2] Average includes fiction or nonfiction with a moderate number of elements, comprising three to six levels of heads, tabular matter, extracts, footnotes, and simple back matter.

[3] Complex designs require special treatment for each page, two- or four-color printing, or other books of greater complexity than average, including coffee table books and cookbooks.

FIGURE 8—8a

back matter such as bibliography and index. The design, excluding the front matter, is set in sample pages for the publisher and approved before the complete manuscript is typeset.

Complex: Books that require special treatment of each page or more complex printing techniques, such as four-color books, cookbooks, workbooks, catalogs, and elaborate art or picture books.

COLLEGE-LEVEL TEXTBOOK

The design of college-level textbooks involves three phases: presentation of concept, full design of all elements, and final design with style sheets for the compositor.

Simple: These are mostly straight text with up to three levels of heads, simple tables, and/or art.

Average: These have up to six levels of heads, tables and/or charts, extracts, footnotes, and illustrations, diagrams, and/or photographs laid out on a grid system.

Complex: These are usually foreign language texts, or two-, three-, or four-color texts, complicated workbooks, catalogs, or illustrated books that require special treatment of each page.

ELEMENTARY THROUGH HIGH SCHOOL-LEVEL (EL-HI) TEXTBOOK

El-hi textbooks tend to be more visually oriented than college-level texts and, therefore, more design-intensive.

The design transmittal

Before the designer can begin, the manuscript must be reviewed to ascertain how many elements will need to be designed and how the hierarchy of the various heads should be organized. This is done in the form of a design transmittal, which lists all elements in the manuscript along with the page number of the first instance. Design transmittals are often prepared by the publisher's editorial department and will accompany the design packet supplied to the designer. However, some designers reported that they are often handed a manuscript and have to go through it themselves to find the elements. This is also common practice in self-publishing projects.

The design transmittal includes a copy of the manuscript or a selection of representative copy for sample pages, a summary of all typographic elements, and a description of the book's production specifications (trim size, desired number of pages, number of ink colors, and so on). The publisher should also reiterate the design directives discussed during the consultation. It is really important at this stage for the designer to get a clear idea of what the client wants, in order to avoid time-consuming revisions. To prevent problems later on, some designers show a preliminary page or two, to make sure they are going in the right direction.

The design fee is based on the complexity of manuscript as demonstrated primarily by the number of elements listed on the design transmittal.

If the designer finds additional elements during the design process or if the transmittal otherwise misrepresents the complexity level of the manuscript, the design fee may be increased accordingly to compensate for the additional work necessary. The publisher should also indicate whether any particular visual style is desired. The designer's pricing is based on the publisher's preparation of the design transmittal. When the designer's assignment includes this responsibility, it is usually reflected in a higher fee.

Book design fees

MASS MARKET, TRADE, & COLLEGE TEXTBOOK

The design fee reflects design complexity. A basic fee for mass market, trade, or college textbooks includes the following services:

- Initial consultation with the publisher, packager, or other contractor to discuss the project. This consultation can be accomplished in person or by phone or e-mail.
- Analysis of the manuscript to confirm that the scope of work complies with the publisher's design transmittal.
- Castoff of the manuscript. Casting-off is estimating the number of pages in the final book by performing an in-depth character count of the manuscript. Sometimes the cast-off has to wait until the final manuscript is ready and all or most of the graphics are acquired. Sometimes the design has to be adjusted at this stage in order to make the page count correct.
- Sample layouts showing principal elements.
- Speccing /markup of the manuscript.
- Preparation of templates for the approved layouts. Digital files with style sheets may be provided by the designer for use by the compositor, or a comp order may be supplied, which contains all specs necessary for the compositor to create his/her own style sheets.
- Follow-through, including a check of first-pass pages.

If a publisher requests minor changes in the design, revisions are included in the basic design fee. If major changes are requested, the design fee may have to be renegotiated, or changes may be billed at the designer's hourly rate. The prices in Figure 7-8a are based on the preparation of as many layouts as the designer feels are necessary to show major design elements. When the client wishes to see highly detailed layouts, a higher fee is usually charged.

EL-HI TEXTBOOK

El-hi textbook design and production are structured a bit differently. Four-color basal math, reading, science, social studies, etc., generally follow this course:

- Meeting of designers, editors, and photo researchers: with sample manuscript in hand, they sketch out what the pages should look like prior to delivery of the full manuscript.
- Concept sketches: usually thumbnail size, 30 to 50 percent of the actual page size.
- Design prototypes: the specs are sometimes included, but if they are extremely complicated, there could be an additional fee for the specs/design brief.
- Page production: includes three rounds of proofing and all associated proofreading fees. Additional steps (charged separately) may include:
  + Art or photo research or acquisition.
  + Art or photo database management/trafficking.
  + Photo shoot set-up, including props, styling, and so on.

Additional charges

Project management; supervision or art direction of an art program, including hiring and coordinating illustrators or photographers; extra conference time; trips to the publisher; page makeup or dummying; and time spent doing other production work, are billed in addition to the design fee. The cost of specially commissioned work and other supplies is traditionally a billable expense.

Design process

After the fee is agreed upon, the designer prepares layouts. These typically include the title page, a sample of frontmatter heads such as "Introduction," a sample chapter opener, a sample part title (if applicable), and double-page spreads showing the text setting along with most or all text elements. These may include extracts, poetry, sidebars, and so forth. These examples are needed for the publisher to evaluate and approve the design and are used as a guide during production.

Designers were once expected to supply a composition order (comp order) for the typesetter that detailed all type specifications based on the layouts. Today, the trend is away from writing formal type specs and more toward setting up style sheets, master pages, and sample pages that hopefully cover all contingencies.

Publishers may use an in-house or a compositor's production facility to take the book from layout to page makeup. In those cases, the designer will be required to check the first set of page proofs to make sure the compositor has followed all design specifications. Other publishers may give designers electronic files of type and art and have them make up the pages electronically. The designer charges an additional per-page rate for type composition or page layout if that is part of the job. See the following section on dummy/page makeup for details.

DUMMY / PAGE MAKEUP

After the book design is approved, the design is applied via style sheets to the text manuscript—

either by the copy editor, compositor, or production person. Next, the dummy or first-pass pages will be created by either the compositor or designer. Some publishing projects require special coding, such as XML and ETM, and this work may be done by software specialists. However, many books are still produced by typesetting houses, production artists, or freelancers.

Dummy/page makeup is charged on a per-page rate, which includes one round of minor corrections. See Figure 8-8b for typical page rates. Author's alterations (AAs) and editor's alterations (EAs) after page makeup are usually charged at an hourly rate in addition to the page rate. However, some publishers require that all revision cycles be included in the page price. Final pages are created after first-pass pages are proofread and reviewed by the publisher.

Book Packaging

Occasionally, a writer and book designer collaborate to create a "package" that is then sold to a publisher. Such a package includes completely finished digital files, relieving the publisher of any production responsibilities. Generally, this way of working is most common when the idea for the book originates with a writer or designer who wishes to maintain control over the book.

With the emergence of self-publishing companies on the Internet, there is an increased demand for book packaging. Online companies that specialize in "one off" publishing (printing one copy at a time) make it easier and more affordable for an author to publish. However, to achieve a professional look, authors still need the services of a professional designer. One designer who has found a niche catering to the self-publishing market describes book packaging as "the art of packaging an author's writing appropriately in book format. It encompasses the cover and interior design and layout; cover materials (e.g., paperback, hardcover); enhancements, such as embossing; trim size, etc. The packaging designer considers the genre and intended audience, among other factors, when making packaging decisions. It is a service that is especially needed for first-time authors. The charge for this service may be included in a designer's fees for book design."

Lettering & Typeface Design

Lettering or typography is used for both text and headlines in all areas of the communications and entertainment industries: advertising and promotion, corporate identity, packaging, publishing, greeting cards, and TV programs and movies. Many lettering artists also offer graphic design services.

Lettering

The computer has had a major impact on lettering, since graphic designers can now manipulate and customize fonts on a computer. Some designers still specialize in the field of lettering, creating various unique headlines used in magazines, books, packaging, and movies. Some designers

Comparative Fees for Book Page Makeup (Per Page)

Trade

	SIMPLE[1]	AVERAGE[2]	COMPLEX[3]
ADULT	$6–12	$7–16	$17–50

Textbook

	SIMPLE[1]	AVERAGE[2]	COMPLEX[3]
College	$12–14	$15–17	$18–25
El-hi	-	-	$75–110[4]

Rush page rates - 20 to 40 percent higher

[1] Simple includes novels and nonfiction, with two to four elements, chapter number, text, extract.

[2] Average includes fiction or nonfiction with a moderate number of elements, comprising three to six levels of heads, tabular matter, extracts, footnotes, and simple back matter.

[3] Complex designs require special treatment for each page, two- or four-color printing, or other books of greater complexity than average, including coffee table books and cookbooks.

[4] Additional fees:
Art or photo research or aquisition: $45 per image (usage additional)
Art or photo database management/trafficking: $25 per image
Photoshoot set-up, including props, styling, etc: $90 per image

FIGURE 8—8b

Comparative Fees for Lettering & Typeface Design

Usual and customary creative fees. Reimbursable expenses not included

Masthead

DISTRIBUTION	SKETCHES/ROUGHS[1]	FINISHED WORK[2]
NATIONAL	$1,500–3,500	$2,000–6,500
REGIONAL	$1,250–2,000	$1,750–4,000
LOCAL	$850–1,250	$1,150–2,750
CORPORATE OR IN-HOUSE	$650–1,250	$850–2,500

[1] Includes up to three sketches; does not include usage rights.

[2] Includes finished art, unlimited rights.

Logotype

Based on 3 to 6 sketches, one finish, unlimited rights.

NATIONAL/LARGE COMPANY	$7,500–15,000
REGIONAL/SMALL COMPANY	$2,500–7,500
INDIVIDUAL	$1,000–5,000

Headlines

Lettering for magazines, brochures, shopping bags, etc.: limited rights, one comp, one finish.

DISTRIBUTION	COMPLEX	SIMPLE
CONSUMER/WIDE	$1,000–5,000	$1,000–5,000
TRADE/MEDIUM	$750–1,500	$500–1,250
SPECIAL INTEREST/NARROW	$750–1,250	$500–1,000
CORPORATE OR IN-HOUSE	$500–1,000	$300–750

Hardcover Book Jacket

Lettering used as a design component; one-time rights only for the specific edition; one comp, one finish.

DISTRIBUTION	COMPLEX	AVERAGE	SIMPLE
MASS MARKET	$1,250–2,500	$1,000–2,000	$750–1,500
MAJOR TRADE	$1,000–2,000	$850–1,750	$650–1,500
MINOR TRADE	$850–2,000	$750–1,500	$500–1,250
TEXTBOOK	$750–1,500	$650–1,250	$500–1,000
YOUNG ADULT	$750–1,200	$600–1,000	$500–850

ALTERNATE PRICING METHOD – ALL GENRES: $1,200–2,200

Price affected by usage; print or print & Internet; author brand and importance; new book or rerelease of an old book.

Paperback Cover

Lettering used as a design component; one-time rights only for the specific edition; one comp, one finish.

MASS MARKET	$1,250–2,000	$1,000–1,500	$750–1,250
MAJOR TRADE	$1,000–1,750	$750–1,500	$650–1,200

(Continues on next page)

FIGURE 8—9

Comparative Fees for
Lettering & Typeface Design (Continued)

Paperback Cover (Continued)

Lettering used as a design component; one-time rights only for the specific edition; one comp, one finish.

DISTRIBUTION	COMPLEX	AVERAGE	SIMPLE
MINOR TRADE	$750–1,500	$600–1,250	$500–1,000
TEXTBOOK	$750–1,500	$600–1,250	$500–1,000
YOUNG ADULT	$750–1,500	$600–1,250	$500–1,000

ALTERNATE PRICING METHOD: ROMANCE & DETECTIVE	
TITLE ONLY	$500–800
TITLE & AUTHOR	$600–2,500*

*Higher price for well-known author or franchise where type is main art on the cover.

Handwriting Campaigns

MAGAZINE & NEWSPAPER ADS
Casual or calligraphic style, integrated with photos and illustration. $700–5,000 per ad

Price affected by usage: U.S. only vs international and if it includes Internet as well as print.

Typeface Design

Assumed that work will be delivered as font software, not as a set of analog drawings.

COMMISSIONED WORK

HOURLY RATE: $75–300 (depends on work involved and variables such as
                      glyph set, script, language support, OpenType features, etc.)

ORIGINAL TYPEFACE DESIGN: Single Weight or Style
(standard glyph set, Latin script, Western European Language support)

EDITORIAL	$5,000–20,000
CORPORATE	$10,000–30,000

Price affected by usage: U.S. only vs international and if it includes Internet as well as print.

ORIGINAL TYPEFACE DESIGN: Multiple Weight/Style Type Families

Generally priced at a lower per font price depending on how many weights and styles are ultimately created.

Including additional scripts, such as Cyrillic, Greek, Hebrew, Arabic, Chinese, Japanese, Indic, or Thai, to a design is a highly specialized skill and is priced on a case-by-case basis.

Generally, commissioned work remains exclusive to the client for a short period of time, usually one year. Prices can be affected by different exclusivity arrangements. Longer exclusivity would increase the price. No exclusivity could reduce the price. A buyout, where the client obtains all rights, would increase the price dramatically.

NONCOMMISSIONED WORK

FONT LICENSING

Fonts developed without commissions and offered to the design public for sale. Some type designers choose to license their fonts to large font houses or resellers rather than sell the licensing themselves. Royalty rates paid to the typeface designer for these arrangements range from 15% to 50% of the retail price.

FONT ENGINEERING

Fonts modified to function optimally in low resolution environments such as computer screens and hand-held devices requires many hours of additional work, separate from the original design and font making. This work is generally referred to as Hinting, and is priced on a case-by-case basis. It is a highly specialized skill and not offered by every typeface designer.

The price ranges in the chart do not constitute specific prices for particular jobs. The buyer and seller are free to negotiate, with each designer independently deciding how to price the work, after taking all factors into account.

FIGURE 8—9

render the many aspects of lettering entirely by hand, although increasingly lettering designers draw sketches manually and then complete the work digitally. Letters may be drawn first and then refined; they may be outlined and then filled in; they may begin with an already drawn form or typeface and then be altered, either manually on paper or digitally after the work is scanned into a computer; or they may be started on a computer and then customized.

A designer who is currently making a living from lettering design is likely to do a mix of calligraphy and lettering, all loosely called "letterform design." Traditionally, calligraphic letters are formed with a broad-edged pen or a brush. Hand-rendered lettering includes handwriting campaigns, created using a casual script or calligraphic style. Handwriting is used in advertising and packaging design. Sometimes the product name is hand-written (e.g., Gardenburger®); in other instances, handwriting is reserved for sub-branding (e.g. light carb, vanilla, etc.).

SPECIFIC TRADE CUSTOMS
The work of lettering artists is similar to that of illustrators. Upon agreement of the terms, usage rights, and fee for the project, a letterer prepares a sketch or sketches of possible solutions to a specific problem. Sketch fees alone usually do not include usage rights that must be transferred in writing. Upon acceptance of the sketches or comp, the lettering artist prepares finished art for reproduction.

PRICING
Many factors affect the pricing of lettering work. A primary factor is usage, which may be further broken down into international, national, regional, buy out, Internet, or print and Internet.

In the publishing field, pricing is affected by whether the lettering is being done for a new release or the re-release of an old book and whether it's a hardcover or a paperback book, with romance being its own category. Hardcovers pay more than paperbacks. The fame of the author and the use of the cover are other pricing considerations. A new title for a well-known, best-selling author commands a higher fee than for an unknown author. The highest prices are paid when the cover becomes a product—the style of the lettering becomes the author's brand or franchise. Likewise, the lettering of a TV show or movie title may also become a brand or franchise.

When pricing headlines designed for advertising, the lettering artist may take into account the size of the ad and the relative size of the headline and refer to advertising illustration fees based on ad size (1/4-page, 1/2-page, etc.). See Figure 10-1 for Comparative Fees for Advertising Illustration.

Artists usually receive half of the total fee upon delivery of sketches. (Increasingly, more time is spent on sketches and less on completing the digital finish.) "Buyouts" (all-rights transfers) currently cost up to 50 percent or more above the original price of the art. Fees for lettering done as part of a package design, depend on, among other factors, whether the client hired the artist directly, which is unusual, or a design firm or advertising agency hired the artist, which is more common. In the latter case, the fee is usually significantly less, reflecting in-house input into the design and the agency's reluctance to part with any more of the client's fee for services than is absolutely necessary. See Figure 8-9 for lettering fees.

Typeface design

Digital typefaces are the foundation for today's printed and broadcast communications. Perhaps because of their constant use and exposure, they tend to be taken for granted by most of the viewing public. Thousands of typefaces exist today, giving graphic designers the ability to depict the feeling, mood, tone, and very essence of a message through type.

The OpenType standard is becoming widely adopted, and there is now a bit of a niche area developing for those who are both talented type designers and programmers. The process of producing a viable OpenType font with OpenType "features" requires knowledge not only of type design, but also of programming and code. It is currently a highly technical and emerging area, as there's a very small group of people who actually know how to do it. However, when used to its full capacity, OpenType can allow for some amazing context-sensitive design possibilities, including interlocking letters, etc. It is helping digital font design to transcend the stigma of feeling too "computerized" compared with hand lettering.

SPECIFIC TRADE CUSTOMS
Each year, hundreds of new typefaces are created, ranging from simple, trendy fonts to complex, sophisticated font families. The designers who create these fonts are often self-employed, or they may be staff designers working at the larger type houses. Typeface design work can be either commissioned or non-commissioned (produced independently, or speculation).

Designers are sometimes asked to modify existing typefaces (fonts). Before doing this, one must always check the End User License Agreement (EULA) that governed the sale of the font license to be sure such modifications are legal. More and more, this kind of work is not allowed by type designers and font resellers. If this work is allowed by the EULA, it is generally priced at an hourly fee based on the type of modifications needed. Persons hiring type designers to perform this type of work are required to present the type designer with valid authorizations to do the work.

PRICING
Non-commissioned work Many fonts are developed without commissions and offered to the design public for sale. Some type designers choose to license their fonts to large font houses

or retailers rather than sell the licenses themselves. Royalty rates paid to the typeface designer for these arrangements range from 15 to 50 percent. The higher figure comes from smaller distributors, or those who have only an online presence. Interfacing with other type designers through online forums is the best way to find out what is going on in the field and who the most favorable distributors are.

Commissioned work Pricing for commissioned typeface design is based on the following factors that make up a commission:

Glyphs are the basic building blocks of a font. They are the shapes that comprise a character, like "ñ"-composed of a lower case "n" and a tilde. Glyphs can be reused multiple times throughout a font to compose larger character sets. The type designer and/or the client decide how many characters are to be included in a single font.

Fonts include the complete **set of characters** in a single typeface: letters, numbers, punctuation marks, ligatures, alternate characters (like special initial caps and swashes), foreign or mathematical symbols, and accent marks. Attention to **kerning** (spacing definitions for specific letter combinations) is integral to the overall quality of the font.

Families are clusters of related fonts that bear the names of their parent typefaces. The fonts in a family vary only in style (roman or italic) and/or weight (bold, regular, light).

Display faces differ from **text faces** in that they are suitable only for headlines or callouts rather than large passages of text. Display faces are usually set in 14 point or larger.

Typeface design for text faces involves creating the upper and lowercase letters, numbers, ligatures, punctuation, as well as alternate and special characters. Creating complete font families requires multiple rounds of finished drawings or printouts, with minute adjustments between rounds. Setting text in a range of sizes and outputting to a variety of devices to insure legibility takes time and patience.

The fee for a typeface commission should reflect the required number and variation of styles, weights, and alternate sets (small caps, lining figures, symbols). Multiple weight/style type families will generally be priced at a lower per font price depending on how many weights and styles are ultimately created. Creating additional scripts, such as Cyrillic, Greek, Hebrew, Arabic, Chinese, Japanese, Indic, or Thai, for a design is a highly specialized skill and is priced on a project-by-project basis.

The exclusivity period for a typeface also affects pricing, as the licensing value of a font may be higher after a period of exposure as a corporate exclusive. Generally, commissioned work remains exclusive to the client for a short period of time, usually one year. Longer exclusivity periods demand a higher price, and a design with no exclusivity would be priced lower. A buyout, where the client retains all rights, would increase the price dramatically. Type designers may also offer clients services that were once provided by type foundries: modification of spacing metrics, creation of custom kerning, expansion of existing character sets to include special characters, and coding for specialized language uses. These services are priced according to the client's intended use and vary widely. Type designers should also consider which operating systems will be supported by their typeface.

Font engineering Fonts modified to function optimally in low resolution environments, such as the screens on computers and hand-held devices, require many hours of additional work separate from the original design and font making. This work is generally referred to as *hinting* and is a highly specialized skill within the type design community that not every typeface designer possesses. It is often contracted out to a hinting specialist, who commands a high fee for the service, due to its painstaking and time-consuming nature.

Photo Retouching, Restoration & Illustration

Today's technology enables graphic artists to become experts at manipulating and altering photographs and other images to better meet a client's needs. Photo manipulation includes such skills as color correcting, distorting, or enhancing an image; replacing backgrounds; and creating complex composites.

Photo retouchers are graphic artists who alter an existing photograph by removing undesirable blemishes, objects, and dust to enhance the image. Traditionally, retouching has been done manually, by applying bleach, dyes, gouache, or transparent watercolor to the photograph or transparency/chrome with a paintbrush or airbrush.

Comparative Fees for **Photo Retouching/ Restoration**

All Markets

	HOURLY
NATIONAL/ GENERAL CONSUMER	$65-200
	PERCENT OF FEE ADDED
RUSH FEE	50%-200%

FIGURE 8—10

Today, it also is done electronically, using special software such as Adobe Photoshop. The resulting image usually appears untouched. This "invisible art" requires a highly skilled hand and eye to be successful. Therefore, the retoucher most often specializes in one area of retouching and concentrates on the skills and technical knowledge of that area.

Photo restoration involves using manual or digital tools to add or subtract areas of a damaged or faded photograph in order to return the image to its original condition. The artist may have to remove scratches, stains, or tears; adjust the color balance and contrast; and even recreate missing sections of the image. Old photographs are irreplaceable. To avoid possible further damage or reducing the value of a collectible or antique, manual work is not done on the original. A copy negative is made first, and the restoration work is done on a work print that may be larger than the original. From the work print, a final negative and prints at requested sizes are made for the customer. Today, most restoration work is done digitally by scanning the photograph into an image editing program and modifying the scanned image file, then outputting that digital file to photo paper on a high quality printer.

Photo illustrators specialize in creating composite images—compilations of multiple images. They may use some of the same artistic treatments employed by retouchers and restorers. Photo illustration may be done digitally, by hand, or by using a combination of both. Photo Illustration is a powerful tool that can have dramatic consequences; for example, evidence that published photographs of a 2006 bombing in Lebanon had been digitally manipulated to make the damage seem more severe caused outrage in the United States press.

Pricing

When pricing a photo retouching, restoration, or illustration project, the artist must take several factors into account.

Complexity: The work required can run the gamut in changes to the photo from simply adding a few highlights to actually creating realistic hand-wrought backgrounds, shapes, or figures or stripping two or more photos together to create a montage. The complexity of the work results in a wide range of hourly rates for these services. Lower fees are charged for simple retouching, such as removing telephone lines from the sky behind a building or removing blemishes and acne from a face. Fees at the higher end of the range would be charged for such jobs as restoring an old photo that has missing areas or has been ripped or stained across the eyes, mouth, ears of a person's face. Also commanding a higher fee would be a job

combining two photos into one, for example, a group shot in which one or more persons is added or subtracted, requiring that the body parts of others are moved around.

Expenses: Typography, photography, props, and other out-of-pocket expenses are generally billed as additional expenses. Artists should also take into consideration the initial cost of hardware and software.

Rush Work: Retouching, by its nature, should not be rushed. It is important to know how much retouchers charge for accelerated schedules. Normal turnaround time for an average project is three days, and "rush" rates usually go into effect for projects with less than three days' turnaround. Rush work is usually billed at 1.5 to 2 times the normal rate.

Rights: Unlike other graphic artists, photo retouchers and restorers always work with an existing piece of art and are not usually entitled to copyright or reuse fees. The fee that they charge, usually based on an hourly rate, represents the total income from that project—unlike other artists who may benefit from future uses of a work (see Figure 8-10 for Photo Retouching & Restoration Fees). On the other hand, photo illustrators are creators who, like other artists, control all the rights to their creations. Photo illustration is priced more akin to other forms of illustration (see Chapter 10).

Environmental Graphic Design

Environmental graphic designers plan, design, and specify communications in the built and natural environment. Today, the field is also referred to as "Wayfinding Graphic Design" to avoid confusion over the term "environmental," which many people think of as "green" design (the use of recycled paper, soy inks, etc.). The discipline merges the communication skills of a graphic designer with the architect's understanding of space and structure. The profession is approached from either the science of "wayfinding" and/or the art of "place-making." Design solutions are most often three-dimensional and expressed visually, but many projects integrate dynamic sensory experiences that might include tactile, audio, and motion graphics, etc. This vital field offers a rich diversity of projects in many environments from offices, campuses, hospitals, airports, cities, parks, transportation and sports facilities, to hotels, museums, zoos, retail stores, theme parks, and cruise ships, to name a few.

Wayfinding is an industry term referring to the design and implementation of directional systems that guide people through complex spaces. Wayfinding can be broken down into several areas: information and interpretation; direction and orientation; identification and regulation. Design elements as sculptural or architectural features

Comparative Fees for Environmental Graphic Design

Based on research and design of all exterior and interior signage systems, excluding tenant signage (if applicable). Includes presentation of three concepts showing format, comprehensive layouts, up to two revisions, and final art. Does not include any reimbursable or out-of-pocket expenses such as service bureau output or production expenses, which may be billed separately.

Commercial Real Estate

PROJECT SCALE	COMPREHENSIVE SIGNAGE
CORPORATE CAMPUS	$42,000–120,000
CLASS "A" OFFICE BUILDING	$40,000–60,000
CLASS "B" OFFICE BUILDING	$5,000–30,000

The pricing ranges in the chart do not constitute specific prices for particular jobs. Depending on the practice of the studio principals, the printing or manufacturing part of the project may be billed directly to the client. The buyer and seller are free to negotiate, with each designer independently deciding on how to price the work, after taking all factors into account. Figures are from the 12th Edition.

FIGURE 8—11

and such aids as color-coding and graphic symbols may be used to increase ease in navigation. A growing field within wayfinding is Interpretive Design. A key component created by designers in this field is the interpretive panel which may cover, among other things, scientific, environmental, historical, or cultural themes.

Placemaking is about the creation of comprehensive environments that may teach through interpretative graphics, project a corporate identity, or create visually arresting places that elevate moods or inspire action. Art, color, pattern, texture, ornament, identity, and landmarks are just a few elements of placemaking.

Environmental graphic designers come predominantly from the fields of graphic, industrial, architectural, interior, and landscape design. Currently the industry reports that clients are equally represented from the public and private sectors, such as governmental agencies and municipalities, to real estate developers and owners. Environmental graphic designers work closely with architects, engineers, city planners, fabricators, and construction firms.

Education & skills required

Projects vary widely in scale and size; consequently, environmental graphic designers need extensive knowledge of building design, project management, codes and regulations, fabrication shop practices, and construction. Also, knowledge of design possibilities and limitations, such as how materials react to weather or how distance, lighting, and speed affect the legibility of type, is crucial.

Designers seeking employment in environmental graphic design should try to apprentice either with someone already working in the field or in the graphics department of an architectural firm. They must be able to read working drawings and understand architectural scale. Useful study also includes architectural drafting, 2-D and 3-D design software, corporate identity and information systems design, packaging, psychology, fine art, literature, and cultural anthropology.

Specific trade customs & pricing

An environmental graphic design team is multidisciplinary and often includes a principal of the firm, a senior project designer, assistant designers, and additional artists and consultants who are often hired freelance for specific skills when needed. Since these projects frequently involve long-term research and development, environmental graphic designers are often brought in at the earliest stages. In addition, many environmental graphic design offices work on retainer and act as design consultants in peripheral areas in addition to their main projects.

According to an industry survey, two-thirds of environmental graphic design firms range in size from one to 15 people, with annual design fees ranging from $100,000 to over $2 million. Project specifications range on average from $250,000 to over $7.5 million. For example, a large, internally illuminated exterior sign may cost $30,000 or more. See Figure 8-11 for comparative fees for environmental graphic design.

In the specific design of signage, often professional and governmental codes regulate and guide the design and where the signage must be located. Consequently, environmental graphic designers are required to know and follow standards established by the Society for Environmental Graphic Design (SEGD), the American Institute of Architects (AIA), and the Construction Specifications Institute (CSI), as well as local zoning laws, municipal sign ordinances, state and local building codes, fire codes, and other government regulations. A significant example of such regulations is the Americans with Disability Act (ADA), which affects the interior and exterior signs of all public facilities in the United States. The ADA calls for the removal of all architectural and communications barriers to those with special needs. ADA Accessibility Guidelines are available from the U.S. Department of Justice (800–514-0301; 800–514-0383; and www.usdoj.gov/crt/drssec. htm). SEGD educates and helps define the practice of environmental graphic design. It also monitors and provides members with updates on related ADA regulations.

The Graphic Artists Guild Foundation and the National Endowment for the Arts published the "Disability Access Symbols Project," a graphics package that is available digitally and as hard copy. The project collected and standardized a graphic vocabulary of 12 symbols indicating accessibility, such as wheelchair access for mobility-challenged people, audio description services for visually challenged people, and listening devices for the hard of hearing. The symbols may be used in signage, floor plans, and other materials promoting the accessibility of places, events, or programs. SEGD also offers tested symbol sets such as healthcare and safety symbols.

Project proposals

The project begins once a client accepts a design proposal, which outlines the scope of the project, the services to be provided, consultant/client responsibilities, project fees, schedule, and terms and conditions under which it will be executed, including ownership, usage, and liability. Most environmental graphic design projects are quoted and billed by phase, with an initial fee representing 10 to 30 percent of total fees and reimbursable expenses.

Phase 1. Programming: Concerned with gathering information and establishing design criteria, this phase often requires spending a great deal of time with the client or on site to define the needs and problems to be solved.

Phase 2. Schematic design: After the designer and client have reached an agreement concerning the basic program, design solutions are pursued that solve the stated problems. Much of this phase involves concept development and investigation of the functional aspects with consulting fabricators. This process results in a presentation showing only those ideas that the design team feels are viable and appropriate and meet the prescribed criteria. Preliminary expectations for factors such as electrical, lighting, and structural details are coordinated with the other consultants.

Phase 3. Design development: At this stage, the design team refines the accepted design, and a final presentation is made, explaining the applications. Once the client and designer have chosen a definite direction, specific information is sought from the fabricator including preliminary cost and schedule estimates.

Phase 4. Contract documentation: The project is fully documented for implementation, which includes preparing working drawings, specifications, and reproducible artwork, where appropriate. Decisions are final at this point. Any changes made by the client after this point are billable as additional work, although designer errors are not.

Phase 5. Contract administration (including pre-bid qualification and bid assistance): This phase involves quality checking and coordinating product manufacturing. Oversight is key to this phase, since so much depends on the precision and quality achieved in this final step. Fabrication is usually billed on approved phased performance benchmarks. After the end product is approved, the project is paid in full. The designer normally retains the right to execute any design intent corrections in the fabrication process.

Billing

Billing expenses and fees may be handled in a number of ways. Early in the project, the designer should arrange to bill as a lump sum or on an hourly, progressive, or project basis. If clients prefer to be billed on a project basis, the client usually establishes an acceptable cap on the total amount billed, although the designer must make it clear that the client is not entitled to unlimited revisions.

Expenses for work done directly with clients are usually billed with markups, including costs incurred for client-approved travel. Client alterations are usually billed at the firm's predetermined hourly rates.

The fabricator is accountable to the designer and is ethically bound to follow the designer's intent and direction while working on the project. This, of course, becomes a matter of practicality, since the designer orchestrates many elements and must oversee them all to ensure consistency. However, final fabrication and installation of the project is normally handled in a separate contract for direct billing between the client and the fabricator.

Resources for Environmental Graphic Design Section: SEGD Process Guide and SEGD Member Survey 2004: The Changing Practice of Environmental Graphic Design.

Exhibit & Display Design

Exhibit and interior display design are growing specialties. The field includes permanent installation work in natural history and art museums, science and technology education centers, and travel and tourism information centers, as well as temporary exhibits and promotional venues such as trade shows, conventions, conferences, other special events, and window and interior displays in retail stores and boutiques. Many companies are solely devoted to the unique design, production, and logistical problems related to these assignments.

Corporate exhibits & displays

Exhibit and display design in the corporate setting includes on-site signage for conferences and events and displays of corporate initiatives or sponsored projects. Corporate displays can be found in-house or at a traveling venue.

Educational exhibits

Developing permanent installations whose main purpose is to educate rather than promote or sell is one example of this type of interpretive design. Exhibit designers work closely with an architect or planning firm to customize the space to meet the project's particular communications needs. Exhibit designers may have other specialists on staff or consult with graphic designers, signage experts, lighting designers, photography and film output vendors, and illustrators. These jobs are generally estimated on a project basis by the design firm. The permanence of the display is often a factor in negotiating prices.

It is critical for the exhibit designer to establish the scope of the work before negotiating a contract. The scope of work should identify the approximate size (square footage) of the exhibit; all likely elements such as cases/objects, graphics, vignettes, audio-visual, or computer components; and the persons who will be responsible for various input, including

Comparative Fees for Exhibit & Display Design

Based on research, consultation, and design of an exhibit, including all structural forms and organization of illustrative, photographic, and editorial material; presentation of up to 3 layouts showing format; and final art. Supervision of execution and billable expenses are billed separately. Simple refers to basic panel or case displays; complex refers to architectural work, reconstruction, large 3-D features, extensive detailing.

Corporate, Large Company

	1,000-2,500 SQ. FT.	3,000-5,000 SQ. FT.	6,000+ SQ. FT.
SIMPLE	$3,500–15,000	$15,000–25,000	$35,000–50,000
COMPLEX	$7,500–50,000	$30,000–75,000	$75,000–125,000

Corporate, Small Company

SIMPLE	$1,750–7,500	$3,500–15,000	$10,000–35,000
COMPLEX	$3,500–15,000	$5,000–25,000	$15,000–50,000

Large Museum

SIMPLE	$5,000–15,000	$10,000–25,000	$20,000–50,000
COMPLEX	$10,000–30,000	$15,000–50,000	$25,000–100,000

Small Museum

SIMPLE	$5,000–15,000	$7,000–20,000	$10,000–40,000
COMPLEX	$9,000–25,000	$4,000–30,000	$15,000–70,000

Trade Show Exhibit

	200 SQ. FT.	1,000 SQ. FT.	2,500+ SQ. FT.
LARGE COMPANY	$3,500–10,000	$6,250–15,000	$15,000–50,000
SMALL COMPANY	$2,500–5,000	$7,500–10,000	$10,000–40,000

Note: Total design fees usually can be derived from the overall exhibit budget—typically from 15 to 30 percent.

FIGURE 8–12

research, curating, scriptwriting, architectural and engineering services, new illustration or photography, photo research, obtaining objects and negotiating loans, and construction supervision. If the client is an established museum, it will likely provide the majority of these functions, while organizations new to doing exhibitions may want the designer to assemble a team to perform all such functions.

As organizations weigh the actual costs of realizing their needs, they may also hire exhibit designers to do feasibility studies to determine the scope of work for a prospective project. A feasibility study includes doing a site survey of existing conditions, developing a narrative or story line, locating sources of images and information, and assembling a firm description of, and bid on, the project so the prospective client may seriously consider what they can afford to spend. The only caution for the exhibit designer is to conduct the study under a separate contract and not as part of the potential project, in case the client decides to cancel it as a result of the study.

Trade show exhibits

In trade show exhibit design, a client usually has a group of specialists (an "exhibits group") design the traveling exhibition, taking into consideration the detailed and specific needs of the design message, the need to customize the exhibit from venue to venue, and the unique traveling and setup/breakdown requirements. Freelance artists are often hired to fulfill particular graphic design needs, such as typography, photography, illustration, and overall creative direction. Printed collateral materials are often needed at the show sites and are prepared in parallel with the overall exhibition design.

Specific trade customs & pricing for exhibits

Project proposals follow the phases previously outlined for environmental graphic design. Fees for exhibit projects are usually negotiated with a "not to exceed" figure. They generally range from 15 to 25 percent of the total project budget, with 20 percent the most common figure. As with other types of design involving construction, change orders are customary as the scope of work evolves. Expenses are generally added to the negotiated fees. Specific contract terms may depend on the client, so determining the client's needs and establishing a collegial working relationship are important from the start.

When pricing trade show exhibits, the artist-designer should consider not only the specific nature of the usage but also that such shows have a limited calendar life of a year or two. Advertising and institutional pricing guidelines should be the starting points for negotiating prices, with the understanding that exhibit usages are not as extensive as those for advertising and broadcast.

For traveling exhibits—which can include many other kinds of exhibits beside trade show exhibits—additional factors affect pricing. If an exhibition is to travel, then it must be designed with that in mind; materials, durability, shipping weight, and ease of assembly and disassembly need to be considered. Generally, designing an exhibit to travel involves additional work and thus a higher fee. Venues often need aspects of the traveling exhibit to be tailored to their particular spaces, so space planning and trimming to fit are also involved. If future venues are scheduled and the designer knows about them at the start of the project, then some of the cost may be included in the initial fee. If venues are added later, an additional fee is charged by the designer. See Figure 8-12 for Exhibit Design fees.

Window & interior displays

For window and interior displays in retail stores and boutiques that change on a monthly or more frequent schedule, designers usually work on a per-project basis, though many have contracts for a specified period of time or number of projects.

SPECIFIC TRADE CUSTOMS & PRICING

While there are no industry standards for this specialty, certain conditions generally prevail. Designers customarily present sketches or drawings on spec for a proposed project. The price of the sketches, generally between $200 and $300, may be figured into the overall budget, which includes the cost of materials (a 50 percent deposit is standard for materials). Display designers are responsible for providing all materials, props, and backgrounds to be used in displays (except permanent fixtures such as mannequins). Unless otherwise specified, these become their property (except permanent fixtures), even if they were built or purchased for a specific project. Designers may subsequently rent or sell these materials, though not to a competing retail outlet unless they are significantly altered first. Designers are responsible for the durability of all displays; any repairs due to weak or faulty construction are assumed to be the designer's responsibility.

Broadcast Design

The work of a broadcast designer involves all aspects of traditional graphic design plus the added dimensions of motion and sound. In one sense, it is a combination of graphic design and filmmaking.

The demands of television, which is in 98 percent of American homes, present unique challenges to broadcast designers. Designers in this field, especially those working on live programming, must have the ability and temperament for working in an extremely fast-paced, deadline-driven environment. Their work is visible in all sports, news, music, and network programming. Broadcast design includes creating the look for an entire show, channel, or network with opening graphics and bumpers (shorter clips of an opening animation that identifies a broadcast). Some examples include the on-air look and sound of any television station or network as well as the logo, ID, lead-ins for movies, and graphics that promote shows. Most television programs begin with a title sequence designed by a broadcast designer. News and sports programs are packed with the work of broadcast designers. Almost every commercial includes some work by a broadcast designer; sometimes, entire commercials are created by broadcast designers. Now that the medium of television has extended into home videos, kiosks, and even web sites, the work of broadcast designers is ever present.

Skills required

The development of computer graphics has greatly expanded the design, art direction, and execution of television graphics and animations. This capability now requires broadcast designers to keep up with hardware and software capabilities, enabling them to combine live-action direction with synthetic imagery. In many cases, it places the designer in the role of a producer/director, making him or her responsible for coordinating a crew, combining all video and audio production elements, and supervising the project through postproduction.

For on-air functions, broadcast designers are required to be illustrators, animators, and type designers. They must be knowledgeable about animation techniques and, on occasion, must prepare and shoot animation on both film and tape. Knowledge of both stand photography (which uses a computerized table-top machine that permits zooms, pans, and other special effects) and remote still photography (filming that occurs outside of the plant or studio) is essential.

Broadcast designers are also responsible for devising off-air collateral—everything from small-space program-listing ads to full-page newspaper ads for print media, as well as trade publication ads, booklets, brochures, invitations, posters, and other material. In that capacity, they double as corporate designers, coordinating everything from the on-air look to the application of identity logos/marks from stationery, memo pads, and sales promotion materials to new vehicle or even helicopter markings.

Scenic design may be another area of responsibility. It requires understanding construction techniques, materials, and paints, and an awareness of staging, furnishing, lighting, spatial relationships, and camera angles.

Art directors in this field must be skilled managers, proficient in organization, budgeting, purchasing, directing staff, and working with upper management. The most effective broadcast designers are those who combine great creative talent with numerous specific skills. Because television is a technological medium, there is a strong benefit to having an affinity toward technological creative tools and techniques. Important

skills beyond those of traditional graphic design include the ability to direct a live-action shoot; a working knowledge of a variety of animation techniques; video editing; compositing; and straight computer graphics. Broadcast designers use a variety of software programs, such as After Effects (animation and effects), Final Cut Pro and Avid (editing; motion and animation effects), DVD Studio Pro (DVD production), and Flash (Web design). For compositing, it's valuable for designers to know the abilities of Discreet Logic products (Flame, Inferno, etc.).

Job titles

Production artist: An expert on a particular system, such as After Effects, Henry, or Flame.
Designer: Handles specific design assignments, such as creating graphics and bumpers under supervision. Develops design solutions and implements them.
Creative director: Has creative skills, assigns work to designers, supervises their work, and screens job applicants. The creative director may also take on the role of designer on specific projects.

Greeting Card & Novelty Design

Greeting card and novelty design is often done by graphic designers, surface designers, and illustrators, although some artists specialize in this field. Opportunities abound to have art or design published on greeting cards as well as on holiday decorations, posters, magnets, mugs, T-shirts, stationery, and gift or boutique-type products.

Naturally, not all designs can make the transition from card to mug to paper plate, but many of them do, making them profitable ventures for their creators. Some leading art licensors in the stationery and gift industry develop their own brands and license their designs to a broad range of product manufacturers to maximize their income potential. Some top leading licensors command good advances, royalty percentages, and project art fees. Commissioned licensed work is also done as well. Since manufacturing materials, resources, and requirements for production of various items often limit their display and design, research into those factors is extremely important for artists who are considering a career designing for this industry or for those who are interested in it as another outlet for licensing their art. While this section will focus on greeting card design, the general information is applicable to novelties as well. (For more information on licensing, see Chapter 5, Essential Business Practices.)

Greeting card design

Greeting cards touch the lives of millions of people each day. They comfort, inspire, celebrate, and communicate a range of emotions. Greeting cards

Comparative Fees for
Greeting Card & Novelty Design

Based on concept, 3 to 5 layouts, comprehensive, supervision of illustration and photography, and final art for each component. Does not include fabrication, supervision of execution, and other production expenses that may be billed separately.

Point-of-Purchase Display Material

ITEM	EXTENSIVE USE	LIMITED USE
BANNERS	$1,000–6,250	$1,000–5,000
COUNTER CARDS	$1,500–10,000	$1,500–7,500
COUNTER DISPLAY	$3,000–5,000	$2,500–5,000
POSTERS	$2,500–7,500	$2,500–5,000
SHOPPING BAGS	$1,250–5,000	$1,250–5,000

Merchandising

	FLAT FEE	ADVANCE	% ROYALTY
CALENDARS	$6,250–13,500	$2,000–5,000	6%
CONSUMER STATIONERY	$500–2,000	$400–800	5-12%
GIFT WRAP (NO REPEAT)	$800–1,400	$200–400	6%
GIFT WRAP (REPEAT)	$800–2,000	$200–400	6%
GREETING CARDS	$250–900	$100–800	5-8%
KITCHEN PRODUCTS	$900–1,600	$250–500	3-10%
MUGS	$250–800	$200–400	4-10%
PAPER PRODUCTS	$500–1,000	$250–500	4-6%
T-SHIRTS	$250–2,500	$250–2,000	4-6%

The price ranges in the chart do not constitute specific prices for specific jobs. The buyer and seller are free to negotiate, with each artist independently deciding how to price the work, after taking all factors into account. (Refer to related material in other chapters in this book, especially the Greeting Cards section in Chapter 10, Illustration Prices & Trade Customs.)

FIGURE 8—13

are one of our culture's foremost tools of communication, and the greeting card industry has a constant, continual need for art. Approximately half of the cards sold each year are designed by freelancers.

Before embarking on a freelance career as a greeting card designer, it is important to understand certain facts about the product and the industry. A great greeting card is a marriage of art and verse—a card's message is communicated through both the design and the verse. The design makes a customer pick up a card, but the verse will make her either purchase the card or return it to the rack and search for one that better expresses what she wants to say. Thus the designer needs to create an illustration eye-catching enough to capture the customer's attention, and the art needs to reflect the card's message. Greeting cards, like other products which feature copy and are designed to touch someone's heart, are part of the industry's "social expressions" category.

INDUSTRY OVERVIEW

Today the greeting card industry generates more than $7.5 billion in retail sales from consumer purchases of more than 7 billion cards. Of the total greeting cards purchased annually, roughly half are seasonal, and the remaining half are for everyday card-sending occasions. Christmas is the most popular card-sending holiday; sales of Christmas cards account for over 60 percent of all seasonal card purchases. Sales of Valentine's Day cards (the next most popular seasonal occasion) account for 25 percent of seasonal card sales. In terms of everyday card sales, birthday cards account for 60 percent of the sales volume, with anniversary cards following at a distant 8 percent.

Most American households purchase 35 greeting cards each year, and the average American receives 20 cards, of which one-third are birthday cards. Women purchase more than 80 percent of all greeting cards. There are over 3,000 greeting card publishers in America, ranging from small family businesses to major corporations, many of which license designs from freelance artists.

GETTING STARTED

When creating designs to license in the greeting card industry, it is advisable to stick with the more popular and saleable categories, such as birthday and Christmas. The chances of getting a design published increase substantially when artists concentrate their designs efforts on high-volume cards. For a list of card-sending occasions and the percentage of sales of each one, visit the Greeting Card Association's web site: www.greetingcard.org.

TIPS OF THE TRADE

Many card stores still use racks that obscure the bottom half of the card, so it is important to get the message—"Happy Birthday," "Merry Christmas," or other text—into the top third of the card. If the design does not have words, try to place the strongest design element where it will be seen. Also, be aware that most racks do not accommodate horizontal cards, so artists who are designing on spec are advised to use a vertical 5 x 7-inch format. When creating work on spec, it's not necessary to design the inside of the card. The cover illustration is enough for art directors to decide if the look and feel are appropriate for their company. Artists who provide layered PhotoShop or InDesign files have a definite advantage over those who submit original artwork. Network with other greeting card designers by joining an online group (e.g. greetingcardillustrators@yahoogroups.com) that focuses on greeting cards.

Marketing designs for cards & novelties

Some artists use a licensing agent to market their work, while others prefer to represent themselves. (For more information on licensing agents, see Chapter 5, Essential Business Practices.) Artists who represent themselves need to decide which companies to approach. Research is extremely important to learn how their work can translate best to potential clients' product ranges. Shopping the market to see what products are out there and how the art is applied to the product formats can put an artist miles ahead of the equally talented competition. The best way to select a company is to view their complete product line, which is easily done by attending one of the national or regional stationery and gift shows, such as the National Stationery Show, which is held in New York City every May, or the Atlanta Gift Show, which is held in January and July. SURTEX, held in May in New York City, is an international show that focuses on selling and licensing art and design for numerous industries, including greeting cards, gift wrap, and other paper products. Reading industry publications, such as *GREETINGS etc.*, the official publication of the Greeting Card Association, is a great way to research different card companies—

and to stay on top of industry trends.

Before making a submission, contact the company and request their artists/photographers guidelines. (Hallmark and American Greetings do not accept unsolicited freelance submissions.) The guidelines will say what to send, to whom to send it, and when to send it. For example, some companies prefer to look at e-mail submissions, some prefer a CD, and others request color photocopies. Some companies will review any work at any time; others have a specific submissions schedule (e.g., they look for Christmas submissions in September and do not want to see Valentine or birthday ideas at that time). Artists who submit their work according to the company guidelines have a better chance of getting their submissions reviewed.

For a first submission, an artist should follow the submission guidelines. Putting his/her art into product prototyping formats can help potential clients see that the artist understands the production process and the value of the art on the client's product. A small package should be sent, along with samples of any published work. Each piece should include the artist's name and contact information, along with a design number and the copyright symbol. Artists should keep a photocopy or digital file of the design. Many art directors keep samples of styles they like on file, so it is appropriate to mention that they are welcome to keep the samples. It is okay to send identical packages out to several companies at the same time.

Pricing

Most greeting card designers license their work either on a flat fee basis or for an advance against royalties. Licensing gives a company the right to reproduce a design for a certain product (e.g., greeting cards or mugs), a specified time period (generally three to five years), and a specific territory (e.g., North America or worldwide). (A more detailed discussion of licensing can be found in the Art Licensing section of Chapter 5, Essential Business Practices.) Some companies attempt to use a "work-for-hire" agreement because they want to own all the rights to the finished design. The Graphic Artists Guild does not recommend creating work under a work-for-hire arrangement because the artist loses all rights to the art and, therefore, all potential future revenue.

The advantage to a flat fee license is that the artist receives money in advance and therefore will not be dependent on the design selling successfully to generate income from it. Also, manufacturers tend to pay a higher flat fee than an advance against royalties. For example, a flat fee for a greeting card design generally ranges between $250 and $800, while an advance—if one is offered—against what is generally a 5- to 8-percent royalty tends to be between $100 and $800. The ranges in pricing reflect differences in the complexity of the design, whether multiple pages (cover and inside) of design are used, and the quantity printed. It's important for artists to know that if the advance against royalty is the amount equivalent to what they would earn if the initial print run sells or if the amount of the flat fee buyout is equivalent to the advance, they are not taking any undue risks to ask for royalties. In fact, it can be a win-win situation: the artist is rewarded for designing great selling art with money on the back half (when the royalties surpass the advance), and the client then has artists devoted to making work that helps their product perform well in the marketplace. This is a team partnership where licensing benefits both parties.

Royalties are paid on the wholesale price of the card. Related products, such as gift wrap and boxed stationery sets, which are more complicated to execute, may command higher prices. To determine if a royalty fee will be profitable, it is best to ask how many pieces the client plans to produce for their initial and ensuing press runs. Then evaluate the options and strike the best deal.

Determining which rights are being acquired is critical when pricing a design. The price should also reflect how complicated a design is and how much time will be required to produce it. Other factors can affect the price, including samples and the artist's credit. Most card companies provide six to twelve free samples of the finished product, but it is possible to negotiate for a larger number. A proper copyright notice should accompany the artwork. Designers should specify in the licensing agreement that name and copyright credit be given to them on both products and packaging. A credit line on all products develops the recognition of the artists and their brands and is essential to building their future as art licensors. Artists just starting out are sometimes willing to accept a smaller fee in return for their credit and extra samples.

The artist should receive a cancellation fee if a project is canceled, either because the artist did not execute the assignment in a satisfactory fashion or because the client changed its mind about the project. If the artist completes the requested assignment but the project does not move forward, a general kill fee is half the flat fee arrangement or all of a royalty advance (since there will be no royalties). If the artist completes the assignment but the design was found lacking, one-quarter to one-third of the agreed-upon price may be more appropriate. (For more discussion of cancellation fees, see the Cancellation & Rejection Fees section of Chapter 3, Professional Issues.)

For fees, advances, and royalties for greeting card and novelty design, see Figure 8-13.

Commissioning procedures

For situations in which a designer is commissioned to create new art for a product according to a client's specifications (as opposed to licensing existing work), most companies will send the artist a commissioning form that spells out all the details of what they want. Many companies also include a contract with the commissioning form, so there is no misunderstanding about what licensing rights they wish to acquire. However, in any client dealings, it is best for artists to have their own standard contracts that they offer to the client first. By offering their own contract first, artists establish their professionalism in the field and let the client know they value their work

The commissioning form should include the due date for the sketches, color comps, and finished art. Many companies include prices for the sketches separately from the finished art. Then, if the project is terminated after the sketch stage, the artist knows how much he or she will be paid. If a company communicates clearly what is expected and the sketches do not reflect those requirements, the firm expects the artist to try again at no additional charge. If, however, the company changes its mind about what is wanted, then it should expect to pay for the artist to rework the sketch.

Contracts

It is essential that artists have a contract, signed by both parties, before beginning work on a project. At the least, artists should have a signed letter of agreement that defines the terms until the exact contract can be signed. If the client insists on using its own contract, artists can still send the client their own contract and suggest that they negotiate a compromise that is mutually fair and beneficial to both parties. Many artists feel that they have no right to ask for changes when they are offered only the client's contract. This is not true—negotiation is key, and artists often cross out wording and terms that they feel are unfair, unacceptable, or unnecessary. Any changes in the contract should be initialed by both parties. If the client does not accept reasonable changes requested by the artist, the artist should consider walking away from the deal. Ultimately, the artist must decide if the deal is worth it and whether or not they can live with the terms of the deal.

Some of the variables in a contract include:

Property: Design(s).
Products: What the company plans to produce or manufacture using the designs.
Territory: Where the company can sell the products. Many companies sell worldwide and therefore need to obtain worldwide rights to the design.
Term: Length of time the company is allowed to manufacture products with this particular design. The average greeting card has a shelf life of three years, but companies usually ask for a five-year term and often an extension term (an additional time period of one to three years).
Renewal fee: Percentage of the original compensation to be paid to the artist if the company wishes to continue to use the design for an additional period. In a flat-fee contract, the artist needs an additional incentive to allow the company to continue to produce the design;

otherwise, the artist could license that design elsewhere. In a royalty contract, a renewal fee clause is optional since the artist is compensated by additional royalties. Designers should ask for a renewal fee of 100% of the original agreed-upon flat fee price. A second advance is not always paid for a renewal, but the royalty is the same.

Automatic renewal clause: It may not be advantageous to the artist to have an automatic renewal clause in the contract because many things can change during the life of a contract, which may not be in an artist's best interest. For example, the client may sell the artist's work to a company that the artist does not want to be associated with, or the client may not produce good sales figures. The artist needs the right to affiliation with that company and enter into an agreement with a company that will be more lucrative.

Out clause: the main reason to have a provision to get out of the contract is if the client does not put the artist's work into commercially feasible quantities within six to eight months of signing the deal. The client should not tie up the rights to the artist's work for three years if it is not going to actually put the art into production. Other reasons for including an out clause are if the client does not pay on time, goes bankrupt, etc.

Two other items are important to include in the contract:

Samples: Companies customarily give artists a number of samples in the quantity in which their product is sold. For example, greeting cards are usually sold in either dozens or half dozens, so the artist ordinarily receives 6 or 12 samples. Mugs and other gift products are sold individually or in lots of two or three, so the artist may receive fewer samples. If more samples are needed as useful giveaways, the artist can request more at the manufacturer's cost. A clause should be added that if the product is liquidated, the artist should be offered the product first at the liquidation price. In any selloff period, artists should still receive their royalty percentage on the selloff, too.

Artist's Credit: Artists should always specify that their name and copyright credit appear on both products and packaging.

Resources

Greeting Card Association Industry Directory. An extremely valuable book that contains information about the industry and gives contact information for over 2,000 greeting card and stationery publishers and industry suppliers. A great marketing tool, the directory is available through the Greeting Card Association at www.greetingcard.org

Art Licensing 101, by Michael Woodward. A well-written, comprehensive handbook on licensing designs, which includes a chapter devoted to greeting cards. From ArtNetwork Press. Available through Amazon.com or www.artmarketing.com. *Artist & Graphic Designer's Market.* Published annually by Writer's Digest Books, it features a section devoted to greeting cards.

Chart & Map Design

Those who produce charts and maps rely upon their pictorial abilities as designers and/or cartographers to satisfy a client's specific needs. Chart design involves presenting, interpreting, and comparing quantitative data in a visual format that makes it easily and more quickly understood. A chart designer might edit and arrange the data using a standard chart or graph format, such as a line graph, bar chart, pie chart, flow chart, etc., or use illustration to visually display the data. Up to about 20–25 years ago, charts, graphs, and maps were still being created by hand, using rulers, ink, color pens, pencils, etc., on paper or vellum. In the 1990s, all that disappeared into the computer, using Illustrator. Today, most charts are done with standard templates inside data-driven applications, such as Excel, so a graphic designer is usually only called upon to do "specialized" stylized charts or illustrations for charts.

Though related, there is a difference between "map design" (or production cartography) and the more complex research-based cartography. Map design generally involves editing, combining, and restyling data from preexisting maps onto a preexisting base. Cartography can include these tasks but can also require collection of data, knowledge of map projections and their spatial uses, and quite often, the creation of all map elements from scratch. Map designers may have an understanding of projections and their implications, but the full range of projections and their uses is better understood and put to correct use by the cartographer.

The chart or map designer frequently works from data based on the client's research, often beginning with general specifications supplied by the client. Map designers may, and cartographers usually do, find it necessary to perform additional research as a supplement to what was provided by the client. Specialized software known as Geographic Information Systems (GIS) is a tool more often used by cartographers to process data and create maps or charts.

Pricing

Chart and map design ranges from the whimsical and highly illustrative to the scientific and highly technical. On the less technical end, the map or chart designer is often treated much like a traditional illustrator. Prices for such work are comparable to pricing for illustration in similar markets. (For more information, see Chapter 10, Illustration Prices & Trade Customs.) Clients usually request artwork to fit a prescribed space; however, the best use of a chart or map requires cartographic input before determining the space.

Comparative Fees for Chart & Map Design

Usual and customary fees based upon client consultation, research, presentation of tight color sketch, and typography in position; one revision, and finished art. Typically, maps command higher fees than charts because they require more effort.

CLIENT SIZE	CORPORATE ADVERTISING	CORPORATE IN-HOUSE	EDITORIAL	TEXTBOOK
LARGE	$1,000-6,000	$800-3,000	$750-3,000	$400-1,500
MEDIUM	$625-6,000	$400-3,000	$500-3,000	$250-750
SMALL	$500-2,500	$200-2,000	$250-1,500	$100-500

The pricing ranges above do not constitute specific prices for particular jobs. The buyer and seller are free to negotiate, with each designer independently deciding how to price the work, after taking all factors into account.

FIGURE 8—14

Factors that can affect the pricing of map design include:

1. Size of client
2. Usage requested/type of client
3. Size of map
4. Level of detail/complexity
5. Amount of research required.

Ideally, the project directors and art directors treat the designer and cartographer as an integral part of the project team. This involvement can include page layout; determination of style, size, content, and color; and even the printing method. It is generally recognized that map and chart design is not illustration per se, and jobs are more often priced on a per-project basis. The fee generally covers time for design, research, and production. However, some clients may want to be billed hourly for time plus expenses and ask for an estimate. The map or chart designer's responsibilities usually include a color comp or prototype, proofs, revisions, and finished artwork. Billable expenses can include: reference materials, travel, messengers, miscellaneous art supplies, and digital output by an imaging center.

See Figure 8-14 for Chart & Map Design fees.

Production Artist

The role and responsibilities, as well as the mode of work, of the production artist have changed drastically with the introduction of electronic technology into the graphic workplace. Before computers, production artists were responsible for quickly and precisely combining type and art as directed by the designer's specifications and preparing the final forms to go to the camera operator, called mechanicals, based on a knowledge of printing. To accommodate the limits of the print medium, many details, including the kind of overlay used on the keyline to the way the ink sat on the paper, had to be understood and considered in the construction of the mechanicals.

With the advent of computers, typographers, strippers, camera personnel, and others involved in lithographic processes were replaced by computer operators and service bureaus. The latter are companies that translate digital files directly to film, plates, or other necessary hardcopy output. Most print service providers now perform their own prepress operations, rather than relying on dedicated service bureaus. As a result, designers are sometimes required to deal directly with printers, so they should expand their production art skills.

Once the designer and client have agreed upon the final design, the production artist begins preparing the art for the printer. The production artist provides the link between the conceptual design and the tangible result; between the graphic designer and the printer. The essential elements a production artist handles include graphic files; software; fonts; color matching; instructions to the printer for resolution, screens, and trapping; and specific service bureau and printer guidelines.

To ensure the integrity of the final product, the production artist's responsibilities include using appropriate tools (hardware and software); conveying to designers the expense of producing their design electronically and giving them options to be more cost-effective; maintaining the integrity of all the design elements; and completing the work by the deadline. Production artists must be detail-oriented and keep current on technological changes in computing and printing. The scope of knowledge that a production artist must have includes design, both conventional and digital printing processes, and constantly changing computer capabilities.

Where does the production artist's responsibility

Hourly Rates and Rush Fees for Production

Hourly Rate

	LAYOUT COMP	LAYOUT TIGHT	ELECTRONIC PREFLIGHT/PREPRESS
	$30–100	$30–100	$40–100

Rush Fees

	HOURLY RATE	% OF FEE
1-DAY	$88–225	50–200%
HOLIDAY/WEEKEND	$95–225	50–200%

The price ranges in the chart do not constitute specific prices for specific jobs. The buyer and seller are free to negotiate, with each artist independently deciding how to price the work, after taking all factors into account.

FIGURE 8—15

end and the service bureau/printer's begin? Production artists can save designers significant costs if they are skilled in areas where printers traditionally have expertise, such as high-end scanning and photo retouching. A production artist who can assume one or more of these responsibilities should be appropriately compensated for providing such service. While imposition and trapping are best left to the print service provider, the production artist should be knowledgeable about both processes. Production artists provide different levels of skills and services based on their level of expertise and training. For example, a production artist working at a printer or service bureau has skills and responsibilities that are different from a production artist working at a design firm. Fees are determined in part by the level of services provided.

Pricing

The complexity of the job determines the production artist's pricing. Some factors production artists should take into account include:

- Level of complexity in preparing electronic files (a 4-page newsletter compared with a 100-page catalog).
- Scanning (low-end, high-end), speccing photography, handling digital photographs.
- Tint building.
- Clipping paths and other masking techniques.
- Page layout (simple to complex).
- File conversions (Mac to PC or PC to Mac).
- On-site or off-site work.
- Last-minute decisions/rush jobs.
- Preparation of all paperwork: a comp to show

how finished piece should look, specifications for printer, composite laser proof (marked up), and laser proof separations.
- Production of rough color proof versus high-quality color proof.

See Figure 8-15 for hourly rates and rush fees for Production.

WEB DESIGN & OTHER DIGITAL GRAPHIC ARTS

This chapter focuses on the newest and continually evolving area of graphic art: creating an ever-expanding array of digital media and the support marketing required to promote these applications, which include website design, media such as digital games, mobile device software, rich Internet applications (RIA), e-commerce, and other stand-alone multimedia software applications.

CHAPTER 9

THE INTERNET

and online media services, as well as other digital and electronic media products, are the fastest-growing commercial markets in the world today. Forrester Research reported that online retail sales (excluding online purchases of autos, travel, and prescription drugs) in the United States alone surged to $155 billion in 2009, an 11 percent increase over 2008 (compared to a 2.5 percent increase for all retail sales). The research group also predicted that, despite the sluggish economy, online sales would continue to climb 10 percent a year for the next five years, reaching nearly $250 billion in 2014. While $155 billion worth of consumer goods were bought online in 2009, a far larger portion of offline sales—$917 billion—were influenced by online research.

With this burgeoning growth comes a ballooning need for fresh content to keep people clicking away—videos, photos, illustrations, multimedia presentations, and animations. Digital media and web designers lead this field by creating content for these new markets. These creators work for a range of industries, including commerce, publishing, marketing, entertainment, and education.

Since the technological means of protecting copyright and reuse are developing simultaneously with the digital market, and since trade practices for traditional media may not always apply, this chapter offers some of the terms and protective mechanisms that artists themselves have developed in response to this new market. No doubt design and business practices in this new arena will continue to change as rapidly as the industry.

The Digital Marketplace

While many digital content providers are extensions of traditional businesses, universities, print/book publishers, media companies, and advertising agencies, the digital marketplace is increasingly populated by startup as well as established online companies. The scope of interests, professions, and products that these providers represent is truly diverse. For instance, software designers create programs that allow prospective real-estate clients and homebuilders to view simulated living spaces and property online. Corporations build data-driven web applications that can be automatically updated to display only the most current inventories and information. Advertisers can publish whole catalogs on removable media or on a web site; these must constantly be updated as stock is depleted or added. These markets also need to advertise their new services via radio commercials, TV trade publication advertisements, brochures, and direct mailers. The demand for images to illustrate new products, such as applications (apps) for hand-held devices, provides steady work for freelance artists. In many respects, the digital marketplace has created a whole new market for the graphic artist.

Industrial applications include designing a network of personal computers (an intranet) so that people in widely separated places can communicate and work together. Human resources and offsite training are other uses. For instance, the Defense Department is the largest user of digital media within the federal government; all training programs in most branches of the military services are conducted with digital media and accessed via personal computers both on- and off-site.

Compressing time and eliminating distance

Digital materials offer numerous advantages. Because the Internet can be accessed from anywhere in the world, electronic files speed communication and information exchange across borders. In fact, the Internet provides a safe, easy way for physically challenged individuals to learn, shop, and communicate, allowing them access to mainstream culture as never before.

Through the use of digital technology, joint research projects, development efforts, and diagnostics are now less constrained by time or distance. For example, hospitals and doctors send image data of medical samples to distant labs for diagnosis, X-ray and MRI results for analysis, and entire chart contents for viewing anywhere in the world via the Internet.

Corporate communications and public relations departments hire digital media professionals to design presentations for product introductions, trade shows, and motivational sales meetings; presentations to the board or shareholders; technical training, distance learning programs, and management development programs; and to design

and implement the office intranet. Designers incorporate illustration, charts, graphs, photography, film, computer graphics, and video. They may also turn print pieces into PDF files for downloading. Sometimes they enhance their work with sound effects, voiceovers, and music. Of course, designers must respect, and therefore purchase, appropriate licenses for materials they have not created or verify that they are in the public domain. (See the Copyright section in Chapter 2, Legal Rights & Issues.)

Great emphasis is placed on developing educational programs—everything from preschool and elementary curricula to college degrees online. Educational materials geared to youngsters are presented in an entertaining format ("edutainment"), such as an animated numbers game that teaches children math or an adventure game that features historical characters or events. Many educational institutions and universities offer fully accredited, distance-learning courses through their web sites, enabling students to earn a college degree in the comfort of their own home and at their convenience. Likewise, employees can receive offsite/onsite job and software applications training through online courses. Museums and zoos routinely use digital media to educate visitors and enhance their experiences.

Reference materials like encyclopedias are compressed, with video, animation, and sound added to text, graphics, and photos. The resulting DVDs are equipped with search engines that help define the subject of interest, pinpoint its location, and cross-reference it with other material on the disk. Development budgets for such reference projects can range from $100,000 to as high as $1 million, with project teams consisting of from 20 to more than 100 people.

Designing for Digital Media

Many clients casually interchange the concepts and challenges of design between print and digital media. And even though both processes begin with concept and content, the functional and production methods of the two are profoundly different. (For helpful books and web sites, see Chapter 15, Resources & References.)

The digital workspace that has evolved using layout programs such as QuarkXPress and Adobe's InDesign came directly from traditional typesetting and film applications and share much of the vocabulary, measuring systems, and printing terms. Amazing tools are available so that the designer can write W3C-approved, flawless code. Optimization and WYSIWYG programs, such as Adobe Fireworks, Dreamweaver, and Adobe Photoshop, help a designer use the appropriate code in partnership with excellent graphics in a non-code, designer-friendly environment. Designers can utilize blogging software such as WordPress, to build basic web sites and can work with back-end programmers utilizing web content management systems (WCMS), such as Joomla or Adobe Contribute. A basic knowledge of such computer languages as HTML, DHTML, XHTML, XML, CSS, JavaScript, JQvery, and PhP is strongly advised if one wishes to know what is possible when producing web sites. Also, designers should have a basic understanding of coding languages and website back-end technologies so as to be able to work effectively with a web developer. Of course, the creative process in digital media, as in print media, requires that a designer thoroughly understand the principles of a visually effective, content-rich result. In order for a designer to move ahead in today's sluggish, highly competitive economy, he or she needs a diverse range of skills.

A few key questions

Designers who are preparing to make the transition to digital media design should ask themselves a few simple questions:

- Do I have the design and information architectural skills needed to produce a multimedia and/or interactive project?
- Do I have the right computer hardware, software, and Internet connection? Am I prepared to purchase what is needed and receive additional training on new applications that are part of the digital design process?
- Do I know how to produce a fully functional web site? Do I know how to optimize graphics and animations for the Web, and upload them onto a remote server utilizing tools such as File Transfer Protocol (FTP) software?
- Do I know how to find a good Web Hosting Provider? Do I understand different hosting options, such as dedicated, virtual, shared servers, and can I recommend the right solution for my client? Do I understand technical specifications, such as bandwidth and targeted browsers, and hit rates?
- Can I develop or direct the development of static and motion graphics that may need to be updated, re-envisioned, or otherwise optimized?
- Do I know how to develop an e-commerce site and implement the technologies to enable secure transactions?
- Do I understand the technologies necessary to develop an interactive offline project, such as a presentation, animation, or slide show auto-running off a DVD?
- Can I afford to take the time to learn these hands-on skills, or can I be an art director on a per-project basis? Do I know what can and cannot be accomplished within a given project or medium? Will I be able to redesign and produce a project based on feedback from the client, provider, and users?
- Have I studied the newest applications, for example, graphic generation/optimization tools such as Adobe Dreamweaver, Fireworks, and Photoshop? Do I have some familiarity with Flash? Am I proficient in at least several of these applications? Do I understand the basics of HTML so that I can instruct a web site coder? If I am coding the web site entirely myself, am I prepared to keep up with the constantly evolving web standards?

- Do I understand user behavior, and the impact of visual and interactive features on the average user? Can I implement usability studies or site testing?
- Do I have experience in organizing and managing the teams of consultants sometimes required to produce large sites/projects in a timely manner? Do I need to subcontract with skilled web or multimedia programmers? Do I know where to find them?

Traditional professional concerns

If you answered yes to the important questions above, you are well on your way to developing a web design or offline digital media project. Remember that traditional concerns and guideposts are still important, including:

- The ability to precisely estimate time and costs to adequately bid on a project.
- The need for clear communication and well-defined contracts between clients and creators.
- An understanding of copyright protection.
- The ability to enforce the essentials of respect and professionalism between client and producers in the face of pressing deadlines. Such practices provide the basis for a successful enterprise, whether it is a 12-month web site contract or designing a set of characters for a new video game.

Website Design

Posting a web site can be like hiding a brochure under a rock. The trick is figuring out how to get as many people as possible to look under that rock for that brochure. With thousands of sites coming online every week—each more elaborate than the next—the pressure to grab someone's attention and effectively communicate a message with good graphic design and illustration is intense. However, effective web design is more than just good visual design—functionality is a key goal. A common misconception is that any graphic designer can design a web site. A web designer has to be a graphic artist as well as a programmer and key word strategist all in one.

Almost all web sites can be categorized as one of the following structures, each serving specific functions:

- **A static site (also known as "brochureware")** includes basic hot links, form submission, and e-mail.
- **A non-static or dynamic site,** which incorporates movement or animation, and/or is interactive. Such sites can be built in a variety of ways,

including: by combining Flash or Flex and actionscript with HTML; by using jquery prototype and other Java-script based libraries; or by using core scripting languages such as PHP, ASP, PERL, etc.

- **A basic e-commerce site** includes a preformed database and online purchasing. These sites are often designed using out-of-the-box software products or freeware cart software to solve initial database and commerce needs.
- **An e-commerce/data mining site** provides a customized, relational database and dynamic purchasing. These sites include customized programming, text, and graphics; multiple browser options; data mining; URL tracking; and a content management system (CMS).
- **A CMS/Blog software-based site,** which does not necessarily have or need e-commerce additions.

Browser-based formats determine how information is shared across a variety of devices and networks, usually using a commonly available browser such as Internet Explorer or Firefox. In some cases, a browser is custom designed for a particular application, such as a company intranet. These formats cover both applications and microsites which may be locally hosted (and not publicly available) or accessible through the Internet. For example, a company may have an internal document-sharing server with graphical user interface (GUI) that resembles a web site; the internal network may only be accessed by employees through the company server. Designers are employed to create the GUIs for these applications. Browser-based formats have also been adapted for at least six different uses:

Internet: Web sites, blogs, podcasts, banners, viral marketing, etc.

Intranet: An internal network used by companies to share files, access web sites, and collaborate on projects. These sites usually cannot be accessed from the Internet.

Extranet: A private network using an Internet protocol and public telecommunication system to securely share part of a business's information or operations with suppliers, vendors, partners, customers, or other businesses.

Reference manual: A resource providing information on products or services packaged with the product or as its own separate product, similar to an instruction manual or reference book. Most software help features are actually browser-based files that provide this type of information.

Kiosk: A terminal-based information interface; examples include ATMs, mall directories, and museum displays.

Mobile devices: mobile and smart phones, handheld devices, laptop computers, GPS devices. (The majority of mobile device applications are browser-based; however, with the advent of new smart phone technologies, more operating system-based applications are running on mobile devices.)

A team approach

Since it is almost impossible for one person to successfully perform all phases of good web product development in a reasonable period of time, most projects require a number of skilled professionals who function as a creative team, headed by a team leader who may be a project manager, art director, or marketing director. A freelance web designer functions as the project manager and is responsible for putting together a team based on the scope of the work. The team leader develops a plan based on the client's vision of the product and determines what features will and will not be included. The team leader, in partnership with the client, needs to understand the average user and how to incorporate that understanding into the scope of the project. The team leader strongly influences the work of programmers, illustrators and animators, and sound technicians, but, as with other markets and product categories, allows craftspeople to carry out their work as independently as possible.

In addition to the team leader, a website development/design project requires the skills of most or all of the following professionals, depending on the size and complexity of the site:

- Information Technology (IT)/Server team who assesses the functionality of the site and delivers diagrams;
- Programmer who assesses the content, creates a site map, and delivers the wireframe, a visual guide to the structure of a site and the relationship between its pages; also approves/declines graphic design and codes the template;
- Graphic Designer who works within the wireframe, following Web Standards;
- Search Engine Optimization (SEO) team who creates keyword strategy and writes content for the web;
- Adwords team who monitors advertising (e-commerce sites).

On smaller projects, multiple tasks may be performed by a single person.

While graphic design is the largest part of a print project, it is just one consideration in a web design project. Web designers, art directors, marketing managers, and clients collaborate to examine and define the overall information structure or architecture, project scope, presentation, and delivery mode needed to achieve the clients' goals for a given site. In fact, many web designers call themselves "information architects" or "interface designers" because they are responsible for the choice of technology, site flow, scope, and deliverables. Similar to architects of three-dimensional space, information architects must coordinate a team of specialists, including graphic designers, illustrators, photographers, copywriters, animators, multimedia experts, and computer programmers well versed in data application languages needed for a data-driven web application.

When pitching to design a web site, a freelance web designer may need to hire consultants on creative deliverables such as mood boards, Photoshop comps, or Flash files and determine if a style guide will be needed. Designers generally create one to three variations for client review. Clients need to know that they will have to buy licenses for any fonts used or transferred to their systems.

Concept and content and how they function determine the success or failure of an increasing number of complex web sites. Visual and behavioral aspects of interface architecture, programming, and code play vital roles. If the web designer only has responsibility for developing the visual interface, not the programming, it is essential that the designer have a clearly structured relationship with a trusted programmer or be familiar with the many existing Web-building applications. The designer is expected to provide the programmer with all the objectives and details for interactivity. The programmer, in turn, is responsible for producing Alpha and Beta site testing versions, and may also be responsible for providing the documentation necessary to implement the work. Thorough advance planning is necessary because once programming has begun, any changes to the program or to the artistic elements will incur high charges.

Web designers should define the ownership rights of the program code (some are in the public domain; some are proprietary) in all contractual arrangements with the programmer, who creates it from a variety of computer languages. Most programmers hired to write code for a proprietary web site are asked to sign a work-for-hire agreement. A programmer rarely maintains ownership of the code for a finished web site, although code is sometimes licensed to the customer, with limited-usage rights, for some highly complex web sites.

Clients should review all materials received at agreed-upon intervals from the project team and give a detailed list of comments and suggestions for revision at specific deadlines. Changes are easiest to implement if they are made before production of the finished work. Designers report treating postproduction changes as author's alterations and charging fees accordingly. Team leaders should be wary of clients who attempt to micromanage the project and should advise them that extra time spent fielding their demands will be tracked and billed accordingly.

The proposal or statement of work

A design proposal or statement of work, including estimated fees and anticipated expenses for each item, is usually presented to the client before work begins (many clients like to work with a bottom-line number). The statement of work is a general agreement that details many of the following factors:

- Project objectives and requirements.
- Project team members with clearly delineated responsibilities.
- Project time frame.
- A visual representation of proposed site architecture, known as a site map.
- Intended use of the work.
- Technical constraints and exclusions.
- Art phases and nature of all deliverables.
- Terms of payment.

In addition, designers frequently describe relationships with subcontractors (such as illustrators, animators or programmers), design specifications (requirements and deliverables for both the client and the designer, milestones for review, and accountability factors), billing procedures, and contract terms. (Refer to the Developing a Design Proposal section in Chapter 1, Professional Relationships.) Also outlined in the statement of work are the number or complexity of the templates, the maximum number of revisions, the way in which comps of project phases will be presented and approved, and the format in which they are needed (static, Photoshop, or HTML).

It is customary for proposals to be submitted to clients as a complimentary service, although fees and expenses accrued thereafter on a client's behalf and with the client's consent are billable. If the client accepts the proposal, the written terms and conditions are confirmed with the signatures of the client, programmer, and designer. Frequently, a deposit is also requested before work begins. Once a client accepts the design proposal and any appropriate deposits have been received, actual work begins.

Questions to ask the client

As part of proposal development, the designer should listen to the client and ask a number of questions to determine the client's goals, design tastes, level of client and anticipated user sophistication, and workflow issues. The following questions may help create a questionnaire that is best suited to specific business needs:

CLIENT GOALS
- What is the client's business and how will the client's web site advance it? What does the client envision? What message should the web site convey?
- Who is the primary audience for the web site? The primary age group of the audience? What are their professions, disciplines, and interests? (Designers should warn clients that if the target is a broad-based, international audience, with potentially slow connections, old browsers, or expensive service, design options may be limited.)
- What are the secondary goals of the web site? Is this an informational site or an avenue for Internet-based marketing or revenue?
- What subjects, in order of priority, does the client want to cover on the web site? Have the client define at least five separate areas of

subject matter and describe in detail the unique qualities of the business.

- What design elements—colors, graphics, animations, logo, consistency of identity, and content parameters—would the client like? What elements does the client feel will be most effective, and why?
- Does the client require original illustration or animation on the site? If so, is the animation going to be entirely original, or will the client be providing imagery (screen shots, product shots, etc.) which need to be animated?

CLIENT EDUCATION

To get a true picture of what the client needs, it is helpful to know how much the client understands about the Internet. Be sure clients accurately describe what they want. For example, with what service does the client have Internet access? What kind of connection does the client have? Does the client have a domain name registered? With which registrar? Does the client have a web hosting account? With which host?

Depending on the answers to these and similar questions, it may be helpful to devote some time to providing basic education about the Internet.

Start-up businesses that want a web site but do not yet have a logo or a comprehensive brand identity may need to be educated about the importance, value, and reusability of a well-planned identity, discrete and separate from the website application. Some web designers recommend that clients without a logo or identity engage with them on an identity design project first, before the creation of a web presence. This practice ensures that the designer is not giving the client a "free" brand identity, and that the client is not using a web site project as a back door to create a holistic identity. Keeping the identity design and web design projects separate avoids potential misunderstandings and dissatisfaction between the client and the designer.

PLANNING

- Who will have final approval of the project? If someone other than the client's team has that authority, then the designer needs to make sure that person has a basic understanding of Web technologies.
- If the client has not already registered a domain name, what top-level domain name would the client like? For example, www.yourwebsite.com, www.yourwebsite.org, or www.yourwebsite.net? What are two or three alternative domain names in case the first choice is already taken?
- Are the client's source materials in a usable electronic form? If not, the designer may need to educate the client about how to submit materials in formats as consistent and compatible as possible. The designer should always request high-resolution versions of files so compression levels can be controlled for final graphics and PDF files. If necessary, the designer should provide the client with a variety of options and be prepared to do conversions.
- Does the site require advanced functionality, such as database functionality? (The database may be written in formats such as Microsoft Access, Filemaker Pro, MySQL, or Oracle Server, among others.) Does the site need to be coded in a special language, such as Cold Fusion, PHP, or ASP? Is the site going to be updated automatically through a server-side database and the implementation of a Common Gateway Interface (CGI) script or does the site need a Content Management System (CMS)?
- Are there requirements for e-commerce, such as the ability to securely process credit card transactions, development of shopping cart strategies, survey forms, advanced configurator sales selectors, online games and interactive demonstrations, and online chat, message boards, user forums, and blogs?
- Will the site be hosted on the client's server or with another provider? If in-house, the client's information technologies department should be included in the planning meetings.

PREPARING TO DESIGN

- Will the web site be designed from scratch, or is it a makeover of an existing site? If a makeover, does the client want any additions or deletions?
- What look and feel would the client like for the web site? The client should show the designer examples of web sites, magazines, publications, or artistic works they like and do not like. Be sure to ask why. Does the client have a specific genre, culture, or style in mind?
- Should the web site be consistent with any existing collateral marketing materials (brochures, publications, corporate identity programs, or posters), preproduction sketches, or media (DVDs, CD-ROMs, video games, or tapes)?
- Does the client desire graphics interactivity and/or multimedia (also involving content development and site mapping)? These typically include JavaScript rollovers and effects, animated GIFs, Quicktime or WMV movies, sound files, PDF downloads, Flash animations, and interactivity. Be sure to advise the client that these features will be estimated/charged in addition to, and not as part of, the basic design proposal.
- Does the client want to incorporate additional publicity for the web site utilizing social media such as Facebook, Twitter, or an online blog?
- Does the client need a new logo or new collateral marketing materials and media, for consistency with the new web site? If so, these design services should be quoted in addition to the proposal.
- Does the designer wish to negotiate a credit link that targets his or her home URL or e-mail?

CLIENT SUPPORT

- Does the client have the staff to respond to an anticipated upsurge in e-mail? If not, the project manager should explain that the client may develop a negative online reputation if people do not receive immediate responses.

- Does the client have the resources to maintain a presence on social networking sites or to keep a blog current, if this is part of the overall website strategy?
- Does the client plan to institute in-house site maintenance, or does the client want the designer to do it? Designers considering site maintenance arrangements should look carefully at the ability of their own organization to do at least biweekly or monthly changes.

Contract terms

Many components of contracts for illustration and design also apply to digital media. The Trade Practices sections in Chapter 8, Graphic Design Prices & Trade Customs, and Chapter 10, Illustration Prices & Trade Customs, as well as the model contracts in the Appendix: Contracts & Forms, give in-depth descriptions of contracts by type of work provided. However, it is important to note terms that are specific to digital media.

DELIVERABLES

Deliverables are all the items that a designer agrees to deliver to the client, including digital files, text, and images. It is important to delineate all the deliverable parts so that both the designer and the client understand the full scope of the project. Depending on the complexity of the project, the designer may divide it into several different phases with corresponding deliverables that will eventually be incorporated in the web site. Things such as content development (copy and graphics), interface design, back-end coding, graphics optimization, search engine optimization, positioning statements, and concepts must be considered separate project modules and priced as different line items.

Many contracts fail to describe deliverables in sufficient detail, leaving both designer and client vulnerable to miscommunication and dissatisfaction during the contract phase and, even worse, with the results. Creating an in-depth specification sheet and flowchart will help the designer avoid major headaches and keep the project on track. A full, clear description includes the size and scope of the work, using appropriate measurements (such as time, file size, number of screens or pages, complexity of linking and navigational elements, segment of programming source code, and site assets); intermediate review timetables and the deliverables required at those stages; the technical needs of the product such as medium, electronic file format, and style guides; copyright ownership of the deliverables; modules that conform to the function specifications; the kinds and types of revisions included in the fee; and the terms of acceptance.

EXPENSES

It is a widespread industry practice for the client to reimburse direct and indirect expenses, as specified in the contract. If precise amounts are not known at the time of signing, they are estimated, and the client should be given the option to approve any costs in excess of those projected in the original agreement. Direct costs include commissioning new or leasing existing images, animation, and sound; hiring voice talent; and signing run-time licenses. Note that use of graphics on printed pieces, such as photos, illustrations, and logos, must be quoted separately. Other expenses include travel, research materials, postage and delivery charges, photocopying, and media costs (such as DVDs). For designers who bill hourly, remember to consider capital investment when establishing fees. (See the Hourly Rate Formula section in Chapter 5, Essential Business Practices.)

PAY RATE

Rates depend upon project scope and complexity. Even if the client wants a bottom-line rate, an estimate must start with the expected hours it will take to complete the project. Most projects are bid in two parts, with an optional third section for 3-D or motion graphics. The first part includes the design, architecture, and user interface, at an average rate of $50–$250 per hour. The second section includes additional back-end programming, at a median rate of $75 per hour. See the Motion Graphics section below for rates.

PAYMENT TERMS

Depending on the length of the project, fees may be paid in a lump sum within a set period (30 days) after completion, or at periodic intervals when the time line is longer. Fees are often tied to acceptance of deliverables, but if there is only one review, payment may also be divided into three increments: a third on signing the contract, a third upon review of deliverables, and the last portion upon completion. Some design firms request up to 50 percent of the payment upon proposal acceptance to cover hiring freelance programmers and coders.

CANCELLATION FEES

A negotiated cancellation fee (also called "kill fee") may range from a portion of the cost to the entire cost of work, depending on the project status at the time of cancellation and the terms of the contract. Terms should stipulate that upon cancellation, all rights—publication and other—revert to the designer; the client shall assume responsibility for all collection and legal fees necessitated by default in payment; and a nondisclosure clause limits the review of the project to the client and specifically prohibits the client from showing the project to other designers.

SCHEDULE

While the timing of deliverables is an important contractual commitment, all digital media projects require specific time frames, including those with intangible deliverables: for example, provision of services. Contracts that include schedules should include contingency provisions to be met in the event deadlines are missed by either designer or client.

COPYRIGHT

For a full discussion of copyright issues, see Chapter 2, Legal Rights & Issues, and Chapter 4, Technology Issues.

One critical copyright concern related to digital media is ownership of the rights to deliverables. Obviously, the creator should ensure that the necessary rights to all work used to create the final product are purchased or confirmed to be in the public domain. Digital media creators often negotiate for the copyright to the final deliverable; if this proves difficult, creators then attempt to retain rights to intermediate deliverables. As noted in Chapters 2 and 4, signing a work-for-hire agreement transfers ownership of all materials and concepts to the client and should be avoided in all circumstances.

NON-COMPETE CLAUSES

Non-compete clauses restrict an artist from creating work perceived to be in competition with a particular client. Non-compete clauses are therefore troublesome for creators, as they limit their potential client base. Clients, however, are legitimately concerned that work resembling theirs will appear in the same market at an overlapping time. A compromise may be a stipulation that the graphic artist will not create work that is in conflict with the client's. If it appears difficult to eliminate a non-compete clause, traditional limitations appropriate to the project may be negotiated, such as time limits, geography, or usage. Occasionally, designers may propose clauses that offer the client the right to refuse new product ideas before they are offered to other clients.

CREDIT

Appropriate attribution and publicizing of credit can enhance a designer's reputation and ability to get work and are therefore important points of negotiation. Production studios, for instance, have initiated negotiations with clients about credits. As in film, video, and television, there are often many creators in web site design, and credit may be difficult to negotiate, at least initially. Credit options may include the creation of a colophon/credit page, a link to the designer's site or e-mail address, or an embedded comment in the HTML code like "Another cool site by The Designer."

DEMONSTRATION RIGHTS

Demonstration rights are essential for self-promotion. They refer to the designer's right to show a client's work as a part of the designer's portfolio. Since the designer is the creator, the designer owns the copyright of the visuals, unless stipulated otherwise in the statement of work. However, clients may raise understandable concerns about preempting launch publicity or revealing work to possible competitors. Compromises may have to be negotiated, such as permitting only portions of the work to be shown, or delaying unlimited rights until after the product is released.

LIABILITY

Liability raises a range of concerns. The client is usually responsible for obtaining permissions for any materials, including code and software, submitted to the designer. Similarly, the designer is usually responsible for obtaining necessary clearances for all subcontracted work (illustration, photography, animation, or any programming—both front-end and back-end), unless the client assumes that responsibility. The designer should also define to what extent the web site will be compatible with existing technologies, software, and platforms and to what extent each party is responsible for the smooth operation of the web site. For instance, subcontracted programmers are responsible for the functionality and legality of their code (they must define all copyright terms relating to their code with the client) and any bugs or incompatibilities. It should be clearly spelled out that any lack of projected hits (number of visits to a site), sales, or awards are not the designer's responsibility. The designer should retain the right to reuse code at a later date. Reuse of photography, motion graphics, and copywriting must also be negotiated.

Pricing

The cost of designing web sites can range dramatically from a limited makeover on the low end to the major launch of an e-commerce site on the high end. Companies often want to pay a flat or hourly fee and have the contractor sign a work-for-hire agreement (for a discussion of work-for-hire, see Chapter 2, Legal Rights & Issues). However, the Guild is opposed to such arrangements. Designers' fees for web work also range widely, depending upon the designer's skill, portfolio, and the complexity of the project. (See Figure 9-1, for Median Hourly Freelance Rates, and Figure 9-2 for Comparative Fees for Website Design.)

Traditional print criteria of size, placement, or number of insertions do not apply to artwork used in digital media, where the end user often

Median Hourly Freelance Rates Web Design

WEB DEVELOPER: FRONT-END/INTERFACE SYSTEMS	$60
WEB DESIGNER	$65
WEB PRODUCER	$70*
WEB PROGRAMMER/DEVELOPER BACK-END SYSTEMS	$75
CONTENT DEVELOPER	$65

*May be much higher if Producer acts as manager and can do the job of a Developer and Programmer/Developer from both a technical and project management standpoint.

FIGURE 9—1

Comparative Fees for
Website Design

A typical project entails concept, site map organization, design of home page and secondary pages under main headings, and supervision/direction of illustration/photography and limited animated and audio elements. Excludes reimbursable expenses. Creative design fees depend on the scope and complexity of assignments, the client's size and budget, production needs and schedules, deadlines, and rights transferred.

ENTIRE WEB SITE/STATIC[1]	ENTIRE WEB SITE/E-COMMERCE[1]	AVERAGE # OF PAGES	PRICE PER ELEMENT[2]	AVERAGE # OF ELEMENTS
$3,000-100,000[3]	$7,000-100,000	5-50	$300-1,500	5-10

[1] The cost of a web site involves more than graphic design. Only 10-50% of the fees for a web site project are graphic design, and the percentage varies by the complexity of the project; the rest of the cost is programming.

[2] Some designers do not separate out the price of elements; they are included/built into the base price.

[3] A full web site can be as inexpensive as $2,000 for a small (3-5 page), static site.

Additional Fees

	% OF ORIGINAL FEE	FLAT RATE	HOURLY RATE
RUSH FEE	50-200%	-	-
MONTHLY MAINTENANCE FEE	50-100%	$150-5,000[4]	$65-100
CONTENT MANAGEMENT SYSTEM[5]	-	$2,000-5,000	$100

[4] Varies by the specific needs of individual clients.

[5] Includes training client. While most reviewers bill CMS as an additional fee, some include CMS training & a user's manual as part of the deliverables of a website design project.

FIGURE 9—2

determines the sequence, timing, and repetitions of the work. The global nature of the Internet eliminates locale as a factor in web site design. Geographic distribution remains relevant for some digital media markets such as games, kiosks, point-of-purchase displays, and training programs.

Recent research indicates that designers transfer rights only for known media delivery, which are specifically listed in the contract. Some payments are made as flat fees; others may be treated as an advance against a royalty, based on total distribution. In rare instances, companies have even allocated royalties to the freelancers they have hired for particular jobs. Beware, however, of the company that promises a percentage of future revenue in lieu of payment for services rendered; that amounts to working on speculation, which is cautioned against in Chapter 3, Professional Issues. An hourly and fixed bid pay rate should be addressed and take precedence over royalties.

The principle of value-based pricing (keying prices to the work's role in the client's business) is as valid in the digital world as in other media. Generally, the wider and greater the benefit of the web site, the higher the value to the client. This may be gauged in relation to projected sales or to the client's track record on previous or similar projects.

Web sites range widely in price because their values range widely. A static site constructed only for functionality is bound to be less effective and less valuable than a static site that also encompasses visual design, including photography, illustration, text, and animation. To accurately estimate a browser-based project, price structures for each component need to be included.

Exposure is another criteria for setting prices. Just as you would price a brochure with a print run of 1,000 lower than you would price a brochure with a print run of 250,000, an in-house manual describing a company's retirement plan should be priced lower than an internationally accessed web site, even though the two may have the same design and layout.

Most designers estimate the hours the job should take as an additional gauge of a job's worth. Fees for meeting time, which may be charged at a lower-than-usual hourly rate, are usually added. Occasionally a client prefers to set a fixed price for a project. In such instances, an accepted industry practice is for designers to increase fees to accommodate unexpected changes, rush work, and overages that can occur during the course of a job. Alterations and changes should also be tracked, charged, and billed separately.

Making site maps, flowcharts, and simple storyboards can help the designer assess the scope of the web design project and serve as an early catalog of the level of graphics required. Web designers often determine file names and sizes on these charts before beginning design concepts. Occasionally, a designer may negotiate payment for a sample to determine the time and therefore the scope of the project. Creating a development (Beta) site based on the mandatory design specifications for any smooth-running web project, with a basic skeleton and outline, is another possibility. Such a site allows the client to review and make changes while the content is easy to manipulate.

Designers should know that although web server software collects data on the number of visits to a site, that number can easily be manipulated and should never be used to establish pricing. The project should be completed and fully paid for by the time a site is launched. If problems need to be addressed after a launch, they should be handled as alterations and changes. Of course, web pages are regularly updated. The person who will be responsible for updating, including all corresponding details, should be described in the contract.

Creative brief

Once the proposal is accepted and all questions satisfactorily answered, the designer should write an internal brief for the creative team, summarizing the client's vision for web site design. This overview of the work should reflect the information obtained from the above questions. Since its purpose is to inform team members about the job, each member should receive a copy and become familiar with it. The team leader also uses it to organize the work flow. Figure 9-3 illustrates a sample brief that can be easily adapted to suit the needs of a particular project.

Copyright protection concerns

From the moment a web site is launched, the information or graphics can be downloaded freely by anyone who wants them. It is all too easy for it to fall prey to illegal copying or element downloading. Even graphics that appear as very-low-resolution images can readily be reused. Using techniques such as Javascript to disable the right-click feature on the mouse makes it more difficult for images to be copied, but there are ways around that.

Software technology enables designers to embed invisible comments (digital watermarks) and numeric signatures in the file's binary data. While this offers minimal protection, it does not prevent copying or swiping. The best way to legally protect graphics on the Web is to clearly spell out any permitted uses of the images and the text on the site. (For more about copyright in the digital environment, see the Digital Millennium Copyright Act section in Chapter 2, Legal Rights & Issues.)

American copyright and libel law is applied to

Sample Creative Brief for **Website Design**

1. ASSESS CURRENT SITUATION
- Is there an existing brand online/offline?
- Define any existing products/offerings
- Is it a relatively competitive/saturated market?

2. ASSIGNMENT
- What is the target goal?
- List adjectives that are descriptive of goal.
- What is the scope of the project?
- How will this be accomplished: what features will need to be included in the website architecture and design to achieve this goal?

3. TARGET AUDIENCE(S)
- List & describe demographics of each.
- Describe target audience's web comfort-level and probable hardware and software usage (e.g., which browser version does it predominantly use? How comfortable is it with interactive online features, etc.?).

4. OBJECTIVES
- Define the specific objectives of the web site.
- Inform the client of the technologies and layout solutions that will achieve the objectives.
- Educate the client on how the website design and technologies will be implemented.

5. BARRIERS
- Define barriers that could hinder achieving the objectives of the web site (e.g., competition, inadequate web technologies, etc.).
- Educate the client about technologies and solutions which can be utilized to mitigate or overcome barriers (e.g., search engine optimization to counter lack of awareness of client's web site, utilizing a blog to drive traffic to the site, etc.).

6. STRATEGIES
- Outline how the web site will be designed and implemented, including coordination with backend designers.
- Outline how the web site will be launched, including steps to publicize the launch.
- Outline how the web site will be maintained on an ongoing basis.

7. TAKE AWAY
- What is the desired end result (to do what)?
- What is the manner of achieving it?

8. CREATIVE CONSIDERATIONS
- Logo
- Colors
- Layout
- Tone & manner (descriptive adjectives)
- Navigation
- Interactive features
- Usability

9. LEGAL REQUIREMENTS
- List

FIGURE 9—3

Internet content, but enforcement in the global Internet environment is extremely difficult. If a designer sees one of his or her graphics on someone else's page (the most frequent offense), common practice is to send an e-mail and ask the person to take it down, as web etiquette requires. Most frequently, the offender does not realize it is illegal to use other people's graphics. However, if the user has copied the graphic artist's work without permission and refuses to remove it, this illegal act is grounds for legal action.

Beware of worms, spiders, or search robots. Bitmap worms are programs that scan the Web for graphics, collecting them into icon and so-called clip art collections and then presenting them on a different site as so-called public domain art. The graphic artist can check hit reports to see who is spending time at the site. A single visitor downloading several megabytes of images is a warning that something illegal has been going on.

Protecting and enforcing one's legal rights in the digital world is easier said than done. Designers and artists are encouraged to register the site's content and images with the U.S. Copyright Office (for information on registration procedures, see Chapter 2, Legal Rights & Issues).

NOTE: Thanks to Tad Crawford for use of pricing perspectives from his *Legal Guide for the Visual Artist*, 4th ed., Allworth Press, 1999.

Motion Graphic Design

When you watch the opening titles of a movie or a TV show, you are seeing the work of Motion Graphic Designers. Motion Graphic Design (or simply Motion Graphics or Mograph) is graphic design for media that has motion. Motion graphics artists create imagery for television, video, film, computers, web sites, cell phones, and mobile devices—any media that has a screen. Motion graphics use video and/or animation technology to create the *illusion* of motion or a transforming appearance. According to Steve Curran, the author of *Motion Graphics: Graphic Design for Broadcast and Film*, "The art of motion graphics combines the arts of design, filmmaking, sound, music design, and animation in solutions that solve communication problems, educate an audience, add to the entertainment experience, or extend the value of a brand." Motion graphics is not the same as animation, although software, such as Adobe Flash is used to create motion design and add animation, video, and interactivity to Web pages. Computer animation may focus on using animated characters to tell a story, while motion graphics utilize type, photography, video, 2-D elements, and 3-D objects to communicate messages.

Motion graphics may be billed as high as $10,000 per on-screen minute, with an average billing rate of $65 to $85 per hour.

Motion Graphics done specifically for television is called Broadcast Design. However, Broadcast Design includes the design of all the print collateral used by a TV station as well as motion graphics. For a more detailed description of Broadcast Design, see Chapter 8, Graphic Design Prices & Trade Customs.

Video Game Art

Video game artists bring to the player the vision set out by the designers, art directors, and producers. Whether the virtual worlds inhabited by the characters and objects are highly realistic, futuristic, fantastic, or mythical, they need the imagination and artistic and technological skills of 2-D and 3-D artists and animators to bring them to life. From the concept artist, who works with the art director to establish the game's style, to the 3-D modeler who brings those concepts into existence, artists play a crucial role in the creation of a game. There are many other positions in the video game industry; however, this section is only concerned with those that require the skills of a graphic artist. It should be noted that a game designer is not a graphic designer; a game designer typically determines the overall vision of the game, similar to the role of the director in the film industry, and is responsible for writing the game design document, which consists of text and diagrams.

Despite the slow economy, video games continued to sell at record numbers in 2008. According to data from market researcher NPD Group, Americans bought $21.33 billion worth of video game systems, software, and accessories. Game software alone accounted for $11 billion in sales in 2008. While revenues fell throughout most of 2009, proving that the industry was not recession proof after all, they exploded at the end of the year. December 2009 was the best month ever in the industry with U.S. revenues a record breaking $5.53 billion—up 4% from December 2008.

The video game industry is a huge market, fueled by its customers' craving for new entertainment and fascination with technology. It is also an evolving and quickly changing industry. There are games that can be played remotely by multiple players scattered all over the world who can talk to each other while playing. There are the wireless motion sensing controller games, such as Wii, that simulate the swing and the sound of a tennis racket, golf club, or other sports equipment. One of the newer genres is the episodic game, which is produced and sold in small units that build into a recognizable series. Play is no longer limited to a video console or a handheld device designed solely for gaming—games are played on computers, online, on social networking sites, and on the iPhone. The ever-increasing types of games and platforms on which to play them have expanded the demographics of those who play as well as created numerous opportunities for artists.

Careers in video game art

Artists work on video games as **3-D Environment Artists, Animators, Character Animators, Special**

Effects Animators, Modelers, Character Modelers, Character Riggers, Concept Artists, Storyboard Artists, Flash Developers, Level Designers, Motion Capture Artists, Technical Directors, and Texture Map Artists, as well as Art Directors.

JOB DESCRIPTIONS

Art Director improves the process, quality, and productivity of art development while promoting artistic and job harmony.

Concept/Layout/Storyboard Artist creates original environments, objects, and storyboards under the guidance of the visual effects art director.

3-D Environment Artist designs and constructs 3D environments for game landscapes including the terrain, buildings, and vehicles.

Texture Map Artist creates 2-D graphic art used to define the surface qualities of a 3-D computer model.

Animator creates movement for characters, objects, and natural phenomenon.

Character Animator specializes in the creation of realistic character movement.

Character Modeler utilizes concept art to create and build 3-D computer-modeled characters.

In the past few years, artists working in the video game industry have had to deal with diminished opportunities due to outsourcing. Art can easily be created and refined outside the main studio, so it's easy for companies to send art-based work overseas, where labor is cheaper. There are still many opportunities for artists in the United States, but the desired skill set for full-time, in-house artists is changing. Art managers, who can speak the language of artists and who have an artistically trained eye, are needed to supervise the flow of outsourced work in and out of the studio. Concept artists, technical artists, riggers, and animators are among the other art jobs that need to stay in house.

Skills needed

Artists who have some technical knowledge, especially a scripting language or a general knowledge of programming, are more desirable job candidates than artists who have none. Nor is artistic talent alone enough to stay in demand in the game industry. To become invaluable to the team and company they work for, artists must be able to creatively collaborate with others, as well as be talented. The spectacular visuals of a game require technical wizardry, artistic persistence, and clever design—all working together. To deal with the endless number of problems inherent in the process of making a game and to keep the game going forward in a creative, productive way, artists must also be creative problem solvers. Other important skills required of artists in this field are a consistent, solid work ethic and the ability to deliver clean, organized work.

For artists working in this ever-evolving field, it is extremely important to develop and hone their traditional artistic skills and at the same time keep ahead of technology. They need to know the media they are creating art for by having a deep understanding of the hardware, tools, and engines they use to produce it.

Game artists and animators should be familiar with at least one 3-D software application, such as Autodesk's 3ds Max, Maya, and Softimage XSI; and Blender, as well as 2-D graphic tools, especially Photoshop. They should have a foundational knowledge of fine arts first, upon which they can build additional digital skills. Some game artists have additional experience in Web design, others have studied hand-drawn animation, and some are former sculptors and painters. Becoming more common in art departments as technology becomes more advanced are technical artists—artists who specialize in the software and hardware side of things. They are typically mid- to senior-level positions. Smaller game studios may prefer generalists who can work in different roles when necessary.

Salaries

According to the *Game Career Guide—Fall 2009* published by *Game Developer* magazine, the average annual salary of all entry-level artists (less than 3 years of experience) in the video game industry in 2008 was $47,692 (up about $4000 from 2007). Artists and Animators earned $45,985 for less than 3 years experience; $59,017 for 3-6 years; and $79,221 for over 6 years. Lead Artists and Technical Artists earned an average of $56,290 for less than 3 years; $70,333 for 3-6 years; and $88,929 for over 6 years. Art Directors, who have over 6 years experience, averaged $105,536. Of all the artists surveyed, 75% reported receiving additional compensation, amounting to an average of $16,130 per year. The types of additional compensation included bonuses (annual and project/title), royalties, pensions/employer contributions to retirement plans, stock options/equity, and profit sharing. Benefits were received by 91% of the artists; of those who reported benefits, 99% get medical, 93% dental, and 80% receive 401K/retirement plans.

There are regional differences in salary in the United States. The ten highest paying states across all disciplines and levels of experience in the industry are located along the East and West Coasts, as well as Illinois and Wisconsin. The highest salaries were paid in California. For art and animation jobs by region, the West paid the best ($76,115), followed by the East ($64,519), with the Mid-West and South almost equally the lowest ($59.500 and $59,250 respectively).

A highly noticeable gender gap exists in the industry: 90% of artists and animators are male and only 10% are female. However, this is slowly changing—from 2007 to 2008, there was a 2% increase in females. Unfortunately, this gender gap affects salaries. Male artists and animators earned an average of $70,385 in 2008, while females earned $61, 929.

Freelance opportunities

Although many assets in the video game industry are now being produced outside the United States, there are still opportunities for freelance/independent artists and animators in the field. However, opportunities vary by both position and company. In the past, freelancers were hired for the length of a project, but today they are increasingly being offered shorter contracts. Freelancers generally charge by the hour. The most important factor that determines their fee is time, but skill, quality, and complexity should be considered as well. Independent artists and animators do not retain the rights to the art they create for a game, and they seldom receive any royalties or additional compensation, so freelance work is basically a work-for-hire arrangement.

Education

Higher education programs to prepare students for careers in the video game industry have popped up all over in the last few years. Educational avenues for those who wish to work in art and animation positions include community colleges, online learning institutions, art or film schools, game-specific schools, game schools within universities, and traditional universities. Degrees are available at the Associate, Bachelor, and Master levels. Some typical degree programs that prepare artists and animators (as well as other positions in the industry) include a BS or BFA in Computer Animation, a BS in Game Art, a BFA or BS in Game Design and Development, BA in Visual Art with Game Art Major, etc.

In a survey *Game Developer* magazine conducted in May 2008 of students pursuing careers in the video game industry, 37% of those interested in art or animation jobs attended art or film schools, while 25% were enrolled in game-specific schools, 18% in game schools within universities, and almost 12% in traditional universities.

Design & Illustration for Other Digital Media

Digital technology has proven to be a double-edged sword for graphic artists. Certain print media and markets in which designers and illustrators have traditionally worked, such as publishing, are shrinking as their digital counterparts expand. We are seeing the demise of long-established major newspapers and magazines as subscribers turn to the Internet for news that is updated hourly instead of daily or weekly. Amazon.com reported that its e-reader, Kindle, was the biggest selling item of all of its products during the 2009 holiday season, signaling a change in books and how we've read them for over 500 years. Up until recently, e-readers could not compete with printed books on aesthetics, but that all changed in early 2010 when Apple launched its iPad with full-screen color.

While work in certain print media may be drying up, the need for illustration and design skills is being transferred to the digital arena. In the past, other than website design, work for digital media was often viewed (and priced) as add-ons to, or as additional usages of, larger print projects. Today, designers and illustrators are increasingly being asked to produce work directly for digital platforms as standalone projects, not tied to print. Advances in technology also have opened up opportunities for artists in digital media that didn't even exist 10 years ago. Described below are some of the areas in digital media not already discussed that need the skills of designers, illustrators, and animators.

Offline

EVENTS, PRESENTATIONS, DISPLAYS
Graphic artists are creating ambient graphics (still or motion) and Flash animation for all types of events and displays. These uses may be commercial—to advertise, promote, demonstrate, and launch products and books—or they may be simply to enhance the experience at events such as art openings. Artists and programmers are needed for touch screen displays, kiosk systems at shopping malls and tradeshows, and large-scale permanent installations that can be found in museums.

MOBILE TECHNOLOGY
In recent years, there has been a proliferation of choices and platforms available for advertising campaigns and programs with a mobile component. Graphic artists are needed to design and illustrate content that will be effective on miniature screens held at arm's length as well as on the vast screens of electronic bulletin boards seen from moving cars and every size in between. There are thousands of apps available now for mobile phones and other handheld devices, including smart phone and mini-game apps, photo and ringtone managers, etc. All these apps are represented onscreen by icons, which have created a demand for icon design beyond those used for web sites. Designers and programmers are also needed for navigational and Global Positioning Systems (GPS), such as an auto GPS or a GPS application on smart phones.

With Apple's introduction of the iPad tablet (with color, video, and audio as well as Wi-Fi and 3G capability), it is expected that its competitors will follow suit with similar products; and e-readers, in order to survive, will expand their content capabilities and increase the sophistication of screen content.

COMPUTER SOFTWARE APPLICATIONS
As more and more service businesses and government agencies, such as banking, medicine, the Department of Motor Vehicles, and the Internal Revenue Service, switch from print to electronic records and services, there will be a greater need for computer software applications that are designed and programmed to make the experience easy and user-friendly for the consumer. There will also be a greater need for information worker software

Comparative Fees for
Graphic Design for Digital Media

OFFLINE MEDIA

A typical project entails concepts; design; layout; and management of illustration, photography, and/or animated elements for "offline" products (CD-ROM, CD-Interactive, DVD, other portable media). Assumes first English language publication rights; excludes reimbursable expenses. Creative design fees depend on the scope and complexity of assignments; the client's size and budget; the number of screens (pages/templates); production needs and schedules; deadlines; and rights transferred.

	NATIONAL DISTRIBUTION	LIMITED DISTRIBUTION
ADVERTISING/PROMOTION	$10,000–85,000	$2,000–40,000
CONSUMER/GENERAL INTEREST	$3,500–35,000	$1,500–30,000
BUSINESS/SPECIAL INTEREST	$5,500–45,000	$3,500–40,000
OTHER	$4,000–35,000	$3,500–25,000

Closed Source Licensed Computer Applications[1,2]

COMPUTER SOFTWARE APPLICATIONS (Microsoft Visual Studio apps; cellular & mobile device apps; gaming engines; video games; and navigations, navigational, & GPS systems)	$10,000–1,000,000+
MOBILE DEVICE & SMART-PHONE APPLICATIONS (standalone) (Ringtone & photo managers; mini-game apps & other internal apps)	$1,500–3,500
SOFTWARE DEVELOPMENT KITS (SDK) (Allows software to be developed within a kit environment for an already existing system, such as the Sony PSP, Nokia N800, iPhone, etc.)	$25,000–500,000
KIOSK SYSTEMS (Touch screens [allow single hitstates]—$5,000–50,000; multi-lib touch screens [allow multiple hitstates]--$15,000–100,000; standalone tradeshow display systems; full-production, large scale permanent installations)	$20,000–750,000
OPEN SOURCE GNU OR MIT STYLE LICENSED APPLICATIONS[1] (May have distribution/sale rights/royalties associated)	$5,000–500,000

[1] 25% of fees are for graphic design and 75% is for programming.

[2] Fees do not include royalties, rights, licensing for development team.

Additional Fees

	PERCENT OF ORIGINAL FEE
Transfer of original files	10–125%
Reuse for indicated uses in this market	100–150%
Rush fee	50–200%
Unlimited use (no time or geographical limits)	100–400%
Unlimited use for 1 year (with geographical limits)	100–150%
Work-for-hire (transfer of legal authorship)	100–500%

(Continues on next page)

FIGURE 9—4

Comparative Fees for
Graphic Design for Digital Media (Continued)

ONLINE MEDIA

Advertising & Promotion

A typical project entails concept and management of design/illustration/photography and limited animated and audio elements. This assumes some knowledge of current programming applications. Excludes reimbursable expenses. Creative design fees depend on the scope and complexity of assignments, the client's size and budget, production needs and schedules, deadlines, and rights transferred.

WEB SITE CAMPAIGN	$5,000–50,000
SPLASH PAGE (per page)	$500–4,000
BANNERS, BUTTONS, FLASH ANIMATION	$375–50,000
3-D ANIMATION & MOTION GRAPHICS	$10,000–150,000
BLOG DESIGN	$2,000–10,000
SOCIAL MEDIA (ex. Twitter background; Facebook, Vimeo, & YouTube pages)	
SET-UP	$400–2,500
DESIGN	$800–3,500[3]

[3] Excludes Facebook application design.

FIGURE 9—4

for the employees who are creating, processing, and managing all this electronic data, as well as software to train them. Software applications include Customer Resource Manager (CRM), used internally to track sales and customer information in a database, and Content Management Systems (CMS), which may be internal intranet and extranet based.

The proliferation of digital entertainment also requires software for those who create it as well as for the user to access and consume it. Entertainment software includes gaming engines and video games. Software Development Kits (SDK) allow software to be developed within a kit environment for an already existing system, such as the Sony PSP and even the iPhone.

Online

E-COMMERCE

E-commerce has evolved to include enhancements to, and applications beyond, web sites. Survey respondents report that advertising is becoming more sophisticated. In addition to the obvious forms, such as Web banners and pop-up ads, more subtle forms are being designed as part of a site's background or content.

Joining e-mail & viral marketing is the personalized URL (PURL). A PURL is a web page or microsite that is tailored to an individual visitor through the use of variable fields and pages that are linked to a database that contains information about each potential visitor. For each recipient on the database's list, the web address is unique, as is the content of the web page. For example, a college could send out an HTML e-mail inviting potential students to visit its web site. After clicking on the link to the site, a student who has an interest in science would see lots of photos of labs, etc.; another student interested in theatre would see the same web site, but the photos and text would talk about the theatre department. Both web pages would have a personal greeting such as, "Welcome to XXX U., John Doe" (or whatever the name is), and the URLs would also be personalized with the recipient's name, such as "www.xxx-university.edu/johndoe." The high degree of personalization involved in creating PURLs requires additional Web design and a great quantity and variety of visual content.

BLOGS & SOCIAL NETWORKING SITES

More and more businesses and organizations have realized the value of hosting blogs and joining social networking sites to promote their products and services or to advance their causes. Graphic artists are being asked to design and illustrate pages for these sites.

E-GREETINGS

There are numerous companies, including the major greeting card companies, that offer online e-greetings for every occasion—many of them free. The offerings include static cards or Flash-animated cards with music and sound, "delivered" via an e-mail to the recipient which includes a web address where the card can be accessed. The greeting can be personalized by whatever message the sender composes. Some companies specialize in corporate e-greetings for business-to-business and customer relationships. They offer additional services such as address books, calendars, and e-mail reminder notifications, as well as the ability to customize cards with a company logo.

Like their printed counterparts, e-greetings require the skills of writers, designers, and illustrators, as well as animators.

Comparative fees for graphic design and illustration for some of the digital media applications mentioned in this chapter are found in Figures 9-4 and 9-5. It should be noted that graphic design and illustration comprise only a percentage of the cost of a digital project and the percentage varies by the type of media or application and the specifics, scope, and complexity of the project.

NOTE: All prices for the design of digital media in this book are based on independent surveys of the United States and Canada that were reviewed by experienced professionals in the various disciplines in which they work. These figures, reflecting the responses of established professionals, are meant as a point of reference only and do not necessarily reflect such important factors as deadlines; job complexity; reputation and experience of a particular designer; research; technique or unique quality of expression; and extraordinary or extensive use of the finished design. (See related material in other sections of this book, especially in Chapter 5, Essential Business Practices, and Chapter 6, Standard Contracts & Business Tools.)

★　　★　　★

Comparative Fees for Illustration for Digital Media

OFFLINE MEDIA

	INTERNATIONAL	NATIONAL	LIMITED	BUNDLED WITH PRINT
SPLASH SCREEN	$1,500-6,000	$1,000-3,000	$875-2,025	$500-2,650
FULL SCREEN	$1,000-3,250	$1,300-3,250	$700-2,075	$500-2,650
HALF SCREEN	$700-2,100	$750-2,100	$500-1,950	$150-1,500
ICON/BUTTON	$525-1,200	$550-2,250	$150-2,250	$150-1,500

			ENTIRE PROJECT	% OF COST FOR ILLUSTRATION
EVENTS MARKETING / LIVE ART & KIOSKS			$30,000-200,000	7-15%
GAME DEVELOPMENT			$10,000-500,000	35%

ONLINE MEDIA

Web site Illustration & Animation

STATIC WEB SITE	E-COMMERCE WEB SITE	AVERAGE # OF PAGES	PRICE PER ELEMENT	AVERAGE # ELEMENTS
$3,500-30,000	$5,000-22,500	10-40	$200-5,000	5-25

			ENTIRE PROJECT	% OF COST FOR ILLUSTRATION
WEB BANNERS			$10,000-60,000	20-50%
ANIMATION & MOTION			$10,000-500,000	35-50%
ANIMATION (per completed second) - $50-500				

Additional Fees

	PERCENT OF ORIGINAL FEE
Stock sale of existing art	50-150%
Rush fee	25-150%
Unlimited use for 1 year	50-400%
Work-for-hire (transfer of legal authorship)	100-400%

FIGURE 9—5

ILLUSTRATION PRICES & TRADE CUSTOMS

This chapter details the different markets where illustrators, mainly independent contractors, sell their creative product and reproduction rights to their artwork. The accepted trade practices that govern the buying and selling of artwork are provided for each market.

ILLUSTRATORS

ILLUSTRATORS are graphic artists who create artwork for any number of different markets. Most illustrators are freelancers (independent contractors) who maintain their own studios and work for a variety of clients, rather than salaried staff artists working for one employer. Some fields in which illustrators work on staff include animation studios, comic books, greeting cards, and clip art production houses. While some freelance illustrators hire representatives or agents to promote their work to art buyers, many do their own promotion and marketing. (For a thorough discussion of artist's representatives, see Chapter 1, Professional Relationships.)

Illustrators use a variety of traditional and new techniques and tools, including pen and ink, airbrush, acrylic and oil painting, watercolor, collage, multidimensional structures, and computers. Most have a signature style, while some are sought for their versatility. Illustrators are responsible for knowing the technical requirements of color separation and printing, including trapping and other production technologies, that are necessary to maintain the quality of the final printed piece (see Chapter 4, Technology Issues).

Original or specially commissioned illustration is sold primarily on the basis of usage and reproduction rights, but other factors are important (see Chapter 5, Essential Business Practices). Original artwork, unless sold separately, usually remains the property of the illustrator.

Usage rights are generally sold according to the client's needs. Other uses for a work may be sold to other clients as long as they are noncompetitive or do not compromise the commissioning client's market. Clients that manage their businesses well only buy rights particular to the project, since it is not economical to pay for additional rights that are not needed and that will not be used.

A Note about Pricing in the Current Economy

—As with advertising and corporate, many editorial budgets are tightening and fees have been decreasing over the past year...more evident over the past 6 months.

—Due to the economy, I have experienced a large drop in the prices my clients are willing to pay for fashion illustration and illustration in general.

—The economy has really hit the business hard and people are hungry and are working for less. There are more of these stupid web sites where people can post a job and dozens will give quotes and they're getting the work done very cheap.

Many illustrators have reported tighter client budgets and stagnant or even declining fees since the last edition of this book was published. Factors negatively affecting pricing include the recessionary economy which has impacted many areas of illustration since late 2008. Other factors, such as the increasing transition from print to electronic-based media, the proliferation of stock images on the Internet, and the outsourcing of work overseas, have slowly eroded specific industries, such as publishing, for several years now. Print versions of daily newspapers and well-established magazines are folding. Illustrators working in these fields are not only being asked by their clients to do the same work for less payment, but they are seeing less and less work coming their way. Some illustrators who sell both original work and stock are seeing a shift in the ratio of original commissioned work versus stock sales: as requests for commissioned work decline, stock illustration usage has risen.

While some illustrators may feel pressured to lower fees to keep work coming in, it is not recommended. Once fees are reduced, it is difficult to justify raising them again when the economy rebounds and fees stabilize. Plus, illustrators who do this are not only devaluating their own worth, but the worth of the entire graphic arts profession. Some artists are reporting being asked to do work at fees that make it impossible to make a living. When the cost of living is steadily climbing, it is financial suicide to start charging less for services. Except for the occasional, temporary discount, what other professional service industry has lowered its fees in the present economy? Artists have to charge rates that realistically account for their own cost of living needs. While they need to be aware of their clients' shrinking budgets and increased costs, they can't always be the party that makes all the concessions.

Illustrators who feel they cannot compete in today's economy without lowering their fees need to make up the difference by negotiating more favorable terms, such as higher royalty rates, increased usage fees, more visible credit, promo-tional opportunities, etc. Educating clients and savvy negotiating are more crucial than ever in the present economic climate. Illustrators are professionals who provide a valuable service that helps clients succeed in business.

It is inevitable that electronic media will continue to make inroads into print media. Opportunities for illustration work are already shifting from print to digital formats. Illustrators are encouraged to seek out and take advantage of new opportunities in digital media (refer to Chapter 9, Web Design & Other Digital Graphic Arts) as well as explore new markets for the re-use of their art, such as selling stock and licensing their images for use on products (see the Maximizing Income section in Chapter 5).

The information in this book is intended to encourage illustrators to evaluate the true worth of their work and seek it aggressively. The value of intellectual property has ballooned as markets have become global. According to Secretary of Commerce Carlos M. Gutierrez in an essay for the *Kauffman Thoughtbook 2009,* "Innovation and entrepreneurship flourish when our nation is open to new people and ideas and engages with the world through commerce. U.S. intellectual property today is worth more than $5 trillion. Intellectual property industries contribute some 40 percent of U.S. economic growth and represent 18 million well-paid workers." Intellectual property is such a valuable commodity that its protection, a major issue in current international trade relations, is critical to the strength and continued expansion of the U.S. economy.

While artists are making persistent, concerted efforts to educate clients about the true value of what they do, it is in the clients' best interest to see artists as partners in creating their message, to treat artists with respect, and to reward artists with the compensation their work deserves.

General Trade Practices for Illustration

The following general trade practices have been used historically and thus have become accepted as standard. Please see individual market sections for additional trade practices specific to those markets.

1. The intended use of the art, the price, and terms of sale must be clearly stated in a contract, purchase order, or letter of agreement.
2. The artwork cannot be altered in any way, except for what occurs during the normal printing process, without the written consent of the artist. Since it is very easy to alter art electronically these days, the client should inform the artist if he or she wishes to alter the artwork and then do so only with the permission and supervision of the illustrator. Anything less is a violation of professional good faith and ethical practice.
3. Return of original artwork "unaltered and undamaged except for normal use and wear" to the artist is automatic unless otherwise negoti-

ated or noted in the individual market sections in this chapter.

4. If artwork will be used for something other than its original purpose, such as for an electronic database or a web site, that fee is usually negotiated as early as possible. Note that secondary use of an illustration may be of greater value than the primary use. Reuse fees vary according to the individual market. (See individual market sections.)

5. Illustrators should negotiate reuse arrangements with the original commissioning party with speed, efficiency, and respect for the client's position.

6. Artists charge higher fees for rush work, and they vary according to the individual market. (See individual market sections.)

7. If the illustrator satisfies the client's requirements but the finished work is not used, full compensation should be made. If a job is canceled after the work has begun, through no fault of the artist, a cancellation or kill fee is often provided. Depending upon the stage at which the job is terminated, this fee must cover all work done, including research time, sketches, billable expenses, and compensation for lost opportunities resulting from the artist's refusing other offers in order to make time available for the commission. In addition, clients who put commissions on hold or withhold approval for commissions for longer than 30 days should secure the assignment by paying a deposit up front.

8. A rejection fee is agreed upon if the assignment is terminated because the preliminary or finished work is found to be unsatisfactory and steps to correct the problem have been exhausted. The rejection fee for finished work often has been over 50 percent of the full price, depending upon the reason for rejection and the complexity of the job. When the job is rejected at the sketch stage, surveys indicate that the customary fee is 20 to 50 percent of the original price. This fee may be less for quick, rough sketches and more for highly rendered, time-consuming work.

9. Artists considering working on speculation assume all risks and should evaluate the risks carefully when offered such arrangements. For a thorough discussion of the risks, see the Speculation section in Chapter 3, Professional Issues.

10. The Graphic Artists Guild is unalterably opposed to the use of work-for-hire contracts, in which authorship and all rights that go with it are transferred to the commissioning party and the independent artist is treated as an employee for copyright purposes only. The independent artist receives no employee benefits and loses the right to claim authorship or to profit from future use of the work forever. In the Guild's view, advertising is not eligible as work-for-hire, as it does not fall under any of the eligible categories defined in the law. Additional information on work-for-hire can be found in Chapter 2, Legal Rights & Issues.

11. Customary and usual out-of-pocket expenses such as props, costumes, model fees, travel costs, production costs, shipping, picture reference, and consultation time are billed to the client separately. An expense estimate is usually included in the original written agreement or as an amendment to the agreement.

NOTE: All prices for illustration in this book are based on independent surveys of artists in the United States and Canada and were reviewed by experienced professionals in the various disciplines in which they work. These figures, reflecting the responses of established professionals, are meant as points of reference only and do not necessarily reflect such important factors as geographic differences in cost of living; deadlines; job complexity; reputation and experience of a particular illustrator; research; technique or unique quality of expression; and extraordinary or extensive use of the finished art. (See related material in other sections of this book, especially in Chapter 5, Essential Business Practices, and Chapter 6, Standard Contracts & Business Tools.)

Advertising Illustration

Illustrators are hired to provide visuals for products or services for specific advertising needs. The illustrator's first contact in this market is usually an art buyer, who solicits and receives portfolios and often, especially in the larger agencies, remains the primary conduit for the flow of work. For creative guidance, however, illustrators usually work with art directors, account executives, copywriters, and heads of the agency's creative group. The terms and fees for art are normally negotiated with the agency's art buyer or art director by the illustrator or the artist's representative.

Traditionally, premium prices for illustration have been paid in the advertising field, where the highest degree of professionalism and performance is expected from artists working within unusually strict time demands. However, illustrators are reporting that advertising seems especially affected by the current economy, with budgets tightening and fees decreasing. Generally, advertising illustration prices are negotiated strictly on a use basis, with extra pay added for the sale of residual or all rights, complexity of style, or extra-tight deadlines. Most magazines have set prices in their budgets, with children's magazines paying at the low end and business magazines somewhat higher.

Advertisements are usually thought of in terms of the number of times they run. Therefore, sale of usage rights may refer to limited or unlimited use in a specific media and geographic area within a specified time period; for example, they may be "limited to one to five insertions in consumer magazines in the United States for one year." The media, distribution area, and time period for which advertising rights are sold should be clearly defined and the price agreed upon before the project starts.

Agencies expect illustrators to work in a specific style represented in their portfolios and to follow a sketch supplied by the agency and approved by the client. Changes and last-minute alterations are common, since many advertisements are created by committee and illustrators may need to please several people of varying opinions. Many illustrators set fees that include a finite number and type of alterations, such as "one reasonable revision."

Comparative Fees for
Advertising Illustration

Fees listed in the following charts are average fees that cover limited use—from one to five insertions for a period of one year. Fees range from a simple single image illustration to complex compositions and highly rendered styles. In many cases, assignment fees can be much higher than are reflected here.

Consumer Magazines including Special Advertising Sections

	SPREAD	FULL PAGE	HALF PAGE	QUARTER PAGE/SPOT
GENERAL INTEREST OR LARGE CIRCULATION *(Readers Digest, Time, Women's Day, The New Yorker, Vanity Fair)*				
Color	$4,500–20,000	$3,000–10,000	$1,500–8,000	$600–5,000
B & W	–	–	–	$500–1,000
SPECIAL INTEREST OR MEDIUM CIRCULATION *(Rolling Stone, Atlantic Monthly, Discover, Wired, Food & Wine)*				
Color	$3,500–20,000	$2,500–10,000	$1,200–8,000	$600–5,000
B & W	–	–	–	$500–1,000
SMALL CIRCULATION *(Scientific American, Mother Jones)*				
Color	$2,500–20,000	$1,500–10,000	$1,000–8,000	$500–5,000
B & W	–	–	–	$450–700

Business Magazines

	SPREAD	FULL PAGE	HALF PAGE	QUARTER PAGE/SPOT
GENERAL BUSINESS OR NATIONAL CIRCULATION *(Business Week, Forbes, Fortune)*				
Color	$3,500–20,000	$2,000–10,000	$1,500–8,000	$600–5,000
B & W	–	–	–	$500–850
MEDIUM TO SMALL CIRCULATION (Trade, institutional, or professional magazines)				
Color	$2,500–20,000	$1,500–10,000	$1,000–8,000	$500–5,000
B & W	–	–	–	$400–750

Newspaper & Newspaper Supplements

	SPREAD	FULL PAGE	HALF PAGE	QUARTER PAGE/SPOT
NATIONAL, MAJOR METRO, OR LARGE CIRCULATION				
Color	$2,000–4,000	$1,500–3,000	$1,200–2,000	$500–1,000
B & W	–	–	$1,000–1,500	$400–750
MIDSIZE METRO				
Color	$1,800–3,000	$1,200–2,000	$850–1,500	$500–750
B & W	–	–	$700–1,200	$400–650
SMALL METRO OR LOCAL WEEKLY				
Color	$1,500–2,500	$850–1,500	$750–1,200	$450–600
B & W	–	$650–1,200	$500–1,000	$350–500

(Continues on next page)

FIGURE 10—1

Comparative Fees for
Advertising Illustration (Continued)

Collateral

	COVER	FULL PAGE	HALF PAGE	QUARTER PAGE/SPOT
PRODUCT/SERVICE CATALOG: EXTENSIVE USE				
Color	$3,500-12,000	$2,500-3,000	$1,000-2,000	$750-1,000
B & W	$1,500-3,000	$1,200-2,000	$750-1,500	$450-600
PRODUCT/SERVICE CATALOG: LIMITED USE				
Color	$2,500-3,500	$2,000-3,000	$850-1,500	$600-850
B & W	$1,700-2,500	$1,500-2,200	$700-1,000	$300-450
PRESS OR MEDIA KIT: EXTENSIVE USE				
Color	$2,500-5,000	$2,000-4,000	$1,000-2,500	$600-1,000
B & W	–	$1,500-2,500	$1,200-2,000	$500-800

PRESS OR MEDIA KIT: LIMITED USE

Average fees are 20-25% less than Extensive Use

	COVER	FULL PAGE	HALF PAGE	QUARTER PAGE/SPOT
BROCHURE*: PRINT RUN OVER 100,000				
Color	$2,000-12,000	$1,500-4,000	$1,000-2,500	$700-1,200
B & W	–	–	$1,200-2,000	$650-1,200
BROCHURE*: PRINT RUN 10,000-100,000				
Color	$2,000-4,000	$1,500-3,000	$1,000-2,000	$600-1,000
B & W	–	–	$1,000-1,200	$600-750
BROCHURE*: PRINT RUN UNDER 10,000				
Color	$1,500-3,000	$1,000-3,000	$700-2,000	$700-1,000
B & W	$1,500-2,500	$1,000-2,000	$700-1,500	$450-750

*8.5" x 11" or 6" x 9" including gate fold, accordion fold, etc.

	COVER	FULL PAGE	HALF PAGE	QUARTER PAGE/SPOT
DIRECT RESPONSE MAILER: PRINT RUN OVER 100,000				
Color	$4,000-6,500	$2,500-3,500	$1,500-2,500	$750-1,200
B & W	–	–	–	$650-1,000
DIRECT RESPONSE MAILER: PRINT RUN 10,000-100,000				
Color	$2,500-4,000	$2,000-3,000	$1,200-2,000	$700-1,000
B & W	$1,500-2,500	$1,000-2,000	$850-1,500	$500-750

DIRECT RESPONSE MAILER: PRINT RUN UNDER 10,000

Average fees are 20-25% less than Print Run 10,000—100,000

(Continues on next page)

FIGURE 10—1

Comparative Fees for
Advertising Illustration (Continued)

Point of Sale, Displays, & Exhibits

	WALLS	BANNER OR POSTER	BOOTH SURFACE	FLOOR DISPLAY	TABLE TOP
ONE-YEAR SHOW LICENSE, MAJOR CLIENT					
	$4,500–30,000	$2,500–8,000+	$1,700–6,000+	$2,000–5,000	$1,000–3,500
SINGLE TRADE SHOW, MAJOR CLIENT					
	$3,500–10,000	$2,800–5,000+	$1,800–5,000	$2,000–5,000	$1,200–3,000
ONE-YEAR SHOW LICENSE, SMALL CLIENT, DEPARTMENT STORE OR BOUTIQUE					
	$3,000–8,000	$2,500–4,500	$2,000–5,000	$1,700–3,500	$1,200–3,000
SINGLE TRADE SHOW, SMALL CLIENT, DEPARTMENT STORE OR BOUTIQUE					
	$2,000–6,500	$2,000–3,500	$1,500–4,000	$1,500–3,000	$1,000–2,500

POINT OF SALE: MULTIPLE USES, ONE YEAR:

WALL/SHELF	FLOOR/TABLETOP/POSTER
$4,000–5,000	$4,500

OTHER	WINDOW DISPLAY	SHOPPING BAG
Color	$2,000–5,000	$1,000–5,000
B & W	–	$850–2,000

Outdoor Advertising

	LARGE AD	MEDIUM AD	SMALL AD
BUS, CAR, & TRANSIT: MAJOR			
Color	$4,500–25,000	$3,000–10,000	$1,800–7,500
B & W	–	–	–
BUS, CAR, & TRANSIT: REGIONAL			
Color	$3,000–7,000	$1,800–5,000+	$1,200–4,000
B & W	–	–	$1,200–3,000
BUS, CAR, & TRANSIT: LOCAL			
Color	$2,200–6,000	$1,500–4,000	$1,000–3,000
B & W	–	–	$1,000–2,000
STATION/KIOSK POSTER			
Color	$3,000–6,000+	$1,800–4,500	$1,200–3,500
B & W	–	–	$1,000–2,500

OUTDOOR BILLBOARD	Major Campaign*	Regional Campaign**	Local Campaign***
	$5,000–25,000	$4,000–10,000	$2,200–5,000

(Continues on next page)

*Major = 40 or more installations   **Regional = approximately 25 installations   ***Local = up to 5 installations

FIGURE 10—1

Comparative Fees for
Advertising Illustration (Continued)

Animated Television Commercials

	COMPLEX	SIMPLE
Original Design/Development: 30 seconds	$20,000-60,000	$10,000-20,000
Licensing of Character: 30 seconds	$12,000-25,000	$8,000-15,000
Styling of Key Frames: 15 seconds	$10,000-25,000	$7,000-12,000
Styling of Key Frames: 30 seconds	$25,000-40,000	$15,000-25,000
TV per frame	$130-250	$100-225

Motion Picture Posters

	PRODUCED POSTER	FINISHED ART-UNUSED
Major Production	$7,500-25,000	$5,000-7,000
Limited Production	$4,500-18,000	$2,500-4,000

Theater & Event Posters*

	COMPLEX	SIMPLE
LARGE PRODUCTION		
Color	$3,000-10,000	$1,500-4,000
B & W	–	$1,500-3,500
SMALL PRODUCTION		
Color	$1,000-5,000	$500-4,000
B & W	–	$1,250-3,000

*A common practice for artists making screen-printed event posters is to charge the client a lower art fee, then sell a full edition of the poster elsewhere, generating additional revenue of several thousand dollars.

Online Advertisement

WEBSITE ADS (PART OF CONTENT): LIMITED USE, ONE YEAR:	$2,000-4,000

Additional Fees

	PERCENT OF ORIGINAL FEE
Rush Fee	25-40%
Sale of original art	50-200%
Stock sale of existing art	65-100%
Unlimited use in print media only (no time or geographical limits)	50-100%
Unlimited use, any media for 1 year	50%+
Total copyright transfer (excluding original art)	100-300%
Work-for-hire transfer of legal authorship and all rights	150-200%+

Fees in Figure 10-1 do not reflect any specific trade practices and do not constitute specific prices for particular jobs. The buyer and seller are free to negotiate, with each artist independently deciding how to price the work, after taking all factors into account.

FIGURE 10—1

Additional changes, especially significant ones, necessitate additional charges, and artists tend to be flexible, giving valued and responsible clients some leeway.

Specific trade practices for advertising illustration

In addition to the general trade practices listed in the beginning of this chapter, the following trade practices for advertising illustration have been used historically and thus are accepted as standard:

1. Illustrators working in advertising normally sell rights to one to five insertions of their artwork, within a given medium and a given market, for one year from date of first use, unless otherwise stated.
2. Return of original artwork "unaltered and undamaged except for normal use and wear" to the artist is automatic unless otherwise negotiated. The advertising agency must be responsible for the art while it is in its possession; the artist should place a value on the artwork to cover loss or damage.
3. Reuse fee: from 50 to 100 percent of the fee that would have been charged had the illustration been commissioned for the new use.
4. Charge for rush work: an additional 25 to 40 percent.

See Figure 10-1 for Comparative Fees for Advertising Illustration.

Preproduction Illustration

Artists who specialize in preproduction art service the advertising, television, and motion picture industries and usually are called upon to produce high-caliber professional work within tight deadlines.

Types

Although some artists specialize, nearly all are engaged in three areas of preproduction art: comps (common abbreviation for "comprehensives"), storyboards, and animatics or "Pre-Viz" (Pre-Visual).

COMPS
Comps are visual renderings of proposed advertisements and other printed promotional materials, usually consisting of a "visual" (a rendering of the illustration or photo to be used in the finished piece), headlines, and body text. Comps may also include character turnarounds, attitudes, and expression sheets.

STORYBOARDS
A storyboard is a visual presentation of a proposed television commercial, program, or feature film, using sequential frames. They are sometimes drawn on a telepad, which is a preprinted matrix with frames that are usually 2.75 x 3.75 inches, although some agencies supply their own telepads in larger formats.

In advertising, storyboards are generally used in-house (within an agency) to present the concept of the proposed commercial to the client. An important component of preproduction artwork in advertising is the "key" frame, a large single frame used with other frames to establish the overall mood or to portray the highlight or key moment of the commercial. The key frame must be given extra attention—and compensation—since it carries most of the narrative burden.

For feature films or television, storyboard renderings are used by producers to envision creative concepts and to evaluate a concept's visual qualities and continuity. Used most often as a reference to an accompanying script, the storyboards and text are filmed as a "photoplay," a critical element in determining a property's value as entertainment and as a visual production. Storyboards are the visual blueprint producers rely upon to budget and help avoid cost overruns. Most animated TV show production is now paperless and all art is drawn on cintiq interactive tablets, which make editing and correcting easier.

Artist fees for television or feature-film storyboards have historically been based on the production's budget and its intended distribution. Fees for high-budget productions, which usually require more complex storyboard renderings, generally are higher than fees for low-budget productions.

Storyboards for motion picture and television features are generally black-and-white and emphasize camera angles and moves. Because a larger number of frames are generally produced for feature-length storyboards, the rendering style that is the most in demand is quick, clean, and realistic. Artists who create storyboards for motion picture and television features must work more closely with other members of the creative team than is customary in advertising preproduction. And artists often scout locations or work on location.

ANIMATICS
An *animatic* is a limited-animation video using camera movements, a select number of drawings, some animation, and a sound track. An animatic is usually produced to test a proposed "spot" or TV commercial. The need for animatics has increased due to the demand for test marketing by advertisers. An animatic must "score" well on such factors as audience recall to go into full production.

Video storyboards are also used frequently in other markets as well, especially motion pictures for television, because of the wider availability of relatively inexpensive video equipment. Video storyboards use only storyboard art (no moving parts), and movement is achieved with simple camera moves. Often a tighter-than-normal style is required, which many artists have used to explain fees that are somewhat higher than for regular storyboards.

Comparative Fees for Preproduction Illustration

HOURLY RATE $75-125+

DAY RATE $650-1,000+

Advertising Comps

	COMPLEX*	SIMPLE*
MAJOR CAMPAIGN**		
Spread	$600-2,500+	$450-1,800+
Full page	$400-2,000+	$250-1,500+
MINOR CAMPAIGN**		
Spread	$500-2,000+	$350-1,200+
Full page	$300-1,500+	$200-1,000+

Story Boards (per frame)***

TV ADVERTISING TEST MARKETING		
Miniboards (1 x 1.5")	$50-150+	$40-75+
Telepads (2.75 x 3.75")	$85-450+	$65-200+
3 x 4"	$125	$50-85
4 x 5"	$150-250+	$65-175+
5 x 7"	$175-420+	$90-200+
8 x 10" key frame	$250-875	$140-495
9 x 12" key frame; presentation board	$300-700+	$200-450+

TV PROGRAMMING		
Major Production		
3 x 4"	$125	$50-85
4 x 5"	$75-125+	$65-100+
5 x 7"	$100-150+	$75-125+
9 x 12"	$450-700+	-
Concept key frame	$175-300+	$125-250+
Character Turnaround	$1,000	-

Minor or Independent Production

Fees average 10-15% less than for major production

Animatics (per frame)

TV COMMERCIAL TEST MARKETING	
5 x 7" (8 x 10" bleed)	$150-450+
8 x 10" (11 x 14" bleed)	$175-500+

* For advertising comps, complexity is determined by such criteria as the number of colors, layers, and elements, as well as the time involved. For example, in addition to the base art, there can be many moving elements, all drawn seperately—arms, legs, head movement, different gestures, etc.

** Major vs. minor is determined by the market the illustration appears in. A major campaign would be national or global. An example of a minor campaign might be a mailer with a limited purpose sent to a small or local market.

*** Storyboards are often a set price, determined by size, complexity, and style. Scanning costs are included in the price. "Complex" vs. "simple" also may be considered "color" vs. "B&W or tone."

NOTE: The price ranges in 10–2 do not reflect specific trade practices and do not constitute specific prices for particular jobs. The buyer and seller are free to negotiate, with each artist independently deciding how to price the work, after taking all factors into account.

FIGURE 10—2

Artists must know in advance whether film or videotape will be used, since each has its own special requirements. A good grasp of current TV commercial, film, and music-video styles is crucial to success in this field. Most files are now digitally submitted after being digitally shot and edited. Preproduction artists generally receive taped copies of their work from production houses so they can compile a reel of sample commercials for their portfolios.

Fees & pricing factors

Fees in this field depend upon job complexity, including factors such as the degree of finish required, number of subjects in a given frame, type of background required, and the tightness of the deadline. In pricing animatics, one background illustration and one to one-and-a-half cut-out figures comprise one frame. Two figures and their moving parts can constitute one frame when backgrounds are used for several scenes.

Some agencies, production companies, producers, and individuals may request that artists sign nondisclosure or non-compete agreements to protect trade secrets and creative properties for specified periods. These conditions may restrict an artist's opportunities for future work; this is a factor that should be seriously considered when negotiating fees. Some agencies also request that artists work in-house, and this should be taken into account when establishing a fee.

Hourly rates, although rarely used, range from $75 to $125 per hour. Flat per-frame rates more accurately reflect all the factors involved in the job, although hourly rates may be appropriate for consultation time if the artist participates in the design of the scene or sequences.

In some cases, a per-diem rate of $650 to $1000 is paid when the artist works on site for extended periods. Be aware that these conditions may open an artist to reclassification as an employee rather than as an independent contractor; that may put the client and the artist at risk, depending on how the client treats the artist. If an artist does not work for other clients, on-site work may endanger an artist's home office deduction. (See the Employment Issues section in Chapter 3, Professional Issues.)

A growing trend in large city markets is for advertising agencies to have exclusive contracts with artists' representatives and preproduction art studios in exchange for lower fees but more-or-less steady work. Artists who are not represented by a designated studio cannot work with a particular ad agency, regardless of past affiliations with art directors. Exclusive ad agency/studio contracts therefore force artists to work with a particular representative, thereby forfeiting a percentage of their income and jeopardizing the artist's status as an independent contractor. The consequent reduction in competition among studios and artists raises concerns about restraint-of-trade issues.

Another factor affecting ad agency practices is cost consultants. Many ad agency clients retain the services of consultants who control agency expenditures and seek to define suppliers' fees. Artist suppliers are rarely able to negotiate directly with these cost consultants but must work through the agencies. This situation makes it important for artists to marshal a firm negotiating stance with agencies in order to maintain industry standards.

If a project is for a Hollywood studio, an artist is required to join the union in order to work. Therefore, artists need to subtract union dues when figuring the actual total compensation for a job.

Specific trade practices for preproduction illustration

In addition to the general trade practices listed in the beginning of this chapter, the following trade practices for preproduction illustration have been used historically and thus are accepted as standard:

1. Return of original artwork to the artist is not automatic unless otherwise negotiated. Artists who work for a Hollywood studio may have to sign over all rights to art, since the property belongs to the studio.
2. Preproduction artists usually sell all rights for preproduction work. Since this work is very product specific (campaigns are often confidential, and the media used—for example, markers—are fugitive, or impermanent), frames are almost never reusable. Higher fees for this work have compensated for the loss of rights, though many art directors will return artwork for an artist's self-promotional use.
3. Reuse fee: from 20 to 100 percent of the fee that would have been charged had the illustration been commissioned for the additional use.
4. Charge for rush work: an average of an additional 70 percent over the regular fee, but it can range from 50 to 100 percent. When time is an issue, instead of a rush fee, an illustrator may negotiate the level of finished work, suggesting black and white rather than color, pencil rather than ink, or loose rather than tight. The reality is that no matter how much financial compensation is offered, there is only so much volume and so much "finished" work an illustrator can do under a tight deadline.

See Figure 10-2 for Comparative Fees for Preproduction Illustration.

Artwork Used in Motion Pictures, Television, & Video

Producers of audiovisual works, including motion pictures, television or video programs, and advertisements generally must obtain a license to use copyright-protected illustrations, drawings, paintings, or other two- or three-dimensional works of graphic or visual art as recognizable set decorations or props. If the average lay observer cannot identify the work in the background, the use may be considered "incidental" or "fair use," not requiring any payment or permission.

Licenses to use art for a specific program, movie, or video can be obtained either from the artist or the artist's representative or gallery. According to interview responses, reuse fees or additional royalties are not usually paid to artists for reruns of commercial television programs or when motion pictures are released on DVD or shown on commercial television. However, new media uses such as Internet, mobile, video games, and other merchandise, not contemplated by the parties at the time a media-specific license was granted, constitute copyright infringement, not merely breach of contract, warranting payment of additional license fees for each new media use.

Commercial use

License practices for the use of artworks as set decorations vary greatly. A four-tier approach is often applied to commercial uses with license fees increasing as onscreen time increases: "minor" or background uses (2-5 aggregate seconds on screen), "medium" uses (5-9 aggregate seconds on screen), "major" uses (10 aggregate seconds or more on screen) and "featured" uses (artwork handled on screen, mentioned in script, used as a plot point, or "morphed"). Higher royalties or license fees are payable for productions with higher budgets, with the lowest fees payable for independent or student short or feature films with no distribution and noncommercial educational programming. License fees for using artwork as set decoration generally increase along with production budgets in the following approximate ascending order:

- Low budget independent, student or short films without national distribution
- Local or regional dramatic TV programs
- Cable reality programs
- Network reality programs
- Local or regional TV commercials
- National cable dramatic programs
- Music videos (under $50,000)
- Network dramatic programs
- Premium pay TV dramatic programs (HBO, Showtime, etc.)
- Pay TV movies
- Music videos (over $50,000)
- Internet advertising
- Feature films (non-U.S. or direct to video)
- Feature film (with U.S. theatrical distribution)
- National TV commercials

Licensing rates depend on numerous factors including the extent of the use, the production budget, type of media, and the prestige of the artist. For representative licensing fees for a feature-length motion picture distributed theatrically or over premium subscription television, a network prime-time dramatic television program, or a national TV commercial, refer to Figure 10–3.

Screen credit for the art and artist can be obtained in special cases. When art is accidentally used without permission, retroactive licenses in the ranges given in Figure 10–3, plus an additional amount for the infringer's profits, are charged to discourage infringements, making it cheaper to license the art than to risk using it without permission. Some licensing reps demand up to ten times the license fee if the infringement is willful, repeated, or the services of an attorney are required.

Noncommercial use

At the low end of the licensing spectrum, copyright owners and broadcasting entities are encouraged to negotiate a royalty for use of artwork in noncommercial educational public broadcasting programs. In the absence of such a negotiated license, federal regulations require public broadcasting companies to pay royalties fixed by a copyright royalty arbitration panel convened by the Librarian of Congress every five years, for use of published artwork in noncommercial educational programming (see Figure 10–3). As with commercial uses, lower fees are payable for "background" or "montage" uses (any display less than full-screen or substantially full-screen, or full-screen for three seconds or less); higher royalties are required for "featured" uses (a full-screen or substantially full-screen display appearing on the screen for more than three seconds).

Royalties for the "thematic use" of a work in an entire series (i.e., utilization of the works of one or more artists where the works constitute the central theme of the program or convey a story line) are double the single program theme rate. If the work is first used other than in a PBS-distributed program and later distributed by PBS, an additional royalty payment shall be made equal to the difference between the rate specified for other than a PBS-distributed program and the rate specified for a PBS-distributed program. The rates of this schedule are for unlimited use for a period of three years from the date of the first use of the work under this schedule. For details about additional payment for succeeding use periods, refer to Figure 10–3.

Low-budget production companies sometimes attempt to cut costs by buying or renting so-called "pre-cleared" art from prop houses for which no license fee is payable, either because the art is in the public domain or because the use was pre-approved by the copyright owner. But if the artist/copyright owner has not given her or his permission, the use is infringing, creating liability for the prop house, its customers, and every company distributing the infringing program. In some cases, art licensing agents charge flat fees for using art, regardless of the extent of the use. Rental fees range from 10 to 100 percent of the retail price of the art for each week (or part of a week) the art is used by the production company.

Trade practices for artists whose artwork is used onscreen in motion pictures, television, and video follow the same general protocols as other areas of illustration.

Corporate, Organizational, & Institutional Illustration

An illustrator creating corporate or institutional illustrations works with a graphic designer, art director, or in-house personnel such as writers, advertising/marketing managers, or communication service directors to create visuals for annual reports, in-house publications, and other material targeted to internal or specific audiences. The assignment is generally made by the editorial department or an outside agency, and the illustrator is often called upon to determine the concept and design of the art. Particularly in annual reports, illustrations are "think pieces" that contribute substantially to enhancing the corporation or institution's public image.

Illustrators who do corporate work are reporting that more and more emphasis is being directed to Web-only projects, such as PDF "booklets" and PDF "brochures," that function much like print pieces but are strictly electronic. Some companies are even replacing their printed annual reports with online versions. Since these electronic pieces are not add-ons to a print project, it is felt by some illustrators that pricing should be at least equal to print for these jobs. If clients resist paying print prices and want to pay less, it can be argued that the Web has more distribution potential than print.

Comparative Fees for Art used in Motion Pictures, Television, & Video

Licensing Fees for Commercial Use

(Feature-length motion picture distributed theatrically or over premium subscription television, network prime-time dramatic television program, or national TV commercial)

USE	AGGREGATE SECONDS ON SCREEN	LICENSING FEES
Minor or background	2-5	$0-1,500
Medium	5-9	$500-3,500
Major	10 or more	$2,000-10,000
Featured*		$5,000-25,000

*Artwork handled on screen, mentioned in script, used as a plot point, or "morphed."

Royalties for Noncommercial Educational Programming

(Royalties are fixed by agreement between the copyright owner and the broadcasting entity. In the absence of a negotiated royalty agreement, at five year intervals the Librarian of Congress convenes a copyright royalty arbitration panel to set new minimum royalties)**

USE	SECONDS ON SCREEN	PBS-DISTRIBUTED PROGRAM	NON PBS-DISTRIBUTED PROGRAM
Featured display of work	More than 3	$68.67	$44.47
Background or montage display	3 or less	$33.49	$22.80
Program ID or thematic use (in entire series)		$135.37	$90.91
Display of an art reproduction copyrighted separately from the work of fine art from which the work was reproduced***		$44.47	$22.80

**Royalty figures listed are for 2003–2007; however, they were still in effect as of April 2010. Royalties are paid twice a year on January 31 and July 31, each for the previous six months of use. The rates of this schedule are for unlimited use for a period of three years from the date of the first use of the work under this schedule. Succeeding use periods will require the following additional payment: additional one-year period—25 percent of the initial three-year fee; second three-year period—50 percent of the initial three-year fee; each three-year period thereafter—25 percent of the initial three-year fee; provided that a 100 percent additional payment prior to the expiration of the first three-year period will cover use during all subsequent use periods without limitation. Such succeeding uses which are subsequent to December 31, 2007, shall be subject to the rates established in this schedule.

***Irrespective of whether the reproduced work of fine art is copyrighted so as to be subject also to payment of a display fee under the terms of this schedule.

FIGURE 10—3

Clients include Fortune 500 companies and smaller companies, as well as educational institutions, government agencies, and not-for-profit groups and associations. An organization with a "not-for-profit" designation does not operate at a deficit; some, in fact, such as AARP, with approximately 40 million members, have enormous resources. Other examples of not-for-profits include trade associations and business leagues, hospitals and health-service organizations, professional membership societies, trade unions, philanthropies, museums and other arts groups, and charitable and educational organizations. Whether a client is for-profit or not-for-profit, pricing varies according to its size, resources, and profitability.

Annual reports

An annual report—the yearly fiscal report by a corporation to its stockholders and the financial community—is an important means for a company to promote itself. Designers of annual reports often seek thoughtful, provocative illustrations to offset the written and financial material while projecting the company's public image powerfully and effectively.

Illustration fees are usually based on the corporation's size and the nature of the annual report and are usually negotiated on a one-time-use basis only. When dealing with large assignments in this area, artists should be prepared to set a fee for selling original art, since annual report clients frequently make such requests.

Comparative Fees for
Corporate, Organizational, & Institutional Illustration

Annual Reports

	COVER	FULL PAGE	HALF PAGE	QUARTER PAGE/SPOT
LARGE CORPORATION OR LARGE DISTRIBUTION (20,000+)				
Color	$2,000-8,000	$1,000-5,000	$750-3,500	$500-2,000
B & W	–	–	$850-2,000	$650-1,500
MEDIUM CORPORATION OR MEDIUM DISTRIBUTION (OVER 5,000, UP TO 20,000)				
Color	$2,000-5,000	$1,000-4,000	$750-3,000	$500-1,500
B & W	–	–	$700-2,000	$450-1,000

SMALL OR NONPROFIT CORPORATION OR LIMITED DISTRIBUTION (UP TO 5,000)

Average fees are 10-50% less than Medium Corporation

In-house Newsletters

	COVER	FULL PAGE	HALF PAGE	QUARTER PAGE/SPOT
LARGE CORPORATION OR LARGE PRINT RUN (5,000+)				
Color	$1,500-3,500	$1,000-3,000	$700-2,000	$450-1,000
B & W	$2,600	–	$500-1,200	$350-850
MEDIUM CORPORATION OR MEDIUM PRINT RUN (OVER 1,000, UP TO 5,000)				
Color	$1,200-2,500	$850-2,000	$550-1,500	$400-800
B & W	–	$700-1,200	$500-1,000	$300-500

SMALL OR NONPROFIT CORPORATION OR SMALL PRINT RUN (UP TO 1,000)

Average fees are 10-25% less than Medium Corporation

(Continues on next page)

FIGURE 10—4

In-house newsletters

Corporate in-house newsletters are distributed at no charge to company employees, retirees, and supporters. Traditionally printed, newsletters today may be print, a downloadable PDF, or both. Illustrators may be hired to illustrate a feature article or story, if not handled by an agency using royalty-free material. Usually the work involves spot illustration which is charged as a flat fee.

Corporate magazines

Corporate magazines, including university and alumni magazines, are distributed to shareholders, policy-makers, industry members, customers, and students at no charge. They may be available as a printed publication, an online downloadable PDF, or in both formats.

Corporate magazine illustration pays similar to editorial magazine prices (see Figure 10-8) but usually on the low end of the pricing scale. Fees include one-time rights. Corporate magazines also buy more stock illustration than mainstream editorial magazines.

Comparative Fees for
Corporate, Organizational, & Institutional Illustration (Continued)

Corporate Magazines & Other Uses

	COVER	SPREAD	FULL PAGE	HALF PAGE	QUARTER PAGE/SPOT
BUSINESS-TO-CONSUMER MAGAZINES					
	$2,000–3,500	$1,800–4,000	$1,200–3,000	$700–1,500	$350–850

CALENDARS

Exterior Use (color)*	$5,000+ (9 x 12")	–	–	–	$450–900
Internal Use $2,000 per image (less if commissioned to do most or all illustrations for calendar)					

*Based on exclusive one-time rights; print & website use for 15 months.

WEBSITE USE (NON-ADVERTISING)

		$750–2,500			$350–1,500

SPECIAL EVENT INVITATIONS

Simple to Complex		$600–3,500+			

Corporate Logos

Major Corporation	$4,000–25,000+
Minor Corporation	$1,200–12,000
Very Small Businesses (e.g. law firms, wineries, "Mom & Pop" retail, etc.)	$1,200–3,000 (simple logo; all rights included)

Additional Fees

	PERCENT OF ORIGINAL FEE
Sale of original art	50–250%
Stock sale/limited use	50–100%
Rush fee	25–100%
Unlimited use in print media only (no time or geographical limits)	50–100%
Unlimited use, any media, including digital, for 1 year	75–200%
Total copyright transfer (excluding original art)	250–300%

NOTE: The price ranges in Figure 10—4 do not reflect any specific trade practices and do not constitute specific prices for particular jobs. The buyer and seller are free to negotiate, with each artist independently deciding how to price the work, after taking all factors into account.

FIGURE 10—4

Corporate calendars

Illustration prices for company calendars can vary greatly and usually depend upon the size of the company, the complexity of the subject, and the intended use. Calendars designed for internal use only generally pay less than calendars distributed to consumers for promotion or sale.

Non-advertising website illustration

Corporate illustration work for non-advertising purposes on a web site includes presenting information that is primarily aimed to educate the consumer and promote the company's products, services, and reputation. This type of illustration pays similar to or slightly lower than editorial magazines.

Specific trade practices for corporate, organizational, & institutional illustration

In addition to the general trade practices listed in the beginning of this chapter, the following trade practices have been used historically and thus are accepted as standard:

1. Artists working in these fields normally sell only first reproduction rights unless otherwise stated.
2. Reuse fee: from 50 to 100 percent of the fee that would have been charged had the illustration been commissioned for the new use.
3. Charge for rush work: an additional 25 to 100 percent.

See Figure 10-4 for Corporate, Organizational, & Institutional Fees.

Book Illustration

The publishing business has undergone tremendous growth and change in the last 20 years. Most well-known publishing houses have been acquired by multinational conglomerates here and abroad, and many smaller houses have been either eliminated or incorporated as imprints. Worldwide paper prices continue to increase the pressure on publishers' bottom lines. A few giant bookstore chains, which often negotiate heavy discounts, dominate the industry, and a growing percentage of bookselling is now handled electronically. Both these factors contribute to the demise of independent bookstores.

Publishers vs packagers: a brief explanation

The use of book packagers has grown but leveled off in recent years, particularly for novelty books, such as pop-up books and book-and-craft-kit combinations. These independent suppliers take over for publishers some or all of the functions of preparing a book. Often they initiate a project, find writers and illustrators, arrange for whatever extras may be involved, and strike a deal with a publisher, usually supplying a set number of bound books at a set price. When a book is conceived by the packager rather than the publisher, the artist will be asked to sign a contract with the packager rather than the publisher, even before the packager has contracted for the project with a publisher.

Book jackets & covers

Book jacket and cover illustration or design is the second most important ingredient in the promotion and sale of a book, superseded only by the fame and success of the author. Pricing illustration in the book publishing market is complex, so all the factors involved need serious attention. Romance, science fiction, and other genre paperback covers can command higher fees than some hardcover jackets, especially when the projected audience is very large. Artists who design and illustrate jackets may approach their work differently from other graphic artists. (See the Book Jacket Design section in Chapter 8, Graphic Design Prices & Trade Customs.)

Illustrators who are selected for occasional cover assignments receive higher fees than illustrators who specialize only in book jackets. In addition, artists recognized for their painterly, highly realistic, or dramatic studies have commanded much higher fees than those whose styles are more graphic and design-oriented. Although this practice is prevalent in the entire illustration field, it is particularly so in publishing.

Some paperback publishers give very specific instructions on assignments, sometimes including the art director's rough notes from a cover conference. If an illustrator is required to read a lengthy manuscript in search of illustrative material and then produce sketches subject to approval by editors, this factor is traditionally taken into account when negotiating the fee.

Other factors that prompt additional fees and that are negotiated before the assignment is confirmed include changes in approach and direction after sketches are completed, requiring new sketches; additional promotional uses above and beyond what is common trade practice (using the art separately from the cover without the title or author's name); and extremely tight color comps done for sales meetings and catalogs.

MASS MARKET & TRADE BOOKS

Mass-market books have large print runs and appeal to a wide audience. They include best sellers, mysteries, thrillers, gothics, fantasy, science fiction, historical novels, and modern romance novels. Trade books include poetry, serious fiction, biography, how-to books, and more scholarly works that appeal to a special audience. When pricing work in these areas, the size of the print run is traditionally taken into account.

Because of their larger print runs and higher gross sales, mass-market books very often generate higher fees for illustrators. A hardcover assignment might also include paperback rights, for which an additional 50 percent of the original fee is customarily charged. Occasionally, the fee for a book with a very large paperback print run may amount to an additional 75 percent of the original fee, or possibly more.

Currently, publishers like Knopf Doubleday/ Random House rarely do wraparound covers. The backs are usually reserved for quotes from book reviews. Advertising rights for the book are included with no extra payment as long as the image is used in context of the book. Otherwise, an extra payment can be negotiated with credit given to the illustrator. See Figure 10-5 for Book Jacket/Cover Illustration fees.

Comparative Fees for Book Jacket/Cover Illustration

Hardcover Jackets[1]/Trade[2]

	FRONT COVER	WRAPAROUND
Major trade[2]	$3,000–4,750+	$3,000–5,000+
Small print run	$2,000–3,000+	$2,000–4,000+
Small press	$1,200–2,800+	$1,500–3,000+
Textbook	$1,200–2,000+	$1,200–2,500+
Young adult/chapter	$2,000–3,000+	–

Paperback Covers[1]

	FRONT COVER	WRAPAROUND
Mass market[3]/major distribution (4 x 7")	$2,500–5,000+	$3,000–7,500+
Major trade[2] (5.5 x 8.5")	$4,000–4,750+	–
Average trade[2]	$2,000–4,000+	$2,000–4,000+
Textbook	$1,200–2,500+	$1,800–3,000+
Young adult/chapter	$2,500–4,000+	$3,500–4,500+
Comic book (major publisher)	$1,500–1,900	–

Additional Fees

	PERCENT OF ORIGINAL FEE
Sale of original art	25–100%
Stock sale of existing art	50–100%
Unlimited use any media, including digital, for 1 year	50–100%
Foreign or world publication rights	25–50%

SUBSIDIARY RIGHTS SALES

Audio	20–30% ($500 max.)
Foreign publisher, translation, or English language edition	20–30%
First serial, dramatic TV, motion picture	50–100%
Domestic reprint, paperback, book club, digest, anthology, or serial; merchandising, audiovisual; sound recording	50–75%
Large print edition	30%

NOTE: Approximate sizes of print runs are as follows:
Mass market: 100,000-1,000,000+ (bestsellers can be in the millions)
Major trade: 25,000-200,000+ (bestsellers can be in the millions)
Average trade: 10,000-20,000
Small print run (hardcover): 3,000-7,000
Minor trade, small press: 2,000-8,000

[1] Advertising rights included

[2] Trade books are sold to bookstores and libraries

[3] Mass market books appeal to a large audience and are sold at all major retail markets: bookstores, supermarkets, drugstores, magazine stands.

FIGURE 10—5

SECONDARY RIGHTS USE

Another way illustrators earn additional fees is to license a cover illustration for use on foreign editions of a book. This type of secondary rights usage is growing; however, fees vary widely from country to country and use to use, with few standards. Most artists or their representatives usually negotiate fees for such rights and not simply accept what is offered. Breaking down the fee for each use (both hardback and paper back, for example) and stipulating a particular length of time for the sale, with an option to renew, are ways to boost and maximize fees. By also specifying "up to x number of copies" in their contracts, illustrators can bill extra if the book becomes a much bigger seller than originally anticipated.

Domestic book club rights are usually included in the original hardcover fee; however, in some instances a book club edition might be huge and make the book into a bestseller—for example, books chosen for the Oprah book club. CD-ROM covers are negotiated as separate subsidiary rights. All other residual rights, especially movie and television rights, are reserved by the artist and transfer of those and all other rights is negotiated by the artist and the client. The original artwork is always returned to the artist.

To ensure that illustrators are compensated for any additional editions and secondary rights beyond those included in the original fee, it is advisable to specify the ISBN number in the terms of the contract. Since each edition has a different ISBN number, the publisher cannot assume additional usage of artwork in subsequent editions if the contract is clearly limited to a specific edition.

Book interiors

Illustrations have long been recognized as an important ingredient in the editorial and market-

Comparative Fees for Book Interior Illustration

	SPREAD	FULL PAGE	HALF PAGE	QUARTER PAGE/SPOT
ADULT HARDCOVER				
Color	$700-2,000	$500-1,500	$350-1,000	$200-400
B & W	$500-1,500	$500-900	$350-800	$100-350
YOUNG ADULT* INCLUDING CHAPTER BOOKS**				
Color	$700-2,000	$500-1,500	$350-1,000	$200-400
B & W	$500-1,500	$500-1,000	$350-800	$100-350
TEXTBOOKS				
Color	$1,000-1,800	$500-1,000	$650-850	$250-500
B & W	$1,000-1,500	$750-1,000	$500-700	$250-450
JUVENILE WORKBOOKS				
Color	$700-1,200	$500-700	$350-500	$200-400
B & W	$500-1,000	$400-650	$250-450	$175-250

*Over age 12   **Ages 8-12

Additional Fees

	PERCENTAGE OF ORIGINAL FEE
Sale of original art	100-200%
Stock sale of existing art for use in books only	50-100%
Foreign or world publication rights	50-100%
Work-for-hire transfer of legal authorship; all rights	100-300%

NOTE: The price ranges in Figure 10—6 do not reflect considerations on the following page and do not constitute specific prices for particular jobs. The buyer and seller are free to negotiate, with each artist independently deciding how to price the work, after taking all factors into account.

FIGURE 10—6

ing value of a book. Book illustrators work with editors, art directors, book designers, or book packagers to create anything from simple instructional line drawings to full-color-spread illustrations for textbooks, picture books, children's and young adult books, novelty books, and special reprints of classics, among other trade genres. The importance of illustration to a specific book may be significant or limited, depending on needs determined by the publisher.

PRICING

Pricing for book illustration is figured as either a flat fee or a royalty arrangement. Outside of children's books, it is exceedingly rare for royalties to be paid for book illustration. (If such an opportunity arises, check Figure 10–7, Children's Picture Book Illustration, for details on an appropriate royalty.) A one-time flat fee is usually paid for interior illustrations for all other books (see Figure 10-6).

Packagers vs publishers Book packagers often offer illustrators either a flat fee or a 10 percent royalty. This royalty is not figured on the book's list price, as with some publishers' contracts, but on what the packager will receive from the publisher for the finished books ("base selling price"). Since publishers generally set a book's retail price at four to five times the cost of its production, illustrators should be aware that 10 percent of the base selling price amounts to a 2 to 2.5 percent royalty of the list price.

Publishers generally allot 10 percent (or 5 percent, in the case of mass-market material) of list price for the author's and illustrator's royalties. When a publisher uses a packager to produce a book, that 10 percent may be absorbed by the publisher or may be paid to the packager in addition to the base selling price. Sometimes that share is paid to a licenser in exchange for the right to publish a book about a popular property (cartoon characters, for instance), and a packager is hired to create the book. In some cases, particularly where the project originates with the author-artist, all or some of those list-price royalties may be paid to the artist. It is the publisher's choice to do so; the packager is not likely to promise an artist any of the publisher's royalties.

Thus, the compensation offered to artists who work through packagers is generally at a lower rate than work that comes directly from publishers, although two factors may somewhat mitigate this difference. Because a packager's contract with a publisher is indexed to the sale of a predetermined number of books, paid up-front, the packager will pay the artist's royalty on the full print run before publication. If a second printing is ordered, royalties on that print run will again be paid in full, rather than if and when the books are sold. This arrangement brings payment to the artist somewhat sooner than the standard publisher's contract. Rights to reuse the artwork (in other editions or promotions, for example) are often considered when negotiating the advance or the fee.

Other factors affecting pricing Other factors affecting advances and fees in this complex area include the type of book and the importance of the author, the artist's reputation and record of commercial success, the size of the print order, and the length of time estimated for the total project.

Historically, illustrators receive partial payment for long projects; for example, a third of the total fee is customarily paid upon approval of sketches, a third upon delivery of half of the finished art, and the remainder within 30 days of delivery of the finished art. Some artists report payments of 50 percent for sketches and 50 percent for final art.

Children's books

The illustrator's contribution to a children's book can range widely, from the entire contents of a wordless picture book to a jacket illustration for a young adult novel. Pricing usually falls into two categories: a flat fee, for books in which the illustrator's contribution is usually substantially less than the author's, or a royalty contract, in which the contributions of author and illustrator are comparable or in which the illustrator is also the author. Publishers will pay more plus royalties to successful writer/illustrator teams.

Packagers often pay a flat fee, but most publishers will negotiate a royalty reflecting the percentage of art versus text. The artist's share can range from 2 to 5 percent, depending upon the reputation of the artist versus the author.

FLAT-FEE CONTRACTS

Publishers' flat-fee contracts tend to stipulate all possible rights to the art in return for a one-time fee. Illustrators should negotiate to retain rights or negotiate additional payment for additional uses, such as the sale of paperback rights. Holding non-book or merchandising rights is particularly vital; otherwise, illustrators will not be able to retain the rights to a copyrighted character.

Chapter books for ages 8 to 12 and young adult books for children over 12 usually are illustrated for a flat fee. A typical flat-fee book contract commissions a full-color wraparound jacket. From 1 to 14 black-and-white interior illustrations of various sizes may be included in a chapter book.

One category of children's books—the juvenile workbook—is handled quite differently from others. Workbooks are assigned through brokers or publishers' agents, representing many illustrators working in varied styles, who have historically established pricing for each book with the publisher. Budgets for workbooks vary considerably, depending on the size of the publisher, the location, publication schedules, and the artist's experience. Illustrator fees for these projects may also vary considerably, and it is always preferable to work directly with the publisher. Workbooks are usually priced per page, per half page, or per spot. Although fees are traditionally quite low, an entire workbook can add up to a considerable amount of work. Artists who are able to produce this kind of artwork quickly may find this field quite lucrative and feel secure knowing that months of work lie ahead. Artists should note that in order to meet increasingly rushed publishing deadlines, a book with a considerable amount of illustration may be divided among several illustrators. See Figures 10-6 and 10-7 for flat fees paid for children's book illustration.

ROYALTY CONTRACTS

An advance against royalties is paid for most children's picture books (see Figure 10-7), storybooks, and middle-grade readers. However, overseas publishers tend to pay a flat rate, usually in three installments. If the author and the artist are different people, a full royalty on the book's list price is commonly split 50-50 between the two creators. The royalty and the size of the advance are based on the illustrator's reputation, experience, and the publisher's budget.

The advance is designed to reflect the anticipated earnings of the book and will rarely exceed the royalty due on the sales of the book's entire first printing. Frequently, 50 percent of the advance is paid upon signing the contract and the remaining 50 percent is paid on delivery of the artwork. Recently, publishers have been negotiating to pay advances in thirds—on signing, on delivery of the finished art, and on publication date of the book. (All the artist's out-of-pocket expenses should be paid in addition to the advance.) An appropriate advance will be earned back within two (and up to ten) years after publication. If the advance is

---

Comparative Fees for Children's Picture Book Illustration

Royalty Contracts

	ILLUSTRATION ONLY	ILLUSTRATION & TEXT
ORIGINAL HARDCOVER EDITION (32 pages)		
Advance*	$3,000-40,000	$10,000-60,000
Royalty (percent of list)	3-5%	10%
Sales point** (net copies sold)	25,000	30,000-50,000
Royalty escalation***	6%	12.5%
Publisher's paperback edition, royalty	3%	5-6%
Publisher's paperback edition, sales point	–	50,000

Flat Fee Contracts****

ORIGINAL HARDCOVER EDITION (32 pages)	$5,000-20,000
TODDLER BOOKS (6 pages: front & back covers and 2 double-page spreads)	$1,700

*Advances are based on the author's reputation and experience and the publisher's budget.

**When royalty escalation takes effect.

***Percent to which royalty increases after sales point is reached.

****Some children's book contracts are based on flat fees, rather than a royalty structure. Foreign publishers tend to pay a flat rate (often paid in three installments).

Subsidiary Rights Sale (percent of net receipts)

Foreign language edition by another publisher	37.5%	75%
First serial, dramatic TV, motion picture	25%	60-100%
Domestic reprint, paperback, book club, digest, anthology, or serial	25%	50-75%
Publisher's direct sales	5-25%	50-55%
Canadian sales	25%	50%
Electronic books	25%	–
Merchandising, audiovisual, sound recording	25-37%	50-75%

NOTE: The price ranges in Figure 10-7 do constitute specific prices for particular jobs. The buyer and seller are free to negotiate, with each artist independently deciding how to price the work, after taking all factors into account.

FIGURE 10—7

earned back after only three months of release, either the advance was too low or the book was an unanticipated good seller.

It is to the illustrator's advantage to obtain as large an advance as possible, since it may not be earned back by sales, or it may take considerable time before any royalties are actually paid. If an advance is earned back very quickly (within the first six-month royalty period), it is a sign that a higher advance would have been more appropriate, a point to consider when negotiating future contracts.

It is customary for a nonrefundable advance to be paid against royalties; it is to the illustrator's advantage to secure only nonrefundable advances. Artists should scrutinize contracts to confirm that the advance does not have to be refunded if a sufficient number of books are not sold. The publisher's right to reject the art should be clearly defined and limited in the contract, and any changes requested by the publisher should be defined as "reasonable." If the artist has submitted pencil drawings that were approved and has not deviated from them in creating the finished art, the artist should be paid the complete advance for the time spent—even if the art is rejected.

Royalty contracts are complicated and vary from publisher to publisher. "Boilerplate" authors' contracts rarely are written with artists in mind, and they can be difficult to comprehend. The Graphic Artists Guild strongly recommends that an attorney or agent with a track record in publishing children's books review any contract if it contains terms about which the illustrator is uncertain, especially if it is the artist's first book contract. Even publishers' boilerplate contracts can be amended if the changes are agreeable to both parties. Among sections of a royalty contract that are often negotiated are the lists of the royalty percentages for the publisher's uses of the work ("publisher's direct") and for the sale of subsidiary rights. In Figure 10-7, see the royalties for uses beyond the original hardcover edition.

Royalty contract terms

Grant of rights: The illustrator grants to the publisher the right to use the art as specified within the contract.

Alterations: The art cannot be altered in any way by the publisher, except as part of the normal printing process, without the written consent of the artist. (It is all too easy to alter art electronically, but this should not be allowed.)

Delivery: Sets deadlines for finished art and sometimes for rough sketches. Often this clause has also specified what payments are due the artist if the project is canceled or rejected (see the Cancellation & Rejection Fees section in Chapter 3, Professional Issues).

Warranty: This states that the illustrator has not infringed copyrights or broken any other laws in granting rights to the publisher.

Indemnity: The illustrator shares the cost of defending any lawsuit brought over the art.

An artist who is found to have broken the terms of the warranty bears the entire cost of the lawsuit and any damages that may result. The indemnity provision might present more risk than the illustrator is willing to accept, but without an attorney, it is difficult to counter this provision effectively. An illustrator should request to be indemnified by the publisher for any suits arising from a request on the publisher's part, such as making a character look like a famous person.

Copyright: The publisher agrees to register the copyright to the work in the artist's name.

Agreement to publish: The book will be published within a specific period of time, usually 18 months from receipt of finished art. If the publisher fails to do so, the rights should revert back to the artist (reversion rights).

Additional points to consider are:

Paperback advance: If an advance against royalties is to be paid for the original publisher's paperback edition, that is usually negotiated at the time of the original contract. The royalty rate is usually less than for the hardcover edition.

Escalation: For trade books, royalties of 10 percent (for author and illustrator combined) are often raised to 12.5 percent after sales reach 30,000 or more copies. Though mass-market books usually have lower royalty rates, these also can be raised based on sales.

De-escalation: Some publishers' contracts stipulate that royalty rates may decrease dramatically under two conditions: when high discounts are given to distributors or other buyers, or when book sales from a low-quantity reprint are slow. Not all publishers include these clauses in their contracts; it is in the artist's interest to strike them or at least to try to negotiate better terms.

There can be some justification for the illustrator to accept a lower royalty rate for a book whose sales are vastly increased by a high discount negotiated between the publisher and booksellers, such as bookstore chains. It is also common practice for the royalty to decline incrementally once discounts exceed 50 percent. It is less favorable for the artist to accept the terms offered by some publishers whereby any discount above 50 percent, for example, produces royalties based on the "amount received" (the wholesale price) rather than the book's list price. This arrangement immediately reduces the royalty rate by at least half.

Illustrators have found it desirable to ensure that this deep discount is given only for "special sales" and is not part of the publisher's normal trade practice. The latter could mean that the publisher uses these discounts to gain sales at the expense of the artist and/or author. Be aware that as giant retail and bookstore chains' domination of the book market has grown, deep discounts have as well. Deep discounts are also customary in book-fair sales and publishers' own book clubs. The artist should try to limit or eliminate all special sales. The artist's royalty payments will decline when books are discounted and the backlist is diminished.

By accepting a royalty decrease for a slow-selling reprint, the illustrator may give the publisher incentive to keep the book in print, but the terms of the decrease should have limitations. For instance, the book should have been in print at least two years, be in a reprint edition of 2,500 or fewer copies, and have sales of fewer than 500 copies in one royalty period. Under these conditions, the royalty might drop to 75 or even 50 percent of the original rate.

A foreign-language edition to be sold domestically may also be published with a lower royalty rate, as it is costlier to produce than a simple reprint and may have limited sales potential. Terms may be set, however, to escalate to a normal royalty rate if sales exceed low expectations.

Subsidiary sales: Income derived from the publisher selling any rights to a third party is divided between publisher and artist and/or author, depending on whether the rights involve art, text, or both. The percentage earned by the illustrator for each type of use is variable and is determined by negotiation. The possible use of a character in a greeting card or poster, for example, can be a valuable source of additional income for the artist. The relatively new area of electronic rights, either as a subsidiary right or as income derived from the publisher's own electronic products, is still ambiguous and changes constantly. Some publishing contracts leave the category unresolved, stating specifically that terms for electronic rights will be agreed upon mutually when and if the need arises. If that is not possible, the artist should limit those rights to three to five years, with an automatic reversion to the artist whether or not they are used by that time. (For a more detailed discussion of these concerns, see Chapter 4, Technology Issues.)

Author's copies: Publishers' contracts usually provide 10 free copies to the author, but 20 free copies are often negotiated. Most publishers offer the artist a 40 to 50 percent discount off the list price on purchases of their book. Some publishers will pay royalties on these sales; others do not.

Schedule of statements and payments: This defines when and how accounting will be made. Normally, a royalty period is six months, with the appropriate royalty payment made four months and one day after the period closes. A useful clause found in many contracts allows access by the artist or a designated accountant to examine the publisher's books and records. If, in a given royalty period, errors of 5 percent or more are found in the publisher's favor, the publisher will correct the underpayment and pay the cost of the examination up to the amount of the error.

If an audit costs more than the error, the artist must pay the difference.

Pass-through clause: This takes effect when the illustrator's share of a subsidiary sale exceeds $1,000. The publisher will then send payment within 30 days of receipt rather than holding it until the semiannual royalty reporting date.

Remaindering: If the book is to be remaindered (sold at a huge discount, often at the end of a print run), the publisher should notify the illustrator and allow him or her to buy any number of copies at the remaindered price.

Return of artwork: Since the art remains the property of the artist, it should be returned "unaltered and undamaged except for normal use and wear" after publication, if not sooner. Since publishers are responsible for the art while it is in their possession, a value should be placed on the cover and inside illustrations in the event of possible loss, damage, or negligence by the publisher. (With children's book art now in demand by galleries and museums, a lost or damaged piece will deny the artist a possible sale of original art.)

Termination of agreement: This states that if a work is not, or will not be, available in any edition in the United States, it is out of print. At that time, the illustrator may request in writing that all rights return to the artist. The publisher usually has six months to declare an intent to reprint and a reasonable amount of time in which to issue a new edition. Failing this, the agreement is terminated, and all rights return to the artist.

In some boilerplate contracts, "out-of-print" is defined too narrowly, or the time allowed the publisher is unreasonably long. Some contracts also grant the illustrator the right to purchase any existing film, plates, or die stamps within 30 days after termination.

Quality control: Occasionally a provision is added to contracts that allows the illustrator to consult on the design of the book and to view bluelines, color separations, and proofs while corrections can still be made. A good working relationship and an informal agreement with the art director are probably as good as a guarantee of this actually occurring.

Revisions without the artist's consent: A clause prohibiting this from occurring is good insurance for protecting the integrity of the work.

Many of these contractual points may not add up to much money for any one book, or even a lifetime of books. However, illustrators can effectively manage their careers only if they retain control over their work. Therefore it makes sense to negotiate the best possible contract, not merely the best possible advance.

Specific trade practices for book illustration

In addition to the general trade practices listed in the beginning of this chapter, the following trade practices have been used historically and thus are accepted as standard:

1. Book illustrators normally license only first reproduction rights for one edition unless otherwise stated.
2. If artwork will be used for a purpose other than the original, such as for an electronic database, a web site, or additional editions of the book, the price for that usage is usually negotiated as early as possible. Reuse fee: from 50 to 100 percent of the fee that would have been charged had the illustration been commissioned for the new use.
3. Charge for rush work: an additional 20 to 100 percent.
4. When satisfactory art has been produced but the publisher, for whatever reason, decides not to use it, the full payment customarily goes to the artist, and rights to the unused work are not transferred to the publisher.

Editorial Illustration

Editorial illustrators are commissioned by art directors and editors of consumer and trade magazines and newspapers to illustrate specific stories, covers, columns, or other editorial material in print or electronic media. Usually the art director, editor, and illustrator discuss the slant and intended literary and graphic impact of a piece before the artist prepares sketches. Unlike other illustration jobs, editorial assignments often offer an illustrator much creative freedom in determining the concept behind the illustration. For some, if not many illustrators, this opportunity is worth a fee lower than what advertising agencies frequently pay. Often illustrators prepare several sketches that explore a range of approaches to the problem. Editorial art is often commissioned under tight deadlines, especially for news publications and weekly magazines and newspapers.

Some editorial illustrators have encountered an unethical problem now that all work is handled digitally. Some unscrupulous art directors and editors have digitally altered the illustrator's work without permission. Be sure to stipulate in any written agreement that artwork may not be cropped or altered in any way without first obtaining the artist's permission.

The Internet has created additional factors that illustrators need to consider when pricing a job. For projects that originate as print, some publishers are trying to get secondary Web use for free. Illustrators need to make it perfectly clear in their contracts or letters of agreement that additional usage in any media, including the Web, will require additional permission and compensation. It is up to the individual illustrator to determine if posting illustration on the Web, only within the context of the original article, is included or not in the fee charged for a print project. Illustrators also are encountering situations in which art directors are trying to negotiate print as secondary usage for Internet-driven assignments in which the primary market is online because they think it will be cheaper.

Magazines

Fees for editorial assignments have historically been tied to the magazine's circulation and geographic distribution, which in turn determine its advertising rates and therefore its income. A magazine's prestige, as well as its circulation and ad revenue, can affect illustration rates. For example, *Time, Reader's Digest,* and *Bloomberg Business Week,* pay some of the industry's highest rates for illustration, while *Family Circle* only pays average rates, yet all four magazines have national circulation. Circulation and distribution information is usually available from advertising and subscription departments of magazines.

Editorial magazine illustration is also priced by what fraction of a magazine's page it occupies. Spread illustrations occupy two facing pages. If a spread illustration occupies only half of each page, one historical basis for fee negotiation has been to add the partial page rate. Keep in mind that if only the title or very little text is used on the spread, it could be interpreted as a full-spread illustration. In these cases, discretion should be used.

Spot illustrations are usually one column wide and simple in subject. Judging the complexity of the assignment may help determine if a spot rate is appropriate. Although quarter-page illustrations are not spots, some magazines (particularly those with lower budgets) make no distinction between the two. In recent years art directors have tended to call any illustration that is less than half a page a spot illustration. This practice fails to accurately describe the commissioned illustration and undermines established trade practices to the artist's detriment.

Newspapers

For pricing purposes, some newspapers, such as *The New York Times, The Washington Post,* and *The Wall Street Journal* are considered large-circulation national publications. They carry national and international news and are distributed both nationally and internationally. Medium-circulation newspapers are generally regional in nature, sell outside the city where they are published, often carry national news, and publish four-color supplements and weekend magazines. Local newspapers, naturally, have the lowest circulation, and their size of readership varies widely and is usually taken into account when determining fees. It is worth noting that this is one of the lowest-paying fields of illustration and is valued, especially for new and emerging talent, as a trade-off for providing exposure and published portfolio pieces.

Comparative Fees for
Editorial Illustration

Magazine

	COVER	SPREAD	FULL PAGE	HALF PAGE	QUARTER PAGE/SPOT
HIGHEST & ABOVE AVERAGE RATES* *(Reader's Digest, Time, Entertainment Weekly, Bloomberg, Sports Illustrated, Money, Business Week, Playboy, The New Yorker, GQ, etc.)*					
	$2,500-4,000	$2,000-4,000	$850-2,500	$700-1,800	$300-1,000
AVERAGE RATES *(Family Circle, Atlantic Monthly, New Republic, Mother Jones, MORE, Women's Health, etc.)*					
	$1,700-4,000	$1,500-3,500	$1,000-2,000	$600-1,500	$300-1,000
LOWER-THAN-AVERAGE & LOWEST RATES (Single Interest, Trade, Institutional, or Professional: *Field & Stream, Outdoor Life, Institutional Hospitals, Architectural Record, etc.)*					
	$1,200-3,500	$1,000-3,000	$700-1,800	$600-1,200	$300-800

*Editorial Illustration rates are determined by the prestige, circulation, and ad revenue of the magazine.

Newspaper & Newspaper Supplements

	SECTION COVER	FULL PAGE	HALF PAGE	QUARTER PAGE/SPOT
NATIONAL, MAJOR METRO, OR LARGE CIRCULATION				
Color	$1,200-2,000	$850-2,000	$600-1,200	$400-850
B & W	$1,200-1,500	–	$550-1,000	$500-800*
MIDSIZE METRO				
Color	$1,000-1,500	$750-1,200	$600-850	$500-600
B & W	–	–	$500-700	$500*

NOTE: Small Metro or Local Weekly average fees are approximately 25-30% less than Midsize Metro and historically do not play an important role in fee structure.

*Minimum fees are usually $500

Additional Fees

	PERCENT OF ORIGINAL FEE
Rush fee	20-150%
Sale of original art	100-300%
Stock sale of existing art	50-100%
Unlimited use in print media only (no time or geographical limits)	100-200%
Unlimited use, any media for 1 year	150-200%
Total copyright transfer (excluding original art)	200-300%
Royalties per 1000 reprints	10-25%

NOTE: The price ranges in Figure 10–8 do not reflect specific trade practices and do not constitute specific prices for particular jobs. The buyer and seller are free to negotiate, with each artist independently deciding how to price the work, after taking all factors into account.

FIGURE 10—8

Specific trade practices for editorial illustration

In addition to the general trade practices listed in the beginning of this chapter, the following trade practices have been used historically and thus are accepted as standard:

1. Editorial illustrators normally sell only first reproduction rights unless otherwise stated.
2. Reuse fee: from 50 to 100 percent of the fee that would have been charged had the illustration been commissioned for the new use.
3. Charge for rush work: an additional 20 to 150 percent, although reviewers are reporting rush fees are more difficult to get.

See Figure 10–8 for Editorial Illustration fees.

Package Illustration

Package illustrators create art for the packaging used for all types of retail products, some of which include apparel, electronics, food and beverages, health and beauty aids, toys and games, and music and film recordings. The illustrator's contribution to packaging consists of pieces of the final package that are revised many times and may be manipulated by both the designer and the client. Some package illustrations become part of the product's branding.

Music recordings

The demand for engaging, forceful, highly creative packaging for recordings has attracted the best of talented editorial and advertising illustrators, who in turn have created a new art form. Many record album covers have become collector's items. Several books have been published on record album cover art, and an ongoing market is active in collecting and selling.

Commissions for record cover illustration can be lucrative. Based on current data, fees vary widely, depending on the recording artist, the particular label and recording company, and the desirability and fame of the illustrator.

With the growth of independent record companies specializing in specific genres, there are many modest-budget, total-package assignments (including illustration, type treatment, and overall design) for diligent creators willing to search for them. Fees for complex recording packages have gone to higher than $10,000. This kind of assignment, however, requires many meetings, sketches, and changes.

Most recording companies have subsidiary labels, featuring various recording artists and types of music. The minor labels of major recording companies are usually reserved for less commercial works and re-releases of previous recordings. According to current survey data, mergers and acquisitions in the recording industry have all but eliminated any discernible differences in fees based on geographic location. In all cases, only recording company publication rights are transferred, and the original art is returned to the artist. Tie-in poster rights are sometimes included.

It is common in the music packaging market for the musicians, their management, or the project's producers to purchase the original art. The artist should be prepared with a dollar amount in case this happens. Possible tie-ins with DVD marketing should also be kept in mind when considering an appropriate fee for the image.

One illustrator who has worked extensively with major recording companies advises artists working in the field to employ a lawyer experienced in the entertainment industry to negotiate contracts for them. Otherwise, the artist may be unknowingly exploited because of lack of experience. The contract should contain a clause clearly spelling out that additions and alterations will lead to extra charges.

Other products

While packaging for the music and film recording industries is somewhat standard, packaging for other industries varies widely in size, shape, and the materials used. Pricing is determined by the complexity of the illustration, the size and prominence of the printed illustration on the package, the size and importance of the client, and the number of usage rights needed.

Clients from the Food/Beverage and Health/Beauty industries almost always request a full buyout of rights. Instead, it is in the best interest of both parties for the illustrator to specify exactly the rights that the client needs so that the illustrator retains unused rights and markets for possible future revenue, and the client is not wasting money on rights it doesn't need. For example, acceptable rights might include "unlimited, exclusive packaging rights in the U.S. for the specified product only. Original artwork belongs to the artist."

Specific trade practices for package illustration

In addition to the general trade practices listed in the beginning of this chapter, the following trade practices have been used historically and thus are accepted as standard:

1. Package illustrators normally sell only first reproduction rights unless otherwise stated.
2. Reuse fee: from 30 to 100 percent of the fee that would have been charged had the illustration been commissioned for the new use.
3. Charge for rush work: an additional 20 to 150 percent. However, with digital delivery expectations, rush fees are more difficult to get.

See Figure 10-9 for Comparative Fees for Packaging Illustration.

Comparative Fees for
Package Illustration

Music Recordings*

	POPULAR & ROCK	CLASSICAL & JAZZ
Major studio or distribution	$1,500–6,500	$1,200–3,500
Small studio or distribution	$1,200–3,000	$1,200–2,500
Re-released property	$750–2,000	$500–1,500

DVDs & Videos*

	SPECIAL INTEREST	GENERAL INTEREST
Major studio or distribution	$1,200–3,500	$2,500–6,000
Small studio or distribution	$750–1,500	$1,000–3,000

Software*

	BUSINESS	EDUCATIONAL	VIDEO GAMES
International distribution	-	-	$14,000[1]
National distribution**	$3,500-10,000	$1,500-4,000	$2,000-7,500
Limited distribution**	$2,000-4,000	$1,000-3,000	$1,500-3,500
Re-released	$1,500-3,000	-	$1,500-2,500

[1] Multiple use: package and advertising/promotion

Retail Products

NATIONAL DISTRIBUTION**

Apparel	$1,800-6,000	Home furnishings	$1,500-2,700
Electronics	$1,200-3,500	Housewares	$1,500-3,000
Food/beverages[2]	$1,000-4,500	Infant products	$1,300-5,000
Footware	$1,700-2,500	Pet food	$1,200-5,000
Gifts/novelties	$1,200-3,000	Sporting goods	$750-5,000
Health/beauty aids[2]	$1,500-5,000	Toys/games	$2,500-6,000

[2] Generally, rights are unlimited, exclusive packaging rights in the U.S. for the specified product only. Original artwork belongs to artist.

Additional Fees

	PERCENT OF ORIGINAL FEE
Rush fee	20-150%
Sale of original art	25-250%
Stock sale of existing art	30-100%
Total copyright transfer (excluding original art)	100-200%
Work for hire (transfer of legal authorship and all rights)	125-300%

* One piece of art used on DVDs, videos, or CDs.

** Test market and limited distribution products usually have a short shelf life or a smaller market share. National distribution indicates an extended shelf life and larger market share.

NOTE: The price ranges in Figure 10-9 do not reflect specific trade practices and do not constitute specific prices for particular jobs. The buyer and seller are free to negotiate, with each artist independently deciding how to price the work, after taking all factors into account.

FIGURE 10—9

Fashion & Lifestyle Illustration

Fashion illustrators specialize in drawing clothed figures and accessories in a specific style or "look" for use by retailers, advertising agencies, graphic design studios, corporations/manufacturers, and in editorials for magazines and newspapers. Sometimes fashion illustrators are required to create an illustration with only a photo or *croquis* (working sketch) of the garment for reference; the illustrator must invent the drape of the garment on a model, the light source, or even the garment itself.

The application of the techniques and styles exclusive to fashion illustration have also been used to create Lifestyle Illustration. These illustrations may be general in appearance but have a stylization that reflects a background in fashion illustration. Due to the nature of lifestyle illustration, artists will need to research, find, and/or create reference to suit the needs of a particular assignment. Lifestyle illustration is priced the same as fashion.

Although the advertising market for apparel and accessory illustration has declined in recent years, illustrations are still commissioned for work with a fashion theme in the growing beauty and cosmetic areas, as well as in the development of crossover markets that are well suited to an illustrative style. Such illustration is generally used as comp or finished art for magazine or newspaper editorial, print advertising, storyboards, television/video, packaging, display, collateral material, and product development or test presentations. Internet displays and sales venues are relatively new markets.

In addition to creating work for publishing, fashion illustrators also are commissioned to appear at various fashion-related events to create fashion drawings and portraits on the spot. These assignments usually involve fashion illustrators booking a two- or three-hour session and drawing during that timeframe. They receive a flat rate for their participation in the event.

Illustrators should be wary of projects that require far more technical details and revisions than normal for fashion illustration. There are unscrupulous clients who pose as designers, but actually use the illustrator to design their lines for them. These types of projects, which might include shoes, handbags, hats, gloves, and other accessories, border on product development and should be priced accordingly

Pricing

Current data indicate that the two most important factors determining fees are the type and extent of usage and the complexity of the job. Other factors that affect pricing are market (such as corporate, advertising, or editorial), size and prestige of the account, volume of work, the illustrator's experience and desirability, and deadlines.

Most apparel illustration is paid on a per-figure basis, with an additional charge for backgrounds. When more than three figures are shown (four to ten), a group rate can be charged at a lower rate, usually 80 to 90 percent of an artist's single-figure rate. In volume work (considered any amount over ten figures), such as catalog, brochure, or instructional use, the per-figure price is negotiated at a volume rate, usually 75 percent of an artist's single-figure rate. Mailers and catalogs also have been a part of a larger package where if the client is cosmetics, then the use of the illustration will be negotiated for a usage fee for display/in-store signage, advertising, and mailers. Accessory illustration is generally paid on a per-item basis. With the exception of specialized work, accessory illustration rates are generally 50 to 75 percent of an artist's per-figure prices. When more than three items are shown, additional items can be charged at a lower unit price.

Fashion illustrators are also hired to create covers and fully illustrated books. These projects are usually negotiated with a flat fee and royalty for the use of the illustrator's work.

Specific trade practices for fashion & lifestyle illustration

In addition to the General Trade Practices listed in the beginning of this chapter, the following trade practices have been used historically and thus are accepted as standard:

1. Fashion/lifestyle illustrators normally sell first reproduction rights unless otherwise stated.
2. Additional uses of artwork in the same (or other) media entail fees ranging from 20 to 100 percent of the standard initial fee for the same medium usage.
3. Reuse fee: from 20 to 100 percent of the fee that would have been charged had the illustration been commissioned for the new use.
4. If a client wishes to purchase all reproduction rights or original artwork, current data indicate that a typical charge is 100 percent of the assignment price or higher, depending on the value of the original art for the individual artist. The artist retains the copyright.
5. If a client wishes to purchase all reproduction rights and original artwork, current data indicate that a typical charge is 200 percent of the assignment price or higher, depending on the value of the original art for the individual artist. The artist retains the copyright.
6. Charge for rush work: an additional 20 to 150 percent.
7. All corrections/revisions should be made in the preliminary sketch stage. All client changes, particularly in finished art, historically require an additional charge; the amount depends on the extent and complexity of the change.

See Figure 10-10 for Fashion & Lifestyle Illustration fees.

Comparative Fees for
Fashion & Lifestyle Illustration

Advertising

	SPREAD	FULL PAGE	HALF PAGE	QUARTER PAGE/SPOT	PER FIGURE/ ILLUSTRATION
MAGAZINE: NATIONAL OR LARGE CIRCULATION					
Color	$5,000–10,000	$3,500–5,000	$2,400	$1,500–1,800	-
B & W	$3,300–8,000	$2,200–4,000	$1,500	$1,000	-
MAGAZINE: SPECIFIC TRADE OR SMALL CIRCULATION					
Color	$2,500	$1,500–2,000	$750–1,500	$500–1,000	-
B & W	$1,500	$1,000	$650	$400-500	-
NEWSPAPER: NATIONAL, MAJOR METRO, OR LARGE CIRCULATION					
Color	$4,000–5,000	$2,600–3,000	$1,500–1,800	$1,100-1,250	-
B & W	$2,500–3,500	$1,600–1,800	$1,000–1,200	$700-800	-
NEWSPAPER: REGIONAL/LOCAL OR SMALL CIRCULATION					
Color	$1,500–2,500	$1,500–1,800	$1,200	$800	-
B & W	$1,700	$1,200	$800	$500	-

	COVER	QUARTER PAGE/SPOT	PER FIGURE/ ILLUSTRATION
DIRECT MAIL BROCHURES & CATALOGS: PRINT RUN GREATER THAN 100,000			
Color	$2,300–4,000	$700–1,000	$1,000–2,000
B & W	$1,500–2,500	$400–750	$750-1,200
DIRECT MAIL BROCHURES & CATALOGS: PRINT RUN 10,000-100,000			
Color	$1,500–2,000	$500	$900–1,000
B & W	$900–1,000	$300-500	$400-750

IN-HOUSE ADVERTISING MOCK-UP	$800 per illus.
INTERNET	
Video Advertisement	$500-750 per illus.
Web Banner (static) (Pricing depends on brand and usage period)	$500-2,000 per illus.
Web Banner (animated) (Pricing depends on complexity and duration of animation, specs, output, file size limitation, and necessary work time)	$1,200 and up
Web site	$500 per illus.

Fashion-Related Events

FASHION DRAWING & PORTRAITS (Supplies & transportation are negotiated as additional fees)	$1,000-2,000 per event (min. 2 hrs.)

(Continues on next page)

FIGURE 10—10

Comparative Fees for
Fashion & Lifestyle Illustration (Continued)

Editorial

	SPREAD	FULL PAGE	HALF PAGE	QUARTER PAGE/SPOT	PER FIGURE/ ILLUSTRATION
MAGAZINE: NATIONAL OR LARGE CIRCULATION					
Color	$3,500	$2,000	$450-2,000	$750	$2,000
B & W	$1,500	$750-1,000	$500	$400	$1,000
MAGAZINE: SPECIFIC TRADE OR SMALL CIRCULATION					
Color	$1,000-1,800	$600-1,500	$300-500	$200-350	-
B & W	$750	$375	$250	$150	-
NEWSPAPER: NATIONAL, MAJOR METRO, OR LARGE CIRCULATION					
Color	$4,000-6,000	$2,600-3,500	$1,600-1,750	$750-1,200	-
B & W	$2,500-4,000	$1,600-2,500	$1,000	$350-800	-
NEWSPAPER: REGIONAL/LOCAL OR SMALL CIRCULATION					
Color	$2,500	$1,800	$750-1,200	$500-800	-
B & W	$1,800	$1,000	$800	$100-500	-

NOTE: The price ranges in Figure 10-10 do not constitute specific prices for particular jobs. The buyer and seller are free to negotiate, with each artist independently deciding how to price the work, after taking all factors into account.

FIGURE 10—10

Greeting Card & Retail Product Illustration

The greeting card and paper novelty fields continue to be highly competitive cost-driven markets. New greeting card companies and fresh card lines constantly enter—and exit—the industry, while the largest card publishers continue to hold the lion's share of the market. Since success or failure in this business is based largely on the public's buying habits, greeting card designs lend themselves particularly well to royalty or licensing arrangements.

Artwork for retail products such as novelty merchandise, apparel, china, giftware, toys, and other manufactured items is traditionally purchased through licensing agreements. Calendars and posters for retail sale may also use licensing or royalty agreements. For more information about uses of this type of illustration, see the Greeting Card & Novelty Design section in Chapter 8, Graphic Design Prices & Trade Customs; the Licensing & Merchandising section in Chapter 5, Essential Business Practices; and the Book Illustration section earlier in this chapter.

Greeting cards

Greeting card sales in such mass-market outlets as supermarkets and big box retailers helped fuel sales growth over the past decade. The benefits of royalty agreements cannot be overstated, although the major card companies (Hallmark and American Greetings) are resistant to outsourcing creative work, keeping it in-house or with "first look" independent contractors who work at high volume. New market niches, such as cards for Hispanics, working women, and seniors, have been introduced, with anticipated sales growth during the next decade.

Although the major companies generally publish cards developed by staff artists, they do commission or buy some outside work. The rest of the industry, however, depends heavily on freelance illustration and design. Freelancers may earn income both from creating an inventory of their own illustrations and designs, which they license to producers/manufacturers and by selling commissioned works. They usually develop different styles for different clients in order to minimize competition.

Designs, usually created in full color, generally fit into everyday or seasonal lines. Everyday cards include birthday, anniversary, get well, friendship, juvenile, religious/inspirational, congratulations, sympathy, and other occasions. Christmas cards comprise the vast majority of seasonal greetings, making up more than a third of all cards sold and as much as 50 to 100 percent of some card companies' offerings. Other seasonal cards include Valentine's Day, Easter, Mother's and Father's Day, Hanukkah, and other holidays. Current survey data indicate that cards with special effects, such as embossing, die-cuts, or pop-ups, command larger fees.

Artists whose cards sell well may propose that the company commission them to develop an entire line of cards, which involves from 20 to 36 stylistically similar cards with a variety of greetings. In cases where an artist's cards become top sellers and the style is strongly identified with the company, the value of the artist's work to the company is recognized with equity and other compensation. Exclusive arrangements providing royalties are negotiated on occasion; artists are advised, however, to develop a solid relationship with the

Comparative Fees for
Greeting Card & Retail Product Illustration[1]

	FLAT FEE	ADVANCE ON ROYALTY	ROYALTY PERCENT[2]
GREETING CARD			
Original design	$500–1,500	$400–1,000	3-10%
Licensing of character	$500–3,500	$500–3,500	5-20%[3]
Pop-up or specialty card	$1,000–3,000	$700–1,500	5-10%
POSTER			
Original design	$1,600–7,000	$500–3,500	10%
Licensed artwork	$1,600–7,000	$500–3,500	10%
CALENDAR			
Original design (whole calendar)	$6,000–12,000	$4,000–10,000	5-10%
Licensed artwork (per page)	$850–3,500	$500–2,500[3]	5-10%[3]
DISPLAY/NOVELTY PRODUCT[4]			
Original design	$1,000–2,500	$750–2,500	5-10%
Trading card game (per illustration)	$800–1,000	–	-
Licensed artwork	$1,000–2,500	$750–2,500	5-12%[3]
GIFT BAG			
Original design	$500–3,500	$500–2,500	5-10%
Licensed artwork	$500–3,500	$500–2,500	5-12%[3]
DOMESTIC PRODUCT[5]			
Original design	$1,000–5,000	$1,000–2,000	5-10%
Licensed artwork	$1,000–2,500	$1,000–2,500	4-12%[3]
PAPER PRODUCT[6]			
Original design	$800–2,500	$800–2,500	5-10%
Licensed artwork	$800–2,500	$800–2,500	5-12%[3]

[1] Assume limited license of 3 years for indicated use. See also Chapter 13, Surface Design Prices & Trade Customs.

[2] Royalties are based on the wholesale price of item.

[3] For all brand character licensing, the percentage can go as high as 20%.

[4] T-shirt, gift, cap, mug, game board, tote bag, key chain, etc.

[5] Sheet, towel, wallpaper, tablecloth, napkin, fabric, window treatment.

[6] Gift wrap, gift card, paper napkin, plate, tablecloth

NOTE: The price ranges in Figure 10–11 do not constitute specific prices for particular jobs. The buyer and seller are free to negotiate, with each artist independently deciding how to price the work, after taking all factors into account.

FIGURE 10—11

client before considering such an agreement.

Greeting card designs are licensed either on an advance-against-royalty basis or for a flat fee (artists should not do revisions on a proposed design before a contract, describing payment and terms, is signed by both client and artist). The royalty is usually a percentage of the wholesale price, unless the company sells retail or online retail as well, in which case the royalty can be a combination of wholesale and retail. In most cases a nonrefundable advance is paid in anticipation of royalties. This reflects the fact that production and distribution schedules require a year to 18 months before a design reaches the marketplace. Royalties and licensing are discussed further in Chapter 5, Essential Business Practices.

Many greeting card companies purchase rights in the greeting card product category only, for a specified period of time (usually three to five years), in a specific market (e.g., North America or worldwide), with the artists retaining rights in all the other product categories (e.g., apparel, home furnishings, etc.). Unlike smaller companies that only seek rights to a design for one or two product categories, larger greeting card companies like Hallmark and American Greetings tend to look for buying a design outright.

Artists should not accept contract terms that they are uncomfortable with or that are not in their best economic interest. All contracts are open to changes and negotiation. Savvy artists can negotiate for themselves to use their own contract, or they can make changes in the company's contract. However, artists who find contracts confusing or overwhelming should consult a lawyer or a consultant who reviews contracts before signing.

Retail products

A wide array of designs and illustrations are in demand for T-shirts, towels, mugs, tote bags, and other novelty items. Whether a design or illustration is specifically developed by the artist for marketing as a product or sold as a spin-off of a nationally known character, it is usually done under a licensing agreement.

In such agreements, an artist, designer, or owner of artwork rights permits ("licenses") another party to use the art for a limited specific purpose, for a specified time, in a specified territory, in return for a fee or royalty. For a detailed discussion of licensing, see Chapter 5, Essential Business Practices. An excellent book on the subject is *Licensing Art and Design,* by Caryn Leland, published by Allworth Press (see Chapter 15, Resources & References). Model licensing agreements, reprinted with permission of the author, appear in the Appendix: Contracts & Forms.

Specific trade practices for greeting card & retail product illustration

In addition to the general trade practices listed in the beginning of this chapter, the following trade practices have been used historically and thus are accepted as standard:

1. Artists illustrating greeting cards and retail products normally sell only first reproduction rights, unless otherwise stated.
2. Reuse Fees: Although there is no set formula, current surveys indicate up to 100 percent of the fee that would have been charged had the illustration been commissioned for the new use.
3. Charge for rush work:, an additional 20 to 150 percent.

See Figure 10-11 for Greeting Card & Retail Product Illustration fees.

Medical Illustration

Medical illustrators train extensively to work in a surprisingly broad range of fields, including medicine, research, art, design, visual technology, media, communication, education, and management. Their job is to translate complex technical information into simple images to clearly convey how bodies work, how medicines interact, what happens under stress or trauma, or any of a nearly endless range of conditions that may need to be expressed.

The market for accurate and well-rendered medical depictions is strong. Medical illustrators may be employed by medical, dental, and veterinary schools, as well as teaching and research medical centers. Animation studios and multimedia production houses also hire medical illustrators on a freelance or full-time basis, as do medical publishers, pharmaceutical houses, advertising agencies, and lawyers. Most medical artists create two-dimensional illustrations in Photoshop, Illustrator, or Painter and three-dimensional models and animation using Maya, Cinema 4D, and SoftImage.

Training & certification

Not surprisingly, anatomical accuracy is critical to success. To achieve this degree of verisimilitude, most medical artists earn a Master's Degree from an accredited graduate program. There are currently four very competitive programs in the United States and one in Canada that are accredited by the Commission on Accreditation of Allied Health Education Programs (CAAHEP), regarded as the premier sanctioning body. Course work includes human gross anatomy (with detailed dissection); histology; physiology; embryology; neuroanatomy; pathology; illustration techniques; anatomical and surgical illustration; modeling; prosthetics; graphic and exhibit design and construction; medical photography; television and multimedia production;

computer graphics; business management; instructional design; and production technology.

Some medical illustrators demonstrate competency and improve their work prospects by becoming board certified. A Certified Medical Illustrator (CMI) is tested on subjects covering business practices, ethics, biomedical science, and drawing and undergoes a rigorous portfolio review. To maintain certification, they must continue their education and must have their certification renewed every five years. The National Commission for Certifying Agencies (NCCA) establishes the standards by which all medical illustrators are evaluated.

Specific trade practices for medical illustration

In addition to the General Trade Practices listed in the beginning of this chapter, the following trade practices have been used historically and are accepted as standard:

1. Medical illustrators and employers should have a signed formal contract, purchase order, or letter of agreement, which states the intended use for the artwork, reproduction rights, and all related terms.
2. Illustrators normally sell only first reproduction rights unless otherwise stated. Additional rights are traditionally licensed on a one-time basis, with separate payment for each and every use.
3. Re-use fee: from 50 to 150 percent of the fee that would have been charged had the illustration been commissioned for the new use.
4. Fees for licensed medical animation are based on final rendered frames. Artists retain copyright to all three-dimensional models and scenes.
5. Due to the proprietary nature of much of the work associated with medical illustration, artists frequently sign nondisclosure agreements prohibiting discussion of work-in-progress and prohibiting exhibit or display of art until a specified date.
6. Charge for rush work: often an additional 20 to 150 percent.

See Figure 10-12 for Medical Illustration Fees.

Natural Science Illustration

Natural science illustrators create accurate and detailed images of scientific subjects, including anthropology, astronomy, botany, cartography, geology, paleontology, and zoology, often working

Comparative Fees for Medical Illustration

The wide ranges reported here represent average fees, depending on complexity and usage which includes exclusive and non-exclusive use, local, national or global rights, and period of use or duration of time granted. More importantly, fees depend on degree of talent and perceived excellence of the creator, not unlike other disciplines in the illustration field.

Advertising

	SIMPLE	COMPLEX
CONCEPTUAL		
Spread	$2,000–5,000	$4,000–12,000
Full Page	$1,500–3,000	$3,000–10,000
1/4 to 1/2 Page	$700–1,500	$2,000–3,500
ANATOMICAL & SURGICAL		
Spread	$1,700–5,000	$4,000–8,000
Full Page	$1,500–4,000	$2,500–6,000
1/4 to 1/2 Page	$600–1,700	$750–2,500
Posters	$3,500–5,000	$7,500–20,000
PRESENTATIONS & TRADE SHOWS		
Conceptual	$1,000–3,000	$4,500–10,000+
Anatomical & Surgical	$700–2,500	$2,000–5,000

(Continues on next page)

FIGURE 10—12

directly with scientists and designers to illustrate books and journals or to create exhibits and educational materials for universities, research centers, state and federal government departments, museums, zoos, botanical gardens, and aquaria. Natural science illustration is expanding into all areas of graphic communications and commercial applications, such as special interest magazines, environmental design, merchandise and package illustration, advertising, computer graphics, audiovisuals, and model-making and murals for museums and zoos.

Education and skills

Scientific illustrators must be versatile in more than one technique or medium, using everything from traditional pencils and paints to digital media; often they must be skilled in using optical equipment and precision measuring devices. A thorough understanding of the subject matter is essential. Many scientific illustrators have advanced degrees or strong backgrounds in science as well as art. The illustrator must often pictorially reconstruct an entire object from incomplete specimens

Comparative Fees for
Medical Illustration (Continued)

Editorial

	SIMPLE	COMPLEX
PROFESSIONAL PUBLICATIONS & MEDICAL JOURNALS		
Cover	$1,000–3,000	$3,000–5,000
Spread	$1,200–1,700	$2,000–4,000
Full Page	$700–1,500	$1,700–3,000
1/4 to 1/2 Page	$350–600	$500–2,000
CONSUMER PUBLICATIONS (Health & Science Magazines)		
Cover	$1,500–4,000	$3,500–8,000
Spread	$1,500–3,500	$1,800–6,500
Full Page	$1,000–2,000	$1,500–3,700
1/4 to 1/2 Page	$350–700	$750–1,200
INSTRUCTIONAL TEXTS (College, Medical and Surgical Textbooks, Patient Educational Manuals)		
Cover	$250–600	$700–2,000

Exhibits

LEGAL EXHIBITS (Often 30" x 40" presentation boards)	$700–1,200	$1,500–4,500
OTHER EXHIBITS	$450–1,000	$1,200–2,500
COMPUTER ANIMATION/MULTI-MEDIA (per completed minute)		$10,000–20,000
CONSTRUCTION OF MODELS FOR MEDICAL USE (depending on complexity)		$3,500–10,000

Additional Fees

	PERCENT OF ORIGINAL FEE
SALE OF ORIGINAL ART	125–250%
STOCK SALE OF EXISTING ART	50–150%
RUSH FEE	20–150%
UNLIMITED USE IN PRINT MEDIA ONLY	100–400%
UNLIMITED USE, ANY MEDIA, 1 YEAR	150–250%
TOTAL COPYRIGHT TRANSFER OF RIGHTS (Excludes original art)	200–700%

FIGURE 10—12

and poor-quality photographs or conceptualize an informed interpretation. Specimens must be correctly delineated to show proportion, coloration, anatomical structures, and other diagnostic features. The illustrator may clarify complex three-dimensional structures, emphasize important details, and idealize an individual specimen in ways not possible by photography. Scientific illustrations are judged for their accuracy, readability, and beauty.

Pricing factors

Scientific illustrators who create works for books and journals report that work-for-hire contracts are unfortunately all too common in the field, especially in the textbook industry. Because more and more works are computer generated, the illustrator's function is frequently viewed as mere data entry, and although their work is integral to the scientific data provided, illustrators are often not even credited. To protect illustrators' rights in this field, and because it may take years for the work to be accepted for publication, practitioners recommend pricing work appropriately for first (and probably only) use, requesting final payment upon submission of the work, and providing scanned images rather than original artwork. In addition to intended usage and rights transferred, the factors found by Guild research to affect pricing in this field include research and consultation time, travel, reference materials, and the complexity of the project, which sometimes requires extra stages of concept development and approvals. Scientific illustrations may contain extremely fine details and communicate complex ideas and therefore may command higher prices than less "information dense" work of the same printed size.

Comparative Fees for Natural Science Illustration

Editorial (HOURLY RATE $60-75)

	COVER	SPREAD	FULL PAGE	SPOT
PROFESSIONAL SCIENTIFIC PEER-REVIEW PUBLICATIONS				
Tone/Color	$1,200–4,000	$1,000–4,000	$600–2,000	$250–750
Line	$500–850	$500–2,000	$400–1,000	$100–300
CONSUMER PUBLICATIONS (Books, magazines, e.g., *Scientific American, National Geographic*)				
Tone/Color	$1,200–3,000	$1,200–3,500	$1,000–2,500	$300–500
Line	$750–2,500	$700–2,000	$600–1,200	$250–450
TEXTBOOKS AND SCIENCE PUBLICATIONS FOR THE SCHOOL MARKET				
Simple	$1,000–1,500	$1,000–2,000	$500–800	$300–400
Moderate	$1,200–2,500	$800–2,500	$600–1,000	$400–600
Complex	$1,200–5,000	$1,200–3,000	$800–2,000	$500–750

Advertising (HOURLY RATE $85-150)

	COMPLEX	MODERATE	SIMPLE
PRODUCT			
Tone/Color	$1,500–4,500	$1,200–3,200	$750–1,500
Line	$1,200–3,000	$1,000–2,000	$600–1,200
Sketch/Comp	$1,200–2,000	$800–1,000	$400–600
POSTER			
Tone/Color	$2,500–8,000	$2,000–5,000	$1,200–4,000
Line	$1,200–4,000	$1,000–3,000	$750–2,500
Sketch/Comp	$1,700–4,500	$1,000–3,000	$750–2,500

(Continues on next page)

FIGURE 10—13

Specific trade practices for natural science illustration

In addition to the general trade practices listed in the beginning of this chapter, the following trade practices have been used historically and thus are accepted as standard:

1. Natural science illustrators normally sell only first reproduction rights, unless otherwise stated.
2. Reuse fee: from 50 to more than 200 percent of the fee that would have been charged had the illustration been commissioned solely for the original use.
3. Charge for rush work: an additional 20 to 150 percent.

See Figure 10-13 for Natural Science Illustration fees.

Technical Illustration

Technical illustrators create highly accurate renderings of machinery, instruments, scientific subjects (such as biological studies, geological formations, and chemical reactions), space technology, or virtually any subject that requires precise interpretation in illustration. Technical illustrators often work directly with a scientist, engineer, or technician to achieve the most explicit and accurate visualization of the subject and/or information. Being trained in mechanical drafting, mathematics, diagrams, blueprints, and production gives technical illustrators specific and required skills.

Technical illustration is used in all areas of graphics communication in this age of sophisticated technology. Some of the areas which most commonly require this specialized art are industrial publications,

Comparative Fees for
Natural Science Illustration (Continued)

Consultation/Research/Alterations (HOURLY RATE $50-125)

Animations (HOURLY RATE $65-85)

	COMPLEX	MODERATE	SIMPLE
Storyboards (per image/panel)	$750–3,000	$575–1,600	$200–1,000
Computer production	$2,600	$1,300	$650

Exhibits/Museums* (HOURLY RATE $65-125)

	COMPLEX	MODERATE	SIMPLE
Model construction	$3,500–6,000	$2,500–4,000	$700–2,000
Exhibit panel illustration	$1,000–6,000	$500–3,000	$350–1,000
Murals (per square foot) $60-70			

* Rights granted are usually one-time rights for the life of the exhibit, to include all promotional usages of the exhibit. All merchandising rights are negotiated separately.

Additional Fees

	PERCENT OF ORIGINAL FEE
Rush fee	20-150%
Sale of original art	100-200%
Stock sale of existing art	50-200%
Unlimited use in print media only (no time or geographical limits)	50-200%
Unlimited use, any media for 1 year	50-150%
Total copyright transfer (excluding original art)	80-300%
Work for hire (transfer of legal authorship and all rights)	100-300%+

NOTE: The price ranges in Figure 10-13 do not reflect specific trade practices and do not constitute specific prices for particular jobs. The buyer and seller are free to negotiate, with each artist independently deciding how to price the work, after taking all factors into account.

FIGURE 10—13

Comparative Fees for Technical Illustration

Cutaway

	VERY COMPLEX	SIMPLE TO MODERATE COMPLEXITY/INFOGRAPHIC
Engine	$12,000-15,000	-
House/Building	$17,000-80,000	$2,000-5,000
Vehicle	$30,000-45,000	-
Ship	$106,000-120,000	-
Industrial Subjects (for advertising)		$1,500-3,000+

Infographics

MAJOR COMPLEXITY	MODERATE COMPLEXITY
$10,000-15,000+	$2,000-6,000

Editorial

	COVER/ SECTION	SPREAD	FULL PAGE	HALF PAGE	QUARTER PAGE/SPOT
MAGAZINES					
Tone/color	$1,700-5,000	$1,500-4,500	$1,000-2,800	$600-1,500	$300-1,000
Line	-	-	$850-2,500	$800-1,500	$350-750
NEWSPAPERS					
Tone/color	$1,500-2,800	$1,200-2,500	$900-1,500	$700-1,000	$400-750
Line	-	$750-1,200	$600-1,000	$500-1,000	$350-650
BOOKS					
Tone/color	$1,700-2,500	$1,000-3,000	$500-1,500	$400-1,000	$350-650
Line	-	-	$400-1,000	$300-700	$200-300

Advertising

	SPREAD	FULL PAGE	HALF PAGE	QUARTER PAGE/SPOT
MAGAZINES: NATIONAL CIRCULATION (Reader's Digest, Time, People, Women's Day, The New Yorker, Atlantic Monthly)				
Simple to complex	$2,500-10,000	$2,000-7,500	$1,000-5,000	$500-5,000
MAGAZINES: SMALL CIRCULATION (Golf Digest, Scientific American)				
Tone/color	$1,500-5,000	$1,500-4,000	$1,000-3,000	$500-2,500
Line	$800-1,500	$700-1,200	$450-850	$300-650

(Continues on next page)

FIGURE 10—14

Comparative Fees for
Technical Illustration (Continued)

Other Publications

	COVER	SPREAD	FULL PAGE	HALF PAGE	QUARTER PAGE/SPOT	PER ILLUSTRATION
EMPLOYEE PUBLICATIONS						
Tone/ Color	$2,000-3,000	$1,200-2,000	$700-1,500	$600-1,000	$500	$1,000
Line	$1,300-2,000	$850-1,500	$700-1,000	$400-700	$350	$250-500
INSTRUCTION MANUAL						
Tone/ Color	$1,200-2,000	$1,700-2,500	$850-1,500	$600-1,200	$500-800	-
Line	$1,000-1,500	$1,200-2,000	$700-1,000	$400-750	$200-300	-
COLLATERAL/DIRECT RESPONSE MAILERS						
Tone/ Color	$2,000-3,500	$1,700-3,500	$1,500-2,500	$700-1,500	$450-750	-
Line	-	$1,200-2,500	$850-1,200	$500-1,000	$300-400	-

PRESENTATIONS

	COLOR FLIP CHARTS	TRADE SHOW EXHIBITS
Tone/Color	$750-2,500	$1,500-4,700

	HOURLY RATE	DAY RATE	FLAT FEE
INSTRUCTION ON PACKAGING	-	-	$250-1,000
DATA SHEETS	$50-100	-	-
PRODUCT USER & SERVICE MANUALS	$50-150	-	-
INSTRUCTIONAL CONSULTATION	$45-125	$500-2,000	-

Additional Fees

	PERCENT OF ORIGINAL FEE
Rush fee	25-100%
Sale of original art	75-200%
Stock sale of existing art	50-100%+
Unlimited use in print media only (no time or geographical limits)	50-150%
Unlimited use, any media for 1 year	50-175%
Total copyright transfer (excluding original art)	75-200%
Work for hire (transfer of legal authorship and all rights)	200-300%

NOTE: The price ranges in Figure 10-14 do not reflect specific trade practices and do not constitute specific prices for particular jobs. The buyer and seller are free to negotiate, with each artist independently deciding how to price the work, after taking all factors into account.

FIGURE 10—14

technical manuals, annual reports, special or single-interest magazines, packaging, advertising, corporate, editorial, web graphics, and audiovisuals. These artists most often create their work digitally.

Information graphics or *infographics* are often employed by technical illustrators. These visual representations of information, data, and knowledge, are used where complex information must be explained quickly and clearly. They include maps, charts, diagrams, and graphs. Infographics can be found everywhere and in all types of media. They have both everyday and scientific uses. While they often serve as visual shorthand in everyday life (traffic signs), in science and technical literature they are used to illustrate physical systems, especially ones that cannot be photographed, such as cutaways, astronomical diagrams, and images of microscopic systems.

It is common for technical illustrators to keep their original art and retain control of the copyright, building a library of their own work that can later be reused with alterations in new work. Given the complexities of some assignments, this practice can help illustrators complete jobs faster.

In addition to intended usage and rights transferred, the factors that affect pricing in this field include research and consultation time, travel, reference materials, and project complexity.

The fees and completion time for technical illustration vary considerably according to the complexity of the assignment. A single complex illustration, such as a cutaway of a ship, can sometimes take six weeks to three months to complete, while simpler cutaways of common household items, such as the interior of a mattress, are done in hours. Many illustrators prefer to shoot their own photographs for reference but often work from reference materials supplied by the client. Using references such as "off angle" photos and blueprints will increase the fee.

Specific trade practices for technical illustration

In addition to the general trade practices listed in the beginning of this chapter, the following specific trade practices have been used historically and thus are accepted as standard:

1. Technical illustrators normally sell only first reproduction rights unless otherwise stated.
2. Reuse fee: from 50 to 100+ percent of the fee that would have been charged had the illustration been commissioned for the new use.
3. Charge for rush work: often an additional 25 to 100 percent.

See Figure 10-14 for Technical Illustration fees.

Architectural/Interior Illustration

Architectural/interior illustrators (also known as renderers or perspectivists) are hired by an architect, designer, or real estate developer to create accurate representations (sketches, drawings, or paintings) of exterior or interior design projects. The original illustration itself is often sold for design presentation purposes, but the copyright and the reproduction rights are usually retained by the artist. Increasingly, artists provide their drawings to clients on a temporary "use basis," with eventual return of the original.

Illustrators are also commissioned by real estate developers and/or their advertising agencies to create art for promotional purposes. Advertising and promotional reproduction rights are negotiated separately from the sale or primary use of the original art, and surveys indicate that the intended uses for the work will affect the fee. (For more information, see Advertising Illustration earlier in this chapter.) When the artist is asked to provide renderings to be used by the client in a design competition, the artist may be asked to provide them at a lower fee. In this speculative arrangement the artist usually negotiates additional compensation or a bonus if the client wins the competition. The amount of the bonus depends on the size of the original discount and the value of the contract the client will secure from winning the competition.

The finished art is in the form of one or a combination of several media: watercolor, colored pencil, marker, gouache, pen and ink, airbrush, pastel, and/or digital. Many illustrators take advantage of computer-aided design (CAD) programs in ways that range from preliminary perspective layouts to complete final renderings. Not only are they extremely useful for their speed and accuracy, but also they allow the artist to quickly choose views that serve the client's needs.

Architectural/interior artists are hired for their unique illustrative styles and their accuracy in depicting the building, space, color, and/or materials. They usually have a background in architectural, interior, or industrial design and have chosen this specialized field after part-time or freelance experience in the business. As a result of these unique qualifications, they are often hired to work in a client's office on a rendering project while the design is in progress. In this situation, it is customary for the renderer to bill hourly (from $90 to $250 per hour), plus expenses. Illustrators often work from a variety of reference materials, depending on the end use and the level of detail required by the client, ranging from rough schematic design sketches with verbal descriptions to completely detailed working drawings.

Recent surveys show that factors involved in pricing include the complexity of the design project (which depends upon the views and amount of detail required), the number of images, the media to be used, and the amount of time required for travel and consultation for the project. While the size of the finished piece may be a consideration when pricing hand-rendered work, it is irrelevant when pricing computer-generated images.

Specific trade practices for architectural/interior illustration

In addition to the general trade practices listed in the beginning of this chapter, the following trade practices have been used historically and thus are accepted as standard:

1. Return of original artwork to the artist is automatic unless otherwise negotiated.

2. Architectural illustrators normally sell only first reproduction rights unless otherwise stated.

3. Reuse fee: from 20 to 100 percent of the fee that would have been charged had the illustration been commissioned for the new use.

4. Charge for rush work: often an additional 20 to 150 percent.

5. A client may request that the illustrator enter into a nondisclosure agreement that would prevent the artist from showing or publishing (for self-promotion) the artwork for a specific period of time. Any conditions limiting an artist's ability to exploit artwork are factors in negotiating fees. Nondisclosure agreements should always be in print.

See Figure 10-15 for Architectural Illustration fees.

Dimensional (3-D) Illustration

Dimensional illustration includes, but is not limited to, paper, soft, or relief sculpture; paper/photo collage; assemblage; plastic, wood, and/or metal fabrications; clay imagery; food sculpture; fabric/stitchery; and other types of mixed media. Dimensional illustrators create original three-dimensional (3-D) artwork, varying from low-relief collage to sculptural assemblage that is usually shown from one vantage point. This genre includes traditional illustrators, model makers, paper sculptors, and fabric artists whose work is created for a wide range of uses in the same markets as that of other illustrators, predominantly in advertising and editorial. Some dimensional illustrators also seek work in related markets creating architectural models; window displays; museum exhibits; convention display booths; prototypes for toys and giftware; sculpture for building interiors; food styling; animation; and sets, props, costumes, and puppets for TV commercials and performances.

Any 3-D illustration to be used in print must have two images: the original dimensional artwork and a photograph (transparency or slide) or digital image to be submitted for reproduction. Typically, the client buys one-time usage rights.

Comparative Fees for Architectural & Interior Illustration (Computer Generated)[1]

SKETCH PERSPECTIVE

(Based on a two-point perspective of a single building or interior with no background or environmental context; simple exteriors, elevations, etc.) — $500-1,000[2]

FORMAL ILLUSTRATION

(Based on exteriors and perspectives of several buildings or interiors with environmental context site plans, etc.) — $2,000-3,500[2]

COMPLEX PRESENTATION ILLUSTRATION

(Based on elaborate architectural detailing with complex perspectives: cityscapes, aerial views, fully illustrated exteriors or interiors, etc.) — $3,000-6,000[2]

EXTREMELY COMPLEX ILLUSTRATION

(Highest level of detail and complexity) — $6,500-12,000[2]

[1] The finished printed size/dimensions of computer illustration do not affect the cost. A major factor determining cost is the work/time involved.

[2] Pricing is per illustration. Illustrator retains copyright of commissioned images.

NOTE: The price ranges in Figure 10-15 do not constitute specific prices for particular jobs. The buyer and seller are free to negotiate, with each artist independently deciding how to price the work, after taking all factors into account.

FIGURE 10—15

Photographing the artwork

Because many dimensional illustrators like to maintain control over the entire process, they choose to photograph their own work. In addition to making the final image, they may take preliminary photos, often digital, to establish camera angles or to submit as sketches or comps. Another advantage of photographing the artwork is that it may be constructed without regard to permanence or the need for transportation or reassembly. Dimensional illustrators thereby eliminate the expense of hiring a photographer, scheduling such services under deadline pressure, and any possible confusion over copyright. The 3-D illustrator who chooses to do his/her own photography is obligated to make a considerable investment in equipment and supplies and in mastering the techniques needed to produce suitable high-quality reproductions.

Dimensional illustrators who opt to use the services of a professional photographer must consider copyright issues carefully. As the creator of the original work, 3-D illustrators implicitly grant authorization to create a two-dimensional (2-D) derivative of their work. Frequently, however, once artwork is photographed for use, it is difficult for 3-D illustrators to control uses and distributions or even obtain copies of their work. This situation can occur under the most ordinary arrangements: when the client hires both the artist and the photographer, when the photographer hires the artist, and even when the artist hires the photographer.

Fortunately, most art directors and photographers function under the assumption that the final photographic image does not belong to either the dimensional illustrator or the photographer, but to both. The reasons for this are logical: the photo could not have been created without the dimensional illustration and is therefore a derived image. The same logic applies in reverse situations. In the well-known case of *Rogers v. Koons*, photographer Art Rogers successfully sued sculptor Jeff Koons for producing unauthorized life-size dimensional derivatives of Rogers' photograph. Earlier cases, in which sculptors who sued photographers were vindicated, provided precedents for Rogers' suit. Therefore photographers should not assume ownership and full rights to an image when that image is derived fully from a dimensional illustrator's work. In most relationships involving model makers, a photographer or client who wants to assume all rights to the work and the derivative photograph will offer to buy out the artist for a fee significantly higher than that offered for first rights. It is sound practice, as always, to ascertain in advance the client's and the photographer's rights.

The best protection dimensional illustrators have is a written agreement; a simple letter to the other party is needed to confirm basic terms.

3-D ILLUSTRATOR & PHOTOGRAPHER HIRED BY CLIENT

Dimensional illustrators should consider the following in situations where the client hires both the illustrator and the photographer:

License: Specify the precise scope of the license granted to the client for use of the illustration and its photographic reproductions.

Assignments: Limit the client's agreements with all third parties (including the photographer) for use of any reproductions of the illustration, photographic and otherwise.

Rights reserved: Obtain permission to make unfettered use of the photograph (a transparency is preferable so additional reproductions can be made).

Credit: Require the client and the photographer to provide a specific credit to the artist whenever the photograph is used (i.e., Photography © 2000 John Photographer, Artwork © 2000 Jane Artist).

PHOTOGRAPHER HIRED BY 3-D ILLUSTRATOR

In cases where a dimensional illustrator hires the photographer, the illustrator should specify the following:

Grant of rights: The rights granted the photographer and the limits of the photographer's exercise of copyright in the photograph.

Permission: The anticipated use of the photograph.

Credit: The credit to be used at all times with the photograph.

Access: If the illustrator is free to reproduce the photograph without using the photographer's services. If so, a negative or a transparency that can be duplicated should be obtained.

3-D ILLUSTRATOR HIRED BY PHOTOGRAPHER

In situations where a dimensional illustrator is retained by the photographer, the illustrator should consider the following:

License: Specify the rights granted to the photographer and the photographer's permitted uses of the photograph depicting the illustrator's work.

Authorship: Retain the copyright of the illustration and, if possible, share joint copyright of the photograph.

Rights reserved: Specify that the illustrator may use his/her illustration freely and without restriction (including having it re-photographed by another photographer).

Credit: Specify the credit that the photograph must carry.

Access: Obtain rights to use the photograph and to obtain a transparency or copy of the negative.

Pricing

Pricing ultimately depends on the client's intended use. Typically, as with 2-D illustration, clients buy one-time publication rights. Artwork created for permanent exhibit or for broadcast media is priced relative to those markets.

Guild surveys show several factors that specifically affect pricing for three-dimensional illustration and should be considered when negotiating with a client. In today's cost-cutting environment, 3-D illustrators are often asked to price their work on a scale similar to that for 2-D art (work painted, drawn, or bitmapped on a flat surface). Because of the complexity of 3-D versus 2-D art, the materials and techniques needed to create a 3-D piece may require considerable investment on the artist's part, because photo-graphing the artwork requires an extra process and expense, and because the 3-D illustrator offers the client greater potential for use (since the lighting and perspective can be varied when photographing it), the comparison of 3-D to 2-D art is not realistic.

Often 3-D pieces are used to promote the client's product in a public place: a shop window or a counter display. Generally, a 3-D display is more valuable to a client than a flat picture because of the number of opportunities to exploit the work. (For example, see Packaging Illustration earlier in this chapter.)

MATERIALS, EQUIPMENT, & SUPPORT SERVICES

The materials used to build a 3-D project can be much more expensive than art supplies used in 2-D illustration. Model-making materials used in miniature sets or architectural models, real objects used in assemblages, rare fabrics used in fabric collages, and casting resins for molded sculpture can add significantly to the cost of a job. It is up to the individual artist to determine if expenses for materials will be included in the original creator's fee or billed separately. If included, the artist should consider unforeseen circumstances that might lead to additional expenses and include an allowance for changes.

Model makers in particular must maintain large facilities and extensive equipment to produce their work—often not just a single piece of sculpture but also a complete setting. And they may need to hire extra help for especially detailed or large projects. If the deadline is short, the model maker may not only have to hire help but may also have to refuse other valuable work in order to meet the client's needs. The client should be aware that giving the artist sufficient time to complete the project is an important factor in controlling costs. Because the model maker's overhead is higher than that for the typical 2-D illustrator, these added expenses are generally reflected in a model maker's fees. A client who requests a piece of sculpture that has been cast from a living model, molded on a vacuum-forming unit, and "gold" plated should expect to pay a considerably higher price than for digitally produced flat art.

If cost is a primary concern to the client, dimensional illustrators frequently offer options, such as simplifying the artwork or, if possible, creating a smaller original.

PHOTOGRAPHY COSTS

In order to photograph 3-D pieces, the dimensional illustrator also must invest in photography and lighting equipment or pay for the services of a photographer. The costs of lab services must also be factored into the illustrator's fees. Another pricing consideration is the number of different photographic images that may be needed for a variety of uses.

Billing

Few clients like surprises, so it is advisable to estimate costs as closely as possible at the time of the agreement. Clients should be informed of the potential for additional expenditures for supplies and alerted in advance when photographic expenses and materials will be billed separately. It is good practice, when billing separately, to submit receipts and/or an itemized list with the invoice. Expenses for projects that require support services (mold making, vacuum forming, plating, engraving, or foundry casting) can increase significantly. The client should be fully informed of any such antic-ipated expenses, which, again, can either be billed separately or reflected in the artist's creative fee.

Specific trade practices for dimensional illustration

In addition to the general trade practices listed in the beginning of this chapter, the following trade practices have been used historically and thus are accepted as standard:

1. The intended use of the art must be stated clearly in a contract, purchase order, or letter of agreement stating the price and terms of sale. This contract should be signed by both parties before the artist begins the work. The agreement should state the usage rights; for example, "For one-time, nonexclusive, English-language, North American print rights only, in one hardcover edition, to be published by XXX, entitled 'YYY.' All additional requests for usage by [client] or any other publication, except as specified above, are to be referred to [name of artist] to determine the appropriate reprint fee."

2. The artwork (photograph of the 3-D art) cannot be altered in any way, except for what occurs during the normal printing process, without the written consent of the artist. Since it is very easy to alter art electronically, the client should inform the artist if he or she wishes to alter the artwork and then do so only with the permission and supervision of the illustrator. Anything less is a violation of professional good faith and ethical practice.

3. Return of original artwork to the illustrator is automatic unless otherwise negotiated. If the client wishes to display the artwork, dimensional illustrators have reportedly charged fees ranging from 100 to 200 percent, in addition to the base one-time use price. The display usage should be agreed upon in the initial purchase order.

4. The payment terms should be negotiated prior to the sale, and these terms should be stated on the invoice, including provisions for late payment. As they largely reflect the graphic artist's labor, invoices should be made payable upon receipt.

5. An advance payment, termed a "material advance," may be requested for large projects.

6. Guild surveys show that additional payment is routinely paid to an artist when (a) the client requests artwork changes that were not part of the original agreement, and (b) sales taxes must be collected on all artwork, except when original work is returned to the dimensional illustrator.

7. Terms of joint authorship and ownership of the photographic image should be accepted by all parties (the dimensional illustrator, the photographer, and, where applicable, the client) and stated in the agreement. The Guild's survey data indicate that a dimensional illustrator who allows the copyright to become the property of the photographer receives substantially higher compensation than for work with shared copyright.

8. Charge for rush work: often an additional 20 to 150 percent.

9. If the illustrator satisfies the client's requirements and the finished work is still not used, full compensation should be made. If a job is canceled after the work has begun, through no fault of the artist, a cancellation or kill fee is often provided. Depending upon the stage at which the job is terminated, the fee must cover all work, including research time, sketches, billable expenses, and compensation for lost opportunities resulting from the artist's refusing other offers in order to make time available for the commission. Ownership of all artwork and copyright is retained by the artist. If a job based on "documentary" work or other original art belonging to a client is canceled, recent surveys reveal that payment of a time and/or labor charge is common.

10. Customary and usual expenses, such as travel costs, consultation time, shipping and mailing charges, and other out-of-pocket expenses for materials (film, model-making supplies, casting resins, and fabric), as well as fees for production services not performed by the dimensional illustrator (such as vacuum forming), outside services such as photography and processing, model fees, and additional production staff are usually billed to the client separately as they occur. An expense estimate, which states that the estimate is subject to amendment, can be included in the original written agreement with the client.

Postage Stamp Illustration

There are several markets for stamp illustration, including the United States Postal Service (USPS), the United Nations, European nations, and small-country stamp producers. Stamps are often offered to collectors; the USPS has a very active branch that caters specifically to philatelists (people who collect and study postage stamps and postmarked materials such as first-day-of-issue envelopes, postcards, and stamps canceled by a specific post office). Sometimes the debut of a postage stamp will be accompanied by a media campaign, as with the release of the Elvis Presley stamp, where the public was asked to vote on which of two images (the young Elvis or the old Elvis) would be produced.

United States stamp program

The commission to do a stamp can come from the USPS directly or from one of the many designers who work with the Postal Service. U.S. postage stamp illustrations are normally priced per image. The contract usually calls for the artist to produce up to three sketches per image, which are priced at $1,500, regardless of whether the project is completed by the USPS. The normal total fee per final stamp image is $5,000. The USPS demands that artists do commissions on a work-for-hire basis, relinquishing both copyright and original artwork for the one-time fee.

If the stamp is a popular issue, the artist may be asked to sign an open or a limited edition series for sale to collectors, although only one or two stamps per year are offered with artists' signatures. The artist may be asked to sign from 5,000 to 20,000 uncut sheets. An uncut sheet consists of six sets of usually 20 stamps per "pane" (a stamp sheet normally purchased from the post office), which is the way the stamps come off the printer's press before they are cut for retail sale. The fee paid to the artist for signing the uncut sheets ranges from $1 to $4 per signature, depending on the edition and the number of sheets being signed.

Because the USPS insists on retaining the copyright and artwork, it perpetuates the worst possible business terms (work-for-hire) for artists. In addition, work-for-hire terms allow the USPS to license stamp images to for-profit companies to produce product spin-offs such as mugs or T-shirts—with the USPS collecting all the profits. Some artists have been able to negotiate control over secondary rights, and the use of Warner Bros. cartoon characters could only have been negotiated through some sort of licensing arrangement. Although the artist cannot sign the image created for the stamp, he or she may be attributed as the creator on materials printed about the stamp.

In 1997 the Guild initiated a campaign to make the USPS change its artist-unfriendly practices. Finally, in 1999 the Guild was invited to a meeting with the creative director of stamp development at the USPS, where a number of issues were discussed, including credit and recognition, compensation and authorship rights, and third-party licensing. The USPS agreed to publicize artists' and designers' names in press releases, program yearbooks, USA Philatelic catalogs and newsletters, and stamp sheets (depending on subject matter), but it did not agree to change its work-for-hire practices.

United Nations stamp program

The United Nations (UN) maintains a stamp program through the United Nations Postal Administration (UNPA). Fees average $2,000 for a single image and $1,000 each for multiple images, with a maximum fee of $12,000 for a series. The UN usually retains the copyright, but the artwork belongs to the artist. The UN seeks out artists from around the world to maintain a global profile.

Foreign stamp programs

EUROPEAN

European stamp programs pay up to $6,000 per stamp image. Each country offers slightly different rights belonging to the artist, but the contracts are unfortunately quite similar to those used in the United States. Some European countries—Great Britain, for example—require stamp illustrators to be citizens of the country for which the stamp will be produced.

SMALL COUNTRY

Small countries that have stamp programs presently pay a rate for a stamp image that is far below any reasonable fee for artists working in the U.S. economy. Fees usually include full copyright to the work, original art, design, and all camera-ready art with typesetting.

INTERGOVERNMENTAL PHILATELIC CORP.

Some foreign stamps are commissioned through Intergovernmental Philatelic Corporation (IGPC), which has about 70 client nations. Although IGPC paid $400–500 per image years ago, now they mostly create images digitally "in house." When IGPC does commission outside illustrators/designers, it pays approximately $40 per stamp image. For this absurdly low compensation, IGPC expects a production-ready disk, along with type layout, etc. The only way an artist can work profitably within this pricing structure is by "manufacturing" an enormous volume of product in record time.

See Figure 10-16 for Postage Stamp Illustration Fees.

Fantastic Art

Although all illustration is imaginative, much of it, inspired by everyday experience and culture, reflects the real world. Illustrators who specialize in fantastic art help us view the world in an extraordinarily different way—they create the unimaginable, the unknown, and the futuristic. Creators of fantasy, science fiction, space fantasy, horror, the grotesque, and the surreal produce images that amaze, delight, enchant, enthrall, and sometimes scare us. Traditionally, fantastic art has been largely confined to illustration and painting. Today, it is commonly found in films, TV programs, comic books and graphic novels, children's literature, video games, and collectible card games, but it

Comparative Fees for Postage Stamp Illustration

Original Art

	UNITED STATES*	UNITED NATIONS*	EUROPEAN**
Per image	$5,000	$2,000	$6,000

Additional Fees

Signing limited numbers of stamps	$1-4 per signature
Sketch fee (U.S.)	$1,500

* Includes original art.

** Usually a set of 4 stamps. $6,000 per stamp, $3,000 per comp. Fee includes original artwork, all original sketches, and comps.

NOTE: No new data was available when this handbook went to press. The data in Figure 10-16 is reprinted from the 12th edition (2007). The price ranges do not constitute specific prices for particular jobs. The buyer and seller are free to negotiate, with each artist independently deciding how to price the work, after taking all factors into account.

FIGURE 10—16

may also be used for editorial and advertising purposes for a variety of media and products. The genre includes elements of magic, mysticism, the occult, and supernatural forces. Stories are often set in exotic and alien fantasy worlds or based on tales from mythology and folklore.

Fantastic art is generally priced according to the market for which it is commissioned, such as children's book illustration, comic book art, video game art, etc. Some illustrators working in this genre also sell their originals as fine art and limited edition prints of the originals to collectors. They promote and market their art online via personal web sites and blogs and social networking sites, as well as at comic and science fiction conventions. An annual juried art contest devoted to fantastic art is sponsored by and published as *Spectrum: The Best in Contemporary Fantastic Art*.

★　　★　　★

Cartooning Prices & Trade Customs

This chapter discusses the many markets available for both staff and freelance cartoonists. While the market is highly competitive, especially for newspaper syndication, new opportunities are opening up in electronic publishing, alternative comic books, and graphic novels.

CARTOONISTS

create single- or multi-panel cartoons, comic strips, comic books, or book-length graphic novels and may specialize in types of cartoons that range from a gag (a visual joke with the punch line in the caption) to editorial, political, or adult subject matter, among other topics. Cartoons appear to be easy to create because they are relatively simple in style, but in fact creating cartoons is a highly demanding specialization that usually requires a long apprenticeship.

Most cartoonists are freelancers, though some work as staff cartoonists at newspapers. Cartoons are used by magazines; web sites; advertising agencies; greeting card publishers; television, animation, and motion picture studios; and commercial art studios. Cartoons are also sought by editors and art directors to enhance textbooks, training materials, in-house publications, novelty items, and posters. Although the field has historically been dominated by men, the number of published works by women is on the rise.

Magazine Cartooning

The magazine cartoon is probably the most popular of the graphic arts; media surveys invariably place cartoons among readers' first preferences. Magazine or gag cartoons are created by freelance cartoonists who usually conceive the idea, draw the cartoon, and then offer it for sale to appropriate magazines. Magazine cartoonists bring a unique blend of writing and drawing skills to every piece. A magazine cartoon must be staged as graphic theater that instantly communicates a situation and characters. A good cartoon says it faster and with more impact than a paragraph of descriptive words and, most importantly, makes you laugh.

Pricing

The pricing of freestanding magazine cartoons is different from that of other forms of illustration. Cartoons are purchased as a complete editorial element, similar to a freelance feature article, at fixed rates determined by each publication. It should also be noted that it is often an editor, rather than an art director, who is responsible for selecting or assigning cartoons. A handful of magazines (such as *The New Yorker*) give additional compensation to those cartoonist contributors who are closely identified with that particular magazine. In those instances, the cartoonist may have a contract providing an annual signature fee, bonuses, and, in a few cases, fringe benefits in return for first look at the cartoons. (When a cartoonist works with a writer, often called a "gagman," the writer gets 25 percent of the fee paid by the publication. Future payments for re-use of cartoons are usually worked out between the writer and artist, especially if they work together regularly.)

Among the factors affecting prices for magazine cartoons are whether the cartoon is black and white or color; the size of reproduction; the magazine's geographical distribution, circulation, impact, and influence; the importance of cartoons as a regular editorial element; the extent of the rights being purchased; and the national reputation of the cartoonist. Since the list is composed of objective and subjective factors and the mix in each case is different, rates vary considerably. Because many cartoonists and humorous illustrators work in overlapping markets, readers should also refer to Chapter 10, Illustration Prices & Trade Customs, for related topics.

Representative fees for original cartoons are listed by publication in Figure 11-1. The fees are meant as points of reference only and do not necessarily reflect such important factors as deadlines, job complexity, the reputation and experience of a particular cartoonist, research, technique, the unique quality of expression, and extraordinary or extensive use of the finished cartoon. The buyer and seller are free to negotiate, taking into account all the factors involved. Representative fees for specific categories of cartoons were collected from the responses of established professionals who have worked for the publications, directly from the publications themselves, or from current resource directories such as *The Artists' and Graphic Designers' Market*. See Chapter 15, Resources & References, for more information.

Representative Fees for Original Cartoons

	B&W	COLOR
AIR & SPACE	$300	
BARRON'S	$375	
BUSINESS LAW TODAY	$200	
FIRST FOR WOMEN	$150	
GOOD HOUSEKEEPING	$300	
HARVARD BUSINESS REVIEW	$700	$800
MEDICAL ECONOMICS	$115	
NATIONAL LAW JOURNAL	$150	
THE NEW YORKER	$675	
PLAYBOY	$400	$450
READER'S DIGEST	$650	$650
SATURDAY EVENING POST	$125	
WALL STREET JOURNAL	$150	
WOMAN'S WORLD	$125	

	SPOT	FULL PAGE
EASY RIDER	$40	$200

FIGURE 11—1

Submitting art

Unless a cartoonist is under contract to a magazine, art submission is normally done on a speculative basis, which means the artist assumes all risks with no promise of payment unless the work is bought. It is important to have an organized plan. Artists should review cartoons found in their targeted publications and submit work that reflects that style. It is helpful to check first with a magazine to find out if it is still looking at unsolicited material.

Most publications will send a copy of their submission guidelines if they receive a self-addressed stamped envelope, while others may charge a small fee. Following are general guidelines for submissions:

• Send between 10 and 20 single- or multi-panel cartoons to a magazine at one time. Each cartoon should fill the center of an 8 1/2 x 11-inch sheet.

- Send good-quality photocopies. Do not send originals!
- Never send the same cartoon to more than one U.S. publisher at a time. Multiple submissions, however, are acceptable to many European and other overseas publishers.
- Label the back of each cartoon with your name, address, phone number/fax, and e-mail address. For personal inventory control, discreetly number each piece.
- To have cartoons returned, include a self-addressed stamped envelope.
- Keep good records about what was sent to whom, and when. See the Appendix for a sample artwork inventory form.

Trade practices

In the ideal relationship between cartoon buyer and seller, the following trade practices would be accepted as standard. Unfortunately, in actuality, many transactions do not go smoothly, and the artist must be prepared to adapt when problems arise. It is up to artists to behave in their best self-interest and even be prepared to lose a sale if conditions do not meet their expectations.

1. Payment is due upon acceptance of the work, net 30 days; never on publication.
2. Artists normally sell only first reproduction rights unless otherwise stated.
3. Under copyright law, cartoonists retain copyright ownership of all work they create. Copyright can be transferred only in writing.
4. Purchasers should make selections promptly (within two to four weeks) and promptly return cartoons not purchased.
5. Return of original artwork to the artist is expected unless otherwise negotiated.
6. The Graphic Artists Guild is unalterably opposed to the use of work-for-hire contracts, in which authorship and all rights that go with it are transferred to the commissioning party and the independent artist is treated as an employee for copyright purposes only. The independent artist receives no employee benefits and loses the right to claim authorship or to profit from future use of the work forever. In any situation, cartoons created by the initiative of the artist are ineligible to be work-for-hire.
7. The terms of sale should be specified in writing in a contract or on the invoice.

Editorial Cartooning

Editorial cartoonists are traditionally salaried staff artists on individual daily newspapers, which provide a base for further syndication. Salaries vary greatly with the circulation and status of the paper and the reputation and experience of the cartoonist. Three factors combine to make editorial cartooning probably the most competitive subspecialty in all cartooning: (1) the number of newspapers, especially major dailies, is shrinking; (2) there are ever-increasing budget constraints at the remaining papers; and (3) syndicated editorial cartoons, even those of very high quality (sometimes Pulitzer Prize-winning quality), have been priced as a cheap commodity by cartoon syndicates for many years, making it the de facto standard.

Some editorial cartoonists are syndicated nationally while on staff with a base paper. Usually the papers require that they produce two locally oriented cartoons per week, while the syndicates want at least three cartoons a week relating to national issues. As with comic strips, the earnings received by editorial cartoonists from syndication depend on the terms of their particular contracts and the number and size of the newspapers buying their work (see the Newspaper Syndication section below).

Although editorial cartoonists are generally paid less than illustrators in other markets, the job is salaried and provides both fringe benefits and more stability than freelancing. Some editorial cartoonists can compensate for the disparity in income by selling reprints. Other advantages afforded editorial cartoonists are that they often have significant creative freedom, exposure, and name recognition by being published in a widely circulated newspaper.

Sometimes freelance cartoonists sell their work to major, daily newspaper op-ed pages or to weekly newsmagazines. Rates vary, but they are generally based on the placement (leisure or advertising section) of the work, the column width of the piece, whether the drawing is an original or a reprint, and the reputation of the artist. Well-known artists generally are sought for large commissions such as covers. Freelance editorial cartoonists without national recognition are rarely even considered. Artists should check with individual papers regarding their interest in freelance contributions before sending work.

Newspaper Syndication

Many freelance cartoonists develop comic strips, panels, or editorial cartoons for major national and international syndicates that edit, print, package, market, and distribute them to newspapers throughout the world. Since the number of newspapers using syndicated material is limited, the field is highly competitive. Few new strips are introduced in any given year by the major syndicates (perhaps only one or two per syndicate), and sales of these new features are usually limited to the somewhat rare instance of an existing feature being dropped. The more numerous smaller syndicates typically offer better contract terms but provide fewer services and much less sales support. The last alternative, self-syndication, can be difficult because newspapers prefer to buy comics from dependable syndicates that screen and manage the artists. Secondary markets such as weekly newspapers are less dependent on the major syndicates and more agreeable to working with self-syndicated cartoonists. Because of the intense competition to become syndicated, it is very tempting for cartoonists whose strips or panels are accepted by a major syndicate to sign the first contract offered. As always, the cartoonist should carefully consider the terms of the agreement before signing and use the services of a syndication lawyer when negotiating.

Submissions

Most syndicates have very specific guidelines for submissions, which vary by syndicate. Syndicate submission guidelines are available on the company's web site or may be obtained by sending a request with a self-addressed stamped envelope. The following are generally accepted guidelines for syndicate submissions, but artists should check the individual syndicate's requirements before submitting:

- Most major syndicates prefer that submissions be mailed, but some now allow online submissions as well.
- Submissions usually include a presentation kit comprised of a "character sheet" (drawings of all characters, their names, and perhaps a descriptive paragraph) and a minimum of 24 daily strips and 2 Sunday strips.
- It is customary practice to send the same strip submission package to all syndicates simultaneously. Acceptance by more than one may add to the artist's negotiation leverage.

Trade practices

When a cartoonist sells a strip, it is tempting to sign the first contract offered. However, cartoonists owe it to themselves to prepare to negotiate contracts as well as they can and to understand all terms thoroughly. (A free, in-depth analysis of syndicate contracts and the syndication business is available at www.stus.com/thesis.htm.) There is no substitute for knowledgeable legal counsel in contract negotiations. A syndication lawyer with expertise in cartooning, visual arts, copyright, and/or literary property contracts is recommended.

Foremost among the terms that are changing in the field are the monetary split between the syndicate and the artist, ownership of the feature, and the length of the contract. The split for newly syndicated cartoonists is still fixed at the customary 50/50, but it is more common for artists renewing their contracts to achieve a better split, such as 60/40 or even higher. A few artists are winning a percentage of gross rather than net receipts.

Syndicates in the past have demanded copyright ownership of the feature, and a few still begin negotiations by requesting it. However, artists benefit so much more economically and artistically from retaining ownership that over the last decade it has become standard for artists to win this point in negotiations. Artists must be alert to the many contract terms syndicates promote to undercut the value of the artists' copyright. For example, most syndicates demand a right of first refusal for renewals, and some major syndicates even require that they be paid their income split for some period of time after termination of the contract.

Contracts for newly syndicated artists that formerly ran for 20-year terms are being negotiated with much shorter renewal dates that are based on the syndicate achieving satisfactory sales of the feature. The flexibility created by ownership of the feature and periodic renegotiations benefit the cartoonist, whose bargaining leverage may increase considerably over the contract period if the work is successful and who may therefore be able to negotiate better terms upon renewal. Depending on the other contract terms and the attitude of the syndicate (which varies considerably), the initial contract term, plus a fairly easy-to-achieve renewal, can be expected to last for a combined 10 to 15 years (3,650 to 5,475 cartoons). Under these circumstances, artists should not sign syndicate contracts unless the terms are acceptable for the long-term.

A number of well-known cartoonists have negotiated or renegotiated contracts with major syndicates on terms more favorable to the artist, such as shorter contracts, better income splits, guaranteed minimums, signing bonuses, and the right of the cartoonist to own and manage their potentially lucrative licensing rights. Cartoonists who are offered a syndicate contract should keep these terms in mind.

Syndicated cartoonists' earnings are based on the number of newspapers who carry their strips or panels and the circulation levels of these papers. This does not mean, however, that syndicates use standardized contracts. Syndicate contracts are complicated and vary considerably among the major firms. The capabilities of the syndicates' sales forces and licensing departments also vary.

Other negotiated terms include the syndicate's and artist's respective roles in securing merchandising and licensing contracts (with the best solution being that the syndicate has the limited right to sell the strip only to newspapers and periodicals, with the artist retaining all other rights); the artist's share of merchandising and licensing revenues should they be entered jointly; assurance of quality control over products and derivative versions of the feature (such as an animated version); the editorial role of the syndicate; what expenses the syndicate may legitimately deduct before the income split; and the ability to leave an unsatisfactory contractual relationship. All terms of a contract are negotiable.

A situation in which a syndicate offers a contract for a particular strip indicates serious interest. The syndicate should be willing to negotiate, however reluctantly. And if one syndicate recognizes that a strip is marketable, chances are good that other syndicates will too. Therefore it may be worth walking away from an unsatisfactory contract offer to seek another syndicate as your partner. Before negotiating a syndication contract, an artist should do as much research on syndication agreements as possible and/or consult with an attorney who is knowledgeable about their conventions and the current market.

Progressive changes in syndicated contract terms reflect the decision of individual cartoonists to fight for more control over their creations and the increasing importance of character licensing in today's markets. In their contracts, savvy artists stipulate that the syndicate has the right to sell the strip only to newspapers and periodicals, with the artist retaining all other rights, including book rights. Cartoonists who negotiate effectively can benefit from their cartoon's success in the marketplace and can establish the potential for an ongoing stream of revenue in the future.

Syndicated cartoonists typically earn between $20,000 and $150,000 per year, depending on the number of newspapers that subscribe to the strip and the number of products that are made from the licensing of characters. Of course, a handful of superstar cartoonists can make hundreds of thousands and even millions of dollars each year. Aspiring cartoonists should also recognize that more than 50 percent and as high as 70 percent of newly launched syndicated cartoons fail and are canceled within the first five years, resulting in very little income for the artist.

A list of syndicates is below. For the most current information, visit the web sites of the individual syndicates. Other sources of information include the Syndicate World column in *Editor & Publisher* (www.editorandpublisher.com) and local libraries.

North American comic syndicates

MAJOR SYNDICATES

Creators Syndicate, Inc.
Editorial Review Board—Comics
5777 West Century Blvd., Suite 700
Los Angeles, CA 90045
310-337-7003 | www.creators.com
Home to *Heathcliff, Speed Bump,* and *Momma*

King Features Syndicate, Inc.
(North America Syndicate, Cowles Syndicate)
Attn: Editor-in-Chief
300 West 57th St., 15th Fl.
New York, NY 10019
212-969-7550 | www.kingfeatures.com
Home to *Bizarro* and *Zits*

Tribune Media Services, Inc.
435 N. Michigan Ave., Suite 1400
Chicago, IL 60611
312-222-2725 | www.tms.tribune.com
tmssubmissions@tribune.com
Home to *Pluggers* and *Dick Tracy*

United Media (United Feature Syndicate & Newspaper Enterprise Association)
200 Madison Ave., 4th Fl.
New York, NY 10016
212-293-8500 | www.unitedmedia.com
Home to *Pearls Before Swine, Get Fuzzy,* and *Dilbert*

Universal Press Syndicate
Attn: John Glynn, Acquisitions Editor
1130 Walnut St.
Kansas City, MO 64106 | 816-581-7300
upssubmissions@amuniversal.com
Home to *Garfield, Non Sequiter,* and *Doonesbury*

Washington Post Writers Group
Attn: Comics Editor
1150 15th St., NW, 4th Fl.
Washington, DC 20071-9200
(800) 879-9794 ext. 2 | 202-334-6375
cartoonsubmission@washpost.com
www.postwritersgroup.com/comicsubmiss ionguide.html
Home to *Pickles* and *Candorville*

SMALLER SYNDICATES

Cartoonists & Writers Syndicate/
Cartoon Arts International (CAI)
67 Riverside Dr., Suite 1D
New York, NY 10024
212-227-8666 | 212-595-4218 (fax)
CWStoons@aol.com

Copley News Service
(see Creators Syndicate, Inc. above)

Online Cartoon Sales

Online syndication of print cartoons, as well as syndication of cartoons that appear exclusively online, is a rapidly expanding market for cartoon material. Cartoons are now often offered as content on advertising-supported web sites, or as opt-in syndicated content from search engines and content portals. Innovations such as animated and interactive editorial cartoons have also been introduced. While the market develops, there is real income potential here, and one encouraging trend is the development of online sites, such as goats (www.goats.com), Uclick (www.uclick.com), and Cartoon Resource (www.cartoonresource.com), to name a few, that sell to a variety of markets and/or hire cartoonists.

Many online purchasers of cartoon rights offer very different business terms in their contracts than traditional print syndicates do. Artists should consider very carefully the specific rights they grant and how those rights are likely to be used in the electronic world. Like many publishers today, syndicates are attempting to retain exclusive electronic publication rights, and artists should consider this carefully when granting rights and negotiating fees. For more information on copyright and the Internet, see Chapter 2, Legal Rights & Issues, and Chapter 4, Technology Issues.

Webcomics

Self-syndication online is fast becoming a legitimate way to market a comic strip or graphic feature. Several comic strips have created financially sustainable web sites by utilizing a free content model which is then subsidized through the selling of advertising, books, and other merchandising. In addition, whereas mainstream print syndication has editorial control of content, the Web allows for unlimited creative freedom and the ability to easily reach both broad and niche audiences.

Successful webcomics include *Penny Arcade* (www.penny-arcade.com/), *Schlock Mercenary* (www.schlockmercenary.com/), *PvP* (www.pvponline.com/), and *Achewood* (http://achewood.com/).

Comic Books

In 2005 and 2006, the sale of comic books experienced a dramatic turnaround from the long slump that began in the mid-1990s. The overall comics market (which includes comic books, trade paperbacks, graphic novels, and magazines) finished 2005 with a 7.3% sales increase over 2004. Comic-book orders in the direct market in May 2006 were higher than they had been in nearly a decade, according to *Comics Buyer's Guide*. Sales continued to climb through 2008. In 2009, during the recession in the general economy, sales were $429.47 million, a 2% decrease from 2008, yet still 30% higher than they were five years earlier. Revenue would have been lower if cover prices had not increased to the highest they've been in the 75-year history of comic books.

Licensing prospects in TV, movies, video games, toys, and consumer products have emerged as the driving factors in determining if a comic book series will be continued. Sales rates that would have seemed low or of marginal profitability in the past are accepted today because of fear that discontinuation would affect licensing possibilities. For further information, see the Licensing and Merchandising section later in this chapter and the Maximizing Income section of Chapter 5, Essential Business Practices.

Comic books, which are cinematic in style, lend themselves to film adaptation and have become a popular source of movie concepts. Writers conceive a story and develop a script or plot, often indicating specific views of the action to be portrayed. Some companies use a style in which scene descriptions and full dialogue are given just like in a screenplay. Others do not indicate panel breaks or even specify the number of panels and may or may not indicate page breaks, giving the artist much more freedom in which to make a graphic statement.

Each monthly comic book (averaging 22 pages of story, with another ten pages of ads and letters) is produced in 28 days to meet distribution deadlines. (Some contracts used in the industry may contain a clause that penalizes the artist if deadlines are missed.) Such high-pressure working conditions mean that comic books are mass-produced in assembly-line fashion. Publishers divide production among people with special skills who complete a specific component in the process and then pass the work on to the next stage of production.

Artistic specialties and job roles

Specialists in comic books generally include writers, pencil artists (pencilers), lettering artists (letterers), ink artists (inkers), and coloring artists (colorists). The editor generally assumes a tracking role, guiding the work along the path from freelancer to freelancer, to meet the company's deadlines and, on rare occasions, also serving as art director. The trend in at least the last decade shows an increasing number of comic book artists who write, draw, and ink their own stories, but even for such specialists, the rigors of the four-week deadline require severe discipline.

When comic books are created traditionally, pencilers lay out the action from the typewritten script and finish the art on bristol board. The penciled board is passed on to the letterer, who letters the balloon text in ink and inks the balloon and panel borders. Next, the board goes to the inker, who inks the figures and backgrounds on each panel. (Background artists, if used, are usually subcontractors, assistants, or interns.) After the boards are reduced to 6 x 9-inch or 8.5 x 11-inch Strathmore paper, they are passed on to the colorist, who hand-colors and color-codes the photocopies of all 22 pages of the book. The boards and coded reductions are then sent to the separator, and finally the colored photocopies are sent to the printer for manufacture.

Digital technology has changed much of this process. Today, lettering is done exclusively on the computer, using font programs capable of approximating a letterer's handwriting. Both Marvel and DC Comics now have in-house lettering departments. A fairly recent trade practice, which is becoming more widespread, is inking pages on a blueline print. The pencilers scan their pencil drawings and transmit them digitally to the inker who then prints them out onto a sheet of bristol board to ink. Once the inking is done, the inker scans the finished page and transmits them digitally to the publisher, whether the inks are on blueline printout or over the original pencils. Like lettering, coloring is also done exclusively on the computer. Color artists are still needed to do the computer coloring, but due to the necessary learning curve and the cost of the equipment, a more sizable initial investment is needed to become a colorist than in the past. Colorists submit their work on disk, which is then "edited" at the publishing company before being sent to a separator for creation of the final film.

Pricing

Freelance artists working in this industry are expected to meet minimum production quotas. They report being paid a page rate set by the publisher for each page completed. Page rates vary according to specialization. Contract artists at many companies still enjoy all the benefits of being salaried employees, including medical and dental insurance.

Since comic books are paid on the piecework system, the faster an artist works, the more he or she will earn, although, in order to meet production deadlines, artists are expected to complete a minimum number of pages in each production cycle. Letterers, for example, are expected to complete at least 66 pages over three weeks but strive to complete ten pages per day, five days a week. Many artists must work ten hours a day, six days a week, to make a living wage. Comic book publishers generally pay artists a lower page rate for reprinting an original publication.

As in other genres, the more popular an artist or writer, the higher the company's projected sales. Therefore all aspects of compensation, including royalties, are open to negotiation.

If a comic book's net domestic sales exceed 75,000 copies, a royalty on the excess is usually paid to the writer, penciler (or other layout artist), and inker. However, few titles actually earn royalties. In the last decade, it's been a general practice to give royalties only to the top ten selling comic books. If royalties are paid, they are usually graduated according to the degree of creative input and the number of units sold, but generally range from 2 to 5 percent of the cover price. Artists who perform more than one function receive a higher royalty; if several creators are involved in a project, they all share the royalties.

Freelance agreements with the major comic book publishers provide for the return of original art. The artist(s) may assign, sell, or transfer ownership only of the physical original. Since several artists work on a given piece, ownership of the original art must be negotiated; normally only the penciler and inker receive original artwork, though a hand-painted piece is given to the colorist. In the traditional process, the penciler receives two-thirds of the originals, and the inker receives one-third. When the pages have been inked on blueline, the penciler retains the pencil drawings, and the inker keeps the inked pages. The artists, however, do not retain any of the copyrights to the work, as the contracts usually contain a work-for-hire clause, which transfers legal authorship and all rights to the publisher. For more information about work for hire, see Chapter 2, Legal Rights & Issues.

Figure 11-2 lists page rates for comic book art by type of skill. The price ranges in the chart do not reflect any of the above considerations and do not constitute specific prices for particular jobs. The buyer and seller are free to negotiate, with each artist independently deciding how to price the work, after taking all factors into account.

Alternative comic books

Alternative comics, while not new, became very popular in the late 1990s and have led to a burgeoning interest in longer comic stories, including book-length graphic novels (see later in this chapter). Alternative comics promote the comic-book medium as an art form for creative expression rather than as an assembly-line business. The result has been a form of comic books more highly regarded as an adult form of literature. With editors and art directors counted as fans, small-press or self-published creators of comic books have found inroads into commercial and editorial illustration.

Unlike other cartooning markets, the alternative comic book market is not dominated by work-for-hire contracts. Usually, the artist also writes the stories and frequently acts as the publisher and distributor. Or, creator-owned art may be done speculatively and submitted to publishers on a freelance basis similar to the way gag cartoons are. Often, these stories are bought by small presses at a low page rate, such as $50 a page. In some cases, they may be contributed to smaller presses that cannot afford to pay but give artists the opportunity to have their work in print and circulation. For artists who feel strongly about their work, the major advantage of working this way is the ability to maintain full control of the content and the copyrights.

Trade practices

The following trade practices for comic book art have been used historically and thus are accepted as standard.

1. The intended use of the art must be stated clearly in a contract, purchase order, or letter of agreement stating the price and terms of sale.

Comparative Page Rates for Comic Book Art

ORIGINAL PUBLICATION*

WRITING (PLOT & SCRIPT)	$75–120
PAINTED ART	$200–750
PENCIL ART	$100–400
INK ART	$75–300
LETTERING**	$40–50
COLORING ART**	$100–150

* Cover Art: fees vary widely. 20–50 percent is generally added to the fee for cover art use. Some artists receive a flat rate for cover art.

** Lettering and coloring art are done exclusively on the computer.

FIGURE 11—2

2. Artists normally sell first North American reproduction rights only unless otherwise stated. Ancillary rights (TV, movie, foreign distribution, paper or hardback printing, or character licensing) are negotiable and are often shared by the publisher and the artist for a fixed period of up to five years, at which time full rights revert to the artist. (It is wise for creators of alternative comics to retain ancillary rights, especially for TV and movies, since there is a growing interest in these rights.)

3. If the artwork is to be used for other than its original purpose, the price for that usage should be negotiated as soon as possible. The secondary use of the art may be of greater value than the primary use. Although there is no set formula for reuse fees, current surveys indicate that artists add a reuse fee in the range of 25 to 75 percent of the fee that would have been charged had the art been originally commissioned for the anticipated usage. Artists should negotiate reuse arrangements with the original commissioning party with speed, efficiency, and respect for the client's position.

4. Deadlines for delivery of finished art and rough sketches should be outlined in the contract. The clause should also specify what payments are due to the artist in the event the project is canceled or rejected. For negotiable fee suggestions, see the sections describing cancellation ("kill") and rejection fees in Chapter 3, Professional Issues.

5. The artist guarantees that the art is original and does not infringe on the copyrights of others and that the artist has the authority to grant rights to the publisher.

6. An artist can request to be indemnified by the publisher for any suits arising from the use of the art by the publisher that might infringe on the rights of others and also against any suits arising from a request on the publisher's part, such as making a character look like a famous person or existing image.

7. In the case of creator-owned art (versus work-for-hire), the publisher agrees to copyright the work in the artist's name.

8. For non-work-for-hire contracts, revisions without the artist's consent are unacceptable; artists should be consulted to protect the integrity of their work.

9. Fees should be established to be paid to the artist in the event artwork is lost or damaged due to the publisher's negligence.

10. The publisher agrees to publish the book within a specific period of time, and upon failure to do so, the rights revert back to the artist (sometimes called reversion rights).

11. Royalties are graduated according to the degree of creative input and the units sold, but they generally range from 2 to 5 percent of the cover price. Royalties are paid quarterly or semi-annually, at which time the artist receives a statement of sales.

12. Return of original artwork to the artist is automatic unless otherwise negotiated. The artwork is often divided between the artists working on the project (primarily the penciler and inker). Most artists view original artwork as a subsidiary income, selling it either directly to collectors or through an agent.

13. Publishers usually provide the artist with 10 free copies of the book, but 20 to 50 copies are often negotiated. Most publishers offer the artist a 40 to 50 percent discount off the list price on purchases of the book.

14. Artists considering working on speculation often assume all risks and should take these into consideration when offered such arrangements; for details, see the Speculation section in Chapter 3, Professional Issues.

15. Although work-for-hire contracts dominate most areas of this field (except for alternative comics), the Graphic Artists Guild is unalterably opposed to their use because authorship and all rights that go with it are transferred to the commissioning party and the independent artist is treated as an employee for copyright purposes only. The independent artist receives no employee benefits and loses the right to claim authorship or to profit from future use of the work forever. Furthermore, comic books are not eligible to be work-for-hire, as they do not fall under any of the eligible categories defined in copyright law. Additional information on work-for-hire can be found in Chapter 2, Legal Rights & Issues.

Book-Length Formats

Several different types of comic-strip products in book-length form are found on the market.

Cartoon and comic collections

The traditional book format for cartoons or comic strips is the collection or anthology, in which cartoons that were originally published in newspapers or magazines are collected into a single volume.

Similarly, comic books are often reprinted as a collection of stories in book format. In the comics industry, they are referred to as *trade paperbacks,* but they may have either a soft or hard cover. Trade paperbacks feature either one story arc from a single title or a common theme or story arc connecting stories from several titles. The collection often includes additional art, such as alternate cover art, that did not appear in the original serialized comic books.

For reprints in book format, major comic book publishers pay artists a rate equal to either one half of the original page rate or a royalty based on the type of original work performed. The royalty is divided among the contributing artists and pro-rated by the portion of original art an artist did. For example, if the book has 100 pages and the royalty rate is 1%, an artist who created 10 of those 100 pages will receive a royalty of .10%.

Graphic novels

A graphic novel (GN) is a book-length narrative in comic strip form, published as a book. GNs are published as trade paperbacks or hard covers by comics publishers and, increasingly, by mainstream publishing houses. The term "graphic novel" is evolving and generally refers to either a collection of stories initially published serially in comic books or an original, long-form narrative. The term is frequently used to differentiate works from comic books designed for children or juveniles and to imply that the work is of a more serious, literary nature.

In the publishing trade, the term graphic novel is sometimes extended to material that would not be considered a novel if produced in another medium. Collections of comic strips that do not form a continuous story, anthologies, collections of loosely related pieces, and even non-fiction comics are categorized by libraries and bookstores as "graphic novels" (similar to the manner in which dramatic stories are included in "comic" books).

A comic created and published as a single narrative without prior appearance in a magazine, comic book, or newspaper is sometimes identified as an original graphic novel (OGN).

Overall sales of graphic novels in the U.S. and Canada in 2008 were $395 million. The largest segment of the GN market ($175 million) is the graphic novel's Japanese cousin, *manga*. Outside of Japan, manga refers to comics originally published in Japan or works derivative of their artistic style. Literally translated as "whimsical pictures," manga has a long tradition dating back to the late 1800s and today represents a multi-billion-dollar global market. Wildly popular in Japan, manga encompasses a very diverse range of subjects and themes for readers of all ages and interests. Popular manga, aimed at mainstream readers, frequently involves science fiction, action, fantasy, and comedy. According to Time.com, manga is credited with expanding the traditionally male-dominated American comics market: 60% of all manga readers in the U.S. are female. This trend has caused major publishing houses to eagerly embrace the genre.

France and Belgium also have a long tradition in comics and comic books. Known by the French term, *bande dessinée* (literally "drawn strip"), Franco-Belgian comics are often viewed in the U.S. as equivalent to graphic novels, due to their more serious subject matter. However, they may be long or short, bound, or in magazine format.

Pricing and trade practices

In the case of cartoon collections and graphic novels, book contracts vary widely—by publisher, genre, success of author, and individual book—so it is advisable to consult a qualified literary agent or lawyer.

TRADITIONAL BOOK PUBLISHERS

Contracts for graphic novels published by major book publishers are structured like other book deals: the contract specifies an advance and a royalty percentage. Once the royalties have paid back the advance, then the artist starts receiving the royalties. Advances can be as low as $5,000 and as high as $40,000; royalties range from 3% to 10%, sometimes with escalators up to 15%. An illustrator who is also the author receives a higher royalty than an artist who does only the illustration. Higher royalties are given for hardcover books than for paperbacks. A first-time cartoonist-author cannot expect a very high advance. Very successful graphic novelists such as Chris Ware (*Jimmy Corrigan: Smartest Kid on Earth*) are able to negotiate higher rates.

COMIC BOOK COMPANIES

Rates for graphic novels published by comic book companies are determined by either the page or the book (with covers sometimes negotiated separately). Arrangements vary by publisher, and royalties vary by book contract, even within the same publisher. Generally, royalties tend to be much lower than those paid by traditional book publishers.

To show the diversity of contract arrangements within the industry, the following is an example of the experiences of one graphic novelist. At one comic-book company, the artist/writer receives an amount equal to the total net profit, minus 15%, and a fee off the top of $2,000. Working on an original graphic novel for another comic book company, the same artist is paid a page rate of $350 for pencils and inks and a royalty to be split 50/50 with the author. The royalty rate starts at .8% for the first 100,000 copies and escalates to .9% for up to 250,000 copies and 1% above 250,000 copies. The artist does not receive royalties until *after* the publisher has recouped all costs.

At the latter company, copyrights are retained by the creator, but the publisher has most if not all media rights. On some contracts, the company buys media rights for a separate fee, usually around $7,500 to be split between writer and artist. Depending on the contract, the company may own the trademark as well. The creators of graphic novels, like those of other alternative comics, should retain ancillary rights—TV/movie especially.

When negotiating a GN contract, it is important for the artist to establish expectations up front on such matters as page length, the party responsible for production (scanning, book design, etc.), and the form in which the finished book will be delivered (original art or on disk). More and more publishers look for all aspects of production to be done by the artist. While this arrangement allows the artist to control the end product, it is a huge additional workload, which should be factored into the artist's overall fee.

Authors of graphic novels need to follow through on all aspects of publication, such as getting the publisher to show them proofs, and be involved at all levels of promotion to ensure that the book is accurately described. Many big publishers are still new to the idea of comics with adult themes and serious subject matter. Authors can expect that much of the promotion will fall on them, for example, book parties and promotion after publication. Taking on this responsibility can make a big difference in book sales. It is in the creator's best interest to find out who follows foreign and domestic sales and establish relationships with those departments to ensure these aspects of promotion are addressed.

To help maximize sales, it is also worth getting the publisher to assign a specific category to a book-length comic—memoir, politics, fiction, adaptation, etc.—in addition to the general genre of graphic novel. For example, a comic categorized as "autobiography" is more likely to be placed in multiple sections of a bookstore, which is more desirable than simply being relegated to a mixed together graphic novel/manga section.

For further information, refer to the Newspaper Syndication section earlier in this chapter and to the Children's Book Illustration section in Chapter 10, Illustration Prices & Trade Customs.

Reuse

Although revenues from advertising and subscriptions have increased significantly over the last 20 years, magazines have not proportionately increased payments to cartoonists and other artists. To make a viable income, cartoonists try to sell drawings repeatedly to secondary markets for use either in merchandising (T-shirts or coffee mugs) or in books as part of an anthology, textbook, or collection, which in turn will usually generate more reprints. Reuse sales can be made in the United States and worldwide. For further information, see the Maximizing Income section of Chapter 5, Essential Business Practices, as well as Chapter 10, Illustration Prices & Trade Customs, "Additional Fees" charts, for examples of the percentages added for "Stock sales of existing art."

Trade practices

Each publication has its own criteria for establishing a fee for reprints. Obviously, some drawings will generate additional fees, and others will not. Rarely, one will turn out to be immensely popular and more than cover the meager earnings from the others.

Artists should be sure to specify the terms of the sale in a contract or on the invoice. For example, if the work is to appear in traditional print media, such as a textbook, the following should be included:

For one-time, nonexclusive, English language, North American print rights only, in one hardcover edition, to be published by [name of publisher], entitled [title of publication]. All additional requests for usage by your organization or any other publication, except as specified above, are to be referred to [name of artist] to determine the appropriate reprint fee.

Trade practices allow for additional printings of the same edition without additional fees, but any change in the content of a book or in the arrangements of its elements would constitute a new edition that would be considered an additional use. If the publisher wishes to purchase electronic publishing rights, which allow for the easy manipulation and arrangement of materials, the cartoonist should limit the license for use of the work to a specific period of time, such as a year, after which any additional or continued rights would be renegotiated. Of course, no changes should be made to a work without the artist's approval and supervision.

Licensing & Merchandising

According to *Licensing Letter,* entertainment/character licensing and merchandising accounted for almost $10 billion in North American sales in 2008, which accounted for nearly 17 percent of all licensed products that year. When characters such as Dilbert, the Simpsons, Snoopy, or TeleTubbies are licensed for a range of products, from toys and apparel to designer sheets and stationery, their creators can earn considerable additional income if they retain all or a significant percentage of the subsidiary rights in the property. In fact, for a few select properties, income from licensing can earn much more than sales of the original character to newspapers and television broadcasters. For less successful properties, even very limited supplemental income may make the crucial difference in making a project sustainable.

It is sometimes assumed that only nationally known syndicated characters are sought by licensing agents or manufacturers. With the tremendous growth in this area, however, there are now possibilities for cartoonists to develop characters specifically for product use. Cartoonists interested in pursuing this potentially lucrative application of their work should consult an attorney specializing in this field to ensure adequate copyright protection before presenting work to licensers or manufacturers.

Trade shows for character licensing and merchandising are held several times a year around the country. They provide a place for creators, licensors, syndicates, and manufacturers to explore business opportunities. (To obtain a list of shows, see Chapter 15, Resources & References or contact the International Licensing Industry Merchandisers Association at www.licensing.org.) For an extensive discussion of these opportunities, consult the Maximizing Income section of Chapter 5, Essential Business Practices.

Animation Prices & Trade Customs

This chapter discusses the growing number of jobs involving animation. Thanks to the computer, animated special effects are increasingly used in a wide range of applications—everything from TV commercials and video games to biomedical research and simulator rides in theme parks.

CHARACTER

animation as entertainment—such as flip books—started long before motion picture film was produced in the late 19th century. Film animation was introduced in 1900 and was effectively adapted for industrial uses in 1917 and for commercial uses in 1921. It has since been adapted for educational uses as well. In recent years, computers have enabled animation artists, who are skilled at creating the illusion of movement, to create images never before seen outside the imagination.

Today, there is a huge demand for computer animation and effects. Applications for animation span varied fields and interests, such as biomedical research; scientific and educational films; litigation arts (forensic animation); television commercials, titles, and station IDs; feature films; visual effects in motion pictures, interactive games, and mobile devices; CD-ROM books, virtual-reality software; and simulator rides for theme parks; spot sequences created for broadband Internet; and much more. Animated films (*Shrek 2, Ice Age: Dawn of the Dinosaurs,* and *Finding Nemo*) figure prominently in the lists of the top 20 box-office-earning films of all time.

Animation is also in demand as an art form. Independent animated films, in a broad spectrum of styles and with their own markets and distribution channels, are usually shown at film festivals or competitions that showcase the artist's work. Independent filmmakers often create production companies to solicit development funds, which can range from $5,000 to over $100,000.

Animation Today

Traditional animators once worked with line drawings that were inked and then painted onto cels (celluloids, or cellulose acetate sheets) with watercolor or gouache. The process was difficult, time-consuming, and expensive. Often several animators were assigned to specific characters, backgrounds, or other segments of a project. The end result was almost always a team effort by a number of artists, each with his or her own area of expertise. Computer animation has increased the level of sophistication, as in such recent mass-market movie successes as Disney/Pixar's *Cars* and *Up*, DreamWorks' *Shrek* films, and Twentieth Century Fox/Blue Sky Studio's *Ice Age* series. However, traditional hand-drawn 2-D animation endures and continues to delight viewers as evidenced in both films—Cartoon Saloon's *The Secret of Kells* and Disney Animation's *The Princess and the Frog*—and TV shows—Nickelodeon's *Avatar: The Last Airbender* and Cartoon Network's *Chowder.*

To be successful in today's market, an animator must be able to tell a story, have an in-depth understanding of creating lifelike movement, be proficient in traditional and computer animation techniques, and understand filming techniques, including timing, staging, texture mapping, lighting, squashing and stretching, and easing in and out. Animation artists may also work as illustrators, cartoonists, and designers for film. Although occasionally cartoonists or illustrators who supply artwork may want to try animating it, most are satisfied with seeing their drawings animated by someone else.

Many animated features are sold internationally and dubbed in any number of foreign languages. So much of animation is based on action, movement, and physical humor that it works well in many different cultures and can be easily dubbed when necessary. Artists must anticipate international markets for their work and need to pay particular attention to such details as avoiding the use of written words or signs in the background to explain the story. Writers must be aware of slang or colloquial expressions in the dialogue that may be difficult to translate.

Computer Animation

High-quality computer animation formerly required access to sophisticated and expensive equipment, but with recent technological advances, broadcast-quality output (used primarily for TV commercials and video games) is readily available, though by no means inexpensive. Full-feature quality is equally attainable, but it takes more time to render. Graphics software now available off the shelf is designed to run on different platforms, including Windows, Mac OS, and Linux. The software used includes Alias Wavefront and Softimage products. Most large motion picture studios work with Maya from Autodesk. 3-D Studio Max by Autodesk is a very popular 3-D application used in games and films. LightWave is another 3-D application that is used in the industry. Cinema 4-D, Houdini, and Softimage XSI are used extensively in film. There are also open source applications available that have been used to create high-quality films, most prominently the 3-D content creation suite Blender (www.blender.org).

2-D animation

2-D animation created for TV, film, etc., can be hand-drawn in the traditional style, using pen and ink, or created with computer-generated imagery (CGI)—images produced digitally using a software program. However, today even drawings done by hand, as well as the backgrounds, are scanned into a computer program. In 2-D computer animation, characters are created and/or edited using either 2-D bitmap or 2-D vector graphics. 2-D computer animation is used for cartoons and some special effects. 2-D morphing tools allow for the integration of dissimilar imagery into cohesive visuals. Software commonly used for 2-D animation includes Toki Line Test, TVP Animation, Plastic Animation Paper, and Toon Boom Harmony.

Artists who create storyboards (visual presentations using sequential frames) for commercials and movie effects sequences can enhance the impact of their storyboards with programs such as DigiCel's FlipBook, which allows them to create simple movement and effects with still images. A moving storyboard, called an animatic, is a video using camera movements, a select number of drawings, a limited amount of 2-D animation, and a sound track (for a detailed explanation of storyboards and animatics, see the Preproduction Illustration section in Chapter 10, Illustration Prices & Trade Customs). For compositing storyboards into animatics, Adobe After Effects and Toon Boom are used. After Effects also is used heavily to create TV commercials in the motion graphics industry and for corporate sales presentations, as well as for some Web animations and feature films.

2.5-D *animation* is a relatively new term that, among other things, refers to 2-D animation that is created using a computer-based production pipeline with mainly flat 2-D techniques, such as Flash or Toon Boom, to create a 3-D look. The animation is not necessarily drawn.

3-D animation

3-D animation uses modeling and/or digitizing to create objects that not only have shape and dimension but also can be viewed from any angle. Computer-generated imagery is commonly used in 3-D computer graphics when doing special effects. With the help of a complex rendering program, the artist can project the object onto a screen or into a virtual environment. Then 2-D texture maps (a surface pattern like wallpaper) are often applied to the 3-D image to give it a realistic surface.

Architectural animation, called Architectural Previsualization or PreViz, allows artists to create realistic simulations of environments, which clients can "walk through" even though they have not yet been built. An efficient design tool, it helps the architect avoid expensive construction mistakes by making alterations before work begins.

Motion picture computer animation is the highest echelon of the field. Perhaps the most well known of all animation houses today are Industrial Light and Magic (ILM) and Pixar. These studios write a great deal of their own software because so much of what they produce is unprecedented in the industry. See Figure 12-1 for examples of computer animation fees.

Other Forms of Animation

Stop-motion animation, using clay figures (claymation), puppets, and any other 3-D objects can also be used to narrate a story. Puppet animation often requires the artist to create movie sets to scale that depict the story line and can be filmed from many angles. Many 3-D claymation animators have also moved into 3-D computer graphics illustration because of their skill at perceiving movement and form in 3-D space. Aardmann Animation (creators of Wallace and Gromit) in Bristol, UK, and former Vinton Studios, now Laika/house (*Coraline*), in Portland, OR, are the better known practitioners of stop-motion animation techniques.

Careers in Animation

Animation companies are growing, and movie studios and game companies are adding computer animation divisions. As more and more interactive services are put online, there will be an even greater demand for designers, animators, directors, and programmers. Mobile devices, as well as the Internet, have spawned numerous opportunities for Flash-based 2-D projects.

Education and training for a career in animation can be found at universities and colleges, as well as at professional schools. The level of education offered ranges from certificate programs and associate degrees (two to three years) to a Bachelor of Arts Degree in Animation (four years). It also is possible to earn a degree in animation online. Educational preparation includes a combination of academic and hands-on learning experiences in animation drawing and practices, 3-D programming, computer graphics, video effects, and graphic design, as well as courses geared to specific positions on the animation team and to specific industries.

Having a solid background in all types of animation techniques only enhances an artist's chances for employment. Many animation studios prefer to hire artists who have traditional animation and fine artistry skills and the ability to tell a story, in addition to computer training and experience, since the technology changes so quickly. Programmers and technical directors are responsible for the technological aspects. Today's cutting-edge techniques can be outdated almost before a project is completed, so it may sometimes feel that a significant part of a computer animator's job is keeping current with the evolution of animation technology.

Animation artists generally work for studios, but some members of the animators' union, the

Comparative Fees for Computer Animation (Per Completed Second)*

	2-D	FLASH	3-D
ADVERTISING	$300-2,000	$80	$1,000-3,000
ARCHITECTURAL	-	-	$300
BROADCAST	$175-500	$25-40	$1,000-3,000
CORPORATE	$150-2,500	$300	$275-3,000
EDUCATIONAL	$125-1,000	$25	-
INDUSTRIAL	$150-1,000	-	$135-335
LEGAL	$100-500	-	-
MEDICAL/SCIENTIFIC IMAGING	$215-2,500	-	$165-2,000
WEB, LARGE CLIENT	$200-1,000	-	$300-2,000
WEB, SMALL CLIENT	$120-800	$80	$325-1,500

* Some animators charge per completed minute; their pricing has been converted to a per-second figure.

FIGURE 12—1

Motion Picture Screen Cartoonists (MPSC) of the International Alliance of Theatrical Stage Employees (IATSE), work freelance. Various locals of the union are located in different cities; for instance, Los Angeles is home to Local 839, also known as the Animator's Guild (www.animationguild.org). There are also nonunion animation artists, but most artists employed by animation studios are covered by the collective bargaining agreements negotiated by MPSC. Some of the big-name studios with which Local 839 has negotiated contracts include Cartoon Network; DreamWorks, SKG; Fox TV Animation; Nickelodeon Animation Studios; Sony Pictures Animation; Universal Cartoon Studios; Walt Disney Pictures and Television; and Warner Bros. Animation.

The animation team

Almost all animation is created by a team in a studio. The team consists, among others, of the following players:

Producer: Hires the team, locates investors, manages expenses, handles distribution, and is responsible for the overall development of the film.

Writer: Identifies the subject of the film, defines the characters, and develops the story line and dialogue.

Character developer: Makes models based on the designer's concepts (often supplied by an advertising agency when the product is a television commercial).

Visual development artist: Provides early inspirational work to help define the look and style of the film and visualize more complex shots. The artist must be facile in both traditional skills and current software such as Photoshop. Some larger motion picture studios may hire a sculptor to create clay maquettes of characters for visual reference for traditional animators and for digitizing purposes. Many vis-dev artists later move into the art direction/production designer roles.

Art director: Oversees creation of the project's visual style, supervises visual development artists in the preproduction phase, and in consultation with the director, oversees functions from the color-modeling process to color timing the film prints. Some projects hire a separate production design supervisor so the art director can focus on color and lighting.

Storyboard/layout artist: Creates storyboards representing the scope of the film's action, breaking the story down into specific scenes and showing the film's sequential development in proper scale. (In feature animation, the storyboard artist is separate from the layout artist.)

Layout artist: Creates the environment or background layout (exterior and interior spaces) in which animated characters function. The category is divided into three parts: character, clean-up, and background layout.

Background artist/matte painter: Paints/color-styles the background layout. This job is now done both with traditional tools and digitally.

Digital matte painter: Colors visual effects scenery.

Color stylist: Chooses colors for the characters; works in conjunction with the art director and background artist.

Director: Responsible for the overall coordination of all animated characters within a project. All elements must work together, including layouts, storyboards, and voice talent. Although there may be some interaction with the "environment" (background), the director is usually concerned only with the actions of the characters, timing, and supervision of the project.

Animator: Creates "roughs," thumbnail sketches, and models of the characters depicting their range of movement, key poses, expressions, and emotions. The 3-D animator creates the actual motion of the pre-built models, often working with low-resolution proxies of the high-quality models to expedite the production process.

Assistant animator (inbetweener): Prepares drawings to fill the intervals between key poses or frames. Inbetweeners also refine the sketches, clean and tighten lines, and darken shadows.

Junior Animator: The entry-level job in 3-D computer animation (the role of Assistant Animator rarely exists in CGI).

Inker/opaquer: Creates the outline of each character based on a scanned sketch and then paints in the character. (These functions are separated in traditional animation, with the inker outlining a character on an acetate sheet and the opaquer painting in the character on the opposite side.) Almost all of this work is now done on computer, except for some gallery cels created for collectors.

Compositor: Puts together matte paintings, live action, and 3-D renders to craft a visual effects shot. Uses tools such as Autodesk Inferno, Flame, Flint, Toxik, and Combustion; Adobe After Effects; Apple Shake; and some proprietary compositing software in major studios.

Checker: Checks that all the cels, layers, exposure sheets, bar sheets, and backgrounds are executed, marked, and registered prior to filming; checks camera mechanics.

Camera operator/scene planner/film transfer technician: Films the movie. Cinematographers are **commonly used in 3-D productions today.** In motion picture production, a scene planner, formerly a traditional camera operator, digitally refines the more sophisticated camera movements to accent the action. The film transfer technician oversees the transfer of digital images to film stock. (As digital projection technology develops, film transfer may prove to be a transitory role.)

Film editor: Cuts together the pieces of exposed film, matching the images to the sound track. Prepares footage for duplication and printing.

Production Assistant: Responsible for assisting in the smooth running of the production. This position can be found in most all departments of a computer animation studio.

Renderer: A position in 3-D animation, involving the process of converting computer data and outputting it as a sequence of viewable images.

Render wrangler: A quality-control position in the computer graphics field, this person makes sure the animation is rendered correctly. The wrangler is the last person to view the animation before its final output to film or video.

Job Markets & Salaries

The job market for animation is varied, highly competitive, and rapidly growing, with over a quarter of a million artists working in the field.

The U.S. Bureau of Labor Statistics projects an additional 30,000 jobs or a 26% increase in animator employment opportunities by 2016. Aspiring animators must have a good knowledge of the industry in general and, more specifically, the target employer's place within that industry.

According to U.S. Bureau of Labor Statistics for 2008, most multi-media and animator jobs were in the motion picture and video industries. Many large production houses have entry-level positions for production assistants and junior animators, and many of these people later become animators and, eventually, directors. TV commercial work usually lasts a few weeks to a few months, while television series projects can take from several months to three years to produce. Artists working in this area should think about where to line up their next job because layoffs are common when a project ends.

Weekly Salaries of Animation Artists

CLASSIFICATION	JOURNEY MINIMUM	MINIMUM[1] REPORTED	MEDIAN AVERAGE[2]	MAXIMUM REPORTED
STAFF WRITER	$1,535	$1,446	$2,573	$9,600
PRODUCER[3]	$1,765	$2,750	$3,000	$4,000
DIRECTOR, THEATRICAL[3]	-	$2,300	$3,284	$9,600
DIRECTOR, TV/INTERACTIVE	$1,794	$1,600	$2,500	$3,800
SHEET TIMER	$1,442	$1,063	$1,900	$2,369
STORY ARTISTS (Feature)	$1,379	$1,535	$2,500	$3,368
PRODUCTION BOARD (TV, etc.)	$1,765	$857	$1,800	$3,000
CHARACTER LAYOUT	$1,535	$1,144	$1,811	$2,909
BACKGROUND PAINTER	$1,535	$1,200	$1,800	$2,875
ART DIRECTOR	$1,765	$1,200	$2,764	$4,211
VISUAL DEVELOPMENT	$1,535	$1,000	$1,818	$3,000
MODEL DESIGNER	$1,535	$1,150	$1,800	$2,518
COLOR KEY/STYLIST	$1,313	$1,125	$1,550	$2,925
TECHNICAL DIRECTORS	$1,535	$807	$1,790	$2,600
VISUAL EFFECTS	$1,535	$1,110	$2,500	$2,938
COMPOSITOR	$1,373	$1,313	$2,000	$2,925
SUPERVISING ANIMATORS	$1,765	$1,853	$2,182	$3,245
3-D ANIMATORS	$1,535	$948	$1,700	$3,700
3-D MODELERS	$1,535	$1,123	$1,470	$2,947
2-D ANIMATORS	$1,535	$1,150	$2,000	$5,000
EFFECTS ANIMATORS	$1,535	$1,110	$1,640	$3,250
ASSISTANT ANIMATORS	$1,313	$1,264	$1,313	$2,900
FLASH ANIMATION/PROCESSORS	$1,110	$1,078	$1,350	$1,600
ANIMATION CHECKERS	$1,313	$1,313	$1,450	$1,850

Reprinted with permission from the Animation Guild, Local 839, IATSE, Member Salary Survey, March 2009. All salaries are computed on a 40-hour week. The listing of "Journey minimum" shows the union minimums for the various job categories. Figures have been rounded to the nearest dollar.

[1] Many of the minimums listed are for people working at non-union shops or those working at less than journey level.

[2] The median average represents the middle rate when the results were listed in order from lowest to highest. The numbers should be viewed in the context of the minimums and maximums reported.

[3] Not all persons working in this category are under Local 839 jurisdiction; results should be judged accordingly.

FIGURE 12—2

Examples of Unit Journeyman Minimum Weekly Salary Rates*
Writing & Storyboard

TV OR THEATRICAL	SYNOPSIS & OUTLINE	STORYBOARD ONLY	TELEPLAY OR SCREENPLAY
4 TO 7 MINUTES	$869	$1,205	$2,076
OVER 7 TO 15 MINUTES	$877	$1,459	$2,859
30 MINUTES	$1,560	$2,771	$5,480
60 MINUTES OR MORE	$2,321	$4,132	$8,244

* For 8/01/10-7/30/11.

Reprinted from Motion Picture Screen Cartoonists (MPSC), Local 839, IATSE. Figures are rounded to nearest dollar. For further information on the above rates, see Animation TAG Minimums 2009-2012 at www.animationguild.org.

FIGURE 12—3

In showing work, portfolios of storyboards, backgrounds, model sheets, and similar items are useful. Artists seeking entry-level positions should include samples of their basic artistic skills, especially life drawing. Almost every employer has a printed summary of portfolio requirements. It pays for artists to do some research into what kind of images a company has used in the past and then make sure their portfolios reflect both their strengths and the company's focus. To show the true nature of their ability to animate movement, animation artists can often submit samples of their work on a film reel or videocassette.

Computer animation companies look for three types of employees: artists to do animation, visual development, storyboards, design, and the more technical artistic skills, such as modeling and lighting; technical directors/technicians who support the artists by writing code and adjusting CG tools to find technical solutions for what they are trying to achieve; and engineers for technical support and maintenance. Many traditionally trained animators are hired by computer companies to do drawings on paper that are then scanned into the computer. Technical operators and directors take over at this point to complete the project. College graduates with a background in computers who do not draw well often become technical directors. Special skills are needed on almost every computer project, and the average artist rarely possesses the technical background to create new effects and other special elements.

Trained computer animators will find positions with film and video production studios, special effects production houses, television stations, and video game producers. Companies seek artists with experience in ball-and-socket puppets, set and model building (creating highly realistic miniatures used in special effects), armatures, mold making, and costume design for puppets.

Though it may be difficult to win, artists should try to include a clause in their contracts that gives them the right to use their work for self-promotion. It is difficult for an artist to have the time to create a demo reel of his or her most current techniques and accomplishments, so retaining the right to show already produced work can be a tremendous advantage. However, in feature films, competition is very high, and some studios will refuse to look at reels that include scenes from non-released productions. Artists who post a studio's proprietary work on their web sites without prior agreement are asking for trouble.

In the CGI industry, it is common for artists to do additional work on their own time to create demo reels for applying to studios. Web sites, such as The 11 Second Club (www.11secondclub.com), provide a free platform to test and train skills for animation. Similar web sites are devoted to specific skills, such as lighting and rigging.

According to the MPSC, going rates for animation artists have increased dramatically in the past decade. The weekly salary levels in Figure 12-2 were supplied by the Animation Guild, Local 839, IATSE, and represent the anonymous poll of its members taken in March, 2009. Review the Animation Guild web site (www.animationguild.org) for the latest contract provisions and wage scales. By contrast, artists and animators working in the video game industry make considerably less—an average annual salary of $45,985 to $79,221—according to *Game Developer* magazine's Salary Survey conducted in 2008.

More information about salaries, career prospects, and animation companies can be found in *Animation Magazine* (www.animation-magazine.net), on Animation World Network (www.awn.com), and Animation Industry Database (www.aidb.com). Some cities also have regional directories covering film, video, and computer production companies. Trade magazines and newsletters also carry job listings. Chapter 7, Salaries & Trade Customs, also lists job descriptions and salary ranges for web animation. Chapter 9 discusses artist and animation jobs in the video game industry.

Pricing

A key factor affecting pricing is whether one is working freelance or on staff. If the animation artist is freelancing, pricing is affected by the animation's category. That is determined by how much movement there is, the intricacy of the movement, and how intricate the drawings must be. Pricing is set before work is begun.

A good starting point for determining freelance fees for animation is to look at the union wage scale for the same type of work. The Animation Guild Local 839, IATSE web site (www.animationguild.org) includes detailed information on its latest collective bargaining agreement, including wage scales, hours of employment, working conditions, and general employment practices found in the industry. The contract provides for several levels of experience; experienced artists, known as journeymen, enjoy a higher wage scale than artists who have been in the business for less than a year or two. See Figure 12-3 for examples of minimum weekly salary rates for unit journeyman writers and storyboard artists.

Wage scales are not the only factor freelance animators should look at when establishing fees. They must take into consideration the benefits they must cover for themselves, such as health, disability, and life insurance; paid holidays and vacation days; 401(k) plans; retirement benefits; etc. Freelancers must pay for these expenses themselves, so they should be factored into their rates. Freelancers also should adjust their rates for taxes—automatically deducted from a staff animator's salary—that they will have to pay at the end of the year.

Surface Pattern Design Prices & Trade Customs

This chapter focuses on decorative graphic designs/patterns created primarily for printed products that are mass manufactured. Once exclusively rendered by hand, some segments of the industry now use fully computer-generated designs. Although computer use has been integrated into the entire process—from design concept to retail sale—there remains a demand for the creative artistic skills or "hand" of the traditional designer.

SURFACE

pattern designers, also often referred to as *surface designers* and *textile designers,* create repetitive and non-repetitive or engineered decorative graphics or patterns used to adorn products for the apparel, home fashions, paper product, giftware, and craft industries. Surface pattern designers create single designs or groups of coordinating designs purchased, commissioned, and sometimes licensed by a company. This work is further developed for specified or cross-product end uses in the pre-production phase, forming the foundation used by textile mills, converters, printers, and product manufacturers for the mass production of decorative retail products with consumer appeal.

Trend & Color Forecasting

Design trends and color palettes are of the utmost importance in dictating consumer appeal of decorative graphic designs. Prior to the influx of technology, the American garment industry was based on the European market, with American designers studying the European trade shows to identify trends and, where possible, purchase designs for the upcoming season. After being applied to apparel products, these "looks" would then appear in home fashions and other industry segments. Technology has changed this, effectively dissolving creative borders. Whereas Europe once set and led design trends, in today's global marketplace, American design plays an important role in driving trends. Companies who are able to respond quickly to "what is selling" have changed the "Europe-first" design aesthetic of the industry. European studios have sold work in America for years; today the competition with American studios has paralleled.

Being aware of future trends and the consumers' color "tastes" is a vital part of creating successful decorative graphic designs. Trend and color forecasts are compiled from research conducted by professional organizations, individual design consultants, or a company's in-house stylist/senior stylist. Trend forecasts mainly contain imagery but can also include color palettes, both resulting from analyzing consumer preferences and other factors influencing changes in taste. Political and social climates, major art exhibits, movies, music, trade journals, magazines, and research done at the national and international trade shows that everyone involved in the industry attends can all have a bearing on what kind of "imagery" or "theme" will be the next hot trend. Color forecasts usually do not include imagery; the palettes are derived from trend projections that define the palettes of colors that can be expected to rise, fall, or maintain popularity in coming seasons.

These projections are condensed by design firms in the form of story, presentation, or "mood boards," as they are referred to in fashion. The boards serve as communication tools to "tell the story" of the upcoming design group, line, or collection. On the whole, trends and color palettes change more rapidly for apparel than for interior products as changes in home decor entail a more serious financial investment for the consumer. A freelance designer may be privy to some of this information when commissioned by a company to develop work with a particular look and specified palette. Professional decorative graphic designers who are accustomed to following trends and color fluctuations are often able to predict with amazing accuracy when the consumer will tire of a particular motif, look, or color palette.

The Design Process

Surface pattern designers create speculative work—original designs sold at trade shows, by an agent, or directly to studios or design firms. When commissioned, they work as problem solvers to create designs conceptualizing solutions to a client's specifications. Designs are executed in a variety of techniques and media, usually on paper, digitally, or both, and accompanied by computer printouts and disks. They can be as simple as a one-color single pattern, a highly illustrative piece, or a collection. Designs for prints are often presented with color *gams,* or color chips, which consist of each color in the design. The gams or color chips are created in different manners, depending on the media used and the production method. Designs for woven or knitted textiles may be accompanied by yarn samples for color matching. Designs for printed, woven, and knitted products go through several phases during production, but the steps are similar—regardless of end use.

Designs for textiles in the apparel industry are created in the form of a *croquis,* a full-color design concept or sketch. The croquis is purchased by a firm and later developed into repeats to meet the technical specifications of the textile or garment manufacturer. Home fashion products are generally designed in a specific repeat relative to the end use or *engineered,* a full-color design created to fit a specific product's dimensions. Hard goods, such as bathroom accessories, may begin as a black and white sketch that is developed with color and mechanicals that show 3-D views of the product. Paper products, crafts, and giftware may begin with a pencil sketch, an engineered design, or a repeated design; depending on the product, they also may require mechanicals.

Surface pattern designers work either as independent freelancers, freelancers in service studios, or as freelancers or full-time employees in the studios of design companies, converters, and manufacturers. Service studios include art directors, a full-time in-house creative staff, CAD designers, and, depending on size, a sales staff. Converters and manufacturers have creative, production, and sales staffs. Design companies have the largest number of employees depending on their product line(s) and size. Employees can range from entry-level colorists/CAD assistants to stylists/senior stylists up to vice-presidents of design, prop stylists, and sales teams. Factors that can determine a designer's fee include track record of success, research, complexity of the rendering technique, number of colors, size of croquis, whether the design is engineered or repeat, design revisions, turn-around time, and transfer of copyright and usage rights.

Computer-Aided Design & the Industry

Computer-aided design (CAD) has had a profound effect on surface pattern design as it has on many other fields of graphic art. The Internet now makes it possible for an individual or corporation to work worldwide in a matter of seconds, and computer-aided manufacturing (CAM) is becoming more digital and global. Many time-consuming tasks, such as layout revisions and creating new colorways (color combinations) by hand, have been virtually eliminated, speeding up the process from design creation to retail sale.

Formerly, a stylist in the home furnishings industry would provide the designer with visual references, color direction, and other relevant technical design information with written instructions. Many hours or days were spent creating a design based on the stylist's instructions. After the initial design layout, color palette, and rendered technique sample were reviewed, revisions were frequently needed. Finally, the design layout and color palette were approved and the design's engraving area was rendered. The process had a particularly long timeline if the design was a large repeat, contained multiple colors, or had a unique rendering technique.

Then the design was further developed in the company's studio to create coordinates and colorways. The production process was often time-consuming. The design(s) had to be color separated and engraved, colorants had to be mixed, and printing machinery prepared. The stylist would then have to approve the "strike-offs," (printed samples) for accuracy; again, revisions would be made and the production process would halt until the revisions were complete.

Today, digital methods have cut out many laborious procedures. Now companies subscribe to online trend and color services, and many have digitized their design archives. A stylist can now provide freelance designers with reference and technical information via e-mail, or the in-house CAD designer can research independently and create original designs. Revisions are done quickly. Although there are many fully digital designs, hand-rendered designs are still in demand. Hand-painted coordinates and colorways have become obsolete and are now done in-house by the studio's CAD staff. Designers and CAD assistants execute design work under the supervision of a stylist, senior stylist, or design manager. Once a design has been approved, everything moves to a digital format. The design(s) are scanned, color reduced, cleaned, and then repeated. Design concepts would be further developed to include coordinates and colorways. All of the design components are then color separated; the type of separation depends on the production method. The separated digital files are then used for engraving.

Many studios use the Pantone color system, now digital, to insure continuity of color in a product line. All the preproduction and postproduction information about the design is entered into a database, which can easily be referenced if further revisions, color palettes, or coordinate designs are needed. Color printouts on paper are used to check color balance, layout scale, etc. Digitally printed fabric samples are now available immediately, so the stylist no longer needs to make regular mill visits. The time-consuming, costly mill runs, which now necessitate trips overseas, are monitored via e-mail to insure production specifications are met. Digitally printed fabric samples are used for product prototypes and go directly to the showroom. Designs are also digitally mapped onto a product for display on a web site or for presentation to buyers. Orders, including different sizes and colors, require a much shorter sales cycle. And with the sales cycle reduced, much more customization of a design can be accommodated in relatively little time.

The many graphic software programs—off-the-shelf, industry level, and proprietary (software developed for a specific company)—that drive CAD are becoming more complex and sophisticated. Designers who know how to use such CAD packages appropriately are increasingly sought out in the digital marketplace. Industry-level and proprietary software is often too expensive for a freelancer to afford. Therefore, it is important for any freelance designer wishing to enter the field today to become proficient in using the Adobe software suites and be familiar with the technical aspects of digital design. Even though this software can be used to develop repetitive designs, if a designer is not fully versed in color theory, repeats, and layouts, computer usage only serves to create a lot of unmarketable digital designs quickly.

Jobs available for someone with CAD experience are varied and include both in-house and freelance positions. For example, during a rush, a freelancer might be hired by a studio to paint a rough design, scan it, and refine it digitally. Although CAD designers are generally pushing salaries higher, salaries or rates can vary widely from industry to industry (see Surface Pattern/Surface/Textile Design Salaries at the end of this chapter).

Types of Surface Pattern, Surface, & Textile Design

Surface patterns are two-dimensional designs applied to surfaces through printing; they are also used for decorative knitted and woven textile products. Due to the variety of designs created, each segment of the industry has creative parameters dictated by consumer appeal and technical specifications required for mass production. In contrast, **surface designs** are applied through surface manipulation, dyeing, painting, embroidery, etc., to a product blank, such as a scarf, and are not intended for mass production but for direct sale at craft fairs, boutiques, and specialty stores. A surface technique could be developed on a fabric swatch or other substrate, scanned in and developed digitally to be part of a printed line; many special looks, textures, etc., are often derived from this method. **Textile designs** are three-dimensional and refer to the creation of a woven or knit structure. Even with modern technology, good design requires skills and knowledge. Freelance designers, regardless of the industry, must be cognizant of trends at all times. For trends and inspiration, they may research online; subscribe to trade publications or design magazines; and visit trade shows, museums, libraries, fabric stores, bookstores, or retail shops.

Printed products

FABRICS

Fabrics (printed decorative) are one of the products produced for the largest segments of industry that utilizes the skills of the surface pattern, surface, and textile designers. The apparel industry has the most market segments and uses the largest quantity of fabric prints for products ranging from yard goods and garments to accessories for personal, corporate, and athletic use. Printed decorative fabrics are produced for both indoor and outdoor use for the residential segment (home/personal) as well as for the commercial segments (hospitality, institutional, corporate, educational, and transportation). Computers are being used more and more for the initial design as software programs are now simulating looks that originally could only be done using hand techniques. Still, as each design is unique, the concept often is still rendered by hand in repeat or engineered, using assorted media: gouache, dye, watercolor, collage, etc., on paper.

Studios that produce prints for the fashion industry create four seasonal collections a year, often devising as many as 250 designs or color variations a month to sell to textile or garment manufacturers. Studios that produce prints for home fashions do not always follow such a schedule, as each product area is different, depending on the market. For example, collections for novelty table linens could include fall/winter, spring/summer, and holiday/seasonal, whereas, collections for bedding, carpeting, or upholstery would not.

DOMESTICS

Domestics include printed fabrics for bath, kitchen, and bed as well as printed fabric and vinyl shower curtains. The designs used for soft goods are translated and developed mostly by CAD for use on hard goods (bath and kitchen accessories). These products are considered 3-D and are executed in much the same way as products for giftware.

TABLETOP

Tabletop includes table linens and dinnerware. Table linens are either printed fabric or vinyl. They may be cut and sewn from a repeated fabric or engineered. Dinnerware designs can be applied to fine china, stoneware, melamine, etc.

WALLCOVERING

Wallcovering is largely printed on a paper substrate for residential use, but there also are fabric- and vinyl-based wallcoverings for both residential and commercial use. The popularity of wallcovering fluctuates frequently in industry. In the past few years, several American manufacturers have closed due to low sales. Just as many American textile printing facilities have closed. One difference is that while the production of textiles has gone overseas, wallcovering production has not followed.

FLOORCOVERING

Floorcovering products are those other than bath mats/rugs. They are used in both residential and commercial settings and include wall-to-wall carpeting, area rugs, and runners, which often coordinate and come in specific industry sizes. There are also custom area rugs sold exclusively to individual clients. Wall-to-wall carpeting comes in either continuous rolls to cover floors from wall to wall or in squares. Most residential carpet rolls do not contain a pattern, whereas commercial carpet rolls or squares almost always do, in order to hide traffic patterns.

PAPER PRODUCTS

Paper Products are largely driven by seasons, holidays, special events, and celebrations. Today, at larger companies, there are specialized teams/departments that cater to ethnic groups and various religious holidays, since worldwide, there is more than Christmas celebrated, and the industry has responded to this. Designs are used for gift wrap, gift bags, party goods, paper tableware, paper decorations, invitations, and stationery. Other areas, sometimes referred to as "personal expression" or "memory keeping," could include album covers, picture frames, note cards, scrapbooking papers, etc. There are also novelty products, such as magnets, mouse pads, bookmarks, recipe boxes, notepads, etc. Extensive knowledge of graphic software is a necessity for freelancing in this industry.

CRAFT

Craft includes products such as quilting fabrics, which have imagery that ranges from simple geometrics to extremely detailed, intricate holiday prints. Most quilting fabrics are printed and are often sold in packs with a central theme. The craft industry uses much the same range of imagery as paper products. Recently, quilting has become quite popular with consumers, and there are companies who only produce fabrics for this purpose. Hobby-based crafts include needlepoint, embroidery, and latch hook kits. The role of the designer here is to create designs that are printed on a base fabric or mesh that is then completed with the needlework technique designated. These images can be simple or complex, and are usually multi-colored. Both of these areas utilize computer-generated work depending on the company's needs.

GIFTWARE

Giftware is probably the one area where the skills of the surface pattern designer are used solely for 3-D products, such as ornaments, figurines, decorative boxes, etc. There is a unique skill set required to design for this area; since many products are three-dimensional, the designer must be able to visually represent to the client different views or mechanicals of the design placement on the product. The ability to use 3-D rendering software is a plus, but not a necessity.

Woven products

Woven fabrics are created by interlacing two sets of yarns—a warp and a weft—on a loom. The patterns created can be very simple or extremely complex, requiring expert knowledge of weave structure. Color, texture, density, and number of yarns used are also necessary design decisions. The woven design industry has become highly computerized (the first computer was the jacquard loom with punch cards), and it is essential for anyone in the field to be computer literate. Woven designs can be visualized on a computer screen or by weaving an actual sample on a handloom (though that term is deceptive because most handlooms are computerized today). Some software packages simulate yarn type and weave textures so finely that they look real.

Most CAD software packages have programs, both proprietary and off-the-shelf packages, supplied by companies working with woven textile requirements that can turn any design sketch or squiggle into a woven fabric. Hand-rendered designs are often used for producing decorative woven jacquard fabrics for residential and commercial upholstery. The design, depending on complexity, may be rendered in highly contrasting colors. The design is then scanned, color reduced, and a weave is specified (plotted) for each color throughout the design. For example, the red in a design could be a twill, the blue a satin, etc. The digital file is then downloaded to the loom and woven.

Most studios specializing in woven fabrics have a creative staff. If the studio has its own loom, a sample weaver, also known as a hand weaver, will execute the designer or stylist's directions. Between the designer/stylist and the sample weaver, there may be many levels and titles, depending on the responsibilities, abilities, and experience of the weaver. The designer and the weaver may be the same person in a small studio. Some studios may not have their own looms and may distribute the work to independent contractors. Despite the predominance of CAD in production, CAD designers have not replaced hand-weavers.

UPHOLSTERY

Upholstery design development work is widely available, particularly in the commercial furnishing market.

DOMESTICS

Domestics include woven fabrics for bath, kitchen, and top-of-bed. Some woven bedding and bath products are embellished with embroidery, fringe, appliqué, etc. Due to the global marketplace, the bedding industry has seen a surge in embellishments for top-of-bed products. There are also tufted bath products such as rugs and mats.

TABLETOP

Tabletop includes wovens for table linens which may also be further embellished with embroidery, beading, etc.

FLOORCOVERING

Floorcovering products that are woven are either produced manually or by machine. They are used in commercial and residential settings and include wall-to-wall carpeting, area rugs, and runners with designs ranging from abstract to traditional.

Knitted products

Knitting yarn or thread into fabric on a machine is based on the same principle as knitting by hand—loops of material are interlocked horizontally and vertically so they make a continuous fabric. Different combinations of loops create different knit structures. Before computers existed, a knit pattern was programmed on punch cards, which directed a knitting machine to reproduce it. Today, as with woven textiles, knits are increasingly produced by CAD programs, and hand-rendered designs are also developed into knitted fabrics.

Knits are usually used predominately in the apparel industry; knit designers develop stitch structures and color combinations for four seasons. They either work as staff designers for knitwear companies, which have their own showrooms, or work as independent contractors through studios that act as brokers and take swatches on consignment. Buyers purchase knit designs from the studios and produce their own original knitted garments. The design process is increasingly computerized, speeding up the entire cycle, and large companies tend to dominate the production end of the business.

Embroidery, the most popular of current embellishment techniques, is often used on knits. Just think of the many different logos embroidered on knitted designer golf shirts. The introduction of high-speed, multi-head, computerized embroidery machines in the late 1970s opened up the industry just when hand-embroidered jeans became popular, and knit designers have taken advantage of the new opportunities to include embroidery in their designs. Knit designers may find it helpful to have a basic understanding of embroidery stitches or to consult a specialist in order to successfully incorporate the work in their designs.

With the bulk of manufacturing handled abroad, most studios rely on design work created here; therefore, since enough handwork is still required, CAD does not dominate the design phase of the business. That leaves the field, driven by the American market, wide open for independent knit designers who choose to pursue their own artistic vision.

Licensing & Royalties

Licensing agreements through which a graphic artist who owns the reproduction rights to a piece of art or design permits another party, usually a client, to use the art or design for a limited, specific purpose, for a specified time, and throughout a specific geographical area in return for a fee or royalty are common in this industry. For example, imagery may be licensed to one party for a wallcovering border and to others for paper products or dinnerware. Upon expiration of the license, the right to use the design reverts to the graphic artist or designer unless another contract is negotiated. (More thorough discussions of licensing can be found in Chapter 2, Legal Rights & Issues, and Chapter 5, Essential Business Practices. Model licensing agreements appear in the Appendix: Contracts & Forms. *Licensing Art & Design,* by Carol LeLand, is listed in Chapter 15, Resources & References.)

In the surface pattern, surface, and textile design industries, licensing agreements are normally negotiated for an entire line, collection, or group of products for a particular market. For example, a licensing agreement for bedding could include designs for a number of entire "beds" (top-of-bed comforter, duvet covers, and shams and inner bed sheets and pillowcases, and so on). A license for bath products could include a shower curtain, rugs/bath mats, towel sets, and accessories. Licenses are not usually granted for a single product, such as a shower curtain or beach towel. Any design can be licensed; in the apparel market, it is rare because designs have such a short life. The home fashions industry tends to license with a brand to produce products under their label as consumer awareness directly impacts revenue.

Graphic artists/designers and clients work together to determine whether a royalty arrangement is in the best interests of both parties in relation to use of the designs. Arrangements may include a non-refundable advance payment to the designer called "an advance against royalties," paid before the product is sold. At minimum, many designers negotiate advances to cover their expenses. Often advances are equal to the price of the work if it were sold outright. Royalties are a percentage of total sales paid to the designer, based on the product's wholesale price. The advance is deducted from sales; once the entire advance has been realized by the licensor, then the designer will begin to receive royalties. Royalty percentages and advances vary from industry to industry; high-volume items may be as low as a fraction of a percent. Percentages are negotiated individually and will vary with the designer or brand's reputation or significance to the consumer. They can range from 1 to 5 percent of the wholesale price and can differ from product to product. See Figure 13-1 for Sample Advances & Royalties by product type.

Working with Representatives

Surface pattern, surface, and textile designers frequently work with representatives or agents who have the legal right to act on behalf of the designers they represent only in the manner agreed to by both parties. A model Surface/Textile Designer-Agent Agreement can be found in the

Sample Advances & Royalties for Surface Pattern/Surface/Textile Design

PRODUCT	ADVANCE AGAINST ROYALTIES	ROYALTY PERCENT*
Domestics: Bath Products (3-pc. towel group)	$5000-10,000	5%
Table Top Products (3-4 pc. dinnerware group)	$500-1500	5%
Paper Products: Greeting Cards/Stationery	$200-350	3-5%
Paper Products: Party Goods (cup, plate, napkin, etc.)	$1,000	5%

* Royalty percents reflect arrangements with department stores and are based on the wholesale price. For mass distribution (chain & discount stores), percentages may be 2 points less.

NOTE: The advance ranges and royalties in Figure 13-1 do not constitute specific prices for particular jobs. The buyer and seller are free to negotiate, with each designer independently, deciding how to price the work after taking all factors into account.

FIGURE 13—1

Appendix: Contracts & Forms. A complete discussion of the artist/representative relationship is found in Chapter 1, Professional Relationships.

Trade Practices

The following trade practices have guided the industry and are particularly relevant to freelance surface pattern, pattern, and textile designers. The Graphic Artists Guild strongly recommends confirming all agreements in writing. Designers should read any agreement carefully and should consider the benefits of restricting the sale of rights to specific markets. See Figure 13–2 for Hourly & Day Rates. (For detailed information on negotiating and model contract provisions, see Chapter 3, Professional Issues; Chapter 5, Essential Business Practices; and the surface design business and legal forms in the Appendix: Contracts & Forms.)

Hourly & Day Rates for Surface Pattern/Surface/Textile Design

PRODUCT	HOURLY RATE	DAY RATE[1]
ON–SITE: HAND WORK[2]		
Apparel	$60-80	
Home Fashions	$70-80	$400-800
Paper Products	$25-40	
ON–SITE: CAD WORK[2]		
Apparel	$60-80	$400-800
Home Fashions	$45-50	$300–500 (depends on experience)
Home Fashions: Colorwork	$50	$300–400
Paper Products	$25-40	
OFF-PREMISES: HAND WORK[2]		
Apparel	$60-80	$400-800
Home Fashions	$75-150	
Paper	$30-50	
OFF-PREMISES: CAD WORK[2]		
Apparel	$60-80	$400-800
Home Fashions	Off-site CAD is usually project-based on invoices, not hourly	
Paper	$30-50	
MILL WORK[3]		
Home Fashions	N/A (handled internally or through vendors)	$400 (8 to 12-hour shift)
TREND/COLOR FORECASTING[4]		
Paper Products	$35-50	
PRODUCT DEVELOPMENT[5]		
Paper Products	$40-50	

[1] Based on an 8-hour day; expenses for travel are generally billed in addition to the day rate. Types of work may include, but are not limited to:

[2] Creation of original designs; design development from original design work; archives; purchased designs for printed, knitted, & woven products; CAD cleaning; separations; colorways; and product mappings.

[3] Approval of engraving, strike-offs, color. Little used in USA. Usually Involves international travel. Travel time is often billed in addition to the day rate.

[4] Future trend reports/market analysis, story/trend boards, color palettes. Apparel and Home Fashion companies are more likely to purchase a package/service or subscribe online with professional forecasting companies/studios to meet this need. Usually involves international travel. Travel time is often billed in addition to the day rate.

[5] For Apparel and Home Fashions, this usually occurs as part of a consultant agreement covering a broad range of responsibility for an entire brand and is more project-fee based.

FIGURE 13—2

Speculation: Speculative ventures, whether in financial markets or in the creative industries, are fraught with risk. Individuals who choose this course risk loss of capital and all expenses. Designers who create speculative work with the hope of selling at a trade show or accept speculative assignments (whether directly from a client or by entering a contest or competition) risk the loss of fees, expenses, and the potential opportunity to pursue other compensated assignments. In most circumstances, all the risks are placed on the designer, with the client or contest holder assuming none. For example, some buyers will decide whether or not to purchase a design only upon approval of finished work. Each designer should make an independent decision about acceptance of speculative assignments based upon a careful evaluation of the risks and benefits of accepting them and of the designer's particular circumstances.

Many surface pattern, surface, and textile designers, choosing to act as entrepreneurs, create original design collections or groups and try to market them in a variety of ways. For example, if a designer develops a collection for the domestic market and enters into a licensing agreement with a manufacturer who agrees to pay an advance against royalty sales, the designer and the manufacturer share the risk in the mutual investment. The compensation to both parties is speculative, meaning both are dependent on the sale of the product.

Designers who create works on assignment or commission always receive payment for their work. (To help ensure payment, see the Estimate and Confirmation Form in the Appendix: Contracts & Forms.)

Billing for a Sale: When a sale is made, a receipt or invoice is presented by the designer that states the terms of the sale and is signed by the client. The terms of payment should be negotiated prior to the sale, and these terms should be stated on the invoice. Because invoices largely reflect the designer's labor, they should be made payable upon receipt. Companies often take 30 days to pay invoices. If payment is legitimately delayed, the designer may wish to accommodate the buyer and grant a reasonable extension, but the new deadline should be presented in writing. Any transfer of copyright or usage rights should be contingent upon full payment of the designer's invoice.

Granting extensions should be viewed as a professional courtesy on the part of the designer, not the buyer's right. Some designers may demand a late fee—usually a percentage of the outstanding balance—as compensation for a delay in payment. Designers who employ this practice usually notify their clients of the policy in writing before any work is accepted. This practice should be used particularly when longer extensions are granted.

Cancellation (kill) Fees: Clients usually pay the designer a cancellation fee if the assignment is cancelled for reasons beyond the designer's control. The amount of the fee varies considerably, ranging from 30 to 100 percent, depending upon the percentage of work completed. (See Chapter 3, Professional Issues, for a detailed discussion of kill fees.)

Unless otherwise agreed to, the client usually obtains all the originally agreed-upon rights to the use of the artwork upon payment of the cancellation fee. Under a royalty arrangement, all rights to the artwork, as well as possession of the original art, generally revert to the designer upon cancellation.

If a job based on documentary work or other original art belonging to a client is canceled, payment of a time and/or labor charge is a widely accepted industry custom.

Client Responsibilities: It is common practice for a client to approve a layout with a "technique sample," a portion of the design rendered on the paper, in the technique, showing the full color palette and the medium proposed for the finished design. Designers may request additional payment when the client requires major changes and/or additions to the design that were not part of the original approved design. Designers should be flexible enough to accept the working procedures with clients from different markets as the design needs, time-lines, etc., vary within the industry. A design for apparel, for example, requires a different procedure and creative needs than that for a wallcovering. Sales taxes, if due in accordance with state laws, must be collected on all artwork.

Credit to Designer: In the past, in acknowledgement of the creative work designers provide, many received credit and their copyright notice printed on the selvage of the fabric or somewhere else on the product other than the fabric. Today this practice is virtually non–existent and only occurs when negotiated as part of a licensing agreement.

Expenses: Additional expenses outside of the agreed-upon design fee, such as travel, accommodations, consultation time, shipping and mailing charges, and other out-of-pocket expenses if applicable, could be billed to the client separately or included in the original work agreement. Regardless, clients should be made fully aware of these possible charges, and they should be included in the original agreement to be billed separately, as they occur or as part of the "design project." Designers should always save receipts whenever possible and submit copies with their invoice to avoid any disputes.

Holding Work: In the past, the practice of holding work was pertinent only to speculative work. Although previous experience with a client who wished to hold work prior to purchase was generally the guide for allowing this practice, designers today usually do not consent to any holding period. In addition to risking that the work may be damaged or lost, with today's technology designers run the risk of their design being digitally appropriated, for want of a better term. Most stylist and design directors have the authority to purchase designs on the spot, and they normally do so. When that is impossible, having a signed holding form with a disclosure agreement is recommended. The length of the holding period of three days is permitted by some designers, but most limit this time to several hours or one day.

Knockoffs: A knockoff is a design that is adapted or taken directly from another. Designers who know they are being hired to create a knockoff should request that the client indemnify them from any legal action that may arise from such work; if the design is copied without recognizable changes, it may be considered a copyright infringement, illegal, and subject to legal action by the copyright owner. Decorative designs throughout the years have been re-invented over and over again. Surface pattern/surface/ textile designers should never copy or plagiarize a design by another even if that work is in the public domain. Designers should possess enough self-worth and talent to use an existing design as an inspiration only and create their own interpretation with the same feel as the original.

Quantity Orders: Each design is unique, and its creation is labor intensive, a factor in pricing that in the view of many designers should not be discounted if a number of designs are purchased at the same time. The exception to this may occur if a designer has created a group of coordinating designs; the designer may sell them individually, but would have better luck selling them as a group with a break in price. Nevertheless, designers should decide independently how to price their work.

Return of Original Work: Commissioned designs or those sold without a licensing agreement are very rarely returned as the production process often mutilates the work to the point that it is rendered useless. Surface pattern, surface, and textile designers should negotiate to obtain samples of their printed designs or finished products for display and portfolio use.

Rush Work: Expedited or rush work will usually increase the original fee, and as with all charges, the parties to the transaction must agree upon a fair rush fee.

Uses and Limitations: The intended use of commissioned or licensed work is generally stated clearly in a contract, purchase order, invoice, or letter of agreement that states the price and terms of sale. If a company commissions a design, it usually holds the copyright and can use the design as it wishes. If a client decides to use a previously commissioned design for products other than originally stated in the contract, the designer is customarily offered the opportunity to redesign the artwork to fit the new format. An example of this would be selecting a design to use as a wall covering that was originally for a printed fabric. Common practice is for the designer to receive additional compensation

for such extended uses. If no specific limits on usage were stated in the original contract and changes do not have to be made to the artwork to render it usable for a new product, the designer usually will not be offered additional payment for the new use of the design. If a designer enters into a licensing agreement to use a design specifically for bedding, the designer should ensure in the agreement with the client that the same design can be licensed in another uncompetitive market, such as paper products, dinnerware, etc.

Specific uses, and terms for uses other than those initially specified, should be negotiated in advance whenever possible. Secondary use of a design can sometimes be of greater value than its primary use. Therefore, there is no set formula for reuse fees.

Surface Pattern/ Surface/Textile Design Salaries

Colorist/CAD Assistant is an entry-level designer, one to two years out of college. Colorists/CAD assistants are guided by the designer/assistant stylist to develop CAD repeats from original or purchased croquis to meet manufacturers' technical specifications and develop coordinating design color combinations or "colorways" for design groups, using CAD software. They may also follow up on lab dip submits and color readings from seasonal color palettes picked by in-house brand teams and develop trend, color, or story boards. $30,000 to $35,000 +/-.

Designer/Assistant Stylists. In addition to possessing the skills of the colorist/CAD assistant, designer/assistant stylists are guided by the stylist/ senior stylist to create original designs for a target market derived from provided reference materials, ranging from color swatches, fabric swatches, design archives/ documents, trend reports, etc. They also create a design collection from re-working/adapting purchased designs for a target market or independently for a target market upon approval of original concepts presented to the stylist/senior stylist. They also develop product and pattern designs and maintain correspondence with suppliers/manufacturers on design instructions relevant to production revisions. $35,000 to $47,000 +/-.

CAD Designer. In addition to possessing the skills of the colorist/CAD assistant and designer/ assistant stylist, CAD designers should be able to multi-task in whatever design capacity is needed in the studio at any given time as directed by the stylist/senior stylist. The position requires creative talent, as well as speed and proficiency in the use of prevalent off-the-shelf graphic software, industry software, or proprietary software developed for a specific company.

They create product mappings showing end uses and store shelving display renderings to assist sales teams. They also may maintain technology. $50,000 to $75,000 +/-.

Stylist/Senior Stylist. In addition to possessing pattern development and CAD skills to support the training and mentoring of the Designer/Assistant Stylist and CAD Designer, stylists/senior stylists are responsible for "styling a line," often traveling abroad to trade shows to purchase designs for development or for creative inspiration, in addition to reading design magazines and trade publications. They initiate original design collections; ensure that the overall quality of the designs developed are on strategy with the target market; and approve design repeats, the original color palette, and new colorways pre-production. They communicate with overseas manufacturers on product production via mail/e-mail to insure the final product is manufactured to the specifications of the director of design. $50,000 to $65,000 +/-.

Design Manager. Design managers report to the director of design and are responsible for creative leadership. They have one or more stylists/assistants reporting to them. They keep abreast of current trends to stay well informed of changes in the marketplace, ensuring that the right creative path is determined months in advance to meet a client's needs. Due to their experience level, they know the current assortment of the client's brand/item/price point and sales activity. They assume more responsibility to assure appropriate product development for the resulting end products. In addition to developing one or more brands, they have budget responsibilities and must possess excellent communication skills when presenting new products to clients to secure accounts. $65,000 to $85,000 +/-.

Director of Design (DOD). The DODs report to the Vice President of design and oversee all activities of one or more design teams or a whole department. They delegate and oversee

Comparative Fees for
Surface Pattern/Surface/Textile Design

APPAREL (FLAT FEES)[1]

	HAND-RENDERED	
	SIMPLE DESIGN (2-6 colors)	COMPLEX DESIGN (6+ colors)
PRINTED ACCESSORIES (Scarves, shawls, ties, etc.)		
Croquis	$100-225	$250-500
Engineered Design	$200-375	$350-675
KNITTED ACCESSORIES		
Engineered Design	$200-400	$400-650
PRINTED GARMENT DESIGNS		
Croquis	$200-375	$350-675
Croquis Developed	$200-375	$350-675
Design in Repeat	$450-1000	$450-1500
WOVEN GARMENT DESIGNS		
Design in Repeat	$100-200	$250-400
CAD COLORWAYS		
	$100-200 each	$150-300 each

[1] Fees are for each design; ranges reflect design complexity.

Croquis = Rendered color concept/sketch.

Croquis Developed = Rendered color concept/sketch repeated and traced; engraving area rendered.

Engineered Design = Full-color design created to fit specific product(s) dimensions.

Design in Repeat = Full-color design repeated for a continuous pattern.

CAD Designs: Additional fees may include: disk(s) with completed art files ($25-50 per disk depending on source).

CAD Colorways: May include scanning, cleaning, coloring. Price increases with # of colors and amount of editing.

FIGURE 13—3

all responsibilities of the studio. They are expected to encompass styling duties, particularly to be a trend leader and set design direction. They also have budget responsibilities. Depending on the size of the company and amount of creative responsibility in addition to design studio oversight and direction, the DOD may also be responsible for overseeing advertising, packaging, showrooms, etc. $100,000 to $175,000+/-.

Vice President of Design (VP). VPs delegate and oversee all studio activities and report to management. They are responsible for ensuring that work is produced on time and on budget, working with merchandising and sales to set the direction and fulfill the sales goals for the company. They may also be responsible for overseeing licensing activities. Depending on the size of the company and amount of creative responsibility in addition to design studio oversight and direction, the VP also may be responsible for overseeing advertising, packaging, showrooms, etc. $120,000 to $250,000 +/-.

Comparative Fees for Surface Pattern/Surface/Textile Design

HOME FASHIONS: DECORATIVE FABRIC (FLAT FEES)[1]

	HAND-RENDERED DESIGNS		CAD DESIGNS	
	SIMPLE	COMPLEX	SIMPLE	COMPLEX
PRINTED ACCESSORIES				
Pillows (engineered)	$150-200	$250-350	$200-250	$300-350
CAD Colorways	-	-	$100 each	$250 each
Throws/Coverlets (design in repeat)	$400-450	$500-700	$400-450	$500-700
CAD Colorways	-	-	$200 each	$350 each
DRAPERY FABRICS Print Repeat Sizes				
27"	$600-700	$700-1200	$700-750	$1200-1250
25.25"	$500-600	$1000-1100	$600-650	$1100-1150
18"	$400-500	$900-1000	$500-550	$1000-1050
13.5"	$200-300	$400-500	$300-350	$500-550
6.75-9"	$100-200	$300-450	$150-200	$450-500
CAD Colorways	-	-	$100-200 each	$150-250 each
UPHOLSTERY FABRICS Print Repeat Sizes				
27"	$700-1200	$1500-2000	$700-1250	$1500-2050
18"	$600-1100	$1300-1850	$600-1150	$1300-1900
13.5"	$500-1000	$1200-1750	$500-1050	$1200-1800
6.75-9"	$350-500	$550-700	$350-550	$550-750
3-4.5"	$250-300	$350-500	$250-350	$350-550
CAD Colorways				
27", 18", 13.5"	-	-	$200-300+/- each	$250-400+/- each
9", 6.75", 4.5", 3"	-	-	$25+/- each	$50+/- each

[1] Fees are for each design; ranges reflect design complexity.

Engineered Design = Full-color design created to fit specific product(s) dimensions.

Design in Repeat = Full-color design repeated for a continuous pattern.

CAD Designs: Additional fees may include: disk(s) with completed art files ($25-50 per disk depending on source).

CAD Colorways: May include scanning, cleaning, coloring. Price increases with # of colors and amount of editing.

FIGURE 13—4

Pricing

The Comparative Fees for Surface Pattern/ Surface/Textile Design provided in Figures 13-3 through 13-9 reflect input from established professionals in the United States and are meant as a point of reference only. They do not necessarily reflect such important factors as geographic differences in cost of living, deadlines, research, job complexity, technique or unique quality of expression, extraordinary or extensive use of the finished design(s) and reputation of a particular freelance designer. Nor do the ranges constitute specific prices for speculative or commissioned design work. The buyer and seller are free to negotiate, with each designer independently deciding how to price the work after taking all the factors into account.

Comparative Fees for
Surface Pattern/Surface/Textile Design
HOME FASHIONS: BATH PRODUCTS (FLAT FEES)[1]

	HAND-RENDERED DESIGNS		CAD DESIGNS
ACCESSORIES (toothbrush holder, lotion dispenser, soap dish, tumbler tissue cover, and wastebasket)			
Single Pieces			
B&W Concept Sketches (2-D)	$35-100 each		$100-150 each
Croquis (2-D)	$75-100 each		$150-175 each
Mechanicals (3-D)	$150-300 each		-
4 & 6-Piece Ensembles – Full-scale color renderings (2-D) with production-ready mechanicals (3-D)			
Toothbrush holder, lotion dispenser, soap dish, tumbler (4)	-	Simple	$1200-1500
+ tissue cover & wastebasket (6)	-	Complex	$1500-2000
B&W Shape concepts / Thumbnails on 8 x 10	$100-150		-
Client (Company) Concept: Full-Color Rendering (2-D)	$300-350		-
Designer Concept: Full-Color Rendering (2-D)	$600-700		-
PRINTED TEXTILES			
Wash Cloth; Hand, Guest/ Face & Bath Towels (B&W Concept Sketches)	$150–200 each	-	
Single full-color motifs: Purchased for specific needs to assist in-house studio with layouts for Wash Cloth; Hand, Guest/Face & Bath Towels	$80–150 each / -	Simple / Complex	$150–200 each / $250–400 each
Single Engineered Designs/ Repeated Designs Purchased and developed via CAD in-house for Wash Cloths; Hand, Guest/ Face & Bath Towels	$700–1200 each		-

[1] Fees are for each design; ranges reflect design complexity and number of colors.

(Continues on next page)

FIGURE 13—5

Comparative Fees for
Surface Pattern/Surface/Textile Design

HOME FASHIONS: BATH PRODUCTS (FLAT FEES)[1] (Continued)

	HAND-RENDERED DESIGNS		CAD DESIGNS	
	SIMPLE	COMPLEX	SIMPLE	COMPLEX
Croquis Developed				
Wash Cloth; Hand, Guest/Face Towels	$100-150 each	$200-350 each	$150-200 each	$250-400 each
Bath Towel	$300-350	$350-450	$350-400	$400-500
Design in Repeat/Engineered				
Wash Cloth; Hand, Guest/Face Towels	$400-450 each	$450-500 each	$450-500 each	$500-550 each
Bath Towel	$500-650	$750-900	$550-700	$800-950
3-Piece Ensemble: Bath, Hand, Wash	$400-700	$700-900	$450-750	$750-950
CAD Colorways	-	-	$300 +/-	$300 +/-
SHOWER CURTAINS (fabric/vinyl)				
B&W Concept Sketches	$150-200 each	$150-200 each	-	
Croquis Developed	$300-450	$500-1200	$350-500	$550-1250
Design in Repeat (fabric 25.25"/vinyl 24")	$500-800	$600-1200	$750-925	$800-1000
Engineered	$750-875	$900-1000	$800-950	$900-1200
CAD Colorways	-	-	$100-175	$200-250
WINDOW TREATMENTS				
Croquis Developed	$450-650	$500-700	$500-700	$550-750
Engineered	$500-700	$700-1000	$550-750	$750-1050
BATH RUGS/MATS				
B&W Concept Sketches	$150-200 each	$150-200 each	-	
Croquis Developed	$200-300	$250-350	$250-350	$300-400
Engineered	$300-500	$500-650	$350-550	$550-700
WOVEN/TUFTED TEXTILES (+$50 if showing woven or tufted texture)				
Design in Repeat/Engineered				
Wash Cloth, Hand Towel, Guest/Face Towel		$150-200 each		$200-250 each
Bath Towel		$350-400 each		$400-450 each
3-Piece Ensemble (bath, hand, wash)		$400-800 each		$450-850 each
Bath Mats/Rugs		$300-600 each		$350-650 each
EMBROIDERY (Color Concepts)		$150-300 each		$200-350 each

[1] Fees are for each design; ranges reflect design complexity and number of colors.

Croquis = Rendered color concept/sketch.

Croquis Developed = Rendered color concept/sketch repeated and traced; engraving area rendered.

Engineered Design = Full-color design created to fit specific product(s) dimensions.

Design in Repeat = Full-color design repeated for a continuous pattern.

CAD Designs: Additional fees may include: disk(s) with completed art files ($25–50 per disk depending on source).

CAD Colorways: May Include scanning, cleaning, coloring. Price increases with # of colors and amount of editing.

FIGURE 13–5

Comparative Fees for
Surface Pattern/Surface/Textile Design

HOME FASHIONS: BED PRODUCTS (FLAT FEES)[1]

	HAND-RENDERED DESIGNS		CAD DESIGNS	
	SIMPLE DESIGN	COMPLEX DESIGN	SIMPLE DESIGN	COMPLEX DESIGN
ACCESSORIES (Boudoir, Breakfast Pillows, Neck Roll, Table Round/Square)				
Croquis Developed	$25–50	$50–75	-	-
Engineered	$75–100	$125–200	-	-
OUTER/TOP OF BED (Comforter Face/Duvet)				
Croquis	$100–300	$200–300	$100–300	$200–850
Croquis Developed	$500–700	$600–800	$175–375	$500–850
36" Repeat	$1000–1100	$1200–1800	$500–700	$700–1000
Engineered	$1200–1800	$1800–2200	$500–850	$1000–1500
INNER BED				
Standard Pillow Case				
Croquis Developed	$125–350	$395–500	$150–175	$200–500
Engineered	$200–250	$250–400	$200–250	$250–400
Flat Sheet, Fitted Sheet				
Croquis Developed	$125–350	$395–500	$150–175	$200–500
36" Repeat	$500–700	$700–1000	$450–650	$700–950
CAD Colorways	-	-	$75–125	$375–650

CONCEPT DEVELOPMENT EMBELLISHMENTS	HAND-RENDERED/CAD
Croquis (Mini Samples, Decorative Pillows, Pillow Cases, Shams)	$100–300 each
Technique Pieces (Quilted, Embroidered, Pleated, etc.)	$80–200 each
5-piece Ensemble	$500
Straight Sample Sewings (Cut & sew of existing print or woven yardage)	$12–50+ per hour (based on experience/expertise)

[1] Fees are for each design; ranges reflect design complexity and number of colors.

Croquis = Rendered color concept/sketch.

Croquis Developed = Rendered color concept/sketch repeated and traced; engraving area rendered.

Engineered Design = Full-color design created to fit specific product(s) dimensions.

Design in Repeat = Full-color design repeated for a continuous pattern.

CAD Designs: Additional fees may include: disk(s) with completed art files ($25–50 per disk depending on source).

CAD Colorways: May Include scanning, cleaning, coloring. Price increases with # of colors and amount of editing.

FIGURE 13—6

Comparative Fees for
Surface Pattern/Surface/Textile Design

HOME FASHIONS: KITCHEN & TABLETOP PRODUCTS (FLAT FEES)[1]

	HAND-RENDERED DESIGNS		CAD DESIGNS	
	SIMPLE	COMPLEX	SIMPLE	COMPLEX
KITCHEN PRODUCTS (Rendered designs purchased & developed via CAD in-house, for printed or woven kitchen towels, dish cloths, pot holders, or oven mitts)				
Engineered	-	-	$ 100–300 each	$ 300–400 each
Croquis Developed	$400–500	$500–700	-	-
Design In Repeat	$500–900	$900–1200	-	-
CAD Colorways	-	-	$50–100 each	$50–100 each
TABLETOP PRODUCTS				
Soft Goods: Textiles (Designs purchased & developed via CAD in-house, for printed or woven tablecloths, runners, placemats, or napkins)				
Croquis	$400–600	$600–900	-	-
Croquis Developed	$450–600	$600–1200	$500–700	$700–1200
Tablecloths (design in repeat or engineered)				
Designs for Prints	$400–800	$800–1250	$500–700	$700–1200
Designs for Wovens	$900–1000	$1000–1300	$900–1000	$1000–2000
Placemats (engineered)				
Designs for Prints	$350–450	$450–750	$300– 350	$350–400
Designs for Wovens	$300–500	$550–800	$300–500	$550–800
CAD Colorways	-	-	$70–120	$100–150
Hard Goods: Dinnerware				
Serveware* - Charger; Dinner, Luncheon, Salad/Dessert, Bread & Butter Plates; Soup & Cereal Bowls; Cup & Saucer.				
Engineered/ Croquis Developed	$300–600 each	$600–1000 each	-	-
Croquis/ Design in Repeat (2–3)			$650–700 Sm Scale	$700–800 Lg Scale
5-Piece Place Setting (Dinner & salad plates; soup/cereal bowl; cup & saucer)				
Engineered/ Croquis Developed	$1000–3000	$3000–5000	-	-
Serviceware** - Tea/coffee set; sugar bowl; creamer; butter, casserole & vegetable dishes; gravy boat; platters; salt & pepper, etc.				
	$300–600 ea.	$600–1000 ea.	-	-

[1] Fees are for each design; ranges reflect design complexity and number of colors.

Croquis = Rendered color concept/sketch.

Croquis Developed = Rendered color concept/sketch repeated and traced; engraving area rendered.

Engineered Design = Full-color design created to fit specific product(s) dimensions.

Design in Repeat = Full-color design repeated for a continuous pattern.

CAD Designs: Additional fees may include: disk(s) with completed art files ($25–50 per disk depending on source).

CAD Colorways: May Include scanning, cleaning, coloring. Price increases with # of colors and amount of editing.

***Serveware** - Refers to an individual place setting.

****Serviceware** - Refers to components used to "service" an entire table.

FIGURE 13—7

Comparative Fees for
Surface Pattern/Surface/Textile Design
HOME FASHIONS: FLOORCOVERING & WALLCOVERING (FLAT FEES)[1]

	HAND-RENDERED DESIGNS		CAD DESIGNS	
	SIMPLE	COMPLEX	SIMPLE	COMPLEX
FLOORCOVERING (Designs for printed, hand & machine woven/tufted rugs)				
Croquis				
3 x 5'	$200 +/-	$250 +/-	$300 +/-	$300 +/-
4 x 6'	$250 +/-	$300 +/-	$450 +/-	$500 +/-
6 x 9', 8 x 10'	$300 +/-	$350 +/-	$500 +/-	$600 +/-
9 x 12'	$350 +/-	$400 +/-	$600 +/-	$700 +/-
10 x 14', 12 x 18'	$350 +/-	$400 +/-	$700 +/-	$800 +/-
2'6" x 8' Runner	$200 +/-	$250 +/-	$300 +/-	$400 +/-
Croquis Developed				
3 x 5', 4 x 6'	$500 +/-	$600 +/-	$600 +/-	$700 +/-
6 x 9'	$700 +/-	$800 +/-	$800 +/-	$900 +/-
8 x 10', 9 x 12'	$800 +/-	$900 +/-	$900 +/-	$1000 +/-
10 x 14', 12 x 18'	$850 +/-	$950 +/-	$1000 +/-	$1200 +/-
2'6" x 8' Runner	$500 +/-	$600 +/-	$400 +/-	$800 +/-
Engineered				
3 x 5', 4 x 6'	$700 +/-	$800 +/-	$800 +/-	$900 +/-
6 x 9', 8 x 10'	$800 +/-	$900 +/-	$900 +/-	$1000 +/-
9 x 12', 10 x 14'	$900 +/-	$1000 +/-	$1000 +/-	$1200 +/-
12 x 18'	$950 +/-	$150 +/-	$1000 +/-	$1700 +/-
2'6" x 8' Runner	$700 +/-	$800 +/-	$900 +/-	$950 +/-

	HAND-RENDERED DESIGNS	CAD DESIGNS
WALLCOVERING		
Repeated Small Scale Simple Patterns (Textural/Commercial End Use)	$500 +/-	$200 +/-
Repeated Medium Scale (Residential End Use)	$1000 +/-	$700–800 +/-
Repeated Fine Rendering, Complex/Special Technique (Residential End Use)	$1200–1800 +/-	$1200–1500 +/-

[1] Fees are for each design; ranges reflect design complexity and number of colors.

Croquis = Rendered color concept/sketch.

Croquis Developed = Rendered color concept/sketch repeated and traced; engraving area rendered.

Engineered Design = Full-color design created to fit specific product(s) dimensions.

Design in Repeat = Full-color design repeated for a continuous pattern.

CAD Designs: Additional fees may include: disk(s) with completed art files ($25–50 per disk depending on source).

FIGURE 13—8

Comparative Fees for
Surface Pattern/Surface/Textile Design
PAPER & NOVELTY PRODUCTS

	CONCEPTS	HAND/CAD DEVELOPED DESIGN
PAPER PRODUCTS (flat fees)[1]		
Gift Tags	$100 each	-
Gift Wrap Sheet/Roll	$250-800	$250-800
Gift Bag	$300-800	$300-800
Greeting Cards/Note Cards	$150-250	$400-600

	HAND-RENDERED	CAD DESIGNS
Purchased/Commissioned Designs Developed In-House	$1200 +/-	$550-1000
NOVELTY PRODUCTS (flat fees)[2]		
T-Shirt Graphics		
Croquis: Rendered Concept	$150-250	$250-500
Engineered Designs	$250-900	$350-1000
Beach Towels		
For Print	$650	
For Woven	$600	
Beach Blanket	$700	
Beach Hoodies (Engineered)	$650-750	

[1] Fees are for each design; ranges reflect design complexity and number of colors.

[2] Fees are for each design; ranges reflect design complexity, size, and number of colors.

Croquis = Rendered color concept/sketch.

Engineered Design = Full-color design created to fit specific product(s) dimensions.

Design in Repeat = Full-color design repeated for a continuous pattern.

CAD Designs: Additional fees may include: disk(s) with completed art files ($25-50 per disk depending on source).

FIGURE 13—9

THE GRAPHIC ARTISTS GUILD

This chapter describes the Graphic Artists Guild's mission and its vision for the visual communications industry as well as the Guild's history and accomplishments over the past four decades. The many services and benefits that come with Guild membership are also detailed.

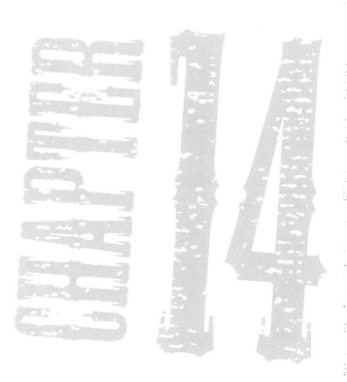

CHAPTER 14

14

PROMOTING

and protecting the economic interests of its members is the mission of the Graphic Artists Guild. It is committed to improving conditions for all graphic art creators and to raising standards for the entire industry. The Guild's vision for the future includes:

- Graphic artists are recognized, respected, and fairly compensated for their work. Baseline fee levels that protect all graphic artists are established. Art and design buyers recognize the value of graphic art to their businesses, and their relationships with graphic artists are fair and ethical.
- The Guild is recognized widely as the leading organization working on behalf of graphic artists. Through its active and involved membership, the Guild has substantial impact on legislative issues and in the global marketplace.
- Because of Guild programs and services, its members enjoy recognition, prosperity, and security.

Long-Range Goals

FINANCIAL AND PROFESSIONAL RESPECT
To ensure that our members are recognized financially and professionally for the value they provide.

EDUCATION AND RESEARCH
To educate graphic artists and their clients about ethical and fair business practices. To educate graphic artists about emerging trends and technologies that have an impact on the industry.

VALUED BENEFITS
To offer programs and services that anticipate and respond to the needs of our members, helping them prosper and enhancing their health and security.

ADVOCACY
To advocate for the interests of our members and the industry as a whole in the legislative, judicial, and regulatory arenas.

ORGANIZATIONAL DEVELOPMENT
To be responsible trustees for our members by building an organization that works proactively on their behalf.

The methods used to accomplish these goals correspond to our members' needs. For the majority of our members, who work for themselves, we work hard to help them improve the skills necessary to compete more effectively in today's volatile markets. This book, for example, helps artists, designers, and clients manage their businesses better.

History of the Guild

1967

- Independent national Guild and local Guild branch (chapter) organized in Detroit, with 113 initial members who signed the charter on November 2, 1967. Graphic Artists Guild Constitution patterned after that of the Screen Actors Guild.

1968

- Organizing of Guild chapters initiated in Cleveland, Chicago, New York, and San Francisco.
- First issue of a Graphic Artists Guild newsletter, *To Date,* published in February 1968.
- First annual Guild Art Show in Detroit.

1970

- New York branch (chapter) charter signed March 7, 1970.
- Guild's Detroit Chapter called strike against Campbell Ewald, an automotive industry advertising agency with ties to Chevrolet/General Motors.

1971-72

- Detroit Chapter's strike against Campbell Ewald proved unsuccessful due to lack of solidarity among local-area artists and pressure from some Detroit art studios.
- National Guild office in Detroit declined rapidly after failure of strike, while chapters elsewhere continued to build and function independently.

1972

- New York Chapter became *de facto* national Guild headquarters, leading efforts to organize Guild chapters in other cities.

1973

- First edition of the *Graphic Artists Guild Handbook: Pricing & Ethical Guidelines* published as a 20-page booklet.
- First publication of *Flash,* forerunner of current national Guild News newsletter.

1974

- Illustrators Guild founded after a group of independent illustrators successfully negotiated higher page rates with Children's Television Workshop, publishers of *Sesame Street* magazine.

1975

- Formation of Professional Practices Committee to help Guild members resolve disputes with clients.
- Second edition of the *Graphic Artists Guild Handbook: Pricing & Ethical Guidelines* published as a 40-page booklet.

1976

- First publication of the *Graphic Artists Guild Talent Directory* (later known as the *Directory of Illustration*), the first sourcebook to serve the needs of illustrators.
- Illustrators Guild merged with Graphic Artists Guild.
- Major medical coverage added to benefits program.
- Guild staged its first business seminars for graphic artists: "How to Run Your Own Business" and "Artists & Agents."

1978

- Graphic Artists for Self-Preservation (GASP) merged with Graphic Artists Guild.
- National Guild office organized in New York.
- New York Chapter became a co-sponsor of the independent Joint Ethics Committee (JEC) to promote the industry's oldest ethical arbitration for industry practitioners.
- Atlanta Chapter chartered.
- Creative Designers Guild merged with Graphic Artists Guild.
- Favorable decision obtained from Copyright

Royalty Tribunal that raised fees and improved reporting procedures for 260 PBS stations regarding use of previously published art for broadcasting.

- Guild published *Visual Artists' Guide to the New Copyright Law,* by Tad Crawford.

1979

- First National Board of Directors elected.
- Third edition of the *Graphic Artists Guild Handbook: Pricing & Ethical Guidelines* published as a 48-page booklet.
- Second edition of the *Graphic Artists Guild Directory of Illustration* published as a 156-page book.
- Textile Designers Guild merged with the Graphic Artists Guild.
- Long-term legislative drive initiated that targeted federal copyright and tax laws and promoted model legislation to establish legal rights for artists at federal and state levels.
- Model business forms drafted for various graphic art disciplines.
- Negotiation with a number of publishers resulted in their withdrawal of work-for-hire contracts.

1980

- First National Board Convention.
- Boston Chapter chartered.
- Good Works (no-fee job referral program) initiated.
- Class was begun at Graphic Artists Guild's Business School, geared towards professionals and taught by professionals.
- Guild assisted a group of textile designers in obtaining a National Labor Relations Board investigation and in filing an unfair labor practices complaint against Print-a-Pattern after the designers were terminated subsequent to seeking to negotiate an employment contract. The designers were able to obtain unemployment insurance and entered into a private settlement regarding monies due.
- Favorable ruling from IRS provided Guild with nonprofit status as a labor organization, which allowed flexibility and broader activities as a professional association beyond those of purely educational or philanthropic associations.
- Guild published *Protecting Your Heirs and Creative Work,* by Tad Crawford.
- Guild assisted with formation of Children's Book Artists & Author Association (CBAAA).

1981

- Professional Education Program started by New York Chapter.
- Oregon passed an artists' fair practices law (Sects. 359.350-359.365 of Rev. Stat.), based on the Guild's model law.
- Third edition of the *Graphic Artists Guild Directory of Illustration* was published as a 272-page book, becoming the largest reference book of its kind in the United States at the time.

1982

- Indiana Chapter chartered.
- Fourth edition of the *Graphic Artists Guild Handbook: Pricing & Ethical Guidelines* published as a 136-page book.
- Guild succeeded in passing California artists' fair practices law (Sect. 988 of Civil Code).
- Assistance provided in the formation of the National Writers Union.
- Responding to Guild opposition, IRS withdraws proposed rule that would have disallowed a home studio deduction where artist has a primary source of income at another location and from other type of work.
- Guild formed the Copyright Justice Coalition, an alliance of creators' groups, including photographers and writers, to lobby for work-for-hire reform in U.S. Congress. Forty-two organizations joined coalition efforts, the largest creators' advocacy coalition in history.
- Graphic Artists Guild Foundation organized and received National Endowment for the Arts (NEA) grant for study.
- New York Chapter succeeded in passage of New York State artists' fair practices law (Sects. 1401 & 1403 of Arts & Cult. Affairs Law) and artists' authorship rights law (Art. 12-J of General Business Law).

1984

- Cartoonist Guild merged with the Graphic Artists Guild.
- Fifth edition of the *Graphic Artists Guild Handbook: Pricing & Ethical Guidelines* published as a 194-page book.
- Fourth edition of the *Graphic Artists Guild Directory of Illustration* published.
- Testimony was presented before the Democratic National Platform Committee on professional issues.
- Guild proposed a Copyright Justice Act to reform work-for-hire provision of the copyright law by eliminating instances in which artists lose rights and benefits as creators of their work.

1985

- Guild Foundation drafted ethical guidelines for contests and competitions.
- Boston Chapter succeeded in passage of state's Arts Preservation Act.
- Formation of Giolito Communications Center, a specialized reference library operated by the Guild Foundation.
- National Legal Referral Network established.
- Traveling education workshops established.

1986

- Contract terms renegotiated with Children's Television Workshop concerning low pay and work-for-hire issues.
- Testimony presented before Congressional

Office of Technology Assessment regarding impact of technology on the profession.
- Guild members testified before U.S. Congress in support of Berne Convention (international copyright agreement concerning moral rights).

1987

- At-Large Chapter organized to provide members outside chapter regions with National Board representation.
- National Professional Practices (currently called Grievance) Committee organized.
- Sixth edition of the *Graphic Artists Guild Handbook: Pricing & Ethical Guidelines* published as a 208-page book.
- Coalition of Designers merged with the Graphic Artists Guild.

1988

- Albany Chapter chartered.
- Guild spearheaded formation of Artists for Tax Equity (AFTE) coalition to confront intended application of uniform tax capitalization requirements to all artists and designers. Coalition grew to 75 organizations representing nearly one million artists and designers.
- Fifth edition of the *Graphic Artists Guild Directory of Illustration* released in 9 x 12-inch format and began annual publication thereafter.

1989

- Guild's leadership helped AFTE win necessary exemption from uniform tax capitalization for all artists and graphic designers through a "technical correction" to the tax law.
- Guild, through the Copyright Justice Coalition, helped convince the Supreme Court to decide in favor of sculptor James Earl Reid in the landmark decision that virtually ended work-for-hire for freelancers in the absence of a written agreement.
- Testimony presented on work-for-hire abuses to Senate Judiciary's Subcommittee on Patents, Copyrights, and Trademarks.

1990

- Atlanta Chapter helped win protection for artists in Georgia, requiring printers to obtain written authorization of copyright clearance for all print orders over $1,000.
- Guild, together with the AIGA (American Institute of Graphic Arts) and the SEGD (Society for Environmental Graphic Design), began working to clarify sales tax collection guidelines for illustrators and graphic designers in New York State.

1991

- Expanded and updated 7th edition of the *Graphic Artists Guild Handbook: Pricing & Ethical Guidelines* published as a 240-page book. Three

printings brought the total number of copies in circulation to 53,000.
- Guild took leadership role in addressing health-care crisis for artists and designers, formally endorsing universal health-care legislation in Congress. Steps were taken to organize Artists United for Universal Health, a coalition of arts and artists organizations dedicated to this goal.

1992

- Guidelines for the Interpretation of Sales Tax Requirements for Graphic Designers and Illustrators, formulated by the Guild, AIGA, and SEGD, were approved by New York State Department of Taxation.
- Guild organized "Eye to Eye," its first national conference and trade show, celebrating 25 years of advancing the interests of creators.

1993

- Chicago Chapter chartered.
- National Labor Relations Board certified the Guild as the exclusive bargaining agent for the graphic artists employed at Thirteen/WNET (Educational Broadcasting Corporation), a publicly funded television station in New York City.
- Immigration and Naturalization Service relies upon the Guild to provide references for foreign artists seeking temporary work visas.
- The Guild Foundation, with the support and technical assistance of the NEA's Office for Special Constituencies, produced an award-winning set of disability access symbols, "Disability Access Symbols Project: Promoting Accessible Places and Programs." The Disability Access Symbols Project (available in both disk and hard-copy formats) was distributed to hundreds of government and nonprofit organizations.

1994

- Seattle's Society of Professional Graphic Artists, founded in the 1950s, merged with the Guild as the SPGA/Seattle Chapter.
- Eighth edition of the *Graphic Artists Guild Handbook: Pricing & Ethical Guidelines* was published. Updated in design, organization, and information, it had grown to nearly 300 pages, with an initial printing of approximately 30,000 copies.
- Guild and ASMP backed widow of illustrator Patrick Nagel in copyright ownership lawsuit against Playboy (*Dumas v. Playboy*), concerning after-the-fact work-for-hire contracts stamped on the back of artist's payment checks. (See Chapter 2, Legal Rights & Issues.)

1995

- Northern California Chapter chartered.
- Guild took proactive lead on electronic rights issues, organizing "Clients vs Creators: The Struggle Over E-Rights," an industry roundtable

featuring Bruce Lehman, U.S. Commissioner of Patents and Trademarks.

- Guild successfully negotiated its first collective bargaining agreement with Thirteen/WNET on behalf of the staff designers it represents, improving hours, pay, and other working conditions.

1996

- Guild organized coalition of 16 industry organizations and launched "Ask First," a copyright awareness campaign intended to end unauthorized use of images for client presentations.
- Guild reached understanding with American Society of Media Photographers (ASMP), National Writers Union (NWU), and Copyright Clearance Center (CCC) to establish digital licensing agency.
- Guild reached agreement with Kopinor, the Norwegian reprographic rights organization, to accept distribution of royalties attributed to U.S. illustrators and designers.
- Guild adopted its first strategic plan to adapt to changing industry conditions.
- Guild's web site on the Internet was activated: www.gag.org.

1997

- Portland, Oregon, Chapter chartered.
- The Graphic Artists Guild Legal Defense Fund founded.
- Ninth edition of the *Graphic Artists Guild Handbook: Pricing & Ethical Guidelines* was published with 313 pages. More than 70,000 copies sold.

1998

- Southern California (now called LA) Chapter chartered.
- *Thirty Years of Raising Standards* was published, a compendium of Guild history, archival material, and information about the Guild's mission and services.
- First Walter Hortens Distinguished Service Award presented to illustrator Milton Glaser for his "unswerving devotion to the issues confronting the profession and for focusing wide public attention on those issues" (specifically his public stand against the Chrysler Corporation's preemptive editorial policy).
- First Lifetime Achievement Award presented to Simms Taback for more than 20 years of service to the Guild.
- Guild launched *Contract Monitor,* an electronic newsletter analyzing industry contracts.
- Guild opposed projected raises in copyright fees and launched copyright registration campaign.
- Revised Code of Ethical Practice adopted.

1999

- After a nearly 20-year search for an appropriate union, Guild membership voted by three-to-one margin to affiliate with the United Auto Workers, creating UAW Local 3030.
- Guild negotiated its second collective bargaining agreement with Thirteen/WNET on behalf of the staff designers it represents, improving pay and working conditions.
- 1999 Walter Hortens Distinguished Service Awards: graphic designer and writer D.K. Holland won Professional Practices Award; Robert Kanes, art director of *PCWorld,* won Outstanding Client Award; and Marybeth Peters, U.S. Register of Copyrights, was given a Special Award for the Advancement of Creators' Rights.
- Copyright rate hike contained to $30 rather than $45, due to lobbying efforts of Guild and others.
- The Guild Legal Defense Fund supported two potentially groundbreaking cases: photographer Leslie Kelly's case against Arriba Soft Corporation and the lawsuit by 18 medical illustrators against Advanstar Communications, Inc. (*Teri J. McDermott, et al. v. Advanstar Communications, Inc.*).
- First president from the West Coast elected: illustrator Jonathan Combs of the SPGA/Seattle Chapter.
- The Campaign for Illustration (C4I) was initiated to preserve the economic well-being of illustrators, to help artists defend and control their rights, and to make the illustration community a truly cohesive business and creative force. Its three components are education, action, and community.

2000

- Walter Hortens Distinguished Service Awards: illustrator Brad Holland won Professional Practices Award; Steven Heller, art director of *The New York Times Book Review,* won Outstanding Client Award; and Jonathan Tasini, president of the National Writers Union and lead plaintiff in the groundbreaking electronic rights lawsuit *Tasini, et al. v. The New York Times, et al.,* was given a Special Award for the Advancement of Creators' Rights.
- Philadelphia and DC/Baltimore Chapters chartered.

2001

- Guild supported the Boston Globe Freelancers Association in their fight against *The Boston Globe* "master contract."
- In February 2001, Guild joined with The Illustrators Partnership in a letter-writing campaign protesting Condé Nast's retroactive all-rights grab contracts. Over 400 protest letters were delivered to Condé Nast.
- Tenth edition of the *Graphic Artists Guild Handbook: Pricing & Ethical Guidelines* was published with more than 400 pages.
- The Northern California Chapter of the Guild achieved a victory for state tax reform when illustrator Heather Preston won her tax case against the California Board of Equalization in April 2001. The Chapter, which had been pursuing sales tax reform in the state since

1996, provided direct support to Preston throughout her ordeal and filed an *amicus curae* with the court.

2002

- The Guild supported the "Freelance Writers and Artists Protection Act" (HR 4643), introduced in the House of Representatives by Rep. John Conyers, which would allow artists to bargain collectively. Guild members around the country raised awareness and support for H.R. 4643 by writing and visiting their local Congresspersons.
- The Guild, in association with the Copyright Society of the USA, participated in Copyright Awareness Week, April 22-28, 2002. The event was a first of its kind for the Guild and a major success.
- The Northern California Chapter celebrated a long-awaited victory for the California arts community when the California Board of Equalization voted to clarify the sales tax regulations affecting illustrators, photographers, cartoonists, and designers.
- A copyright case supported by the Guild, *Kelly v. Arriba Soft, Inc.,* won in the Ninth Circuit Court of Appeals. The case was remanded back to the U.S. District Court, Santa Ana, California, for determination of damages.
- The Guild met with other leading organizations representing graphic artists and photographers to discuss common problems in the marketplace, possible legislative solutions to those problems, and how best to work together toward relieving them.
- The Guild joined the Author's Coalition, a group of independent authors' organizations incorporated to work together to repatriate and distribute foreign non-title-specific royalty payments for American works photocopied abroad. These non-title-specific royalty monies are distributed to the Coalition member organizations to be used for educational and advocacy projects that will benefit the industry as a whole.

2003

- The eleventh edition of the *Graphic Artists Guild Handbook: Pricing & Ethical Guidelines* was published.
- The Guild submitted *amicus* briefs in support of two artists' rights cases: the estate of cartoonist/comic book artist Daniel S. DeCarlo in *Archie Comic Publications, Inc. (Publica) v. Daniel S. DeCarlo* and *MGM Studios, et. al in Metro-Goldwin-Mayer Studios, et. al. v. Grokster, Ltd., et. al.*
- Then Guild president, Lloyd Dangle, responded to work-for-hire contracts being forced on journalists at *Ski and Skiing* magazine by parent company AOL/TIME Warner. A press conference was also held on April 23 in New York City on the steps of City Hall, about the issue. Representatives from the Guild, National Writers Union, American Society of Media Photographers, Editorial Photographers, Author's Guild, Society of American Travel Writers, freelancers, and Council members from New York City were in attendance.

2004

- After much discussion by the Guild's Board of Directors, membership voted to end the Guild's affiliation with the UAW in May 2004. Expectations associated with the affiliation were never realized, and the Guild's Board decided it was best to put the matter before the membership for a vote.

2005

- The Guild continued to support the plaintiffs in the Grokster case by joining a community *amicus* brief for presentation before the Supreme Court.
- The Guild submitted a commentary letter in response to the Copyright Office notice asking for comments regarding the issue of "Orphan Works," copyrighted works whose owners may be impossible to identify or locate. (See Chapter 2, Legal Rights & Issues and the Guild's web site, www.graphicartistsguild.org, for more information.)
- The Guild participated in the Copyright Office's two-day roundtable discussions on possible solutions to the "Orphan Works" issue in Washington, D.C.
- The Guild contributed to the "Illustration Growers of America" campaign in two ways: a $2,500 contribution for campaign advertising costs and a page in the *Guild Directory of Illustration.* (See Chapter 2, Legal Rights & Issues and the Guild's web site, www.graphicartistsguild.org, for more information.)
- Membership voted to simplify the Guild's dues structure, eliminating the various income levels that determine applicable dues owed, and moving to a flat fee that varies according to membership category: Full Membership, Associate Membership, Lifetime/Retired (with ten-year Guild membership), and Student.

2006

- The "Orphan Works" issue continued as a major issue for visual artists with the introduction of a Congressional bill in the House of Representatives. The Guild joined forces with other visual artists' organizations to fight the sections of the bill that would be detrimental to the livelihood of all visual artists. (See Chapter 2, Legal Rights & Issues and the Guild's web site, www.graphicartists-guild.org, for more information.)
- The Guild supported photographer Thomas Dallal in his copyright infringement lawsuit against *The New York Times*. The Guild, in conjunction with the American Society of Media Photographers (ASMP), submitted an *amicus* brief in support of Dallal's appeal of an earlier court decision in favor of *The New York Times*. The Second Circuit Court of Appeals vacated the earlier decision and the judges ordered The New York Times to negotiate a settlement payment for usage fees of over 1,000 images created by Tom Dallal.
- The Guild joined the International Council of Graphic Design Associations (ICOGRADA), the

world body for professional graphic design and visual communication. Founded in 1963, ICOGRADA is a voluntary assembly of associations concerned with graphic design, visual communication, design management, design promotion, and design education. ICOGRADA promotes graphic designers' vital role in society and commerce and unifies the voices of graphic designers and visual communicators worldwide. The Guild attended the ICOGRADA regional meeting in Seattle, held in conjunction with the ICOGRADA Design Week, July 9-15, 2006.

2007

- The Graphic Artists Guild joined the Authors Guild in warning members about the all-rights, print-on-demand contracts being forced on authors and illustrators by Simon and Schuster.
- The Guild joined the Copyright Alliance and participated in its Copyright Expo.
- The 12th Edition of *Pricing and Ethical Guidelines* was published and distributed to members.
- Representatives of the Executive Committee of the Graphic Artists Guild, Executive Director Tricia McKiernan and Ex Com member Rebecca Blake, attended the World Design Congress in Havana, Cuba, to accept the Guild's permanent membership in ICOGRADA.

2008

- The Graphic Artists Guild worked with the Guild lobbyist to coordinate with the Copyright Office and Congressional staff regarding proposed orphan works legislation. Also representing the National Textile Association, the American Craft & Hobby Association, and George Little Management, these organizations collaborated, along with the American Society of Media Photographers (ASMP) and the Professional Photographers of America (PPA).
- Participated in a roundtable discussion in Washington, DC, with the Copyright Office regarding revision of a section of U.S. Copyright Law on "Compilations" and provisions for counting damages for infringing use of works registered as compilations. Testimony submitted on behalf of illustrators and other graphic artists.
- The Graphic Artists Guild and ASMP filed an *amicus curiae* in support of the owner of the Perfect 10 Web site in his appeal of the lower court's denial of his copyright infringement suit against Google.
- Guild President John Schmelzer and Advocacy Chairperson Lisa Shaftel attended the 2008 Annual General Meeting of the International Federation of Reproduction Rights Organisation (IFRRO) in Jamaica, as Guild representatives.

2009

- The Graphic Artists Guild joined several other visual arts rights holders' trade groups and prominent individual photographers in filing objections to the $125 million class action settlement with Google Books for copyright infringement.
- The American Society of Media Photographers (ASMP), joined by the Graphic Artists Guild, the Picture Archive Council of America, and the North American Nature Photography Association, filed a statement for the U.S. House of Representatives Judiciary Committee hearing on "Competition and Commerce in Digital Books." The statement, which has been added to the hearing record, represents the interests of thousands in the visual artist community.
- Guild Executive Director Tricia McKiernan briefed the Senate Small Business Committee about the importance of copyright to the livelihood of graphic artists as part of a panel of Copyright Alliance members.
- Coinciding with the 2009 IFRRO Annual General Meeting in Oslo, Norway, an International Authors Forum was held in Oslo on Tuesday, October 20. The meeting focused on media concentration, authors' rights, and contracts—the same issues the Graphic Artists Guild has promoted in the United States since its inception in 1967 and supported by the Guild via its presence at the meeting.
- Guild member Chad Cameron was part of a delegation of emerging artists in The Copyright Alliance's grassroots network of creators who delivered to the White House a letter signed by more than 11,000 artists nationwide asking President Obama and Vice President Biden to pursue policies supportive of artists' rights.

Taking Action

The Graphic Artists Guild is an organization whose headquarters is located in New York City. Local chapters of the Guild exist in Boston, Massachusetts; Chicago, Illinois; Los Angeles, California; New York City; San Francisco, California; and Seattle, Washington. The At-Large Chapter serves those individuals who do not reside in or near a geographic chapter.

The Guild is mandated by its constitution "to advance and extend the economic and social interests of [our] members" and to "promote and maintain high professional standards of ethics and practice and to secure the conformance of all buyers, users, sellers, and employers to established standards."

Foremost among the Guild's activities is the ongoing effort to educate members and non-members alike about the business of being a graphic artist. Through its chapter network, the Guild organizes programs on negotiation and pricing strategies, tax issues, self-promotion, time management, and other essential business skills that are not, by and large, taught in art schools. The Guild provides a means for experienced artists to share their understanding of advertising, publishing, and corporate markets with young artists and a way for artists at every level to share concerns and information. In fact, many artists join the Guild for the information and networking it offers and are drawn into other activities as well.

The bottom line, though, is work—the more the better. The Guild wants to help members get jobs that recognize, financially and otherwise, the valuable contributions of graphic artists. One means is through the Member Portfolios section of the Guild web site (www.graphi-cartistsguild.org/theguild/member-portfolios/) whose purpose is to promote artists' work and make it easier for advertising agencies, marketing executives, art directors, and design firms to find the right artist for the right assignment. Through its lobbying, the Guild has helped strengthen copyright laws and ease the tax burden on freelancers. The Grievance Committee helps members resolve grievances, which in turn helps reinforce industry standards. Since knowledge is power, especially in the communication industries, the Guild makes special efforts to keep members informed through newsletters, programs, and events.

Active membership in the Graphic Artists Guild is the best way to ensure the advancement of creators' interests and equitable professional conditions for all. Joining the Guild gives graphic artists an avenue to work as a group acting to protect their professional integrity and their art by sharing information, discussing problems in the industry, and working to improve the profession. Guild members share and communicate with each other to take advantage of the experiences of the group on contract issues, pricing, and artists' rights legislation.

Member Benefits & Services

The needs and concerns of members dictate all Guild projects, benefits, and services. Each chapter of the Guild organizes its own programs to serve the needs of its region. When an issue is recognized as a concern that extends beyond any one chapter, it is often referred to the Guild Board for assessment and possible action or, in the case of successful events, implementation in all chapters.

The Guild web site

The Guild launched a new web site in 2009 at www.graphicartistsguild.com. The site features a portfolio area where full professional members are listed by discipline with a link (where applicable) to their own web sites; news briefs; a listing of member benefits; an advocacy section packed with information about the various industry issues affecting the Guild's membership; links to related organizations; and individual chapter home pages highlighting chapter-based events and programs.

The site also has a new "members only" area with a forum for discussion of topics of particular interest to graphic artists, access to assets available only to members, access codes for benefits, and other areas of interest to the Guild's members.

Newsletters

The Guild News, a bi-monthly print newsletter, is distributed to members and teaching institutions with art and design programs. It features a wide variety of issues affecting graphic artists and how they work. It also provides updated information on Guild programs; legislative initiatives; legal issues; chapter news and event calendars; and other items of interest. Submission of articles and artwork from members is welcome (subject to the editor's discretion). Subscriptions are available at $12 per year for nonmembers (contact the Guild office, 212-794-3400 or sales@gag.org, for further information).

Most chapters publish their own monthly or quarterly e-newsletters that cover issues of regional interest, announce meetings and programs, and report on members' activities.

Job referral systems

The Guild offers both formal and informal job referral systems. *JOBline News,* a weekly e-newsletter of the New York Chapter, is a benefit available to all Guild members free of charge. The publication includes national job opportunities for both freelance and staff in all areas of the graphic arts. Members can subscribe to *JOBline* by e-mailing jobline@gag.org.

Plans are underway to morph *JOBline News* into an online JobBoard available only to Guild members through a password-protected section on the Guild's web site. An announcement will appear on the Guild web site (www.graphi-cartistsguild.org) once JobBoard is launched.

Other job referral systems offered by the chapters are tailored to meet the needs of the geographic areas they serve and depend on the structure and character of the chapter. Several chapters maintain informal systems and publicize opportunities online or via e-mail regarding positions referred by members or clients. Chapters are encouraged to contact local art directors, design firms, and other potential clients to let them know they can contact the Graphic Artists Guild for referrals.

Professional education programs

The Graphic Artists Guild offers a variety of audio teleclasses on issues of importance for graphic artists— for members and non-members alike. De-signed to educate artists on subjects that can im-prove their skills, prospecting, operations, and un-derstanding of legislation related to the industry, transcripts for teleclasses are also available to anyone unable to attend the class itself. The Graphic Artists Guild web site lists the topics avail-able for download and/or live participation; visit www.graphicartistsguild.org for more information.

Whether promoting the business of art or up-dating skills needed to compete effectively in the market, Guild chapters offer events throughout the year on topics of special interest. Some are discipline-specific, related to graphic design, illustration, surface/ textile design, multimedia, cartooning, or web design; others, such as negotiation, marketing, self-promotion, and financial planning, appeal to the broad spectrum of Guild members. Members receive announcements for general and discipline-specific meetings from individual chapters and through the *Guild News*.

Other components of the program include Guild volunteers speaking at area art schools about the Guild and the benefits of joining; copyright and how it protects the artists' work; contracts and why using them is important, and teachers who are Guild members sharing information about professional practices on the undergraduate level.

Professional practices monitoring & dispute resolution

The Guild monitors problems that occur throughout the industry and tracks member complaints on issues concerning standards, practices, and pricing. The Guild's Grievance Committee offers a grievance procedure for members who have contractual or professional disputes with clients. The committee meets on an ad hoc basis and reviews grievances, makes recommendations for further action, communicates with clients if necessary on behalf of members, and may also provide support letters if a member decides to take a case to court.

Legal referral network

Because independent contractors often face legal questions particular to their type of business, the Guild has a referral system listing attorneys around the country who have been selected because of their familiarity with artists' issues. Network attorneys are available in Albany, New York; Boston, Massachusetts; Chicago, Illinois; Indianapolis, Indiana; Los Angeles, California; Miami, Florida; New York City; Portland, Oregon; San Francisco, California; and Washington, D.C. (referrals may not be available in all areas of the country).

Discounts

Through various agreements, the Guild offers members numerous discounts on goods and services such as art and office supplies, car rentals, and listings in talent directories and sourcebooks, as well as books and subscriptions to trade publications. Current discounts are listed on the Guild's web site, www.graphicartistsguild.org. You may also contact the Guild's office at 212-791-3400, or e-mail membership@gag.org.

Meetings & networks

Regular membership meetings are hosted by most Guild chapters and include programs on such issues as negotiating, pricing, resource sharing, and self-

promotion. Members can confer directly with peers on business issues, keep updated on the latest developments in the field, and socialize. Some chapters also offer monthly get-togethers for members of a particular discipline, such as children's book illustrators or cartoonists.

Graphic Artists Guild Board of Directors

The Board of Directors, which has oversight responsibility for the organization, consists of elected artist members. Each local chapter has representatives on the Board. The full Board meets in person once a year, and by phone when necessary, to establish goals and priorities, share information on program development, and approve the organization's budget.

Graphic Artists Guild Foundation

The Graphic Artists Guild Foundation was formed in 1983 to "foster, promote, and advance greater knowledge, appreciation, and understanding of the graphic arts...including the presentation and creation of the graphic arts; activities designed to promote, aid, and advance the study of existing works, and to promote the creation, presentation, and dissemination of new works; to sponsor workshops, training sessions, symposia, lectures, and other educational endeavors." The Foundation's constitution states among its goals "to help monitor and establish rules governing industry practices and to contribute to modifying these when necessary."

The Foundation receives grants and donations to conduct studies that will benefit the industry, the public, and the arts in general. For instance, it undertook a two-year study, partially sponsored by the National Endowment of the Arts (NEA), of art-related contests and competitions. The study assessed the nature of contests and competitions and developed a set of ethical guidelines and standards for these events.

In 1993, with the support and assistance of the NEA's Office for Special Constituencies, the Foundation developed the Disability Access Symbols Project: Promoting Accessible Places and Programs. The 12 graphic symbols that were created help solve the communications needs of design firms, agencies, not-for-profits, and other entities who need to show that programs and services are accessible to people with mobility, sight, or hearing impairments. To achieve standardization, the symbols and accompanying text were reviewed by more than 15 organizations representing people with various disabilities, in connection with the design community. The symbols are available for downloading from the Guild's web site, www.graphicartists-guild.org/resources/disability-access-symbols/. Please call 212-794-3400 for more information.

The Graphic Artists Guild Foundation provides an avenue for donations and bequests to advance the interests of artists. Donations, which are deductible as allowed by tax law, can be sent to the Foundation in care of the Graphic Artists Guild. Please make checks payable to the "Graphic Artists Guild Foundation." Call 212-794-3400 for further information.

Graphic Artists Guild Legal Defense Fund

The purpose of the Guild's Legal Defense Fund, founded in June 1997, is to support cases that may have industry-wide impact or may set a precedent that could affect the working lives of graphic artists. Requests for assistance are referred to the Guild's Advocacy Committee, which makes recommendations to the Executive Committee. The Executive Committee decides which cases will receive support from the Fund.

Some past cases supported by the Fund include the *National Association of Freelance Photographers v. the Associated Press, Kelly v. Arriba Soft*, and *Teri J. McDonald, et al. v. Advanstar Communications, Inc.*

Contributions to the Fund are gladly accepted; checks should be made out to the "Graphic Artists Guild," with a note in the memo section indicating Legal Defense Fund. For further information, call 212-791-3400.

Joining the Guild

Often, graphic artists resist joining the Guild until they get into some sort of difficulty: legal trouble, a client who will not pay, a client who demands electronic files, questions about how to competitively quote a job. The Guild's mission is to help artists avoid problems, and the Guild believes that membership is a wise business investment.

Membership in the Guild benefits the artist's business because the Guild works toward the following goals:

- Protecting and improving business conditions for professional creators—as well as art buyers–and helping them succeed in business.
- Improving necessary skills for members to compete more effectively in today's volatile markets. *The Graphic Artists Guild Handbook: Pricing & Ethical Guidelines* helps creators and clients manage their businesses better.
- Advancing and extending the economic and social interests of members; promoting and maintaining high professional standards of ethics and practice; and securing the conformance of buyers, users, sellers and employers to established standards.
- Striving to educate members and non-members alike about the business of being an artist. The Guild offers programs on negotiation and pricing strategies, tax issues, self-promotion, time management, and other essential business skills that are not, by and large, taught in art schools.
- Providing a means for experienced artists to share their understanding of advertising, publishing, and corporate markets with young artists and a way for creators at every level of development to share concerns and information.
- Fighting for all creators' rights. When the market stacks the deck unfairly against artists, the Guild is determined to do something about it, whether through education, legislative advocacy, or other means. Guild members have established a strong track record of successful lobbying on behalf of artists at state and federal levels; developing trail-blazing publications on professional practices and pricing strategies; establishing educational seminars; and offering group health, life, and disability insurance plans.

After joining the Guild, each member is assigned to a local chapter: Boston, Massachusetts; Chicago, Illinois; New York, New York; Northern California; Seattle, Washington; Los Angeles, California; or members who do not reside near a geographic chapter are served by the At-Large Chapter.

A community of artists

Members report that the most important benefit of belonging to the Guild is the direct connection to other graphic artists, the collective wisdom and experience of the Guild's members. Chapter meetings and workshops offer opportunities to meet potential team members, employees, and employers. Our active members appreciate having a community in which to share information about advocacy, business practices, clients, vendors, and technology.

Promoting positive change

The vitality of any member organization lies in its members, and the Guild enjoys a large membership. As the most vocal advocate for graphic artists, the Guild works hard to establish and protect ethical business practices and standards. The larger the membership is, the stronger the Guild's representation is.

Join the Guild to work with other artists to promote positive change in the marketplace and in society.

Membership application

Membership is effective once the Guild receives a completed, signed application, the application fee, and the appropriate dues amount. New members should allow three to four weeks to receive membership materials.

For questions about membership, call the Membership Department at 212-791-3400 x 12 or e-mail membership@gag.org.

A membership application is located at the end of this book and is also available online at www.graphicartistsguild.org. Applicants should complete all portions of the application, sign it, and return it with the application fee and dues payment to Graphic Artists Guild, 32 Broadway, Suite 1114, New York, NY 10004. If paying by credit card, the complete application can be faxed to 212-791-0333.

★　　★　　★

RESOURCES & REFERENCES

This chapter lists the many valuable resources and references—books, publications, directories, related organizations, conferences, trade shows, merchandise markets, and web sites—that the Guild recommends.

ACCESS

to a wide range of resources helps graphic artists keep up with the demands of their profession. The Graphic Artists Guild has collected the information in this chapter over the course of its four decades and offers it as a service to the visual communications industry. Though every effort has been made to provide the most up-to-date contact information, some listings will have changed. Please notify the Guild of additional resources that should be included in the next edition.

Recommended Books

Battle, Carl W.
The Retirement Handbook.
New York, NY: Allworth Press, 1998.

Benun, Ilise.
The Art of Self Promotion.
Hoboken, NJ: Marketing Mentor Press, 2007.

Caplin, Lee Evan.
The Business of Art.
Englewood Cliffs, NJ: Prentice Hall, Inc., 1998.

Craig, James; Bevington, William;
and Scala, Irene Korol.
Designing with Type:
The Essential Guide to Typography, 5th ed.
New York, NY: Watson-Guptill, 2006.

Crawford, Tad, and Bruck, Eva Doman.
Business & Legal Forms for
Graphic Designers, 3d ed.
New York, NY: Allworth Press, 2003.

Crawford, Tad.
Business & Legal Forms for Illustrators, 5th ed.
New York, NY: Allworth Press, 2010.

Crawford, Tad.
Legal Guide for the Visual Artist, 5th ed.
New York, NY: Allworth Press, 2010.

Cusack, Margaret.
Picture Your World in Appliqué:
Creating Unique Images with Fabric.
New York, NY: Watson-Guptill, 2005.

Dougherty, Brian.
Green Graphic Design.
New York, NY: Allworth Press, 2008.

Evan, Poppy.
Designer's Survival Manual: The Insider's Guide
to Working with Illustrators, Photographers,
Printers, Web Engineers, and More.
Cincinnati, OH: North Light Books, 2001.

Fleishman, Michael
How to Grow as an Illustrator.
New York, NY: Allworth Press, 2007.

Fleishman, Michael.
Starting Your Career as a Freelance
Illustrator or Designer, rev. ed.
New York, NY: Allworth Press, 2001.

Fleishman, Michael.
Starting Your Small Graphic Design Studio.
Cincinnati, OH: North Light Books, 1993.

Foote, Cameron S.
The Creative Business Guide to Running
a Graphic Design Business, Updated Edition.
New York, NY: W.W. Norton & Company, 2009.

Harris, Leslie Ellen.
Digital Property: Currency of the 21st Century.
Canada: McGraw-Hill Ryerson, 1998.

Heller, Steven.
The Education of a Design Entrepreneur.
New York, NY: Allworth Press, 2002.

Heller, Steven.
The Education of an e-Designer.
New York, NY: Allworth Press, 2002.

Heller, Steven, and Arisman, Marshall, eds.
The Education of an Illustrator.
New York, NY: Allworth Press, 2000.

Heller, Steven, and Arisman, Marshall.
Inside the Business of Illustration.
New York, NY: Allworth Press, 2004.

Heller, Steven and Arisman, Marshall.
Marketing Illustration: New Venues,
New Styles, New Methods.
New York, NY: Allworth Press, 2008.

Heller, Steven, and Womack, David.
Becoming a Digital Designer: A Guide to
Careers in Web, Video, Broadcast, Game
and Animation Design.
Hoboken, NJ: John Wiley and Sons, Inc., 2008.

Hodges, Elaine R.S., ed.
The Graphic Artists Guild Handbook of
Scientific Illustration, 2d ed.
New York, NY: John Wiley and Sons, 2003.

Jenkins, Sue.
How to Do Everything Illustrator CS4.
Columbus, OH: McGraw-Hill, 2009.

Jenkins, Sue.
Web Design for Dummies All-in-One
Desk Reference.
Hoboken, NJ: John Wiley and Sons, Inc., 2009.

Lee, Marshall.
Bookmaking: Editing, Design, Production
(Third Edition).
New York, NY: W.W. Norton & Co., 2009.

Leland, Caryn R.
Licensing Art & Design: A Professional's Guide
to Licensing and Royalty Agreements.
New York, NY: Allworth Press, 1995.

Levine, Mark L.
Negotiating a Book Contract: A Guide for
Authors, Agents and Lawyers.
Hubbardston, MA: Asphodel Press, 2007.

McCann, Michael.
Artist Beware, Updated and Revised: The Hazards and Precautions of Working with Art and Craft Materials and the Precautions Every Artist and Craftperson Should Take.
Guilford, CT: The Lyons Press, 2005.

Metzdorf, Martha.
The Ultimate Portfolio.
Cincinnati, OH: North Light Books, 1991.

Michels, Caroll.
How to Survive and Prosper as an Artist.
New York, NY: Owl Books (Henry Holt), 2001.

Newberry, Betsy.
Designer's Guide to Marketing.
Cincinnati, OH: North Light Books, 1997.

Oldach, Mark.
Creativity for Graphic Designers.
Cincinnati, OH: North Light Books, 2000.

Piscopo, Maria.
The Graphic Designer's and Illustrator's Guide to Marketing and Promotion.
New York, NY: Allworth Press, 2004.

Rixford, Ellen.
3-Dimensional Illustration: Designing with Paper, Clay, Casts, Wood, Assemblage, Plastics, Fabric, Metal, and Food.
New York, NY: Watson-Guptill, 1992.

Roberts, Jason.
Director Demystified.
San Francisco, CA: Peach Pit Press, 2000.

Rossol, Monona.
The Artist's Complete Health & Safety Guide, 3d ed.
New York, NY: Allworth Press, 2001.

Sedge, Michael.
Successful Syndication: A Guide for Writers and Cartoonists.
New York, NY: Allworth Press, 2000.

Sellers, Don.
ZAP! How Your Computer Can Hurt You—and What You Can Do About It.
San Francisco, CA: Peach Pit Press, 1994.

Sparkman, Don.
Selling Graphic and Web Design, 3d ed.
New York, NY: Allworth Press, 2006.

Tholenaar, Jan, Purvis, Alston W., and Cees De Jong.
Type: A Visual History of Fonts and Graphic Styles, Volume 1: 1628–1900.
Los Angeles, CA: Taschen America, 2009.

Wilde, Judith, and Wilde, Richard.
Visual Literacy: A Conceptual Approach to Graphic Problem Solving.
New York, NY: Watson-Guptill, 2000.

Williams, Theo Stephan.
The Streetwise Guide to Freelance Design & Illustration.
Cincinnati, OH: North Light Books, 1998.

Wilson, Lee.
The Copyright Guide.
New York, NY: Allworth Press, 2003.

Woodward, Michael.
Licensing Art, 101, Third Edition: Publishing and Licensing Your Artwork for Profit.
Nevada City, CA: ArtNetwork Press, 2007.

Useful Publications

Graphic arts & communication

3 x 3 Magazine
244 Fifth Avenue, Suite F269
New York, NY 10001
212-591-2566 | Fax: 212 537 6201
www.3x3mag.com

Advertising Age
Crain Communications
740 Rush Street, Chicago, IL 60611
312-649-5200 | www.adage.com

Adweek
1515 Broadway
New York, NY 10036-8986
212-536-5336 | 800-722-6658
www.adweek.com

AIGA Journal of Graphic Design
American Institute of Graphic Arts
164 Fifth Avenue
New York, NY 10010
212-807-1990 | www.aiga.org

Airbrush Action
P.O. Box 2052
Lakewood, NJ 08701
732-364-2111 | 800-876-2472
www.airbrushaction.com

American Printer
29 N. Wacker Drive
Chicago, IL 60606
312-726-2802 | www.americanprinter.com

Animation Magazine
30941 West Agoura Road, Suite 102
Westlake Village, CA 91361
818-991-2884 | www.animationmagazine.net

Archive
American Showcase
584 Broadway, Suite 303
New York, NY 10010
212-941-2496 | 800-894-7469
www.showcase.com

The Artist's Magazine
F&W Publications
4700 Galbraith Rd.
Cincinnati, OH 45236
513-531-2690 | www.fwpublications.com

Communication Arts
110 Constitution Road
Menlo Park, CA 64025
800-258-9111 | www.commarts.com

Creative Business
29 Temple Place
Boston, MA 02111
617-451-0041 | www.creativebusiness.com

Dynamic Graphics
6000 N. Forest Park Drive
Peoria, IL 61614
1-888-698-8642 | www.dgusa.com

Folio
11 Riverbend Drive S.
P.O. Box 4272
Stamford, CT 06907-0272
203-358-9900 | www.foliomag.com

Graphic Design: USA
Kaye Publishing
79 Madison Avenue, Suite 1202
New York, NY 10016
212-696-4380 | www.gdusa.com

Graphis Journals
307 Fifth Avenue, 10th Floor
New York, NY 10016
212-532-9387 | www.graphis.com

HOW
F&W Publications
4700 Galbraith Rd.
Cincinnati, OH 45236
513-531-2690 | www.howdesign.com

ID: Magazine of International Design
116 E 27th Street
New York, NY 10016
212-447-1402 | www.idonline.com

Letter Arts Review (formerly *Calligraphy Review*)
P.O. Box 9986
Greensboro, NC 27429
336-272-6139 | www.johnnealbooks.com/lar/

Macworld
Subscriptions
P.O. Box 37781
Boone, IA 50037-0781
515-243-3273 | 800-288-6848
www.macworld.com

PC Magazine
Ziff Davis Media, Inc.
28 E. 28th Street, 8th Fl.
New York, NY 10016
212-503-5340 | www.pcmag.com

PC World
Subscription Department
P.O. Box 37571
Boone, IA 50037-0571
415-243-0500 | 800-234-3498
www.pcworld.com

Photo District News
770 Broadway, 7th Floor
New York, NY 10003
646-654-5780 | www.pdnonline.com

Print
116 E. 27th Street
New York, NY 10016
212-447-1430 | www.printmag.com

Printing News
Cygnus Publishing
445 Broad Hollow Road, Suite 21
Melville, NY 11747
631-845-2700 | 800-308-6397
www.printingnews.com

Publish!
462 Boston Street
Topsfield, MA 01983
978-887-2246 | www.publish.com

Publishers Weekly
360 Park Avenue South
New York, NY 10010
646-746-6758 | www.publishersweekly.com

Sign Business
National Business Media
2800 W. Midway Blvd.
Broomfield, CO 80020
303-469-0424 | www.nbm.com/signbusiness/

STEP Inside Design (formerly *Step-by-Step*)
6000 N. Forest Park Drive
Peoria, IL 61614
888-698-8543 | www.stepinsidedesign.com

Surface Design Journal
Surface Design Association
P.O. Box 360
Sebastopol, CA, 95473-0360
707-829-3110 | surfacedesign@mail.com

Women's Wear Daily
Fairchild Publications
750 Third Avenue
New York, NY 10017
212-630-4000 | www.wwd.com

Trade publications of interest

ART/WALL DÉCOR
Art Business News
One Park Avenue, 2nd Floor
New York, NY 10016-5802
212-951-6646
Fax: 212-951-6671
www.artbusiness.com

Arttrends
225 Gordons Corner Road
PO Box 420
Manalapan, NJ 07726
732-446-4900 | 800-969-7176
Fax: 732-446-5488
E-mail: arttrends@hobbypub.com
www.arttrendsmagazine.com

DÉCOR
1801 Park 270 Drive
Maryland Heights, MO 63146
314-824-5500 | Fax: 314-824-5640
E-mail: DÉCOR@pfpublish.com
www.decormagazine.com

CRAFTS & HOBBIES
CNA
700 East State Street
Iola, WI 54990
800-258-0929
E-mail: cna@krause.com
www.cnamag.com

Craftrends
741 Corporate Circle, Suite A
Golden, CO 80401
303-278-1010
Fax: 303-277-0370
www.craftrends.com

Somerset Studio
(numerous arts & crafts publications)
22992 Mill Creek, Suite B
Laguna Hills, CA 92653
949-380-7318 | 877-782-6737
Fax: 949-380-9355
www.somersetstudio.com

GIFT & STATIONERY INDUSTRY
Giftbeat
317 Harrington Ave.
Closter, NJ 07624
201-768-3890 | 800-358-7177
Fax: 201-768-3894
E-mail: editors@giftbeat.com
www.giftbeat.com

Gifts & Decorative Accessories
360 Park Avenue South
New York, NY 10010
646-746-6400
www.giftsanddec.com

Giftware Business
770 Broadway, 5th Floor
New York, NY 10003-9595
646-654-5000 | Fax: 646-654-4978
E-mail: gwb@halldata.com
www.giftwarebusiness.com

Giftware News
20 North Wacker, Suite 1865
Chicago, IL 60606
312-849-2220 | Fax: 312-849-2174
E-mail: giftwarenews@talcott.com
www.giftwarenews.com

Greetings etc.
4 Middlebury Boulevard
Randolph, NJ 07869-1111
973-252-0100 | Fax: 973-252-9020
E-mail: dvanhouten@edgellmail.com
www.greetingsmagazine.com

Party & Paper
107 Mill Plain Road
Danbury, CT 06811
203-730-4090
E-mail: party@partypaper.com

Souvenirs, Gifts & Novelties
7000 Terminal Square, Suite 210
Upper Darby, PA 19082
610-734-2420 | Fax: 610-734-2423
E-mail: SouvNovMag@aol.com

HOME ACCENTS
Home Accents Today
7025 Albert Pick Road, Suite 200
Greensboro, NC 27409
336-605-0121 | Fax: 336-605-1143
www.homeaccentstoday.com

Home Décor Buyer
7400 Skokie Boulevard
Skokie, IL 60077-3339
847-675-7400 | Fax: 847-675-7494
www.HomeDecorBuyer.com

Home Fashions & Furniture Trends
20 North Wacker Drive, Suite 1865
Chicago, IL 60606
312-849-2220 | Fax: 312-849-2174
E-mail: hfft@talcott.com
www.hfft.com

Home Textile Exports
Ihas Medya Plaza
29 Ekim Cad.
34520 Yenibosna
Istanbul, Turkey
90.212 454 25 30 pbx
Fax: 90.212 454 25 55
E-mail: img@img.com.tr
www.img.com.tr

Home Textiles Today
360 Park Avenue South
New York, NY 10010
646-746-7290 | Fax: 646-746-7300
www.hometextilestoday.com

LICENSING
Art Buyer
The magazine of licensed art and images
A4 Publications
The Hogarth Centre
Hogarth Lane
London, W4 2QN, UK
Phone: +44 (0)20 8742 3636
Fax: +44 (0)20 8995 1350
www.a4publications.com

License!
One Park Avenue
New York, NY 10016
888-527-7008
E-mail: license!@advanstar.com

LTW Licensing Today Worldwide
A4 Publications
The Hogarth Centre
Hogarth Lane
London, W4 2QN, UK
Phone: +44 (0)20 8742 3636
Fax: +44 (0)20 8995 1350
www.a4publications.com

The Licensing Book
1501 Broadway, Suite 500
New York, NY 10036
212-575-4510 | 212-575-4521
www.LICENSINGBOOK.com

The Licensing Letter
EPM Communications
160 Mercer Street, 3rd Fl.
New York, NY 10012
212-941-0099 | www.epmcom.com

PET INDUSTRY
Pet Age
200 S. Michigan Avenue, Suite 840
Chicago, IL 60604
312-663-4040 | Fax: 312-663-5676
E-mail: petage@hhbacker.com

Pet Business
233 Park Avenue South, 6th Floor
New York, NY 10003
212-979-4800 | Fax: 212-228-3142
E-mail: request@petbusiness.com
www.petbusiness.com

Pet Product News Magazine
PO Box 6050
Mission Viejo, CA 92690
949-855-8822 | Fax: 949-855-3045
E-mail: ppneditor@fancypubs.com
www.petproductnews.com

MISCELLANEOUS
Brandweek; Adweek; Mediaweek
770 Broadway
New York, NY 10003
646-654-5518 | 800-562-2706
www.brandweek.com

Christian Retailing
Strang Communications Company
600 Rinehart Road
Lake Mary, FL 32746
407-333-0600
www.christianretailing.com

Museums & More
343 S. Union
PO Box 128
Sparta, MI 49345
616-887-9008
Fax: 616-887-2666
E-mail: circulation@museumsandmore.com
www.museumsandmore.com

Industry Directories

Artist's & Graphic Designer's Market
F&W Publications
4700 Galbraith Rd.
Cincinnati, OH 45236
513-531-2690 | www.writersdigestshop.com

Children's Writers & Illustrator's Market
F+W Publications, Inc.
4700 Galbraith Road
Cincinnati OH 45236
cwim@fwpubs.com

Gale Directory of Publications
Gale Research
27500 Drake Road
Farmington Mills, MI 48331-3535
248-699-4253 | www.galegroup.com

Gift and Decorative Accessory Buyers' Directory
360 Park Avenue South
New York, NY 10010
646-746-6400 | www.giftsanddec.com

National Association of Schools of
Art & Design Directory
11250 Roger Bacon Drive, Suite 21
Reston, VA 20190
703-437-0700 | www.arts-accredit.org

O'Dwyer's Directory of
Public Relations Firms
J. R. O'Dwyer
271 Madison Avenue, #600
New York, NY 10016
212-679-2471 | www.odwyerpr.com

Standard Directory of
Advertising Agencies
(Red Book series)
121 Chandon Road
New Providence, NJ 07974
908-464-6800 | www.redbooks.com

Standard Periodical Directory
Oxbridge Communications
186 Fifth Avenue, 6th floor
New York, NY 10010
212-741-0231 | www.mediafinder.com

Thomas Register of Manufacturers
Thomas Publishing
5 Penn Plaza, 12th floor
New York, NY 10001
212-290-7277 | www.thomasregister.com

Ulrich's International
Periodicals Directory
R.R. Bowker
630 Central Avenue
New Providence, NJ 07974
800-340-3244 | www.ulrichsweb.com

Writer's Market
F&W Publications
4700 Galbraith Rd.
Cincinnati, OH 45236
513-531-2690 | www.writersdigest.com

Buyer Databases & List Services

ADBASE online custom lists
877-500-0057 | www.adbase.com
Quick access to thousands of new creative service buyers—online! Select by location, job position, or type of work, and then create customized lists as often as you like during the year. Print labels, download names, or send out e-mail promotions. All contact information updated six times a year.

Animation Industry Database
www.aidb.com
The ultimate resource for the professional animation, visual effects, and gaming-related communities. Includes free downloadable directories to find animation, visual effects, and related companies located worldwide. Covers almost 5,000 companies and schools. Useful as a buyer's guide, a way to find clients, get work, and obtain products and services.

Creative Access
415 West Superior Street
Chicago, IL 60610
312-440-1140 | 800-422-2377
www.bigroster.com
Graphic design firms, art buyers, corporations, ad agencies, illustrators, graphic designers, film directors, photographers, artist representatives, and production houses.

Steve Langerman Lists
36 Mussey Road
Scarborough, ME 04074
207-396-5674 | www.langermanlists.com
Art directors in public relations firms, cosmetic companies, department stores, consumer magazines, and advertising agencies.

Talent Source Books & Annuals

AIGA Design Annual
www.aiga.org
AIGA
164 Fifth Avenue
New York, NY 10010
212-807-1990 | 212 807 1799

The Alternative Pick / Altpick.com
http://altpick.com
1123 Broadway, Suite 716
New York, NY 10010
212-675-4176 | Fax: 212-675-4403

American Illustration
American Photography
www.ai-ap.com
1140 Broadway, 4th Floor
New York, NY 10001
917-408-9944 | Fax: 212-691-6609

The Art Directors Annual
www.adcglobal.org
Art Directors Club
106 West 29th Street
New York, NY 10001
212-643-1440

The Black Book
www.blackbook.com
740 Broadway, Suite 202
New York, NY 10003
212-979-6700 | 212-979-4266

Communication Arts Annuals
www.commarts.com
110 Constitution Drive
Menlo Park, CA 94025
650-326-6040 | Fax: 650-326-1648

Directory of Illustration
www.directoryofillustration.com
Serbin Communications
813 Reddick Street
Santa Barbara, CA 93103
805-963-0439 | 800-876-6425
Fax: 805-965-0496

Graphis Annuals
www.graphis.com
Graphis Inc.
307 Tenth Ave., 5th Floor
New York, NY 10016
212-532-9387 | 212-213-3229

PRINT Regional Annual
www.dexinger.com
1230 Avenue of the Americas, 7th Floor
Rockefeller Plaza Center
New York, NY 10020
917-639-4074 | Fax: 917-639-4005

Society of Illustrators Annual
www.societyofillustrators.org
128 East 63rd Street
New York, NY 10065
212- 838-2560 | Fax: 212- 838-2561

Spectrum: The Best in Contemporary Fantastic Art
www.spectrumfantasticart.com
PO Box 4422
Overland Park, KS 66204

theispot
www.theispot.com
53 West 36th St., Suite 306
New York, NY 10018
800-838-9199 | Fax: 212-502-0925

Workbook
www.workbook.com
6762 Lexington Ave.
Los Angeles, CA 90038
800-547-2688 | 323-856-0008
Fax: 323-856-4368

Organizations

Artists' health and safety

Arts, Craft and Theater Safety
181 Thompson St., #23
New York, NY 10012-2586
212-777-0062 | www.caseweb.com/acts
Publishes newsletter and books about artists' health hazards and safe working conditions.

Communication Workers of America (CWA)
District 1, Health and Safety Program
80 Pine St., 37th floor
New York, NY 10005
212-344-2515 | www.cwaunion.org
Publishes "VDT Work Station Checklist" and related data sheets with complete information on safe workstation setup.

New York Committee for Occupational Safety and Health (NYCOSH)
275 Seventh Ave., 8th floor
New York, NY 10001 |212-627-3900
www.nycosh.org | nycosh@nycosh.org
NYCOSH is one of 26 COSH coalitions around the country that provide information on VDT safety and other health topics.

Occupational Safety and
Health Administration (OSHA)
U.S. Department of Labor
200 Constitution Ave., NW
Washington, DC 20210
202-693-1999 | www.osha.gov
Provides the global picture, including the graphic arts industry.

Graphic arts & related occupations

Advertising Photographers of New York
27 W. 20th Street, Suite 601
New York, NY 10011
212-807-0399 | www.apany.com

American Institute of Graphic Arts (AIGA)
164 Fifth Avenue
New York, NY 10010
212-807-1990 | www.aiga.org

American Society of Architectural Illustrators (ASAI)
5310 E. Main Street, #104
Columbus, OH 43213
614-552-3729 | www.asai.org

American Society of
Media Photographers (ASMP)
150 N. Second Street
Philadelphia, PA 19106
215-451-2767 | www.asmp.org

The Animation Guild, Local 839 IATSE
1105 N. Hollywood Way
Burbank, CA 91505
818-845-7500 | www.animationguild.org

Art Directors Club
106 W. 29th Street
New York, NY 10001
212-643-1440 | www.adcglobal.org

Association of Science Fiction & Fantasy Artists (ASFA)
P.O. Box 65011
Phoenix AZ 85082-5011
www.asfa-art.org

Association of Theatrical Artists & Craftspeople (ATAC)
48 Fairway St.
Bloomfield, NJ 07003-5515
ATACBiz@aol.com

Freelancers Union
20 Jay St., Suite 700
Brooklyn, NY 11201
800-856-9981 | Fax: 718-228-9580
www.freelancersunion.org

Graphic Artists Guild
32 Broadway, Suite 1114
New York, NY 10004
212-791-3400 | Fax: 212-791-0333
www.graphicartistsguild.org

Museum of Comic & Cartoon Art (MoCCA)
32 Union Square East, Suite 600
New York, NY 10003
212-254-3511 | www.moccany.org

National Cartoonists Society
NCS Membership Committee
PO Box 713
Suffield, CT 06078
www.reuben.org

National Endowment for the Arts (NEA)
1100 Pennsylvania Ave., NW
Washington, DC 20506
202-682-5400 | www.arts.gov

The Newspaper Guild-CWA
501 3rd Street, NW, Suite 250
Washington, DC 20001
202-434-7177 | www.newsguild.org

New York Foundation for the Arts
155 Avenue of the Americas, 14th Fl.
New York, NY 10013-1507
212-366-6900 | www.nyfa.org

Society for Environmental
Graphic Design (SEGD)
1000 Vermont Avenue, NW, Suite 400
Washington, DC 20005
202-638-5555 | www.segd.org

Society for News Design
1130 Ten Rod Road, Suite F-104
North Kingstown, RI 02852-4177
401-294-5233 | www.snd.org

Society of Children's Book Writers
& Illustrators
8271 Beverly Blvd.
Los Angeles, CA 90048
323-782-1010 | Fax: 323-782-1892
www.scbwi.org

Society of Illustrators
128 E. 63rd Street
New York, NY 10021
212-838-2560
www.societyillustrators.org

Society of Photographers &
Artists Representatives (SPAR)
60 E. 42nd Street, Suite 1166
New York, NY 10165
212-779-7464 | www.spar.org

Society of Publications Designers (SPD)
60 E. 42nd Street, Suite 721
New York, NY 10165
212-983-8585 | www.spd.org

Software & Information Industry Association
1090 Vermont Avenue NW, 6th Fl.
Washington, DC 20005
202-289-7442 | www.siia.org

Stencil Artisans League
P.O. Box 3109
Los Lunas, NM 87031
505-865-9119 | www.sali.org

Surface Design Association (SDA)
P.O. Box 360
Sebastopol, CA 95473-0360
707.829.3110 | www.surfacedesign.org

Type Directors Club
60 E. 42nd Street, Suite 721
New York, NY 10165
212-983-6042 | www.tdc.org

Visual Artists & Galleries Association (VAGA)
350 Fifth Ave., Suite 6305
New York, NY 10118
212-736-6666

Women in Production
276 Bowery
New York, NY 10012
212-334-2106 | www.wip.org

Intellectual property

U.S. Copyright Office
101 Independence Ave., SE
Washington, DC 20559-6000
202-707-3000 (pre-registration questions)
202-707-6737 (TTY)
202-707-9100 (to request registration forms
or information circulars)
202-707-5959 (help line for registration
questions); 8:30am–5:00pm EST (M-F)
www.copyright.gov
Publishes circulars regarding copyright basics and
directions for registering; all registration forms
available by mail. Maintains an up-to-date web site
with all the information artists need for registering
(see Useful Web Sites section).

U.S. Patent and Trademark Office
Commissioner for Trademarks
P.O. Box 1451
Alexandria, VA 22313-1451
800-786-9199 (24-hour technical & general support)
571-272-9950 (TTY customer assistance)
www.uspto.gov
Source of information, support, and forms for
registering patents and trademarks. Maintains
up-to-date web site (see Useful Web Sites section).

Related trade organizations

Craft & Hobby Association
319 East 54th Street
Elmwood Park, NJ 07407
201-835-1200 | 201-797-0657
www.hobby.org

Direct Marketing Association
1120 Avenue of the Americas
New York, NY 10036
212-768-7277 | www.the-dma.org

Greeting Card Association
1156 15th Street, NW, Suite 900
Washington, DC 20005
202-393-1778 | www.greetingcard.org

Volunteer lawyers for the arts

ARIZONA
Volunteer Legal Assistance for Artists
P.O. Box 877906
Tempe, AZ 85287
www.artsadvocacy.org/

AUSTRALIA
Arts Law Centre of Australia
The Gunnery
43-51 Cowper Wharf Road
Woolloomooloo, Sydney NSW 20111-800- 221-457
(toll-free from Australia)
Local: 02- 9356-2566 | Fax: 02- 9358-6475
artslaw@artslaw.com.au
www.artslaw.com.au/

CANADA
CARFAC – Canadian Artists' Representation
410 Richmond St. West, Suite 440
Toronto, Ontario M5V 3A8
416-340-8850 | carfac@carfac.ca
www.carfacontario.ca/

CALIFORNIA
California Lawyers for the Arts (Statewide)
cla@calawyersforthearts.org
http://www.calawyersforthearts.org

Beverly Hills Bar Association Barristers
Committee for the Arts
300 S. Beverly Dr., Ste. 201
Beverly Hills, CA 90212
(310) 601-2422
http://www.bhba.org

California Lawyers for the Arts (Sacramento)
1127 11th Street, Ste. 214
Sacramento, CA 95814
916-442-6210 | Fax: 916-442-6281
clasacto@aol.com

California Lawyers for the Arts (San Francisco)
Fort Mason Center, Building C, Rm 255
San Francisco, CA 94123
415-775-7200 | Fax: 415-775-1143
cla@calawyerforthearts.org

California Lawyers for the Arts
(San Jose/South Bay)
c/o Arts Council Silicon Valley
4 North 2nd Street
San Jose, CA 95113
408-998-2787 x216 | Fax: 408-971-9458
sanjose@calawyersforthearts.org

California Lawyers for the Arts (Santa Monica)
1641 18th St.
Santa Monica, CA 90404
310-998-5590 | Fax: 310-998-5594
UserCLA@aol.com
www.calawyersforthearts.org

COLORADO
Colorado Lawyers for the Arts
P.O. Box 48148
Denver, CO 80204
303-722-7994 | Fax: 303-778-0203
info@lawyersforthearts.org
www.lawyersforthearts.org

CONNECTICUT
Connecticut Volunteer Lawyers for the Arts
Connecticut Commission on the Arts
One Financial Plaza
755 Main St.
Hartford, CT 06103
860-256-2800 | Fax: 860-256-2811
artsvla@ctarts.org

DISTRICT OF COLUMBIA
Washington Area Lawyers for the Arts (WALA)
901 New York Avenue, NW, Suite P1
Washington, DC 20001-4413
202-289 4440 | Fax: 202-289 4985
legalservices@thewala.org
www.thewala.org

FLORIDA
Volunteer Lawyers for the Arts / ArtServe
(Ft. Lauderdale)
1350 East Sunrise Blvd.
Ft. Lauderdale FL 33304
954-462-8190
ArtServeFl@aol.com
www.artserve.org

Volunteer Lawyers for the Arts of Pinnellas County
14700 Terminal Blvd., Suite 229
Clearwater, FL 33762
Fax: 727-453-7855
http://pinellasarts.org/smart_law.htm

GEORGIA
Georgia Lawyers for the Arts
887 W. Marietta Ave., Ste: J-101
Atlanta, GA 30318
404-873-3911 | Fax: 404-817-6827
gla@glarts.org | www.glarts.org

ILLINOIS
Lawyers for the Creative Arts
213 W. Institute Pl., Suite 403
Chicago, IL 60610
312-649-4111 | Fax: 312-944-2195

KANSAS
Kansas City Volunteer Lawyers &
Accountants for the Arts
PO Box 413199
Kansas City, MO 64104
816-977-3587
www.kcvlaa.org | info@kcvlaa.org

LOUISIANA
Louisiana Volunteer Lawyers for the Arts
818 Howard, Suite 300
New Orleans, LA 70113
504-523-1465 | Fax: 504-529-1465
www.artscouncilofneworleans.org

MAINE
Maine Lawyer Referral & Information Service
Maine State Bar Association
800-860-1460 (toll-free) | 207- 622-7523 (local)
Fax: 207-623-0083
www.mainebar.org/

MASSACHUSETTS
Volunteer Lawyers for the Arts of
Massachusetts, Inc.
249 A Street, Studio 14
Boston, MA 02110
617-350-7600 | 617-350-7600 TTY
Fax: 617-350-7610
mail@vlama.org | www.vlama.org

MICHIGAN
ArtServe Michigan
Volunteer Lawyers for the Arts & Culture
Riley Broadcast Court
1 Clover Court
Wixom, MI 48393
248-912-0760 | Fax: 248-912-0768
neeta@artservemichigan.org
www.artservemichigan.org

MINNESOTA
Springboard for the Arts
Resources and Counseling for the Arts
308 Prince St., Suite 270
St. Paul, MN 55101
651-292-4381 | 800-546-2891 x.1
Fax: 651-292-4315
www.springboardforthearts.org

MISSOURI
Kansas City Volunteer Lawyers &
Accountants for the Arts
115 W. 18th St.
Kansas City, MO 64108
(816) 472-3535
info@kcvlaa.org | www.kcvlaa.org

St. Louis Volunteer Lawyers &
Accountants for the Arts
3540 Washington
St. Louis, MO 63103
314-652-2410 | Fax: 314-652-0011
vlaa@stlrac.org

MONTANA
Montana Arts Council
(Note: No more pro bono for arts-related issues)
Postal Address:
P.O. Box 202201
Helena, MT 59620-2201
Street Address:
830 N. Warren St., 1st Floor
Helena, MT 59601
406-444-6430 | Fax: 406-444-6548
mac@mt.gov | www.art.mt.gov

NEW HAMPSHIRE
Lawyers for the Arts—New Hampshire
One Granite Pl.
Concord, NH 03301
603-224-8300 | Fax: 603-226-2963
arts@nhbca.com
www.nhbca.com/lawyersforarts.php

NEW JERSEY
New Jersey Volunteer Lawyers for the Arts
P.O. Box 1520
Laurel Springs, NJ 08021
856-963-6300 | Fax: 856-963-6301
info@njvla.org | www.njvla.org

NEW YORK
Volunteer Lawyers for the Arts
1 E. 53rd St., 6th Fl.
New York, NY 10022
212-319-2787 x1 | Fax: 212-752-6575
www.vlany.org | vlany@vlany.net

NORTH CAROLINA
North Carolina Volunteer Lawyers for the Arts
(NCVLA)
PO Box 26513
Raleigh, NC 27611
919-491-4625 | Fax: 775-255-5286
info@ncvla.org | www.ncvla.org

OHIO
Volunteer Lawyers & Accountants
for the Arts—Cleveland
c/o The Cleveland Bar Association
1301 East 9th St., 2nd Level
Cleveland, OH 44114
216-696-3525 (Lawyer referral service)
www.clevelandbar.org

Toledo Volunteer Lawyers &
Accountants for the Arts
c/o Arnold Gottlieb, Esq.
608 Madison, Suite 1523
Toledo, OH 43604
419-255-3344 | Fax: 419-255-1329

OKLAHOMA
Oklahoma Accountants & Lawyers for the Arts
c/o Eric King, Gable & Gotwals
One Leadership Sq., 15th Fl.
211 N. Robinson
Oklahoma City, OK 73102
405-235-5518 | Fax: 405-235-2875
eking@gablelaw.com

OREGON
Northwest Lawyers for the Arts
621 SW Morrison Street, Suite 1417
Portand, Oregon 97205
503-295-2787 | artcop@aol.com

PENNSYLVANIA
Philadelphia Volunteer Lawyers for the Arts
The Bellevue Offices of the Philadelphia
Chamber of Commerce
200 South Broad St., Suite 700
Philadelphia, PA 19102
215-545-3385 | Fax: 215-545-4839
pvla@libertynet.org

Pittsburgh Volunteer Lawyers for the Arts
Greater Pittsburgh Arts Council
707 Penn Ave., 2nd Floor
Pittsburgh, PA 15222
412-391-2060 | Fax: 412-394-4280
info@pittsburghartscouncil.org
www.pittsburghartscouncil.org

RHODE ISLAND
Ocean State Lawyers for the Arts
PO Box 19
Saunderstown, RI 02874
401-789-5686|
dspatt@artslaw.org | www.artslaw.org

TENNESSEE
Tennessee Volunteer Lawyers for the Arts
1507 16th Ave., South
Nashville, TN 37212
615-298-9309 | Fax: 615-298-9353

TEXAS
Artists' Legal and Accounting Assistance
205 West 9th St., Suite 233
Austin, TX 78701
512-476-4458 | Fax: 512-478-4269

Texas Accountants & Lawyers for the Arts
1540 Sul Ross
Houston, TX 77006
800-526-8252 (toll-free)
713-526-4876 x201 (local) | Fax: 713-526-1299
info@talarts.org

UTAH
Utah Lawyers for the Arts
PO Box 652
Salt Lake City, UT 84110
801-482-5373 | 801-521-3200
Contact: Andrew Deiss
adeiss@joneswaldo.com

WASHINGTON
Washington Lawyers for the Arts
1525 4th Avenue, Suite 800
Seattle, WA 98101
206-328-7053 | Fax: 206-545-4866
info@thewla.org | www.wa-artlaw.org

WISCONSIN
Wisconsin Volunteer Lawyers for the Arts
P.O. Box 1054
Madison, WI 53701
608-255 8316
akatz@artswisconsin.org
www.artswisconsin.org

Conferences, Trade Shows, & Merchandise Markets

NOTE: Information is subject to change.

America's Mart, Atlanta
240 Peachtree Street, Suite 2200
Atlanta, GA 30303
404-220-3000 | www.americasmart.com

Boston Gift Show*

Chicago Gift Show
The Merchandise Mart
701 Michigan Avenue, Suite 470
Chicago, IL 60654
800-677-6278 | www.merchandisemart.com

Comic-Con
Comic Con International
P.O. Box 128458
San Diego, CA 92112-8458
619-491-2475
www.comic-con.org

Dallas Market Center
2100 Stemmons Freeway
Dallas, TX 75207
800-DALMKTS
www.dallasmarketcenter.com
www.glmshows.com

Game Developers Conference
www.gdconf.com

George Little Management, Inc.
10 Bank Street
White Plains, NY 10606
914-421-3200 | www.glmshows.com

Gourmet Products Show*
San Francisco, CA

HOW Design Conference
www.howconference.com
800-436-8700 or 513-531-2690, ext. 11450

ICON: The Illustration Conference
1140 Broadway, 4th Floor
New York, NY 10001
917-408-9944 | Fax 212-691-6609
www.theillustrationconference.org

International Surface Design
Association Conference
SDA
P.O. Box 360
Sebastopol, CA 95473-0360
707.829.3110 | www.surfacedesign.org

Los Angeles Merchandise Mart (including Invite,
L.A. Stationery Show, and Western Tabletop Fair)
1933 South Broadway Los Angeles, CA 90007
213-749-7911 | 800-LAMART4
www.merchandisemart.com/lamart/

Merchandise Mart Properties, Inc.
200 World Trade Center Chicago, Suite 470
Chicago, IL 60654
312-527-7600 | www.merchandisemart.com

National Stationery Show*
New York, NY

New York Home Textiles Show*
(America's Premier Bed, Bath, and Linen Show)
New York, NY
New York International Gift Fair*
(including Accent on Design and American
and International Crafts)

San Francisco International Gift Fair*
(including Accent on Design West, American
and International Crafts West, Just Kidstuff West,
and the Museum Source West)

San Francisco Mart*
1355 Market Street, Suite 294
San Francisco, CA, 94103
415-552-2311 | www.sfmart.com

Society of Children's Book Writers
& Illustrators Conference
323-782-1010 | Fax: 323-782-1892
www.scbwi.org

Surtex Show*
New York, NY
www.surtex.com

Toy Industry Association
1115 Broadway, Suite 400
New York, NY 10010
(212) 675-1141 | www.toy-tia.org

Washington DC Gift Show*

* See: George Little Management, Inc. for contact information.

Useful Web Sites

Adobe
www.adobe.com
Tutorials, free newsletters, and free technical announcements via e-mail.

Animation World Network
www.awn.com
The largest animation-related publishing group on the Internet, providing a wide range of interesting, relevant, and helpful info pertaining to all aspects of animation. It covers areas as diverse as animator profiles, independent film distribution, commercial studio activities, licensing, CGI and other animation technologies, as well as in-depth coverage of current events in all fields of animation.

artBizcoach.com
www.artbizcoach.com
Articles on new marketing ideas, time management and productivity, getting organized for art shows, etc.

Creative Eye
www.creativeeyecoop.com
A cooperative for photographers and illustrators created to increase the competitiveness of its members through purchasing and licensing programs.

CNET Builder
www.builder.com
A site full of web site construction tips and tricks.

Copyright Alliance
www.copyrightalliance.com
The website and blog of a group of institutions and individuals who have chosen to work together to champion copyright as fundamental to the United States' creativity, jobs, and growth. The Alliance represents all creative industries. The site is a good source for information about copyright, news about the latest copyright issues and legislation, and curriculum resources for educators. It also includes a glossary of copyright and computer-related terms.

Domtar Designer Corner
www.domtardesignercorner.com
An inspirational and informative online design source from Domtar Paper. Created by designers for designers, it covers everything from industry news and events to designer profiles, eco-smart design options, and tips for selecting the best paper to bring designs to life.

Dynamic Drive.com
dynamicdrive.com/dynamicindex1/index.html
Help creating DHTML menus in the browser, pull down menus, cascading menus, etc.

Graphic Artists Guild
www.graphicartistsguild.org
Numerous resources for graphic artists and art buyers: copyright and contract information; updates on the latest legislation affecting creative professionals; archived issues of *Guild News;* and portfolio section, organized by artistic discipline, with live links to graphic artists' web sites. Members-only section has numerous community forums where members can communicate and consult with each other.

Library of Congress/Copyright Office
www.loc.gov | www.loc.gov/copyright
Home of the U.S. Copyright Office as well as online exhibitions and access to several digital collections.

lynda.com
www.lynda.com
Online subscription software training in Web design and development, digital photography, motion graphics, etc. All major software represented. Free video tutorials to preview training courses. Subscriptions available by month or year.

Macintosh information
www.Macfixit.com | www.macintouch.com
Technical information, tips, news, etc., for Mac users.

Matt's Script Archive
www.scriptarchive.com
This is the place to go to tame your CGI and PERL script nightmares!

morgueFile
www.morguefile.com
A public image archive for creatives by creatives. Free photos for inspiration, reference, and use (even commercial). Very flexible usage terms and no licensing fees.

MyFonts
http://new.myfonts.com/
World's largest collection of fonts: find fonts for a project, identify fonts that you've seen, try fonts before buying. Site also includes the newsletter Rising Stars featuring popular new fonts.

Neenah Paper
www.neenahpaper.com
Resource center contains great information on paper, postal requirements (size standards, business reply mail, etc.) and glossary of paper terms.

Search Engine Watch
searchenginewatch.com
Want to know how all those search engines really work? Danny Sullivan's site has the answers.

Skillset: The Sector Skills Council
for Creative Minds
www.skillset.org
Although a British web site, Skillset has a wealth of information about creative occupations. For example, for animation, it describes the phases of the animation process in great detail, defines specific jobs in the industry, and explains the differences among traditional 2-D, computer 2-D, 3-D, and stop-motion animation. Other industries included are computer games, film, interactive media, photo imaging, publishing, radio, and TV.

Tax and Accounting Sites Directory
www.taxsites.com
One-stop shopping for all types of tax information, this is an extremely easy-to-use site with direct links to international, federal, state, and local tax web sites, organized in chart form. It includes tax law and regulations, rates and tables, forms and publications, news, and updates. Also has sections relating to accounting and payroll. A service of AccountantsWorld, LLC.

The 11 Second Club
www.11secondclub.com
Sponsored by animationmentor.com, The 11 Second Club is a monthly character animation competition open to everyone. It provides a free platform to train and test animation skills.

The Copyright Society of the U.S.A.
www.csusa.org
A not-for-profit corporation, the Society works to advance the study and understanding of copyright law and related rights, the scope of rights in literature, music, art, theater, motion picture, television, computer software, architecture, and other works of authorship, and their distribution via both traditional and new media. Sponsors of Copyright Awareness Week. Site includes curricula for teaching copyright awareness in schools, including history and interesting facts.

U.S. Copyright Office
www.copyright.gov
An extremely well-organized and helpful site that includes copyright basics and history; frequently asked questions section; step-by-step instructions on how to register; help via e-mail; and the publications, circulars, and forms needed for registering, which can be downloaded. The Office offers online registration at a reduced fee of $35. Paper registration is still available at $65.

U.S. Patent and Trademark Office
www.uspto.gov
Online trademark searches and application filing for trademark registration. Includes basic information and FAQs about trademarks and step-by-step directions for filing. Forms available for downloading and printing.

Visibone
www.visibone.com/swatches
Get web-safe palettes for Photoshop and ImageReady.

Web Design Group
htmlhelp.com
The Web Design Group was founded to promote the creation of non-browser-specific, non-resolution-specific, creative and informative sites that are accessible to all users worldwide.

WebMonkey
www.webmonkey.com
A killer web-site-building site from *Wired* magazine.

William House
www.williamhouse.com
Information about paper resources, envelopes, sizes for booklets, etc.

CONTRACTS & FORMS

This Appendix contains standard Graphic Artists Guild contracts and other useful forms for doing business. Also included is the U.S. Copyright Office Form VA for registering a work of the Visual Arts. The forms appear in order from general (all purpose or for use by most graphic artists) to specific (by discipline).

How to Use These Forms

It should be noted that while these forms are as comprehensive as possible, some terms might not be suited to a given assignment. However, these forms can be used as starting points for your own customized contracts. Be aware that legal language is written to be precise, and attempts to simplify contract terms into "plain English" or delete contract terms altogether may leave the artist exposed to misinterpretation and misunderstanding of important aspects of an agreement.

Form VA
For a Work of the Visual Arts
UNITED STATES COPYRIGHT OFFICE

REGISTRATION NUMBER

_____

VA   VAU

EFFECTIVE DATE OF REGISTRATION

_____

Month   Day   Year

DO NOT WRITE ABOVE THIS LINE. IF YOU NEED MORE SPACE, USE A SEPARATE CONTINUATION SHEET.

Title of This Work ▼   **NATURE OF THIS WORK ▼** See instructions

Previous or Alternative Titles ▼

Publication as a Contribution If this work was published as a contribution to a periodical, serial, or collection, give information about the collective work in which the contribution appeared. **Title of Collective Work ▼**

If published in a periodical or serial give: **Volume ▼**   **Number ▼**   **Issue Date ▼**   **On Pages ▼**

2

a

NAME OF AUTHOR ▼   **DATES OF BIRTH AND DEATH**
Year Born ▼   Year Died ▼

NOTE

der the law,
e "author" of
work made
hire" is
nerally the
ployer, not
e employee
ee instruc-
ns). For any
rt of this
rk that was
ade for hire"
eck "Yes" in
e space
ovided, give
e employer
other
rson for
om the work
s prepared)
"Author" of
at part, and
ve the
ace for dates
birth and
ath blank.

Was this contribution to the work a "work made for hire"?   Author's Nationality or Domicile   Was This Author's Contribution to the Work
☐ Yes   ☐ No   Name of Country   **OR** { Citizen of _____ / Domiciled in _____   Anonymous? ☐ Yes ☐ No   Pseudonymous? ☐ Yes ☐ No   If the answer to either of these questions is "Yes," see detailed instructions.

Nature of Authorship Check appropriate box(es). **See instructions**
☐ 3-Dimensional sculpture   ☐ Map   ☐ Technical drawing
☐ 2-Dimensional artwork   ☐ Photograph   ☐ Text
☐ Reproduction of work of art   ☐ Jewelry design   ☐ Architectural work

b

Name of Author ▼   **Dates of Birth and Death**
Year Born ▼   Year Died ▼

Was this contribution to the work a "work made for hire"?   Author's Nationality or Domicile   Was This Author's Contribution to the Work
☐ Yes   ☐ No   Name of Country   **OR** { Citizen of _____ / Domiciled in _____   Anonymous? ☐ Yes ☐ No   Pseudonymous? ☐ Yes ☐ No   If the answer to either of these questions is "Yes," see detailed instructions.

Nature of Authorship Check appropriate box(es). **See instructions**
☐ 3-Dimensional sculpture   ☐ Map   ☐ Technical drawing
☐ 2-Dimensional artwork   ☐ Photograph   ☐ Text
☐ Reproduction of work of art   ☐ Jewelry design   ☐ Architectural work

---

3

a   **Year in Which Creation of This Work Was Completed**   This information must be given   _____ Year   in all cases.

b   **Date and Nation of First Publication of This Particular Work**   Complete this information ONLY if this work has been published.   Month _____ Day _____ Year _____   Nation

---

4

instructions
ore completing
space.

COPYRIGHT CLAIMANT(S) Name and address must be given even if the claimant is the same as the author given in space 2. ▼

Transfer If the claimant(s) named here in space 4 is (are) different from the author(s) named in space 2, give a brief statement of how the claimant(s) obtained ownership of the copyright. ▼

DO NOT WRITE HERE
OFFICE USE ONLY

APPLICATION RECEIVED

ONE DEPOSIT RECEIVED

TWO DEPOSITS RECEIVED

FUNDS RECEIVED

MORE ON BACK ▶   • Complete all applicable spaces (numbers 5-9) on the reverse side of this page.
   • See detailed instructions.   • Sign the form at line 8.

DO NOT WRITE HERE
Page 1 of _____ pages

EXAMINED BY

CHECKED BY

CORRESPONDENCE
☐ Yes

FORM VA

FOR
COPYRIGH
OFFICE
USE
ONLY

DO NOT WRITE ABOVE THIS LINE. IF YOU NEED MORE SPACE, USE A SEPARATE CONTINUATION SHEET.

PREVIOUS REGISTRATION Has registration for this work, or for an earlier version of this work, already been made in the Copyright Office?

☐ **Yes** ☐ **No** If your answer is "Yes," why is another registration being sought? (Check appropriate box.) ▼

a. ☐ This is the first published edition of a work previously registered in unpublished form.

b. ☐ This is the first application submitted by this author as copyright claimant.

c. ☐ This is a changed version of the work, as shown by space 6 on this application.

If your answer is "Yes," give: **Previous Registration Number** ▼   **Year of Registration** ▼

5

DERIVATIVE WORK OR COMPILATION Complete both space 6a and 6b for a derivative work; complete only 6b for a compilation.

a. Preexisting Material Identify any preexisting work or works that this work is based on or incorporates. ▼

b. Material Added to This Work Give a brief, general statement of the material that has been added to this work and in which copyright is claimed. ▼

6

a

b

See instructions
before completi
this space.

DEPOSIT ACCOUNT If the registration fee is to be charged to a Deposit Account established in the Copyright Office, give name and number of Account.

Name ▼   **Account Number** ▼

CORRESPONDENCE Give name and address to which correspondence about this application should be sent. Name/Address/Apt/City/State/Zip ▼

7

a

b

Area code and daytime telephone number   (   )   Fax number   (   )

Email

CERTIFICATION* I, the undersigned, hereby certify that I am the

check only one ▶ {
☐ author
☐ other copyright claimant
☐ owner of exclusive right(s)
☐ authorized agent of
}

Name of author or other copyright claimant, or owner of exclusive right(s) ▲

of the work identified in this application and that the statements made by me in this application are correct to the best of my knowledge.

Typed or printed name and date ▼ If this application gives a date of publication in space 3, do not sign and submit it before that date.

Date

Handwritten signature (X) ▼

X

8

Certificate
will be
mailed in
window
envelope
to this
address:

Name ▼

Number/Street/Apt ▼

City/State/ZIP ▼

YOU MUST:
· Complete all necessary spaces
· Sign your application in space 8
**SEND ALL 3 ELEMENTS
IN THE SAME PACKAGE:**
1. Application form
2. Nonrefundable filing fee in check or money order payable to *Register of Copyrights*
3. Deposit material
MAIL TO:
Library of Congress
Copyright Office
101 Independence Avenue SE
Washington, DC 20559-6000

9

*17 *USC* §506(e): Any person who knowingly makes a false representation of a material fact in the application for copyright registration provided for by section 409, or in any written statement filed in connection with the application, shall be fined not more than $2,500.

Form VA – Full   Rev: 07/2006   Print: 07/2006–30,000   Printed on recycled paper   U.S. Government Printing Office: 2004-320-958   60

"Cease & Desist" Letter

Artist s Letterhead

[Date]
[First & Last Name]
[Address]
RE: [List project or issue]

Dear [name]:

It has come to my attention that you have made an unauthorized use of my copyrighted work entitled [name of work] (the "Work") in the preparation of a work derived there from. I have reserved all rights in the Work, first published in [date], [and have registered copyright therein]. Your work entitled [name of infringing work] is essentially identical to the Work and clearly used the Work as its basis. [Give a few examples that illustrate direct copying.]

As you neither asked for nor received permission to use the Work as the basis for [name of infringing work] nor to make or distribute copies, including electronic copies, of same, I believe you have willfully infringed my rights under 17 U.S.C. Section 101 et seq. and could be liable for statutory damages as high as $150,000 as set forth in Section 504(c) (2) therein.

I demand that you immediately cease the use and distribution of all infringing works derived from the Work, and all copies, including electronic copies, of same, that you deliver to me, if applicable, all unused, undistributed copies of same, or destroy such copies immediately and that you desist from this or any other infringement of my rights in the future. If I have not received an affirmative response from you by [date give them about 2 weeks] indicating that you have fully complied with these requirements, I shall take further action against you.

Very truly yours,

Artist-Agent Agreement

Remove all language in italics before using this form.

FRONT

Artist's Letterhead

Agreement, this _____ day of _____ , 200___ , between _____

(hereinafter referred to as the "Artist"), residing at _____

and _____ (hereinafter referred to as the "Agent"), residing at _____

Whereas, the Artist is an established artist of proven talents; and

Whereas the Artist wishes to have an agent represent him or her in marketing certain rights enumerated herein; and

Whereas the Agent is capable of marketing the artwork produced by the Artist; and

Whereas the Agent wishes to represent the Artist;

Now, therefore, in consideration of the foregoing premises and the mutual covenants hereinafter set forth and other valuable consideration, the parties hereto agree as follows:

1. Agency
The Artist appoints the Agent to act as his or her [non-] exclusive representative: **(A)** in the following geographical area:

_____

_____

(B) for the markets listed here *(specify publishing, advertising, etc.)*:

_____

_____

The Agent agrees to use his or her best efforts in submitting the Artist's work for the purpose of securing assignment for the Artist. The Agent shall negotiate the terms of any assignment that is offered, but the Artist shall have the right to reject any assignment if he or she finds the terms thereof unacceptable.

2. Promotion
The Artist shall provide the Agent with such samples of work as are from time to time necessary for the purpose of securing assignments. These samples shall remain the property of the Artist and be returned within 30 days of termination of this Agreement. The Agent shall take reasonable efforts to protect the work from loss or damage, but shall be liable for such loss or damage only if caused by the Agent's negligence. Promotional expenses, including but not limited to promotional mailings and paid advertising, shall be paid _____% by the Agent and _____% by the Artist. The Agent shall bear the expenses of shipping, insurance, and similar marketing expenses.

3. Term
This Agreement shall take effect on the _____ day of _____ , 200___ , and remain in full force and effect for a term of one year, unless terminated as provided in Paragraph 9.

4. Commissions
The Agent shall be entitled to the following commissions: **(A)** On assignments secured by the Agent during the term of this Agreement, 25% of the billing. **(B)** On house accounts, 10% of the billing. For purposes of this Agreement, house accounts are defined as accounts obtained by the Artist at any time or obtained by another agent representing the Artist prior to the commencement of this Agreement and are listed in Schedule A attached to this Agreement. It is understood by both parties that no commission shall be paid on assignments rejected by the Artist or for which the Artist fails to receive payment, regardless of the reason payment is not made. Further, no commissions shall be payable in either **(A)** or **(B)** above for any part of the billing that is due to expenses incurred by the Artists in performing the assignment, whether or not such expenses are reimbursed by the Client. In the event that a flat fee is paid by the Client, it shall be reduced by the amount of expenses incurred by the Artist in performing the assignment, and the Agent's commission shall be payable only on the fee as reduced for expenses.

5. Billing
The [ ] Artist [ ] Agent shall be responsible for all billings.

6. Payments
The party responsible for billing (the "Billing Party") agrees to hold all funds due to the other party as trust funds in an account separate from the Billing Party's funds prior to making payment to the other party. The Billing Party shall make all payments due within 10 days of receipt of any fees covered by this Agreement. Late payments shall be accompanied by interest calculated at the rate of _____% per month thereafter.

7. Accountings
The Billing Party shall send copies of invoices to the other party when rendered. If requested, that party shall also provide the other party with semiannual accountings showing all assignments for the period, the Clients' names, the fees paid, expenses incurred by the Artist, the dates of payment, the amounts on which the Agent's commissions are to be calculated, and the sums due less those amounts already paid.

8. Inspection of the Books and Records

The Billing Party responsible shall keep the books and records with respect to commissions due at his or her place of business and permit the other party to inspect these books and records during normal business hours on the giving of reasonable notice.

9. Termination

This Agreement may be terminated by either party by giving 30 days written notice to the other party. If the Artist receives assignments after the termination date from Clients originally obtained by the Agent during the term of this Agreement, the commission specified in Paragraph 4(A) shall be payable to the Agent under the following circumstances. If the Agent has represented the Artist for 6 months or less, the Agent shall receive a commission on such assignments received by the Artist within 90 days of the date of termination. This period shall increase by 30 days for each additional 6 months that the Agent has represented the Artist, but in no event shall such period exceed 180 days.

10. Assignment

This Agreement shall not be assigned by either of the parties hereto. It shall be binding on and inure to the benefit of the successors, administrators, executors, or heirs of the Agent and Artist.

11. Arbitration

Any disputes in excess of $ _____ (*maximum limit for small-claims court*) arising out of this Agreement shall be submitted to binding arbitration before a mutually agreed-upon arbitrator pursuant to the rules of the American Arbitration Association. The Arbitrator's award shall be final and judgment may be entered in any court having jurisdiction thereof. The Agent shall pay all arbitration and court costs, reasonable attorney's fees, and legal interest on any award of judgment in favor of the Artist.

12. Notices

All notices shall be given to the parties at their respective addresses set forth above.

13. Independent Contractor Status

Both parties agree that the Agent is acting as an independent contractor. This Agreement is not an employment agreement, nor does it constitute a joint venture or partnership between the Artist and Agent.

14. Amendments and Merger

All amendments to this Agreement must be written. This Agreement incorporates the entire understanding of the parties.

15. Governing Law

This Agreement shall be governed by the laws of the State of _____.

In witness whereof, the parties have signed this Agreement as of the date set forth above.

SCHEDULE A: HOUSE ACCOUNTS

Date _____

1. *name and address of Client* _____

2. _____

3. _____

4. _____

5. _____

6. _____

7. _____

8. _____

9. _____

10. _____

11. _____

12. _____

Artist _____   Agent _____

Artwork Inventory Form

Remove all language in italics before using this form.

Artist's Letterhead

ID#

Final or Rough

Name of Publication

Date Sent

Date Accepted

Date Final Due *(if applicable)*

Fee Negotiated

Date Rejected

Date Artwork Returned

All-Purpose Purchase Order

Remove all language in italics before using this form.

FRONT

Art Buyer's Letterhead

TO

Commissioned by _____

Date _____

Purchase Order Number _____

Job Number _____

ASSIGNMENT DESCRIPTION *(Indicate any preliminary presentations required by the buyer.)*

Delivery date _____

Fee _____

BUYER SHALL REIMBURSE ARTIST FOR THE FOLLOWING EXPENSES

Messengers _____   Models _____   Props _____

Travel _____   Telephone _____   Proofs _____

Transport disks _____   Transparencies _____   Film output _____

Other _____

RIGHTS TRANSFERRED. BUYER PURCHASES THE FOLLOWING EXCLUSIVE RIGHTS FOR USAGE:

Title or Product *(name)* _____

Category or Use *(advertising, corporate, promotional, editorial, etc.)* _____

Medium of Use *(consumer or trade magazine, annual report, TV, book, etc.)* _____

Edition (if book) *(hardcover, mass-market paperback, quality paperback, etc.)* _____

Geographic Area *(if applicable)* _____

Time Period *(if applicable)* _____

Artist reserves any usage rights not expressly transferred. Any usage beyond that granted to buyer herein shall require the payment of a mutually agreed-upon additional fee. Any transfer of rights is conditional upon receipt of full payment.

TERMS

1. Time for Payment
All invoices shall be paid within 30 days of receipt. The grant of any license or right of copyright is conditioned on receipt of full payment.

2. Default in Payment
The Buyer shall assume responsibility for all collection of legal fees necessitated by default in payment.

3. Changes
Buyer shall make additional payments for changes requested in original assignment. However, no additional payment shall be made for changes required to conform to the original assignment description. The Buyer shall offer the Artist first opportunity to make any changes.

4. Expenses
Buyer shall reimburse Artist for all expenses arising from this assignment, including the payment of any sales taxes due on this assignment. Buyer's approval shall be obtained for any increases in fees or expenses that exceed the original estimate by 10% or more.

5. Cancellation
In the event of cancellation of this assignment, ownership of all copyrights and the original artwork shall be retained by the Artist, and a cancellation fee for work completed, based on the contract price and expenses already incurred, shall be paid by the Buyer.

6. Ownership of Artwork
The Artist retains ownership of all original artwork, whether preliminary or final, and the Buyer shall return such artwork within 30 days of use.

7. Credit Lines
The Buyer shall give Artist and any other creators a credit line with any editorial usage. If similar credit lines are to be given with other types of usage, it must be so indicated here:

_____

_____

_____

[ ] If this box is checked, the credit line shall be in the form: © 200___ _____.

8. Releases
Buyer shall indemnify Artist against all claims and expenses, including reasonable attorney's fees, due to uses for which no release was requested in writing or for uses which exceed authority granted by a release.

9. Modifications
Modification of the Agreement must be written, except that the invoice may include, and Buyer shall pay, fees or expenses that were orally authorized in order to progress promptly with the work.

10. Warranty of Originality
The Artist warrants and represents that, to the best of his/her knowledge, the work assigned hereunder is original and has not been previously published, or that consent to use has been obtained on an unlimited basis; that all work or portions thereof obtained through the undersigned from third parties is original or, if previously published, that consent to use has been obtained on an unlimited basis; that the Artist has full authority to make this agreement; and that the work prepared by the Artist does not contain any scandalous, libelous, or unlawful matter. This warranty does not extend to any uses that the Buyer or others may make of the Artist's product that may infringe on the rights of others. Buyer expressly agrees that it will hold the Artist harmless for all liability caused by the Buyer's use of the Artist's product to the extent such use infringes on the rights of others.

11. Limitation of Liability
Buyer agrees that it shall not hold the Artist or his/her agents or employees liable for any incidental or consequential damages that arise from the Artist's failure to perform any aspect of the Project in a timely manner, regardless of whether such failure was caused by intentional or negligent acts or omissions of the Artist or third party.

12. Dispute Resolution
Any disputes in excess of $ _____ *(maximum limit for small-claims court)* arising out of this Agreement shall be submitted to binding arbitration by a mutually agreed-upon arbitrator pursuant to the rules of the American Arbitration Association. The Arbitrator's award shall be final, and judgment may be entered in any court having jurisdiction thereof. The Buyer shall pay all arbitration and court costs, reasonable attorney's fees, and legal interest on any award of judgment in favor of the Artist.

13. Acceptance of Terms
The signature of both parties shall evidence acceptance of these terms.

Consented and agreed to

Artist's signature/date _____

Authorized signature/date _____

Buyer's name and title _____

Nondisclosure Agreement for Submitting Ideas

FRONT

Illustrator's or Designer's Letterhead

Agreement, entered into as of this _____ day of _____, 200__, between _____

(hereinafter referred to as the "Illustrator" or "Designer"), located at _____

and _____ (hereinafter referred to as the "Recipient")

located at _____

Whereas, the Illustrator (or Designer) has developed certain valuable information, concepts, ideas, or designs, which the Illustrator (or Designer) deems confidential (hereinafter referred to as the "Information"); and

Whereas, the Recipient is in the business of using such Information for its projects and wishes to review the Information; and

Whereas, the Illustrator (or Designer) wishes to disclose this Information to the Recipient; and

Whereas, the Recipient is willing not to disclose this Information, as provided in this Agreement;

Now, therefore, in consideration of the foregoing premises and the mutual covenants hereinafter set forth and other valuable considerations, the parties hereto agree as follows:

1. Disclosure
Illustrator (or Designer) shall disclose to the Recipient the Information, which concerns _____

_____

_____

_____

2. Purpose
Recipient agrees that this disclosure is only for the purpose of the Recipient's evaluation to determine its interest in the commercial exploitation of the Information.

3. Limitation on Use
Recipient agrees not to manufacture, sell, deal in, or otherwise use or appropriate the disclosed Information in any way whatsoever, including but not limited to adaptation, imitation, redesign, or modification. Nothing contained in this Agreement shall be deemed to give Recipient any rights whatsoever in and to the Information.

4. Confidentiality
Recipient understands and agrees that the unauthorized disclosure of the Information by the Recipient to others would irreparably damage the Illustrator (or Designer). As consideration and in return for the disclosure of this Information, the Recipient shall keep secret and hold in confidence all such Information and treat the Information as if it were the Recipient's own property by not disclosing it to any person or entity.

5. Good-Faith Negotiations
If, on the basis of the evaluation of the Information, Recipient wishes to pursue the exploitation thereof, Recipient agrees to enter into good-faith negotiations to arrive at a mutually satisfactory agreement for these purposes. Until and unless such an agreement is entered into, this nondisclosure Agreement shall remain in force.

6. Miscellany
This Agreement shall be binding upon and shall inure to the benefit of the parties and their respective legal representatives, successors, and assigns.

© Tad Crawford 1990

In witness whereof, the parties have signed this Agreement as of the date first set forth above.

Illustrator (or Designer) _____

Recipient _____

Company name _____

By _____

Authorized signatory, title _____

Licensing Agreement (Short Form)

FRONT

Licensor's Letterhead

1. _____ (The "Licensor") hereby grants to _____ (the "Licensee") a nonexclusive license to use the image _____ _____ (the "Image") created and owned by Licensor on ("Licensed Products") and to distribute and sell these Licensed Products in _____ *(territory)* for a term of ____ years commencing _____ 200__, in accordance with the terms and conditions of this Agreement.

2. Licensor shall retain all copyrights in and to the Image. Licensee shall identify the Licensor as the artist on the Licensed Products and shall reproduce thereon the following copyright notice: © 200__ _____.

3. Licensee agrees to pay the Licensor a nonrefundable royalty of _____(_____%) percent of the net sales of the Licensed Products. "Net Sales" as used herein shall mean sales to customers less prepaid freight and credits for lawful and customary volume rebates, actual returns, and allowances. Royalties shall be deemed to accrue when the Licensed Products are sold, shipped, or invoiced, whichever first occurs.

4. Licensee shall pay Licensor a nonrefundable advance in the amount of $ _____ upon signing of this Agreement. Licensee further agrees to pay Licensor a guaranteed nonrefundable minimum royalty of $ _____ every month.

5. Royalty payments shall be paid on the first day of each month commencing _____, 200__, and Licensee shall furnish Licensor with monthly statements of account showing the kinds and quantities of all Licensed Products sold, the prices received therefor, and all deductions for freight, volume rebates, returns, and allowances. The first royalty statement shall be sent on _____, 200____.

6. Licensor shall have the right to terminate this Agreement upon 30 days' notice if Licensee fails to make any payment required of it and does not cure this default within said 30 days, whereupon all rights granted herein shall revert immediately to the Licensor.

7. Licensee agrees to keep complete and accurate books and records relating to the sale of the Licensed Products. Licensor shall have the right to inspect Licensee's books and records concerning sales of the Licensed Products upon prior written notice.

8. Licensee shall give Licensor, free of charge, _____ *(number)* samples of each of the Licensed Products for Licensor's personal use. Licensor shall have the right to purchase additional samples of the Licensed Products at the Licensee's manufacturing cost. "Manufacturing cost" shall be $ _____ per Licensed Product.

9. Licensor shall have the right to approve the quality of the reproduction of the Image on the Licensed Products and on any approved advertising or promotional materials and Licensor shall not unreasonably withhold approval.

10. Licensee shall use its best efforts to promote, distribute, and sell the Licensed Products, and said Products shall be of the highest commercial quality.

11. All rights not specifically transferred by this Agreement are reserved to the Licensor. Any transfer of rights is conditional upon receipt of full payment.

12. The Licensee shall hold the Licensor harmless from and against any loss, expense, or damage occasioned by any claim, demand, suit, or recovery against the Licensor arising out of the use of the Image.

13. Nothing herein shall be construed to constitute the parties hereto joint ventures, nor shall any similar relationship be deemed to exist between them. This Agreement shall not be assigned in whole or in part without the prior written consent of the Licensor.

14. This Agreement shall be construed in accordance with the laws of *(state)*; Licensee consents to jurisdiction of the courts of *(state)*.

15. All notices, demands, payments, royalty payments and statements shall be sent to the Licensor at the following address: _____ and to the Licensee at: _____

16. Any disputes arising out of this Agreement shall be submitted to binding arbitration before a mutually agreed-upon arbitrator pursuant to the rules of the American Arbitration Association in the city of _____. The Arbitrator's award shall be final, and judgment may be entered in any court having jurisdiction thereof. The Licensee shall pay all arbitration and court costs, reasonable attorney's fees, and legal interest on any award of judgment in favor of the Licensor.

17. This Agreement constitutes the entire agreement between the parties hereto and shall not be modified, amended, or changed in any way except by written agreement signed by both parties hereto. This Agreement shall be binding upon and shall inure to the benefit of the parties, their successors, and assigns.

In witness whereof, the parties have executed this Licensing Agreement on the day _____, 200__.

Licensee *(company name)* _____

By *(name, position)* _____

Licensor _____

© Caryn Leland 1990

Licensing Agreement (Long Form)

FRONT

Licensor's Letterhead

1. Grant of License

Agreement made this _____ day of _____, 200_

between _____ *(the "Licensor")*,

having an address at _____

_____ *(address)*, and

_____ *(the "Licensee")*,

located at _____

_____ *(address)*, whereby

Licensor grants to Licensee a license to use the designs listed on the attached Schedules A and B (the "Designs") in accordance with the terms and conditions of this Agreement and only for the production, sale, advertising, and promotion of certain articles (the "Licensed Products") described in Schedule A for the Term and in the Territory set forth in said Schedule. Licensee shall have the right to affix the Trademarks: _____ and _____ on or to the Licensed Products and on packaging, advertising, and promotional materials sold, used, or distributed in connection with the Licensed Products.

2. Licensor's Representation and Credits

A. Licensor warrants that Licensor has the right to grant to the Licensee all of the rights conveyed in this Agreement. The Licensee shall have no right, license, or permission except as herein expressly granted. All rights not specifically transferred by the Agreement are reserved to the Licensor.

B. The Licensee prominently shall display and identify the Licensor as the designer on each Licensed Product and on all packaging, advertising, and display and in all publicity therefor and shall have reproduced thereon (or on an approved tag or label) the following notices: "© (Licensor's name), 200____. All rights reserved." The Licensed Products shall be marketed under the name _____

_____

for _____. The name shall not be co-joined with any third party's name without the Licensor's express written permission.

C. The Licensee shall have the right to use the Licensor's name, portrait, or picture, in a dignified manner consistent with the Licensor's reputation, in advertising or other promotional materials associated with the sale of the Licensed Products.

3. Royalties and Statements of Account

A. Licensee agrees to pay Licensor a nonrefundable royalty of _____ (_____%) of the net sales of all of the Licensed Products incorporating and embodying the Designs. "Net sales" is defined as sales direct to customers less prepaid freight and credits for lawful and customary volume rebates, actual returns, and allowances; the aggregate of said deductions and credits shall not exceed 3% of accrued royalties in any year. No costs incurred in the manufacture, sale, distribution, or exploitation of the Licensed Products shall be deducted from any royalties due to Licensor. Royalties shall be deemed to accrue when the Licensed Products are sold, shipped, or invoiced, whichever first occurs.

B. Royalty payments for all sales shall be due on the 15th day after the end of each calendar quarter. At that time and regardless if any Licensed Products were sold during the preceding time period, Licensee shall furnish Licensor an itemized statement categorized by Design, showing the kinds and quantities of all Licensed Products sold and the prices received therefor, and all deductions for freight, volume rebates, returns, and allowances. The first royalty statement shall commence on: _____ 200__.

C. If Licensor has not received the royalty payment as required by the foregoing paragraph 3B within 21 days following the end of each calendar quarter, a monthly service charge of 1 1/2% shall accrue thereon and become due and owing from the date on which such royalty payment became due and owing.

4. Advances and Minimum Royalties

A. In each year of this Agreement, Licensee agrees to pay Licensor a Guaranteed Minimum Royalty in the amount of $_____, of which $_____ shall be deemed a Nonrefundable Advance against royalties. The difference, if any, between the Advance and the Guaranteed Minimum Royalty shall be divided equally and paid quarterly over the term of this Agreement commencing with the quarter beginning _____ 200__.

B. The Nonrefundable Advance shall be paid on the signing of this agreement. No part of the Guaranteed Minimum Royalty or the Nonrefundable Advance shall be repayable to Licensee.

C. On signing of this Agreement, Licensee shall pay Licensor a nonrefundable design fee in the amount of $_____ per Design. This fee shall not be applied against royalties.

D. Licensor has the right to terminate this Agreement upon the giving of 30 days' notice to Licensee if the Licensee fails to pay any portion of the Guaranteed Minimum Royalty when due.

5. Books and Records

Licensee agrees to keep complete and accurate books and records relating to the sale and other distribution of each of the Licensed Products. Licensor or its representative shall have the right to inspect Licensee's books and records relating to the sales of the Licensed Products upon 30 days' prior written notice. Any discrepancies over 5% between the royalties received and the royalties due will be subject to the royalty payment set forth herein and paid immediately. If the audit discloses such an underpayment of 10% or more, Licensee shall reimburse the Licensor for all the costs of said audit.

6. Quality of Licensed Products, Approval, and Advertising

A. Licensee agrees that the Licensed Products shall be of the highest standard and quality and of such style and appearance as to be best suited to their exploitation to the best advantage and to the protection and enhancement of the Licensed Products and the good will pertaining thereto. The Licensed Products shall be manufactured, sold, and distributed in accordance with all applicable national, state, and local laws.

B. In order to ensure that the development, manufacture, appearance, quality, and distribution of each Licensed Product is consonant with the Licensor's good will associated with its reputation, copyrights, and trademark, Licensor shall have the right to approve, in advance, the quality of the Licensed Products (including, without limitation, concepts and preliminary prototypes, layouts, or camera-ready art prior to production of first sample and revised production sample, if any) and all agreements. No part of the Guaranteed Minimum Royalty or the Nonrefundable Advance shall be repayable to Licensee.

C. On signing this agreement, Licensee shall be responsible for delivering all items requiring prior approval pursuant to Paragraph 6B without cost to the Licensor. Licensor agrees not to withhold approval unreasonably.

D. Licensee shall not release or distribute any Licensed Product without securing each of the prior approvals provided for in Paragraph 6B. Licensee shall not depart from any approval secured in accordance with Paragraph 6B without Licensor's prior written consent.

E. Licensee agrees to expend at least _____% percent of anticipated gross sales of the Licensed Products annually to promote and advertise sales of the Licensed Products.

7. Nonexclusive Rights

Nothing in this Agreement shall be construed to prevent Licensor from granting other licenses for the use of the Designs or from utilizing the Designs in any manner whatsoever, except that the Licensor shall not grant other Licenses for the use of the Designs in connection with the sale of the Licensed Products in the Territory to which this License extends during the term of this Agreement.

8. Nonacquisition of Rights

The Licensee's use of the Designs and Trademarks shall inure to the benefit of the Licensor. If Licensee acquires any trade rights, trademarks, equities, titles, or other rights in and to the Designs or in the Trademark, by operation of law, usage, or otherwise during the term of this Agreement or any extension thereof, Licensee shall forthwith upon the expiration of this Agreement or any extension thereof or sooner termination, assign and transfer the same to Licensor without any consideration other than the consideration of this Agreement.

9. Licensee's Representations

The License warrants and represents that during the term of this License and for any time thereafter, it, or any of its affiliated, associated, or subsidiary companies will not copy, imitate, or authorize the imitation or copying of the Designs, Trade names, and Trademarks, or any distinctive feature of the foregoing or other designs submitted to the Licensee by Licensor. Without prejudice to any other remedies the Licensor may have, royalties as provided herein shall accrue and be paid by Licensee on all items embodying and incorporating imitated or copied Designs.

10. Registrations and Infringements

A. The Licensor has the right but not the obligation to obtain, at its own cost, appropriate copyright, trademark, and patent protection for the Designs and the Trademarks. At Licensor's request and at Licensee's sole cost and expense, Licensee shall make all necessary and appropriate registrations to protect the copyrights, trademarks, and patents in and to the Licensed Products and the advertising, promotional, and packaging material in the Territory in which the Licensed Products are sold. Copies of all applications shall be submitted for approval to Licensor prior to filing. The Licensee and Licensor agree to cooperate with each other to assist in the filing of said registrations.

B. Licensee shall not at any time apply for or abet any third party to apply for copyright, trademark, or patent protection that would affect Licensor's ownership of any rights in the Designs or the Trademarks.

C. Licensee shall notify Licensor in writing immediately upon discovery of any infringements or imitations by others of the Designs, Trade names, or Trademarks. Licensor in its sole discretion may bring any suit, action, or proceeding Licensor deems appropriate to protect Licensor's rights in the Designs, Trade names, and Trademarks, including, without limitation, for copyright and trademark infringement and for unfair competition.

If for any reason Licensor does not institute any such suit or take any such action or proceeding, upon written notice to the Licensor, Licensee may institute such appropriate suit, action, or proceeding in Licensee's and Licensor's names. In any event, Licensee and Licensor shall cooperate fully with each other in the prosecution of such suit, action, or proceeding. Licensor reserves the right, at Licensor's cost and expense, to join in any pending suit, action, or proceeding.

The instituting party shall pay all costs and expenses, including legal fees, incurred by the instituting party. All recoveries and awards, including settlements received, after payments of costs and legal fees, shall be divided 75% percent to the instituting party and 25% percent to the other party

11. Indemnification and Insurance

A. The Licensee hereby agrees to indemnify and hold the Licensor harmless against all liability, cost, loss, expense (including reasonable attorney's fees), or damages paid, incurred, or occasioned by any claim, demand, suit, settlement, or recovery against the Licensor, without limitation, arising out of the breach or claim of breach of this Agreement; the use of the Designs by it or any third party the manufacture, distribution, and sale of the Licensed Products; and for any alleged defects in the Licensed Products. Licensee hereby consents to submit to the personal jurisdiction of any court, tribunal, or forum in which an action or proceeding is brought involving a claim to which this foregoing indemnification shall apply.

B. Licensee shall obtain at its sole cost and expense product liability insurance in an amount providing sufficient and adequate coverage, but not less than $1 million combined single limit coverage protecting the Licensor against any claims or lawsuits arising from alleged defects in the Licensed Product.

12. Grounds for and Consequences of Termination

A. Licensor shall have the right to terminate this Agreement by written notice, and all the rights granted to the Licensee shall revert forthwith to the Licensor and all royalties or other payments shall become due and payable immediately if:

i. Licensee fails to comply with or fulfill any of the terms or conditions of this Agreement;

continued…

ii. The Licensed Products have not been offered or made available for sale by Licensee _____ months from the date hereof;

iii. Licensee ceases to manufacture and sell the Licensed Products in commercially reasonable quantities; or

iv. The Licensee is adjudicated a bankrupt, makes an assignment for the benefit of creditors, or liquidates its business.

B. Licensee, as quickly as possible, but in no event later than 30 days after such termination, shall submit to Licensor the statements required in Paragraph 3 for all sales and distributions through the date of termination. Licensor shall have the right to conduct an actual inventory on the date of termination or thereafter to verify the accuracy of said statements.

C. In the event of termination, all payments theretofore made to the Licensor shall belong to the Licensor without prejudice to any other remedies the Licensor may have.

13. Sell-off Right

Provided Licensee is not in default of any term or condition of this Agreement, Licensee shall have the right for a period of _____ months from the expiration of this Agreement or any extension thereof to sell inventory on hand subject to the terms and conditions of this Agreement, including the payment of royalties and guaranteed minimum royalties on sales that continue during this additional period.

14. Purchase at Cost

A. Licensor shall have the right to purchase from Licensee, at Licensee's manufacturing cost, such number of Licensed Products as Licensor may specify in writing to Licensee, but not to exceed _____ for any Licensed Product. For purposes of this Paragraph, "manufacturing cost" shall mean $ _____ per Licensed Product. Any amounts due to Licensee pursuant to this Paragraph shall not be deducted from any royalties, including any minimum royalties, owed to Licensor.

B. Licensee agrees to give the Licensor, without charge, _____ each of the Licensed Products.

15. Miscellaneous Provisions

A. Nothing herein shall be construed to constitute the parties hereto partners or joint ventures, nor shall any similar relationship be deemed to exist between them.

B. The rights herein granted are personal to the Licensee and shall not be transferred or assigned, in whole or in part, without the prior written consent of the Licensor.

C. No waiver of any condition or covenant of this Agreement by either party hereto shall be deemed to imply or constitute a further waiver by such party of the same or any other condition. This Agreement shall be binding upon and shall inure to the benefit of the parties, their successors, and assigns.

D. Whatever claim Licensor may have against Licensee hereunder for royalties or for damages shall become a first lien upon all of the items produced under this Agreement in the possession or under the control of the Licensee upon the expiration or termination of this Agreement.

E. This Agreement shall be construed in accordance with the laws of _____. The Licensee hereby consents to submit to the personal jurisdiction of the _____ Court, _____ County, and Federal Court of the District _____ for all purposes in connection with this Agreement.

F. All notices and demands shall be sent in writing by certified mail, return receipt requested, at the addresses above first written; royalty statements, payments, and samples of Licensed Products and related materials shall be sent by regular mail.

G. This Agreement constitutes the entire agreement between the parties hereto and shall not be modified, amended, or changed in any way except by written agreement signed by both parties hereto. Licensee shall not assign this Agreement.

In witness whereof, the parties have executed this Licensing Agreement as of the date first set forth above.

Licensee (company name) _____

By *(name, position)* _____

Licensor _____

© Caryn Leland 1990

Graphic Designer's Estimate & Confirmation Form

Remove all language in italics before using this form.

FRONT

Designer's Letterhead

TO

Date _____

Commissioned by _____

Assignment Number _____

Client's Purchase Order Number _____

ASSIGNMENT DESCRIPTION

Delivery Date *(predicated on receipt of all materials to be supplied by Client)* _____

Materials Supplied by _____

Assignment Number _____ Fee _____

FEE PAYMENT SCHEDULE

ESTIMATED EXPENSES

Client shall reimburse the Designer for all expenses. Expense amounts are estimates only.

Illustration _____ Printing *(if brokered by Designer)* _____

Photography _____ Client's Alterations _____

Models & Props _____ Toll Telephone Calls _____

Materials & Supplies _____ Transportation & Travel _____

Messengers _____ Shipping & Insurance _____

Copies _____ Other Expenses _____

Subtotal _____

Sales Tax _____

Total _____

RIGHTS TRANSFERRED

The Designer transfers to the Client the following exclusive rights of usage:

Title or Product *(name)* _____

Category of Use *(advertising, corporate, promotional, editorial, etc.)* _____

Medium of Use *(consumer or trade magazine, annual report, TV, book, etc.)* _____

Edition (if book) *(hardcover, mass-market paperback, quality paperback, etc.)* _____

Geographic Area *(if applicable)* _____ Time Period *(if applicable)* _____

Any usage rights not exclusively transferred are reserved to the Designer. Usage beyond that granted to the Client herein shall require payment of a mutually agreed-upon additional fee subject to all terms. Any transfer of rights is conditional upon receipt of full payment.

TERMS

1. Time for Payment
All invoices are payable within 30 days of receipt. A 1 1/2% monthly service charge is payable on all overdue balances. The grant of any license or right of copyright is conditioned on receipt of full payment.

2. Default in Payment
The Client shall assume responsibility for all collection of legal fees necessitated by default in payment.

3. Estimates
The fees and expenses shown are minimum estimates only. Final fees and expenses shall be shown when invoice is rendered. The Client's approval shall be obtained for any increases in fees or expenses that exceed the original estimate by 10% or more.

4. Changes
The Client shall be responsible for making additional payments for changes requested by the Client in original assignment. However, no additional payment shall be made for changes required to conform to the original assignment description. The Client shall offer the Designer the first opportunity to make any changes.

5. Expenses
The Client shall reimburse the Designer for all expenses arising from this assignment, including the payment of any sales taxes due on this assignment, and shall advance $_____ to the Designer for payment of said expenses.

6. Cancellation
In the event of cancellation of this assignment, ownership of all copyrights and the original artwork shall be retained by the Designer, and a cancellation fee for work completed, based on the contract price and expenses already incurred, shall be paid by the Client.

7. Ownership and Return of Artwork
The Designer retains ownership of all original artwork, whether preliminary or final, and the Client shall return such artwork within 30 days of use unless indicated otherwise below:

_____

_____

8. Credit Lines
The Designer and any other creators shall receive a credit line with any editorial usage. If similar credit lines are to be given with other types of usage, it must be so indicated here:

_____

_____

9. Releases
The Client shall indemnify the Designer against all claims and expenses, including reasonable attorney's fees, due to uses for which no release was requested in writing or for uses that exceed authority granted by a release.

10. Modifications
Modification of the Agreement must be written, except that the invoice may include, and the Client shall pay, fees or expenses that were orally authorized in order to progress promptly with the work.

11. Uniform Commercial Code
The above terms incorporate Article 2 of the Uniform Commercial Code.

12. Code of Fair Practice
The Client and the Designer agree to comply with the provisions of the Code of Fair Practice *(which is in the Ethical Standards section of Chapter 1, Professional Relationships).*

13. Warranty of Originality
The Designer warrants and represents that, to the best of his/her knowledge, the work assigned hereunder is original and has not been previously published, or that consent to use has been obtained on an unlimited basis; that all work or portions thereof obtained through the undersigned from third parties is original or, if previously published, that consent to use has been obtained on an unlimited basis; that the Designer has full authority to make this agreement; and that the work prepared by the Designer does not contain any scandalous, libelous, or unlawful matter. This warranty does not extend to any uses that the Client or others may make of the Designer's product that may infringe on the rights of others. Client expressly agrees that it will hold the Designer harmless for all liability caused by the Client's use of the Designer's product to the extent such use infringes on the rights of others.

14. Limitation of Liability
Client agrees that it shall not hold the Designer or his/her agents or employees liable for any incidental or consequential damages that arise from the Designer's failure to perform any aspect of the Project in a timely manner, regardless of whether such failure was caused by intentional or negligent acts or omissions of the Designer or a third party.

15. Dispute Resolution
Any disputes in excess of $_____ *(maximum limit for small-claims court)* arising out of this Agreement shall be submitted to binding arbitration before a mutually agreed-upon arbitrator pursuant to the rules of the American Arbitration Association. The Arbitrator's award shall be final, and judgment may be entered in any court having jurisdiction thereof. The Client shall pay all arbitration and court costs, reasonable attorney's fees, and legal interest on any award of judgment in favor of the Designer.

16. Acceptance of Terms
The signature of both parties shall evidence acceptance of these terms.

Consented and agreed to

Designer's signature/date _____

Authorized signature/date _____

Client's name and title _____

Noncompetition Clause

This clause and its explanatory text have been supplied by Tad Crawford, the author of Legal Guide for the Visual Artist *and* Business and Legal Forms for Graphic Designers *(Allworth Press), and are used here by permission.*

Often a designer working with an illustrator, photographer, or even another designer will place that supplier in direct contract with a client. In such a case, the normal expectation would be that the supplier would not then go directly to the client seeking business that the original designer might have been able to handle for the client. However, this expectation may not always be realized and sometimes it becomes wise to include the expectation as a clause in the contract with the supplier. Such a clause might read as follows:

> Supplier understands that in the course of working for the Designer, the Supplier may sometimes have direct contact with the clients of the Designer or access to confidential information such as lists of the Designer's clients. The Supplier agrees not to seek work from such clients of the Designer without the Designer's express, written permission. This clause shall include but not be limited to the following clients of the Designer:
>
> _____
>
> _____
>
> _____
>
> _____
>
> In the event of any breach of this clause, the Supplier shall pay the Designer _____ as liquidated damages and shall also be responsible for the Designer's reasonable attorneys' fees and court costs.

The amount of the liquidated damages might be two or three times the fee paid to the supplier if the supplier is doing an assignment for the designer. If the supplier is not working for the designer but gains access to confidential client lists, the liquidated damages might be an amount per client contacted. The clause should serve as a warning to any supplier that the designer considers clients to be proprietary and will not tolerate any attempts by suppliers to compete for the designer's clients.

Graphic Designer's Invoice

FRONT

Designer's Letterhead

TO

Date _____

Commissioned by _____

Assignment Number _____

Invoice Number _____

Client's Purchase Order Number _____

ASSIGNMENT DESCRIPTION

_____

FEE PAYMENT SCHEDULE

_____

ITEMIZED EXPENSES (OTHER BILLABLE EXPENSES)

Illustration _____	Printing *(if brokered by Designer)* _____
Photography _____	Client's Alterations _____
Models & Props _____	Toll Telephone Calls _____
Materials & Supplies _____	Transportation & Travel _____
Messengers _____	Shipping & Insurance _____
Copies _____	Other Expenses _____
	Subtotal _____
	Sales Tax _____
	Total _____

RIGHTS TRANSFERRED

The Designer transfers to the Client the following exclusive rights of usage.

Title or Product *(name)* _____

Category of Use *(advertising, corporate, promotional, editorial, etc.)* _____

Medium of Use *(consumer or trade magazine, annual report, TV, book, etc.)* _____

Edition (if book) *(hardcover, mass-market paperback, quality paperback, etc.)* _____

Geographic Area *(if applicable)* _____

Time Period *(if applicable)* _____

Any usage rights not exclusively transferred are reserved to the Designer. Usage beyond that granted to the Client herein shall require payment of a mutually agreed-upon additional fee subject to all terms. Any transfer of right is conditional upon receipt of full payment.

TERMS

1. Time for Payment
All invoices are payable within 30 days of receipt. A 1 1/2% monthly service charge is payable on all overdue balances. The grant of any license or right of copyright is conditioned on receipt of full payment.

2. Default in Payment
The Client shall assume responsibility for all collection of legal fees necessitated by default in payment.

3. Expenses
The Client shall reimburse the Designer for all expenses arising from this assignment, including the payment of any sales taxes due on this assignment.

4. Changes
The Client shall be responsible for making additional payments for changes requested by the Client in original assignment. However, no additional payment shall be made for changes required to conform to the original assignment description. The Client shall offer the Designer the first opportunity to make any changes.

5. Cancellation
In the event of cancellation of this assignment, ownership of all copyrights and the original artwork shall be retained by the Designer, and a cancellation fee for work completed, based on the contract price and expenses already incurred, shall be paid by the Client.

6. Ownership and Return of Artwork
The Designer retains ownership of all original artwork, whether preliminary or final, and the Client shall return such artwork within 30 days of use unless indicated otherwise below:

_____

_____

7. Credit Lines

The Designer and any other creators shall receive a credit line with any editorial usage. If similar credit lines are to be given with other types of usage, it must be so indicated here:

_____

_____

8. Releases

The Client shall indemnify the Designer against all claims and expenses, including reasonable attorney's fees, due to uses for which no release was requested in writing or for uses that exceed authority granted by a release.

9. Modifications
Modification of the Agreement must be written, except that the invoice may include, and the Client shall pay, fees or expenses that were orally authorized in order to progress promptly with the work.

10. Uniform Commercial Code
The above terms incorporate Article 2 of the Uniform Commercial Code.

11. Code of Fair Practice
The Client and the Designer agree to comply with the provisions of the Code of Fair Practice *(which is in the Ethical Standards section of Chapter 1, Professional Relationships)*.

12. Warranty of Originality
The Designer warrants and represents that, to the best of his/her knowledge, the work assigned hereunder is original and has not been previously published, or that consent to use has been obtained on an unlimited basis; that all work or portions thereof obtained through the undersigned from third parties is original or, if previously published, that the consent to use has been obtained on an unlimited basis; that the Designer has full authority to make this agreement; and that the work prepared by the Designer does not contain any scandalous, libelous, or unlawful matter. This warranty does not extend to any uses that the Client or others may make of the Designer's product that may infringe on the rights of others. Client expressly agrees that it will hold the Designer harmless for all liability caused by the Client's use of the Designer's product to the extent such use infringes on the rights of others.

13. Limitation of Liability
Client agrees that it shall not hold the Designer or his/her agents or employees liable for any incidental or consequential damages that arise from the Designer's failure to perform any aspect of the Project in a timely manner, regardless of whether such failure was caused by intentional or negligent acts or omissions of the Designer or a third party.

14. Dispute Resolution
Any disputes in excess of $ _____ *(maximum limit for small-claims court)* arising out of this Agreement shall be submitted to binding arbitration before a mutually agreed-upon arbitrator pursuant to the rules of the American Arbitration Association. The Arbitrator's award shall be final, and judgment may be entered in any court having jurisdiction thereof. The Client shall pay all arbitration and court costs, reasonable attorney's fees, and legal interest on any award of judgment in favor of the Designer.

Computer-Generated Art Job Order Form

Remove all language in italics before using this form.

FRONT

Illustrator's Letterhead

TO

Date _____

Commissioned by _____

Purchase Order Number _____

Job Number _____

For Use in Issue _____ Date _____

DEFINITION/TYPE OF ASSIGNMENT/NATURE OF MARKET

_____

_____

Additional Uses *(promotional, packaging, etc.)* _____

Number of Screens or Images Still Frame *(single frame, multiple frame)* _____

Sector Length Per Screen _____ Maximum Preferred _____ Minimum _____

Copy to Read (The Artist is not responsible for any copy other than what appears below; be sure copy is spelled and titled correctly.)

Disk(s) may be used only for the purposes stated below. All other use(s) and modification(s) is (are) prohibited. Disk(s) may not be copied without the Artist's permission and must be returned after use.

RIGHTS TRANSFERRED

Any transfer of rights is conditional upon receipt of full payment.

Type of Use *(game program, advertising, etc.)* _____

Medium of Use *(floppy, documentation, packaging, promotion, etc.)* _____

Distribution/Geographical Area *(method of distribution, electronically downloaded, floppy disk, store distribution)* _____

_____

Time/Number of Printings *(one-time use, etc.)* _____

System Applications *(for use on specific machine, or compiled into other operation languages)* _____

PRODUCTION SCHEDULE

First Showing _____

Review _____

Final Acceptance _____

Purchase Price _____

Payment Schedule _____

continued...

TERMS

1. Time for Payment
All invoices are payable within 30 days of receipt. A 1 1/2% monthly service charge is payable on all overdue balances. The grant of any license or right of copyright is conditioned on receipt of full payment.

2. Default in Payment
The Client shall assume responsibility for all collection of legal fees necessitated by default in payment.

3. Estimates
If this form is used for an estimate or assignment confirmation, the fees and expenses shown are minimum estimates only. Final fees and expenses shall be shown when invoice is rendered. The Client's approval shall be obtained for any increases in fees or expenses that exceed the original estimate by 10% or more.

4. Expenses
The Client shall reimburse the Artist for all expenses arising from this assignment, including the payment of any sales taxes due on this assignment and shall advance $ _____ to the Artist for payment of said expenses.

5. Artist's Guarantee for Program Use
The Artist guarantees to notify the Client of any licensing and/or permissions required for art generating/driving programs to be used.

6. Changes
The Client shall be responsible for making additional payments for changes requested by the Client in original assignment. However, no additional payment shall be made for changes required to conform to the original assignment description. The Client shall offer the Artist the first opportunity to make any changes.

7. Cancellation
In the event of cancellation of this assignment, ownership of all copyrights and the original artwork shall be retained by the Artist, and a cancellation fee for work completed, based on the contract price and expenses already incurred, shall be paid by the Client.

8. Ownership and Return of Artwork
The Artist retains ownership of all original artwork, whether preliminary or final. The Client waives the right to challenge the validity of the Artist's ownership of the art subject to this agreement because of any change or evolution of the law and will return all artwork within 30 days of use.

9. Copy-Protection
The Client must copy-protect all final art that is the subject of this agreement against duplication or alteration.

10. Credit Lines
The Artist shall be given credit in (**a**) floppy disk, (**b**) documentation, (**c**) packaging, (**d**) Artist's mark on art.

[ ] If this box is checked, the Artist shall receive copyright notice in this form: © 200 ___ _____ .

11. Alterations
Any electronic alteration of original art (color shift, mirroring, flopping, combination cut and paste, deletion) creating additional art is prohibited without the express permission of the artist. The artist will be given first opportunity to make any alterations required. Unauthorized alterations shall constitute additional use and will be billed accordingly.

12. Other Operating Systems Conversions
The Artist shall be given first option at compiling the work for operating systems beyond the original use.

13. Unauthorized Use and Program Licenses
The Client will indemnify the Artist against all claims and expenses arising from uses for which the Client does not have rights to or authority to use. The Client will be responsible for payment of any special licensing or royalty fees resulting from the use of graphics programs that require such payments.

14. Warranty of Originality
The Artist warrants and represents that, to the best of his/her knowledge, the work assigned hereunder is original and has not been previously published, or that consent to use has been obtained on an unlimited basis; that all work or portions thereof obtained through the undersigned from third parties is original or, if previously published, that consent to use has been obtained on an unlimited basis; that the Artist has full authority to make this agreement; and that the work prepared by the Artist does not contain any scandalous, libelous, or unlawful matter. This warranty does not extend to any uses that the Client or others may make of the Artist's product that may infringe on the rights of others. Client expressly agrees that it will hold the Artist harmless for all liability caused by the Client's use of the Artist's product to the extent such use infringes on the rights of others.

15. Limitation of Liability
Client agrees that it shall not hold the Artist or his/her agents or employees liable for any incidental or consequential damages that arise from the Artist's failure to perform any aspect of the Project in a timely manner, regardless of whether such failure was caused by intentional or negligent acts or omissions of the Artist or a third party.

16. Dispute Resolution
Any disputes in excess of $ _____ *(maximum limit for small-claims court)* arising out of this Agreement shall be submitted to binding arbitration before a mutually agreed-upon arbitrator pursuant to the rules of the American Arbitration Association. The Arbitrator's award shall be final, and judgment may be entered in any court having jurisdiction thereof. The Client shall pay all arbitration and court costs, reasonable attorney's fees, and legal interest on any award of judgment in favor of the Artist.

17. Acceptance of Terms
The signature of both parties shall evidence acceptance of these terms.

Consented and agreed to

Artist's signature/date _____

Authorized signature/date _____

Client's name and title _____

Computer-Generated Art Invoice

This invoice form is a sample of a possible contract for computer-generated art. Artists should view this as a model and amend it to fit their situations and the needs of their Client, based on a negotiated agreement.
Remove all language in italics before using this form.

FRONT
Illustrator's Letterhead

TO

Date _____

Authorized Buyer _____

Artist's Job Number _____

Client's Job Number _____

For Use in Issue _____ Date _____

DEFINITION/TYPE OF ASSIGNMENT/NATURE OF MARKET

_____

Additional Uses *(promotional, packaging, etc.)* _____

Number of Screens or Images Still Frame *(single frame, multiple frame)* _____

Sector Length Per Screen _____ Maximum Preferred _____ Minimum _____

Copy to Read (The Artist is not responsible for any copy other than what appears below; be sure copy is spelled and titled correctly.)

Disk(s) may be used only for the purposes stated below. All other use(s) and modification(s) is (are) prohibited.
Disk(s) may not be copied without the Artist's permission and must be returned after use.

RIGHTS TRANSFERRED
Any transfer of rights is conditional upon receipt of full payment.

Type of Use *(game program, advertising, etc.)* _____

Medium of Use *(floppy, documentation, packaging, promotion, etc.)* _____

Distribution/Geographical Area *(method of distribution, electronically downloaded, floppy disk, store distribution)* _____

Time/Number of Printings *(one-time use, etc.)* _____

System Applications *(for use on specific machine, or compiled into other operation languages)* _____

ITEMIZED EXPENSES (other billable items)

Client's Alterations _____

Sale of Original Art _____

Miscellaneous _____

Subtotal _____

Sales Tax _____

Payments on Account _____

Balance Due _____

Original artwork, including sketches and any other preliminary materials, remains the property of the Artist unless purchased by payment of a separate fee subject to terms appearing herein.

TERMS

1. Time for Payment

All invoices are payable within 30 days of receipt. A 1 1/2% monthly service charge is payable on all overdue balances. The grant of any license or right of copyright is conditioned on receipt of full payment.

2. Default in Payment

The Client shall assume responsibility for all collection of legal fees necessitated by default in payment.

3. Expenses

The Client shall reimburse the Artist for all expenses arising from this assignment, including the payment of any sales taxes due on this assignment.

4. Artist's Guarantee for Program Use

The Artist guarantees to notify the Client of any licensing and/or permissions required for art generating/driving programs to be used.

5. Ownership and Return of Artwork

The Artist retains ownership of all original artwork, whether preliminary or final. The Client waives the right to challenge the validity of the Artist's ownership of the art subject to this agreement because of any change or evolution of the law, and will return all artwork within 30 days of use.

6. Copy-Protection

The Client must copy-protect all final art that is the subject of this agreement against duplication or alteration.

7. Credit Lines

The Artist shall be given credit in: (**a**) floppy disk, (**b**) documentation, (**c**) packaging, (**d**) Artist's mark on art

[ ] If this box is checked, the Artist shall receive copyright notice in this form: © 200 _____ _____ .

8. Other Operating Systems Conversions

The Artist shall be given first option at compiling the work for operating systems beyond the original use.

9. Alterations

Any electronic alteration of original art (color shift, mirroring, flopping, combination cut and paste, deletion) creating additional art is prohibited without the express permission of the Artist. The Artist will be given first opportunity to make any alterations required. Unauthorized alterations shall constitute additional use and will be billed accordingly.

10. Unauthorized Use and Program Licenses

The Client will indemnify the Artist against all claims and expenses arising from uses for which the Client does not have rights to or authority to use. The Client will be responsible for payment of any special licensing or royalty fees resulting from the use of graphics programs that require such payments.

11. Arbitration

Any disputes in excess of $ _____ *(maximum limit for small-claims court)* arising out of this Agreement shall be submitted to binding arbitration before a mutually agreed-upon arbitrator pursuant to the rules of the American Arbitration Association. The Arbitrator's award shall be final, and judgment may be entered in any court having jurisdiction thereof. The Client shall pay all arbitration and court costs, reasonable attorney's fees, and legal interest on any award of judgment in favor of the Artist.

12. Acceptance of Terms

The signature of both parties shall evidence acceptance of these terms.

Consented and agreed to

Artist's signature/date _____

Authorized signature/date _____

Buyers's name and title _____

Digital Media Invoice

Remove all language in italics before using this form.

FRONT

Designer's Letterhead

TO

Date _____

Commissioned by _____

Purchase Order Number _____

Job Number _____

DESCRIPTION OF ASSIGNMENT

Primary Use _____

Additional Uses _____

Number of Screens or Images Still Frame *(single frame, multiple frame)* _____

Sector Length Per Screen _____   Maximum Preferred _____   Minimum _____

Description of Materials to Be Supplied by Client _____

Date Due _____

Disk(s) may be used only for the purposes stated below. All other use(s) and modification(s) is (are) prohibited. Disk(s) may not be copied without the Developer's permission and must be returned after use.

RIGHTS TRANSFERRED

Any transfer of rights is conditional upon receipt of full payment.

Distribution/Geographical Area _____

System Applications *(for use on specific machine, or compiled into other operation languages)* _____

PRODUCTION SCHEDULE (Including milestones, dates due, and appropriate fees.)

Milestone	Due Date	Payment upon Acceptance
Contract Signing	_____	$ _____
Delivery of Web Site Design	_____	$ _____
Delivery of Beta Version	_____	$ _____
Delivery of Final Version (includes return of source materials to Client)	_____	$ _____
Acceptance of Final Version	_____	$ _____
Total	_____	$ _____

Bonus: Client agrees to pay Developer a bonus of _____ payable to the Developer in the event an acceptable Final Version of the Web site is delivered to the Client prior to _____ (date).

continued...

TERMS

1. Time for Payment

Each milestone is payable upon the Client's acceptance of the Deliverables. All invoices are payable within 30 days of receipt. A 1 1/2% monthly service charge is payable on all overdue balances. The grant of any license or right of copyright is conditioned on receipt of full payment.

2. Default in Payment

The Client shall assume responsibility for all collection of legal fees necessitated by default in payment.

3. Estimates

If this form is used for an estimate or assignment confirmation, the fees and expenses shown are minimum estimates only. Final fees and expenses shall be shown when invoice is rendered. The Client's approval shall be obtained for any increases in fees or expenses shall be shown when invoice is rendered. The Client's approval shall be obtained for any increases in fees or expenses that exceed the original estimate by 10% or more.

4. Expenses

The Client shall reimburse the developer for all expenses arising from this assignment, including payment on any sales taxes due on this assignment and shall advance $_____ to the Developer for payment of said expenses.

5. Internet Access

Access to Internet will be provided by a separate Internet Service Provider (ISP) to be contracted by the Client and who will not be party to this agreement.

6. Progress Reports

The Developer shall contact or meet with the Client on a mutually acceptable schedule to report all tasks completed, problems encountered, and recommended changes relating to the Development and testing of the Web site. The Developer shall inform the Client promptly by telephone upon discovery of any event or problem that may significantly delay the development of the work.

7. Developer's Guarantee for Program Use

The Developer guarantees to notify the Client of any licensing and/or permissions required for art generating/driving programs to be used.

8. Changes

The Client shall be responsible for making additional payments for changes requested by the Client in original assignment. However, no additional payment shall be made for changes required to conform to the original assignment description. The Client shall offer the Developer the first opportunity to make any changes.

9. Testing and Acceptance Procedures

The Developer will make every good-faith effort to thoroughly test all deliverables and make all necessary corrections as a result of such testing prior to handing over the deliverables to the Client. Upon receipt of the deliverables, the Client shall either accept the deliverable and make the milestone payment set forth or provide the Developer with written notice of any corrections to be made and a suggested date for completion, which should be mutually acceptable to both the Developer and the Client. The developer shall designate _____ (name) and the Client shall designate _____ (name) as the only designated persons who will send and accept all deliverables, and receive and make all communications between the Developer and the Client. Neither party shall have any obligation to consider for approval or respond to materials submitted other than through the designated person listed above. Each party has the right to change its designated person upon _____ day(s) notice to the other.

10. Web Site Maintenance

The Developer agrees to provide the Client with reasonable technical support and assistance to maintain and update the Web site on the Internet during the Warranty Period of _____ (dates) at no cost to the Client. Such assistance shall not exceed _____ hours per calendar month. After the expiration of the Warranty Period, the developer agrees to provide the Client with reasonable technical support and assistance to maintain and update the Web site on the Internet for an annual fee of $_____ for a period of _____ years after the last day of the Warranty Period, payable 30 days prior to the commencement date of each year of the Maintenance Period. Such maintenance shall include correcting any errors or any failure of the Web site to conform to the specifications. Maintenance shall not include the development of enhancements to the originally contracted project.

11. Enhancements

Under the maintenance agreement, if the Client wishes to modify the Web site, the Developer shall be given first option to provide a bid to perform such enhancements.

12. Confidential Information

The Developer acknowledges and agrees that the source materials and technical and marketing plans or other sensitive business information, including all materials containing said information, that are supplied by the Client to the Developer or developed by the Developer in the course of developing the Web site are to be considered confidential information. Information shall not be considered confidential if it is already publicly known through no act of the Developer.

13. Return of Source Information

Upon the Client's acceptance of the Final Version, or upon the cancellation of the project, the Developer shall provide the Client with all copies and originals of the source materials provided by the Developer.

14. Cancellation

In the event of cancellation of this assignment, ownership of all copyrights and any original artwork shall be retained by the Developer, and a cancellation fee for work completed, based on the pro-rated portion of the next payment and expenses already incurred, shall be paid by the Client.

15. Ownership of Copyright

Client acknowledges and agrees that the Developer retains all rights of copyright in the subject material.

16. Ownership and Return of Artwork

The Developer retains ownership of all original artwork, in any media, including digital files, whether preliminary or final. The Client waives the right to challenge the validity of the Developer's ownership of the art subject to this agreement because of any change or evolution of the law and will return all artwork within 30 days of use.

17. Ownership of Engine
The Developer retains ownership of all engines that are created by Developer for used in the production of the product unless those engines are provided by the Client.

18. Copy-Protection
The Client must copy-protect all final art that is the subject of this agreement against duplication or alteration.

19. Credit Lines
The Developer shall be given credit in (**a**) floppy disk, (**b**) documentation (**c**) packagine (**d**) Developer's mark on art.

[ ] If this box is checked, the Developer shall receive copyright notice in this form: © 200 ____ _____.

20. Alterations
Any electronic alteration of original art (color shift, mirroring, flopping, combination cut and paste, deletion) creating additional art is prohibited without the express permission of the Developer. The Developer will be given first opportunity to make any alterations required. Unauthorized alterations shall constitute additional use and will be billed accordingly.

21. Other Operating Systems Conversion
The Developer shall be given first option at compiling the work for operating systems beyond the original use.

22. Unauthorized Use and Program Licenses
The Client will indemnify the Developer against all claims and expenses arising from uses for which the Client does not have rights to or authority to use. The Client will be responsible for payment of any special licensing or royalty fees resulting from the use of graphic programs that require such payments.

23. Warranty of Originality
The Developer warrants and represents that, to the best of his/her knowledge, the work assigned hereunder is original and has not been previously published or that consent to use has been obtained on an unlimited basis; that all work or portions thereof obtained through the undersigned from third parties is original or, if previously published, that consent to use has been obtained on an unlimited basis; that the Developer has full authority to make this agreement; and that the work prepared by the Developer does not contain any scandalous, libelous, or unlawful matter. This warranty does not extend to any uses that the Client or others may make of the Developer's product that may infringe on the rights of others. Client expressly agrees that it will hold the Developer harmless for all liability caused by the Client's use of the Developer's product to the extent such use infringes on the rights of others.

24. Limitation of Liability
Client agrees that it shall not hold the Developer or his/her agents or employees liable for any incidental or consequential damages that arise from the Developer's failure to perform any aspect of the project in a timely manner, regardless of whether such failure was caused by intentional or negligent acts or omissions of the Developer or a third party. Furthermore, the Developer disclaims all implied warranties, including the warranty of merchantability and fitness for a particular use.

25. Dispute Resolution
Any disputes in excess of $ _____ *(maximum limit for small-claims court)* arising out of this Agreement shall be submitted to binding arbitration before a mutually agreed-upon arbitrator pursuant to the rules of the American Arbitration Association. The Arbitrator's award shall be final, and judgment may be entered in any court having jurisdiction thereof. The Client shall pay all arbitration and court costs, reasonable attorney's fees, and legal interest on any award of judgment in favor of the Developer.

26. Acceptance of Terms
The signature of both parties shall evidence acceptance of these terms.

Consented and agreed to

Developer's signature/date _____

Authorized signature/date _____

Client's name and title _____

Web Site Design & Maintenance Order Form

This job order form is a sample of a possible contract for Web site development and maintenance. Since the field is changing very rapidly, artists should view this as a model and amend it to fit their particular circumstances. Remove all language in italics before using this form.

FRONT

Developer's Letterhead

TO

Date _____

Commissioned by _____

Purchase Order Number _____

Job Number _____

DESCRIPTION OF ASSIGNMENT

Primary Use _____

Additional Uses _____

Number of Individual Screen Pages *(if the page is a frame page, the number of frames per page)* _____

Pixel Length per Screen _____ Maximum Preferred _____ Minimum _____

Description of Materials to Be Supplied by Client _____

Date Due _____

RIGHTS TRANSFERRED

The material on the disk can be used only for the purposes stated below. All other use(s) and modification(s) is (are) prohibited. The material on the disk may not be copied without the Developer's permission and must be returned after use. Any transfer of rights is conditional upon receipt of full payment.

SYSTEM APPLICATIONS

(For use on specific machine or compiled into other operation languages)

PRODUCTION SCHEDULE (Including milestones, dates due, and appropriate fees.)

Milestone	Due Date	Payment upon Acceptance
Contract Signing	_____	$ _____
Delivery of Web Site Design	_____	$ _____
Delivery of Beta Version	_____	$ _____
Delivery of Final Version (includes return of source materials to Client)	_____	$ _____
Acceptance of Final Version	_____	$ _____
Total	_____	$ _____

Bonus: Client agrees to pay Developer a bonus of _____ payable to the Developer in the event an acceptable Final Version of the Web site is delivered to the Client prior to _____ (date).

TERMS

1. Time for Payment

Payment is due at each milestone upon the Client's acceptance of the Deliverables. All invoices are payable within 30 days of receipt. A 1 1/2% monthly service charge is payable on all overdue balances. The grant of any license or right of copyright is conditioned on receipt of full payment.

2. Default in Payment

The Client shall assume responsibility for all collection of legal fees necessitated by default in payment.

3. Estimates

If this form is used for an estimate or assignment confirmation, the fees and expenses shown are minimum estimates only. Final fees and expenses shall be shown when invoice is rendered. The Client's approval shall be obtained for any increases in fees or expenses that exceed the original estimate by 10% or more.

4. Expenses

The Client shall reimburse the Developer for all expenses arising from this assignment, including the payment of any sales taxes due on this assignment, and shall advance $ _____ to the Developer for payment of said expenses.

5. Internet Access

Access to Internet will be provided by a separate Internet Service Provider (ISP) to be contracted by the Client and who will not be party to this agreement.

6. Progress Reports

The Developer shall contact or meet with the Client on a mutually acceptable schedule to report all tasks completed, problems encountered, and recommended changes relating to the development and testing of the Web site. The Developer shall inform the Client promptly by telephone upon discovery of any event or problem that may delay the development of the work significantly.

7. Developer's Guarantee for Program Use

The Developer guarantees to notify the Client of any licensing and/or permissions required for art-generating/driving programs to be used.

8. Changes

The Client shall be responsible for making additional payments for changes in original assignment requested by the Client. However, no additional payment shall be made for changes required to conform to the original assignment description. The Client shall offer the Developer the first opportunity to make any changes.

9. Testing and Acceptance Procedures

The Developer will make every good-faith effort to test all deliverables thoroughly and make all necessary corrections as a result of such testing prior to handing over the deliverables to the Client. Upon receipt of the deliverables, the Client shall either accept the deliverable and make the milestone payment set forth herein or provide the Developer with written notice of any corrections to be made and a suggested date for completion, which should be mutually acceptable to both the Developer and the Client. The Developer shall designate _____ (name) and the Client shall designate _____ (name) as the only designated persons who will send and accept all deliverables and receive and make all communications between the Developer and the Client. Neither party shall have any obligation to consider for approval or respond to materials submitted other than through the designated persons listed above. Each party has the right to change its designated person upon _____ day(s) notice to the other.

10. Web Site Maintenance

The Developer agrees to provide the Client with reasonable technical support and assistance to maintain and update the Web site on the Internet during the Warranty Period of _____ (dates) at no cost to the Client. Such assistance shall not exceed _____ hours per calendar month. After the expiration of the Warranty Period, the Developer agrees to provide the Client with reasonable technical support and assistance to maintain and update the Web site on the Internet for an annual fee of $ _____ for a period of _____ years after the last day of the Warranty Period payable 30 days prior to the commencement date of each year of the Maintenance Period. Such maintenance shall include correcting any errors or any failure of the Web site to conform to the specifications. Maintenance shall not include the development of enhancements to the originally contracted project.

11. Enhancements

Under the maintenance agreement, if the Client wishes to modify the Web site, the Developer shall be given first option to provide a bid to perform such enhancements.

12. Confidential Information

The Developer acknowledges and agrees that the source materials and technical and marketing plans or other sensitive business information, as specified by the Client, including all materials containing said information, that are supplied by the Client to the Developer or developed by the Developer in the course of developing the Web site are to be considered confidential information. Information shall not be considered confidential if it is already publicly known through no act of the Developer.

13. Return of Source Information

Upon the Client's acceptance of the Final Version, or upon the cancellation of the project, the Developer shall provide the Client with all copies and originals of the source materials provided to the Developer.

14. Ownership of Copyright

Client acknowledges and agrees that Developer retains all rights to copyright in the subject material.

15. Ownership and Return of Artwork

The Developer retains ownership of all original artwork, in any media, including digital files, whether preliminary or final. The Client waives the right to challenge the validity of the Developer's ownership of the art subject to this agreement because of any change or evolution of the law and will return all artwork within 30 days of use.

16. Cancellation

In the event of cancellation of this assignment, ownership of all copyrights and any original artwork shall be retained by the Developer, and a cancellation fee for work completed, based on the prorated portion of the next payment and expenses already incurred, shall be paid by the Client.

17. Copy-Protection

The Client must copy-protect all final art that is the subject of this agreement against duplication or alteration.

18. Credit Lines

The Developer shall be given credit on: (**a**) floppy disk, (**b**) documentation, (**c**) packaging, (**d**) Developer's mark on art.

☐ If this box is checked, the Developer shall receive copyright notice in this form: © 200__ _____ .

19. Alterations

Any electronic alteration of original art (color shift, mirroring, flopping, combination cut and paste, deletion) creating additional art is prohibited without the express permission of the developer. The Developer will be given first opportunity to make any alterations required. Unauthorized alterations shall constitute additional use and will be billed accordingly.

20. Other Operating Systems Conversions

The Developer shall be given first option at compiling the work for operating systems beyond t he original use.

21. Unauthorized Use and Program Licenses

The Client will indemnify the Developer against all claims and expenses arising from uses for which the Client does not have rights to or authority to use. The Client will be responsible for payment of any special licensing or royalty fees resulting from the use of graphics programs that require such payments.

22. Warranty of Originality

The Developer warrants and represents that, to the best of his/her knowledge, the work assigned hereunder is original and has not been previously published, or that consent to use has been obtained on an unlimited basis; that all work or portions thereof obtained through the undersigned from third parties is original or, if previously published, that consent to use has been obtained on an unlimited basis; that the Developer has full authority to make this agreement; and that the work prepared by the Developer does not contain any scandalous, libelous, or unlawful matter. This warranty does not extend to any uses that the Client or others may make of the Developer's product that may infringe on the rights of others. CLIENT EXPRESSLY AGREES THAT IT WILL HOLD THE DEVELOPER HARMLESS FOR ALL LIABILITY CAUSED BY THE CLIENT'S USE OF THE DEVELOPER'S PRODUCT TO THE EXTENT SUCH USE INFRINGES ON THE RIGHTS OF OTHERS.

23. Limitation of Liability

Client agrees that it shall not hold the Developer or his/her agents or employees liable for any incidental or consequential damages that arise from the Developer's failure to perform any aspect of the Project in a timely manner, regardless of whether such failure was caused by intentional or negligent acts or omissions of the Developer or a third party. Furthermore, the Developer disclaims all implied warranties, including the warranty of merchantability and fitness for a particular use.

24. Dispute Resolution

Any disputes in excess of $ _____ *(maximum limit for small-claims court)* arising out of this Agreement shall be submitted to final binding arbitration before a mutually agreed-upon arbitrator pursuant to the rules of the American Arbitration Association. The Arbitrator's award shall be final, and judgment may be entered in any court having jurisdiction thereof. The Client shall pay all arbitration and court costs, reasonable attorney's fees, and legal interest on any award of judgment in favor of the Developer.

25. Acceptance of Terms

The signature of both parties shall evidence acceptance of these terms.

Consented and agreed to

Developer's signature/date _____

Authorized signature/date _____

Client's name and title _____

Magazine Purchase Order for Commissioned Illustration

FRONT

Magazine's Letterhead

This letter is to serve as our contract for you to create certain illustrations for us under the terms described herein

1. Job Description

We, the Magazine, retain you, the Illustrator, to create _____ illustration(s) described as follows (indicate if sketches are required: _____

_____

_____

to be delivered to the Magazine by _____

200___ for publication in our magazine titled _____

_____.

2. Grant of Rights

The Illustrator hereby agrees to transfer to the Magazine first North American magazine rights in the illustration(s). All rights not expressly transferred to the Magazine hereunder are reserved to the Illustrator.

3. Price

The Magazine agrees to pay the Illustrator the following purchase price: $ _____ in full consideration for the Illustrator's grant of rights to the Magazine. Any transfer of rights is conditional upon receipt of full payment.

4. Changes

The Illustrator shall be given the first option to make any changes in the work that the Magazine may deem necessary. However, no additional compensation shall be paid unless such changes are necessitated by error on the Magazine's part, in which case a new contract between us shall be entered into on mutually agreeable terms to cover changes to be done by the Illustrator.

5. Cancellation

If, prior to the Illustrator's completion of finishes, the Magazine cancels the assignment, either because the illustrations are unsatisfactory to the Magazine or for

any other reason, the Magazine agrees to pay the Illustrator a cancellation fee of 50% of the purchase price. If, after the Illustrator's completion of finishes, the Magazine cancels the assignment, the Magazine agrees to pay 50% of the purchase price if cancellation is due to the illustrations not being reasonably satisfactory and 100% of the purchase price if cancellation is due to any other cause. In the event of cancellation, the Illustrator shall retain ownership of all artwork and rights of copyright, but the Illustrator agrees to show the Magazine the artwork if the Magazine so requests so that the Magazine may make its own evaluation as to the degree of completion of the artwork.

6. Copyright Notice and Authorship Credit

Copyright notice shall appear in the Illustrator's name with the contribution. The Illustrator shall have the right to receive authorship credit for the illustration and to have such credit removed if the Illustrator so desires due to changes made by the Magazine that are unsatisfactory to the Illustrator.

7. Payments

Payment shall be made within 30 days of the billing date.

8. Ownership of Artwork

The Illustrator shall retain ownership of all original artwork and the Magazine shall return such artwork within 30 days of publication.

9. Acceptance of Terms

To Constitute this a binding agreement between us, please sign both copies of this letter beneath the words "consented and agreed to" and return one copy to the Magazine for its files.

Consented and agreed to

Artist's signature/date _____

Magazine _____

Authorized signature/date _____

Name and title _____

Illustrator's Estimate & Confirmation Form

Remove all language in italics before using this form.

FRONT

Illustrator's Letterhead

TO

Date _____

Commissioned by _____

Illustrator's Job Number _____

Client's Job Number _____

ASSIGNMENT DESCRIPTION

DELIVERY SCHEDULE

FEE PAYMENT SCHEDULE

ESTIMATED EXPENSES (OTHER BILLABLE ITEMS)

Toll Telephone Calls _____

Transit & Travel _____

Messengers _____

Cancellation Fee *(percentage of fee)* _____

Shipping & Insurance _____

Client's Alterations _____

Other Expenses _____

Before Sketches _____ After Sketches _____

After Finish _____

Sale of Original Art _____

RIGHTS TRANSFERRED

Any usage rights not exclusively transferred are reserved to the Illustrator. Usage beyond that granted to the Client herein shall require payment of a mutually agreed-upon additional fee subject to all terms.

For use in magazines and newspapers, first North American reproduction rights unless specified otherwise here:

For all other uses, the Client acquires only the following rights:

Title or Product *(name)* _____

Category of Use *(advertising, corporate, promotional, editorial, etc.)* _____

Medium of Use *(consumer or trade magazine, annual report, TV, book, etc.)* _____

Geographic Area *(if applicable)* _____

Time Period *(if applicable)* _____

Number of Uses *(if applicable)* _____

Other *(if applicable)* _____

Original artwork, including sketches and any other preliminary material, remains the property of the Illustrator unless purchased by a payment of a separate fee. Any transfer of rights is conditional upon receipt of full payment.

TERMS

1. Time for Payment

Payment is due within 30 days of receipt of invoice. A 1 1/2% monthly service charge will be billed for late payment. Any advances or partial payments shall be indicated under Payment Schedule on front.

2. Default in Payment

The Client shall assume responsibility for all collection of legal fees necessitated by default in payment.

3. Grant of Rights

The grant of reproduction rights is conditioned on receipt of full payment.

4. Expenses

The Client shall reimburse the Illustrator for all expenses arising from the assignment.

5. Estimates

The fees and expenses shown are minimum estimates only. Final fees and expenses shall be shown when invoice is rendered. The Client's approval shall be obtained for any increases in fees or expenses that exceed the original estimate by 10% or more.

6. Sales Tax

The Client shall be responsible for the payment of sales tax, if any such tax is due.

7. Cancellation

In the event of cancellation or breach by the Client, the Illustrator shall retain ownership of all rights of copyright and the original artwork, including sketches and any other preliminary materials. The Client shall pay the Illustrator according to the following schedule: 50% of original fee if canceled after preliminary sketches are completed, 100% if canceled after completion of finished art.

8. Alterations

Alteration to artwork shall not be made without consulting the initial Illustrator, and the Illustrator shall be allowed the first option to make alterations when possible. After acceptance of artwork, if alterations are required, a payment shall be charged over the original amount.

9. Revisions

Revisions not due to the fault of the Illustrator shall be billed separately.

10. Credit Lines

On any contribution for magazine or book use, the Illustrator shall receive name credit in print. If name credit is to be given with other types of use, it must be specified here:

_____

_____

[ ] If this box is checked, the Illustrator shall receive copyright notice adjacent to the work in the form: © 200___ _____.

11. Return of Artwork

The Client assumes responsibility for the return of the artwork in undamaged condition within 30 days of first reproduction.

12. Loss or Damage to Artwork

The value of lost or damaged artwork is placed at no less than $ _____ per piece.

13. Unauthorized Use

The Client will indemnify the Illustrator against all claims and expenses, including reasonable attorney's fees, arising from uses for which no release was requested in writing or for uses exceeding the authority granted by a release.

14. Warranty of Originality

The Illustrator warrants and represents that, to the best of his/her knowledge, the work assigned hereunder is original and has not been previously published, or that consent to use has been obtained on an unlimited basis; that all work or portions thereof obtained through the undersigned from third parties is original or, if previously published, that consent to use has been obtained on an unlimited basis; that the Illustrator has full authority to make this agreement; and that the work prepared by the Illustrator does not contain any scandalous, libelous, or unlawful matter. This warranty does not extend to any uses that the Client or others may make of the Artist's product that may infringe on the rights of others. Client expressly agrees that it will hold the Illustrator harmless for all liability caused by the Client's use of the Illustrator's product to the extent such use infringes on the rights of others.

15. Limitation of Liability

Client agrees that it shall not hold the Illustrator or his/her agents or employees liable for any incidental or consequential damages that arise from the Illustrator's failure to perform any aspect of the Project in a timely manner, regardless of whether such failure was caused by intentional or negligent acts or omissions of the Illustrator or a third party.

16. Dispute Resolution

Any disputes in excess of $ _____ *(maximum limit for small-claims court)* arising out of this Agreement shall be submitted to binding arbitration before a mutually agreed-upon arbitrator pursuant to the rules of the American Arbitration Association. The Arbitrator's award shall be final, and judgment may be entered in any court having jurisdiction thereof. The Client shall pay all arbitration and court costs, reasonable attorney's fees, and legal interest on any award of judgment in favor of the Illustrator.

17. Acceptance of Terms

The signature of both parties shall evidence acceptance of these terms.

Consented and agreed to

Illustrator's signature/date _____

Authorized signature/date _____

Client's name and title _____

All-Purpose Illustrator's Letter of Agreement

This letter of agreement is a model, which should be amended to fit the artist's particular circumstances. Remove all language in italics before using this form.

FRONT

Illustrator's Letterhead

TO

Commissioned by _____

Date _____

Job/Invoice Number _____

Shipping Number _____

Illustrator's Tax ID *(Social Security)* Number _____

THIS AGREEMENT MUST BE SIGNED AND RETURNED BEFORE ARTIST CAN SCHEDULE OR BEGIN THIS JOB.

Project title *(if any)* _____   Client's purchase order number *(if available)* _____

DESCRIPTION

Subject matter _____

Size _____

Color or black & white _____

Media _____

Any relevant production information _____

DUE DATES

Sketch _____   Final _____

COPYRIGHT USAGE

Rights transferred _____

Duration of usage _____

Limitations on media in which used *(print rights only, no electronic usage)* _____

Limitations on number of insertions *(if appropriate)* _____

Limitations on geographical use *(North American, English editions)* _____

Owner of original art *(only if different from Credits below)* _____

Fee for rights granted _____

TERMS

1. Reservation of Rights
All rights not expressly granted above are retained by the Artist, including any electronic rights or usage and including, but not limited to, all rights in sketches, comps, or other preliminary materials. Any use additional to that expressly granted above requires arrangement for payment of a separate fee.

2. Revisions
(**A**) Preliminary Work/Sketches: Artist agrees to submit _____ [insert studio standard] rough sketches and/or _____ [insert studio standard] finished sketches for Client's approval. Additional fees will be charged to Client for revisions made after such sketches and for all revisions that reflect a new direction for the assignment or new conceptual input. (**B**) Finished Art: Client agrees to pay Artist an additional fee, to be negotiated separately, for changes requested to final art where Client asked Artist to proceed directly to final art. No additional fee shall be billed for changes required to bring final artwork up to original specifications or assignment description. Client agrees to offer Artist the first opportunity to make any changes to final artwork.

3. Cancellation and Kill Fees
Cancellation ("kill") fees are due based on the amount of work completed. Fifty percent (50%) of the final fee is due within 30 days of notification that for any reason the job is canceled or postponed before the final stage. One hundred percent (100%) of the total fee is due despite cancellation or postponement of the job if the art has been completed. Upon cancellation or kill, all rights to the art revert to the Artist, and all original art must be returned, including sketches, comps, or other preliminary materials.

4. Credits and Copies
A credit line suitable to the design of the page will be used. Client agrees to pay an additional 50% of the total fee, excluding expenses, for failure to include credit line. Credit line is required independent of Artist's signature, which shall be included at Artist's discretion unless otherwise agreed in writing above. Client agrees to provide Artist with [insert studio standard] sample copies of any printed material.

5. Payment
Payment for finished work is due upon acceptance, net 30 days. The Client's right to use the work is conditioned upon receipt of payment within 30 days of acceptance and upon Client's compliance with the terms of this agreement. A 1 1/2% monthly service charge will be billed against late payment.

6. Original Art
Original art remains the property of the Artist unless expressed otherwise in the agreement. Client is responsible for return of original art in undamaged condition within 30 days of first reproduction.

7. Additional Expenses
If Client does not provide a courier/shipping number in the space provided above, shipping charges will be added to the final invoice. Client agrees to reimburse Artist for the following expenses:

Messengers _____	Models _____
Props _____	Travel _____
Telephone _____	Proofs _____
Transport disks _____	Transparencies _____
Film output _____	Other _____

8. Permissions and Releases
The Client agrees to indemnify and hold the Artist harmless against any and all claims, costs, and expenses, including attorney's fees, due to materials included in the Work at the request of the Client for which no copyright permission or privacy release was requested or for which uses exceed the uses allowed pursuant to a permission or release.

9. Miscellany
This Agreement shall be binding upon the parties, their heirs, successors, assigns, and personal representatives. This Agreement constitutes the entire understanding of the parties. Its terms can be modified only by an instrument in writing signed by both parties, except that the Client may authorize expenses or revisions orally. No terms attached to any check for payment under this Agreement can modify the Agreement except under an independent instrument in writing signed by both parties. Any dispute regarding this agreement shall be arbitrated in [your city and state] under the rules of the American Arbitration Association and the laws of [state of arbitration] . A waiver of a breach of any of the provisions of this Agreement shall not be construed as a continuing waiver of other breaches of the same or other provisions. This Agreement shall be governed by the laws of the State of [name of your state] and courts of such State shall have exclusive jurisdiction and venue.

Consented and agreed to

Artist's signature/date _____

Authorized signature/date _____

Buyer's name and title _____

Accounts payable contact name/phone _____

Illustrator's Release Form for Models

Illustrator's Letterhead

In consideration of _____ dollars ($_____), receipt of which is acknowledged,

I,_____, do hereby give _____, his or

her assigns, licenses, and legal representatives the irrevocable right to use my name (or any fictional name),

picture, portrait, or photograph in all forms and media and in all manners, including composite or distorted

representations, for advertising, trade, or any other lawful purposes, and I waive any right to inspect or

approve the finished version(s), including written copy that may be created in connection therewith.

I am of full age.* I have read this release and am fully familiar with its contents.

Witness _____

Model _____

Address _____

Address _____

Date _____, 200___

CONSENT *(if applicable)*

I am the parent or guardian of the minor named above and have the legal authority to execute the above release.
I approve the foregoing and waive any rights in the premises.

Witness _____

Parent or Guardian _____

Address _____

Address _____

Date _____, 200_____

Delete this sentence if the subject is a minor. The parent or guardian must then sign the consent.

Reproduced with permission from Business and Legal Forms for Illustrators by Tad Crawford (Allworth Press).

Illustrator's Invoice

Remove all language in italics before using this form.

FRONT

Illustrator's Letterhead

TO

Date _____

Commissioned by _____

Illustrator's Job Number _____

Client's Job Number _____

ASSIGNMENT DESCRIPTION

_____

FEE PAYMENT SCHEDULE

_____

ITEMIZED EXPENSES (OTHER BILLABLE ITEMS)

Toll Telephone Calls _____

Transportation & Travel _____

Messengers _____

Shipping & Insurance _____

Client's Alterations _____

Sale of Original Art _____

Cancellation Fee _____

Miscellaneous _____

Subtotal _____

Sales Tax _____

Payments on Account _____

Balance Due _____

RIGHTS TRANSFERRED

Any usage rights not exclusively transferred are reserved to the Illustrator. Usage beyond that granted to the Client herein shall require payment of a mutually agreed-upon additional fee subject to all terms.

For use in magazines and newspapers, first North American reproduction rights unless specified otherwise here:

[   ]   [   ]

For all other uses, the Client acquires only the following rights:

[   ]   [   ]

Title or Product *(name)* _____

Category of Use *(advertising, corporate, promotional, editorial, etc.)* _____

Medium of Use *(consumer or trade magazine, annual report, TV, book, etc.)* _____

Geographic Area *(if applicable)* _____

Time Period *(if applicable)* _____

Number of Uses *(if applicable)* _____

Other *(if applicable)* _____

Original artwork, including sketches and any other preliminary materials, remains the property of the Illustrator unless purchased by payment of a separate fee subject to all terms.

Any transfer of rights is conditional upon receipt of full payment.

TERMS

1. Time for Payment
Payment is due within 30 days of receipt of invoice. A 1 1/2% monthly service charge will be billed for late payment.

2. Default in Payment
The Client shall assume responsibility for all collection of legal fees necessitated by default in payment.

3. Expenses
The Client shall reimburse the Illustrator for all expenses arising from the assignment.

4. Sales Tax
The Client shall be responsible for the payment of sales tax, if any such tax is due.

5. Grant of Rights
The grant of reproduction rights is conditioned on receipt of payment.

6. Credit Lines
On any contribution for magazine or book use, the Illustrator shall receive name credit in print. If name credit is to be given with other types of use, it must be specified here:

_____

_____

[ ] If this box is checked, the Illustrator shall receive copyright notice adjacent to the work in the form:

© 200___ _____.

7. Additional Limitations
If the Illustrator and the Client have agreed to additional limitations as to either the duration or geographical extent of the permitted use, specify here:

_____

_____

_____

8. Return of Artwork
The Client assumes responsibility for the return of the artwork in undamaged condition within 30 days of first reproduction.

9. Loss or Damage to Artwork
The value of lost or damaged artwork is placed at no less than $ _____ per piece.

10. Alterations
Alteration to artwork shall not be made without consulting the initial Illustrator, and the Illustrator shall be allowed the first option to make alterations when possible. After acceptance of artwork, if alterations are required, a payment shall be charged over the original amount.

11. Unauthorized Use
The Client will indemnify the Illustrator against all claims and expenses, including reasonable attorney's fees, arising from uses for which no release was requested in writing or for uses that exceed the authority granted by a release.

12. Warranty of Originality
The Illustrator warrants and represents that, to the best of his/her knowledge, the work assigned hereunder is original and has not been previously published, or that consent to use has been obtained on an unlimited basis; that all work or portions thereof obtained through the undersigned from third parties is original or, if previously published, that consent to use has been obtained on an unlimited basis; that the Illustrator has full authority to make this agreement; and that the work prepared by the Illustrator does not contain any scandalous, libelous, or unlawful matter. This warranty does not extend to any uses that the Client or others may make of the Illustrator's product that may infringe on the rights of others. Client expressly agrees that it will hold the Illustrator harmless for all liability caused by the Client's use of the Illustrator's product to the extent such use infringes on the rights of others.

13. Limitation of Liability
Client agrees that it shall not hold the Illustrator or his/her agents or employees liable for any incidental or consequential damages that arise from the Illustrator's failure to perform any aspect of the Project in a timely manner, regardless of whether such failure was caused by intentional or negligent acts or omissions of the Illustrator or a third party.

14. Dispute Resolution
Any disputes in excess of $ _____ *(maximum limit for small-claims court)* arising out of this Agreement shall be submitted to binding arbitration before a mutually agreed-upon arbitrator pursuant to the rules of the American Arbitration Association. The Arbitrator's award shall be final, and judgment may be entered in any court having jurisdiction thereof. The Client shall pay all arbitration and court costs, reasonable attorney's fees, and legal interest on any award of judgment in favor of the Illustrator.

Surface/Textile Designer–Agent Agreement

FRONT

Designer's Letterhead

Agreement, this _____ day of _____, 200___, between _____

(hereinafter referred to as the "Designer"), residing at: _____

_____ and _____ (hereinafter referred to as the "Agent"),

residing at: _____

Whereas, the Designer is a professional surface/textile designer; and

Whereas, the Designer wishes to have an Agent represent him or her in marketing certain rights enumerated herein; and

Whereas, the Agent is capable of marketing the artwork produced by the Designer; and

Whereas, the Agent wishes to represent the Designer;

Now, therefore, in consideration of the foregoing premises and the mutual covenants hereinafter set forth and other valuable consideration, the parties hereto agree as follows:

1. Agency

The Designer appoints the Agent to act as his or her representative for:

❑ Sale of surface/textile designs in apparel market,

❑ Sale of surface/textile designs in home furnishing market,

❑ Securing of service work in apparel market. Service work is defined to include repeats and colorings on designs originated by the Designer or other designers,

❑ Securing of service work in home furnishing market

❑ Other_____

The Agent agrees to use his/her best efforts in submitting the Designer's artwork for the purpose of making sales or securing assignments for the Designer. For the purposes of this Agreement, the term artwork shall be defined to include designs, repeats, colorings, and any other product of the Designer's effort. The Agent shall negotiate the terms of any assignment that is offered, but the Designer shall have the right to reject any assignment if he or she finds the terms unacceptable. Nothing contained herein shall prevent the Designer from making sales or securing work for his or her own account without liability for commissions except for accounts that have been secured for the Designer by the Agent. This limitation extends only for the period of time that the Agent represents the Designer. Further, the Designer agrees, when selling his or her artwork or taking orders, not to accept a price that is below the price structure of his or her Agent.

After a period of _____ months, the Designer may remove his or her unsold artwork form the Agent's portfolio to do with as the Designer wishes.

2. Artwork and Risk of Loss, Theft, or Damage

All artwork submitted to the Agent for sale or for the purpose of securing work shall remain the property of the Designer. The Agent shall issue a receipt to the Designer for all artwork that the Designer submits to the Agent. If artwork is lost, stolen, or damaged while in the Agent's possession due to the Agent's failure to exercise reasonable care, the Agent will be held liable for the value of the artwork. Proof of any loss, theft, or damage must be furnished by the Agent to the Designer upon request. When selling artwork, taking an order, or allowing a client to hold artwork for consideration, the Agent agrees to use invoice, order, or holding forms that provide that the client is responsible for loss, theft, or damage to artwork while being held by the client, and to require the client's signature on such forms. The Agent agrees to enforce these provisions, including taking legal action as necessary. If the Agent undertakes legal action, any recovery shall first be used to reimburse the amount of attorney's fees and other expenses incurred and the balance of the recovery shall be divided between Agent and Designer in the respective percentages set forth in Paragraph 5. If the Agent chooses not to require the client to be responsible as described herein, then the Agent agrees to assume these responsibilities. If the Agent receives insurance proceeds due to loss, theft, or damage of artwork while in the Agent's or client's possession, the Designer shall receive no less than that portion of the proceeds that have been paid for the Designer's artwork.

3. Term

This Agreement shall take effect on the _____ day of _____, 200__, and remain in full force and effect for a term of one year, unless terminated as provided in Paragraph 10.

4. Prices

At this time the minimum base prices charged to clients by the Agent are as follows:

Sketch (apparel market)

_____

Repeat (apparel market)

_____

Colorings (apparel market)

_____

Sketch (home furnishing market)

_____

Repeat (home furnishing market)

_____

Colorings (home furnishing market)

_____

Other

_____

_____

The Agent agrees that these prices are minimum prices only and shall be increased whenever possible (i.e., when the work is a rush job or becomes larger or more complicated than is usual.) The Agent also agrees to try to raise the base price to keep pace with the rate of inflation.

The Agent shall obtain the Designer's written consent prior to entering into any contract for payment by royalty.

No discounts shall be offered to clients by the Agent without first consulting the Designer.

When leaving a design with the Agent for possible sale, the Designer shall agree with the Agent as to the price to be charged if the design should bring more than the Agent's base price.

5. Agent's Commissions
The rate of commission for all artwork shall be _____. It is mutually agreed by both parties that no commissions shall be paid on assignments rejected by the Designer or for which the Designer does not receive payment, regardless of the reasons payment is not made.

On commissioned originals and service work, expenses incurred in the execution of a job, such as phone calls, shipping, etc., shall be billed to the client in addition to the fee. No Agent's commission shall be paid on these amounts. In the event that a flat fee is paid by the client, it shall be reduced by the amount of expenses incurred by the Designer in performing the assignment, and the Agent's commission shall be payable only on the fee as reduced for expenses. It is mutually agreed that if the Agent offers a client a discount on a large group of designs including work of other designers, then that discount will come out of the Agent's commission since the Agent is the party who benefits from this volume.

6. Commissioned Work
Commissioned work refers to all artwork done on a nonspeculative basis. The Agent shall provide the Designer with a copy of the completed order form that the client has signed. The order form shall set forth the responsibilities of the client in ordering and purchasing artwork. To this the Agent shall add the date by which

the artwork must be completed and any additional instructions that the Agent feels are necessary to complete the job to the client's satisfaction. The Agent will sign these instructions. Any changes in the original instructions must be in writing, signed by the Agent, and contain a revised completion date.

It is mutually agreed that all commissioned work generated by the Designer's work shall be offered first to the Designer. The Designer has the right to refuse such work.

The Agent agrees to use the order confirmation form of the Graphic Artists Guild, or a form that protects the interests of the Designer in the same manner as that form. The order form shall provide that the Designer will be paid for all changes of original instructions arising through no fault of the Designer. The order form shall also provide that if a job is canceled through no fault of the Designer, a labor fee shall be paid by the client based on the amount of work already done and the artwork will remain the property of the Designer. In a case in which the job being canceled is based on artwork that belongs to the client, such as a repeat or coloring, a labor fee will be charged as outlined above and the artwork will be destroyed. If the artwork is already completed in a satisfactory manner at the time the job is canceled, the client must pay the full fee.

7. Holding Policy
In the event that a client wishes to hold the Designer's work for consideration, the Agent shall establish a maximum holding time with the client. This holding time shall not exceed 5 working days. Any other arrangements must first be discussed with the Designer. The Agent agrees to use the holding form of the Graphic Artists Guild, or a form that protects the interests of the Designer in the same manner as that form. All holding forms shall be available for the Designer to see at any time.

8. Billings and Payments
The Agent shall be responsible for all billings. The Agent agrees to use the invoice form of the Graphic Artists Guild, or a form that protects the interests of the Designer in the same manner as that form. The Agent agrees to provide the Designer with a copy of all bills to clients pertaining to the work of the Designer. The Designer will provide the Agent with a bill for his or her work for the particular job. The Designer's bill shall be paid by the Agent within 1 week after the delivery of artwork or, if the Agent finds it necessary, within 10 working days after receipt of payment from the client. The terms of all bills issued by the Agent shall require payment within 30 calendar days or less. If the client does not pay within that time, the Agent must immediately pursue payment and, upon request, inform the Designer that this has been done. The Agent agrees to take all necessary steps to collect payment, including taking legal action if necessary. If either the Agent or Designer undertakes legal action, any recovery shall first be used to reimburse the amount of attorney's fees and other expenses incurred and the balance of the recovery shall be divided between the Agent and Designer in the respective percentages set forth in Paragraph 5. The Agent agrees, whenever possible, to bill in such a way that no single bill exceeds the maximum that can be sued for in small-claims court.

continued...

Under no circumstances shall the Agent withhold payment to the Designer after the Agent has been paid. Late payments by the Agent to the Designer shall be accompanied by interest calculated at the rate of 1 1/2% monthly.

9. Inspection of the Books and Records
The Designer shall have the right to inspect the Agent's books and records with respect to proceeds due the Designer. The Agent shall keep the books and records at the Agent's place of business and the Designer may make such inspection during normal business hours on the giving of reasonable notice.

10. Termination
This Agreement may be terminated by either party by giving 30 days' written notice by registered mail to the other party. All artwork executed by the Designer not sold by the Agent must be returned to the Designer within these 30 days. In the event of termination, the Agent shall receive commissions for all sales made or assignments obtained by the Agent prior to the termination date, regardless of when payment is received. No commissions shall be payable for sales made or assignments obtained by the Designer after the termination date.

11. Assignment
This Agreement shall not be assigned by either of the parties hereto. It shall be binding on and inure to the benefit of the successors, administrators, executors, or heirs of the Agent and Designer.

12. Arbitration
Any disputes in excess of $ _____ *(maximum limit for small-claims court)* arising out of this Agreement shall be submitted to binding arbitration before a mutually agreed-upon arbitrator pursuant to the rules of the American Arbitration Association. The Arbitrator's award shall be final and judgment may be entered in any court having jurisdiction thereof. The Agent shall pay all arbitration and court costs, reasonable attorney's fees, and legal interest on any award of judgment in favor of the Designer.

13. Notices
All notices shall be given to the parties at their respective addresses set forth above.

14. Independent Contractor Status
Both parties agree that the Agent is acting as an independent contractor. This Agreement is not an employment agreement, nor does it constitute a joint venture or partnership between the Designer and Agent.

15. Amendments and Merger
All amendments to this Agreement must be written. This Agreement incorporates the entire understanding of the parties.

16. Other Provisions
_____
_____
_____
_____

17. Governing Law
This Agreement shall be governed by the laws of the State of _____.

18. Acceptance of Terms
The signature of both parties shall evidence acceptance of these terms.

In witness whereof, the parties have signed this Agreement as of the date set forth above.

Designer _____

Agent _____

Surface/Textile Designer's Estimate and Confirmation Form

FRONT

Designer's Letterhead

TO

Date _____

Pattern Number _____

Due Date _____

ESTIMATED PRICES

Sketch _____

Repeat _____

Colorings _____

Corners _____

Tracings _____

Other _____

DESCRIPTION OF ARTWORK

Repeat _____

Size _____

Colors _____

Type of Printing _____

1/2 Drop _____ ❑ Yes _____ ❑ No _____

SPECIAL COMMENTS

_____

_____

_____

_____

_____

_____

_____

continued...

TERMS

1. Time for Payment
Because the major portion of the above work represents labor, all invoices are payable 15 days net. A 1 1/2% monthly service charge is payable on all unpaid balances after this period. The grant of textile usage rights is conditioned on receipt of payment.

2. Default of Payment
The Client shall assume responsibility for all collection of legal fees necessitated by default in payment.

3. Estimated Prices
Prices shown above are minimum estimates only. Final prices shall be shown in invoice.

4. Payment for Changes
Client shall be responsible for making additional payments for changes requested by Client in original assignment.

5. Expenses
Client shall be responsible for payment of all extra expenses rising from assignment, including but not limited to mailings, messengers, shipping charges, and shipping insurance.

6. Sales Tax
Client shall assume responsibility for all sales taxes due on this assignment.

7. Cancellation Fees
Work canceled by the client while in progress shall be compensated for on the basis of work completed at the time of cancellation and assumes that the Designer retains the project, whatever its stage of completion. Upon cancellation, all rights, publication and other, revert to the Designer. Where Designer creates corners that are not developed into purchased sketches, a labor fee will be charged, and ownership of all copyrights and artwork is retained by the Designer.

8. Insuring Artwork
The client agrees when shipping artwork to provide insurance covering the fair market value of the artwork.

9. Uniform Commercial Code
The above terms incorporate Article 2 of the Uniform Commercial Code.

10. Warranty of Originality
The Designer warrants and represents that to the best of his/her knowledge, the work assigned hereunder is original and has not been previously published, or that consent to use has been obtained through the undersigned from third parties is original or, if previously published, that the consent to use has been obtained on an unlimited basis; that the Designer has full authority to make this agreement; and that the work prepared by the Designer does not contain any scandalous, libelous, or unlawful matter. This warranty does not extend to any uses that the Client or others may make of the Designer's product that may infringe on the rights of others. Client expressly agrees that it will hold the Designer harmless for all liability caused by the Client's use of the Designer's product to the extent such use infringes on rights of others.

11. Limitation of Liability
Client agrees that it shall not hold the Designer or his/her agents or employees liable for any incidental or consequential damages that arise from the Designer's failure to perform any aspect of the Project in a timely manner, regardless of whether such failure was caused by intentional or negligent acts or omissions of the Designer or a third party.

12. Dispute Resolution
Any disputes in excess of $ _____ *(maximum limit for small-claims court)* arising out of this Agreement shall be submitted to binding arbitration before a mutually agreed-upon arbitrator pursuant to the rules of the American Arbitration Association. The Arbitrator's award shall be final, and judgment may be entered in any court having jurisdiction thereof. The Client shall pay all arbitration and court costs, reasonable attorney's fees, and legal interest on any award of judgment in favor of the Surface/Textile Designer.

13. Acceptance of Terms
The signature of both parties shall evidence acceptance of these terms.

Consented and agreed to

Designer's signature/date _____

Authorized signature/date _____

Client name and title _____

Surface/Textile Designer's Holding Form

Designer's Letterhead

TO

Date _____

Pattern number _____

NUMBER OF DESIGNS HELD

Sketch _____

Design _____   Number of designs held _____

Sketch _____

Design _____   Number of designs held _____

Sketch _____

Design _____   Number of designs held _____

Sketch _____

Design _____   Number of designs held _____

Sketch _____

Design _____   Number of designs held _____

Sketch _____

Design _____   Number of designs held _____

The submitted designs are original and protected under the copyright laws of the United States, Title 17 United States Code. These designs are submitted to you in confidence and on the following terms:

1. Ownership and Copyrights
You agree not to copy, photograph, or modify directly or indirectly any of the materials held by you, nor permit any third party to do any of the foregoing. All artwork and photographs developed from these designs, including the copyrights therein, remain my property and must be returned to me unless the designs are purchased by you. Any transfer of rights is conditional upon receipt of full payment.

2. Responsibility for Artwork
You agree to assume responsibility for loss, theft, or any damage to the designs while they are being held by you. It is agreed that the fair market value for each design is the price specified above.

3. Holding of Artwork
You agree to hold these designs for a period not to exceed _____ working days from the above date. Any holding of artwork beyond that period shall

constitute a binding sale at the price specified above. You further agree not to allow any third party to hold designs unless specifically approved by me.

4. Arbitration
Any disputes in excess of $ _____ *(maximum limit for small-claims court)* arising out of this Agreement shall be submitted to binding arbitration before a mutually agreed-upon arbitrator pursuant to the rules of the American Arbitration Association. The Arbitrator's award shall be final, and judgment may be entered in any court having jurisdiction thereof. The party holding the designs shall pay all arbitration and court costs, reasonable attorney's fees, and legal interest on any award of judgment in favor of the Surface/Textile Designer.

5. Uniform Commercial Code
The above terms incorporate Article 2 of the Uniform Commercial Code.

6. Acceptance of Terms
The signature of both parties shall evidence acceptance of these terms.

Consented and agreed to

Designer's signature/date _____

Authorized signature/date _____

Client's name and title _____

Surface/Textile Designer's Invoice

Designer's Letterhead

TO

Date _____

Invoice Number _____

Purchase Order Number _____

Stylist _____

Designer _____

DESCRIPTION

Pattern Number _____

Price _____

Subtotal _____

ITEMIZED EXPENSES

Subtotal _____

Sales Tax _____

Payments on Account _____

Balance Due _____

TERMS

1. Receipt of Artwork
Client acknowledges receipt of the artwork specified above.

2. Time for Payment
Because the major portion of the above work represents labor, all invoices are payable 15 days net. The grant of textile usage rights is conditioned on receipt of payment. A 1 1/2% monthly service charge is payable on unpaid balance after expiration of period for payment.

3. Default in Payment
The Client shall assume responsibility for all collection of legal fees necessitated by default in payment.

4. Adjustments to Invoice
Client agrees to request any adjustments of accounts, terms, or other invoice data within 10 days of receipt of the invoice.

5. Uniform Commercial Code
These terms incorporate Article 2 of the Uniform Commercial Code.

6. Dispute Resolution
Any disputes in excess of $ _____ *(maximum limit for small-claims court)* arising out of this Agreement shall be submitted to binding arbitration before a mutually agreed-upon arbitrator pursuant to the rules of the American Arbitration Association. The Arbitrator's award shall be final, and judgment may be entered in any court having jurisdiction thereof. The Client shall pay all arbitration and court costs, reasonable attorney's fees, and legal interest on any award of judgment in favor of the Designer.

7. Acceptance of Terms
The signature of both parties shall evidence acceptance of these terms.

Consented and agreed to

Designer's signature/date _____

Authorized signature/date _____

Client's name and title _____

Glossary

2-D animation: Any hand-drawn graphic created for TV, film, etc., using either pen and ink or computer-generated imagery.

3-D animation: Use of modeling and/or digitizing to create objects that not only have shape and dimension but also can be viewed from any angle.

A

account executive: Representative of an advertising agency who handles specific accounts and acts as a client liaison to the art director, creative director, and others creating advertising for the account.

advance: Amount of money paid prior to the commencement of work or in the course of work. It may be intended to cover expenses, or it may be partial payment of the total fee. An advance as partial payment is common for a time-consuming project.

advance on royalties or **advance payment against royalties:** Amount paid prior to actual sales of the commissioned item or work; sometimes paid in installments. Advances are generally not expected to be returned, even if unearned in sales. Both the terms and the size of the advance are negotiable.

agreement: See *contract.*

all-media rights: A contract term that asks the graphic artist, in essence, to allow the buyer to distribute work in all media (often it includes the clause "now known or invented in the future"). Media that convey art or design can take many forms: print media are books or magazines; electronic media are CDs or multimedia presentations; other media are television, radio, and the web.

all-rights contract: A contract that purchases all rights of usage for reproduction of an artwork forever. All-rights contracts are different from work-for-hire contracts, which strip away not only the graphic artist's rights but the graphic artist's authorship. Under an all-rights contract, the artist still retains statutory termination right. See also *perpetuity, termination rights,* and *work-for-hire.*

arbitration: Negotiation in a legal dispute by a neutral party that results in a binding decision, enforced by a court.

art director: Usually an employee of an advertising agency, publishing house, magazine, or other user of a graphic artist's work. Some organizations hire freelance art directors to perform these duties. Responsibilities include selection of talent, purchase of visual work, and supervision of the quality and character of visual work.

art staff: Group of artists working under an art director's supervision for a company such as an advertising agency, publisher, magazine, or large design studio.

artwork: Any finished work of a graphic artist.

assigning (transferring): Term commonly used for reselling or relicensing signed-over rights to artwork.

attribution: Basic artist's right whereby the artist retains authorship of a work and is acknowledged properly for its creation. Attribution ensures that an artist's name not be used on works he or she did not create. Also called *paternity.*

author's alterations: Any changes requested by the client in service or responsibility beyond the scope outlined in the design proposal; these are billable expenses.

B

back end: In website development, the back end delivers the content which populates the front end, and provides the functionality not visible to the website visitor. It is the software and database that support a site, including advanced search mechanisms, built-in security, payment processing, audio and video streaming, etc.

bailment: Obligation on the part of the individual(s) with whom art is left to take reasonable care of it. This is a legal requirement and applies to situations such as a portfolio left for review.

Berne Convention: Worldwide multinational treaty for the protection of literary and artistic works that accepts moral rights as a matter of course. Member nations participating in Berne are required to frame their copyright laws according to certain minimum standards and to guarantee reciprocity to citizens of any other member nation.

bid: To offer an amount as the price one will pay or accept.

blanket contract: Contract kept on file by a publishing firm covering all future, and sometimes past, assignments.

blog (a contraction of Web log): A web site or web page, usually maintained by an individual, that allows users to reflect, share opinions, and discuss various topics in the form of an online journal; readers may comment on posts written by others.

blues: Nonreproducible photographic prints made from negatives, used in platemaking (also known as browns, ozalids, or silvers), which enable an editor to verify that all art and text are in proper position and that pages are in sequence.

boilerplate: Contract or document containing formulaic language that can be used for a number of purposes or similar circumstances, requiring only minor alterations.

book packagers: Independent suppliers who take over some or all of the functions for publishers of preparing a book. Functions include initiating projects, finding writers and illustrators, arranging for whatever extras may be involved, and striking deals with publishers.

broker: Agent or representative.

buyout: Imprecise term for an all-rights transfer.

C

cancellation fee: A fee paid as compensation for the artist's or studio's effort in developing an illustration or design when a project is terminated or not used by the client for reasons outside the artist's control. See also *kill fee*.

cartoonist: Professional artist who works in a humorous and satirical style, including political commentary.

cast off: In publishing, to estimate the typeset number of pages based on the manuscript length.

CGI (Common Gateway Interface): A standard for running external programs from a World Wide Web HTTP server. CGI specifies how to pass arguments to the executing program as part of the HTTP request. It also defines a set of environment variables.

check with conditions: Attempt to add terms to contract or change terms after the work is completed by listing conditions on the check.

claymation: Three-dimensional animation using clay figures or puppets.

client accommodation: To work at fees below the normal rate in order to accommodate budgetary restrictions and to preserve a long-term working relationship.

clip art: Public domain line art specifically designed for royalty-free reuse.

Code of Fair Practice: A code, drafted in 1948, to uphold existing laws and traditions and to help define an ethical standard for business practices and professional conduct in the graphic communications industry. The code has been used successfully since its formulation by thousands of industry professionals to create equitable business relationships.

collateral: Materials created to support or reinforce a design or promotional concept.

color proofs: First full-color printed pieces pulled off the press for approval before the press is considered ready to roll for the entire press run. Sometimes called *simple colored proofs,* these proofs are useful for making on-press corrections, particularly for problems resulting from improper registration and the effects of overprinting. Progressive proofs are the preferred method of accurately checking color.

color separation: A photographic process that breaks up colors into basic components or separate pieces of film, which are later recombined to recreate the original image.

commission: (n) Percentage of a fee paid by an artist to an artist's agent or gallery for service provided or business transacted. (v) The act of giving an artist an assignment to create a work of art.

comprehensive/comp: Visualization of the idea for an illustration or a design, usually created for the client and artist to use as a guide for the finished work. "Tight comps" and "loose comps" refer to the degree of detail, rendering, and general accuracy used to create the comprehensive.

confidentiality: Standard clause in contracts that prevents disclosure of company secrets and information concerning the job; may include a clause to prevent discussion of the contract terms.

confirmation form: Contract used by an artist when no purchase order has been given or when the purchase order is incomplete with respect to important terms of the contract, such as amount of fee, rights transferred, and so on.

contingency fee: Fee dependent on or conditioned by other circumstances.

contract: Agreement, whether oral or written, whereby two parties bind themselves to perform certain obligations. Synonyms: *agreement* or *letter of agreement* if the contract takes the form of a letter.

copy: Text of an advertisement, editorial content of a magazine or newspaper, or the text of a book.

copyright: Authorship of a creative work that provides the exclusive legal right to reproduce, publish, and sell that work. Any artist creating artwork automatically owns the copyright to that work unless provisions have been made prior to the start of the project to transfer authorship to the buyer (see *work-for-hire*).

copyright registration: The establishment of a public record of the artist's claim to authorship and a necessary prerequisite to asserting any copyright claim in court.

copywriter: Writer of advertising or publicity copy.

Copyright Royalty Tribunal Reform Act: Passed by Congress on December 17, 1993, the act established copyright arbitration royalty panels (CARPs) that set rates of compensation for the use of musical, graphic, sculptural, and pictorial works by noncommercial educational broadcasting stations. Also allows interested parties to negotiate voluntary agreements instead of invoking a CARP.

creative director: Usually an employee or officer of an advertising agency; his or her responsibilities include supervision of all aspects of the character and quality of the agency's work for its clients.

croquis: 1) In fashion illustration, a rough sketch made by an artist. 2) In textile design for the apparel industry, a full-color design concept or sketch that is developed into repeats to meet the technical specifications of the manufacturer.

cure provision: Clause in a contract that gives an infringing party a certain amount of time to "fix" a mistake before any legal action is taken.

D

de-escalation: A clause in a contract that allows for a decrease in extent, volume, or scope.

derivative work: One based on one or more preexisting works; may be a modification, adaptation, or translation, and applies to a work that, according to copyright law, is "recast, transformed or adapted."

design brief: Analysis of a project prepared by either the client or the designer. When the designer assumes this responsibility, it should be reflected in the design fee. The design brief for the design of a book, for example, may include 1) a copy of the manuscript, with a selection of representative copy for sample pages and a summary of all typographical problems, copy areas, code marks, and so on; 2) an outline of the publisher's manufacturing program for the book: compositor and composition method, printer and paper stock, binder and method of binding; 3) a description of the proposed physical characteristics of the book, such as trim size, page length, list price, quantity of first printing, and whether the book will print in one color or more than one. The publisher should also indicate whether any particular visual style is expected.

director: In animation, the person who oversees an animated picture from conception to finish and has complete control over all phases: character design (usually supplied by an agency), layout, sound, and so on.

distribution right: The right to control distribution of a work that is held by the copyright holder, unless sold.

documentary design: Design adapted from a historical document or plate, usually in public domain because of its age, such as Art Deco, Art Nouveau, and Egyptian.

droit de suite: A provision that grants creators a share in the value of their works by guaranteeing a certain percentage of the sale price every time a work is resold. In the United States, also known as *resale royalties.*

dummy: 1) In book design and production, first-pass pages. 2) Book, brochure, or catalog idea in a roughly drawn form, usually made up to contain the proper number of pages and used as a reference for positioning and pagination.

E

electronic rights: Rights specified in a contract to control electronic publication in addition to other media, often for no additional compensation. Graphic artists should make every effort to retain them or negotiate higher fees.

e-mercial: A marketing tool that delivers its commercial message within a client's e-mail and often employs e-mail's ability to play animation and sound. Sophistication may range from the simple, such as a static business card, to an animated cartoon.

exclusive unlimited rights: Usage rights granted by an artist in which the artist may not sell any use to anyone else. The artist retains authorship rights and may reclaim these rights after thirty-five years. The artist may display the work or use it for self promotion. Sale of the original art is a separate transaction.

exclusive use: A usage right by which no one except the purchaser of the image may use the image without permission of the purchaser.

F

fair use: A use of a copyrighted work not specifically defined, but resolved by courts by examining the purpose and character of the use; the nature of the copyrighted work; the amount and substantiality of the portion used in relation to the copyrighted work as a whole; and the effect of the use on the potential market for, or value of, the copyrighted work

finished art: Usually an illustration, photograph, or layout that is prepared and ready for the printer.

first North American serial rights: The right to be the first magazine to publish art for use in one specific issue to be distributed in North America.

first right: The right to be the first user of art for a one-time use; frequently describes the right to publish art in a magazine serial or drawn from a book in which the art will appear.

fonts: Individual branches of a typeface design.

format: Arrangement of type and illustration that is used for many layouts; arrangement used in a series.

Fortune 500 company: *Fortune* magazine's annual listing of the 500 largest corporations in the United States, as measured by their gross revenues.

freelance employee: An employee whose work hours are determined by the assignment and who uses his/her own workspace and materials; freelancers generally provide their own benefits. The freelancer often collects state sales tax from clients and pays his or her own income taxes.

front end: In website development, the front end refers to the visual interface the website visitor experiences: the overall aesthetics, the navigation, and the interface layout.

G

gams: Color chips used in surface pattern design consisting of each color in the design. Gams are created in different manners, depending on the media used and the production method. Designs for woven or knitted textiles may be accompanied by yarn samples for color matching.

generic work: Art that has the potential for wide application in a variety of markets.

graphic artist: Visual artist doing commercial work.

graphic designer: Graphic artist and professional problem solver who works with the elements of typography, illustration, photography, and printing to create commercial communications tools such as brochures, advertising, signage, posters, slide shows, book jackets, and other forms of printed, electronic, or graphic communications.

graphic film artist: One skilled in creating special

effects on film by use of computerized stands and/or adding computerized movement to artwork, such as television logos with glows and set movement.

graphics: Visual communications.

group head: Some advertising agencies divide their clients into groups under a group head who supervises the work of art directors on the various accounts.

guild: Association of like-minded professionals seeking to protect and better their status and/or skills. When employees are members in equal proportion to freelancers, such a guild qualifies with the U.S. government as a union. In this capacity, a guild may represent employees who are its members in collective bargaining.

H-I

house accounts: Clients that an artist contacted and developed before signing with a rep. Most artists do not pay commissions on house accounts that they service themselves, and they generally pay a lower commission on house accounts that the rep services.

illustrator: Professional graphic artist who communicates an idea pictorially by creating a visual image for a specific purpose, using paint, pencil, pen, collage, computer, or any other graphic technique except photography.

image: Pictorial idea.

image processing: Manipulation of an image, usually digitally scanned, such as enhancement, colorizing, or distortions.

indemnity: Common clause in contracts that seeks to exempt or protect the client and/or the graphic artist from damages or liability in actions brought by third parties.

invoice: Statement given to a client showing the amount due in payment for an assignment. Usually submitted after work has been completed. If advance payments are made, the invoice should reflect these and show the balance due.

J-K

job ledger: A ledger or journal that contains standard columns for information such as job description, rights granted, fees and expenses, and billing information.

kickback: Sum of money or a large figure paid to an artist by a supplier for the artist's part in passing on work such as printing. May be demanded by art buyers from artists in exchange for awarding commissions. Kickbacks are illegal. Often the supplier's kickback costs are hidden in invoices submitted to the client.

kill fee: Payment by the client to the graphic artist when the client does not use a commissioned work. Includes two types of payments: *cancellation fee* and *rejection fee*.

L

layout: The arrangement of all the design, visual, and text elements of an advertisement, magazine or book page, or any other graphic work (such as brochures and catalogs) intended for reproduction. Usually executed by an art director or graphic designer to be used as a guide in discussions with the client.

layout artist: In animation, one who lays out and arranges backgrounds.

letter of agreement: See *contract*.

licensee: The entity that acquires the rights to use the design or property.

license: Right to sell or rent artwork or design for a specific use and period of time. It is in the graphic artist's interest to license use of work, rather than sign all-rights or work-for-hire contracts. See also *sublicensing rights*.

licensing agent: An agent who usually handles marketing, contract negotiation, billing, and paperwork concerned with licensing art. Licensing agents should have contacts at a number of companies.

licensor: The artist or owner/creator of a design or property.

ligatures: Letter combinations used in type design.

limited rights: Specific usage rights that may range from one time to extensive use. Should be clearly detailed in the purchase order and should include market, medium, time period, and geographic region.

limited-edition print: A print made by lithography or serigraphy in a limited quantity, numbered and signed by the artist. May be created independently by graphic artist or under contract with a gallery or publisher; payment made on commission or royalty basis.

logo: Mark or symbol created for an individual, company, or product that translates its use, function, or essence into a graphic image.

logotype: Any alphabetical configuration that is designed to identify by name a producer, company, publication, or individual.

M

markup (n)/mark up (v): (n) Service charge added to an expense account to reimburse the artist for the time needed to process the billing of items to the client and the cost of advancing the money to pay such expenses; (v) the process of adding such a charge.

mechanical: Layout created by a production artist for the printer to use in the printing process.

mediation: Negotiation in a legal dispute where an impartial person seeks to facilitate an agreement between the two parties. A mediator can be appointed by a judge or another third party, such as an arts mediation service, but the resolution is binding upon the parties only if the parties agree to it in writing.

montage: Image created from a compilation of other images.

mood board: A tool used by a designer at the early stages of a project to convey to the client the overall feel, or emotional and contextual aspects, of a design concept. The board is composed of images and objects that inspire, target desires, and facilitate creativity and innovation.

moonlighting: A situation in which a freelance commission is taken by a salaried person to be completed in the person's spare time.

moral rights: Personal rights of creators in their original (not reproduced) works, regardless of the sale or transfer of copyrights. Specifically, right of identification of authorship, and right of approval, restriction, or limitation on use or subsequent modifications.

motion graphics: Graphics that use video and/or animation technology to create the illusion of motion or a transforming appearance.

multiple rights: Usage rights for artwork on high-exposure products that may need numerous rights over longer periods and more media, regions, and markets. Fees should be adjusted accordingly.

N-O

no-assertion-of-rights clause: Contract item that clarifies that the rights licensed to the client are only the ones specified in the contract and that the artist retains all other rights. This clause should be included in every graphic artist's contract.

noncompeting rights: Uses other than the original commission that do not conflict or compete with the commissioning party's business or market.

nonexclusive use: A usage right in which the purchaser, along with the graphic artist, is allowed to reuse (or resell) a work in specified regions and situations. All uses need to be specified and clarified to avoid any future conflict of interest.

novelties: General term for gift or boutique-type items or for a wide variety of clever decorative or functional items. Some novelties can overlap as home accessories.

optimization tools: Tools that fine tune a program so that it runs more quickly or takes up less space or that configure a device or application so that it performs better.

overhead: Nonbillable expenses such as rent, phone, insurance, secretarial and accounting services, and salaries.

ownership of artwork: The copyright is separate and distinct from the material work in which it is embodied. For example, original artwork is owned by the creator even if rights of reproduction are transferred. Likewise, the artist can sell the original and still keep rights of reproduction.

P

packagers: Companies that coordinate all the components of a book publishing project and either present the finished concepts to publishers for execution or manufacture the books themselves and deliver bound volumes to the publisher.

page makeup: Assembling in sequence all the typographic and/or illustrative elements of a brochure, catalog, book, or similar item.

pass-through clause: Contract term that takes effect when an illustrator's share of a subsidiary sale exceeds a predetermined amount and for which payment is usually received within 30 days of receipt.

patent: Provision of intellectual property law that protects an invention rather than an image or a name.

per diem: Day rate of pay given to a professional by a client to complete an assignment.

perpetuity: Term meaning "forever" that is increasingly used in contracts to define length of usage. It is recommended that graphic artists negotiate rights for a limited time period rather than perpetuity. See also *termination right*.

plagiarism: Act of stealing and passing off as one's own the ideas or words of another; or the use of a created production without crediting the source.

platform: Set of hardware components, operating system, and delivery media that provide specific functions and capabilities for the production or playback of digital programming.

podcast: A series of audio or video digital media files that are released episodically and are downloadable, usually via an automated feed with computer software.

point-of-purchase: A term used for collateral that includes all point-of-sale materials, such as signs, leaflets, shopping cart posters, catalogs, brochures, counter displays, etc.

portfolio/artist's book: Reproductions and/or originals that represent the body of an artist's work.

post-project contracts: Terms introduced after receiving the artist's invoice, listed at the bottom or on the back of invoices, checks, or even purchase orders.

presentation boards: Any preliminary design mounted on boards that the graphic designer shows a client. In the fashion industry, color illustrations of a grouping of styles from the design collection that a manufacturer wishes to feature during market week sales.

printer's error (PE): Mistake made in the film negatives, platemaking, or printing that is not due to the client's error, addition, or deletion. The cost of correction is normally absorbed by the printer.

production artist: Professional artist who works with a designer to take a layout from conception through the printing process.

production coordinator: In animation, one responsible for making sure that everything is in order before it goes under the camera.

profit: The difference remaining (net income) after overhead, expenses, and taxes are subtracted from income received (gross income).

proposal/estimate: Graphic artist's detailed analysis of the cost and components of a project. Used to firm up an agreement before commencing work on a client's project.

public domain: Status of works that have no copyright encumbrances and may be used freely for any purpose.

purchase order (PO): Form given by a client to an artist describing the details of an assignment and, when signed by an authorized person, permitting work to commence.

R

reference file: Clippings compiled by an illustrator or designer from newspapers, magazines, and other printed pieces that are referred to for ideas and inspiration as well as technical information.

rejection fee: Payment made by client to artist when the artwork does not satisfy the client's stated requirements. See also *kill fee.*

remedies: Clauses that map out agreed-upon courses of action by which a disagreement or breach of contract can be resolved.

representative/rep: Professional agent who promotes specific talent in illustration, photography, or surface design and negotiates contracts for fees and commissions. Usually receives a percentage of the negotiated fee as payment for services provided to the talent.

reprint right: Right to print something that has been published elsewhere.

reproduction copy/repro: Proofs printed in the best possible quality for use as camera copy for reproduction. Also called *reproduction proof.*

request for proposal (RFP): A design brief created by a client that contains all the background information, objectives, and specifications for a project that a design firm needs for creating and submitting a proposal.

residuals: Payments received in addition to the original fee, usually for extended usage of a work. See also *royalty.*

retainer agreement: An arrangement by which an artist agrees to work for a client for a specific length of time or on a particular project, for a fee paid according to an agreed-upon schedule. Can take several forms: annual, project-based, or service.

return of artwork: The responsibility of a client to return original artwork undamaged to the graphic artist after using it during a project.

reuse: Sale of additional rights to existing artwork; an opportunity for all illustrators and an important area of income for many.

reversion rights: Book publishing contract provision that protects the artist in the event the publisher fails to publish within a specific period of time; after that, all rights revert back to the artist.

right to modify (alterations): Purchaser of rights to artwork holds the copyright only in the collective work, not in the underlying contribution (the art) itself. Since altered artwork is a derivative work of an original, if the artist does not grant the right to create a derivative work, the client has no right to alter the image. Any alterations to artwork should be made in consultation with the initial artist.

roughs: Loosely drawn ideas, often done in pencil on tracing paper, by an illustrator or designer. Usually several roughs are sketched before a comprehensive is developed from them.

royalty: Payment to the artist that is based on a percentage of the revenue generated through the quantity of items sold, such as books, cards, calendars. See also *advance on royalties.*

royalty-free distribution: Art inventories sold on CD-ROM disks, royalty free. Artist earns royalties on sales of the CD-ROMs but are not paid royalties for additional use, and rights are sold outright.

S

sales tax: The rate of taxation on items sold, established by each state government; in states that charge sales tax, the rate varies between 4 and 9 percent, and the types of products and services for which sales tax should be billed to the client also vary by state. The freelance graphic artist is often required to be licensed to charge, collect, and remit sales tax to the state on a quarterly basis.

second right: Right to use art that has appeared elsewhere. Frequently applied to magazine use of art that has appeared previously in a book or another magazine.

service mark: Provision of trademark law that identifies and protects the source of services rather than goods, indicated by the letters SM or by ᔆᴹ.

simultaneous right: Right to publish art at the same time as another publication. Normally used when two publications have markets that do not overlap.

speculation: Accepting assignments without any guarantee of payment after work has been completed. Payment upon publication is also speculation.

spine: Area between the front and back book bindings, on which the author, title, and publisher are indicated.

storyboards: 1) Series of sketches drawn by artists in scale for a television screen to indicate camera angles, type of shot (close-up, extreme close-up), backgrounds. Essentially a plan for shooting a

TV commercial; often accompanied by announcer's script and actor's lines. 2) Sketches of action for animation. Synonyms: *story* or *story sketches.*

style: Particular artist's unique form of expression; also referred to as "look." In surface design, referred to as *hand.*

stylists: Creative and managerial heads of departments, sometimes referred to as *style directors* or *art buyers.*

sublicensing right: The right of the publisher to sell any of the rights granted to it to third parties. All such terms must be thoroughly spelled out in the contract so that the third party is under the same copyright limitations as any other client and so that the artist receives the same fee as any other client.

subsidiary rights: In publishing, those rights not granted to the publisher but which the publisher has the right to sell to third parties. Proceeds of such sales are shared with the artist.

surface designer: Professional artist who creates art to be used in repeat on such surfaces as fabric, wallpaper, woven material, or ceramics.

syndication: Simultaneous distribution to print or broadcast media of artwork or other creative work. Often refers to sales of cartoons or comic strips.

T

talent: Group of artists represented by an agent or gallery.

tear sheet: Sample of finished work as it was reproduced, usually in print media.

technique: Refers to the way a graphic artist uses a particular media.

termination right: Refers to 1) right provided in copyright law (see *perpetuity*) and 2) right to end a contract, most often with agent or broker.

test-market: (v) To subject (a product) to trial in a limited market. Artwork has been historically purchased at low rates for use in a limited number of markets; additional fees should be stipulated if use is expanded.

textbook: Any book used for educational purposes.

thumbnail or thumbnail sketch: Very small, often sketchy visualization of an illustration or design. Usually several thumbnails are created together to show different approaches to the visual problem being solved.

trade book: Any book sold in bookstores to the general public.

trade dress: Part of trademark law that protects a product's total image and overall appearance. Trade dress is defined by a work's overall composition and design, including size, shape, color, texture, and graphics.

trademark (™): Word, symbol, design, slogan, or a combination of words and designs that identifies and distinguishes the goods or services of one party from those of another.

transparency/chrome: Full-color translucent photographic film positive. Also called *color slides.*

typography: Style, arrangement, or appearance of typeset material.

U-W

union: Group of people in the same profession working to monitor and upgrade business standards in their industry.

unlimited rights: The purchase of all usage rights connected with a product for all media in all markets for an unlimited time. Longstanding trade custom provides that the artwork may be reproduced by the artist for self-promotion, and the artist may display the work. The artist also retains the copyright.

viral marketing: A self-propagating marketing technique aimed at replicating "word of mouth" on the Internet or via e-mail by facilitating and encouraging people to pass along a marketing message.

W3C (World Wide Web Consortium): International organization founded in 1994 that standardizes HTML used by most leading browsers. Its purpose is to develop open standards so the Web evolves in a single direction rather than splintering into different factions.

warranty/indemnification clause: Clause in a contract in which a graphic artist guarantees that the work created will not violate the copyright of any party.

web content management system (WCMS or Web CMS): Software implemented as a web application for creating and managing HTML content. The software provides authoring tools designed to allow users with little knowledge of programming or markup languages to create and manage content with relative ease.

work-for-hire: For copyright purposes, "work-for-hire," or similar terms such as "done for hire" or "for hire," signifies that the commissioning party owns the copyright of the artwork as if the commissioning party had, in fact, been the artist.

working contract: Term referring to a document that everyone recognizes as a contract, complete with legal language and clauses.

wraparound: Book jacket design and/or illustration that encompasses front and back covers, sometimes including book flaps.

Index

NOTE: Page numbers in boldface indicate information contained in tables or figures.

C

California Art Preservation Act, 35

camera operator, 245

Canadian copyright, 41–43

cancellation fees, 54, 86, 113, 172

cartoon collections, 237

cartooning, 229–239

    book-length formats, 237–239

    comic books, 235–237

    editorial, 232

    licensing and merchandising, 239

    magazine, 231–232, **231**

    newspaper syndication, 232–234

    online cartoon sales, 234

    reuse, 239

cartoonist, 230

CCNV v. Reid, 34

Cease and Desist Letter, 307

character animation.
    See animation

character developer, 245

chart and map design, 161–162, **162**

check contracts, 110

checker, 245

checks with conditions, 89–90

children's books, 201–205, **202**

client alterations, 113

client contracts.
    See also contracts, 115–116

client relationships

    for graphic designers, 9, 64–66

    for illustrators, 3, 66

clients, 3

    determining needs, 79–80

    determining real goals of, 116, 170–171

    negotiating offers, 79–83

    researching, 80

    targeting, 95

    web design questions to ask, 170–172

clip art/rights-free art, 101

Code of Fair Practice, 14, **15–16**

collage, 28

collateral design, **137**, 138

collection, 90–95, **92**, **93**

    Graphic Artists Guild Grievance Committee, 93

    legal counsel for, 94–95

    mediation and arbitration, 93–94

    small-claims court, 94

    step-by-step strategy, **92**

    strategies for dealing with nonpayment, 91–95

collective works, 23

color forecasting, 253

color stylist, 245

comic books, 235–237, **236**

commissioned design, 160

commissioned typeface design, 151

commissions/fees, 5

company benefits, 124

company policies, 124

compositor, 245, **246**

comps, 191, **192**

compulsory licensing, 29

computer animation, 243–244, **244**

computer software application design, 178–180

computer-aided design (CAD), 254, 260

Computer-Generated Art Invoice, 325–326

Computer-Generated Art Job Order Form,
    323–324

Conference on Fair Use (COFU), 28

conferences, 298

consultation fees, 131

contact lists, 95

contests and competitions

    awards for excellence in the field, 56

    for commercial purposes, 56

    continuing problems, 57–58

    Guild survey results, 55–56

    for nonprofit purposes, 57

contracts.
    See also agreements, written, 88, 107–118

    boilerplate contracts, 111, 115

    check contracts, 110

    in children's book illustration, 201–204

    client contracts, 115–116

    copyright use and, 112

    demonstration rights, 173

    elements to include, 112–114, 131

    greeting card and novelty design, 160–161

    importance of, 109

    indemnity clauses, 114

    invoice contracts, 110

    lawyer involvement, 117

    legal issues, 113–114

    letters of agreement or engagement, 110

    negotiating, 116–117

I

illustration

　for advertising, 186–191, **187–190**

　architectural/interior, 220–221, **221**

　for books (*see also* book illustration),
　198–205, **199**, **200**, **202**

　cancellation/kill/rejection fees, 186

　corporate, organizational, and institutional,
　195–198, **196–197**

　dimensional (3-D), 221–224

　editorial, 205–207, **206**

　effects of current economy on pricing, 185

　fantastic art, 225–226

　fashion and lifestyle, 209–211, **210–211**

　greeting card and retail products, 211–213, **212**

　medical, 213–214, **214–215**

　for movies, TV, and video, 193–194, **195**

　natural science, 214–217, **216–217**

　package design, 207–208, **208**

　postage stamps, 224–225, **225**

　preproduction, 191–193, **192**

　technical, 217–220, **218–219**

　trade practices, 185–186

　work-for-hire contracts, 186

illustrators

　digital media, **181**

　vs. graphic designers, 2

　job descriptions, 126

　overview, 184

　pricing considerations, 67–68

　professional relationships, 3–7

　salaries, 126

　sources for finding, 13–14

　technology considerations, 66

Illustrator's Estimate and Confirmation Form,
334–335

Illustrator's Invoice, 339–340

Illustrator's Release Form for Models, 338

inbetweener, 245

income maximization, 97–105

independent contractors.
　See also work-for-hire, 52–54

INDUCE Act (Inducing Infringement of Copyrights
　Act), 72

industry directories, 291–292

infringement of copyright.
　See also copyright, 28–29

inker/opaquer, 245

institutional illustration, 195–198, **196–197**

insurance, 52

interactive project manager, 126

Intergovernmental Philatelic Corp. (IGPC), 225

international copyright, 41–43

Internet

　cartoon syndication, 234–235

　digital marketplace, 167

　factors for illustrators, 205

　overview, 166

　as recruitment source, 13

Internet regulation.
　See Digital Millenium Copyright Act (DMCA)

invoice contracts, 110

invoices, tracking, 90

J

job descriptions.
　See also under specific jobs, 124–126

job files, 88–89

job ledgers, 89

job market, 246–247

JOBline News, 14

Joint Ethics Committee, 14

joint works, 70

junior animator, 245

K

Kelly v. Arriba Soft Corporation, 30, 72

kill fees.
　See also cancellation fees, 54–55, 113

knitted textiles, 256–257

L

labor market, 74–75

Lanham Act, 40

late-payment fees, 113

lawyers, 94–95, 118

Lawyers for the Arts, 118

layout artist, 245

legal cases

　regarding copyright, 34

　regarding trade dress, 40–41

　regarding trademarks, 39–40

legal issues

　copyright, 21–32

　digital art, 68–73

　fair practices law, 38

　moral rights, 36–37, 42

Membership Application

Graphic Artists Guild
32 Broadway, Suite 1114
New York, NY 10004-1612
www.gag.org

The Graphic Artists Guild is a national union with local chapters. When you join the Guild, you join the National Organization and are assigned to a local chapter serving your area. If there isn't a local chapter near you, you will be assigned to the At-Large Chapter.

Please complete all portions of this application, sign it, and return it with your application fee and dues payment to the address above.

To pay by credit card, fax the completed form to 212-791-0333, or apply online at www.gag.org.

❑ New Membership   ❑ Renew Membership

Please print legibly and provide a shipping address for UPS deliveries

Name _____

Company _____

Position/Title _____

Street Address _____

City _____ State _____ Zip Code _____

Country _____

Phone (Include area code) _____ Fax Number _____

E-mail _____ Web site _____

Has your work been published, for example, print, web, etc.?
❑ Yes   ❑ No

How did you learn about the Guild?
❑ Direct Mail
❑ Friend / Associate
❑ Guild Meeting
❑ Internet / Website
❑ *Pricing & Ethical Guidelines*
❑ School / Instructor
❑ Trade Show

Discipline
In order of importance, please indicate no more than 3 disciplines. Please mark "1" for your primary discipline, "2" for your secondary discipline, and "3" for your tertiary discipline.

❑ Animation / Multimedia/Online
❑ Art Direction
❑ Artists' Representative
❑ Cartooning
❑ Computer Arts
❑ Dimensional Illustration / Model Making
❑ Fashion Illustration
❑ Graphic Design
❑ Illustration
❑ Marbling
❑ Pre-production (comps, storyboards, animatics)
❑ Surface / Textile Design
❑ Teaching Professional
❑ Video / Broadcast Design
❑ Web site Design
❑ Other: _____

Markets
In order of importance, please indicate no more than 3 markets in which you work. Please mark "1" for your primary market, "2" for your secondary market, and "3" for your tertiary market.

❑ Advertising / Collateral
❑ Architecture
❑ Book
❑ Charts / Maps
❑ Consumer
❑ Corporate
❑ Displays / Exhibits
❑ Editorial
❑ Educational
❑ Entertainment
❑ Fashion
❑ Internet / Online Services / World Wide Web
❑ Licensing / Merchandising
❑ Packaging
❑ Publication
❑ Syndication
❑ Other

Employment Status
❑ Freelance
❑ Staff
❑ Freelance and Staff
❑ Student: expected graduation year _____
❑ Retired Graphic Artist
❑ Business Owner

Please read and complete the 2nd page of this application

☞

MEMBERSHIP STATUS

There are two categories of membership:

Full Member – Only working graphic artists who derive more than 50% of their income from their graphic art are eligible to be full, voting members.

Associate Member – All other interested persons in related fields who support the goals and purposes of the Guild are welcome to join as Associate Members, as are graphic arts students and retired artists. Associate Members may participate in all Guild activities and programs and serve on committees but may not vote or hold office.

DUES (select one)

Full Member Dues Per Year

❏ Professional $200

Associate Member Dues Per Year

❏ Associate $170

❏ Lifetime $75 Age 60 and/or retired with 10 years past membership

❏ Student* $75 (enclose copy of current ID)

*Note: The Student category is available to full-time students carrying at least 12 credit hours. It is valid for one year beyond graduation. A photocopy of your current student ID is required.

Application Fee

Guild dues are based upon your membership category. To offset the administrative expense of processing new or reinstated memberships, the Guild collects a $30 fee with each membership application. Please note that membership dues and application fees are not refundable. $35.00 of your dues is for a copy of the *Graphic Artists Guild Handbook: Pricing & Ethical Guidelines*; $12 is for your subscription to the national *Guild News*.

Method of Payment

❏ Visa   ❏ Check
❏ MasterCard   ❏ Money Order
❏ American Express ❏ Discover

Card Number _____

Expiration Date (Example: 08/09) _____

Name on Card _____

AMOUNT ENCLOSED

Please make a payment of at least one half[1] of the chosen membership category plus $30 initiation fee.

Dues[1] enclosed _____

Initiation/Reinstatement Fee[2]   + **30.00**

Total payment $ _____

1. Any payment of less than one-half of your dues plus the full initiation fee will be automatically returned.
2. One-time fee. However, a $30 reinstatement fee is charged for memberships renewed past 60 days of expiration.
Returned checks are subject to a $25 service charge.

MEMBERSHIP STATEMENT (signature required)

Please read and sign the following. Application will not be entered without acceptance.

For Full Members Only – I derive more income from my own work as a graphic artist than I do as the owner or manager of any business that profits from the buying and/or selling of graphic artwork. I agree to abide by the Constitution and By-Laws* of the Graphic Artists Guild and do hereby authorize the Guild to act as my representative with regard to negotiation of agreements to improve my wages, fees, hours, and conditions of work. I further assign nonexclusive agency rights to the Graphic Artists Guild and extend to it my power of attorney to represent my contractual interests.

I further understand that my membership in the Graphic Artists Guild is continuous and that I will be billed for dues annually in September. If I wish to resign from the Graphic Artists Guild, I understand that I must do so in writing, and that I will be responsible for the payment of any dues owed prior to the date of my resignation.

❏ Accept

Your Signature _____

For Associate Members Only – I agree to abide by the Constitution and By-Laws* of the Graphic Artists Guild. I understand that my membership in the Graphic Artists Guild is continuous and that I will be billed for membership dues, annually in September. If I wish to resign from the Graphic Artists Guild, I understand that I must do so in writing and that I will be responsible for the payment of any dues owed prior to the date of my resignation.

❏ Accept

Your Signature _____

*The Guild's Constitution and By-Laws may be downloaded from our web site: http://www.gag.org/about/constitution.php, or you can request a copy from the National office. The document is also on file at National and Chapter offices. Your membership is effective upon our receipt of this completed and signed application, the application fee, and the appropriate dues amount.

Please allow 3 to 4 weeks to receive membership materials.

For more information, call 212-791-3400, ext. 12, or e-mail membership@gag.org

For office use only

❏ PEGs _____   ❏ CARD _____   ❏ DB _____